CRIMINAL LAW

GREENS CONCISE SCOTS LAW

CRIMINAL LAW

By

Timothy H. Jones, LL.B., M.Phil., Ph.D.,

Lecturer in Law, University of Manchester

and

Michael G. A. Christie, M.A., LL.B., Solicitor,

Lecturer in Private Law, University of Aberdeen

W. GREEN / Sweet & Maxwell
EDINBURGH
1996

First Published 1992
Reprinted 1993
Second edition 1996

© 1996
W. Green & Son Ltd

ISBN 0 414 01146 5
A catalogue record for this book is available from the British Library

Typeset by Trinity Typesetting, Edinburgh
Printed and bound in Great Britain by Redwood Books, Wiltshire

CONTENTS

Page

Preface v
Table of Cases ix
Table of Statutes xxvii
Table of Statutory Instruments xxxi

1. Introduction to Criminal Law 1
2. Nature and Sources of Scots Criminal Law 10
3. Actus Reus and Mens Rea 43
4. Voluntary Acts and Automatism 60
5. Causation 95
6. Attempt 111
7. Complicity and Conspiracy 125
8. Defences 147
9. Crimes Against the Person 180
10. Crimes of Dishonesty 239
11. Crimes Against Property 286
12. Crimes Relating to Public Order and Morality 311
13. Statutory Offences 336
14. Conclusion 354

Appendix A — Select Bibliography of Scots Criminal Law   363
Appendix B — Criminal Law Case Reports 365
Appendix C — The Standard Scale of Fines 367
Appendix D — Scottish Criminal Courts 369

Index 372

PREFACE TO SECOND EDITION

There has been a surprising number of significant developments in the criminal law over the past four years. Indeed, the enactment of the Criminal Procedure (Scotland) Act and correlative legislation of 1995 would alone have made the first edition seriously out of date, but there have been significant advances made by the courts in many areas of the common law too — for example in attempts, voluntary acts, *mentes reae*, causation, assault, homicide (including a case on persistent vegetative state), theft, and rape. In many ways, the High Court under the Presidency of Lords Hope and Ross has continued and accelerated the process of reform which began to be noticed some 20 years ago, and which will doubtless be given additional impetus when (as is anticipated) Lord Rodger assumes the role of Lord Justice-General later in the current year.

The simple object of this new edition has been the incorporation of these developments within the basic pattern of the original work. Teachers, therefore, should find a familiar arrangement of subject matters, and students an up-to-date outline of the common law of crime.

We have tried to state the law at April 1, 1996, although it has been possible to mention some matters which have arisen since then. (Readers may wish to note, however, that the particular aspect of English law referred to in para. 9–37 has now been abolished in terms of the Law Reform (Year and a Day Rule) Act 1996, c. 19.)

We should once again wish to record our gratitude to the whole of the production team at Greens, and especially to Stephen Harvey and Noel Keenan for their particular encouragement, hard work and support.

T.H.J.
M.G.A.C.
August 1996

TABLE OF CASES

ADAM OR REID, WILLIAM, (1829) Bell's Notes 43 .... 10.49
Adam v. MacNeill, 1972 J.C. 1; 1971 S.L.T.(Notes) 80 .... 8.08
Adcock v. Archibald, 1925 J.C. 58; 1925 S.L.T. 258 .... 10.75; 10.76
Advocate, H.M. v. Aitken, 1975 S.L.T.(Notes) 86 .... 4.22; 4.25
——— v. Anderson, 1928 J.C. 1; 1927 S.L.T. 651 .... 6.29
——— v. Bell, 1966 S.L.T.(Notes) 61 .... 11.32
——— v. ———, 1995 S.L.T. 350; 1995 S.C.C.R. 244 .... 2.64
——— v. Bennett, 1996 S.L.T. 662 .... 2.64; 4.21
——— v. Blake, 1986 S.L.T. 661 .... 6.10; 9.70
——— v. Boyd, 1977, unreported 3.27
——— v. Brogan, 1964 S.L.T. 204 .... 8.43
——— v. Browne (1903) 6 F. (J.) 24; (1903) 11 S.L.T. 353 .... 10.62
——— v. Cairns, 1967 J.C. 37; 1967 S.L.T. 165 .... 12.35
——— v. Callander, 1958 S.L.T. 24 .... 9.22
——— v. Camerons (1911) 6 Adam 456; 1911 S.C. (J.) 110; 1911 2 S.L.T. 108 .. 6.18–6.19;
                                                                                                                    7.31
——— v. Carson, 1964 S.L.T. 21 .... 8.32
——— v. Carter, 1990, unreported 9.71
——— v. Coutts (1899) 3 Adam 50 .... 10.16
——— v. Cunningham, 1963 J.C. 80; 1963 S.L.T. 345 .... 4.22; 4.25; 4.30; 4.31;
                                                                                                4.35; 4.40; 4.41; 4.48; 9.23
——— v. Delaney, 1945 J.C. 138; 1945 S.L.T. 25 .... 9.55
——— v. Docherty (1976) S.C.C.R. Supp. 146 .... 8.80
——— v. Doherty, 1954 J.C. 1; 1954 S.L.T. 169 .... 8.21; 8.24; 8.26
——— v. Donoghue, 1971 S.L.T. 2 .... 9.93
——— v. Duffy, 1983 S.L.T. 7; 1982 S.C.C.R. 182 .... 9.83; 14.11
——— v. Fallan, 1996 S.L.T. 314; 1996 S.C.C.R. 80 .... 2.64
——— v. Fletcher (1846) Ark. 171 .... 8.38
——— v. Forbes, 1994 S.L.T. 861; 1994 S.C.C.R. 163 .... 1.05; 2.35; 3.20; 6.06; 9.17;
                                                                                                                    14.02; 14.05
——— v. Fraser and Rollins, 1920 J.C. 60; 1920 2 S.L.T. 77 .... 7.17; 9.46; 9.49
——— v. Gallacher, 1950, unreported; reported on another point, 1951 J.C. 38; 1951
       S.L.T. 158 .... 7.18
——— v. Gilmour, 1938 J.C. 1; 1938 S.L.T. 72 .... 9.64
——— v. Harris, 1993 J.C. 150; 1993 S.L.T. 963; 1993 S.C.C.R. 559 .... 2.31; 3.23; 3.27;
                                                                                                9.07; 9.12; 9.14; 9.24; 9.27; 9.28
——— v. Hartley, 1989 S.L.T. 135 .... 9.48
——— v. Hayes, 1949, unreported 4.41
——— v. Hayes, 1973 S.L.T. 202 .... 9.91
——— v. Hill, 1941 J.C. 59; 1941 S.L.T. 401 .... 9.64
——— v. Innes (1914) 7 Adam 596; 1915 S.C.(J.) 40; 1915 1 S.L.T. 105 .... 6.18
——— v. Johnstone and Stewart, 1926 J.C. 89; 1926 S.L.T. 428 .... 7.15
——— v. Kay, 1970 S.L.T.(Notes) 66 .... 8.38
——— v. Kennedy (1907) 5 Adam 347 .... 9.43

—— v. Kerr (1871) 2 Coup. 334 .... 7.20
—— v. Kidd, 1960 J.C. 61; 1960 S.L.T. 82 .... 8.17; 9.48
—— v. Laing (1871) 2 Coup. 23 .... 8.09
—— v. Lee, 1996 S.L.T. 568 .... 2.64
—— v. Logan, 1936 J.C. 100; 1937 S.L.T. 104 .... 9.81
—— v. McAllister, 1996 S.L.T. 220; 1995 S.C.C.R. 545 .... 2.64; 10.71
—— v. McCallum (1977) S.C.C.R. Supp. 169 .... 8.79; 8.86
—— v. McDonald (1890) 2 White 517 .... 8.72–8.74
—— v. McGinlay, 1983 S.L.T. 562 .... 9.55
—— v. McGlone, 1955 J.C. 14; 1955 S.L.T. 79 .... 8.19
—— v. McGuinness, 1937 J.C. 37; 1937 S.L.T. 274 .... 9.49
—— v. McKean, 1996 S.C.C.R. 402 .... 9.64
—— v. McKenzie, 1990 J.C. 62; 1990 S.L.T. 28; 1989 S.C.C.R. 587 ...... 1.16
—— v. Mackenzie (1913) 7 Adam 189; (1913) S.C. (J.) 107; 1913 S.L.T. 48 .... 3.03;
                                                              6.14; 10.08; 10.25; 10.26
—— v. McPhee, 1935 J.C. 46; 1935 S.L.T. 179 .... 3.11; 9.43
—— v. ——, 1994 S.L.T. 1292; 1994 S.C.C.R. 830 .... 2.64
—— v. Mannion, 1961 J.C. 79 .... 12.36
—— v. Manson (1893) 1 Adam 114 .... 9.43
—— v. Martin, 1956 J.C. 1; 1956 S.L.T. 193 .... 2.35; 12.36
—— v. May, 1995 S.L.T. 753; 1995 S.C.C.R. 375 .... 2.64
—— v. Mitchell, 1951 J.C. 53; 1951 S.L.T. 200 .... 4.40
—— v. Murray, 1969 S.L.T.(Notes) 85 .... 4.31; 8.06
—— v. O'Donnell, 1996 S.L.T. 563; 1995 S.C.C.R. 745 .... 2.64; 9.17
—— v. O'Neill, 1992 J.C. 22; 1992 S.L.T. 303; 1992 S.C.C.R. 130 .... 2.56
—— v. Paxton, 1984 J.C. 105; 1985 S.L.T. 96; 1984 S.C.C.R. 311 .... 9.83; 14.11
—— v. Pearson (1967) S.C.C.R. Supp. 20 .... 8.42
—— v. Peters (1969) 33 J.C.L. 209 .... 8.87
—— v. Phipps (1905) 4 Adam 616 .... 3.27; 9.12.9.14
—— v. R. K., 1994 S.C.C.R. 499 .... 12.28; 14.01
—— v. Raiker, 1989 S.C.C.R. 149 .... 4.16; 8.76; 8.82
—— v. Ritchie, 1926 J.C. 45; 1926 S.L.T. 308 .... 4.19; 4.30
—— v. Robertson (1896) 2 Adam 92; (1896) 3 S.L.T. 264 .... 7.22
—— v. Robertson and Donoghue, 1945, unreported 8.33
—— v. Rutherford, 1947 J.C. 1; 1947 S.L.T. 3 .... 9.51
—— v. Savage, 1923 J.C. 49; 1923 S.L.T. 659 .... 9.23; 9.69
—— v. Semple, 1937 J.C. 41; 1937 S.L.T. 48 .... 2.27; 2.28; 6.29
—— v. Sherman, 1990, unreported 9.41
—— v. Stevenson, July 5, 1985, Appeal Court, unreported (referred to in Jamieson v.
        H.M. Advocate, 1994 S.L.T. 537; 1994 S.C.C.R. 181) 9.82
—— v. Tannahill and Neilson, 1943 J.C. 150; 1944 S.L.T. 118 .... 6.14; 7.62
—— v. Welsh and McLachlan (1897) 5 S.L.T. 137 .... 7.22; 7.23; 7.25; 7.26
—— v. Wilson, 1984 S.L.T. 117; 1983 S.C.C.R. 420 .... 11.08; 11.10; 11.13; 11.14;
                                                              11.19–11.23; 14.02
—— v. Wilson, Latta and Rooney, 1968, unreported 3.24; 7.47; 7.51; 7.54; 7.57
—— v. Wishart (1975) S.C.C.R. Supp. 78 .... 10.43; 10.75; 10.76
—— v. Wood (1903) 4 Adam 150 .... 9.59
—— v. Woods, 1972 S.L.T.(Notes) 77 .... 8.43
Advocate, Lord, v. University of Aberdeen and Budge, 1963 S.C. 533; 1963 S.L.T.
        361 .... 10.13
Advocate's Reference, Lord (No. 1 of 1985), 1986 J.C. 137; 1987 S.L.T. 187; 1986
        S.C.C.R. 329 .... 2.40; 12.35
Advocate's Reference, Lord (No. 2 of 1992), 1993 J.C. 43; 1993 S.L.T. 460; 1992
        S.C.C.R. 960 .... 3.17; 3.20; 3.23; 9.04; 9.07; 9.08; 9.12; 9.14;
                                                              9.15; 9.91

Advocate's Reference, Lord (No. 1 of 1994), 1995 S.L.T. 248; 1995 S.C.C.R.
 177 .... 5.16; 5.20; 9.32; 9.56
Ahmed *v.* MacDonald, 1995 S.L.T. 1094; 1994 S.C.C.R. 320 .... 2.50
Aird, William (1693) Hume i, 248 .... 9.65
Aitken *v.* Wood, 1921 J.C. 84; 1921 2 S.L.T. 124 .... 9.06
Alexander *v.* Smith, 1984 S.L.T. 176 .... 12.16
Allan, Petr., 1993 J.C. 181; 1994 S.L.T. 229; 1993 S.C.C.R. 686 .... 2.68
Allan *v.* Patterson, 1980 J.C. 57; 1980 S.L.T. 77 .... 3.29; 9.58; 11.26; 11.42; 13.02
Allenby *v.* H.M. Advocate, 1938 J.C. 55; 1938 S.L.T. 150 .... 3.27; 10.43
Alphacell Ltd *v.* Woodward [1972] A.C. 824; [1972] 2 W.L.R. 1320 .... 13.13; 13.19
Alston, Peter, and Forrest, John (1837) 1 Swin. 433 .... 10.30; 10.32
Ames *v.* MacLeod, 1969 J.C. 1 .... 4.04; 13.03
Anderson, Elizabeth (1858) 3 Irv. 65 .... 10.06
———, Paul, and Bannatyne (1791) Hume i, 105 .... 10.47
———, Robert (1832) Bell's Notes 73 .... 9.33
Anderson *v.* Allan, 1985 S.C.C.R. 399 .... 12.20
——— *v.* H.M. Advocate, 1974 S.L.T. 239 .... 2.68
——— *v.* ———, 1996 S.L.T. 155; 1996 S.C.C.R. 114 .... 2.18
——— *v.* Rose, 1919 J.C. 87; 2 S.L.T. 86 .... 13.16
Angus *v.* H.M. Advocate (1905) 4 Adam 640; 13 S.L.T. 507; 8 F.(J.) 10 .... 11.29; 11.38
Armitage, George (1885) 5 Coup. 675 .... 9.59
Arthur, John (1836) 1 Swin. 124 .... 11.32
Atkins *v.* London Weekend Television Ltd, 1978 J.C. 48; 1978 S.L.T. 76 .... 9.06
Atkinson *v.* H.M. Advocate, 1987 S.C.C.R. 534 .... 9.08
Attorney-General's Reference (No. 6 of 1980) [1981] Q.B. 715; [1981] 3 W.L.R.
 125; 73 Cr.App.Rep.63 .... 9.18
Attorney-General's Reference (No. 2 of 1992) [1994] Q.B. 91; [1993] 3 W.L.R. 982;
 [1993] 4 All E.R. 683; (1993) 99 Cr.App.Rep. 429; [1993] R.T.R. 337 (C.A.) . 4.21

BALLANTYNE, JOHN (1859) 3 Irv. 352 .... 2.23; 2.27; 2.28
Bannatyne, Alexander (1847) Ark. 361 .... 10.75
Barbour *v.* H.M. Advocate, 1982 S.C.C.R. 195 .... 9.75; 9.78; 10.09
Baron Meats Ltd *v.* Lockhart, 1991 J.C. 129; 1993 S.L.T. 279; 1991 S.C.C.R. 537 ... 2.17
Barr, Archibald (1834) Bell's Notes 47 .... 11.11
——— John (1839) 2 Swin. 282 .... 2.27–2.29; 2.32
——— *v.* H.M. Advocate, 1927 J.C. 51; 1927 S.L.T. 412 .... 10.83
——— *v.* O'Brien, 1991 S.C.C.R. 67 .... 3.26; 10.19
Barrett *v.* Allan, 1986 S.C.C.R. 479 .... 6.20; 6.21
Bassi *v.* Normand, 1992 S.L.T. 341; 1992 S.C.C.R. 413 .... 2.60
Batty *v.* H.M. Advocate, 1995 S.L.T. 1047; 1995 S.C.C.R. 525 .... 9.20
Beattie, John M., 1990 S.C.C.R. 435 .... 13.02
Beattie *v.* Waugh, 1920 J.C. 64; 1920 2 S.L.T. 23 .... 13.19; 13.21
Bell, John and Elizabeth (1736) Hume i, 114 .... 10.54
Bellie, Thomas (1600) Hume i, 124 .... 11.13
Bennett *v.* Houston, 1993 S.L.T. 1182 .... 10.71
Berry *v.* H.M. Advocate (1976) S.C.C.R. Supp. 156 .... 9.52; 9.65
Bird *v.* H.M. Advocate, 1952 J.C. 23; 1952 S.L.T. 446 .... 5.10; 9.55
Black *v.* Allan, 1985 S.C.C.R. 11 .... 3.29; 11.26
——— *v.* Carmichael; Carmichael *v.* Black, 1992 S.L.T. 897; 1992 S.C.C.R. 709 .... 9.93;
 9.94; 10.02; 10.06
——— *v.* Laing (1879) 4 Coup. 276 .... 11.13; 11.17
——— *v.* H.M. Advocate, 1974 J.C. 43; 1974 S.L.T. 247 .... 13.17
Blair, Daniel (1868) 1 Coup. 168 .... 12.02
———, James (1810) Bell's Notes 43 .... 10.50
Blane *v.* H.M. Advocate, 1991 S.C.C.R. 576 .... 3.18; 3.27; 11.35; 11.38

Bonar and Hogg v. Macleod, 1983 S.C.C.R. 161 .... 7.21; 9.06
Boner v. United Kingdom; Maxwell v. United Kingdom, 1995 S.C.C.R. 1 .... 2.18
Bowers v. Tudhope, 1987 J.C. 26; 1987 S.L.T. 748; 1987 S.C.C.R. 77 .... 12.38
Boyle v. H.M. Advocate, 1993 S.L.T. 577; 1992 S.C.C.R. 824 .... 8.34; 9.14; 12.08
Boyne v. H.M. Advocate, 1980 S.L.T. 56; reported on another point, 1980 J.C. 47 ... 7.26
Bradbury, William (1872) 2 Coup. 311 .... 10.78
Bradford v. McLeod, 1986 S.L.T. 244; 1985 S.C.C.R. 379 .... 2.60
Brady v. H.M. Advocate, 1986 J.C. 68; 1986 S.L.T. 686; 1986 S.C.C.R. 191 .. 6.10; 8.38; 9.66
Braithwaite v. H.M. Advocate, 1945 J.C. 55; 1945 S.L.T. 209 .... 9.68
Bratty v. Attorney-General for Northern Ireland [1963] A.C. 386; [1961] 3 W.L.R.
  965; 46 Cr.App.Rep. 1 .... 4.01; 4.10; 4.11; 4.34
Brennan v. H.M. Advocate, 1977 J.C. 38; 1977 S.L.T. 125 .... 4.18; 4.20; 4.22; 4.25;
                                                              8.13; 8.16; 8.66–8.70; 8.72; 8.74; 9.23; 9.46; 9.48; 9.68
Broadley v. H.M. Advocate, 1991 J.C. 108; 1991 S.L.T. 218; 1991 S.C.C.R. 416 ..... 9.49
Brodie, James (1842) 1 Broun 341 .... 10.50
Brown, George (1839) 2 Swin. 394 .... 10.06
——, Lachlan (1842) 1 Broun 230 .... 9.06
——, or Graham, Mysie or Marion (1827) Syme 152 .... 9.17
——, Robert, and Lowson, John (1842) 1 Broun 415 .... 9.29
Brown v. Burns Tractors Ltd, 1986 S.C.C.R. 146 .... 13.17
—— v. H.M. Advocate, 1993 S.C.C.R. 382 .... 7.26
—— v. Hilson, 1924 J.C. 1; 1924 S.L.T. 35 .... 9.07
Bryson v. H.M. Advocate, 1961 S.L.T. 289 .... 9.08
Buchanan, David (1817) Hume, i, 192 n.2 .... 9.58
——, Walter (1728) Hume i, 133 .... 11.33
Buchanan v. Hamilton, 1990 S.L.T. 244; 1989 S.C.C.R. 398 .... 12.11; 13.07
Buchmann v. Normand, 1994 S.C.C.R. 929 .... 3.09; 10.72
Burns, Robert (1855) 2 Irv. 65 .... 9.41
Burns v. Allan, 1987 S.C.C.R. 449 .... 6.06; 6.14; 6.20; 10.35
—— v. H.M. Advocate, 1995 S.L.T. 1090; 1995 S.C.C.R. 532 .... 8.34
Bush v. Commonwealth, 78 Ky. 268 (1880) 5.21
Butcher v. Jessop, 1989 J.C. 55; 1989 S.L.T. 593; 1989 S.C.C.R. 119 .... 12.16

C. v. H.M. Advocate, 1987 S.C.C.R. 104 .... 9.19; 9.76
Cafferata v. Wilson [1936] 3 All E.R. 149 .... 13.03
Cairns, James (1837) 1 Swin. 597 .... 9.05; 12.02
Cairns v. H.M. Advocate (1973) S.C.C.R. Supp. 44 .... 2.48
Cameron v. Normand, 1992 S.C.C.R. 866 .... 12.15
Campbell, Colin (1823) Alison i, 450 .... 11.13
——, J. (1819) Alison i, 147 .... 5.22
——, James (1824) Hume i, 107 .... 10.46
——, John (1836) 1 Swin. 309 .... 9.50
Capuano v. H.M. Advocate, 1985 S.L.T. 196; 1984 S.C.C.R. 415 .... 7.31
Cardle v. David Carlaw Engineering (Glasgow) Ltd, 1992 S.L.T. 1101; 1991 S.C.C.R.
  807 .... 2.17
—— v. Mulrainey, 1992 S.L.T. 1152; 1992 S.C.C.R. 658 .... 4.20; 4.21; 4.25; 8.16
—— v. Murray, 1993 S.L.T. 525; 1993 S.C.C.R. 170 .... 12.18
Carey v. Tudhope, 1984 S.C.C.R. 157 .... 12.16
Carmichael v. Boyle, 1985 S.L.T. 399; 1985 S.C.C.R. 58 .... 4.28; 4.29; 4.48
Carney v. H.M. Advocate, 1995 S.L.T. 1208 .... 3.26; 12.36
Carr v. H.M. Advocate, 1995 S.L.T. 800; 1994 S.C.C.R. 521 .... 3.25; 3.27; 3.29;
                                                              9.24; 11.28; 11.35; 11.42
Carraher v. H.M. Advocate, 1946 J.C. 108; 1946 S.L.T. 225 .... 9.68
Carrick v. H.M. Advocate, 1990 S.C.C.R. 286 .... 7.26
Carrington v. H.M. Advocate, 1994 S.C.C.R. 567 .... 4.26

Casey v. H.M. Advocate, 1993 J.C. 102; 1994 S.L.T. 54; 1993 S.C.C.R. 453 .... 9.41
Cassidy v. McLeod, 1981 S.C.C.R. 270 .... 10.60
Cavanagh v. Wilson, 1995 S.C.C.R. 693 .... 12.19
Cawthorne v. H.M. Advocate, 1969 J.C. 32; 1968 S.L.T. 330 .... 3.25; 4.05; 4.06; 6.10;
                     6.11; 9.43; 9.46; 9.48
Christie, James (1731) Hume i, 245 .... 9.64
City and Suburban Dairies v. Mackenna, 1918 J.C. 105; 1918 2 S.L.T. 155 .. 13.23; 13.24
Clark v. H.M. Advocate, 1965 S.L.T. 250 .... 10.63
—— v. ——, 1968 J.C. 53; 1969 S.L.T. 161 .... 4.45; 4.48; 8.06
—— v. Syme, 1957 J.C. 1; 1957 S.L.T. 32 .... 8.45; 8.49; 8.50; 11.13–11.16
Clerk, Thomas (1805) Hume i, 192 n.2 .... 9.58
Clements v. H.M. Advocate, 1991 J.C. 62: 1991 S.C.C.R. 266 .... 2.42
Coats, J. and P., v. Brown (1909) 6 Adam 19 .... 2.59
Codona v. Cardle, 1989 J.C. 99; 1989 S.L.T. 791; 1989 S.C.C.R. 287 .... 9.07
—— v. H.M. Advocate, 1996 S.C.C.R. 300 .... 7.26
Collins v. H.M. Advocate, 1991 S.C.C.R. 898 .... 6.27; 7.18; 8.87; 9.40
Commonwealth v. Wright, 455 Pa. 480 (1974) 5.17
Connachan v. Douglas, 1990 J.C. 244; 1990 S.L.T. 563; 1990 S.C.C.R. 101 .... 2.43
Connelly v. H.M. Advocate, 1990 J.C. 349; 1991 S.L.T. 397; 1990 S.C.C.R. 504 ..... 9.23;
                                9.69
Cook, Margaret (1897) 2 Adam 471 .... 10.53
Cosgrove v. H.M. Advocate, 1990 J.C. 333; 1991 S.L.T. 25; 1990 S.C.C.R. 358 ...... 9.63;
                                9.65
Costello, Charles (1882) 4 Coup. 602 .... 9.11
Courtney, Rendal (1747) Hume i, 99 .... 10.33
Coventry v. Douglas, 1944 J.C. 13 .... 6.06; 6.08; 6.20; 6.21
Craigie v. H.M. Advocate, 1989 S.L.T. 631; 1989 S.C.C.R. 196 .... 10.57; 10.60
Crawford v. H.M. Advocate, 1950 J.C. 67; 1950 S.L.T. 279 .... 8.31; 9.62
Crofter Hand Woven Harris Tweed Co. Ltd v. Veitch, 1942 S.C. (H.L.) 1; 1943
  S.L.T. 2 .... 7.39
Crossgrove or Bradley, Catherine (1850) J. Shaw 301 .... 10.11; 10.42
Crowe v. H.M. Advocate, 1990 J.C. 112; 1990 S.L.T. 670; 1989 S.C.C.R. 681 .... 3.29
Crown v. Devin and Polin (1829) 5 Deas and Anderson 145 .... 10.32
Cunliffe v. Goodman [1950] 2 K.B. 237; [1950] 1 All E.R. 750 .... 3.24

Davidson v. Brown, 1990 J.C. 324; 1991 S.L.T. 335; 1990 S.C.C.R. 304 .... 10.57
Davies v. Smith, 1983 S.L.T. 644; 1983 S.C.C.R. 232 .... 13.03
Dean v. John Menzies (Holdings) Ltd, 1981 J.C. 23; 1981 S.L.T. 50 .... 2.49; 12.24; 13.24
Derrett v. Lockhart, 1991 S.C.C.R. 109 .... 12.15; 12.16; 12.19
Dewar, John (1777) Burnett 115 .... 10.08; 10.32
Dewar v. H.M. Advocate, 1945 J.C. 5; 1945 S.L.T. 114 .... 8.52; 8.53; 8.57; 8.60;
                         10.13; 10.16; 10.17
Dick v. Walkingshaw, 1995 S.L.T. 1254; 1995 S.C.C.R. 307 .... 13.02
Dickson v. Linton (1888) 2 White 51; 15 R. (J.) 76 .... 13.19; 13.21
Dingwall, Alexander (1867) 5 Irv. 466 .... 9.23; 9.67
Director of Public Prosecutions v. Majewski [1977] A.C. 443; [1976] 2 W.L.R.
  623; 62 Cr.App.Rep. 262 .... 8.65
—— v. Morgan [1976] A.C. 182; [1975] 2 W.L.R. 913; [1975] 2 All E.R. 347; 61
  Cr.App.Rep. 136 .... 9.82
Director of Public Prosecutions for Northern Ireland v. Lynch [1975] A.C. 653;
  [1975] N.I. 35; [1975] 2 W.L.R. 641; 61 Cr.App.Rep. 6 .... 14.04
Dobbs and Macdonald v. Neilson (1899) 3 Adam 10 .... 9.07
Docherty, Francis (1841) 2 Swin. 635 .... 12.06
Docherty v. Brown, 1996 S.L.T. 325; 1996 S.C.C.R. 136 .... 6.24; 6.27; 6.29; 6.31
—— v. H.M. Advocate, 1945 J.C. 89; 1945 S.L.T. 247 .... 7.05; 7.22; 7.26

—— v. Stakis Hotels Ltd; Stakis Hotels Ltd v. Docherty, 1991 S.C.C.R. 6 .... 13.26
Donnelly v. Carmichael, 1996 S.L.T. 153; 1995 S.C.C.R. 737 .... 2.14
Dougal v. Dykes (1860) 4 Irv. 101; 34 J. 29 .... 12.16
Douglas, Captain Charles (1697) Maclaurin's Cases 13 no. 12 .... 9.75
Downie v. H.M. Advocate, 1984 S.C.C.R. 365 .... 10.15
Drew v. H.M. Advocate, 1995 S.C.C.R. 647 .... 10.68
Druce v. Friel, 1994 S.L.T. 1209; 1994 S.C.C.R. 432 .... 10.59; 10.60
Drysdale, Margaret (1826) Alison i, 435 .... 11.33
Duguid v. Fraser, 1942 J.C. 1; 1942 S.L.T. 51 .... 13.24; 13.26
Duthie, Ann (1849) J. Shaw 227 .... 11.13

EBSWORTH v. H.M. Advocate, 1992 S.L.T. 1161; 1992 S.C.C.R. 671 .... 4.20; 4.26; 8.77
Edgar v. Mackay, 1926 J.C. 94; 1926 S.L.T. 446 .... 10.42–10.44
Edmiston, Elizabeth (1866) 5 Irv. 238 .... 9.91
Elliot v. Tudhope, 1987 S.C.C.R. 85 .... 9.02
Elliott v. H.M. Advocate, 1987 S.C.C.R. 278 .... 8.27
—— v. ——, 1995 S.L.T. 612; 1995 S.C.C.R. 280 .... 2.03
Eviot, Patrick (1614) Hume i, 80 .... 10.07
Ewart, Andrew (1828) Syme 315 .... 8.50; 9.50

FAGAN v. Metropolitan Police Commissioner [1969] 1 Q.B. 439; [1968] 3 W.L.R.
  1120; 52 Cr.App.Rep. 700 .... 3.34
Fairweather, William (1842) 1 Broun 309 .... 9.26
Falconer v. Jessop, 1975 S.L.T.(Notes) 78 .... 8.05
Farquhar, James (1861) 4 Irv. 28 .... 12.08
Farrell v. Normand, 1993 S.L.T. 793; 1992 S.C.C.R. 859 .... 12.14
—— v. Stirling, 1975 S.L.T.(Sh.Ct.) 7 .... 4.42
Fay, George (1847) Ark. 397 .... 3.09
Fay v. H.M. Advocate, 1989 J.C. 129; 1989 S.L.T. 758; 1989 S.C.C.R. 373 .... 2.63
Federal Steam Navigation Company Ltd v. Department of Trade & Industry, [1974]
  1 W.L.R. 505; [1974] 2 All E.R. 97; 59 Cr.App.Rep. 131 .... 13.03
Fegen, James (1838) 2 Swin. 25 .... 10.46
Fenning v. H.M. Advocate, 1985 J.C. 76; 1985 S.L.T. 540; 1985 S.C.C.R. 219 .... 8.25;
  9.21; 9.44; 9.60; 9.63
Ferguson, John, and Edie, John (1822) Hume i, 237 .... 9.27
Ferguson v. Carnochan (1889) 2 White 278; 16 R. (J.) 93 .... 12.15
Finlayson v. H.M. Advocate, 1979 J.C. 33; 1978 S.L.T.(Notes) 60 .... 5.25; 5.34; 9.36
Finnigan, Wm., 1958, unreported 9.57
Fitzpatrick v. H.M. Advocate, 1992 S.L.T. 796 .... 8.32
Flynn v. H.M. Advocate, 1995 S.L.T. 1267; 1995 S.C.C.R. 590 .... 10.46
Fontana, Ross, 1990, unreported 9.59
Forbes v. H.M. Advocate, 1995 S.L.T. 627 .... 10.57
—— v. Ross (1898) 2 Adam 513; 6 S.L.T. 12; 25 R. (J.) 60 .... 11.17
Fowler v. O'Brien, 1994 S.C.C.R. 112 .... 10.24
Fox v. Patterson, 1948 J.C. 104; 1948 S.L.T. 547 .... 10.60
Fraser, John (1759) Hume i, 439 .... 9.90
——, John (1831) Bell's Notes 41 .... 10.31
——, Simon (1859) 3 Irv. 467 .... 10.81
——, Simon (1878) 4 Coup. 70 .... 4.37–4.39; 4.41
——, William (1847) Ark. 280 and 329 .... 2.23; 2.29; 9.81; 9.84–9.86;
  10.65; 10.72; 10.76
——, Colin, and Gunn, Daniel (1827) Hume i, 98 .... 10.32
Fraser v. Anderson (1897) 2 Adam 705; 6 S.L.T. 390 .... 10.21
Frew v. Brown, 1996 S.L.T. 282 .... 2.60
Friel v. Docherty, 1990 S.C.C.R. 351 .... 10.56

Fulton *v.* Lees, 1993 S.L.T. 927; 1992 S.C.C.R. 923 .... 2.15
Fulton Jnr, Robert (1841) 2 Swin. 564 .... 9.75

GAMMON (HONG KONG) LTD *v.* Attorney-General For Hong Kong, [1985] A.C. 1;
    [1984] 3 W.L.R. 437; [1984] 2 All E.R. 503; 80 Cr.App.Rep. 194 .... 13.11;
                                                   13.16; 13.20
Gibbs, James (1836) 1 Swin. 263 .... 9.17
Gibson, Rachel (1845) 2 Broun 366 .... 9.26
——, William (1842) 1 Broun 485 .... 12.02
Gill *v.* Lockhart, 1988 S.L.T. 189; 1987 S.C.C.R. 599 .... 13.17
Gilmour, Christian (1844) 2 Broun 23 .... 9.43
Gilmour *v.* McGlennan, 1993 S.C.C.R. 837 .... 6.07; 9.08; 9.09
Girdwood *v.* Houston, 1989 S.C.C.R. 578 .... 10.57; 10.63
Gizzi *v.* Tudhope, 1983 S.L.T. 214; 1982 S.C.C.R. 442 .... 3.30; 9.33
Glass of Sauchie *v.* Monro of Auchinbowie (1712) Hume i, 122 .... 11.09
Gollon, Alexander, or Gollan (1883) 5 Coup. 317 .... 12.04
Gordon or Bryan, Jean, (1841) 2 Swin. 545 .... 11.36
Gordon *v.* Shaw (1908) 5 Adam 469; 1908 S.C. (J.) 17; 15 S.L.T. 792 .... 13.13–13.15;
                                                  13.19; 13.21
Graham, Mathew (1813) Hume i, 192 n.2 .... 9.58
——, Minnie (1897) 2 Adam 412 .... 9.35
Graham *v.* Annan, 1980 S.L.T. 28 .... 8.06
—— *v.* H.M. Advocate, 1987 S.C.C.R. 20 .... 9.60; 9.62
Grant, Laird and Lady (1712) Hume i, 135 .... 9.90
——, Mungo (1712) Hume i, 122 .... 11.09
Grant *v.* Allan, 1987 J.C. 71; 1988 S.L.T. 11; 1987 S.C.C.R. 402 ... 1.05; 2.22; 2.27; 2.35;
                                      10.08; 10.38; 10.61; 14.02; 14.05
Grassom, Archibald (1884) 5 Coup. 483 .... 9.27
Gray, James (1737) Hume i, 441 .... 9.90
Gray *v.* Criminal Injuries Compensation Board, 1993 S.L.T. 28; 1992 S.C.L.R. 777 .. 9.19; 9.84
—— *v.* H.M. Advocate, 1994 S.L.T. 1237; 1994 S.C.C.R. 225 .... 7.24
—— *v.* Hawthorn, 1964 J.C. 69; 1964 S.L.T. 252 .... 9.07
—— *v.* Morrison, 1954 J.C. 31 .... 12.38
Greenhuff, Bernard (1838) 2 Swin. 236 .... 2.22; 2.23; 2.27; 2.29; 2.30; 12.36
Grieve, Peter (1866) 5 Irv. 263 .... 11.32
Guest *v.* Annan, 1988 S.C.C.R. 275 .... 9.07
Guthrie *v.* Friel, 1993 S.L.T. 899; 1992 S.C.C.R. 932 .... 6.12; 6.15; 6.18; 13.02

HAIG *v.* Thompson, 1931 J.C. 29; 1931 S.L.T. 557 .... 13.24
Hall, John (1881) 4 Coup. 438; 8 R. (J.) 28 .... 10.69
——, Robert (1837) 1 Swin. 420 .... 11.13
Hamilton, Elizabeth (1857) 2 Irv. 738 .... 9.56
Hamilton *v.* Mooney, 1990 S.L.T.(Sh.Ct.) 105 .... 10.15
—— *v.* Wilson, 1994 S.L.T. 431; 1993 S.C.C.R. 9 .... 10.15
Hancock *v.* H.M. Advocate, 1981 J.C. 74; 1981 S.C.C.R. 32 ... 12.02; 12.03; 12.06; 12.08
Hardie, Ensign (1701) Hume i, 244 n.2 .... 9.63
——, William (1847) Ark. 247 .... 3.10
Harding *v.* Price [1948] 1 K.B. 695; [1948] 1 All E.R. 283 .... 4.05
Harkin *v.* H.M. Advocate, 1992 S.L.T. 785; 1992 S.C.C.R. 501 .... 2.63
Harrison *v.* Jessop, 1992 S.L.T. 465; 1991 S.C.C.R. 329 .... 10.49
Hart, Michael, and Ors. (1854) 1 Irv. 574 .... 7.19
Haughton *v.* Smith [1975] A.C. 476; [1974] 2 W.L.R. 1; 58 Cr.App.Rep. 198 .... 6.32
Hendry *v.* H.M. Advocate, 1987 J.C. 63; 1988 S.L.T. 25; 1987 S.C.C.R. 394 .... 5.04
Henrie, Johne (1615) Pitcairn's Criminal Trials, III, p. 361 .... 11.28
Herkes *v.* Dickie, 1958 J.C. 51; 1959 S.L.T. 74 .... 2.14

Herron *v.* Best, 1976 S.L.T.(Sh.Ct.) 80 .... 10.22
—— *v.* Diack and Newlands, 1973 S.L.T.(Sh.Ct.) 27 .... 10.16
Heywood *v.* Reid, 1996 S.L.T. 378; 1995 S.C.C.R. 741 .... 6.06; 10.35
Hill *v.* McGrogan, 1945 S.L.T.(Sh.Ct.) 18 .... 9.94
Hinchy, Michael (1864) 4 Irv. 561 .... 10.79; 10.82
Hogg *v.* H.M. Advocate, 1954 S.L.T.(Notes) 52 .... 9.92
—— *v.* MacPherson, 1928 J.C. 15; 1928 S.L.T. 35 .... 3.04; 4.15
—— *v.* Normand, 1992 S.L.T. 736; 1992 S.C.C.R. 26 .... 2.60; 9.20
Hood *v.* Young (1853) 1 Irv. 236 .... 10.71; 10.76
Horne, John (1814) Hume i, 150 .... 10.82
Horsburgh *v.* Russell, 1994 S.L.T. 942; 1994 S.C.C.R. 237 .... 2.18; 2.53; 13.07
Howman *v.* Russell, 1923 J.C., 32; 1923 S.L.T. 336 .... 13.13; 13.19; 13.21
Hughes *v.* Crowe, 1993 S.C.C.R. 320 .... 3.26; 12.18
Humphries *v.* H.M. Advocate, 1994 S.C.C.R. 205 .... 7.22
Hunter, John (1801) Hume i, 99 .... 10.33
Hussain *v.* Houston, 1995 S.L.T. 1060 .... 9.19
Hyam *v.* Director of Public Prosecutions [1975] A.C. 55; [1974] 2 W.L.R. 607; 59
    Cr.App.Rep. 91 .... 3.23; 9.46

INGLIS, HENRY, AND COLVILLES, ANDREW AND ROBERT (1784) Hume i, 237 .... 9.29
Ingram *v.* Macari, 1982 J.C. 1; 1982 S.L.T. 92; 1981 S.C.C.R. 184 .... 12.24
—— *v.* ——, 1983 J.C. 1; 1983 S.L.T. 61; 1982 S.C.C.R. 372 .... 12.24
Innes, Thomas, and Blair, Ann (1834) Bell's Notes 42 .... 10.45
Irvine, Margaret (1784) Burnett 133 .... 2.23
Irving, John (1833) Bell's Notes 88 .... 9.08
Ivers *v.* Normand, 1994 S.L.T. 317 .... 10.28

JAMIESON *v.* Guild, 1989 S.C.C.R. 583 .... 7.20
—— *v.* H.M. Advocate, 1987 S.C.C.R. 484 .... 3.18
—— *v.* ——, 1994 J.C. 88; 1994 S.L.T. 537; 1994 S.C.C.R. 181 ... 2.08; 8.58; 8.60; 8.61;
    9.19; 9.73; 9.76; 9.82; 10.20
Jeffreu, George (1840) 2 Swin. 479 .... 9.93
——, William (1842) 1 Broun 337 .... 10.82
Jessop *v.* Johnstone, 1991 S.C.C.R. 238 .... 4.07; 4.15
—— *v.* Stevenson, 1988 J.C. 17; 1988 S.L.T. 223; 1987 S.C.C.R. 655 .... 2.03; 2.23
Johnstone *v.* Lees, 1995 S.L.T. 1174; 1994 S.C.C.R. 687 .... 6.08; 12.36
—— *v.* Lindsay (1906) 5 Adam 192; 1907 S.C. (J.) 9; 14 S.L.T. 429 .... 12.11
Jones *v.* H.M. Advocate, 1990 J.C. 160; 1990 S.L.T. 517; 1989 S.C.C.R. 726 ... 8.30; 8.61
Joss, James (1821) J. Shaw 29 .... 10.29

KAUR *v.* Lord Advocate, 1980 S.C. 319; 1981 S.L.T. 322; [1980] 3 C.M.L.R. 79 ...... 2.18
Kay *v.* Allan (1978) S.C.C.R. (Supp.) 188 .... 9.10
Keay, David (1837) 1 Swin. 543 .... 9.10; 9.16; 9.56
Keith, William (1875) 3 Coup. 125 .... 10.41
Kelly, Thomas (1837) Bell's Notes 44 .... 10.48
Kelly *v.* MacKinnon, 1982 J.C. 94; 1983 S.L.T. 9; 1982 S.C.C.R. 205 .... 13.03
Kennedy *v.* A., 1993 S.L.T. 1134 .... 9.07
—— *v.* H.M. Advocate, 1944 J.C. 171; 1945 S.L.T. 11 .... 9.48
—— *v.* Young (1854) 1 Irv. 533 .... 9.03; 9.05
Kent *v.* H.M. Advocate, 1950 J.C. 38; 1950 S.L.T. 130 .... 10.40
Kepple *v.* H.M. Advocate, 1936 S.L.T. 294 .... 9.06
Kerr, Elizabeth (1860) 3 Irv. 645 .... 9.43
Kerr (D.A.) *v.* H.M. Advocate, 1986 J.C. 41; 1986 S.C.C.R. 81 .... 2.42
—— (Stephen) *v.* H.M. Advocate, 1986 S.C.C.R. 91 .... 9.17
—— *v.* Hill, 1936 J.C. 71; 1936 S.L.T. 320 .... 2.28; 12.38

Khalid *v.* H.M. Advocate, 1990 J.C. 37 .... 7.04; 7.08; 9.31
Khaliq *v.* H.M. Advocate, 1984 J.C. 23; 1984 S.L.T. 137; 1983 S.C.C.R. 483 .. 2.05; 2.23;
                   2.28; 2.35; 2.53; 5.20; 9.24; 9.30–9.32; 14.02; 14.11
Kidston *v.* Annan, 1984 S.L.T. 279; 1984 S.C.C.R. 20 .... 10.27
Kiely *v.* H.M. Advocate, 1988 S.C.C.R. 120 .... 7.26
—— *v.* Lunn, 1983 J.C. 4; 1983 S.L.T. 207; 1982 S.C.C.R. 436 .... 13.04
Kilpatrick *v.* H.M. Advocate, 1992 J.C. 120 .... 12.02; 12.06
Kimmins *v.* Normand, 1993 S.L.T. 1260; 1993 S.C.C.R. 476 .... 3.06; 9.27
Kippen, George (1849) J. Shaw 276 .... 10.71; 10.76
Kirkwood *v.* H.M. Advocate, 1939 J.C. 36; 1939 S.L.T. 209 .... 9.17
Kivlin *v.* Milne, 1979 S.L.T.(Notes) 2 .... 10.24
Knight *v.* The Queen (1992) 175 C.L.R. 496 .... 6.09
Kokkinakis *v.* Greece (1994) 17 E.H.R.R. 397 .... 14.09

L. *v.* Wilson, 1995 S.L.T. 673; 1995 S.C.C.R. 71 .... 10.49
Lafferty *v.* Wilson, 1990 S.C.C.R. 30 .... 10.32
Laird *v.* H.M. Advocate, 1985 J.C. 37; 1985 S.L.T. 298; 1984 S.C.C.R. 469 .... 10.78
Lambert *v.* H.M. Advocate, 1993 S.L.T. 339 .... 9.26
Lamont *v.* Strathern, 1933 J.C. 33; 1933 S.L.T. 118 .... 6.28; 6.29
Lane, Edward (1830) Bell's Notes 77 .... 9.39
Latta *v.* Herron (1967) S.C.C.R. Supp. 18 .... 10.55–10.57
Lawler *v.* Neizer, 1993 S.C.C.R. 299 .... 7.20
Lawrence, John (1872) 2 Coup. 168 .... 10.40
Lawson, Alexander (1829) Bell's Notes 76 .... 9.27
Lees *v.* Haig, 1993 S.L.T. (Sh.Ct.) 76 .... 13.10
Lennon *v.* H.M. Advocate, 1991 S.C.C.R. 611 .... 9.22
Leper, John (1682) Hume i, 194 .... 9.38
Lewis *v.* Commonwealth, 19 Ky. L. Rep. 1139 (1897) 5.28
Leys, Peter (1839) 2 Swin. 337 .... 9.17
Little *v.* H.M. Advocate, 1983 J.C. 16; 1983 S.L.T. 489; 1983 S.C.C.R. 56 .... 7.14
Lochrie *v.* Jessop, 1992 S.L.T. 557 .... 12.19
Lockhart, Alexander (1746) Hume i, 336 .... 9.22
Lockhart *v.* National Coal Board, 1981 S.L.T. 161; 1981 S.C.C.R. 9 .... 13.13; 13.14;
                   13.16; 13.17
—— *v.* Stephen, 1987 S.C.C.R. 642 (Sh.Ct.) 12.26
Logan *v.* Jessop, 1987 S.C.C.R. 604 .... 12.19
Lourie *v.* H.M. Advocate, 1988 S.C.C.R. 634 .... 5.05; 9.57
Low *v.* H.M. Advocate, 1994 S.L.T. 277; 1994 S.C.C.R. 493 .... 7.31; 9.63
Lundie, Hugh (1754) Hume i, 107 .... 10.49

M. *v.* H.M. Advocate (1980) S.C.C.R. Supp. 250 .... 9.02
McArthur *v.* Valentine, 1990 S.L.T. 732; 1989 S.C.C.R. 704 .... 4.04; 13.03
McBain *v.* Crichton, 1961 J.C. 25; 1961 S.L.T. 209 .... 2.59
MacBean, George (1847) Ark. 262 .... 11.42
McCabe, John (1838) 2 Swin. 20 .... 12.10
McCallum, John, and Corner, William (1853) 1 Irv. 259 .... 9.50; 9.55
McCawley *v.* H.M. Advocate (1959) S.C.C.R. Supp. 3 .... 10.61
McCluskey *v.* H.M. Advocate, 1959 J.C. 39; 1959 S.L.T. 215 .... 8.26; 8.27; 8.39
—— *v.* ——, 1988 S.C.C.R. 629 .... 9.34
MacCormack *v.* H.M. Advocate, 1993 J.C. 170; 1993 S.L.T. 1158; 1993 S.C.C.R.
    581 .... 9.63; 9.64
MacDermid *v.* H.M. Advocate, 1948 J.C. 12; 1948 S.L.T. 202 .... 2.62
McDermott *v.* H.M. Advocate, 1973 J.C. 8; 1974 S.L.T. 206 .... 9.55
McDonald, Charles (1867) 5 Irv. 525 .... 9.43
——, Margaret (1876) 3 Coup. 271 .... 9.91

MacDonald, Marion (1879) 4 Coup. 268 .... 9.92
MacDonald *v.* Cardle, 1985 S.C.C.R. 195 .... 3.26; 12.25
McDonald *v.* H.M. Advocate, 1989 S.C.C.R. 559 .... 10.58
MacDonald *v.* H.M. Advocate, 1996 S.L.T. 723 .... 2.63; 10.66
—— *v.* Howdle, 1995 S.L.T. 779; 1995 S.C.C.R. 216 .... 13.17
McDonald *v.* Mackay (1842) 1 Broun 435 .... 11.17
—— *v.* Smellie (1903) 5 F. 955 .... 5.09
MacDougall *v.* Dochree, 1992 J.C. 154; 1992 S.L.T. 624; 1992 S.C.C.R. 531 .... 12.12;
                                                                    12.15; 12.16; 12.18
—— *v.* Yuk-Sun Ho, 1985 S.C.C.R. 199 .... 11.27
McElhinney *v.* Normand, 1996 S.L.T. 238; 1996 S.C.C.R. 86 .... 12.36
McEwan, Charles (1824) Hume i, 331 .... 9.06
McEwen, James (1838) Bell's Notes 91 .... 9.22
MacGibbon, Finlay (1669) Hume i, 79 .... 10.29
McGlennan *v.* Clark, 1993 S.L.T. 1069; 1993 S.C.C.R. 334 .... 13.10
MacGregor, Thomas, and Inglis, George (1846) Ark. 49 .... 10.71; 10.78
McGregor *v.* H.M. Advocate (1973) S.C.C.R. Supp. 54 .... 4.26; 6.10; 8.41; 8.75
McGuire *v.* H.M. Advocate, 1996 S.L.T. 566; 1995 S.C.C.R. 776 .... 9.41; 9.42
McIntosh *v.* H.M. Advocate, 1994 S.L.T. 59; 1993 S.C.C.R. 464 .... 3.18
Maciver and Macallum (1784) Hume i, 176 .... 10.71
McIver *v.* H.M. Advocate, 1991 S.L.T. 81 .... 8.56
McKay *v.* H.M. Advocate, 1991 J.C. 91; 1991 S.C.C.R. 364 .... 9.64
Mackay Brothers *v.* Gibb, 1969 J.C. 26; 1969 S.L.T. 216 .... 13.28
McKee *v.* MacDonald, 1995 S.L.T. 1342; 1995 S.C.C.R. 513 .... 13.10
McKellar *v.* Normand, 1992 S.C.C.R. 393 .... 10.57
McKenzie (1733), unreported (partial account at (1733) Burnett, 124) 10.16
McKenzie *v.* H.M. Advocate, 1988 S.L.T. 487; 1988 S.C.C.R. 153 .. 6.14; 6.15; 10.71; 10.76
—— *v.* ——, 1983 S.L.T. 220; 1982 S.C.C.R. 499 .... 8.40; 9.08
—— *v.* Maclean, 1981 S.L.T.(Sh.Ct.) 40 .... 10.13
—— *v.* Normand, 1992 S.L.T. 130; 1992 S.C.C.R 14 .... 12.14
—— *v.* Skeen, 1971 J.C. 43; 1972 S.L.T. 15 .... 10.77
McKenzie *v.* Whyte (1867) 4 Irv. 570 .... 12.25
McKew *v.* Holland and Hannen and Cubitts (Scotland) Ltd, 1970 S.C. (H.L.) 20;
   1970 S.L.T. 68 .... 5.27
MacKinnon *v.* Mackenzie, 1987 S.C.C.R. 473 .... 10.59
Mackirdy, John (1856) 2 Irv. 474 .... 11.28; 11.33
McLachlan, Petr., 1987 S.C.C.R. 195 .... 2.67
McLaughlan *v.* Boyd, 1934 J.C. 19; 1934 S.L.T. 629 .... 9.20
—— *v.* H.M. Advocate, 1991 S.L.T. 660; 1991 S.C.C.R. 733 .... 7.18
McLean, Alexander (1886) 1 White 232 .... 12.04
MacLean, John (1828) Bell's Notes 36 .... 10.32
McLean, John (1876) 3 Coup. 334 .... 4.45
McLean *v.* McNaughton, 1984 S.C.C.R. 319 .... 12.16
MacLennan *v.* Mackenzie, 1988 S.L.T. 16; 1987 S.C.C.R. 473 .... 10.57; 10.59; 10.60
McLeod *v.* H.M. Advocate, 1989 S.L.T. 298 .... 2.63
McLeod, John (1858) 3 Irv. 79 .... 10.37
McLeod, Petr. (1975) S.C.C.R. Supp. 93 .... 2.67
MacLeod *v.* MacDougall, 1989 S.L.T. 151; 1988 S.C.C.R. 519 .... 8.88
—— *v.* Mathieson, 1993 S.C.C.R. 488 .... 4.12; 4.20; 4.21; 4.27; 4.42
—— *v.* Napier, 1993 S.C.C.R. 303 .... 4.21; 4.25; 8.77
McManimy and Higgans (1847) Ark. 321 .... 9.26
Macmillan, Duncan (1833) Bell's Notes 82 .... 9.75
——, William, and Gordon, Spence (1829) Alison i, 231 .... 10.49
MacMillan *v.* Lowe, 1991 J.C. 13; 1991 S.C.C.R. 113 .... 10.05
McNab *v.* Guild, 1989 S.C.C.R. 138 .... 8.92

M'Naghten's Case, (1843) 10 C. & F. 200 .... 8.16
McNeil v. H.M. Advocate, 1968 J.C. 29; 1968 S.L.T. 338 .... 10.61; 10.63
MacNeil v. H.M. Advocate, 1986 J.C. 146; 1986 S.L.T. 244, *sub nom.* Socratous v.
    H.M. Advocate, 1986 S.C.C.R. 288 .... 7.37
MacNeil v. Wilson, 1981 J.C. 87; 1981 S.L.T.(Notes) 109; 1981 S.C.C.R. 80.. 13.13; 13.16
MacNeill v. McTaggart (1976) S.C.C.R. Supp. 150 .... 9.21
McNicol v. H.M. Advocate, 1964 J.C. 25; 1964 S.L.T. 151 ....'... 2.63
Macphail v. Clark, 1983 S.L.T. (Sh.Ct.) 37; 1982 S.C.C.R. 395 (Sh.Ct.) .. 3.12; 9.28: 9.30
MacPherson, Angus, and Stewart, John (1861) 4 Irv. 85 .... 9.59
MacPhie, Alexander (1823) Alison i, 512 .... 12.04
MacQueen, Charles, and Baillie, Alexander (1810) Hume i, 102 .... 10.35
McRae, John, or McCrae (1842) 1 Broun 395 .... 9.25; 9.26
Macra or Macrae, Alexander (1841) Bell's Notes 83 .... 9.75
McShane v. Paton, 1922 J.C. 26; 1922 S.L.T. 251 .... 9.07
Makconeill, John (1608) Pitcairn's Criminal Trials III, p. 5 .... 11.28
Malone v. H.M. Advocate, 1988 S.C.C.R. 498 .... 5.04; 7.24
Mann, William (1877) 3 Coup. 376 .... 10.81
Marchbank v. Annan, 1987 S.C.C.R. 718 .... 9.07
Marshall, William (1897) 4 S.L.T. 217 .... 9.48
Martin, Myles (1886) 1 White 297 .... 12.02
——, John (1873) 2 Coup. 501 .... 10.06
Martin v. Hamilton, 1989 J.C. 101; 1989 S.L.T. 860; 1989 S.C.C.R. 292 .... 7.18
Martindale v. H.M. Advocate, 1994 S.L.T. 1093; 1992 S.C.C.R. 700 .... 9.23; 9.69
Mason v. Jessop, 1990 S.C.C.R. 387 .... 3.26; 10.28; 10.35
Mather v. H.M. Advocate (1914) 7 Adam 525; (1914) S.C. (J.) 184; 1914 2 S.L.T.
    212 .... 10.76
Mathieson v. H.M. Advocate, 1981 S.C.C.R. 196 .... 9.56
Mathieson v. H.M. Advocate, 1996 S.C.C.R. 388 .... 7.26
Matthews and Rodden v. Linton (1860) 3 Irv. 570 .... 12.15
Maxwell v. H.M. Advocate, 1980 J.C. 40; 1980 S.L.T. 241 .... 6.29; 7.39; 7.59
Meehan v. Inglis, 1975 J.C. 9; 1974 S.L.T.(Notes) 61 .... 2.59
Meek v. H.M. Advocate, 1983 S.L.T. 280; 1982 S.C.C.R. 613 .... 8.58–8.62; 9.82
Melvin v. H.M. Advocate, 1984 S.L.T. 365; 1984 S.C.C.R. 113 .... 7.24; 7.27; 7.28
Meredith v. Lees 1992 J.C. 127; 1992 S.L.T. 802; 1992 S.C.C.R. 459 .... 9.20
Merrin v. S., 1987 S.L.T. 193 .... 2.46
Millar, Elliott (1847) Ark. 355 .... 10.71; 10.76
—— or Oates, Mary (1861) 4 Irv. 74 .... 10.09
Miller, David (1848) Ark. 525 .... 11.23–11.25
——, James (1862) 4 Irv. 238 .... 9.91; 9.92
Miller and Denovan v. H.M. Advocate, 1960, unreported; noted at 1991 S.L.T.
    211 .... 3.11; 3.28; 9.50
Miln, James (1758) Hume i, 79 .... 10.07
Milne, Alexander (1863) 4 Irv. 301 .... 3.19; 8.74
——, Peter, and Barry, John (1868) 1 Coup. 28 .... 9.29
Milne v. Tudhope, 1981 J.C. 53; 1981 S.L.T.(Notes) 42 .... 10.27
Mitchell, Alexander (1833) Bell's Notes 90 .... 9.29
——, (1874) 3 Coup. 77 .... 10.40
——, Hugh (1856) 2 Irv. 488 .... 4.15
Mitchell v. Morrison, 1938 J.C. 64; 1938 S.L.T. 201 .... 13.12; 13.13; 13.16; 13.26
Moir v. H.M. Advocate, 1993 S.L.T. 1191 .... 7.24
Mongan v. H.M. Advocate, 1989 S.C.C.R. 25 .... 10.48
Montgomery v. McLeod (1977) S.C.C.R. Supp. 114 .... 12.14; 12.15
Mooney, John (1851) J. Shaw 496 .... 10.10; 10.12
Moore v. MacDougall, 1989 S.C.C.R. 659 .... 8.26
Morrison v. Valentine, 1991 S.L.T. 413; 1990 S.C.C.R. 692 .... 8.06; 8.87; 8.92

Morton *v.* H.M. Advocate, 1986 S.L.T. 622 .... 7.22
——— *v.* Henderson, 1956 J.C. 55; 1956 S.L.T. 365 .... 3.03; 6.13; 6.14; 7.62
Moses *v.* Winder [1981] R.T.R. 37 .... 4.28
Muir, Nicolson (1825) Alison i, 450 .... 11.13
Munro, David (1831) Bell's Notes 48 .... 11.13
———, Ensign Andrew (1700) Hume i, 334 n.2 .... 9.22
Murdoch, John E. (1849) J. Shaw 229 .... 11.23; 11.24
Murray *v.* O'Brien, 1994 S.L.T. 1051; 1993 S.C.C.R. 90 .... 10.57; 11.27
——— *v.* Robertson, 1927 J.C. 1; 1927 S.L.T. 74 .... 10.23; 10.26

NAIRNE, CAPTAIN ANDREW (1712) Hume i, 442 .... 9.90
Nicolson, John (1887) 1 White 307 .... 12.08
Niezer *v.* Rhodes, 1995 S.C.C.R. 799 .... 11.05
Niven, James (1795) Hume i, 192 .... 9.56
Niven *v.* Tudhope, 1982 S.C.C.R. 365 .... 12.25
Norman *v.* Smith, 1983 S.C.C.R. 100 .... 9.07
Normand *v.* Donnelly, 1994 S.L.T. 62; 1993 S.C.C.R. 639 .... 13.10
——— *v.* Morrison, 1993 S.C.C.R. 207 (Sh. Ct.) 3.06; 9.28
——— *v.* Robinson, 1994 S.L.T. 558; 1993 S.C.C.R. 1119 .... 3.06; 3.30; 9.28; 14.02
Norrie *v.* MacLeod, 1988 S.C.C.R. 572 .... 12.19
Norris, Joseph and Mary (1886) 1 White 292 .... 5.12; 5.13
Norval *v.* H.M. Advocate, 1978 J.C. 70 .... 9.08

O'BRIEN *v.* Strathern, 1922 J.C. 55; 1922 S.L.T. 440 .... 10.59
O'Connell *v.* H.M. Advocate, 1987 S.C.C.R. 459 .... 7.26
O'Neil, Cornelius (1845) 2 Broun 394 .... 10.19
O'Neill *v.* H.M. Advocate, 1934 J.C. 98; 1934 S.L.T. 432 .... 10.45; 10.46
Oropesa, The [1943] P. 32 .... 5.26
Owens *v.* H.M. Advocate, 1946 J.C. 119; 1946 S.L.T. 227 .... 8.30

PALAZZO *v.* Copeland, 1976 J.C. 52 .... 12.16; 12.19
Parr *v.* H.M. Advocate, 1991 J.C. 39; 1991 S.L.T. 208; 1991 S.C.C.R. 180 . 9.49; 9.61; 9.62
Patchett *v.* MacDougall, 1983 J.C. 63; 1984 S.L.T. 152; 1983 S.C.C.R. 361 .... 13.05
Paterson, George (1897) 5 S.L.T. 13 .... 9.48; 9.50
———, James, and Glasgow, Alexander (1827) Syme 174 .... 10.19
Paterson *v.* Ritchie, 1934 J.C. 42; 1934 S.L.T. 281 .... 10.77
——— *v.* Robertson, 1944 J.C. 168; 1945 S.L.T. 31 .... 11.07
Paton, James (1858) 3 Irv. 208 .... 10.72; 10.76
Paton *v.* H.M. Advocate, 1936 J.C. 19; 1936 S.L.T. 298 .... 3.32; 9.24; 9.58
Peebles *v.* MacPhail, 1990 S.L.T. 245; 1989 S.C.C.R. 410 .... 9.07
People *v.* Fowler, 178 Cal. 657; 174 Pac. 892 (1918) 5.28
——— *v.* Lewis, 124 Cal. 551; 57 Pac. 470 (1899) 5.17
Pepper *v.* Hart, [1993] A.C. 593; [1992] 3 W.L.R. 1032; [1993] 1 All E.R. 42 .... 13.06
Petrovich *v.* Jessop, 1990 S.L.T. 594; 1990 S.C.C.R. 1 .... 3.31; 10.28
Phaup, Archibald (1846) Ark. 176 .... 11.13
Philip, Adam (1818) Hume i, 237 n.a 9.56
Pollock, Alexander (1869) 1 Coup. 257 .... 11.37
Pollok *v.* McCabe (1909) 6 Adam 139; 1910 S.C. (J.) 23; 1910 1 S.L.T. 83 .... 10.14
Priteca *v.* H.M. Advocate (1906) 5 Adam 79; 8 F. (J.) 66; 14 S.L.T. 218 .... 9.93
Purcell Meats (Scotland) Ltd *v.* McLeod, 1987 S.L.T. 528; 1986 S.C.C.R. 672 .... 2.49;
                                                                                      13.27

QUINN *v.* Cunningham, 1956 J.C. 22; 1956 S.L.T. 55 .... 3.22; 9.24; 9.27; 9.45; 14.02
——— *v.* H.M. Advocate, 1990 S.C.C.R. 254 .... 7.20; 8.59
——— *v.* Lees, 1994 S.C.C.R. 159 .... 3.17; 9.10

R. *v.* Ancio (1984) 6 D.L.R. (4th) 577 .... 6.09
—— *v.* Bailey [1983] 1 W.L.R. 760; 77 Cr.App.Rep. 76 .... 4.27; 4.28
—— *v.* Blaue [1975] 1 W.L.R. 1411; 61 Cr.App.Rep. 271 .... 5.11; 5.16; 5.31
—— *v.* Bradish [1990] 1 Q.B. 981; [1990] 2 W.L.R. 223; 89 Cr.App.Rep. 271 .... 13.20
—— *v.* Brown [1994] 1 A.C. 212; [1993] 2 W.L.R. 556; [1993] 2 All E.R. 75;
    (1993) 97 Cr.App.Rep. 44 .... 9.18
—— *v.* Burgess [1991] 2 W.L.R. 1206; 93 Cr.App.Rep. 41 .... 4.11; 4.34; 4.39
—— *v.* Burrow (1868) 11 Cox C.C. 191 .... 9.85
—— *v.* Camplin (1845) 1 Den. 89; 1 Cox C.C. 220 .... 9.80
—— *v.* Charles [1977] A.C. 177; [1976] 3 W.L.R. 431; 68 Cr.App.Rep. 334 .... 10.74
—— *v.* Charlson [1955] 1 W.L.R. 317; 39 Cr.App.Rep. 37 .... 4.44
—— *v.* Cheshire [1991] 1 W.L.R. 844; 93 Cr.App.Rep. 251 .... 5.23
—— *v.* Clarke (1854) 6 Cox C.C. 412; (1854) Dears C.C. 397 .... 9.85
—— *v.* Cogan and Leak [1976] 1 Q.B. 217; [1975] 3 W.L.R. 316; 61 Cr.App.Rep.
    217 .... 7.33; 7.35; 7.36
—— *v.* Cugullere [1961] 1 W.L.R. 858; [1961] 2 All E.R. 343 .... 13.10; 13.12
—— *v.* Cunningham [1982] A.C. 566; [1981] 3 W.L.R. 76; 73 Cr.App.Rep. 253 ..... 9.48
—— *v.* Dudley and Stephens (1884) 14 Q.B.D. 273; 15 Cox C.C. 624 .... 8.92
—— *v.* Dyson [1908] 2 K.B. 454; 21 Cox C.C. 669; 1 Cr.App.Rep. 13 .... 9.37
—— *v.* Falconer (1991) 65 A.L.J.R. 20 .... 4.10
—— *v.* Fletcher (1859) 8 Cox C.C. 131; (1859) Bell C.C. 63 .... 9.80
—— *v.* H.M. Advocate, 1988 S.L.T. 623; 1988 S.C.C.R. 254 .... 12.23; 12.28; 14.02
—— *v.* Hancock and Shankland [1986] A.C. 455; [1986] 2 W.L.R. 357; 82
    Cr.App.Rep. 264 .... 3.23
—— *v.* Hardie [1985] 1 W.L.R. 64; 80 Cr.App.Rep. 157 .... 4.25
—— *v.* Hennessy [1989] 1 W.L.R. 287; 89 Cr.App.Rep. 10; [1989] R.T.R. 153 .... 4.11;
    4.12; 4.27; 4.33; 4.35; 4.42
—— *v.* Instan [1893] 1 Q.B. 450; 17 Cox C.C. 602 .... 3.10
—— *v.* Isitt (1978) 67 Cr.App.Rep. 44; [1978] R.T.R. 211 .... 4.46
—— *v.* Jordan (1956) 40 Cr.App.Rep. 152 .... 5.30
—— *v.* Kemp [1957] 1 Q.B. 399; [1956] 3 W.L.R. 724; 40 Cr.App.Rep. 121 ... 4.24; 4.44
—— *v.* Lambie [1982] A.C. 449; [1981] 3 W.L.R. 88; 73 Cr.App.Rep. 294 .... 10.74
—— *v.* Le Brun [1992] 1 Q.B. 61 .... 3.33
—— *v.* MacDonagh [1974] Q.B. 448; [1974] 2 W.L.R. 529; 59 Cr.App.Rep. 55 ...... 13.03
—— *v.* McPherson [1973] Crim. L.R. 191; (1972) 117 Sol. Jo. 13 .... 10.19
—— *v.* Mitchell [1983] Q.B. 741; [1983] 2 W.L.R. 938 .... 4.03
—— *v.* Moloney [1985] A.C. 905; [1985] 2 W.L.R. 648; 81 Cr.App.Rep. 93 .... 3.22; 9.48
—— *v.* Morris [1983] Q.B. 587; [1983] 2 W.L.R. 768; 77 Cr.App.Rep. 309 .... 10.72
—— *v.* Nedrick [1986] 1 W.L.R. 1025; 83 Cr.App.Rep. 267 .... 9.46
—— *v.* Page [1971] 2 Q.B. 330; [1973] 2 W.L.R. 1308 .... 10.73
—— *v.* Quick [1973] Q.B. 910; [1973] 3 W.L.R. 26; 57 Cr.App.Rep. 722 .... 4.11; 4.29;
    4.34; 4.42; 4.48
—— *v.* R., [1992] 1 A.C. 599; [1991] 3 W.L.R. 767; [1991] 4 All E.R. 481; 94
    Cr.App.Rep. 216 .... 7.35; 9.83
—— *v.* Roberts (1971) 56 Cr.App.Rep. 95 .... 5.15; 5.27
—— *v.* Russell [1933] V.L.R. 59 .... 3.13
—— *v.* Smith [1959] 2 Q.B. 35; [1959] 2 W.L.R. 623; 43 Cr.App.Rep. 121 ..... 5.22–5.24
—— *v.* —— [1974] Q.B. 354; [1974] 2 W.L.R. 20; 58 Cr.App.Rep. 178 .... 8.49
—— *v.* Stable [1965] Qd. R. 86 .... 6.22
—— *v.* Stripp (1978) 69 Cr.App.Rep. 318 .... 4.32
—— *v.* Sullivan [1984] A.C. 156; [1983] 3 W.L.R. 123 .... 4.11; 4.24; 4.35; 4.40
—— *v.* Turner [1971] 1 W.L.R. 901; 55 Cr.App.Rep. 336 .... 10.11
—— *v.* Venna [1976] Q.B. 421; [1975] 3 W.L.R. 737; 61 Cr.App.Rep. 310 .... 9.16
—— *v.* Watson [1989] 1 W.L.R. 684; 89 Cr.App.Rep. 211 .... 5.05
—— *v.* Whybrow (1951) 35 Cr.App.Rep. 141 .... 6.09

—— *v.* Williams and Davis [1992] 1 W.L.R. 380; 95 Cr.App.Rep. 1 .... 5.15
R. H. W. *v.* H.M. Advocate, 1982 S.L.T. 420; 1982 S.C.C.R. 152 .... 3.28; 9.16; 9.27
R. L. *v.* H.M. Advocate, 1969 J.C. 40 .... 9.20
Rae *v.* Donnelly, 1982 S.C.C.R. 148 .... 9.93
—— *v.* Linton (1874) 3 Coup. 67; (1873) 2 R.(J.) 17 .... 10.73
Raffaelli *v.* Heatly, 1949 J.C. 101; 1949 S.L.T. 284 .... 12.13; 12.16
Ralston *v.* H.M. Advocate, 1989 S.L.T. 474; 1988 S.C.C.R. 590 .... 3.20; 12.18
Ramage, Janet (1825) Hume i, 28 .... 6.16; 6.17
Readers' Digest Association Ltd *v.* Pirie, 1973 J.C. 42; 1973 S.L.T. 170 .... 13.25
Redpath, Walter (1810) Hume i, 252 .... 9.61
Rees *v.* United Kingdom (1987) 9 E.H.R.R. 56; [1987] 2 F.L.R. 116; (1987)
    17 Fam. Law 157 .... 9.74
Riccards, Samuel (1710) Hume i, 107 .... 10.49
Richards *v.* H.M. Advocate, 1971 J.C. 29 .... 10.70
Roberts *v.* Hamilton, 1989 J.C. 91; 1989 S.L.T. 399; 1989 S.C.C.R. 240 ... 2.08; 3.35–3.37;
                                                                               8.41; 9.16
—— *v.* Local Authority for Inverness (1889) 2 White 285; 17 R. 19 .... 8.49
—— *v.* Ramsbottom [1980] 1 W.L.R. 823; [1980] R.T.R. 261 .... 4.44
Robertson, John (1854) 1 Irv. 469 .... 5.17
——, John G. (1842) 1 Broun 152 .... 12.03; 12.07; 12.08
—— or Brown, Margaret (1886) 1 White 93 .... 9.48
Robertson *v.* H.M. Advocate, 1994 S.L.T. 1004 .... 9.63
—— *v.* H.M. Advocate, 1990 S.C.C.R. 345 .... 7.26
—— *v.* Smith, 1980 J.C. 1; 1979 S.L.T.(Notes) 51 .... 12.24; 12.27
Robinson, Henry (1843) 1 Broun 590 and 643 .... 12.27
Rodgers *v.* Hamilton, 1994 S.L.T. 822 .... 9.17; 9.87
Ross *v.* H.M. Advocate, 1991 J.C. 210; 1991 S.L.T. 564; 1991 S.C.C.R. 823 .... 4.09;
                         4.18–4.26; 4.29; 4.30; 4.32; 4.34; 4.35; 4.36;
                         4.38; 4.40; 4.43; 4.44; 4.48; 8.08; 8.69; 8.77
Roy, John (1839) Bell's Notes 88 .... 9.12
Russell *v.* H.M. Advocate, 1946 J.C. 37; 1946 S.L.T. 93 .... 4.46
—— *v.* H.M. Advocate, 1991 J.C. 194; 1992 S.L.T. 25; 1991 S.C.C.R. 790 .... 2.60
Ryan *v.* The Queen (1967) 40 A.L.J.R. 488; [1967] A.L.R. 577; 121 C.L.R. 295 . 4.10; 4.13

S. *v.* H.M. Advocate, 1989 S.L.T. 469; 1989 S.C.C.R. 248, *sub nom.* Stallard *v.*
    H.M. Advocate 1.05; 2.05; 7.35; 9.76; 9.83; 14.02; 14.11
S. W. *v.* United Kingdom; C.R. *v.* United Kingdom (1996) 21 E.H.R.R. 363 .... 14.10; 14.11
Salmond *v.* H.M. Advocate, 1992 S.L.T. 156; 1991 S.C.C.R. 43 .... 9.66
Saltman *v.* Allan, 1989 S.L.T. 262; 1988 S.C.C.R. 640 .... 12.16; 12.19
Sandlan *v.* H.M. Advocate, 1983 S.C.C.R. 71; reported on another point, 1983 J.C. 22;
    1983 S.L.T. 519 .... 10.27
Sayers *v.* H.M. Advocate, 1982 J.C. 17; 1982 S.L.T. 220; 1981 S.C.C.R. 312;
    reported on another point, 1981 J.C. 98 .... 3.24; 7.56
Scott *v.* H.M. Advocate, 1996 S.L.T. 519; 1995 S.C.C.R. 760 .... 2.08; 9.44
Shannon *v.* H.M. Advocate, 1985 S.C.C.R. 14 .... 10.56
—— *v.* Skeen (1977) S.C.C.R. Supp. 180 .... 12.14
Sherras *v.* De Rutzen [1895] 1 Q.B. 918 .... 13.19
Sillars *v.* Smith, 1982 S.L.T. 539; 1982 S.C.C.R. 367 .... 13.01
Silverstein *v.* H.M. Advocate, 1949 J.C. 160; 1949 S.L.T. 386 .... 9.94
Simpkins *v.* H.M. Advocate, 1985 S.C.C.R. 30 .... 12.37
Simpson *v.* McClory, 1993 J.C. 110; 1993 S.L.T. 861; 1993 S.C.C.R. 402 .... 13.03
—— *v.* Tudhope, 1988 S.L.T. 297; 1987 S.C.C.R. 348 .... 12.35
Sinclair *v.* Annan, 1980 S.L.T.(Notes) 55 .... 12.15
Skeen *v.* Malik, 1977, unreported 9.31
Skinner *v.* Robertson, 1980 S.L.T.(Sh.Ct.) 43 .... 9.07

Slaven, Patrick (1885) 5 Coup. 694 .... 5.14; 9.55
Sloan *v.* Macmillan, 1922 J.C. 1; 1922 2 S.L.T. 296 .... 12.03; 12.04; 12.07
Smart *v.* H.M. Advocate, 1975 J.C. 30; 1975 S.L.T. 65 .. 2.08; 4.05; 9.04; 9.14; 9.18; 9.19
Smillie, Robert (1883) 5 Coup. 287; 10 R.(J.) 70 .... 11.36; 11.41
Smillie *v.* Wilson, 1990 S.L.T. 582; 1990 S.C.C.R. 133 .... 12.11
Smith or Thom, Jane (1876) 3 Coup. 732 .... 9.17
——, John (1838) 2 Swin. 28 .... 2.05; 10.05; 10.06
——, John (1871) 2 Coup. 1 .... 10.82; 10.83
——, Thomas (1853) 1 Irv. 271 .... 9.27
——, David, and McNeil, William (1842) 1 Broun 240 .... 9.33
——, George (1848) Ark. 473 .... 12.05
Smith *v.* Downie, 1982 S.L.T. (Sh.Ct.) 23 .... 12.27
—— *v.* H.M. Advocate, 1952, unreported; see also 1952 J.C. 66; 1952 S.L.T. 286 ... 9.63
—— *v.* M., 1984 S.L.T.(Sh.Ct.) 28; 1983 S.C.C.R. 67 (Sh.Ct.) 4.18
—— *v.* Paton, 1986, unreported 9.11
Smith of Maddiston Ltd *v.* MacNab, 1975 J.C. 48; 1975 S.L.T. 86 .... 13.14; 13.17
Sneddon *v.* Lees, 1996 S.L.T. 294 .... 2.60
Sommerville, Grizell (1606) Hume i, 135 .... 9.90
Sorley *v.* H.M. Advocate, 1992 J.C. 102; 1992 S.L.T. 867; 1992 S.C.C.R. 396 .... 4.19;
4.20; 4.21; 4.25; 4.47; 8.77
Speid *v.* Whyte (1864) 4 Irv. 584 .... 11.13; 11.16
Spiers *v.* H.M. Advocate, 1980 J.C. 36 .... 7.14
Steele *v.* H.M. Advocate, 1992 J.C. 1; 1992 S.C.C.R. 30 .... 10.49
Steuart, Andrew (1874) 2 Coup. 554 .... 11.18
Stevenson *v.* Beatson, 1965 S.L.T.(Sh.Ct.) 11 .... 4.32
Stewart, Patrick (1602) Hume i, 260 .... 9.50
——, James, and Walsh, John (1856) 2 Irv. 359 .... 11.41
Stewart *v.* Lockhart, 1991 S.L.T. 835; 1990 S.C.C.R. 390 .... 12.16
—— *v.* P. F. Forfarshire (1829) 2 S.J. 32 .... 6.07
—— *v.* Thain, 1981 J.C. 13; 1981 S.L.T.(Notes) 2 .... 9.07
Stillie *v.* H.M. Advocate, 1992 S.L.T. 279; 1990 S.C.C.R. 719 .... 7.20
Stirling *v.* Annan, 1984 S.L.T. 88; 1983 S.C.C.R. 396 .... 4.43
Stobbs *v.* H.M. Advocate, 1983 S.C.C.R. 190 .... 9.60; 9.65; 9.76
Strachan *v.* H.M. Advocate, 1995 S.L.T. 178; 1994 S.C.C.R. 341 .... 6.20; 9.08
Strathearn *v.* H.M. Advocate, 1996 S.C.C.R. 100 .... 9.67
—— *v.* Seaforth, 1926 J.C. 100; 1926 S.L.T. 445 .... 2.28; 2.29; 10.23; 10.26
Strathern *v.* Fogal, 1922 J.C. 73; 1922 S.L.T. 543 .... 10.72
Strowger *v.* John [1974] R.T.R. 124; [1974] Crim.L.R. 123 .... 2.41; 13.11; 13.13
Stuart, Daniel (1829) Bell's Notes 42 .... 10.45
Sugden *v.* H.M. Advocate, 1934 J.C. 103; 1934 S.L.T. 465 .... 2.22; 2.24; 2.28; 2.43
Sumner, Peter A., 1983, unreported 10.40
Surman *v.* H.M. Advocate, 1988 S.L.T. 371; 1988 S.C.C.R. 93 .... 8.43
Sutherland, Williamina (1856) 2 Irv. 455 .... 9.59
Sutherland *v.* H.M. Advocate, 1994 S.L.T. 634; 1994 S.C.C.R. 80 .... 9.56; 9.58
Swan *v.* MacNab, 1977 J.C. 57; 1978 S.L.T. 192 .... 13.12; 13.17; 13.26
Sweeney *v.* X., 1982 S.C.C.R. 504 .... 9.81
Sweenie, Charles (1858) 3 Irv. 109 .... 9.05; 9.74; 9.81; 9.88
Sweet *v.* Parsley [1970] A.C. 132; [1969] 2 W.L.R. 470; 53 Cr.App.Rep. 221 ... 2.41; 13.11
Sze *v.* Wilson, 1992 S.L.T. 569; 1992 S.C.C.R. 54 .... 2.56

Tapsell *v.* Prentice (1910) 6 Adam 354; (1911) S.C. (J.) 67; 1910 2 S.L.T. 330 .... 10.71;
10.76
Taylor, Daniel (1853) 1 Irv. 230 .... 10.76; 10.80
Taylor (1808) Burnett App. No. X 2.22
Tees *v.* H.M. Advocate, 1994 S.L.T. 701; 1994 S.C.C.R. 451 .... 9.37

Thabo-Meli *v.* R. [1954] 1 W.L.R. 228; [1954] 1 All E.R. 373 .... 3.33
Thompson *v.* Carmichael, 1990 S.C.C.R. 51 .... 10.35
Thomson, Archibald (1874) 2 Coup. 551 .... 11.13; 11.14
Thomson *v.* H.M. Advocate, 1983 J.C. 69; 1983 S.L.T. 682; 1983 S.C.C.R. 368 ...... 2.05;
                                                                 8.80; 8.84–8.86
—— *v.* ——, 1986 S.L.T. 281; 1985 S.C.C.R. 448 .... 9.62; 9.63; 9.65
—— *v.* ——, 1995 S.L.T. 827; 3.29; 9.58; 11.42
—— *v.* MacPhail, 1989 S.L.T. 637; 1989 S.C.C.R. 266 .... 12.15
Tobin *v.* H.M. Advocate, 1934 J.C. 60; 1934 S.L.T. 325 .... 7.31
Trotter of Mortonhall (1716) Hume i, 123 .... 11.09
Trotter, Henry, of Mortonhall (1730) Hume i, 123 .... 11.09
Tudhope *v.* Barlow, 1981 S.L.T.(Sh.Ct.) 94 .... 12.24
—— *v.* Grubb, 1983 S.C.C.R. 350 (Sh.Ct.) 8.91
—— *v.* McKee, 1988 S.L.T. 153; 1987 S.C.C.R. 663 .... 13.18
—— *v.* Smellie (1977) S.C.C.R. Supp. 186 .... 10.60
—— *v.* Sommerville, 1981 J.C. 58; 1981 S.L.T. 117 .... 12.27
—— *v.* Taylor, 1980 S.L.T.(Notes) 54 .... 12.27
Tumbleson, Samuel (1863) 4 Irv. 426 .... 6.15
Turnbull *v.* H.M. Advocate, 1953 J.C. 59 .... 12.36
Turner *v.* Kennedy (1972) S.C.C.R. Supp. 30 .... 12.16
—— *v.* Scott, 1996 S.L.T. 200; 1995 S.C.C.R. 516 .... 9.17

ULHAQ *v.* H.M. Advocate, 1991 S.L.T. 614; 1990 S.C.C.R. 593 .... 5.20; 9.31; 9.32
Urquhart, John (1844) 2 Broun 13 .... 12.08

VALENTINE *v.* Kennedy, 1985 S.C.C.R. 89 (Sh.Ct.) 10.14
Vallance, John (1846) Ark. 181 .... 11.32
Vance, Robert (1849) J. Shaw 211 .... 9.55
Vaughan *v.* H.M. Advocate, 1979 S.L.T. 49 .... 7.30

W. *v.* H.M. Advocate, 1995 S.L.T. 685 .... 9.73; 9.76
Waddell *v.* MacPhail, 1986 S.C.C.R. 593 .... 12.36
Walker *v.* MacGillivray (1980) S.C.C.R. Supp. 244 .... 10.29
Walker and Raiker *v.* H.M. Advocate, 1985 J.C. 53; 1985 S.L.T. 245, *sub nom.*
    Raiker *v.* H.M. Advocate, 1985 S.C.C.R. 150 .... 7.26
Walkingshaw *v.* Coid, 1988 S.C.C.R. 454 (Sh.Ct.) 12.38
—— *v.* Marshall, 1992 S.L.T. 1167; 1991 S.C.C.R. 397 .... 2.17
Wallace, Samuel, and Ferguson, Thomas (1839) Bell's Notes 47 .... 11.13
—— *v.* Walsh, 1921, unreported; reported on another point, 1922 J.C. 82; 1922 S.L.T.
    443 .... 7.55
Wan Ping Nam *v.* Federal German Republic, 1972 J.C. 43; 1972 S.L.T. 220 .... 2.66
Ward *v.* Robertson, 1938 J.C. 32; 1938 S.L.T. 165 .... 11.12; 11.14
Watson *v.* H.M. Advocate (1978) S.C.C.R. Supp. 192 .... 5.03
Watt, Robert, and Kerr, James (1868) 1 Coup. 123 .... 9.25
Watt *v.* Annan, 1978 J.C. 84; 1978 S.L.T. 198 .... 1.07; 2.07; 2.35; 12.24; 12.26; 14.04
—— *v.* ——, 1990 S.C.C.R. 55 .... 10.57; 10.59; 10.60
Waugh, John (1873) 2 Coup. 424 .... 10.06
West *v.* H.M. Advocate, 1985 S.C.C.R. 248 .... 7.57; 7.58
Westwater *v.* Thomson, 1993 S.L.T. 703; 1992 S.C.C.R. 624 .... 2.17
Wheatley, Edmund (1853) 1 Irv. 225 .... 9.59
Whitchurch *v.* Millar (1895) 2 Adam 9; 23 R.(J.) 1; 3 S.L.T. 129 .... 12.16
White *v.* MacPhail, 1990 S.C.C.R. 578 .... 7.20
Whiteside *v.* H.M. Advocate, 1996 S.L.T. 299 .... 9.44
Wild, Thomas (1854) 1 Irv. 552 .... 12.04
Williamson, James (1866) 5 Irv. 326 .... 5.14; 5.23; 5.30

Williamson *v.* H.M. Advocate, 1984 S.L.T. 200 .... 9.06; 9.17
—— *v.* ——, 1994 J.C. 149; 1994 S.L.T. 1000; 1994 S.C.C.R. 358 .... 9.23; 9.68; 9.69
Wilson, Petr., 1992 S.L.T. 145; 1991 S.C.C.R. 957 .... 2.68
——, James (1838) 2 Swin. 16 .... 5.22
Wilson *v.* Brown, 1982 S.L.T. 361; 1982 S.C.C.R. 49 .... 12.13
Windsor, Petr., 1994 S.L.T. 604; 1994 S.C.C.R. 59 .... 2.68
Wings Ltd *v.* Ellis, [1985] A.C. 272; [1984] 3 W.L.R. 965; [1984] 3 All E.R. 577 .... 13.12;
13.19
Winnick *v.* Allan, 1986 S.C.C.R. 35 .... 12.11
Wither *v.* Adie, 1986 S.L.T.(Sh.Ct.) 32 .... 11.38
—— *v.* Cowie, 1994 S.L.T. 363 .... 2.17
Woods, Petr., 1994 S.L.T. 197; 1993 S.C.C.R. 106 .... 2.68
—— *v.* Normand, 1992 S.C.C.R. 805 .... 12.18
Wormald, J. D. (1876) 3 Coup. 246 .... 10.42
Wright, Edgar (1788) Hume i, 108 .... 10.51
Wright, Rachel (1809) Burnett 134 and App. No. VII; (1808–9) Hume i, 84 .... 2.23;
2.24; 10.09
Wyness *v.* Lockhart, 1992 S.C.C.R. 808 .... 12.15

X. *v.* Sweeney , 1982 J.C. 70; 1983 S.L.T. 48, *sub nom.* H. *v.* Sweeney, 1982 S.C.C.R.
509 .... 2.59
X. Ltd and Y. *v.* United Kingdom (1982), case no. 8710/79 .... 14.10

YOUNG, ANDREW (1800) Hume i, 79–80 .... 10.07
—— or Gilchrist, Mary, and Hislop, Cecilia (undated) Bell's Notes 34 .... 10.34
Young, Petr., 1994 S.L.T. 269 .... 2.68
Young *v.* Heatly, 1959 J.C. 66; 1959 S.L.T. 250 .... 12.15
—— *v.* McGlennan, 1991 S.C.C.R. 738 .... 9.19
—— *v.* Webster, 1993 S.L.T. 349; 1992 S.C.C.R. 818 .... 10.60

TABLE OF STATUTES

ACTS OF THE PARLIAMENT OF SCOTLAND

Act 1526 (c.8; A.P.S. ii, 316, c.10)
  "Of ... byrningis" 11.28
Act 1540 (c.118; A.P.S. ii, 377,
  c.38) "Anentis birning" 11.28
Act 1592 (c.148; A.P.S. iii, 575,
  c.68) "fyre in coilheuchis". 11.28
Act of Union 1707 (c.7; A.P.S. xi,
  406, c.7) 2.11
Courts Act 1672 (c.16; A.P.S. viii,
  80, c.40) 2.04
Incest Act 1567 (c.14; A.P.S. iii, 26,
  c.15) 7.30; 12.29
Poor's Counsel Act 1424 (c.45;
  A.P.S.ii, 8, c. 24) 2–66
Theft Act 1607 (c.3; A.P.S. iv, 373,
  c.6) 2.11; 10.14

ACTS OF THE PARLIAMENT OF GREAT BRITIAN

Abortion Act 1967 (c.87)
  s.1(1) 9.35
Administration of Justice (Emergency
  Provisions) (Scotland) Act 1939
  (2 & 3 Geo. 6, c. 79)
  s.3(2) 2–62
Adoption (Scotland) Act 1978 (c.28)
  s.41(1) 12.30
Airports Act 1986 (c.31)
  ss.63, 64 .... 2.15

Burgh Police (Scotland) Act 1892
  (55 & 56 Vict. c.55)
  s.381(22) 13.06

Carrying of Knives Etc. (Scotland)
  Act 1993 (c.13) 2.25, 6.06
Children and Young Persons
  (Protection from Tobacco)
  Act 1991 (c.23) 9.32
Children and Young Persons (Scotland)
  Act 1937 (1 Edw. 8 and
  1 Geo. 6, c.37) 3.10

s.12(1) 4.45
s.18 .... 9.32
Children (Scotland) Act 1995 (c.36)
  ss.1–4, 11 .... 10.15
  Pt. II, Chap. 2, Sched.1 .... 2.47
  Pt. II, Chap. 3 .... 2.47
  ss.45(8), 45(9), 51, 52(2), 65(7),
  68, 69, 93(2)(b) 2.47
Civic Government (Scotland) Act
  1982 (c.45)
  s.7 .... 2.19
  s.7(4) 10.72
  s.43 .... 2.19
  s.45 .... 12.27
  s.46 .... 12.20
  s.46(1) 13.06
  s.49(2) 12.20
  s.51(2) 12.27
  s.54(1) 12.20
  s.55(1) 12.20
  s.58 .... 6.06
  s.73 .... 10.13
  ss.112–118 .... 2.16
  s.130 .... 2.49
  Sched. 2, para. 1 .... 12.27
Computer Misuse Act 1990 (c.18)
  ss.1–3 .... 13.20
Consumer Credit Act 1974 (c.39)
  ss.116(3), 117(2), 118(1),
  119(2), 120–122 .... 10.11
Copyright, Designs and Patents Act
  1987 (c.48)
  s.107 .... 10.08
Countryside (Scotland) Act 1967
  (c.86)
  s.58(3) 2.15
Criminal Attempts Act 1981 (c.47)
  s.1(1) 6.09; 6.22
Criminal Justice Act 1982 (c.48)
  ss.53(a), 54 .... Appendix C
Criminal Justice Act 1988 (c.33)
  Sched. 15, para. 58 ...... Appendix C
Criminal Justice Act 1991 (c.53)
  s.17(1), (2) .... Appendix C

Criminal Justice Act 1993 (c.36)
  s.67(1) 2.25
Criminal Justice and Public Order
    Act 1994 (c.33)
  s.61(4), (6) 11.05
  s.61(9) 11.05; 12.20
  s.61(9)(b) 11.05
  s.62 .... 11.05
  s.63 .... 12.21
  s.63(1), (1)(b) 12.20
  s.63(2) 12.20
  s.63(4) 12.20
  s.63(6) 12.20
  s.63(7) 12.20
  s.63(9) 12.20
  s.63(10) 12.20
  s.65 .... 12.20
  s.68, 68(2), 68(5)(A) 11.06
  s.69, 69(4) 11.06
  ss.70, 71 .... 11.07
  s.142 .... 9.74; 9.81
  s.172(8) 11.05
Criminal Justice (Scotland) Act 1980
    (c.62) 11.26
  s.78(1) 11.26
Criminal Justice (Scotland) Act 1995
    (c.20)
  s.63 .... 2.59
Criminal Law Act 1977 (c.45)
  s.63 .... Appendix C
  Sched. 11, para. 5 .... Appendix C
Criminal Law Amendment Act 1885
    (48 & 49 Vict. c.28) 9.85
Criminal Law (Consolidation)
    (Scotland) Act 1995 (c.39)
  s.1 .... 7.30; 12.29
  s.1(1), paras. 1, 2 .... 12.30
  s.1(1)(a)–(c) 12.30
  s.2 .... 12.31
  s.3 .... 12.28; 12.31
  s.5(2), (3) 9.88
  s.6 .... 9.19; 9.20
  s.7(2) 9.88
  s.13 .... 2.10
  s.14 .... 2.53
  s.20(7)(b) 6.20
  s.47(1), (4) 13.10
  s.48(2)(a) 13.09
  s.49 .... 2.25
  s.51 .... 10.52
  s.52 .... 11.26
  s.52(2) 11.30
  s.52(3) 11.27
Criminal Procedure (Consequential
    Provisions) (Scotland)

  Act 1995 (c.40)
  Sched. 2, Pt. III 2.15
Criminal Procedure (Scotland) Act
    1887 (50 & 51 Vict. c.35)
  s.44 .... 2.23
  s.56 .... 11.29
Criminal Procedure (Scotland) Act
    1975 (c.21)
  s.7(2) 10.64
  s.289B .... Appendix C
  s.289D(1), (1A) .... Appendix C
  s.289G .... Appendix C
  292(2) 10.64
Criminal Procedure (Scotland) Act
    1995 (c.46)
  s.3(3), (4), (5) .... Appendix D
  s.3(6) .... 9.88; Appendix D
  s.4(b) 10.64
  s.5(2)(a),(d), (3) .... Appendix D
  s.5(4) 11.30
  ss.6,7 .... Appendix D
  s.7(4) .... 10.29; Appendix D
  s.7(5) .... Appendix D
  s.7(6), (7), (8)–(10) ...... Appendix D
  s.7(8)(b) 9.41
  s.7(8)(b)(iii) 10.64
  s.11, 11(4) 2.42
  s.11(4)(a),(b) 10.36
  s.41 .... 2.46
  s.42 .... 2.47
  s.54(6) 8.11
  ss.54–56 .... 2.51
  s.57 .... 2.51; 4.18
  s.57(1)(a), (2), (3) 8.11
  ss.58–63 .... 4.18
  s.65 .... 2.44
  ss.66(6), 71, 78(1) 8.07
  s.78(2) 4.19; 8.08
  s.78(3) 8.07
  ss.86, 90 .... 2.62
  s.92 .... 2.60
  s.97 .... 2.55
  s.98 .... 2.61
  s.103 .... Appendix D
  s.103(2) 2.23
  s.103(3) .... 2.23; Appendix D
  s.103(4) 2.23
  s.106 .... 2.65
  s.107 .... 2.65
  s.108(a),(b) 2.64
  s.118(1)(c) 2.52
  s.118(7) 2.64
  s.119 .... 2.52
  s.123 .... 2.65
  s.136 .... 2.44

s.138 .... 2.59
s.138(2) 12.20
s.142 .... 2.47
s.147 .... 2.44
s.153 .... 2.60
s.160 .... 2.55
s.161 .... 2.61
ss.173, 173(2) .... Appendix D
s.173(1), (2) 2.23
ss.175, 175(3) 2.65
s.175(3)(b) 2.64
s.175(4) 2.64; 2.65
s.180 .... 2.65
ss.183(1)(d), 185 .... 2.52
s.186 .... 2.65
ss.189(7), 197 .... 2.64
s.195 .... Appendix D
s.205, 205(4) 9.41
s.219(8) .... Appendix D
s.225(2), (4), (8) .... Appendix C
s.255 .... 13.06
s.274(2)(c) 9.87
s.292 .... 2.44
s.294 .... 6.02
s.301 .... 2.58
ss.304, 305 .... 2.13
Sched. 2 .... 10.16; 10.34;
                     11.38; 12.02; 12.06
Sched. 3, para. 2 .... 2.53
——, para. 8 .... 10.65
——, para. 8(1) 10.52; 10.53
——, para. 8(2) 2.53; 10.59;
                          10.60; 10.65
——, para. 8(3) 10.38; 10.45;
                          10.60; 10.65
——, para. 8(4) 2.53; 10.38;
                          10.60; 10.65
——, paras. 9(2) 2.53
——, para. 14 .... 2.18; 2.53
——, para. 14(b) 13.07
Sched. 5 .... 4.18; 10.16;
       10.31; 10.41; 10.68; 11.25; 12.20
Criminal Procedure (Consequential
       Provisions) (Scotland)
       Act 1995 (c.40)
    Sched. 4, para. 17(b) .... Appendix C
Crossbows Act 1987 (c.32) 2.25

Dangerous Dogs Act 1991 (c.65) .. 2.25
District Courts (Scotland) Act 1975
       (c.20) .... Appendix D
    s.5 .... Appendix D

Education (Scotland) Act 1883
       (46 & 47 Vict. c.56)

s.11 .... 13.04
Education Scotland Act 1980 (c.44)
    ss.35(1), 41(2)(b) 13.04
    s.48A 9.07
Environment Act 1995 (c.25),
       Sched. 22, para. 88 .... 10.13
Environmental Protection Act 1990
       (c.43)
    ss.45(9), 60(1), 75(2) 10.13
European Communities Act 1972
       (c.68) 2.17
    s.2, 2(2)(a) 2.17
    Sched. 2, para. 1(1)(d) 2.17

Firearms Act 1968 (c.27)
    s.57(1)(b) 13.03
Firearms (Amendment) Act 1994
       (c.31) 2.25
Food Safety Act 1990 (c.16) 13.20
    ss.8(1), 21 .... 13.21
Forestry Act 1967 (c.10)
    s.46 .... 2.15

Human Fertilisation and Embryology
       Act 1994 (c.37)
    s.37 .... 9.34

Indecent Displays (Control) Act 1981
       (c.42)
    ss.1, 5(4)(a) 12.25
Inshore Fishing (Scotland) Act 1984
       (c.26)
    s.10, Sched. 2 .... 13.15
Interpretation Act 1978 (c.30)
    Sched. 1 .... Appendix C
Intoxicating Substances (Supply)
       Act 1985 (c.26) 9.31

Law Reform (Miscellaneous Provisions)
       (Scotland) Act 1966 (c.19)
    s.10 .... 2.13
Licensing (Scotland) Act 1976
       (c.66) 9.30
    s.67(1), (2) 2.50; 13.25
    Sched. 5 .... 2.50; 13.25
Local Government (Scotland) Act
       1973 (c.65)
    s.201(1), (2) 2.14
Local Government Etc. (Scotland)
       Act 1994 (c.39)
    s.180(1) 2.14
    s.127 .... 2.47
    Sched. 13, para. 92(61) 2.14
    ——, para. 129 .... 12.27

Local Government Finance Act 1992
(c.14)
s.97(4) 2.19
Sched. 3 .... 2.19

Mental Health (Scotland) Act 1984 (c.36)
s.106 .... 9.86
s.106(5) 9.88
Misuse of Drugs Act 1971
(c.38) 3.05; 13.01
s.4(3)(b) 2.42; 13.18
s.5(2) 13.17
s.5(3) 6.27
s.8 .... 13.09
s.19 .... 6.27
s.25 .... 2.25
s.28 .... 13.18
Sched. 4 .... 2.25

Official Secrets Acts 1989 (c.6)
s.16(2) 12.33

Police (Scotland) Act 1967 (c.77)
s.41(1)(a) 4.19; 4.29
Police and Criminal Evidence Act
1984 (c.60)
ss.24, 118 .... 2.38
Preservation of Timber Trees Act
1715 (1 Geo. 1, c.48) 11.29
Protection of Animals (Scotland) Act
1912 (2 & 3 Geo. 5, c.14)
s.1(1)(a) 13.05
Protection of Children (Tobacco) Act
1986 (c.34) 9.32
Public Order Act 1986 (c.64)
s.1 .... 12.03
ss.14A–14C 11.07
s.14A(1)(b), (5)(a)(b), (6), (9),
(9)(b) 11.07

Riot Act 1714 (1 Geo. 1, c.5) 12.03
Road Traffic Act 1988 (c.52) ...13.01; 13.03
s.1 .... 4.02; 4.30; 4.39
s.2 .... 4.02; 13.02
s.3 .... 4.02; 4.20
s.4(1) 3.14; 4.39
s.5(1) 4.31
s.8(9) 3.09
s.28 .... 13.02
s.42(1) 13.19
s.97(3), (7) 4.20
s.143(1)(a), (2) 4.20
s.170 .... 4.02
s.178 .... 4.40; 10.24
s.192(1), (2) 13.02

Road Traffic Act 1991 (c.40) 4.40
ss.1, 2 .... 4.02
Road Traffic Offenders Act 1988 (c.53)
s.6 .... 2.43
s.10 .... Appendix D
s.23 .... 2.53
Sched. 1 .... 2.43
Sched. 2, Pt. I 2.25
Road Traffic Regulation Act 1984 (c.27)
s.89(1) 13.18
Roads (Scotland) Act 1984 (c.54) ... 11.03;
13.02

Sale of Goods Act 1979 (c.54)
ss.17–19, 21 .... 10.12
Sale of Goods (Amendment) Act
1995 (c.28), s.1 .... 10.12
Scotland Act 1978 (c.51) 14.07
Sea Fisheries Regulation (Scotland)
Act 1895 (58 & 59 Vict. c.42)
s.10(4) 13.15
Sexual Offences Act 1956 (4 & 5
Eliz.2, c.69)
s.1 .... 9.81
Sexual Offences (Amendment) Act
1976 (c.82)
s.1 .... 9.80
Statute Law (Repeals) Act 1973 (c.39)
s.1(1) 12.03
Sched. 1, Pt. V 12.03
Statute Law Revision (Scotland) Act
1964 (c.80)
Sched. 2 .... 10.14
Statutory Instruments Act 1946 (9 &
10 Geo. 6, c.36) 2.13
Succession (Scotland) Act 1964 (c. 41)
s.14(1) 10–16

Theft Act 1968 (c.60)
s.1(1) 10.02
s.5(1) 10.11
s.22 .... 6.32
Trade Descriptions Act 1968 (c.29) . 10.65
Treason Act 1708 (7 Anne, c.21)
s.10 .... 11.29; 12.33
Trespass (Scotland) Act 1865 (28 &
29 Vict. c.56) 11.02; 11.04
ss.2–4 .... 11.03

Unsolicited Goods and Services Act
1971 (c.30) 13.25

Vehicles Excise and Regulation Act
1994 (c.22)
s.33 .... 2.41

Video Recordings Act 1984 (c.39)
s.12 .... 12.27

Wireless Telegraphy Act 1949 (12,
13 & 14 Geo. 6, c.54)
s.1(1) 2.41

LOCAL ACT

Edinburgh Municipal and Police Act
1879 (42 & 43 Vict. c.cxxxii)
s.93(3) 3.04

TABLE OF STATUTORY INSTRUMENTS

Act of Adjournal (Criminal Procedure
Rules) 1996 (S.I. 1996 No. 513)
r. 3.1(2) 2.13

Road Vehicles Lighting Regulations
1989 (S.I. 1989 No. 1796) .. 13.19

CONVENTIONS AND TREATIES

European Convention for the Protection
of Human Rights and
Fundamental Freedoms
(1953) (Cmnd. 8969)
Art. 1 .... 2.18
Art. 6.1, 6.3(a),(b),(c) 2.18
Art. 7 .... 14.09–14.11
Art. 7(1) 2.21
Treaty Establishing the European
Economic Community 1957
Art. 189 .... 2.17

CHAPTER 1

INTRODUCTION TO CRIMINAL LAW

WHAT IS CRIMINAL LAW?

The criminal law consists of a series of rules. These rules define what is not   **1–01**
permissible in social conduct according to certain moral principles or
political policies. An example of a moral principle is that "injuring others
in their persons or property is wrong". Accordingly, the criminal law includes
such well known crimes as theft, assault and rape. An example of a political
policy which forms the basis of a criminal offence is that a licence must be
purchased for a television receiver.

Part of public law

It is important to appreciate from the outset that criminal law forms part of   **1–02**
"public law" rather than "private law". Private law (sometimes referred to as
"civil law") is concerned with regulating disputes that do not directly involve
the state. This is not to say that the state does not take an active interest in
areas such as company law or family law. What it does mean is that
governmental agencies are not directly on the side of one of the litigants: the
state does not claim a direct interest in the outcome of a particular court case.

The same cannot be said of public law, which relates directly to the state   **1–03**
in a political and sovereign role. In a broad sense, public law is concerned
with the structure of government, and the powers, duties and obligations of
public officials and private citizens. Criminal law has a public law character.
A crime constitutes an offence not just against an individual, but against
the state. The state must take a direct interest in protecting persons within
its territory from conduct which has been declared to be, or accepted as,
criminal. This feature is reflected in the fact that crimes are generally
prosecuted in the name of the Crown on behalf of the community, rather
than by privately retained lawyers, let alone aggrieved individuals (see para.
2–58, following). Private prosecution indeed is highly exceptional in
Scotland (see para. 2–59, following). Thus it is that reports of criminal
cases are cited as "*Her Majesty's Advocate v. [name of the accused]*" in
serious cases. Her Majesty's Advocate refers to the chief Scottish law officer
of the Crown (more commonly known as the "Lord Advocate"). In less
serious cases, the prosecution will be recorded in the name of the local
procurator fiscal, holding office under the Lord Advocate. It is these public

officials and their deputes who are charged with the task of conducting criminal prosecutions on behalf of the state. Unlike private law litigation, furthermore, where the aggrieved party (the "pursuer" in Scottish terminology) must instigate legal action against the "defender", the Crown, through its appointed representatives, can undertake the prosecution of a person accused of committing a crime, even if this is against the wishes of the victim (or "complainer").

THE PROPER SCOPE OF THE CRIMINAL LAW

1–04 A question which has long been the subject of debate among both criminal lawyers and philosophers is that of the proper scope of the criminal law. In particular, this debate has been concerned with the extent to which the criminal law should be used to enforce moral standards. A number of scholars have argued that society is permitted, and sometimes obliged, to enforce morality by means of the criminal law. The legal philosopher H. L. A. Hart has identified two versions of this argument[1]: the "conservative thesis" and the "disintegration thesis". According to Hart, the conservative thesis stands for "the claim that society has the right to enforce its morality by law because the majority have the right to follow their own moral convictions that their moral environment is a thing of value to be defended from change."[2] Proponents of the disintegration thesis maintain that morality is "the cement of society, the bond, or one of the bonds, without which men would not cohere in society"[3] and that it must be upheld in order to prevent social disintegration. In his book, *The Enforcement of Morals*, the principal advocate of the disintegration thesis, Lord Devlin, argues that: "[T]he law must protect ... the institutions and the community of ideas, political and moral, without which people cannot live together. Society cannot ignore the morality of the individual any more than it can his loyalty; it flourishes on both and without either it dies."[4] Writing more than two centuries earlier, Erskine had similarly argued that crimes should be penalised because they threatened to "loosen the bonds of society".[5]

1–05 In common parlance the criminal law tends to be discussed in terms of serious crimes such as theft, assault and rape. Questions as to the proper scope of the criminal law do arise, even in relation to such long-recognised crimes. Recent issues before the Scottish courts have included whether the

---

[1] "Social Solidarity and the Enforcement of Morality" (1967) 35 *University of Chicago Law Review* 1, drawing upon R. Dworkin, "Lord Devlin and the Enforcement of Morals" (1966) 75 *Yale Law Journal* 986.
[2] *ibid*. p. 2.
[3] *ibid*. p. 1.
[4] *The Enforcement of Morals* (1965), p. 22.
[5] *Institutes*, IV, iv, 2.

law recognises the crime of housebreaking with intent to rape,[6] whether the crime of rape can be committed by a husband against his wife[7] and whether the unauthorised use of confidential information constitutes a form of theft.[8] However, the main focus of the "criminalisation" debate has tended to be elsewhere, involving those crimes intended to protect public morality, for example, "shameless indecency" (see Chapter 12, following).

Scotland would generally be regarded as having a highly moralistic   **1–06** criminal law, but there are types of behaviour which, although generally regarded as immoral, have never been within its scope: for example, breach of contract. Thus, to say that the task of the criminal law is to uphold moral standards is not a sufficient answer to the question as to the proper scope of the criminal law. It merely raises the further issues of how much morality, and whose, the law should uphold. Lord Devlin concedes as much, since he recognises the impossibility of setting theoretical limits on the power of the law to enforce morality. His solution is to apply the standard of the "reasonable" or "right-minded" man, "the man in the jury box", because "the moral judgment of society must be something about which any 12 [presumably 15 in Scotland] men or women drawn at random might after discussion be expected to be unanimous."[9]

The harm principle

A very different approach to that of Lord Devlin can be found in the   **1–07** philosophy of liberalism. The most famous statement of the liberal approach to the role of the law in the maintenance of morality is that of the nineteenth-century philosopher John Stuart Mill. Mill maintained that "the only purpose for which power can be rightfully exercised over any member of a civilized community, against his will, is to prevent harm to others. His own good, either physical or moral, is not a sufficient warrant."[10] An individual is only answerable to society for conduct "which concerns others".[11] The harm principle has been developed by Feinberg, who, as a further justification for criminalisation, puts forward an "offense principle". This principle is based upon the necessity "to prevent serious offense to persons other than the actor".[12] His preferred formulation of the harm principle is:

"It is always a good reason in support of penal legislation that it would probably be effective in preventing (eliminating, reducing) harm to

---

[6]   *H.M. Advocate v. Forbes*, 1994 S.L.T. 861
[7]   *S. v. H.M. Advocate*, 1989 S.L.T. 469.
[8]   *Grant v. Allan*, 1987 J.C. 71.
[9]   *The Enforcement of Morals*, p. 15.
[10]   Mill, *On Liberty* (1974 ed.), p. 68.
[11]   *ibid*. p. 69.
[12]   Feinberg, *Harm to Others* (1985), p. 26.

persons other than the actor (the one prohibited from acting) *and* there is probably no other means that is equally effective at no greater cost to other values."

Applying the harm principle, the individual should be granted the maximum degree of liberty consistent with this end (the rights of others). Thus one might say that an individual should be permitted to behave in a shamelessly indecent fashion, perhaps by showing an obscene film to a number of willing viewers, if no "harm" is caused.[13]

1–08   The harm principle has been very influential among writers on the criminal law. It captures the common feeling that the interests of the state should make accommodation for individual freedom. It also reflects the view that a primary function of the criminal law is the prevention of harm. This approach is very different from that of the disintegration thesis, which asserts that the role of the law is to protect the moral and political institutions of society and the "community of ideas" necessary for society to cohere (see para. 1–04, above). From this perspective, it would be legitimate to criminalise shamelessly indecent behaviour, even though no "harm" has been caused to anyone, because someone who acts in that fashion (for example, exhibiting an obscene film) could be regarded by the members of a jury as posing a threat to society's moral fabric.

PUNISHMENT

1–09   The rules of the criminal law define crimes and can be distinguished from those found in other branches of the law by the way in which it is sought to make them effective. As is well understood, those who contravene criminal rules make themselves liable to *punishment*. Indeed, so varied are the moral principles and political policies (which inspire what is not permitted) that it is usually helpful to focus upon punishment as *the* distinctive characteristic which all crimes share. This, however, leads to the question: "What is punishment?" In times past, the answer would not have proved too difficult — at least in practical terms. When those found to be contraveners of the criminal law were regularly hanged, beheaded, mutilated, branded, whipped or otherwise corporally abused, then punishment clearly entailed the infliction of some kind of physical suffering.[14] But from the nineteenth century onwards, such physical suffering has increasingly come to be regarded as unsuitable in a developed western society. Today, therefore, the principal sanctions for criminal behaviour are expressed as terms of imprisonment or monetary penalties (fines). There are more anodyne

---

[13] But compare *Watt v. Annan*, 1978 J.C. 84.
[14] See Hume, ii, 488 *et seq.*

alternatives available too — which include probation orders, community service orders and awards of compensation to victims. Since awards of compensation (damages) can also be made under quite different branches of the law (for example, for failing to honour an agreement under the law of contract, or injuring someone by carelessness under the law of delict) and civil penalties are not unknown either (see para. 2–19, following), one must endeavour to be much more precise in order to appreciate why punishment is uniquely associated with the criminal law.

This point is taken up by the American scholar, Henry M. Hart. In a **1–10** famous article[15] he states that the differentiating feature of the criminal law is that only criminal sanctions (that is, punishments) are both accompanied and justified by the condemnation of the community (that is, by a finding of guilt, which is referred to as "conviction"). Accordingly, one could say that it is this feature of the criminal law which distinguishes it from the civil law of contract and delict. In support of his contention, Hart cites another author to the effect that:

> "The essence of punishment for moral delinquency lies in the criminal conviction itself. One may lose more money on the stock market than in a court-room; a prisoner of war camp may well provide a harsher environment than a state prison; death on the field of battle has the same characteristics as death by sentence of law. It is the expression of the community's hatred, fear or contempt for the convict which alone characterizes hardship as punishment."[16]

Indeed, Hart's preferred definition of a crime is "an act or omission and its accompanying state of mind which, if duly proven to have taken place, will incur a formal and solemn pronouncement of the moral condemnation of the community."[17]

This definition, however, is only really persuasive in relation to the **1–11** more serious crimes long recognised by the common law (see Chapter 2, following). In modern times the ambit of the criminal law has expanded enormously. Of course, Henry M. Hart was aware of this development. He remarked upon the unfortunate tendency of modern criminal statutes to punish individuals who are not morally blameworthy and considered this to be an abuse because "a criminal conviction carries with it an ineradicable connotation of moral condemnation."[18] Nevertheless, the

[15] "The Aims of the Criminal Law" (1958) 23 *Law and Contemporary Problems* 401.
[16] M. Gardner, "Bailey v. Richardson and the Constitution of the United States" (1953) 33 B.U.L.Rev. 176 at p. 193.
[17] (1958) 23 *Law and Contemporary Problems* 401 at p. 405. The various elements of a crime referred to in this passage are described in detail in Chap. 3, following.
[18] *ibid.* p. 424.

problem with Hart's definition remains that it is difficult to maintain that public condemnation always inheres in a criminal conviction. For example, it would be unrealistic to suggest that every individual convicted of careless driving is subject to denunciation by his community. However, this problem is as much one of the adequacy or suitability of a particular sanction or of the appropriateness of bringing the conduct in question within the scope of the criminal law. The notion of punishment remains central to any plausible and self-contained account of the criminal law; and punishment cannot be imposed without conviction by a competent court.

PRINCIPLES OF CRIMINAL RESPONSIBILITY

1–12 Conviction certainly entails more than a mere finding that, for example, "A killed B." This in itself is a legally neutral statement. To justify punishment, the stage has to be attained where it is possible to conclude, for example, that "A is guilty of murdering B", and clearly that stage is not reached in law if A killed B on the field of battle during, say, the Gulf conflict. The prime function of the criminal law then is that of articulating the circumstances under which it is justifiable to hold a person punishable for his conduct. This entails a two-fold process.

1–13   First, there must be examination of what in general will have to be shown for conviction to be justified, no matter what particular crime is involved. This concerns what are known as the principles of criminal responsibility. Some basic principles of that sort are considered as part of Chapter 2, while the better known and more traditional ones are dealt with in Chapters 3 (*actus reus* and *mens rea*), 4 (voluntariness) and 5 (causation). These principles are regarded as essential moral and legal safeguards to ensure that only those who deserve it are in fact convicted and made liable to punishment. If occasionally adherence to these allows a few, possibly "guilty" persons to escape condemnation, this tends to be regarded as an acceptable price to pay. Different legal systems, however, display varied approaches to the acceptability of allowing such escapes from justice. Scottish criminal law, in particular, is currently in a phase of viewing with suspicion the suggestion that such principles should be weighted in favour of accused persons — as readers will doubtless conclude from their own studies and observations. But where derogations from, or adjustments to, these principles seem to have occurred, it will clearly be necessary to assert some cogent, countervailing justifications. That having been stated, it is also necessary to declare that some of the principles espoused by academic writers and others are controversial — in terms of their interpretation and scope as well as their applicability (see in particular the discussion of the concept of voluntariness in Chapter 4). A fair amount of space, therefore, has been reserved for their discussion. As has been aptly written: "We must not be naive about the subtlety with which the law is capable of reflecting fine moral judgments and distinctions."[19]

Secondly, there must be an examination of what precisely has been made **1–14** or declared punishable under Scots law. The principles referred to in the previous paragraph do not provide any guide to the individual acts and omissions which are not permitted under a particular system of law. Although there may be a basic core of crimes (nominally, at least) common to most legal systems, the totality of criminal acts and omissions is usually unique to a particular country or society. Chapters 9 to 12 are, therefore, devoted to a detailed study of selected acts and omissions proscribed under the law of Scotland. Unless plainly stated to the contrary, what is discussed there has no necessary application to the United Kingdom as a whole or to any other jurisdiction.

AIMS OF THE CRIMINAL LAW

Deterrence

The aims of the criminal law are very much those of its central **1–15** characteristic — namely, punishment. Unlike the branches of the civil law, which are expressed in terms of conditional causes and effects (for example, if one does not make a will, then one's property on death will devolve in certain predetermined ways), the intention is to *prevent* persons acting (or, sometimes, omitting to act) in particular ways. One could envisage this being promoted by a system of incentives and rewards, such as lower insurance premiums for drivers who avoid committing motoring offences. However, this would be regarded as too fragile a method of preventing harmful, injurious, destructive or antisocial behaviour; and, in practice, criminal systems rely on punishment. It would be naive indeed to imagine that the mere threat of punishment could entirely eradicate the sorts of behaviour which have been proscribed by the criminal law. The most that can be hoped for is that the threat will exercise sufficient psychological restraint over the *majority* of the population. The threat itself should be sufficient to deter. For those who were not in fact deterred, punishment within the parameters imposed by the law must actually be imposed with the object of personal deterrence for the future. Publicity for the punishments imposed might also be important in helping to restrain those still wavering on the brink of criminal conduct.

Retribution

Of course, if deterrence was the only aim, then the maximum possible **1–16** penalties would always seem justified, whenever there was an opportunity

---

[19] Lacey, *State Punishment* (1988), p. 71.

to impose punishment in fact. This might well be effective in preventing the individuals who were sentenced from committing further crimes, particularly if life imprisonment or capital punishment were to be meted out to them. However, this policy would be counter-productive as far as the rest of society was concerned if that punishment was not seen to be proportionate to what the individual had actually done. Not only, therefore, should a sentence after conviction aim to deter (both personally and generally); it should also aim to be "just deserts" for what has been done, after all the circumstances have been taken into consideration. This principle of just deserts should not be confused with the biblical enjoinment of an eye for an eye and a tooth for a tooth. Although its advocates do sometimes use it to argue that more punishment than now exists can be justified, modern Scots law has departed from corporal punishments. Further, it is clearly impossible to order the rape of a convicted rapist, or take property from a convicted, but destitute thief. A judge is simply required to do the best he can in the way of proportionality, given the circumstances of the offender, the nature of his offence, and what the law will allow. One might think that a victim's views would be relevant to consideration of sentence under this heading, but Scots law does not currently favour such an approach.[20]

Reformation

1–17   The modern criminal law may also aim to reform or rehabilitate. It is unlikely that the primary punishments (prison or fines) will have any such effect. In particular, an enlightened prison regime is currently the exception rather than the rule in Scotland. However, alternative "punishments" (depending on the significance one cares to give to that term), such as community service and probation, do seem to contemplate more than deterrence or retribution (often, one might add, to the dismay of the victims of the crimes in question).

Public protection

1–18   The notion of deterrence implies that an offender, or a potential offender, will be capable of exercising rational judgment and can be deterred by the threat of punishment from infringing the criminal law. Where this is clearly not so, then measures may have to be taken to protect others from the future conduct of that sort of convicted person — which may entail incarceration, or other restraint, far beyond the requirements of simple deterrence or retribution. When insanity is involved, then the same principle applies — although one might not wish (or indeed have) to register a conviction in

---

[20]   *H.M. Advocate v. McKenzie*, 1990 J.C. 62.

such a case. Scots law certainly appears to adhere to these particular views (see Chapter 4, following).

CRIMINAL PROCEDURE

The criminal law would be quite ineffective in pursuing its aims unless there **1–19** were police to detect and deter the commission of crimes, prosecutors to conduct cases against suspected persons, courts to assess the evidence for and against such suspects, the whole panoply of prisons, social work agencies (for probation and community service schemes) and so on. In brief, criminal law requires complementary procedural devices. The law of criminal procedure is, however, generally beyond the scope of this book. Readers are referred to the relevant standard works noted at the end of this chapter.

CRIMINAL EVIDENCE

The success of criminal prosecutions (on which the efficiency of the law is **1–20** often seen to depend) and the procurement of fair dealing for suspected persons are predicated on the sort of evidence which can be led before a court of law. Again, there are detailed rules, and principles, which operate here; but the law of criminal evidence is generally also beyond the scope of this book. At appropriate points the reader is referred to an introductory text on the law of evidence.

Further reading

Generally

Fletcher, G. P., *Rethinking Criminal Law* (1978), pp. 408–420.
Gordon, G. H., *The Criminal Law of Scotland* (2nd ed., 1978) and Second Cumulative Supplement (1992), paras. 2–09 to 2–17.
Gross, H., *A Theory of Criminal Justice* (1979), Chaps. 1 and 9.
Hart, H. L. A., *Punishment and Responsibility* (1968), Chap. 1.
Lacey, N., *State Punishment* (1988), Chap. 5.
Law Reform Commission of Canada, *Our Criminal Law*, Report No. 3, 1976.
Walker, N., *Punishment, Danger and Stigma: The Morality of Criminal Justice* (1980).

And specifically on procedure or evidence

Field, D., *Law of Evidence in Scotland* (2nd ed., 1996).
Gane, C. H. W., & Stoddart, C. N., *Criminal Procedure in Scotland: Cases & Materials* (2nd ed., 1994).
Macphail, I. D., *Evidence* (1987).
Renton, R. W., & Brown, H. H., *Criminal Procedure According to the Law of Scotland* (6th ed. by G. H. Gordon & Others, 1996).

CHAPTER 2

NATURE AND SOURCES OF SCOTS CRIMINAL LAW

General

2–01   Unlike many European countries (*e.g.* France, Germany) and the USA (both at Federal and individual State levels), there is no criminal code in Scotland. This means that there is no convenient place where any *official* list or description of Scottish crimes can be found. Equally there is no authorised account of the principles which govern the operation of the criminal law. It follows that this area of the law is less certain (but more flexible) in Scotland than may be the case elsewhere. Whether this is an advantageous situation will often depend on the perspective — *i.e.* whether one views the matter from the point of view of the accused or the prosecutor.

2–02   Of course, the absence of a code does not make it impossible to give a perfectly intelligible and pragmatic account of Scots criminal law. Both principles and crime descriptions appear, for example, in modern textbooks (such as this one) and have been compiled from authoritative sources. As textbooks themselves are not normally recognised as being in any way authoritative, it is necessary to appreciate what are the true legal sources on which their authors have relied. These sources must invariably be checked too before any legal opinion based on textbook or periodical literature is ventured. Although legal sources may be described as a constant, interpretation of what they are found to contain is a very real variable of which careful account must be taken.

SOURCES — THE COMMON LAW

2–03   Traditionally, rules pertaining to the "Common Law" are said to be those of such long standing that their origins cannot be traced. Such rules are often described as "consuetudinary" (*i.e.* customary). Alternatively, if a rule does in fact have a clear origin, it is still reckoned as a common law one if it has no *legislative* foundation. More practically, however, it is the criminal law expounded by judges of the superior criminal courts in actual proceedings before them which lawyers are wont to refer to as "Common Law." The superior criminal courts in Scotland for this purpose are the

High Court of Justiciary as a trial court and the High Court of Justiciary as an appeal court (in the widest sense).[1]

The High Court of Justiciary was altered to more or less its modern **2–04** form in 1672,[2] but its authenticated history can be traced for many centuries prior to that. To establish any part of the common law through judicial decisions from earliest times down to the present would thus be a mammoth task involving painstaking research in the records of the High Court (as it is known for short) as these are preserved in the Scottish Record Office in Edinburgh. In practice then, a simpler route has evolved.

Professor (sometimes "Baron") David Hume made a study of what might **2–05** be gleaned from High Court decisions down to 1797. With some (minor) additions of his own, he was thus able to deduce and publish an account of the common law of Scotland pertaining to criminal matters. Two new editions were produced by him which updated the common law to 1819 and 1829. He died in 1838, but a prominent advocate (Benjamin R. Bell) republished the 1829 edition together with updating notes of his own (drawn from High Court decisions) in 1844. This is invariably, though not quite accurately, referred to as the fourth edition of Hume's *Commentaries*. This work has for many decades been accorded authoritative status. Whenever a question relating to the common law of crimes is at issue, the starting point for Scottish lawyers (and sometimes the end point too) is any statement Hume might have made on the matter. Occasionally, judges of the High Court have disagreed with his pronouncements,[3] but more often than not, they have treated his writings with the utmost deference.[4] Hume's *Commentaries* are, therefore, much more than a mere textbook. They are regarded as an important *source* of the common law of crimes at the time they were written, and indeed as the initial point for subsequent research into the present state of that common law.

It is necessary to establish an initial point for research since the common **2–06** law is constantly being developed by High Court judges in actual criminal proceedings before them. So long as there is a common law of crimes in Scotland, this evolutionary process will continue. That process applies to the creation of novel crimes, the definitions of existing crimes, defences to those crimes, evidential and procedural matters, and even to principles. The notion of flexible development is simply inseparable from the notion of common law, in so far as Scots criminal law is concerned.

There are some other text-writings which judges of the High Court have **2–07** looked upon with something of the same favour accorded to Hume. Foremost

---

[1] See *Jessop v. Stevenson*, 1988 J.C. 17, opinion of the court at p. 20; *Elliott v. H.M. Advocate*, 1995 S.L.T. 612, *per* Lord Justice-Clerk Ross at p. 615K–L.
[2] A.P.S., VIII, 80 at 87–88.
[3] *John Smith* (1838) 2 Swin. 28; *S. v. H.M. Advocate*, 1989 S.L.T. 469.
[4] See, *e.g.*, *Khaliq v. H.M. Advocate*, 1984 J.C. 23; *Thomson v. H.M. Advocate*, 1983 J.C. 69.

among these is Archibald Alison's *Principles of the Criminal Law of Scotland*, published in 1832. Although this work relies heavily on Hume's earlier text, it nevertheless "draws freely on [Alison's] own experience as an advocate-depute [*i.e.* criminal prosecutor] and quotes over 1,000 cases in which he was personally engaged and of which there was and is no other published report."[5] It also seems that J. H. A. Macdonald's *Practical Treatise on the Criminal Law of Scotland* (latest edition 1948) may enjoy considerable authoritative status with at least some High Court judges.[6]

2–08   No text-writings, other than those mentioned above, have been regarded as sources of criminal common law. For example, the outstanding work of scholarship in the twentieth century on Scots criminal law, Gordon's *Criminal Law*,[7] contains much lucid, influential and persuasive writing on the subject; but the author's opinions and deductions have very rarely been preferred to those of Hume, Alison and Macdonald.[8]

2–09   The present common law, then, consists of the deductions, conclusions and opinions of Hume, Alison and Macdonald together with such alterations, additions and amendments as have been made to date by judges of the High Court of Justiciary in particular criminal proceedings before them. Since the early nineteenth century, such criminal proceedings have been published in a variety of different law reports (see Appendix B), and these provide the most important modern source of the common law.

SOURCES — LEGISLATION

2–10   Legislation refers to technically written rules promulgated in a predefined way at a particular point in time by a person or body recognised as having the authority to do so. Such rules differ from those of the common law in that they are not subject to similar development — *i.e.* they cannot be added to or altered by judges in actual criminal proceedings before them. They may only be enlarged or amended by subsequent acts of legislation. Of course, judges can interpret the words of such rules. Indeed they must do this if the arid generalisations of legislation are to be made applicable to (and thus decisive of) actual criminal cases. If such interpretations are made by judges of the High Court of Justiciary, then such decisions make law in a very real sense. The interpretations then become part of the legislative

---

[5]   Sheriff J. Irvine Smith at p. vii of his introduction to the 1989 reprint of Alison's *Principles*.
[6]   See the opinion of Lord Cameron in *Watt v. Annan*, 1978 J.C. 84 at pp. 88 *et seq.*
[7]   Gordon, *Criminal Law* (2nd ed., 1978), with second cumulative supplement (1992).
[8]   See *Smart v. H.M. Advocate*, 1975 J.C. 30; *Roberts v. Hamilton*, 1989 J.C. 91; *Scott v. H.M. Advocate*, 1996 S.L.T. 519. Although the trial judge, Lord Osborne, referred to academic writings as part of the reason for the directions he gave the jury in *Jamieson v. H.M. Advocate*, 1994 S.L.T. 537 at p. 539H, those writings were entirely ignored by the Appeal Court in deciding that what he had said amounted to a misdirection in law.

rule itself. But it is not the case that such an interpretation would ever be spoken of as forming part of the common law. Common law and legislation thus remain separate sources of the criminal law; but, although the common law can have no effect on existing legislation, the converse is not true. Legislative rules can radically alter portions of the common law (see, *e.g.*, section 13 of the Criminal Law (Consolidation) (Scotland) Act 1995, which radically alters the common law prohibition against male homosexual practices).

Legislation from Parliament

The supreme source of criminal legislation in Scotland is Parliament.   **2–11** After May 1, 1707,[9] the Scottish Parliament ceased to exist. Its demise was closely followed by that of the Scottish Privy Council on May 1, 1708.[10] Prior to 1707, both these Scottish bodies had produced a mass of legislation, much of it of a criminal law nature. Nor did such legislation perish with the death of its parent. Indeed, the Act of Union[11] assumed that it would continue until altered by the new "Great Britain" Parliament, common to both Scotland and England. Naturally, the Acts (or Statutes — to use a synonymous expression) of the defunct Scots Parliament looked increasingly anachronistic as the eighteenth century ran its course. In the nineteenth century, therefore, the then styled "United Kingdom" Parliament began to remove many of the older Scots statutes by enactments of its own (generally known as "Statute Law (Repeal)" or "Statute Law (Revision)" Acts). Those which remained were heavily amended.[12] In brief, the modern criminal law relies very rarely indeed on pre-Union legislation; the legislation now current (and there is a great deal of it) was created, and continues to be created, by the United Kingdom Parliament at Westminster. Perhaps the most useful repository of criminal legislation is the set of looseleaf volumes known as *Statutes in Force — Official Revised Edition.* This series makes strenuous (though not impeccable) efforts to keep legislation current — *i.e.* to rewrite criminal, and other legislation in accordance with amendments and repeals. Where commentaries are desired on particular Acts of Parliament, the set of statutes known as *Current Law Statutes* (formerly *Scottish Current Law Statutes*) can be recommended. The comments found there, however, have no official status and are in no way to be taken as part of the legislation itself.

---

9 A.P.S., XI, 406 *et seq.*
10 See the Edinburgh History of Scotland, Vol. 4 at pp. 54–55.
11 Art. XVIII, A.P.S., XI, 410.
12 Compare the "Theft" Act 1607 as it appears in A.P.S., IV, 373 with the present version quoted in Statutes in Force 39:6:1.

Non-Parliamentary legislation

2–12   Of no less relevance as a source of criminal law is legislation which
Parliament permits other bodies, or even persons, to create. The power to
make such legislative rules is not, of course, delegated in an unfettered
way. A "parent" statute will make clear the parameters within which the
body or person (almost always a Secretary of State) may legislate; and
what is eventually produced may be attacked if those parameters have been
exceeded. There are two principal types of such "delegated" legislation —
Statutory Instruments and Byelaws.

2–13   A comprehensive definition of "Statutory Instrument" is given in the
Statutory Instruments Act 1946 at section 1. Much of the modern legislative
criminal law (road traffic law, for example) is now to be found in these
"Instruments" (or S.I.s, for short) which may easily be located in any well-
stocked law library. They include legislative powers exercised by Ministers
of the Crown (Secretaries of State) and by the High Court of Justiciary as a
collegiate court.[13] Historically, the High Court probably always had authority
to lay down rules relating to its own procedures — but the power to do so is
now clarified by Act of Parliament.[14] When the court exercises its rule-
making powers, it is said to do so by "Act of Adjournal". That title refers to
the court's records (the Books of Adjournal) where acts and regulations
were (and still are) engrossed[15]; but although the title has been retained, it
is now clear that Acts of Adjournal are to be treated as ordinary S.I.s[16] and
indeed are published as such.

2–14   Byelaws are rules made by a variety of bodies in accordance with powers
specifically given to them by Parliament. In particular, Scottish local
authorities can make these, their powers to do so being apparently very
wide: "A local authority may make byelaws for the good rule and
government of the whole or any part of their area, and for the prevention
and suppression of nuisances therein."[17] Their discretion here, however, is
contained by the requirement that any proposed byelaw should first have
been confirmed by the Secretary of State for Scotland before it acquires the
force of law. Byelaws certainly form a source (although admittedly a minor
source) of criminal law. In 1990, for example, the City of Dundee District
Council (as it then was) banned the consumption of alcoholic drink in
designated public places by this method for a trial period of two years.
(These byelaws were made on April 17, were confirmed on July 6, and

---

[13] See *Stair Memorial Encyclopaedia*, Vol. 22, para. 306.
[14] See the Criminal Procedure (Scotland) Act 1995, s.305. See also s.304 (Criminal Courts
      Rules Council).
[15] Act of Adjournal (Criminal Procedure Rules) 1996 (S.I. 1996 No. 513), r. 3.1(2).
[16] Law Reform (Miscellaneous Provisions) (Scotland) Act 1966, s.10.
[17] Local Government (Scotland) Act 1973, s.201(1) and (2), as amended by the Local
      Government (Scotland) Act 1994, s.180(1), Sched.13, para. 92(61).

became effective on August 20, 1990.) A similar measure was also adopted by other local authorities, such as the (then) Motherwell District Council.[18] Byelaws, however, must be produced in evidence before criminal courts since, unlike Parliamentary legislation, they do not othewise have probative status.[19] At present, the maximum fine for the breach of such a byelaw is usually set at level 2 on the standard scale — see Appendix C.

Bodies other than local authorities can also make byelaws. This is **2–15** common where statutory bodies either own or lease land and generally allow the public to disport themselves there. The Forestry Commission, for example, has power to make rules concerning the use by the public of its camp-sites, nature trails, information centres and other facilities — although curiously the byelaws so made are declared expressly to be statutory instruments.[20] Transport undertakers, such as airport operators have similar byelaw-making powers.[21]

In addition to byelaws, a Scottish local authority can make "Management **2–16** Rules" relating to the conduct of persons in premises which the authority owns or manages. Whilst it is not a crime to contravene such rules, it is an offence (maximum fine — level 2 on the standard scale) to refuse to leave such premises when an authorised officer requires one to do so on the grounds that a breach of the rules has taken place or is likely to happen.[22]

Extra-national legislation

Since the accession of the United Kingdom (and thus Scotland) to the **2–17** European Community (known as the European Economic Community prior to the coming into force of the Treaty on European Union in November 1993),[23] certain community legislation (in particular regulations) promulgated by the Council or the Commission is of direct effect within Scotland, and automatically supersedes any existing (and contrary) national law. Other community legislation (*e.g.* directives) requires express implementation in this country before the expiry of predetermined calendar dates.[24] Where implementation is required, however, this can be achieved by mere (United Kingdom) ministerial regulations or orders in council —

---

18 Motherwell District Council (Prohibition of Consumption of Alcohol) Byelaws 1991.
19 See, *e.g.*, *Donnelly v. Carmichael,* 1996 S.L.T. 153, following *Herkes v. Dickie,* 1958 J.C. 51.
20 See the Forestry Act 1967, s.46, as amended by the Criminal Procedure (Consequential Provisions) (Scotland) Act 1995, Sched. 2, Part 3; the Countryside (Scotland) Act 1967, s.58(3).
21 See the Airports Act 1986, ss.63 and 64. For an example of byelaws made thereunder, see *Fulton v. Lees,* 1993 S.L.T. 927.
22 See the Civic Government (Scotland) Act 1982, ss.112–118.
23 See the European Communities Act 1972, as amended.
24 See the European Community Treaty 1957 (as amended), Art. 189; European Communities Act 1972, s.2.

although no really serious crimes can be created in Scotland in such ways.[25] Nevertheless, the importance of community law as a source of criminal law is constantly increasing, especially in the areas of road traffic law and environmental protection. Where community law is of relevance to the criminal law, questions of interpretation are bound to arise. Under Article 177 of the European Community Treaty, national courts may request preliminary rulings from the European Court of Justice as to the interpretation and validity of community laws, and Scottish courts have made such requests on several occasions.[26] If the meaning of a particular piece of community legislation is plain, however, Scottish courts may give it that meaning without resort to the European Court.[27] Equally, where there are previous rulings of the European Court which are applicable to the case on hand, Scottish courts are bound to follow those rulings.[28]

2–18 By way of contrast, the European Convention on Human Rights (effective since September 3, 1953) is not regarded as source legislation in Scotland.[29] Although it has been both signed and ratified by the United Kingdom, the Convention remains merely an international treaty, and thus will not become part of Scots law until expressly made so by Act of Parliament. The conclusion reached by governments to date appears to be that human rights, as expressed in the Convention and which, by Article 1, the United Kingdom must "secure to everyone" within its jurisdiction, are adequately protected by existing national laws, and that there is accordingly no need actually to incorporate them into domestic law.[30] This may be a justifiable view in relation to certain provisions. Article 6, for example, provides generally that everyone charged with the commission of a crime is entitled to a fair trial, which entails (*inter alia*) certain minimum rights, namely, to be

---

[25] See the European Communities Act 1972, s.2(2)(a) and Sched. 2, para. 1(1)(d).

[26] See, *e.g.*, *Wither v. Cowie*, 1994 S.L.T. 363 (where, *inter alia*, a Council regulation required Member States to notify the Commission of any change to their existing sea-fishing laws, and a sheriff court requested a preliminary ruling on the validity of U.K. fishing laws which had been implemented without such prior notification), and *Walkingshaw v. Marshall*, 1992 S.L.T. 1167 (where certain U.K. legislation, prohibiting the carriage of particular types of nets by British registered fishing vessels in Scottish inshore waters, having been attacked as both discriminatory and contrary to the principle of proportionality and thus contrary to community law, was referred by the High Court of Justiciary to the European Court for a preliminary ruling as to its validity).

[27] See, *e.g.*, *Westwater v. Thomson*, 1993 S.L.T. 703 — although it was emphasised there that the principles to be employed in interpreting community law are those of the European Community and not those of the domestic law of Scotland.

[28] See, *e.g.*, *Baron Meats Ltd v. Lockhart*, 1991 J.C. 129, where the High Court of Justiciary followed a prior decision of the European Court on the meaning of "door to door selling" as applicable to vehicles fitted out as mobile shops.

[29] *Kaur v. Lord Advocate*, 1980 J.C. 319, *per* Lord Ross at pp. 324–326 and 328–330.

[30] Wade and Bradley, *Constitutional and Administrative Law* (11th ed., 1993), p. 421.

informed in detail of the nature of the charge against him,[31] to have sufficient time and facilities to prepare his defence, and to have legal assistance (free of charge where necessary in the interests of justice) in the conduct of his defence.[32] Of these particular provisions it has recently been said that they "are not part of our domestic law, but the principles which they describe have, for a long time, been established as part of the law of this country."[33] Indeed, the case in which these words were uttered arguably parallels the European Court of Human Rights's interpretation of Article 6.3(c) by introducing a (limited) right to *effective* assistance in an accused person's defence, by making it a recognised ground of appeal that the way in which counsel or a solicitor conducted the case deprived the accused of his defence and thus of an essential element in his right to a fair trial.[34] On the other hand, and following from the fact that the United Kingdom has recognised the right of individual petition to the European Commission of Human Rights and accepted the compulsory jurisdiction of the European Court of Human Rights,[35] two persons who were forced to conduct their own appeals before the Scottish Appeal Court (since legal aid had been refused) were considered by the European Court to have had their rights under Article 6.3(c) infringed.[36] Although the terms of the Convention may be used in England as an aid to the interpretation of domestic legislation, the Scottish courts have yet to decide to follow suit, or even to accept that legislative ambiguities (where relevant) may be resolved by considering that Parliament must have intended to legislate in conformity with, rather than against the United Kingdom's treaty obligations.[37]

THE DEFINITION OF CRIME

Among other things, the sources of the criminal law referred to above should   **2–19**
reveal the current catalogue of crimes. A comprehensive yet succinct definition of what makes any particular act or omission or situation criminal rather than not is probably an impossibility, given the enormous range of

---

[31] See, *e.g.*, *Cardle v. David Carlaw Engineering (Glasgow) Ltd,* 1992 S.L.T. 1101; *cf.* *Horsburgh v. Russell,* 1994 S.L.T. 942 (on the effect of the rule now contained in the Criminal Procedure (Scotland) Act 1995, Sched. 3, para. 14).

[32] Art. 6.1 and 6.3 (a), (b), (c).

[33] *Anderson v. H.M. Advocate,* 1996 S.L.T. 155, *per* Lord Justice-General Hope at p. 158B.

[34] See Harris, O'Boyle and Warbrick, *Law of the European Convention on Human Rights* (1995), pp. 264 *et seq.*

[35] See Wade and Bradley, *Constitutional and Administrative Law*, p. 419; but note the imminent changes in the institutions and application procedures of the Convention to be wrought by the Eleventh Protocol — see Harris, O'Boyle and Warbreck, *op. cit.*, Chap. 26.

[36] *Boner v. United Kingdom; Maxwell v. United Kingdom,* 1995 S.C.C.R. 1 (E.C.H.R.).

[37] See *Anderson v. H.M. Advocate,* 1996 S.L.T. 155, *per* Lord Justice-General Hope at p. 158B–C.

matters which are definitely criminal.[38] There seems little to connect (morally or otherwise), for example, the deliberate killing of another human being (murder at common law) and trading as a window cleaner without having obtained a licence.[39] It is possible, of course, to refer to the threat of punishment which is often said uniquely to underlie any truly criminal proscription (see Chapter 1, above). But this raises the problem of what content should be given to the term "punishment". Under the Local Government Finance Act 1992,[40] for example, a failure to supply particular information to a local authority in connection with council tax results in the imposition of a penalty of £50 (rising to £200 for subsequent failures). The imposition of such penalties might well be taken as punishment of a very real sort; but it is abundantly clear that no crime is intended or involved. It is equally possible to stress that crimes are uniquely the objects of a particular type of procedure — involving prosecutors, courts and proceedings which are very definitely different from anything encountered in the civil law field.[41] But such attempts at definition are problematic, often circular and perhaps unnecessary. Modern statutes invariably identify clearly what is intended to be criminal by employing the word "offence" (virtually a legal synonym for "crime") in the context of "summary" or "indictment" (*i.e.* plainly criminal) procedure. The maximum fine or period of imprisonment will also clearly be stated. The identification of what is criminal under legislative provisions is, therefore, unlikely to present difficulties.

2–20　　In the common law field, where inevitably matters are rather more fluid, identification of acts or omissions as criminal or not may indeed pose occasional problems. But even here, resort in practice is not had to any standard definition of the essence of "crime". Such issues of identification are resolved by the "inherent" power of the High Court of Justiciary to declare the common law, which it does from time to time in particular cases according to ad hoc criteria of its own choosing.

THE DECLARATORY POWER OF THE HIGH COURT

2–21　　In "declaring the common law", the High Court may simply be declaring the ambit of a known crime (a function usually accepted as necessary under any common law system), or it may be exercising a distinct power to criminalise what was not formerly known to be criminal. The existence of that distinct power (usually referred to as the "Declaratory Power") is

---

[38] See Gordon, *Criminal Law*, Chap. 1; Smith and Hogan, *Criminal Law* (7th ed., 1992), Chap. 2.
[39] Civic Government (Scotland) Act 1982, ss.7 and 43.
[40] See s.97(4) and Sched. 3.
[41] Gordon, *Criminal Law*, para. 1–04.

probably contrary to the principles of clarity, accessibility and non-retroactivity of criminal provisions — principles which many modern legal systems espouse, and which are expressed in, or implied by Article 7(1) of the European Convention on Human Rights.[42] In more detail, the main principle here (sometimes expressed in Latin as *nullum crimen sine lege*) enjoins that no one should be convicted for an act or omission which was not clearly and knowably criminal at the time it was done. A corollary may also be stated — namely that no one should be denied a defence which was clearly relevant and available in law at the time of commission of some act or omission. In so far, therefore, as it recognises a power to make new crimes or cancel defences in actual cases, Scots criminal law seems unable to adhere to these principles — or at least seems unable to do so in relation to the common law. Adherence to such principles in the matter of legislation is primarily the responsibility of Parliament.

Authority for the existence of the power

It appears that the first written notice of such a power was given by **2–22** Hume in the 1797 edition of the *Commentaries*[43] although he gives few examples of its actual use. That might give rise to the charge that the declaratory power was something of a novelty — if not a product of the author's own imagination — but Alison[44] also refers to it, independently of any reference to Hume, and apparently quotes 16 different instances of its application. The judges of the High Court have also endorsed the existence of the power in many cases.[45] There is also clear confirmation of this situation in Macdonald,[46] although his primary (footnote) authority is given as Hume. There can be little doubt, therefore, that the High Court of Justiciary has authority to enlarge the contents of the common law.

---

[42] See Harris, O'Boyle, and Warbrick, *Law of the European Convention On Human Rights*, Chap. 7.
[43] i, 52; 1844 ed. i, 12.
[44] *Principles*, i, 624 *et seq.*
[45] See *Taylor*, October 19, 1808, Burnett, App., No. X, *per* Lords Craig, Armadale, Meadowbank (by implication) and Lord Justice-Clerk Hope; *Bernard Greenhuff* (1838) 2 Swin. 236, *per* Lords Moncreiff (at p. 265) and Mackenzie (at pp. 268–269), and Lord Justice-Clerk Boyle (at p. 259), who all make reference to Hume, and Lord Medwyn (at p. 270) who favoured Alison's analysis; *Sugden v. H.M. Advocate*, 1934 J.C. 103, *per* Lord Justice-Clerk Aitchison at p. 109, who refers to it as a "prerogative of the Justiciary derived from its history, and coming down from the days of the Justiciar"; and *Grant v. Allan*, 1987 J.C. 71, *per* Lord Justice-Clerk Ross at p. 77, where he asserts that "there are circumstances where it will be appropriate for the court to exercise this power", whilst conceding that great care requires to be taken in its exercise.
[46] *Criminal Law* (5th ed., 1948), p. 193.

Meaning of the "High Court" for this purpose

2–23   It seems agreed that the declaratory power is only possessed by the High Court of Justiciary[47] and not by any lesser court (see Appendix D). What is unclear, however, is what is here meant by the "High Court". According to the court itself in *Jessop v. Stevenson*[48]: "A decision of a judge of the High Court of Justiciary is a decision of the High Court of Justiciary." That does not mean, however, that a single High Court judge can necessarily exercise all the powers of that institution as a "Collegiate Court".[49] Sheriff Gordon opines that a "quorum" of the court must be present,[50] but it is hard to know what that means in the context of this power. Prior to the reforms of the late nineteenth century, when all judges of the Court of Session also became members of the supreme criminal court,[51] it was feasible, and not uncommon, for the whole court of six or seven judges — depending on whether the Lord Justice-General was present — to sit in relation to decisions on *inter alia* the exercise of the power.[52] A possible *de facto* exercise of the power by two judges on circuit at Aberdeen was clearly unusual and required explanation.[53] But the whole court now consists of at least 26 judges; and it is, therefore, not unreasonable to conclude that a minimum of three judges will form a "quorum" for the purposes of the declaratory power. That represents the minimum number for appeal proceedings,[54] and for matters certified to the High Court under the Criminal Procedure (Scotland) Act 1995, section 103(4); and it is by appeal or certification that issues concerning the exercise of the power will come before that court.

Why does the court have this power?

2–24   Both Hume[55] and Alison[56] assume that it will always be necessary to create new crimes; and in fact few would dispute that assumption. They further assume, however, that both Parliament and the High Court are

---

[47] See Gordon, *Criminal Law*, para. 1–43.

[48] 1988 J.C. 17 at p. 20.

[49] See *Stair Memorial Encyclopaedia*, Vol. 6, paras. 859 and 904.

[50] *Criminal Law*, para. 1–43; see also *Khaliq v. H.M. Advocate*, 1984 J.C. 23, *per* Lord Avonside at p. 24.

[51] Criminal Procedure (Scotland) Act 1887, s.44.

[52] See *Rachel Wright* (1809) Burnett 134 and App. No. vii; *Bernard Greenhuff* (1838) 2 Swin. 236; *William Fraser* (1847) Ark. 280; *John Ballantyne* (1859) 3 Irv. 352.

[53] *Margaret Irvine*, September 1784, Burnett 133, commented on in *Rachel Wright, supra, per* Lords Craig, Armadale, Meadowbank and Lord Justice-Clerk Hope.

[54] Criminal Procedure (Scotland) Act 1995, ss.103(2) and 173(1); but note that for appeals against (generally) sentence alone, the quorum of the court falls to two (unless the two are unable to agree) — see ss.103(3) and 173(2).

[55] i, 12.

[56] *Principles*, i, 624.

competent to create such new crimes. But the rationale behind the court's entitlement to do so is simply not revealed. Since Parliament is constitutionally recognised as having legislative functions, it is hardly surprising that it may from time to time increase the stock of available crimes. Courts in the modern world, however, are not generally recognised as having legislative powers co-extensive with those of legislatures, and some explanation for the High Court's continued ability to declare acts (or omissions) to be criminal would seem to be called for. The best explanation which the judiciary themselves have suggested is that the High Court simply occupies a unique constitutional position within the United Kingdom. "I hold it to be law, that the right of enquiring into all injuries to individuals by criminal acts, as well as of defining in such cases the nature and extent of the punishment, is constitutionally entrusted to this Court."[57]

On the assumption that the High Court and Parliament may make acts   **2–25**
(or omissions) criminal which were not so regarded before, the question arises whether one body is to be preferred to the other in the exercise of such a function. Hume[58] certainly addresses himself to this matter, and concludes that the court is definitely preferable, since Parliament is generally too slow in remedying social problems suitable for criminalisation, provides too rigid definitions of what is eventually proscribed (thus encouraging the search for, and exploitation of "loopholes"), and imposes too severe maximum punishments. Only the last of these matters is endorsed by Alison[59]; but whatever the shortcomings of Parliaments of the early nineteenth century, Hume's criticisms are scarcely tenable now. In modern times, there is no reason to suppose that professional legislatures could not (or would not) respond quickly to matters perceived as dangerous to the community or individuals. The Crossbows Act 1987 and the Firearms (Amendment) Act 1988, for example, both represented fairly rapid legislative responses to the problems of controlling the circulation of newly-popular types of lethal weapon; and the Dangerous Dogs Act 1991, the Carrying of Knives etc. (Scotland) Act 1993,[60] and the Firearms (Amendment) Act 1994 represented fairly rapid responses to newly perceived issues of public safety. Also, with only limited exceptions,[61] offences created by Parliament have generally carried more limited

---

[57] *Rachel Wright* (1809) Burnett, App. No. vii, *per* Lord Meadowbank; see also *Sugden v. H.M. Advocate*, 1934 J.C. 103 at p. 109 where Lord Justice-Clerk Alness asserted the power to be a "prerogative right of the Justiciary derived from its history."

[58] i, 12.

[59] *Principles*, i, 625.

[60] Now repealed and re-enacted as s.49 of the Criminal Law (Consolidation) (Scotland) Act 1995.

[61] For example, the Misuse of Drugs Act 1971, s.25 and Sched. 4, as amended by the Controlled Drugs (Penalties) Act 1985, s.1(1).

maximum penalties than corresponding common law crimes. For example, compare the Road Traffic Offenders Act 1988, Schedule 2, Part I ("RTA section 1" entry[62]) — 10 years — with the equivalent maximum punishment for the common law offence of "culpable homicide" (life in prison, if taken before a High Court). Finally, the lack of flexibility in the definitions of statutorily created crimes will be seen by many as a decided advantage. Criminal law ought to be clear and readily understandable. Given the serious consequences of contravening the criminal law, it ought to be abundantly clear how one may remain within the letter of the law.

2–26   It is, therefore, not really clear why the High Court should continue to enjoy the "declaratory power". The fact that it does so continue at least, however, carries the prospect of providing some answers to the troublesome question — "What are the essential characteristics of behaviour deemed to be criminal?" If the court declares some act or omission to be criminal, one would expect to obtain useful information as to why it had done so.

Criteria for the power's exercise

2–27   Hume's view[63] was that the power might be exercised where the act (or omission) in question was "obviously of a criminal nature". In the case of *John Ballantyne*[64] Lord Justice-Clerk Inglis ventured the view that Hume meant by that acts which were *mala in se* — *i.e.* evils in themselves. This, if correct, connotes the criterion of "immorality," with all the vagueness that that implies. Nevertheless, some judges have clearly opined that the perceived immorality of an act (or omission) will suffice to exercise the crime-making power,[65] especially if likely to corrupt the young,[66] or pose "danger" to society.[67] In modern times, however, the High Court appears to have rejected such a criterion. More must be shown than that the act (or omission) was "reprehensible and immoral"[68]; in particular, it might suffice if "injurious consequences to persons or property" could be demonstrated[69] — which itself shows a tendency towards the acceptance of Alison's less vague criterion (see para. 2–28, below). The major problem with any appeal

---

[62] As amended by the Road Traffic Act 1991, Sched. 2, para. 5, and the Criminal Justice Act 1993, s. 67(1).

[63] i, 12.

[64] (1859) 3 Irv. 352 at p. 359.

[65] See *Bernard Greenhuff* (1838) 2 Swin. 236, *per* Lord Justice-Clerk Boyle at p. 258 and Lord Meadowbank at p. 264.

[66] *Bernard Greenhuff, supra, per* Lord Justice-Clerk Boyle at p. 258.

[67] *Bernard Greenhuff, supra, per* Lord Moncreiff at p. 266; *John Barr* (1839) 2 Swin. 282, *per* Lord Mackenzie at p. 310 and Lord Medwyn at p. 315.

[68] *Grant v. Allan,* 1987 J.C. 71, *per* Lord Justice-Clerk Ross at p. 77; *H.M. Advocate v. Semple,* 1937 J.C. 41, *per* Lord Justice-Clerk Aitchison at pp. 45–46 and Lord Fleming at p. 47.

[69] *John Ballantyne* (1859) 3 Irv. 352, *per* Lord Justice-Clerk Inglis at pp. 359–360.

to immorality is, of course, that few people can be found to agree as to what is or is not immoral. And this problem is merely re-phrased by opining that an act (or omission) must be "so grossly immoral and mischievous on its face that no man can fairly be ignorant of it" before the court may exercise its crime-making power.[70]

The other most often-quoted criterion is that proffered by Alison.[71] His   **2–28** view was that the power might be exercised in respect of an act (or omission) which was both in itself wrong (*malum in se*) and hurtful to the persons or property of others. There is a pragmatic flavour to this which almost anticipates the development of the "harm" principle by John Stuart Mill and others[72]; and there has been some judicial acceptance of it.[73] It also may underlie the decisions in *Strathern v. Seaforth*[74] — a decision which definitely involved use of the power, according to *Sugden v. H.M. Advocate*[75] and *Khaliq v. H.M. Advocate*[76] — where use of the power is less certain.

There are various other criteria which have been judicially mentioned   **2–29** as justifying the exercise of the power — for example, that the act was criminal under English common law,[77] that it would be absurd to take any other view,[78] and that there must be something akin to a "public nuisance".[79] None of these, however, really provides any sensible or practical test.

Lord Cockburn as critic

Of the six judicial opinions cast in the case of *Bernard Greenhuff and*   **2–30** *Others*,[80] the only dissenting voice was that of Lord Cockburn. He rejected flatly any suggestion that the court might declare an act (or omission) to be criminal simply on the grounds of its immorality. If immoral acts were to be criminalised, then that was a matter for Parliament and not for the court.[81]

---

[70] *Bernard Greenhuff, supra, per* Lord Mackenzie at p. 268, approved in *John Ballantyne, supra,* by Lord Justice-Clerk Inglis at p. 359.

[71] i, 624.

[72] Mill, *On Liberty* (1859), Chaps. I and IV; Feinberg, *Moral Limits of the Criminal Law,* Vol. 1 — "Harm to Others" (1984).

[73] See *Kerr v. Hill,* 1936 J.C. 71, *per* Lord Justice-General Normand at p. 75; *John Ballantyne* (1859) 3 Irv. 352, *per* Lord Justice-Clerk Inglis at pp. 359–360; *H.M. Advocate v. Semple,* 1937 J.C. 41, *per* Lord Justice-Clerk Aitchison at pp. 45–46 and Lord Moncrieff at p. 48; *John Barr* (1839) 2 Swin. 282, *per* Lord Medwyn at p. 315.

[74] 1926 J.C. 100.

[75] 1934 J.C. 103, *per* Lord Justice-Clerk Alness at p. 109.

[76] 1984 J.C. 23.

[77] See *Bernard Greenhuff* (1838) 2 Swin. 236, *per* Lord Justice-Clerk Boyle at p. 258, Lord Moncreiff at p. 266 and Lord Mackenzie at p. 268; *John Barr, supra, per* Lord Moncreiff at p. 314.

[78] See *Strathern v. Seaforth,* 1926 J.C. 100, *per* Lord Justice-Clerk Alness at p. 102.

[79] *Bernard Greenhuff, supra, per* Lord Medwyn at p. 270.

[80] (1838) 2 Swin. 236.

[81] *ibid.* p. 272.

But the High Court might, he thought, legitimately develop the common law in certain ways since

> "an old crime may certainly be committed in a new way; and a case, though never occurring before in its facts, may fall within the spirit of a previous decision, or within an established general principle ... There is no ... exercise of any extraordinary power needed, in the Court's merely determining that an act that has never presented itself before, comes within the range of a known term, case or principle."[82]

2–31   Clearly, a crime can be committed in a new way.[83] Hume would no doubt have been surprised to learn that a person could be killed by exposure to a radioactive source; but the method employed is hardly of the essence of criminal forms of killing, and death occasioned by deliberate irradiation would hardly excite comment as an example of murder (all other things being equal).

2–32   Equally, it is always possible to argue that some act (or omission) falls within the spirit of a previous decision (meaning, no doubt, that one may extend by analogy the definition, as previously understood by the courts, of any common law crime) and that it ought, therefore, to be considered as an example of that crime. Lord Cockburn himself gave colour to such argument in the case of *John Barr*,[84] where falsely swearing that one was qualified to vote in an election was considered by him to be a species of fraud or of perjury,[85] since it shared the essential characteristics of those crimes. With respect to any common law crime, however, it can be a somewhat arbitrary process to identify what are its essential characteristics — as was amply demonstrated in the case of *William Fraser*.[86] There the accused had intercourse with a married woman by pretending to be her husband. He thus obtained her consent by a trick. Surely the essence of rape was thus satisfied, there being no true consent? Yet the majority of the court (including Lord Cockburn) held that consent had been obtained, that the intercourse had not in fact been "against her will", and that, therefore, rape must be ruled out. It could not thus be extended. Quite apart from the arbitrary way in which these two cases (*Barr* and *Fraser*) were determined, it should be noted that extending crimes to novel situations by means of analogy is considered by some to be as much a breach of the principle *nullum crimen sine lege* (see para. 2–21, above) as declaring acts to be

---

[82] (1838) 2 Swin. 236.
[83] See, *e.g.*, Lord McCluskey's acknowledgement of this in *H.M. Advocate v. Harris*, 1993 J.C. 150 at p.159F.
[84] (1839) 2 Swin. 282.
[85] *ibid.* pp. 316–317.
[86] (1847) Ark. 280.

criminal simply because they offend against some supposed rule of morality or whatever.[87]

Established general principles

Lord Cockburn's third suggestion that a novel act, in so far as the criminal law is concerned, may nevertheless fall within an established general principle is no less perplexing, since he did not explain what was meant by such a principle nor how such principles were to be established.   **2–33**

As Gordon[88] has surely correctly pointed out, principles may be deduced, from existing known crimes, of such generality as to be capable of encompassing many different forms of behaviour. Thus, for example, from the known crimes of theft, fraud and embezzlement, it may be deduced that "dishonest conduct is criminal". If that deduction were then considered as some general principle supporting those known crimes, there could be no limit, on Cockburn's thesis, to the proscription of, say, many supposedly legitimate business activities simply on the basis that they smacked of "dishonesty". This would appear to be a highly questionable process, since it seems perfectly capable of restoring the declaratory power (so heavily criticised by Cockburn) in all but name.   **2–34**

Nevertheless, since Cockburn was apparently offering an alternative to the declaratory power, an alternative which was, therefore, not subject to the rules for the power's operation — *e.g.* only exercisable by a quorum of the High Court (see para. 2–23, above), it has become acceptable for even single judges of the court to "find" general principles in order to justify decisions which otherwise might have entailed the declaration of new crimes. Thus in *H.M. Advocate v. Martin*[89] Lord Cameron was able to invoke the "principle" that conduct which violated the order and course of justice was criminal. That then enabled him (at least in part) to find that helping a prisoner to escape from an extramural working party was indeed a crime, without any resort to the declaratory power. Similarly, in *Khaliq v. H.M. Advocate*,[90] it was possible to determine that the supply of harmful substances to others was criminal, since it fell under the broad criminalising "principle" of "that which was capable of causing real injury". Again, in *Watt v. Annan*,[91] showing an obscene or indecent film to consenting adults was found criminal since it lay within the general "principle" that "all shamelessly indecent conduct is criminal". Where it has suited the High   **2–35**

---

[87] van Dijk and van Hoof, *Theory and Practice of the European Convention on Human Rights* (2nd ed., 1990), pp. 359–361.

[88] *Criminal Law*, para. 1–23.

[89] 1956 J.C. 1 at p. 3.

[90] 1984 J.C. 23.

[91] 1978 J.C. 84.

Court to do so, however, an "obvious" general "principle" (*e.g.* that dishonest conduct is criminal) has been ignored, and the alternative exercise of the declaratory power been deliberately avoided.[92]

2–36   It is, therefore, uncertain whether Lord Cockburn was describing a legitimate developmental facility possessed (relative to the common law) by the High Court, or whether he was drawing attention to another form of the declaratory power, a more acceptable form, perhaps, with the result that the modern picture is rather confused. Certainly, it can be confidently stated that attempts by the High Court to formulate new types of criminal behaviour have done little to answer the general question why certain conduct deserves to be stigmatised as criminal at all. Further, since much of Scots criminal law continues to be drawn from the common law, it must be concluded that some aspects of the current law are, and will remain, somewhat enigmatic. A criminal code would, of course, help to clarify matters; but it would also remove the element of dynamism which many see as the real advantage of the current system.

CLASSIFICATIONS OF CRIMES

2–37   Scots law does not formally group crimes into classes. Thus, the classifying of crimes as "felonies, misdemeanours, petty misdemeanours or violations," as favoured in the American Law Institute's Model Penal Code,[93] is unknown in this country. Nor is any particular distinction made here between the terms "crime" and "offence". It thus makes equal legal sense in Scotland to speak of the "crime" or the "offence" of murder.

2–38   In some legal systems, crimes may be classified according to some attribute which they possess. In England, for example, certain crimes are termed "arrestable offences" since the police have powers of summary arrest in respect of them.[94] Almost all Scottish crimes, however, are probably "arrestable" in that sense, and it is, therefore, pointless to classify in such a way.

2–39   Of course, there are two distinct types of criminal procedure in this country. "Summary" procedure is (supposedly, if not in fact) flexible, quick and relatively informal; involves a non-jury type trial (if a trial is held); and is normally reserved for the less serious type of crime. On the other hand, "solemn" procedure (or procedure "on indictment") is more lengthy and rule-bound, involves a judge and jury trial (if a trial is held), and is supposedly reserved for the more serious type of offence. It might appear,

---

[92]   See *Grant v. Allan*, 1987 J.C. 71. See also *H.M. Advocate v. Forbes*, 1994 S.L.T. 861, where the Crown's argument, that "housebreaking with intent to commit any crime" was a general principle (see p. 863F), was rejected by the court.

[93]   Proposed Official Draft (1962), s.1.04.

[94]   See the Police and Criminal Evidence Act 1984, ss.24 and 118.

therefore, that a classification by way of procedure would be appropriate — crimes being divided into those which were "summary" and those which were "indictable". This is not possible, however. Most common law crimes may be processed by either form of procedure — depending upon the discretion of the prosecutor and the seriousness of the individual case. It is thus generally not the type of crime that is more or less serious, but individual examples of it. Whilst it is true that some statutory offences are designated as attracting only summary procedure, or triable only on indictment, it is equally true that many such offences may be processed in either way, thus equating them with common law offences, from the procedural point of view. There is no satisfactory way, therefore, of classifying crimes in Scotland according to the procedural regime which they attract.

It is traditional, however, and very convenient, particularly for the **2–40** purposes of textbook writing, to group crimes together according to some significant feature that they possess (or, more accurately, appear to possess) in common. Thus, later chapters in this book are headed "Crimes Against the Person", "Crimes of Dishonesty", "Crimes Against Property", and so on: but these groupings have no official basis whatsoever. Sheriff Gordon has stressed a similar (though more general) theme in his useful thesis that there are both conduct and result crimes.[95] His view is that in relation to some crimes, what is forbidden consists primarily of the "result" of conduct, the precise form of conduct employed to achieve that result being of minimal interest to the law. Murder is his stock example here. (One must pause, however, to observe that conduct is still involved in murder — and crucially so, if anyone is to be convicted of such a crime.) The alternative is a "conduct" crime, where the result, if any, of human conduct is in no sense required for conviction.[96] Although it is plain that not all offences can be neatly classified in such a way (see, for example, the offence of being "drunk and incapable of taking care" of oneself in a public place,[97] which seems to involve neither conduct nor result, and which Smith and Hogan[98] would refer to as a "state of affairs" crime), the identification of those crimes which require a result does highlight that area of the criminal law where issues of causation are at a premium (see Chapter 5, below).

There is some judicial support for a classification of crimes based upon **2–41** the Latin tags *mala in se* and *mala prohibita*. *Mala in se* refers to those crimes which are morally reprehensible — evils in themselves; and clearly murder, rape, assault and some other traditional common law crimes would answer to that sort of description. At the opposite end of the scale, *mala*

---

[95] *Criminal Law*, paras. 3–05 and 3–39.
[96] Gordon's initial example being that of perjury — on which see *Lord Advocate's Reference (No. 1 of 1985)*, 1986 J.C. 137.
[97] Civic Government (Scotland) Act 1982, s.50(1).
[98] *Criminal Law* (7th ed, 1992), pp. 43–45.

prohibita are "mere regulatory offences" or "not criminal in any real sense"[99] — offences which have no perceptible moral content, and which may be described as administrative rules given the added efficacy that only criminal sanctions can command. Examples may be seen in the offences of failing to have a television licence (where appropriate receiving apparatus has been installed[1]) and failing properly to display an excise licence disc on a vehicle.[2] This sort of classification is often resorted to in relation to statutory offences — where criteria are being sought to identify offences of strict liability, *i.e.* those not requiring proof or inference of *mens rea* (see Chapters 3 and 13, below). But there are many offences (even common law ones) where it cannot affirmatively be said that moral reprehensibility is always involved. Abortion, culpable homicide, carrying an offensive weapon, incest, having carnal knowledge of a girl under the age of 16, brothel keeping, and so on may or may not involve moral obloquy, depending upon the circumstances: but it is difficult to envisage any of them being described as a mere regulatory offence. Opinions on issues of morality are in any event so hopelessly diverse that this sort of classification is of very limited utility.

BASIC PRINCIPLES OF THE CRIMINAL JUSTICE SYSTEM

JURISDICTION

2–42   No proceedings against a person for a crime can competently be commenced before a Scottish court (see Appendix D) unless that crime and the person alleged to have committed it are subject to the jurisdiction of that court. Diplomatic immunity apart, each "prosecutable person" (see paras. 2–46 *et seq.*, below), whatever his nationality, can be prosecuted before a court within whose territorial area he is alleged to have committed a crime. It is clearly important, therefore, to establish where an alleged crime was committed. If the place of the crime (usually referred to as the "*locus*") is outwith the United Kingdom, then generally there will be no jurisdiction possessed by any Scottish court in respect of that crime. But there are exceptions, mostly statutory. Under section 11 of the Criminal Procedure (Scotland) Act 1995, for example, a British citizen or subject, who commits murder or culpable homicide (as these are understood in Scotland) in a country outwith the United Kingdom, may be prosecuted for what he did before a Scottish court. Other exceptions, such as piracy, may be within the jurisdiction of Scottish courts as a matter of international comity. If the

---

[99] See *Sweet v. Parsley* [1970] A.C. 132, *per* Lord Reid at p. 149.
[1]   See the Wireless Telegraphy Act 1949, s.1(1).
[2]   See the Vehicle Excise and Regulation Act 1994, s.33. See also *Strowger v. John* [1974] R.T.R. 124.

locus is completely or partly outwith Scotland but within the United Kingdom, the issue of jurisdiction may depend on the nature of the crime itself and also whether that crime is of statutory or common law origin. In *Clements v. H.M. Advocate*,[3] for example, the Scottish courts assumed jurisdiction over persons who were based in London and who had furnished their criminal activities only in that city. But the statutory crime in question[4] was one where criminal activities in one location vitally contributed to the end-result of the crime in another — and that other location was Edinburgh. Where, therefore, a crime is of such a nature that chains of interlocking activities in different parts of the United Kingdom are involved in its commission, the Scottish courts may have jurisdiction over persons who never visited Scotland at all (except to be prosecuted) and who were unaware that the end-*locus* was Scotland. The crime in that case was, however, of unusually wide scope.[5] As far as common law crimes are concerned, it seems that a similar rule will pertain where the crime in question involves a scheme of cross-border activities and where a material part of those activities takes place in Scotland.[6] In addition, of course, to a particular court having territorial jurisdiction in respect of the *locus*, it must also be competent to deal with the type of crime involved. Thus, for example, only a High Court can competently try a person accused of murder or rape — even though the crime in question occurred within the territorial area of a sheriff or district court.[7]

PRESCRIPTION

A prosecution will be barred as incompetent if the time-limit laid down by the law has prescribed before commencement of proceedings. There are several aspects to this. First, in relation to common law crimes, there is no period of prescription at all.[8] Whatever may have been the position under Roman law or in Scotland during the eighteenth century, there is now no time-bar on the prosecution of any common law offence (although the lack of availability of witnesses, and diminished powers of recollection by them will obviously put an effective end to proposed prosecutions relating to crimes allegedly committed many years in the past). It is, however, within

2–43

---

[3]   1991 J.C. 62.
[4]   A contravention of s.4(3)(b) of the Misuse of Drugs Act 1971, *i.e.* being concerned in the supplying of a controlled drug to another.
[5]   See *Kerr v. H.M. Advocate*, 1986 J.C. 41.
[6]   See *Laird v. H.M. Advocate*, 1985 J.C. 37. See also the provisions of the Criminal Procedure (Scotland) Act 1995 s.11(4) pertaining to theft and reset.
[7]   For further details, discussion and authorities, see Gane and Stoddart, *Criminal Procedure in Scotland: Cases and Materials* (2nd ed., 1994), Chap. 3; Renton and Brown, *Criminal Procedure* (6th ed., 1996) under the title "Jurisdiction".
[8]   *Sugden v. H.M. Advocate*, 1934 J.C. 103.

a judge's discretion to refuse to allow a prosecution to proceed if
unwarrantable delay is deemed to be oppressive to the accused.[9]

2–44   Second, in relation to statutory offences, each piece of relevant legislation
must be consulted in order to determine if a specific time-limit exists, and,
if so, when the prescriptive period begins to run. The Road Traffic Offenders
Act 1988, Schedule 1, for example, identifies those offences to which the
specific time-limits contained in section 6 apply. If no specific time-limit is
set in relation to a statutory offence which is triable only summarily, then a
general prescriptive period of six months (from the date of the alleged
offence) applies.[10]

2–45   There are also prescriptive time periods, applicable to prosecutions under
either sort of procedure, which are designed to ensure that accused persons
will not remain in custody for too long before being brought to trial, or, in
the case of solemn prosecutions alone, to ensure that accused persons who
are not in custody will be brought to trial within a reasonable space of
time.[11]

PROSECUTABLE PERSONS

2–46   The range of persons who can be prosecuted for an alleged crime is not
confined to human beings, but, on the other hand, does not extend to all
human beings. In particular, a "child" cannot be found guilty of any offence.
Almost all legal systems have a similar rule, probably based on an assumed
lack of capacity of young children for any true criminal appetite, or on
some general notion that young children cannot be expected to exercise
adult restraints. Whatever the basis for the rule, the great difficulty lies in
determining an appropriate age when prosecution will be in order. In fact,
all solutions to this problem involve the assigning of a totally arbitrary age
limit. In England, this has been fixed at 10 years of age; in Scotland, however,
it is taken to be eight.[12] These age limits are clearly intended to refer to
chronological and not mental age. A child under eight years of age cannot,
therefore, be found guilty of any crime, no matter what he may apparently
have done. Nor can this presumption be overcome by resort to "Children's
Hearing" procedure.[13]

---

[9] See *Connachan v. Douglas*, 1990 J.C. 244.
[10] Criminal Procedure (Scotland) Act 1995, s.136. See also s.292, for the meaning of an
offence "triable only summarily".
[11] *ibid*. ss.65 and 147.
[12] *ibid*. s.41.
[13] See *Merrin v. S.*, 1987 S.L.T. 193, and next paragraph for "Children's Hearings".

Older children

Children between the ages of eight and 16 can certainly be prosecuted **2–47** before a criminal court, even though steps may have to be taken to render the proceedings rather less public and awesome than where adult offenders alone are involved.[14] There is no equivalent in Scotland to the English rule that a child between the ages of 10 and 14 must be shown to have had "mischievous discretion" before he can be convicted. The Scottish police, however, do not report most alleged child offenders to the public prosecutors. Instead, they resort to the principal reporter[15] to the children's panel. Under the Children (Scotland) Act 1995, Part 2, Chapter 3, the intention is that most (alleged) child offenders will appear before a body of three specially trained lay-adults, known collectively as a "Children's Hearing".[16] Such a hearing is arranged by the principal (in practice, the local) reporter, and, assuming that the child and any "relevant person"[17] (who must also attend) accept that the alleged crime was committed by that child, the only object is to secure that child's future welfare. The proceedings are not open to the public and may not be reported in the press. If it is not accepted that the child in question committed the crime, then fact finding must be referred to a sheriff of the local sheriff court.[18] Appeal against his findings (or indeed the eventual decision of the hearing) lies ultimately to the Court of Session[19] rather than the Court of Criminal Appeal, since it is not intended that any of this process should be seen as a criminal proceeding and since the process indeed relates to all children thought to be in need of compulsory measures of supervision. That a child is thought to have committed a crime is, therefore, only one of a range of possible reasons for invoking this rather special (if not unique) procedure.[20]

The children's hearing process will probably not be used where a child **2–48** is alleged to have committed an offence which requires solemn procedure — either as a matter of law (*i.e.* in relation to murder or rape, or a select few statutory offences) or because the particular circumstances of the offence

---

[14] Criminal Procedure (Scotland) Act 1995, ss.42 and 142.

[15] See Local Government (Scotland) Act 1994, s.127.

[16] See Children (Scotland) Act 1995, Pt.2, Chap. 2 and Sched.1. Notice that a child for the purposes of Pt.2, Chaps. 2 and 3 means a person who is under 16 years of age, or who is aged between 16 and 18 years if already subject to a supervision requirement: see ss. 93(2)(b) and 69 *et seq*.

[17] Defined *ibid.* s. 93(2)(b) to include any parent enjoying certain rights, any person who has parental responsibilities or rights vested in him, and any person who ordinarily has charge of, or control over, the child. Attendance by such a person is required under s.45(8). It is an offence not to attend, under s.45(9).

[18] *ibid.* ss.65(7) and 68.

[19] *ibid.* s.51.

[20] See *ibid.* s.52(2) for the complete range.

seem to necessitate it.[21] It should be noted that a children's hearing has no powers to impose fines, imprison, disqualify, order forfeiture, or indeed to punish in any conventional sense.

Non-human persons

2–49   A non-human, legal "person" can be prosecuted for at least some forms of crime. In Scotland, certain business organisations — in particular companies incorporated under the Companies Acts — are treated in law as if they were human beings, with an existence (a *persona*) separate from the people who direct them or are employed by them. Such organisations, therefore, can be convicted and punished — again as if they were truly human beings; but there are limits to this process. Some offences (rape, for example) are such that it is difficult to envisage their being committed by a non-human, and it has also been held that a corporate body cannot act "shamelessly" for the purposes of "shamelessly indecent conduct".[22] On the other hand, there are clearly offences involving, for example, dishonest dealings or fraud, which apparently pose no practical or conceptual problems.[23] It must also be understood that a company (as opposed to its directors and staff) could never be imprisoned since it has no physical existence and that it could never, therefore, be prosecuted for an offence which carried a mandatory prison sentence (*e.g.* murder). Exact criteria for the identification of common law crimes "committable" by corporate bodies have not yet clearly evolved in Scotland, where a case-by-case and crime-by-crime approach has so far been adopted; but statutory offences appear to pose fewer problems, particular enactments often making specific provision for corporate prosecutions.[24] The exact theoretical basis for the criminal liability of a non-human person remains, however, unclear in Scots law. Since a company, for example, cannot act at all except through the agency of human beings, it must be questioned why the company, as opposed to the men or women who actually carried out the deeds, should ever be considered for prosecution. Fictions must plainly be employed here — such as, for example, that certain acts of particular individuals (*e.g.* directors and others at a high level in the overall management structure) may be imputed to the company since such individuals in a very real sense control that company. Where *mens rea* (see Chapter 3, below) is also an issue in relation to the particular crime involved, again this will have to be imputed to the corporate body from the individuals who actually were concerned in

---

[21] See *Cairns v. H.M. Advocate* (1973) S.C.C.R. Supp. 44.
[22] *Dean v. John Menzies (Holdings) Ltd*, 1981 J.C. 23.
[23] *Purcell Meats (Scotland) Ltd v. McLeod*, 1987 S.L.T. 528.
[24] See the Civic Government (Scotland) Act 1982, s.130 for a typically worded example.

the matter, provided that such individuals can be said to form the "controlling mind" of that corporate body.[25]

Crimes committed by others

A person may be validly prosecuted for a crime he did not personally **2–50** commit. He may be liable for its commission "art and part" (*i.e.* as an accessory, see Chapter 7, below) or vicariously (usually by being the employer of the person actually responsible). Vicarious liability seems to be confined, however, to statutory offences which make specific provision for it[26] and statutory offences where the courts have decided that it is appropriate (see Chapter 13, below).

Insane persons

A prosecutable person must also be sufficiently sane to understand the **2–51** proceedings against him, and to give instructions for (or be able to conduct personally) his defence. It is a plea "in bar of trial" that such a degree of sanity is lacking.[27] This plea should not be confused with the *defence* of insanity (see Chapter 8, below).

RES JUDICATA

Once a person has been prosecuted for an offence and a verdict has been **2–52** reached of either guilt or acquittal, it is not lawful for him to be re-prosecuted for that same offence. Again, a good plea "in bar of trial" would lie if such a re-prosecution were to be attempted. In Scotland, this plea is sometimes known as that of *res judicata* or "tholed assize", though no jury (assize) need have been involved at all. There is one exception to this in that the Appeal Court may give authority for a new prosecution after hearing an appeal.[28]

CHARGE MUST RELATE TO A KNOWN CRIME

The charging document in a solemn procedure case is known as an **2–53** indictment. The equivalent in a summary procedure case is known as a

---

[25] The theoretical problems here are very troublesome indeed, and for some modern thinking on these see Gordon, *Criminal Law*, paras. 8–84 to 8–93, together with the second cumulative supplement; D. Whyte, "Corporate Criminal Liability," 1987 S.L.T. (News) 348.

[26] See the Licensing (Scotland) Act 1976, s.67(1), (2) and Sched. 5, column 3, and, *e.g.*, *Ahmed v. MacDonald*, 1995 S.L.T. 1094 (where the accused successfully invoked the "all due diligence" defence).

[27] Criminal Procedure (Scotland) Act 1995, ss.54–57.

[28] See *ibid*. ss.118(1)(c), 119, 183(1)(d) and 185.

complaint. These documents must allege that the accused committed a known crime. If they do not, then they may be attacked and disposed of as "irrelevant". There is really no problem in relation to statutory offences, since clearly an existing enactment either is or is not validly referred to. But common law offences do pose difficulties. Some of these offences are "innominate" (*i.e.* having no short, recognisable name — or *nomen juris* — as opposed to the better known crimes with instantly recognisable titles, such as murder, theft and rape), and consequently must be charged by a more or less lengthy description.[29] It will often be a moot point whether the description given is adequate or whether it relates to something entirely novel.[30] The ability of criminal courts to develop the common law, and of the High Court to declare new crimes are clearly live issues in the consideration of any objections to the relevancy of such charges (see paras. 2–20 to 2–36, above). It must also be borne in mind that conviction is possible in respect of any part of a charge, provided that part itself constitutes an identifiable crime,[31] and that specific statutes do allow "hidden" alternative charges to be considered by a judge (summary cases) or a jury (solemn cases).[32]

2–54   There is probably no *de minimis* principle[33] operated in Scots criminal law. It is thus not a competent objection to any criminal charge that the matter is too trivial for consideration by a court. Scottish prosecutors (see para. 2–58, below) are deemed to have considered fully the matter of triviality at a stage prior to the drawing of a complaint or indictment.

ACCUSATORIAL FORM OF PROCEDURE

2–55   The principle followed by Scots criminal law is that the prosecutor, public or private, must not only make the accusation against the person in question, but also prove the matter to the satisfaction of the judge (summary case) or jury (solemn case). On a charge being made by way of complaint or

---

[29] See, for example, the charge in *Khaliq v. H.M. Advocate*, 1984 J.C. 23.

[30] But compare the Criminal Procedure (Scotland) Act 1995, Sched. 3, para. 2, which requires only that the appropriate document sets forth facts relevant and sufficient to constitute a crime.

[31] Criminal Procedure (Scotland) Act 1995, Sched. 3, para. 9(2).

[32] See, *e.g.*, the Criminal Law (Consolidation) (Scotland) Act 1995, s.14 (certain sexual offences); the Criminal Procedure (Scotland) Act 1995 Sched. 3, para. 8(2)–(4) (certain crimes of dishonesty) as also the general provision in the 1995 Act Sched. 3, para. 14 — where a statutory charge may contain a hidden common law one in respect of which conviction may follow (as, *e.g.*, in *Horsburgh v. Russell*, 1994 S.L.T. 942).

[33] The complete Latin tag is *de minimis non curat lex*, *i.e.* the law does not concern itself with trivial matters.

indictment, it is not for the accused to satisfy the judge or jury as to his innocence. To that extent at least, content can be given to the often quoted statement that "there is a presumption of innocence". The prosecutor must, therefore, provide the court with evidence. In Scotland, that generally entails the provision of two independent pieces of evidence in respect of every material issue in the case against the accused. The "evidential burden", therefore, lies on the prosecutor. But he also carries the "persuasive burden". He must persuade the judge (or the jury) that the case against the accused is true beyond reasonable doubt. If he fails on either of these burdens, the case will be lost (perhaps on a plea from the accused that there is "no case to answer"[34]). Precisely what the prosecutor must establish by way of evidence and persuasion depends upon the particular crime charged and its *actus reus* and *mens rea* requirements (see Chapter 3, below). In a result crime (see para. 2–40, above), the issue of causation (see Chapter 5, below) will also have to be addressed.[35]

The Scottish prosecutor is regarded as being "the master of the instance". **2–56** That means he has entire discretion as to whether the case should be prosecuted at all,[36] as to the way in which the case will be prosecuted (the accused, for example, having no right to demand jury trial), and as to the conduct of the case in court before a judge or a judge and jury.[37] He may in particular abandon the case, "desert the diet", either temporarily, *pro loco et tempore*, subject to any prescriptive time periods which apply (see paras. 2–43 to 2–45, above) or permanently, *simpliciter*, or cause the proceedings to be adjourned, or even decline after a verdict of "guilty" to "move", *i.e.* ask, for sentence, in which event (or certainly in an indictment case) no sentence can be passed by the presiding judge.

ADVERSARIAL FORM OF PROCEDURE

In Scotland, as in the Anglo-American family of legal systems, a trial is **2–57** conducted by the opposing parties (*i.e.* the prosecutor and the accused — or more commonly, his lawyer or advocate) before a largely silent judge, or judge and jury. It is not for the judge (or the jury, if present) to question the witnesses. The judge (or jury) must simply follow the questioning and cross-questioning conducted by the two sides, then give a verdict according to

---

[34] See the Criminal Procedure (Scotland) Act 1995, ss.97 and 160.
[35] For detailed information on evidential matters, see Field, *Law of Evidence in Scotland* (2nd ed., 1996).
[36] Thus he may ignore the complainer's wish that the offender should not be prosecuted, see, *e.g.*, *Sze v. Wilson*, 1992 S.L.T. 569.
[37] Thus the Lord Advocate cannot be required to give reasons for any decisions taken which are entirely within the province of the Crown, see, *e.g.*, *H.M. Advocate v. O'Neill*, 1992 J.C. 22.

what has been heard. It is also of the essence of this "adversarial" procedure that the accused (or his lawyer) is entitled to question the prosecutor's witnesses and introduce evidence of his own by way of defence. General and special defences (see Chapter 8, below) are regarded as the accused's responsibility — in the first instance, at least. He will have the "evidential burden" of placing some evidence favouring them before the court — but without assuming any responsibility for persuading the court of their truth. Insanity and diminished responsibility are well known exceptions to these principles, both of these defences requiring that the accused persuade the court that it is more likely than not that they are true. This standard is usually referred to as proof "on the balance of probabilities". It is never for the accused to prove anything on the prosecutorial standard of "beyond reasonable doubt". For the avoidance of doubt, it appears that Scots law subscribes to the Anglo-American rule that ignorance (*i.e.* lack of knowledge) of the strictures of the criminal law is not a defence — although this sits somewhat uneasily alongside the declaratory power (see paras. 2–21 *et seq.*, above, and Chapter 8, below).

PUBLIC PROSECUTION

2–58 The norm, in Scotland, is for criminal prosecutions to be instituted and conducted by the public prosecution service consisting of the Lord Advocate, the Solicitor General for Scotland, advocates-depute, regional procurators fiscal, procurators fiscal and depute-procurators fiscal. The service operates from the Crown Office in Edinburgh and from regional and district fiscals' offices throughout the country. Procurators fiscal and their deputes normally deal with cases set for proceedings before sheriff and district courts. In High Courts (as also before the Appeal Court), advocates-depute (or the Lord Advocate or the Solicitor General in person) normally present cases on behalf of the public.[38] It has become customary to designate public prosecutors as "the Crown".

Private prosecutors

2–59 Since considerable confidence is reposed in the public prosecution service, demand for private prosecution is low. It appears that a private party, wishing to prosecute under solemn procedure, must use the rather archaic and long-winded form of document called "criminal letters" rather than the more modern "indictment", and must apply (by "bill") to the High Court for the issue of such "letters". That court will not normally issue these unless the application for them is supported by the Lord Advocate, although it is possible in

---

[38] Although solicitor-advocates may be permitted to do so, see the Criminal Procedure (Scotland) Act 1995, s.301.

exceptional circumstances for the court to permit their issue without his concurrence.[39] It is essential, however, for the prospective private prosecutor to show that he has been personally wronged by the alleged offence. It is not possible in Scotland to prosecute in respect of a crime that is no more than a general public wrong.[40] It appears, too, that there are crimes which are always to be regarded as primarily public wrongs, in respect of which only public prosecutors can be permitted to take action.[41] Private prosecution under summary procedure is generally not competent.[42]

PUBLIC PROCEEDINGS

It is a principle of Scots criminal law that solemn trials, though not **2–60** necessarily preliminary proceedings, should take place in the presence of the accused and in public (presumably so that justice can be seen to be done). To this principle, there are some exceptions. In particular, the accused may be removed if he "misconducts himself", and the public may be excluded when evidence is being tendered in a trial involving a sexual offence.[43] The position in summary proceedings is broadly similar.[44] That justice must not only be done, but be seen to be done, is both proverbial and a ground of appeal. The test is not whether, for example, the trial judge was in fact impartial or in good faith, but whether any suspicion might linger in the mind of a reasonable person that there might have been a lack of impartial justice.[45] Curiously, there have been more reported cases on this matter since it was stated in *Bradford v. McLeod* that the paucity of recorded examples was a tribute to Scots law.[46] Thus, imposing sentence without giving an opportunity for a plea in mitigation,[47] congratulating the mother of a young complainer who had just given evidence in court,[48] using intemperate language in court,[49] and falling asleep on the bench[50] have all fallen foul of the general principle.[51]

---

[39] See *J. & P. Coats Ltd v. Brown* (1909) 6 Adam 19; *X. v. Sweeney,* 1982 J.C. 70.
[40] See *McBain v. Crichton,* 1961 J.C. 25.
[41] See, *e.g., Meehan v. Inglis,* 1975 J.C. 9.
[42] See s.138 of the Criminal Procedure (Scotland) Act 1995, and the now repealed s.63 of the Criminal Justice (Scotland) Act 1995.
[43] Criminal Procedure (Scotland) Act 1995, s.92.
[44] *ibid.* s.153.
[45] See *Hogg v. Normand,* 1992 S.L.T. 736.
[46] 1986 S.L.T. 244 at p. 248G.
[47] *Bassi v. Normand,* 1992 S.L.T. 341.
[48] *Hogg v. Normand,* 1992 S.L.T. 736.
[49] *Sneddon v. Lees,* 1996 S.L.T. 294.
[50] *Frew v. Brown,* 1996 S.L.T. 282.
[51] By way of contrast, what was alleged to have taken place in the privacy of the jury room was not considered to be covered by the principle — *Russell v. H.M. Advocate,* 1991 J.C. 194.

PROCEEDINGS CONDUCTED FAIRLY

2–61   It is axiomatic that all stages of criminal proceedings should be conducted
fairly and impartially according to predetermined rules of evidence and
procedure. In particular, proceedings must not be conducted according to
arbitrary and ad hoc rules; and Scots law adheres to these principles as well
as any other legal system within the Anglo-American world.[52] Indeed, the
accused or his legal representative always has the right to speak last in a
Scottish criminal trial.[53]

NO RIGHT TO JURY TRIAL

2–62   Unlike the law of England and many States in the USA, Scots law does not
permit accused persons to elect for a jury rather than a bench (*i.e.* judge
alone) trial. They must simply accept what the prosecutor or, unusually, the
law, (*e.g.* in murder and rape cases) dictates. Scottish prosecutors' discretion
is absolute in this matter, which explains why jury trials are much less
common in this country than elsewhere. If jury trial is considered proper,
the accused's case will be determined (unless foreclosed by, for example, a
plea of guilty) by a jury of 15 persons, rather than the more usual six to 12
persons favoured elsewhere in the Anglo-American family of legal systems.[54]
Scottish juries are selected almost totally at random with no recourse to the
extensive *voir dire* processes found in so many American States.[55]

VERDICTS

2–63   In Scottish criminal trials, both judges (in bench trials) and juries may
consider three possible verdicts — guilty, not guilty, and not proven.
Although it is not easy to state or understand the circumstances under which
a not proven verdict will be appropriate,[56] there is no doubt that such a

---

[52]   See generally Renton and Brown *Criminal Procedure*; Field, *Law of Evidence in Scotland*.
[53]   Criminal Procedure (Scotland) Act 1995, ss.98 and 161.
[54]   But it is possible to proceed with a trial where a jury has been reduced to 12, although even
then (as with a full jury) a guilty verdict can only be returned where a majority of eight
favours it — Criminal Procedure (Scotland) Act 1995, s.90. Indeed, juries smaller than 15
are not unknown in Scotland. During the Second World War, and for a short time thereafter,
trials were undertaken before juries of seven persons — see, *e.g.*, *MacDermid v. H.M.
Advocate*, 1948 J.C. 12. See also Administration of Justice (Emergency Provisions)
(Scotland) Act 1939, s. 3(2).
[55]   See, *e.g.*, Whitebread and Slobogin, *Criminal Procedure: An Analysis of Cases and Concepts*
(2nd ed., 1986), para. 27.06, pp. 630–633. All challenges to persons being sworn as jurors
in Scotland require cause to be shown (unless both parties at the trial agree that a particular
person should be "excused") — Criminal Procedure (Scotland) Act 1995, s.86.
[56]   *cf. McNicol v. H.M. Advocate*, 1964 J.C. 25, observations of Lord Justice-General Clyde at
pp 26–27.

verdict effectively acts as one of acquittal.[57] It is also generally a misdirection in law for a judge to discourage a jury from returning a verdict of not proven[58]; yet the view taken is that Scottish juries are so familiar with that "third verdict" that it is not generally a misdirection *not* to draw it specifically to their attention.[59] On the other hand, judges have been advised by the Appeal Court not to attempt to distinguish not proven from not guilty.[60] Nevertheless, it has recently been stated that "it may be that at some stage the High Court will take the view that some guidelines should be given to juries about the difference between the two acquittal verdicts."[60a] Recent attempts to rid Scots law of the not proven verdict have, however, been met by spirited professional opposition: and the latest legislative reforms have left all three verdicts intact.

FAIR SENTENCING

It is also axiomatic that a person who pleads guilty to, or is found guilty of, an offence should be sentenced fairly and impartially within the limits imposed by law. Principles of sentencing in Scotland are, relative to many other legal systems, rather unstructured and loosely defined. Criticisms of particular sentences as either too lenient or too severe are certainly as common in Scotland as elsewhere; but it is inevitable in any system which allows wide discretion to judges (the present norm in the United Kingdom) that not all sentencing exercises will meet with universal approval. Two recent developments, however, may assist in the attainment of greater consistency and fairness in sentencing. First, in the course of deciding appeals against sentence (in a broad sense), the Appeal Court may pronounce an opinion on the sentence or other disposal or order which is appropriate in any similar case[61]; and trial courts in future must consider any such opinion in the course of deciding upon appropriate sentences in individual cases.[62] Secondly, not only may the prosecutor appeal on a point of law against a sentence passed[63] but he may also appeal on the ground that a sentence passed was unduly lenient.[64] There have been several reported decisions

2–64

---

[57] *McLeod v. H.M. Advocate*, 1989 S.L.T. 298.
[58] *McNicol v. H.M. Advocate*, 1964 J.C. 25.
[59] *Harkin v. H.M. Advocate*, 1992 S.L.T. 785, following *MacDermid v. H.M. Advocate*, 1948 J.C. 12.
[60] *Fay v. H.M. Advocate*, 1989 J.C. 129.
[60a] *MacDonald v. H.M. Advocate*, 1996 S.L.T. 723, *per* Lord Justice-Clerk Ross at p. 727E.
[61] Criminal Procedure (Scotland) Act 1995, ss.118(7) and 189(7).
[62] *ibid.* s.197.
[63] *ibid.* ss.108(b) and 175(3)(b).
[64] *ibid.* ss.108(a) and 175(4). Notice, however, that in terms of s.175(4), which relates to summary procedure, the prosecutor is restricted to such classes of case as may be specified by the Secretary of State. No such restriction applies to the Lord Advocate in solemn procedure cases.

relative to sentences alleged to have been unduly lenient, and it has emerged that the proper test in such matters is not whether the Appeal Court itself would have imposed a heavier sentence but whether the trial judge's sentence was outwith the range of sentences which a judge at first instance, applying his mind to all the relevant factors, could reasonably have considered appropriate.[65] "Relevant factors" will obviously vary from case to case; but the gravity of the offence itself, the past criminal record of the accused, the effect of the crime on the victim (psychological as well as physical), and society's need for retribution and/or deterrence have all figured prominently in the Appeal Court's deliberations.[66]

RIGHT OF APPEAL

2–65 Scots law adheres to the principle that a convicted person should have a right of appeal against his conviction, his sentence or both.[67] The single, broad ground is that there has been a miscarriage of justice. But leave of a single judge of the High Court of Justiciary is required.[68] Prosecutors in a summary case may appeal by stated case on a point of law against an acquittal, or against the sentence passed[69] — in addition to appealing against what they consider to have been an unduly lenient sentence.[70] The inviolability of jury acquittals, however, is jealously guarded, since prosecutors are not permitted to appeal against findings of "not guilty" (or "not proven"[71]) in solemn procedure cases. But it is possible for prosecutors to seek clarification of the law as pronounced by the judge in such a case where the accused has been acquitted (or convicted) by referring the legal issues involved to the Appeal Court for a ruling. This is known as a "Lord Advocate's Reference".[72] The outcome of such a reference has no effect on the original acquittal (or conviction).

LEGAL ASSISTANCE FOR THE ACCUSED

2–66 Given the ever-growing complexity of the criminal law and the relative imbalance in resources between the state, in bringing prosecutions through

---

[65] *H.M. Advocate v. Bell*, 1995 S.L.T. 350.
[66] See, *e.g.*, *H.M. Advocate v. McPhee*, 1994 S.L.T. 1292 (unduly lenient); *H.M. Advocate v. O'Donnell*, 1995 S.C.C.R. 745 (unduly lenient); *H.M. Advocate v. May*, 1995 S.L.T. 753 (not unduly lenient), *H.M. Advocate v. McAllister*, 1996 S.L.T. 220 (not unduly lenient), *H.M. Advocate v. Lee*, 1996 S.L.T. 568 (unduly lenient), *H.M. Advocate v. Ross*, 1996 S.L.T. 729 (not unduly lenient). *Cf. H.M. Advocate v Fallan*, 1996 S.L.T. 314 and *H.M. Advocate v. Bennett*, 1996 S.L.T. 662.
[67] Criminal Procedure (Scotland) Act 1995, ss.106 (solemn case) and 175 (summary case).
[68] *ibid.* s.107 (solemn case); ss.180 and 186 (summary case).
[69] *ibid.* s.175(3).
[70] *ibid.* s.175(4): see para. 2–64, above.
[71] See para. 2–63, above.
[72] Criminal Procedure (Scotland) Act 1995, s.123.

its prosecution service, and the accused, in having to defend them, it is imperative that legal assistance should be provided for those who cannot afford to employ a lawyer. Scots law prides itself in having made provision for legal aid since the early fifteenth century,[73] though it is doubtful that criminal cases were then catered for. Certainly the early, simple schemes have given way to much more complicated rules which rely largely on the means of the accused.[74]

PROVISION FOR EXTRAORDINARY CIRCUMSTANCES

It is inevitable in any legal system that situations will arise which have not been foreseen and in respect of which the existing law consequently provides no answer or remedy. It would be possible, of course, for such matters to be resolved eventually by Parliament through legislation; but Scots law provides a quicker solution. Persons aggrieved by some issue, for which the law provides no relief, may apply by petition for the exercise of the *nobile officium* of the High Court of Justiciary. This refers to a broad, equitable power which that court traditionally possesses to effect relief in suitable cases, the suitability of a case being wholly within the discretion of the court. For example, under the extradition legislation in force in the 1970s, it was discovered that Parliament had provided only one way of challenging a person's detention where his extradition had been requested by a foreign state — namely by application for the English prerogative writ of *habeas corpus*. Since that writ was (and remains) unknown in Scotland, a person detained in this country successfully sought a Scottish way of challenging that detention by appropriately petitioning the High Court.[75]

2–67

Since the *nobile officium* power clearly represents an equitable jurisdiction, it would be wrong to regard cases where it had been exercised or denied as necessarily forming precedents for the future in like cases. But equitable decisions have always had a habit of crystallising into "hard" law, and it has become clear that the *nobile officium* power will not be exercised unless the matter in question is truly unforeseeable and extraordinary,[76] there is no other remedy available in law,[77] the petitioner is in good faith,[78] and there will be no conflict with statutory provisions to the contrary.[79] The decided cases certainly suggest that the High Court is

2–68

---

[73] A.P.S., II, 1424, c.24, p. 8.

[74] The details of the present law on criminal legal aid can most easily be found in Stoddart, *The Law and Practice of Legal Aid in Scotland* (4th ed., 1994).

[75] *Wan Ping Nam v. Federal German Republic*, 1972 J.C. 43.

[76] Alison, ii, 23 (at 13).

[77] See, *e.g.*, *Wilson, Pet.*, 1992 S.L.T. 145: *cf. Anderson v. H.M. Advocate*, 1974 S.L.T. 239 (only *one* appeal allowed in Scots law).

[78] *Woods, Pet.*, 1994 S.L.T. 197.

[79] See, *e.g.*, *Young, Pet.*, 1994 S.L.T. 269 (noting that the statutory provisions are now ss.116(1), 124(2) of the Criminal Procedure (Scotland) Act 1995; *Windsor, Pet.*, 1994 S.L.T. 604.

reluctant to use this power save in the clearest instances of oppression or injustice[80] — which will no doubt be welcomed by those who find the continued existence of that power in modern times no less perplexing than the survival of the declaratory power.

Further reading

D. K., "Codifying Criminal Law," 1988 S.L.T. (News) 97.

Duff, P., "The Not Proven Verdict: Jury Mythology or 'Moral Panic'," 1996 J.R. 1.

Fairbairn, Sir N., "The Not Proven Verdict," 1994 S.L.T. (News) 315.

Finnie, W., "European Court of Human Rights & Criminal Legal Aid in Scotland," 1995 S.L.T. (News) 89.

Harris, D.J., O'Boyle, M., and Warbrick, C., *Law of the European Convention on Human Rights* (1995), Chaps. 6 and 7.

Hutton, N. and Tata, C., "Some Options for Sentencing Reform in Scotland," 1993 S.L.T. (News) 89.

McLean, Judge I., (1) "Sentencing Guidelines" and (2) "Judicial Discretion in Sentencing," 1995 S.L.T. (News) 331 and 339.

Murdoch, J. L., "The European Convention on Human Rights in Scots Law" [1991] Public Law 40.

Ross, J., "Corporate Liability for Crime," 1990 S.L.T. (News) 265.

Stair Memorial Encyclopaedia, Vol. 22, title on "Sources".

Stuart, S. L., "The Case of the Shameless Company" (1981) 26 J.L.S. 176 and 222.

Styles, S.C., "Something to Declare: A Defence of the Declaratory Power of the High Court of Justiciary" in Hunter, R.F. (ed.), *Justice and Crime* (1993), pp. 211–231.

Walker, D. M., *The Scottish Jurists* (1985), pp. 316 *et seq.* (on Hume) and 355 *et seq.* (on Alison).

Willock, I.D., "The Declaratory Power — Still Indefensible," 1996 J.R. 97.

---

[80] as, *e.g.*, where the Appeal Court *per incuriam* exceeded its powers — *Allan, Pet.*, 1993 J.C. 181.

CHAPTER 3

ACTUS REUS AND *MENS REA*

BASIC CONCEPTS AND DEFINITIONS

–01   The purpose of this chapter is to provide an introduction to the fundamental principles of criminal liability. The basic rule is commonly expressed in a Latin maxim: *actus non facit reum nisi mens sit rea* — conduct does not make a man guilty unless his mind is also guilty. Generally speaking, a crime will have two features: the *actus reus*, the physical or external component; and *mens rea*, which is the mental element. *Actus reus* and *mens rea* constitute the essential ingredients of criminal liability at common law. There are, however, a large number of statutory offences which do not require proof of *mens rea*. These are the so-called crimes of "strict liability". Strict liability crimes are discussed in Chapter 13. For the time being, the focus will be on more traditional crimes which do require proof of both *mens rea* and *actus reus*.

–02   An understanding of the terminology of *actus reus* and *mens rea* is essential to the student of criminal law. They are the fundamental terms of the criminal lawyer's vocabulary. These terms do not, however, have a fixed meaning. The specific form that *actus reus* and *mens rea* take differs from one crime to another. This point can easily be demonstrated. The *actus reus* of rape is forcible intercourse with a woman. In contrast, the *actus reus* of theft is the taking or appropriating without lawful authority of property which belongs to someone else. Similarly, the *mens rea* involved in murder is different from that involved in culpable homicide. In both crimes someone has been killed, but it is only from looking at the accused's mental state that one can determine whether he is a murderer or not.

ACTUS REUS

CONDUCT REQUIRED

–03   The *actus reus* of a crime is simply the harmful or blameworthy conduct which the law seeks to prevent. It is the "doing something wrong" ingredient of criminal liability. All crimes require conduct or an overt act. Thought crimes are unknown in the Scottish legal system: "No one can be punished for merely what goes on in his own head."[1] The criminal law imposes punishment only for the actions which result from thoughts, not for "unfulfilled intents".[2] As Lord Justice-Clerk MacDonald emphasised in *H.M. Advocate v. Mackenzie*,[3] a "mere expression of willingness" to do something "morally reprehensible" is insufficient. If the prosecution cannot prove the *actus reus* required by the definition of the crime charged, there cannot be a conviction for that crime. An accused has to have performed an "act which falls within the category either of accomplished or attempted crime."[4] As is explained in detail in Chapter 6, if the accused has advanced sufficiently far in his preparations, he can be convicted of an attempt to commit a crime.

3–04   It is also axiomatic that the accused must have actually done something to bring about what the criminal law seeks to forbid. In *Hogg v. Macpherson*[5] the appellant was the driver of a horse-drawn furniture van. While he was driving the van along a street on a very windy day, a "furious" gust of wind blew the van over. The van struck and broke a street lamp. Under legislation then in force, the appellant was liable to make recompense for the damage, whether it was caused by negligence or by accident. The offence of which the appellant had been convicted was that of failing to pay the sum demanded by the local authority.[6] It was accepted that the appellant could have done nothing to avoid causing the damage. Lord Justice-General Clyde observed: "All I can say is that it seems to me as plain as can be from the circumstances of the case that the breaking of the lamp was not the appellant's act at all, either negligent or accidental, and that, accordingly, upon the facts found proved, there was no justification for the award made."[7] Consequently, the conviction could not stand.

CONDUCT CRIMES AND RESULT CRIMES

3–05   A distinction is sometimes drawn between "conduct crimes" and "result crimes" (see para. 2–40, above). On occasion, the law simply forbids a certain form of conduct. A straightforward example would be the possession of a controlled drug under the Misuse of Drugs Act 1971. It is simply the act of possessing the drug which constitutes the *actus reus*. More generally, however, the law requires some forbidden consequence to result from the conduct. Most crimes require as part of their definition some resultant harm.

---

[1]   *Morton v. Henderson*, 1956 J.C. 55, *per* Lord Justice-General Clyde at p. 57.
[2]   *H.M. Advocate v. Mackenzie*, 1913 S.C.(J.) 107, *per* Lord Justice-Clerk Macdonald at p. 111.
[3]   *ibid.* p. 112.
[4]   *ibid.*
[5]   1928 J.C. 15.
[6]   Edinburgh Municipal and Police Act 1879, s.93(3).
[7]   1928 J.C. 15 at p. 17.

The result of the crime of murder is obviously that someone is killed, but it is not really significant *how* the victim dies. The law is concerned here only with penalising the result of the conduct. There are no separate laws governing, for example, murder by stabbing or murder by strangulation.

CAUSATION

In a result crime, it is necessary to prove as part of the *actus reus* both 3–06 conduct and consequences. It is also necessary to prove the existence of a sufficient causal link between the conduct of the accused and the result. In *Kimmins v. Normand*,[8] the appellant had been convicted of the reckless injury of a police officer. Prior to commencing a search for controlled drugs, the officer had asked the appellant whether he was in possession of any needles. He denied that he was. In fact, there was an unguarded needle in the appellant's pocket and an injury was caused to the police officer's hand. The Appeal Court held that there was a sufficient causal connection between the appellant's denial and the resulting injury. The reasoning was that it must have been obvious to the appellant that the explanation for the officer's question was that he was about to put his hand into the appellant's pocket. It was a reasonable inference that the denial would lead to the officer's doing so. The court's conclusion was that "there was a causal connection between the denial and the end result."[9] The issue of causation is examined in detail in Chapter 5.

TYPES OF *ACTUS REUS*

Regardless of whether a particular offence is classified as a conduct crime 3–07 or a result crime, the *actus reus* will be one of three possible types: (1) an overt (or positive) act; (2) an omission — a failure to act where there is a legal duty to act; or (3) a state of affairs.

1. Overt acts

What is meant by an "act" is simply a movement of a part of the body. 3–08 The criminal law excludes consideration of the relevant thought processes from the definition of *actus reus*. What the actor thought or intended will invariably be dealt with under the head of *mens rea*. Generally the relevant act will have a physical or external manifestation, but this need not

---

[8]   1993 S.C.C.R. 476.
[9]   *ibid*. p. 478E. In the absence of injury, the appellant could have been charged with reckless endangerment; see *Normand v. Morrison*, 1993 S.C.C.R. 207. In *Normand v. Robinson*, 1994 S.L.T. 558, there was held to be a sufficient causal link between the organisation of a "rave" on derelict premises and the reckless endangerment of those in attendance.

necessarily involve actual movement of the limbs. Merely speaking to another person could constitute the *actus reus* of a crime (most notably incitement and breach of the peace).

2. Omissions

3–09   The general rule of the common law is that there can be no criminal liability for an omission, unless at the time of the failure to act there was a legal duty to act. It is only in limited circumstances that the criminal law extends to acts of omission as well as acts of commission. But if the law does impose a duty to act, then a failure to comply with that requirement can constitute sufficient conduct for the *actus reus* of the crime.[10] There is no exception for the accused who did not know that he was under a legal duty. This legal duty to act can derive from a number of sources. The obligation to act may be created by statute: there are a number of statutory offences which are specifically defined in terms of an omission to act. One straightforward example is failing to provide a specimen of breath under the breathalyser legislation.[11] As well as conduct crimes of this kind deriving from statute, it is possible to commit a result crime by means of omission. To starve a child to death could be the result of an omission.[12] This might be described as committing a crime of commission by omission.

A duty to act?

3–10   There are also instances where the common law would probably impose a duty to act. This will be the case where an individual has undertaken to do something upon which the health and safety of others depends. Examples of this are the cases of *William Hardie*,[13] where a charge of culpable homicide brought against an Inspector of Poor who had ignored the deceased's application for poor relief was held to be relevant, and an English case, *R. v. Instan*,[14] where a fatal omission by a niece to provide food and medical attention for her invalid aunt resulted in a manslaughter (equivalent to culpable homicide) conviction. The crimes in these two examples were committed by failing to fulfil a legal duty. In *William Hardie* the legal duty was derived from a contract. The failure to act was not just a breach of contract with his employer, however, but provided the basis for a conviction: the duty of care also extended to members of the public he was paid to protect. In *Instan* the duty had been assumed voluntarily. This would seem to imply that if someone agreed to look after a neighbour's child and the

---

[10] See *Buchmann v. Normand*, 1994 S.C.C.R. 929.
[11] Road Traffic Act 1988, s.8(9).
[12] See *George Fay* (1847) Ark. 397.
[13] (1847) Ark. 247.
[14] [1893] 1 Q.B. 450.

child drowned in the bath while that child-minder was watching television, then a conviction for culpable homicide could ensue. This scenario could be analysed either in terms of a voluntary assumption of a duty of care or of a contractual obligation.[15]

The duty to limit the harm caused by a dangerous act

There are also occasions where the accused may have created a dangerous situation and is therefore under a legal duty to do what he can to remedy the situation. If he omits to do so, then this can constitute the *actus reus* of a crime. The accused in *H.M. Advocate v. McPhee*[16] was charged with murder. He had committed a serious assault on a woman and had left her injured and unconscious in an open field. Lord Mackay, the trial judge, upheld the relevancy of the indictment, stating that there could be a murder conviction "if he is proved to have wickedly and feloniously exposed the unconscious woman regardless of consequences to the inclemency of the weather, and if she died in consequence ... both of the beating and the exposure".[17]

3–11

In *MacPhail v. Clark*,[18] the accused was a farmer who was charged with culpable and reckless endangerment. He had set fire to some straw in a field near a public road, but neglected to ensure that no danger was caused. The fire spread to vegetation on the verge of the road with the result that there was a collision on the road which resulted in injuries to people driving there at the time. At no time did the accused make any attempt to remedy the dangerous situation which he had caused. The sheriff held that the accused, as a farmer, was aware of the dangers of straw burning and knew of the presence of the road. He had allowed the fire to spread and had thereby demonstrated a reckless indifference to the consequences of his actions. He was convicted. Where the farmer was at fault was in his omitting to take sufficient precautions to safeguard against the fire spreading.

3–12

No general duty to assist

The law does not, however, impose a general duty to assist another person who is in peril. The criminal law does not maintain that everyone is obliged to be his brother's keeper. There may be a moral duty to act, but this will not necessarily constitute a legal duty. The man who stands by and watches a small child drown in a swimming pool does not commit a crime, even though he might have saved the child with ease and at no risk to himself.

3–13

---

[15] Failure to provide for a child in one's care also constitutes an offence in its own right: see the Children and Young Persons (Scotland) Act 1937.

[16] 1935 J.C. 46. See also *Miller and Denovan v. H.M. Advocate*, 1960, noted at 1991 S.L.T. 211.

[17] 1935 J.C. 46 at p. 50. The accused was convicted of culpable homicide.

[18] 1983 S.L.T.(Sh.Ct.) 37.

The situation would, of course, be very different if the man was the child's father. There would then be a legal duty to act.[19] Similarly, a duty to intervene would arise if the bystander was an attendant employed to ensure the safety of swimmers. In some other jurisdictions, however, there exist specific offences of failing to assist a person who is in peril.[20] This is sometimes described as a duty of "easy rescue" and will be subject to some kind of proviso that the assistance can be rendered without danger. It is thought that the existence of such an offence may be rather more in accord with the moral intuitions of readers than an application of the bare common law principle.

3. A state of affairs

3–14   There are a number of statutory offences which are defined in such a way that they can be committed when a certain state of affairs exists or where the accused is in a particular situation. There is no express requirement of conduct. An example of this type of offence is section 4(1) of the Road Traffic Act 1988. This section makes it an offence for a person to be unfit to drive through drink or drugs while in charge of a mechanically propelled vehicle on the road. The offence is a state of affairs: being in charge of a mechanically propelled vehicle while unfit.

MENS REA

THE MENTAL ELEMENT

3–15   As a general rule, the criminal law does not apply to an individual who has acted without mental fault. The common law draws a general distinction between conduct which is meant and conduct which is not deliberate. This precondition for the establishment of criminal liability has long been part of the Scottish criminal legal heritage. The explanation for this requirement of a blameworthy state of mind is that it serves to justify the imposition of punishment. This mental element is generally referred to as the *mens rea*. It is a presumption of the common law that crimes require *mens rea*. Statutory offences which impose strict liability are by way of an exception to the common law principle.

Mens rea and dole

3–16   *Mens rea* is not the easiest concept to grasp. In the simplest terms, it refers to the mental element required by the definition of a particular crime

---

[19]   As in *R. v. Russell* [1933] V.L.R. 59.
[20]   See, for example, French Penal Code, Article 63(2).

as distinct from the *actus reus*. That is, the *mens rea* is the individual's state of mind at the time that the forbidden conduct took place. (Perversely, and confusingly, some authorities refer to the *actus reus* as containing a form of *mens rea*. What is meant there is that the conduct, amounting to the *actus reus* of a particular crime, should be "voluntary" as a minimum requirement of liability. "True" *mens rea* would still have to be established over and above.) One can identify two distinct meanings attached to the concept of *mens rea* (treated quite separately from the *actus reus*). The first of these is that *mens rea* connotes a general notion of moral blameworthiness. This conception of *mens rea* correlates to the traditional Scottish term for the mental element of "dole", derived from the Latin *dolus* (meaning evil). It is the term dole which is to be found in many of the older cases. Hume defined dole as "that corrupt and evil intention, which is essential ... to the guilt of any crime."[21] He stated that the requirement of dole did not mean that there had to be an intention to do the particular crime. Rather, the *actus reus* "must be attended with such circumstances as indicate a corrupt and malignant disposition, a heart contemptuous of order and social duty."[22] This conception of the mental element indicating an evil character might be appropriate to the most serious offences, such as murder or an aggravated assault, but it is plainly not applicable to the majority of crimes (which are far less serious). For most crimes, especially those created by statute, it is more helpful to think in terms of *mens rea* as a mental state specific to a particular crime.

This is the second meaning of *mens rea* and is the conception which has **3–17** gained prominence. Nevertheless, the traditional approach to *mens rea* does persist. Although the term dole is not in common use today, the moralistic approach reflected in Hume still provides the background to the modern criminal law. The concept of "wicked recklessness" continues to be a significant aspect of the law of murder and "evil intent" features in the crime of assault. It remains unclear whether the adjective "evil" in the latter context has any particular legal significance. In the *Lord Advocate's Reference (No. 2 of 1992)*,[23] Lord Justice-Clerk Ross suggested that it means only "that assault cannot be committed accidentally or recklessly or negligently". If this is correct, the intention behind an assault would not have to accord with the dictionary definition of the word "evil" to attract criminal liability.

---

[21] i, 21.
[22] *Hume*, i, 22.
[23] 1993 J.C. 43 at p. 48, relying upon Gordon, *Criminal Law*, para. 29–30; applied in *Quinn v. Lees*, 1994 S.C.C.R. 159. For a fuller discussion of this issue, see paras. 9–14 *et seq*.

Subjectivity and objectivity

3–18   Criminal lawyers often refer to *mens rea* as being assessed either subjectively or objectively. A subjective approach to *mens rea* requires that the accused had actually foreseen the consequences of his actions. Did he know that the particular result would ensue from his conduct? In contrast, if an objective approach to *mens rea* is adopted, the accused will be judged by the standards of the reasonable man. It will be permissible to conclude that he had the necessary *mens rea* because he really should have known what was going to happen. There is no requirement that the trier of fact put himself in the position of the accused and decide what he (the accused) actually thought at the time of the *actus reus*. It is easier for a prosecutor to prove beyond reasonable doubt the existence of *mens rea* if it is objectively, rather than subjectively, assessed; and in Scotland it is objectively assessed.[24]

Mens rea and motive

3–19   It is important at the outset to distinguish *mens rea* from motive, since the two are not infrequently confused. Motive (sometimes called the ulterior intention) is concerned with the reason why an individual acted as he did. What caused him to act in the way in which the prosecution allege? The substantive criminal law is generally unconcerned with motive in this sense. As Lord Justice-Clerk Inglis observed in the case of *Alexander Milne*[25]: "The motive may remain a mystery, while the murder is an accomplished fact." That said, motive can be very significant in evidential terms.

3–20   The case of *Ralston v. H.M. Advocate*[26] concerned a prisoner who had taken part in a roof-top protest. He was convicted of committing a breach of the peace. He claimed that he did so in order to protest against prison conditions. On appeal, the High Court upheld the sheriff's direction to the jury that, even if Ralston's motives had been blameless, they were irrelevant to determining whether his conduct constituted a breach of the peace. In the *Lord Advocate's Reference (No. 2 of 1992)*,[27] the accused contended that he had pointed a gun at the owner of a shop during an apparent armed robbery as part of a joke. It was held that this was a claim as to the motive or ulterior intention. This was irrelevant if he had been acting deliberately.

[24] A modern authority for this proposition is *Blane v. H.M. Advocate*, 1991 S.C.C.R. 576; see also *Jamieson v. H.M. Advocate*, 1987 S.C.C.R. 484; *McIntosh v. H.M. Advocate*, 1993 S.C.C.R. 464.
[25] (1863) 4 Irv. 301 at p. 345.
[26] 1989 S.L.T. 474; followed in *H.M. Advocate v. Forbes*, 1994 S.L.T. 861.
[27] 1993 J.C. 43.

THE CATEGORIES OF *MENS REA*

The concept of *mens rea* embraces those who have made a decision and **3–21** chosen to break the law. An example would be the person who drives his car towards another with the specific purpose of striking and killing him. *Mens rea* is not limited to this one mental state. The criminal law distinguishes among a number of analytically distinct levels of *mens rea*. This reflects a recognition that some law-breakers act with a greater degree of "evil intent" or "wickedness" than others and can properly be held to a higher degree of culpability. Thus the individual who drives his car at such a speed that any reasonable person would foresee that someone might be killed, but does not aim the vehicle at anyone, would be held to be less culpable (subject to a less severe penalty) than the driver in the previous example.

This second example also illustrates the point that the *mens rea* of some **3–22** crimes can extend to those who do not anticipate causing any harm, but really ought to have realised the risks involved in their actions. *Mens rea* does not refer to any one mental state. It cannot be equated with intent. There are degrees of *mens rea*. In *Quinn v. Cunningham*,[28] Lord Justice-General Clyde observed: "it is an essential element in the constitution of a crime at common law that there should be either an intention to commit a wrong or an utter disregard of what the consequences of the act in question may be". In relation to common law (and statutory) crimes, therefore, there are two significant states of mind: (1) intention; and (2) recklessness. That said, Scottish practice recognises a wide variety of terms to indicate *mens rea* in common law crimes. These include, *inter alia*, knowledge, malice, shamelessness and wilfulness.

1. Intention

Some crimes, most notably assault[29] and theft,[30] can only be committed **3–23** intentionally. This does not mean that there has to have been advance planning or prolonged deliberation. Intention involves no more than a resolve or purposive decision to act in a particular way. The Scottish courts have not progressed very far towards defining the concept of intention. Three reasons for this can be suggested. The first is that the generally objective approach to *mens rea* in Scots law makes it unnecessary to measure with precision the degree of intention present at the time of the *actus reus*. Whilst intention is clearly a subjective state of mind, it is accepted in Scots law

---

[28] 1956 J.C. 22 at p. 24.
[29] *Lord Advocate's Reference (No. 2 of 1992)*, 1993 J.C. 43; *H.M. Advocate v. Harris*, 1993 J.C. 150.
[30] Hume, i, 73 ("felonious purpose" required).

that there can be objective proof (see paras. 3–25 and 3–26, following). The second reason is that there may have been a desire to avoid the difficulties in which the English courts have found themselves as the result of a series of cases on the concept of intention.[31] These problems have arisen as the result of judges attempting to give juries detailed guidance on how intention can be proved. Scottish courts have been more prepared to treat the concept of intention as an ordinary word, the meaning of which will be apparent to juries. A third reason is that the English cases are concerned with intention in the law of murder. Since Scots law recognises the alternative *mens rea* of wicked recklessness, this means that intention is not necessarily the central issue in such cases.[32]

3–24   One useful definition of intention is that adopted by Lord Ross in his charge to the jury in *Sayers v. H.M. Advocate*[33]: "An 'intention' to my mind connotes a state of affairs which the party 'intending' ... does more than merely contemplate; it connotes a state of affairs which, on the contrary, he decides, so far as in him lies, to bring about, and which ... he has a reasonable prospect of being able to bring about, by his act of volition." Although helpful, this definition has to be read in the context of a conspiracy case. It is concerned with an intention to perform a future action.[34] The criminal law is generally concerned with determining what constitutes an intention to effect a result which has actually been brought about. Not all intended actions are preceded by an opportunity for reflection and conscious decision-making. This intuition sits well with the Scottish approach to *mens rea*, which tends not to see *mens rea* as a mental process which can be investigated separately from what the accused has actually done. As Lord Justice-Clerk Grant observed in *H.M. Advocate v. Wilson, Latta and Rooney*[35]: "It is by their acts, as frequently happens in other spheres of life, that we know them."

Proving intention

3–25   Unless the accused has confessed as to his state of mind, intention will have to be proved by inference from the evidence: "His intention must, in the absence of any admissions by him, be derived from the circumstances

---

[31] See the decisions of the House of Lords in *Hyam v. D.P.P.* [1975] A.C. 55; *R. v. Moloney* [1985] A.C. 905 and *R. v. Hancock and Shankland* [1986] A.C. 455.
[32] See *Cawthorne v. H.M. Advocate*, 1968 J.C. 32.
[33] 1981 S.C.C.R. 312 at p. 318. The source of this quotation is *Cunliffe v. Goodman* [1950] 2 K.B. 237, *per* Lord Justice Asquith at p. 253.
[34] For discussion of this issue, see Duff, *Intention, Agency and Criminal Responsibility* (1990), pp. 17 and 44–47.
[35] 1968, unreported, but see Gane and Stoddart, *Casebook on Scottish Criminal Law*, p. 203.

surrounding the incident."[36] In *Cawthorne v. H.M. Advocate*,[37] Lord Avonside pointed out: "It is impossible ... to look into the mind of the man, and when, therefore, you are seeking to evaluate the effect of the evidence in regard to the nature and purposes of the act you can only do so by drawing an inference from what that man did in the background of all the facts of the case which you accept as proved."

This evidence will consist of the words and conduct of the accused and **3–26** the circumstances surrounding the crime. As Lord Justice-General Hope explained in *Hughes v. Crowe*,[38] the actions of the accused have "to be of a sufficient quality to enable the inference to be drawn of mens rea. That is an inference to be drawn from the nature and quality of the acts complained of". In a case of assault, for example, the necessary intention could be inferred from the fact that a punch was thrown. The prosecution would not have to offer specific proof of the accused's intention. In an example such as this, the accused will need to raise a reasonable doubt about the presence of an intention to assault in order to secure an acquittal. He will bear the tactical burden of overcoming the inference that the assault was committed intentionally.[39] Sometimes, however, the conduct of the accused will be consistent with entirely innocent behaviour and a simple inference of intention will be impossible. If this is the case, then some additional evidence will be required from the prosecution for the purpose of proving the presence of a criminal intent. An example might be a charge of shoplifting, since it is possible to mistakenly leave a shop without paying. An intention to steal would also have to be shown to be present (see para. 10–28, following). The prosecution might do so by producing evidence that the accused had acted furtively.[40]

Distinguishing intention from recklessness

Scottish criminal law recognises a distinction between an individual who **3–27** has acted recklessly and one who has purposely brought about a particular

---

[36] *Carr v. H.M. Advocate*, 1995 S.L.T. 800 at p. 804B–C. See also Erskine, *Inst.*, IV, iv, 8: "dole ... can only be discovered from the outward circumstances from which it is presumed."

[37] 1968 J.C. 32 at p. 33.

[38] 1993 S.C.C.R. 320 at p. 323F. See also *MacDonald v. Cardle*, 1985 S.C.C.R. 195 (a rather unusual case); *Mason v. Jessop*, 1990 S.C.C.R. 387; *Carney v. H.M. Advocate*, 1995 S.L.T. 1208.

[39] See Field, *Law of Evidence in Scotland*, para. 2.4.

[40] See Erskine, IV, iv, 8: "and in actions which are either innocent or criminal, according to the good or bad intention of the agent, dole must also in that case be presumed or not, from the circumstances previous to or concomitant with the crime." See *Barr v. O'Brien*, 1991 S.C.C.R. 67, for an example of an intent to steal by shoplifting being proved by inference from the conduct of the accused.

result.[41] In practical terms, it is important to draw a boundary between recklessness and intention because some crimes can only be committed intentionally. On occasion, however, the High Court has been a little careless in its use of language and shown a tendency to blur the distinction between intention and recklessness. In *Blane v. H.M. Advocate*,[42] Lord Justice-General Hope observed: "since the matter must be approached objectively I think it is open to inference, where the accused is shown to have acted with a reckless disregard for the likely consequences of what he does, that he intended those consequences to occur." This is coming very close to merging the concepts of intention and recklessness. How can an individual be said to have intended a consequence as to which he was (objectively) reckless? What a court has to decide is whether the evidence is sufficient to permit an inference of intention to be drawn. But if a judge tells a jury that intention "will be implied" by the fact that the accused acted in a way which evinced an "utter disregard"[43] for the consequences of his actions, this is to blur somewhat the distinction between intention and recklessness. However reckless one may have been as to the consequence of an action, this is quite different to having intended to bring it about.

2. Recklessness

3–28   The criminal law has long regarded the reckless law-breaker as culpable and deserving of punishment. What constitutes criminal recklessness is "a total indifference to and disregard for the safety of the public."[44] The test for establishing recklessness is essentially an objective one. Scots law does not require that the accused has actually and subjectively realised the risk attendant upon his conduct before it can be categorised as criminally reckless. An individual who has given no thought to a risk may be reckless. The argument would be that this very "thoughtlessness" is blameworthy: the accused really *ought* to have given thought to the risks. The two appellants in *Miller and Denovan v. H.M. Advocate*[45] had been convicted of a murder in the course of a robbery. The deceased had been struck on the head with a large piece of wood. The intention of the appellants seems to have been to rob, not kill, and they were convicted on the basis of the alternative *mens*

---

[41] *H.M. Advocate v. Harris*, 1993 J.C. 150, *per* Lord Justice-Clerk Ross at p. 154E, founding upon *H.M. Advocate v. Phipps* (1905) 4 Adam 616.

[42] 1991 S.C.C.R. 576 at p. 581F. See para. 11–35, following.

[43] *H.M. Advocate v. Boyd*, 1977, unreported, *per* Lord Kincraig, cited with approval in *H.M. Advocate v. Blane, supra* at p. 582A. See also *Carr v. H.M. Advocate*, 1995 S.L.T. 800. In *Allenby v. H.M. Advocate*, 1938 J.C. 55 at p. 59, Lord Wark stated that "evidence of dishonest intention may be afforded either by acts which are deliberate or by acts which are reckless."

[44] *R.H.W. v. H.M. Advocate*, 1982 S.L.T. 420 at p. 420.

[45] 1960, noted at 1991 S.L.T. 211. The ensuing discussion of this case draws upon Duff, *supra*, pp. 157–167.

rea for murder of wicked recklessness. Lord Justice General Clyde observed:[46]

> "Both appellants displayed a callous disregard of whatever injuries they may have done him. They centred their whole attention upon snatching all they could from his pockets, rolling his body over ... in order to get easier access to them. Once their purpose was achieved they fled into the night and left him to his fate."

The question which arises is how the appellants could be said to be reckless of their victim's life. They were so intent upon robbery that they did not notice the risk to life which their actions had brought about. Applying a subjective approach to recklessness, one would have to say that they had not been reckless as to the risk of death. Even though the appellants had perpetrated a vicious assault, there was no subjective appreciation or awareness of endangering life. In contrast, the objective approach taken in Scots law focuses upon the indifference to the victim's life demonstrated by the nature of the assault. Miller and Denovan's recklessness was exhibited by what they did. The fact that they failed to appreciate the risk to the victim demonstrated their callous disregard for his life.

The decision in *Allan v. Patterson*[47] concerned the interpretation of the **3–29** concept of recklessness in the context of the now repealed statutory offence of reckless driving. Lord Justice-General Emslie stated that inquiry into the state of knowledge of the individual driver at the time of the offence was not required. In order to be able to "apply the adverb 'recklessly' to the driving in question",[48] it had to be established

> "that it fell far below the standard of driving expected of the competent and careful driver and that it occurred either in the face of obvious and material dangers which were or should have been observed, appreciated and guarded against, or in circumstances which showed a complete disregard for any potential dangers which might result from the way in which the vehicle was being driven."

This suggests that recklessness is a description of behaviour as much as a state of mind, although Lord Emslie did accept that "in reaching a decision upon the critical issue a Judge or jury will be entitled to have regard to any explanation offered by the accused driver designed to show that his driving in the particular circumstances did not possess the quality of recklessness at the material time."[49] It is important, however, to read Lord Emslie's

---

[46] 1991 S.L.T. 211 at p. 211K–L.
[47] 1980 J.C. 57; approved in *Crowe v. H.M. Advocate*, 1990 J.C. 112. See also *Black v. Allan*, 1985 S.C.C.R. 11, discussed in para. 11–26, following.
[48] 1980 J.C. 57 at p. 60.
[49] *ibid*.

judgment in the context of a statute which made it an offence to drive recklessly. The offence was targeted at performing an otherwise lawful activity, but doing so in a way which could be described as reckless. But, as Lord Justice-General Hope explained in *Carr v. H.M. Advocate*,[50] in relation to a common law crime (fire-raising in this instance), "it is not the manner of doing an act which would otherwise be lawful which is in issue but the question whether the accused had the *mens rea* necessary for the commission of a crime." The issue is "whether the accused's actions showed a complete disregard for any dangers which might result from what he was doing".

Objectivity and the reasonable man

3–30   In *Gizzi and Another v. Tudhope*,[51] the two appellants had been convicted of the reckless discharge of firearms. They had gone on a clay pigeon shoot. The two men were "in ignorance of what lay beyond ... or what might lie beyond the screen of trees" over which they discharged their shotguns. Some workmen were injured. On appeal, the opinion of Lord Justice-General Emslie[52] stressed the fact that the appellants had discharged their firearms in a place where "it might reasonably be expected that members of the public ... might come to be" and that they had done nothing to satisfy themselves that no one was within range. The basis of this decision to uphold the convictions seems to have been that *reasonable* men would not have acted as the two appellants did. The risk would have been obvious to a person who exercised a reasonable degree of care. The crucial point to note is that the court was impervious to the fact that the appellants had not actually realised that there might be people behind the trees. It was unconcerned that the appellants had not been subjectively reckless.

3–31   One issue which the Scottish courts have yet to address directly is the position of the accused who would not have appreciated the risk attendant upon his action even had he applied his mind to the issue. The reasonable man would have appreciated the risk, but the accused, perhaps because of immaturity or lack of understanding, could not. His action may have been the result of inadequacy (for which he cannot be blamed), rather than any sort of indifference or disregard on his part. In the context of intention in *Petrovich v. Jessop*,[53] the Appeal Court accepted that transient factors such as lack of sleep and stress could lead to a reasonable doubt as to the normal inference of *mens rea*. It may be that such transient factors could also refute an inference of recklessness. It remains to be seen what the position is as

---

[50] 1995 S.L.T. 800 at p. 803K–L; applied in *Thomson v. H.M. Advocate*, 1995 S.L.T. 827.
[51] 1983 S.L.T. 214. See also *Normand v. Robinson*, 1994 S.L.T. 558.
[52] 1983 S.L.T. 214 at p. 216. See also *H.M. Advocate v. Phipps* (1905) 4 Adam 616.
[53] 1990 S.L.T. 594.

regards the permanent characteristics of the accused (but see para. 4–45, following).

Negligence

Negligence is similar to recklessness in that it also requires an individual **3–32** to have engaged in risk-creating conduct that deviates from the standards of the reasonably careful man. The difference lies in the degree of carelessness exhibited. The common law does not generally regard negligent conduct as sufficiently blameworthy to attract the sanction of the criminal law, although the notion of "gross negligence" is sometimes used as an alternative for recklessness.[54] There are many statutory offences which rely upon negligence.

CONCURRENCE OF *ACTUS REUS* AND *MENS REA*

If the definition of a crime requires both *actus reus* and *mens rea*, then **3–33** there will need to be a concurrence or coincidence of these two elements in order for criminal liability to be established. If there is a *mens rea* without an *actus reus* or an *actus reus* without *mens rea* (unless the offence is one of strict liability), there is again no crime. This requirement of concurrence does not mean, however, that in a result crime the *mens rea* must continue until the result occurs. In a case of murder, for example, an error as to the method or time of death will not affect criminal liability. All that is necessary is that the *mens rea* actuates the conduct which causes the death. This point is illustrated by the decision of the Privy Council in *Thabo-Meli v. R.*[55] The appellants had been convicted of murder before the High Court of Basutoland. They had struck the victim over the head and, believing him to be dead, had thrown the "body" over a cliff. The evidence was that the victim in fact died from exposure from being left at the bottom of the cliff. The appellants argued that the elements of the crime were not satisfied as *mens rea* and *actus reus* did not coincide in time. At the time when the blow had been inflicted death had not occurred, even though *mens rea* was present, and at the time of death the appellants did not have *mens rea*. The Privy Council held that it was not possible to divide up what was in reality one series of acts in the way that the appellants had argued. Lord Reid[56] observed that it would be "too refined a ground of judgment to say that, because they were under a misapprehension at one stage and thought that their guilty purpose had been achieved before, in fact, it had been achieved, therefore they are to escape the penalties of the law."

---

[54] See, for example, *Paton v. H.M. Advocate*, 1936 J.C. 19 at p. 22.
[55] [1954] 1 W.L.R. 228. See also *R. v. Le Brun* [1992] 1 Q.B. 61.
[56] [1954] 1 W.L.R. 228 at p. 230.

3–34		Generally the requirement of concurrence will mean that the *mens rea* must either precede the forbidden conduct or exist contemporaneously with the *actus reus*, but it is possible that in an exceptional case *mens rea* could be superimposed upon it. A decision to this effect is the English one of *Fagan v. Metropolitan Police Commissioner*.[57] The accused had driven his car onto a police officer's foot. The officer asked him to drive off his foot, but for a time the accused refused to do so. It could not be proved that the original driving onto the foot had been accompanied by the requisite *mens rea* for the crime of battery. Nevertheless, the majority of the divisional court took the view that the accused's conduct did constitute a battery. The reasoning was that the driving of the car onto the complainer's foot and allowing it to remain there could be treated as one continuing act of the application of force. On this analysis, the accused's act was not complete by the time his *mens rea* began (which would have been the case if the driving onto the complainer's foot had been treated as a single complete act). The accused's *mens rea* could therefore be superimposed on the existing continuing *actus reus* which he had caused. *Fagan* is thus persuasive authority for the view that, where an *actus reus* can be regarded as a continuing one, it is sufficient if *mens rea* is present at some stage during its continuance.

TRANSFERRED INTENT

3–35	The problem of concurrence does not arise where an individual acts intending to harm one person, but in fact harms someone other than the intended victim. If, as occurred in *Roberts v. Hamilton*,[58] A aims a blow at B, but strikes C instead, A will still be guilty of an assault. Similarly, if A shoots at B intending to kill him, but in fact the bullet hits C, killing him, A will be guilty of the murder of C.[59] Thus the fact that A assaults or kills someone other than his intended victim is not relevant to his criminal liability. This principle is generally referred to as the doctrine of transferred intent or malice. Under this doctrine the intent to injure B is held to have been transferred to the actual victim.

3–36		It is possible to construct an argument that there is little need to utilise the terminology of transferred intent. In *Roberts v. Hamilton*, for example, one might say that the reason why the accused was guilty of an intentional assault was quite simply that she possessed the requisite *mens rea* for the crime. The "evil intent" did not need to be transferred. The intent required to establish fault in that case was to assault a, but not a *particular*, person. The accused intended to assault a person and in fact did so.

---

[57]	[1969] 1 Q.B. 439.
[58]	1989 J.C. 91.
[59]	Erskine, IV, iv, 43.

Transferred intent and *mens rea*

For the doctrine of transferred intent to operate the accused must have   **3–37**
the requisite *mens rea* of the crime for which he is being prosecuted. That
is, the doctrine will not operate where the accused has the *mens rea* for one
crime, but in fact perpetrates the *actus reus* of a crime which requires a
different *mens rea*. If the intention of the accused in *Roberts v. Hamilton*
had been to break a window, the doctrine does not mean that this intention
could be transferred to make her guilty of assault. The *mens rea* of assault
cannot be satisfied by an intention to break a window.[60]

Further reading

Ashworth, A., "The Scope of Criminal Liability for Omissions" (1989)
    105 L.Q.R. 424.
Ferguson, P., "Recklessness and the Reasonable Man in Scots Criminal
    Law," 1985 J.R. 29.
Scottish Law Commission, *The Mental Element in Crime* (Scot. Law Com.
    No. 80, 1983).

---

[60] It is possible that she could be convicted of causing reckless injury. This crime is described
    in detail in Chap. 9. See also para. 11–35, below, for transferred intent relative to fire-
    raising.

CHAPTER 4

VOLUNTARY ACTS AND AUTOMATISM

THE ACADEMIC VIEW

TEXT BOOKS & OTHERS

4–01 "The foundation of criminal liability is conduct, for without an act there can be no liability. But not any act will do. There are qualifications that an act must meet, and the first is that it be *voluntary*."[1] This statement by an academic writer is echoed in major text books around the world. Thus, in Smith and Hogan, *Criminal Law*,[2] it is asserted that there is a "rule requiring proof that a relevant act was voluntary" and also that "the voluntariness of an act is a more fundamental element of criminal liability than ... *mens rea*." The Canadian writers, Mewett and Manning, put the matter even more forcefully when they state that an "essential element of a criminal offence is voluntary conduct on the part of the accused."[3] Gordon appears to take the same view, as the following quotation indicates: "the term 'act' is usually restricted to 'voluntary' acts, so that a man is responsible only for his voluntary acts."[4] Nor is that view confined to textbook writings. Many criminal codes in the United States, for example, have adopted the provision in the Model Penal Code[5] that: "a person is not guilty of an offence unless his liability is based on conduct which includes a voluntary act or the omission to perform an act of which he is physically capable."[6] In the United Kingdom, however, the proposed criminal code for England and Wales[7] makes no mention of the "voluntariness" of an act as an element (essential or otherwise) of criminal liability; and the following judicial opinion is rather *un*-typical: "The requirement that [there] should be a voluntary act is

---

[1] Gross, *A Theory of Criminal Justice* (1979), p. 67.
[2] 7th ed., p. 39.
[3] Mewett and Manning, *Criminal Law*, 2nd ed. (1985), p. 73.
[4] *Criminal Law*, para. 3–08.
[5] Proposed Official Draft (1962), para. 2.01.
[6] LaFave and Scott, *Criminal Law*, p. 197, n. 23.
[7] Law Com. No. 177 (1989).

essential, not only in a murder case, but also in every criminal case."[8] Regrettably, it is not at all immediately apparent what is meant by these various views; and an illustration may help to clarify the issues involved.

Illustration

Suppose that John is seen at the wheel of his car, as it travels from **4–02** Glasgow to Renfrew. On a perfectly straight piece of road, in good daylight conditions of visibility and weather, his vehicle is observed to swerve suddenly to the "wrong" side of the road and collide with an oncoming motorcycle. The motorcyclist is thrown into the air and his bike crushed. John's vehicle pauses for less than two seconds before speeding away from the scene of the incident. Some minutes later, his vehicle knocks down a police officer who had stepped into the road in order to signal him to stop. The police officer is seriously injured. On the face of things, John would seem to have committed a number of offences — since cars (at the time of writing, at least) are incapable of directing their own movements. The offences in question might include dangerous driving under section 2 of the Road Traffic Act 1988 (as substituted by section 1 of the Road Traffic Act 1991), or perhaps the lesser offence of driving without due care and attention under section 3 of the Road Traffic Act 1988 (as substituted by section 2 of the Road Traffic Act 1991), and almost certainly failing to stop after an accident under section 170 of the Road Traffic Act 1988. Were the motorcyclist to die of his injuries, then even more serious charges might possibly apply (*e.g.* culpable homicide at common law, or the offence of causing death by dangerous driving under section 1 of the Road Traffic Act 1988, as substituted by section 1 of the Road Traffic Act 1991). *A propos* the unfortunate police officer, charges of assault or even attempted murder at common law might easily be envisaged.

Acts of an Innocent Agent or Events Beyond Human Control

If in the preceding example, John had been alert and apparently in full **4–03** control of his vehicle "at the relevant time", then one might assume that he had simply been travelling too fast for his own capabilities or the mechanical tolerances of his car (or that he had been paying scandalously little attention to his driving) — and that he had panicked when the "accidents" occurred. One would have little sympathy for his plight. But suppose that he had been driving competently enough at a wholly reasonable speed just before the first "accident", and that events thereafter were directed by a passenger who seized the steering wheel without prior warning and deliberately aimed

---

[8] *Bratty v. Att.-Gen. for Northern Ireland* [1963] A.C. 386, *per* Lord Denning at p. 409.

the vehicle at the passing motorcyclist. The passenger also, one may conjecture (with some suspension of disbelief), caused the car to move off after the initial collision, and thereafter knock down the police officer, by physically forcing John's hands and feet to execute the required movements. If John had no reason to anticipate such behaviour on the part of his passenger, one would probably conclude that he had simply been an innocent agent (see para. 7–34, below) in the execution of the real culprit's plan — no more responsible for the act or its result than a broken glass in the hands of a violent man.[9] John could not reasonably have been said to be "driving" or doing anything at all during the crucial time periods. If the question were to be posed: "Who was driving at the relevant moments?" — one would surely not answer that it was John. No part of the conduct or acts making up the *actus reus* of any of the crimes involved (see para. 4–02, above) could be said to have been his; and the same conclusion would follow, at least in respect of the initial collision, if the car swerved because a sudden defect manifested itself in the steering, or a tyre burst without warning — assuming that either event placed the car beyond any reasonable human control.

ACTING UNCONSCIOUSLY OR SEMI-CONSCIOUSLY

4–04   One might further suppose, however, again in relation to the above example (in para. 4–02), that the car collided with the unfortunate victims because John was "unconscious" at the time, or, was "semi-conscious" or in a state of "impaired consciousness". Perhaps he had had an epileptic fit or a "heart attack" whilst at the wheel and was thus unaware of what he was doing for a particular period of time; or he might have become comatose or semi-conscious because he suffered from a condition (such as diabetes) where full consciousness depended upon a very fine balance being struck between the ingestion of prescribed drugs (such as insulin) and normal foodstuffs — and that balance had ceased to be maintained. Perhaps, again, he might have slept badly or not at all the night before and succumbed to tiredness whilst at the wheel (which might at least explain the initial collision under the postulated non-adverse road and weather conditions). Yet again John might have been drinking alcohol prior to setting out on his journey: he might have been plainly drunk. His less-than-conscious state might even have been due to toxic fumes, leaking into the interior of the vehicle because, for example, of a defective exhaust — either on his own car or on a truck he had happened to be following closely. In all of these possible scenarios, John might nevertheless appear to be driving. It might appear that he was

---

[9]   See, for instance, the contribution of Mr. Smith to Mrs. Craft's death in *R. v. Mitchell* [1983] 2 W.L.R. 938.

manipulating the controls and directing the movements of the vehicle — which is what "driving" amounts to in law.[10] If one was now to ask: "Who was driving at the relevant moments?" it would be difficult to say it was anyone other than John himself — particularly since the vehicle was (apparently) purposefully driven off after the initial collision.

The problem

Where the only person (in retrospect, at least) who could have influenced **4–05** the course of events apparently did things which had a major causal influence over that course of events (as in the illustration set out at para. 4–02, above), then a problem relating to his responsibility for the outcome exists if he "did" those things whilst he was unconscious or only semi-conscious (as in the various scenarios described in para. 4–04, above). If he apparently did those things, then it is very difficult to conclude that he did not do them at all (although some text-writers seem to maintain that in such circumstances there is indeed no human act).[11] That does not lead to the conclusion, however, that he is necessarily criminally responsible for them. The first component of criminal liability, it will be remembered, is not just an "act" (*i.e.* "doing something") but an *actus reus*. It can, therefore, be postulated that it is a "responsible" human act (and not a "bare" act) which the criminal law seeks. The law thus attempts, or should attempt, to give effect to the intuitive feeling that there is a significant difference in responsibility between a driver who collides with another vehicle because he has been wantonly driving too fast and one who (in fact) causes a similar "accident" because he has temporarily, through no fault of his own, lost the ability to comply with the dictates of the criminal law by making, or refraining from making, particular bodily movements. Of course, in many instances that difference in responsibility can be accounted for by the law's taking note that a person so incapacitated lacks *mens rea*. He may have "acted" after a fashion, but not so as to give rise to any inference that he intended the outcome, had knowledge of the criminative circumstances, or foresaw (objectively or subjectively) the risks, such was his lack of awareness of what was happening. To that extent, then, it would hardly be necessary to attempt to distinguish a "bare" act from a "responsible" one. The matter would simply be settled in terms of whether there was or was not *mens rea* — given his personal circumstances at the time.[12]

---

[10] See *Ames v. MacLeod*, 1969 J.C. 1, and *McArthur v. Valentine*, 1990 J.C. 146.

[11] Mewett and Manning, p. 74; Ashworth, *Principles of Criminal Law* (2nd ed., 1995), pp. 95–96, para. 4.2 "Involuntary conduct, (a) Automatism and Authorship."

[12] Of the crimes possibly committed in the scenario depicted in para. 4–02 above, failing to stop after an accident (see *Harding v. Price* [1948] 1 K.B. 695), assault (see *Smart v. H.M. Advocate*, 1975 J.C. 30), culpable homicide (see paras. 9–52 to 9–71, below), and attempted murder (see *Cawthorne v. H.M. Advocate*, 1968 J.C. 32) all require some form of *mens rea*.

The need to distinguish different sorts of act

4–06   There are, however, some crimes (some statutory ones — see Chapter 13, below) where liability is said to be "strict". That means in effect that there is no requirement that the prosecutor should show *mens rea* on the part of the accused, or bring forward evidence from which it might be inferred.[13] In bald terms, proof that the accused brought about the forbidden result or performed the forbidden conduct is quite sufficient for conviction.[14] To take effective cognisance of incapacitating defects (mental or physical) accompanying human conduct, it would be necessary, therefore, in such cases to distinguish between conduct amounting to a "bare" act and that amounting to an *actus reus*.[15] Similarly, with respect to any criminal system which pursues an objective method of proving *mens rea* (as is believed to be the case in Scotland — see Chapter 3, above), it may be necessary to distinguish "responsible" human conduct from "mere" human conduct, since proof of the *actus reus* will very often imply the existence of the required *mens rea*. In the illustration above (see para. 4–02), for example, if John's car was apparently driven at the unfortunate policeman, it would be simple to infer from the facts that the driver intended to kill the officer, or was completely indifferent whether he lived or died — either sufficing for the crime of attempted murder.[16] There is thus a case to be made for marking off "bare" human conduct from the "responsible" sort.

What distinctions can be made?

4–07   With reference once again to the illustration (see paras. 4–02 to 4–04, above), there is plainly a distinction to be made between John's conduct where he willingly courts the risks of an "accident" by wantonly driving too fast, and his conduct where he "drives" in the throes of an epileptic fit or a heart attack. There is also perhaps a further distinction to be made, for example, between his "driving" whilst experiencing such a fit or attack, and his doing so whilst intoxicated — depending to a large extent on the way in which he came to be intoxicated (though other factors are also involved — *e.g.* the type and known effects of the intoxicant). These distinctions, however, are exceedingly difficult to generalise. It is tempting to conclude, for example, that the issue depends on whether or not the apparent actor was conscious (in the sense of "being aware") of what he was doing at the relevant time. But this is not an infallible guide. A person

---

[13] Smith and Hogan, pp. 38–39.
[14] Of the crimes possibly committed in the scenario depicted in para. 4–02 above, dangerous driving, driving without due care and attention, and causing death by dangerous driving are probably all of this type.
[15] *cf.* Ashworth, *Principles of Criminal Law*, p. 96.
[16] *Cawthorne v. H.M. Advocate*, 1968 J.C. 32.

afflicted by cerebral palsy will (usually) be fully conscious of the random movements of his limbs; but it does not follow that one should wish to label such movements as "responsible" acts, even though they might result in prima facie assaults upon others unfortunate enough to be within range. The same might be said of so called "reflex" movements where a human physiological response is triggered automatically by the application of external stimulus.[17]

It has become customary, at least in academic writings, to refer to the **4–08** primary distinction as that between a voluntary (*i.e.* responsible) act and an involuntary (*i.e.* bare) one. This, however, only produces a terminological shift. Meaning must still be given to the replacement terms. Equally, it has become customary to speak of a "voluntary" act as a "willed" bodily movement, or as conduct which flows from an exercise of "will"[18] — which suggests that the presence or absence of some mental process is the issue at stake. If this is correct, then a mental element must be involved in conduct truly amounting to an *actus reus* — although this disturbs the neat symmetry of criminal law theory, namely that the mental element of *mens rea* is separate from the *actus reus*.[19] It is, however, rather uncertain what can be meant by the "will" in such an analysis. Clearly it must be different from "wanting" or "desiring" what one does, since these terms normally connote the seeking of goals well beyond the actions themselves; nor can it be squared with more limited conceptions of "wanting" or "desiring", since one may in fact do something (for example, visit a dentist) which is opposed to one's short-term desires or wants (*cf.* the long-term desire to have attractive and effectively-functioning teeth). The term "will", therefore, seems to be no less obscure than the terms "responsible" or "voluntary".

Legal effect of involuntariness

It is also uncertain what should be the result of making a distinction **4–09** between "bare" acts and "responsible" ones. For the authors of the American Model Penal Code, a person is to be held "not guilty of an offence" unless his conduct includes a voluntary act (see para. 4–01, above). Fletcher,[20] on the other hand, remarks that "we intuitively recoil at the notion of punishing" persons in respect of acts where the "will" was not operative; and LaFave and Scott also suggest that it is punishment which cannot be justified for

---

[17] See *Jessop v. Johnstone*, 1991 S.C.C.R. 238. For a more sophisticated analysis, see Gross, *supra*, n.1, pp. 67–73.

[18] See, for example, Smith and Hogan, p. 37; *cf.* Ashworth, pp. 96 *et seq.* "(b) The Essence of Automatism."

[19] See Williams, *Criminal Law: The General Part* (2nd ed. 1961), p. 12; Williams, *Textbook of Criminal Law* (2nd ed. 1983), p. 147 at para. 7.2. *Cf.* Mewett and Manning, p. 69.

[20] *Rethinking Criminal Law* (1978), p. 426.

"involuntary" acts.[21] Obviously, punishment cannot be imposed unless there is a finding of guilt; but the converse is not necessarily true. A person may be convicted of an offence, but may thereafter be discharged without punishment at all (unless, of course, conviction itself is taken to be a form of punishment). As far as current Scots law is concerned, there is an important matter of public policy here. As will be seen (see para. 4–36, below), Scots criminal law does not always sanction acquittal in cases where there were "involuntary" acts; but it may encourage a special approach to disposal in cases where the policy of safeguarding the public demands conviction — to the point of approving no punishment at all in suitable circumstances. If, then, the theory here does not rule out convictions but draws the line at punishments for at least some "involuntary" acts, then the Scottish approach, whatever other justifications it may claim, is not necessarily as inconsistent with principle as some have thought it to be.[22]

Voluntariness as an essential element of liability

4–10   Regrettably, it is further uncertain whether the "voluntariness" of an act is indeed to be taken as an essential element of criminal liability. If it were to be accepted as an essential element[23] then one would expect "voluntariness" to be something which prosecutors were duty bound to establish at criminal trials. Neither academic writings nor judicial dicta, however, support such a proposition. At best, those who favour a requirement of "voluntariness" take the view that an act will be presumed to be "voluntary" until some evidence to the contrary is presented.[24] This has had the effect of highlighting the issue as one of "*in*voluntariness" and of shifting the emphasis from that of "fundamental element" to that of "defence". Smith and Hogan, for example, remark[25] that "[i]t is a defence known as 'automatism' that this element [that an act was voluntary] has not been proved by the Crown." Some text-writers, therefore, deal with the whole issue here under the heading of "Defences",[26] others tackle it almost

---

[21] pp. 197–198.
[22] See, for example, Gane and Stoddart, *A Casebook on Scottish Criminal Law*, under the heading "(ii) Automatism" at p. 69 — although their criticisms were admittedly made before the case of *Ross v. H.M. Advocate*, 1991 J.C. 210 was decided (see para. 4–19, below).
[23] See para. 4–01, above, "a more fundamental element than ... *mens rea.*" See also Ashworth, pp. 95–96, at para. 4.2, (a).
[24] See *Bratty v. Att.-Gen. for Northern Ireland* [1963] A.C. 386, *per* Lord Denning at p. 413; *Ryan v. The Queen* (1967) 40 A.L.J.R. 488, *per* Barwick C.J. at p. 492, followed in *R. v. Falconer* (1991) 65 A.L.J.R. 20; and Ashworth, p. 96.
[25] Somewhat oddly in its context at p. 39.
[26] See Williams, *Textbook of Criminal Law,* Part 4 — Defences, Chap. 29, pp. 662–684.

exclusively under the title of *"Actus Reus"*,[27] whilst others present it under both such headings.[28]

Involuntariness as a defence — automatism

In English and Scots criminal law, it is now clear that the whole issue **4-11** has become one for the defence in the first instance. The accused must somehow place some evidence before the court or jury which will tend to displace the tacit presumption that his proven conduct was "voluntary". He must, therefore, discharge the initial evidential burden required by the defence of "automatism". He must show that his acts could be construed as "involuntary". If that construction finds favour, it may be that the reason for his involuntariness falls within the definition of insanity accepted in law. In that event, "insane automatism" may be established,[29] although the conventional view in Scotland is that a burden of proof lies with the defence to satisfy the court of the accused's insanity on the balance of probabilities — a burden which exceeds a mere evidential one, and which may be more difficult to discharge. In England, the scope of the independent defence has been narrowed to that of "non-insane automatism"; and that, as has repeatedly been said by English judges, is itself of very narrow scope.[30] The English judiciary, therefore, has taken every opportunity to make the defence difficult to establish; and in practice, pleas of non-insane automatism are seldom successful. The strange practice has also arisen in England of permitting an accused to withdraw his defence of automatism in favour of a guilty plea where the trial judge has ruled that the defence truly amounts to one of insanity.[31] This seems to confound both principle and policy notions of public safety.

The scope of a legally relevant act

An added difficulty for those who favour an "involuntary act" defence **4-12** is that the judiciary has proved more than willing to enlarge the scope of the "acts" in question. In the illustration concerning John (see para. 4-02, above), the incidents (possibly attracting criminal liability) are of fairly short duration. His car was "driven" into the path of a motorcycle, collided with that cycle, and then was "driven" away — all within the space of a

---

[27] See Smith and Hogan, pp. 37–41, who nevertheless also treat it there as the defence of "Automatism".
[28] See Mewett and Manning, pp. 73 *et seq.* and pp. 279 *et seq.*
[29] See, for example, *R. v. Burgess* [1991] 2 W.L.R. 1206, *per* Lord Lane C.J. at p. 1208E.
[30] See *Bratty v. Att.-Gen. for Northern Ireland* [1963] A.C. 383; *R. v. Quick* [1973] Q.B. 910; *R. v. Sullivan* [1984] A.C. 156; *R. v. Hennessy* [1989] 1 W.L.R. 287.
[31] See, for example, *R. v. Sullivan, supra*; *R. v. Hennessy, supra*.

few seconds, no doubt. Similarly, the knocking down of the police officer will have occupied a very short interval of time. If it was established that, during the relevant time periods, John was truly "unconscious" (*i.e.* unaware of his surroundings and his obligations as a driver — even though his eyes may have been open and his behaviour apparently normal), and if his legally relevant acts were to be confined to only those narrow periods of time, then it is certainly possible to conclude that his actions were not "responsible" ones (with whatever effect that is deemed to have in law). He would not be responsible for what he did during those few seconds. It should not then matter what the reason for his unconsciousness was. In any event, if the reason was connected with something which was not his fault and which he could not have anticipated (a stroke or heart attack, for example), one would not wish to enlarge the field of view. But, if John (say) had known himself to be diabetic and had further known that failure to take insulin would lead to the rapid onset of unconsciousness in his case due to hyperglycaemia,[32] then one feels the need to inquire whether he had taken his medication at all that day. If he had not, then his "acts" may be seen as including the fault-ridden ones of failing to take insulin and then driving, all in the knowledge that unconsciousness might well intervene before his destination was reached. One would perhaps not then view the incidents as "involuntary" on his part at all — provided that a wide-angled view of his "actings" can legitimately be taken. Truly, he might have been unaware of what he was doing during an incident and its immediate aftermath; but he was certainly not unaware when he began to drive that his actions might pass beyond his control. This may be enough, therefore, to mark his acts as responsible ones after all (for the purposes of at least some crimes); but this will depend on how widely the law is prepared to look for relevant actings, and how concerned it is whether he should have been able to anticipate precisely what eventually happened. Enlarging the field of view, therefore, can turn unconscious or uncontrolled actions into responsible ones.

Ryan v. The Queen

4–13   A well known illustration here can be found in the Australian case of *Ryan v. The Queen*[33] where the accused set out to rob a petrol filling-station. He carried a loaded, sawn-off rifle with him, and used it as a threat to subdue the person in charge of the cash-box there. The accused ordered that person to face a wall and hold his hands out behind him — so that these could then be tied securely with a piece of rope the accused thought he had in his pocket. Whilst he searched his pocket for that rope, two things

---

[32] See *R. v. Hennessy*, *supra* and para. 4–27, below. *Cf. MacLeod v. Mathieson*, 1993 S.C.C.R. 488 (Sh.Ct.).

[33] (1967) 40 A.L.J.R. 468.

happened. The person being coerced in that way suddenly crouched down and half turned round; and the accused "shot" him in the neck — killing him. The accused claimed that he had been holding the rifle (which did not have its safety catch set) with one hand, and that the act of pulling the trigger had been "involuntary". It was, he said, a reflex action "triggered" by the sudden movement on the part of the victim. Subsequent police tests suggested that there might be some basis for that possibility — which might have been decisive in the later proceedings for criminal homicide. In fact, he was convicted of murder; and his subsequent appeal was dismissed partly on the view that

> "the jury, having concluded that the discharge of the gun was involuntary could have concluded that the act causing death was the presentation of the cocked, loaded gun with a safety catch unapplied and that its involuntary discharge was a likelihood which ought to have been in the contemplation of the applicant when presenting the gun in the circumstances."[34]

Where the focus was widened slightly beyond the mere pulling of the trigger, there was thus produced a voluntary act which the court could have accepted as *the* cause of the death in all the circumstances there.

CONCLUSION

It is theoretically satisfying to conclude that a person can only be criminally **4–14** liable for his "voluntary acts". But it is very difficult to give content to the word "voluntary"; and it is not always easy to identify what is the "act" for the purposes of a particular crime. It seems very generally agreed, however, that a person should not be punished for his involuntary acts. Punishment after all cannot deter a person from repeating his conduct if he did not know or could not help what he was doing at the time. Nor can it deter third parties successfully, since the imposition of punishment will be viewed as simply unfair in the circumstances. Still less would punishment be seen to be merited in such a case; and, therefore, its imposition could not be retributively justified. "Restraint or rehabilitation might be deemed appropriate, however, when individuals are likely to constitute a continuing threat to others because of their involuntary movements, but it is probably best to deal with this problem outside the criminal law."[35] In Scotland, however, the view appears to be taken that any necessary measures of restraint should be taken within the criminal law.

---

[34] (1967) 40 A.L.J.R. 468, *per* Barwick C.J. at p. 494.
[35] LaFave and Scott, p. 198.

THE POSITION UNDER SCOTS LAW

ACTS OF AN INNOCENT AGENT OR EVENTS BEYOND HUMAN CONTROL

4–15   Under Scots law, a person who is physically compelled by another to be the innocent agent of a criminal act is not responsible for that act. Criminal liability clearly remains with the other person — since the act is truly his. It would be absurd and unjust to take any other view (see para. 4–03, above), and the case of *Hugh Mitchell*[36] provides ample authority. There, Mitchell attacked his wife, kicking and punching her whilst she was holding their four-month old baby in her arms. In terms of the indictment, it was alleged that *he* caused his wife, by the assault he made upon her, to compress or squeeze the child so as to obstruct its respiration in some way — by all which, or part thereof, the child was mortally injured and thus culpably killed by *him*. This part of the charge was found relevant by the three-judge High Court; and the jury eventually convicted him of the culpable homicide of the child on the stated basis. There was no question of his wife's having had any liability at all for the child's death. Her contribution to the fatality was recognised as no greater than that of some inanimate object in the hands of her husband. It is equally apparent that Scots law would not hold a person criminally liable for an event which was beyond his power to control (although normally this would be treated as an event he had not caused). Reference may be made here to the decision in *Hogg v. MacPherson*,[37] which is considered at paragraph 3–04, above. It will be seen that Lord Justice-General Clyde held there that "the breaking of the lamp was not the appellant's act at all, either negligent or accidental".[38] It seems that the same view could be taken of genuine reflex actions; but these are difficult to define, and there are few, reported Scottish cases which have featured them. In *Jessop v. Johnstone*[39] Lord Justice-Clerk Ross did say: "We appreciate that there may be cases where a person instinctively reacts to violence in a reflex way, such as if a person is suddenly and without warning struck and turns round sharply so that he comes in contact with his assailant." The Appeal Court held, however, that the facts of the case did not support a finding of "reflex response". Had the facts done so, presumably the court would have endorsed the sheriff's original decision to acquit — although that had been based by him on a consequent lack of *mens rea*.

---

[36] (1856) 2 Irv. 488.
[37] 1928 J.C. 15.
[38] *ibid.* p. 17.
[39] 1991 S.C.C.R. 238 at p. 240E.

Hypnotic or Similar Influences

If a person is forcibly or unwittingly hypnotised by another (assuming **4–16** forcible or unwitting hypnotism of a subject to be possible) and thus made to do that other's bidding, then that person surely becomes an innocent agent — just as much as if he had been physically compelled; and the same conclusion would seem to follow if drugs were to be administered to him by stealth or force, in order to make him comply with the administrator's criminal designs.[40]

Acting Unconsciously or Semi-Consciously

Where a person has apparently acted purposively, and there was no question **4–17** of physical compulsion by another or from natural phenomena (see para. 4–15, above) and no question of hypnotic influence (see para. 4–16, above) then it may be that he did so whilst unconscious, or whilst not fully conscious. He may have been observed in the act of assaulting another, driving a car, or taking things away from a store without paying for them; but it may also be the case that due to some mental dysfunction (going beyond mere inattention) he was not aware (or not fully aware) of what he was doing. His mental condition, then, may have been less than normal at the relevant time. Scots law does not ignore such a mental condition, but inquires into the cause producing it.

Causal factor — mental illness

If that cause is proved on the balance of probabilities to be a "mental **4–18** illness, mental disease or defect or unsoundness of mind"[41] then legal insanity is present, and the person concerned will be acquitted of the assault, the driving offence, the theft, or whatever. Of course, the acquittal will be on the ground of insanity; but that does not commit the court, in either a solemn or a summary case, to order the acquitted person's detention in a mental hospital. The court instead may make a guardianship order, a supervision and treatment order, or make no order at all.[42] The often expressed view, therefore, that an insanity plea holds severe consequences for an accused person,[43] is no longer as compelling as once was the case.

---

[40] See *H.M. Advocate v. Raiker*, 1989 S.C.C.R. 149, *per* Lord McCluskey's charge to the jury at p. 154C — although his approach stressed the consequent lack of *mens rea* of the "innocent agent".

[41] *Brennan v. H.M. Advocate*, 1977 J.C. 38, *per* Lord Justice-General Emslie at p. 45.

[42] Criminal Procedure (Scotland) Act 1995, s.57: and see also ss.58–63, and Sched. 4.

[43] See, *e.g.*, *Ross v. H.M. Advocate*, 1991 J.C. 210, *per* Lord Justice-General Hope at p. 213.

Causal factor — external to the accused — automatism

4–19　　　In *Ross v. H.M. Advocate*[44] a full bench of five appeal court judges decided, for the first time authoritatively,[45] that a straightforward acquittal was competent where an accused person behaved in an apparently criminal fashion after drugs had been administered to him without his knowledge or consent. Ross had been at a party where a can of lager from which he had been drinking was surreptitiously "laced" by others with LSD (lysergic acid diethylamide) and five or six "jellies" of temazepam. Unwitting as to its contents, Ross continued to imbibe from the same can, with the result that his conduct became uncharacteristically bizarre and exceptionally violent. Amongst other things, he then stabbed several persons, inflicting upon them serious, life-threatening injuries. The case was, therefore, concerned with the criminal responsibility of one who knowingly consumes some alcohol whilst unknowingly ingesting hallucinogenic drugs (*i.e.* LSD — temazepam generally, and on its own at least, having a tranquillising effect). The Appeal Court, however, ignored the fact that Ross had knowingly taken drink, and instead was content to emphasise that proof of *mens rea* is essential for conviction,[46] that the burden of proving *mens rea* lies on the Crown throughout a trial,[47] and that some evidence introduced during the trial of an "external factor" operating on the accused's mental condition at the relevant time may prevent the Crown establishing that he had (or must have had) the necessary *mens rea*.[48] On the face of things then, the court treated the issue as one involving "lack of *mens rea*" rather than lack of voluntariness (or responsibility) in relation to the conduct itself. This approach leaves the issue of "strict liability" offences in limbo (see para. 4–06, above); and indeed only Lord McCluskey[49] obliquely acknowledged that such offences might exist. Clearly if the only effect of an "external factor" is to negative *mens rea*, then persons (such as Ross) would have to be convicted of any strict liability offences of which they stood accused. Of course, the majority of the charges in Ross's case were common law ones; and the one statutory accusation (police assault under section 41(1)(a) of the Police (Scotland) Act 1967) did not involve strict liability and had, in any event, dropped from the picture at appellate level. It may well be, therefore, that the court did not address itself to the problem of "strict"

---

[44] 1991 J.C. 210.
[45] See the single judge decision in *H.M. Advocate v. Ritchie,* 1926 J.C. 45, which was approved in *Ross.*
[46] *ibid. per* Lord Justice-General Hope at p. 217; *per* Lord Allanbridge at p. 223; *per* Lord McCluskey at pp. 227–228; *per* Lord Brand at p. 232. Lord Weir, at p. 232, expressed unreserved agreement with the opinion of the Lord Justice-General.
[47] *ibid. per* Lord Justice-General Hope at p. 219; Lord Allanbridge at p. 223; Lord McCluskey at p. 228; and Lord Brand at p. 232.
[48] *ibid. per* Lord Justice-General Hope at p. 221; Lord McCluskey at p. 230.
[49] *ibid.* p. 228.

statutory offences at all since these were simply not germane to the case on hand; and it remains just possible to read parts of the opinions as if something more fundamental than "lack of *mens rea*" was involved — in other words, as if a fundamental element was missing in a case such as that of *Ross* which rendered the *actus* not *reus and* which also had the effect of negativing *mens rea* where that was an essential requirement of the particular crime in question. This, however, is somewhat speculative,[50] and is not a view encouraged by later cases where reference is made to the "defence" of "automatism" consisting of an inability to form *mens rea*.[51] What is clear then is that an external factor affecting the normal mental condition of the accused can lead to an acquittal if certain qualifying conditions are met.

Automatism — qualifying conditions

As is so often the case with landmark decisions, the defence of automatism created in *Ross v. H.M. Advocate*[52] has been clarified in subsequent appeal court rulings. Perhaps the most important of these is *Sorley v. H.M. Advocate*.[53] It is worth reproducing what was said by the Lord Justice-General there in relation to the new defence: **4–20**

> "As the law now stands on this matter, automatism consisting of an inability to form *mens rea*[54] which is due to an external factor,[55] and

---

[50] But see, for example, Lord Justice-General Hope's view at p. 222 that the external factor "must be one which resulted in a total loss of control of his actions in regard to the crime with which he is charged"; Lord Allanbridge's view at p. 223 that "an accused will not have the necessary *mens rea* if his mind is so affected by [an external] factor that the result is a total loss of control over his actions which have led to the alleged crime charged being committed"; and Lord Weir's opinion at p. 232 that "the accused must have been suffering from a total alienation of reason rendering him incapable of controlling or appreciating what he was doing."

[51] See, *e.g.*, *Sorley v. H.M. Advocate,* 1992 J.C. 102, *per* Lord Justice-General Hope at p. 105. See also the Criminal Procedure (Scotland) Act 1995, s.78(2), where "automatism" is treated as if it were a special defence.

[52] 1991 J.C. 210.

[53] 1992 J.C. 102 at p. 105.

[54] At least two of the charges in *Cardle v. Mulrainey,* 1992 S.L.T. 1152 (driving without insurance, contrary to s.143(1)(a), (2), and, as the holder of a provisional driving licence, driving without a supervisor being present, contrary to s.97(3),(7) of the Road Traffic Act 1988) were probably of strict liability — a fact noted by the sheriff but entirely ignored by the Appeal Court. The sheriff considered that, notwithstanding that *mens rea* did not have to be established by the Crown in respect of these offences, it would still on principle have to be shown that the accused's conduct was voluntary.) Also, in *MacLeod v. Mathieson,* 1993 S.C.C.R. 488 (Sh.Ct.), the sheriff assumed (but merely for the sake of dealing with and rejecting the defence arguments) that automatism applied to careless driving under s.3 of the Road Traffic Act 1988, although such an offence is not normally thought of as requiring *mens rea*.

[55] See paras. 4–24 to 4–33, below.

not to some disorder of the mind itself which is liable to recur,[56] is a defence so long as there is evidence that three requirements are satisfied. These are that the external factor must not be self-induced, that it must be one which the accused was not bound to forsee [sic] and that it must have resulted in a total alienation of reason amounting to a total loss of control of his actions in regard to the crime with which he is charged..."

The first of these requirements seems to disqualify an accused person from availing himself of the defence if, for example, he voluntarily pours alcohol down his throat[57] or voluntarily ingests some other substance which has the effect of producing a total alienation of his reason. It has been shown, however, that it is not the voluntariness or deliberateness of the pouring or ingesting which is crucial. In *Ebsworth v. H.M. Advocate*,[58] the accused had broken a bone in his leg. Since the fracture refused to heal, the injury was extremely painful, and the accused's remedy was to take large quantities of proprietary analgesics (on this occasion, 50 tablets of paracetamol) combined with prohibited drugs (on this occasion, 10 tablets of diamorphine). He took these quite deliberately. He then suffered "a total alienation of reason", and committed various offences whilst in that mental state. The trial judge withdrew Ebsworth's defence of automatism from the jury, on the basis that his condition was self induced and his motive irrelevant. The Appeal Court, however, ruled that the first two of the qualifying conditions for the defence should be seen as together reaching out to meet the same goal. As Lord Justice-General Hope put it: "The element of guilt or moral turpitude lies in the taking of drink or drugs voluntarily and reckless of their possible consequences."[59] It is not so much, therefore, that the external factor itself must not be self induced; rather it is the "alienation of reason" produced by that factor which must not have been deliberately or recklessly effected by the accused. In *Ebsworth*, therefore, it was the grossly excessive consumption of drugs — the purpose itself being not perhaps an illegitimate one — which ruled out the defence. Such excess simply courted totally unpredictable mental dysfunction (with concomitant effect on behaviour), and thus showed clear recklessness as to the consequences.

4–21   The third qualifying requirement insists that the external factor should be shown to have caused the total alienation of reason, which should itself

---

[56] See paras. 4–34 to 4–46, below.
[57] In accordance with *Brennan v. H.M. Advocate*, 1977 J.C. 38.
[58] 1992 S.L.T. 1161.
[59] *ibid*. p. 1166F.

be characterised by a total loss of control over what one does.[60] If the alienation or loss of control is not total, this will rule out the defence and prevent acquittal on that ground[61] — although mitigation of punishment after conviction would remain possible.[61a] It is also highly desirable that medical evidence should be available to confirm that the alleged causal link between the external factor and the accused's state of mind (at the time of the offence) was a plausible one, and that that state of mind would reasonably have been describable in the circumstances as one of total alienation of reason.[62] For this purpose it seems that medical expert witnesses are permitted to sit in court during the leading of evidence[63] so that they may comment appropriately during their own evidence on what they have heard.[64]

EFFECT OF *ROSS v. H.M. ADVOCATE* ON SCOTS LAW

Prior to the decision in *Ross*, the authoritative dictum in Scotland was that **4–22** of Lord Justice-General Clyde in his unreserved opinion in the certified case of *H.M. Advocate v. Cunningham*[65] where he said that: "Any mental or pathological condition short of insanity — any question of diminished responsibility owing to any cause, *which does not involve insanity* — is relevant only to the question of mitigating circumstances and sentence."[66] Those, and there were many, who would then have liked Scots law to recognise acquittals in at least some cases of mental dysfunction not related to mental illness, suggested that Lord Clyde's opinion should be seen as advocating extension of the concept of legal insanity.[67] That would at least

---

[60] In England too, it has been held that the loss of control should be total — see, *e.g.*, *Attorney General's Reference (No. 2 of 1992)* [1994] Q.B. 91 (C.A.), *per* Lord Taylor of Gosforth, C.J., at p. 105C.
[61a] See *H.M. Advocate v. Bennett*, 1996 S.L.T. 662, *per* Lord Justice-General Hope at p. 665D.
[61] See *Cardle v. Mulrainey* 1992 S.L.T. 1152, where the suggestion that this was too strict a standard was rejected.
[62] *Sorley v. H.M. Advocate*, 1992 J.C. 102. In *MacLeod v. Napier*, 1993 S.C.C.R. 303, Lord Justice-Clerk Ross at p. 307C indicated that it might be possible to succeed without expert evidence, but considerable detailed evidence would then be essential to convince the court that there was a satisfactory basis for the defence. (According to *Sorley*, if there is no such satisfactory basis, the trial judge should withdraw the defence from the jury, in a solemn case.)
[63] *i.e.* evidence given by eye-witnesses who saw the accused's behaviour and can provide information sufficient to satisfy all the essential elements of the defence: *Sorley v. H.M. Advocate*, 1992 J.C. 102, *per* Lord Justice-General Hope at p. 107.
[64] See, *e.g.*, *Cardle v. Mulrainey*, 1992 S.C.C.R. 1152; *MacLeod v. Mathieson*, 1993 S.C.C.R. 488 (Sh.Ct.).
[65] 1963 J.C. 80 at p. 84.
[66] The phrase in italics reads "short of insanity" in the version given at 1963 S.L.T. 345 at p. 347.
[67] See Gordon, *Criminal Law*, para. 3–18 (in the original 1978 version); W. M. Reid, "Three Steps Back," 1963 S.L.T. (News) 166.

have secured an acquittal — although the then consequences (mandatory incarceration in a mental hospital, for an indictment case at least) were not to their liking and often absurd (*e.g.* that a person suffering from diabetic hypoglycaemia (see para. 4–27, below) should be so incarcerated for wholly pointless psychiatric "treatment").[68] But contrary views (*i.e.* that *Cunningham* really required conviction in non mental illness cases) existed,[69] and prior to *Ross v. H.M. Advocate* (see para. 4–19, above), it seemed certain from cases subsequent to *Cunningham* that these contrary views prevailed. Whatever may have been the case in England, where a very wide view was, and still is, favoured, Scots law has so far not been prepared to extend its notion of legal insanity to mental dysfunctions not clearly related to recognised mental illnesses.[70] Prior to *Ross*, therefore, where an accused person was not fully aware of what he was doing owing to a mental dysfunction, the only question to be answered was whether that mental condition was due to genuine mental illness or not. If it was, then the test for legal insanity would probably have been met, and the accused would have been dealt with according to the law relating to offenders who committed their offences whilst insane (see Chapter 8). If it was not, then conviction seemed inevitable (in the absence of any other line of defence); but the disposal of the convicted person would then have been at large — dependent mainly on what provision should be made for the future safety of the public.

4–23   The full bench in *Ross v. H.M. Advocate*,[71] however, decided that Lord Clyde's opinion, offering only insanity or conviction with mitigation of penalty in all cases of mental dysfunction, was over concerned with public policy or safety, and too little concerned with basic principle.[72] Lord Clyde's opinion was thus overruled to the extent that "it held that *any* mental or pathological condition short of insanity is relevant only to the question of mitigating circumstances and sentence."[73] Straightforward acquittal was possible if the accused's mental dysfunction was not due to insanity, but rather to the effect of an "external factor" — provided certain safeguards were met (see paras. 4–20 to 4–21, above).

---

[68] Acquittal of an accused person on the ground of insanity no longer, of course, necessitates such incarceration: see para. 4–18, above.

[69] See, for example, J. W. R. Gray, "A Purely Temporary Disturbance," 1974 J.R. 227.

[70] See *Brennan v. H.M. Advocate*, 1977 J.C. 38, opinion of the court at p. 46, where the charge to the jury in *H.M. Advocate v. Aitken*, 1975 S.L.T. (Notes) 86, is strongly disapproved.

[71] 1991 J.C. 210, and see para. 4–19 above.

[72] See, for example, Lord Justice-General Hope at pp. 217–218.

[73] See Lord Justice-General Hope at p. 222.

External factors

The court in *Ross v. H.M. Advocate* did not find it necessary to explain   **4-24**
what was meant by "external factor"; nor did it seek to provide illustrations
of the concept. Lord Justice-General Hope[74] did, however, refer to the
English case of *R. v. Sullivan*[75] and, with apparent approval, to that part of
Lord Diplock's opinion there where he said:

> "I do not regard that learned judge [Devlin J. in *R. v. Kemp* [1957] 1
> Q.B. 399 at p. 407] as excluding the possibility of non-insane
> automatism (for which the proper verdict would be a verdict of 'not
> guilty') in cases where temporary impairment (not being self-induced
> by consuming drink or drugs) results from some external physical
> factor such as a blow on the head causing concussion or the
> administration of an anaesthetic for therapeutic purposes."

It would appear, therefore, that the Scottish court had in mind external
physical factors, such as those considered in the paragraphs which follow.

(1) Alcohol and non-prescribed drugs

Whether the effects on the mind of the voluntary ingestion or, as the   **4-25**
case may be, inhalation or injection, of alcohol or non-prescribed drugs
can be taken into account for the purposes of criminal liability would seem
to depend on the "knowledge" of the person concerned.[76] If he knew he
was taking the substance in question, and willingly did so, and knew, or
ought to have known, the effects it might have on him, then it has been
recognised for some time that criminal liability is neither excluded nor
diminished.[77] If the consumption or ingestion was not voluntary, then *Ross
v. H.M. Advocate* clearly allows acquittal — at least in respect of an offence
requiring *mens rea*.[78] Of course, it would not be impossible for a long course
of voluntary consumption of alcohol or drugs to result in a condition of
legal insanity (see para. 4–18, above) or "diminished responsibility"[79]; but

---

[74] 1991 J.C. 210 at p. 216.
[75] [1984] A.C. 156 at p. 172.
[76] See the English case of *R. v. Hardie* [1985] 1 W.L.R. 64, and paras. 8–63 *et seq.,* below.
[77] See *Brennan v. H.M. Advocate*, 1977 J.C. 38, which dealt with gross, self-induced
    intoxication with alcohol and LSD — both substances popularly associated with violent
    and irrational behaviour.
[78] 1991 J.C. 210, *per* Lord McCluskey at pp. 225 to 226; and see para. 4–19 above. See also
    Sorley v. H.M. Advocate, 1992 J.C. 102 (LSD and sleeping pills); *Cardle v. Mulrainey,*
    1992 S.L.T. 1152 (amphetamines); and *MacLeod v. Napier,* 1993 S.C.C.R. 303 ("speed").
[79] Which, as a doctrine, is said to be confined to murder and effects a reduction of that crime
    to culpable homicide — see *H.M. Advocate v. Cunningham*, 1963, J.C. 80, *per* Lord Justice-
    General Clyde at p. 84; and see para. 9–23 below.

occasional episodes of consumption and drunkenness cannot have such legal results.[80]

(2A) Prescribed drugs — general

4–26   Where medically prescribed drugs are taken by the person for whom they were intended (in accordance with medical advice as to dose, contra-indications and circumstances), and have an unforeseen effect on that person's mental condition leading to the alleged commission of a criminal act, then this ought to result in his acquittal.[81] Anaesthetics administered as part of some proper surgical, medical or dental treatment must follow the same rule — as hinted at by Lord Fraser in his charge to the jury in *McGregor v. H.M. Advocate*[82] — a charge approved of generally by Lord Justice-General Hope in *Ross v. H.M. Advocate*.[83]

(2B) Prescribed drugs — insulin

4–27   Diabetes is an illness stemming from an organic malfunction. Sufferers cannot maintain a stable blood-sugar ratio. If the disease is not treated in any way, the level of sugar in the patient's blood rises uncontrollably (hyperglycaemia). Drowsiness, unawareness of actions, and finally unconsciousness (coma) will be the inevitable results. Standard treatment for many diabetics, however, consists of the injection (or ingestion) of insulin, which reverses the rise of sugar in the blood. Carefully managed consumption of food is essential when insulin is being taken, otherwise the insulin on its own will cause the level of sugar in the blood to drop too low, too quickly (hypoglycaemia). Such a condition, if not checked, also has the inevitable outcome of drowsiness, unawareness of actions and coma. Since hypoglycaemic or hyperglycaemic conditions can occasionally result in violent conduct[84] and always affect the ability of the sufferer to drive properly,[85] they are of interest to the criminal law. In particular, for present purposes, it is important to establish whether the condition was caused by the taking of insulin (a plain, external factor) or by the disease itself (considered further at para. 4–42, below).

4–28   Where, for example, a crime is apparently committed by a person experiencing an "attack" of hypoglycaemia due to his intake of prescribed

---

[80] For example, see the rejection of Lord Stewart's charge to the jury in *H.M. Advocate v. Aitken*, 1975 S.L.T. (Notes) 86 by the court in *Brennan, supra*, at p. 46.
[81] See *Ebsworth v. H.M. Advocate* 1992 S.L.T. 1161, *per* Lord Justice-General Hope at p. 1166H-J. *Cf. Carrington v. H.M. Advocate*, 1994 S.C.C.R. 567.
[82] (1973) S.C.C.R. Supp. 54 at p. 57.
[83] 1991 J.C. 210 at p. 217.
[84] See, for example, *R. v. Bailey* [1983] 1 W.L.R. 760; *R. v. Hennessy* [1989] 1 W.L.R. 287.
[85] See, for example, *MacLeod v. Mathieson*, 1993 S.C.C.R. 488 (Sh.Ct.).

insulin, then he should be acquitted if a criminal charge is brought. He would clearly have been suffering from a sufficient mental dysfunction at the relevant time — a mental dysfunction due to an external factor. It does not matter here that the insulin was voluntarily taken by that person. It is the mental dysfunction (and its sufficiency) which counts; and surely no diabetic could be assumed to have taken insulin in order to induce a condition of hypoglycaemia. Of course, the other qualifying conditions for a "defence" based on an external factor still apply (see paras. 4–20 to 4–21, above). In particular, the mental dysfunction and its effects must not be ones the accused had any reason to anticipate. If, for example, the accused had injected himself with the correct dose of insulin, but then neglected to eat food (contrary to medical advice), then normally he should be able to foresee that his motor skills would be adversely affected by the inevitable onset of unconsciousness. It should be plain to him that he ought to avoid driving or operating machinery. If he does not refrain from such activities, then he should not be immune from criminal liability for the consequences.[86] On the other hand, if the accused is alleged to have committed crimes of violence in the course of an insulin-induced, hypoglycaemic episode, then the question arises whether it is common knowledge (and if so, whether apparent to the particular accused person) that failure to take food can have such violent repercussions.[87] If it is common knowledge, and particularly where it was known to the accused, then he surely was bound to anticipate that violence would ensue. The opposite conclusion will obviously be reached if there was no such knowledge. From this point of view, the conviction ordered by the Appeal Court in the case of *Carmichael v. Boyle*[88] must now be doubted.

Carmichael v. Boyle. Boyle was charged with breach of the peace, assault **4–29** and statutory assault under the Police (Scotland) Act 1967, section 41(1)(a). He was a doubly unfortunate individual, in that he suffered from both an abnormally low level of intelligence and an unstable form of diabetes. His form of that disease was particularly difficult to manage, the balance between intake of insulin and food being an extremely critical one. Boyle, in view of his limited intellect, found it very difficult to follow his medically prescribed regime. He frequently omitted to have regular meals, and thus had often become hypoglycaemic. He had also been violent when in such a condition. It was claimed on his behalf, nevertheless, that he should be acquitted of the charges brought against him since he had taken his prescribed insulin on the day in question, but, thereafter, having failed to take sufficient food, had exhibited the classic signs of hypoglycaemia at the time of the alleged offences. It was argued, therefore, that he would probably have

---

[86] See, for example, *Moses v. Winder* [1981] R.T.R. 37.
[87] See, for example, *R. v. Bailey* [1983] 1 W.L.R. 760, *per* Griffiths L.J. at pp. 764H to 765B.
[88] 1985 S.L.T. 399.

been unaware of what he had been doing at the relevant times. There was no question of his mental condition at those relevant times being treated as insanity, of course. Medical evidence simply confirmed that there was no underlying mental illness. The sheriff, who dealt with this case, frankly admitted that he had no sympathy with the then Scots law rule (see paras. 4–22 and 4–23, above), and, therefore, sought to avoid it. He did so by holding (in terms which now seem wholly proper) that the charges against Boyle entailed crimes which required *mens rea* to be established. Since the accused had been seen kicking and punching other people by several witnesses, there was no doubt that there was sufficient evidence from which the *mens rea* of assault could be inferred. Persons who kick and punch can usually be taken to have intended those actions. But the sheriff also considered that the evidence of hypoglycaemia meant that the accused could not in fact have been capable of intending the actions which amounted to the assaults charged. He, therefore, acquitted him on that basis. On appeal by the prosecutor, the Appeal Court simply affirmed that the then existing rule had to be applied — namely, since Boyle had not been insane at the times in question, he had to be convicted. Standing the more modern decision in *Ross v. H.M. Advocate*[89] Boyle was probably entitled to an acquittal. His condition was brought about by the insulin he had legitimately taken — by an external factor. It was true, of course, that he had failed to take sufficient food and had been drinking; but such were his intellectual failings that it could hardly be said that he should have anticipated the consequent mental dysfunction and its violent effects.[90]

(3) Toxic fumes

4–30	Exposure to toxic fumes, which have a sufficient effect on the mental condition of an accused person at a relevant time, must surely result in the acquittal of any relevant criminal charge. This follows from the case of *H.M. Advocate v. Ritchie,*[91] where the accused was charged with culpable homicide. He had been driving a car which had knocked down and killed a pedestrian. He had not stopped at the scene of the incident. There was evidence that his speed had been excessive at the time. His defence, however, was one of "temporary dissociation" due to "toxic exhaustive factors". Although the reports of the case fail to make this clear, it seems that he was alleging that he had been temporarily rendered unconscious, or less than fully conscious, by the inhalation of toxic exhaust fumes (presumably from his own vehicle). The trial judge, Lord Murray, told the jury:

---

[89]	1991 J.C. 210, and para. 4–19 above.
[90]	*cf. R. v. Quick* [1973] Q.B. 910, *per* Lawton L.J. at p. 922E–G.
[91]	1926 J.C. 45.

"[W]here the defence is that a person, who would ordinarily be quite justified in driving a car, becomes — owing to a cause which he was not bound to foresee, and which was outwith his control — either gradually or suddenly not the master of his own actions, a question as to his responsibility or irresponsibility for the consequences of his actions arises, and may form the ground of a good special defence."[92]

By this he must have meant that a good exculpatory plea might then exist.[93] And indeed he went on to say that the jury should acquit if they took the view that "the condition of mental dissociation, which admittedly was present after the accident, was also actively present prior to the accident".[94] The jury did acquit. Although Lord Justice-General Clyde in *H.M. Advocate v. Cunningham*[95] suggested that Lord Murray's charge to the jury, and the subsequent acquittal, had been wrong, both that charge and the verdict were subsequently vindicated in *Ross v. H.M. Advocate*.[96] This is entirely proper since toxic fumes clearly form an "external factor" which should lead to acquittal if the qualifying conditions (in paras. 4–20 to 4–21, above) are met.

It is probable, for example, that the qualifying conditions were not met **4–31** in *H.M. Advocate v. Murray*.[97] There the accused was charged with serious offences — causing the death of three passengers in the car he was driving (when it collided with a parked van), and driving with more than the permitted level of alcohol in his blood (both statutory offences now contained in sections 1 and 5(1) of the Road Traffic Act 1988, as amended). At the trial, Murray attempted to lead evidence that just before he had left his work at a dry-cleaning establishment to drive home on the evening in question, he had been exposed to the toxic fumes of tetrachlorethylene (a chemical used in the dry-cleaning process). He had apparently hoped thereby to convince the jury that he had not been aware of what he was doing and thus secure an acquittal. The trial judge ruled, however, that although the evidence could be heard, it could not lead to an acquittal on the first charge. At best, it could simply lead the jury to make a recommendation for leniency. Of course, the evidence of intoxication by a substance other than alcohol would have gone to the merits of the second charge since it clearly required the intoxicant to be alcohol — but that is a separate issue. The trial judge was no doubt influenced by the now-discredited rule laid down in *H.M.*

---

[92] 1926 J.C. 45 at p. 49.
[93] Since special defences lead to acquittal — see para. 8–08, following.
[94] 1926 J.C. 45 at p. 50.
[95] 1963 J.C. 80 at p. 83.
[96] 1991 J.C. 210, *per* Lord Justice-General Hope at pp. 217–218
[97] 1969 S.L.T. (Notes) 85.

Advocate v. Cunningham[98]; and it must be conceded that the accused's defence did involve an "external factor". But, as he worked in an establishment where toxic chemicals were admittedly used, should he not have been aware of the possibility of exposure to the fumes from those chemicals and of the likely effect on his driving skills? Was what happened not something he was bound to foresee? Were a similar case to arise today, then such matters would perforce require to be investigated before an acquittal could be sustained.

(4) Blows producing concussion

4–32   If a person were to be the victim of an assault which left him dazed and concussed, or if he were to be struck on the head in some accidental way which left him similarly (but temporarily) incapacitated, then an external factor would be present to avoid conviction for any crime apparently committed by him when he was so dazed and concussed. This must follow from the decision in *Ross v. H.M. Advocate*.[99]

(5) Stress, anxiety and depression

4–33   An attempt was apparently made in the English case of *R. v. Hennessy*[1] to argue that stress, anxiety and depression could be external factors if they resulted in some relevant mental dysfunction at the time the defendant was alleged to have committed a crime. It was claimed that the defendant in the case was diabetic, and that psychological stress on such a person could lead to a state of hyperglycaemia (see para. 4–27, above). The defendant, however, had neglected to take any insulin for some days prior to his "committing" the alleged offences; and the Court of Appeal[2] pointed out that: "stress, anxiety and depression can no doubt be the result of the operation of external factors, but they are not, it seems to us, in themselves separately or together external factors of the kind capable in law of causing or contributing to a state of automatism." Indeed, the Court of Appeal also pointed out that the accused's line of defence, if successful, would have amounted to legal insanity, as that concept is defined in England. Despite what is hinted at in *Hennessy*, it is suggested that Scots law would not and should not accept a stressful situation as a sufficient "external factor" since it lacks the direct quality of (apparently required) "physical contact" with the accused, and, in any event is hardly an unforeseeable occurrence with

---

[98] 1963 J.C. 80; see paras. 4–22 and 4–23 above.
[99] 1991 J.C. 210; see para. 4–19 above; *cf. Stevenson v. Beatson*, 1965 S.L.T. (Sh.Ct.) 11, noting that the sheriff there erroneously held that an "onus" lay on the accused; and *cf.* also the English case of *R. v. Stripp* (1978) 69 Cr.App.R. 318.
[1] [1989] 1 W.L.R. 287.
[2] *ibid. per* Lord Lane C.J. at p. 294C.

unforeseeable effects. Stress is a common human experience for which no particular provision should be made by the criminal law unless, of course, that sort of experience is so serious as to lead to diminished responsibility.

Causal factor — internal

If the position of external factors which produce total alienation of reason is reasonably clear, the same cannot be said of non-external (*i.e.* "internal") factors. Lord Justice-General Hope in *Ross*[3] stressed that the court was "not concerned in this case with a pathological condition such as epilepsy or with the questions of public policy which may affect how such cases should be approached." Accordingly, the opinions cast in that case provide no guidance as to the treatment of non-external factor situations, other than to indicate that a problem exists in respect of them. Lord McCluskey makes this plain when he says[4]: "The policy of the law in relation to the criminal responsibility of persons who act under the influence of a continuing or recurrent mental or pathological condition short of insanity which derives from some disease or physical morbidity might have to be different." But how different? If external factors, leading to temporary but total loss of control via total alienation of reason, can lead to straightforward acquittals where certain qualifying conditions are met (see paras. 4–20 to 4–21, above), presumably internal factors leading to a similar loss of control may justifiably have a different outcome — and especially so if there was a risk of recurrence and a consequent issue of public safety. If, for example, such an internal factor were regarded as creating a situation of legal insanity at the time an alleged crime was committed, then the verdict would have to be one of acquittal on the ground of insanity (see para. 4–18, above). This was certainly the favoured approach of Lord Denning in *Bratty v. Attorney General for Northern Ireland*[5] where he said:

> "[A]ny mental disorder [including epilepsy or cerebral tumour] which has manifested itself in violence and is prone to recur is a disease of the mind. At any rate it is the sort of disease for which a person should be detained in hospital rather than be given an unqualified acquittal."[6]

With the modification that genuine external causes of mental dysfunction are to be excluded from that dictum,[7] Lord Denning's formulation has

4–34

---

[3]   1991 J.C. 210 at p. 217.
[4]   *ibid.* p. 231.
[5]   [1963] A.C. 386 at p. 412.
[6]   Echoes of this occur in *Ross v. H.M. Advocate,* 1991 J.C. 210, opinion of Lord Justice-General Hope at p. 213: "We are concerned here only with a mental condition of a temporary nature which was the result of an external factor and not of some disorder of the mind itself which was liable to recur."
[7]   See *R. v. Quick* [1973] Q.B. 910, *per* Lawton L.J. at pp. 917–918 and 922–923.

repeatedly been endorsed in England, most recently in *R. v. Burgess*.[8] The standard English approach, therefore, is to treat internal causes of mental dysfunction leading to total loss of control as examples of legal insanity, and especially so if such mental dysfunction is associated with violence and is likely to recur. Is this, or should this also be the standard approach in Scotland?

4–35   It is suggested that this has not hitherto been, nor should be followed in Scotland. The English definition of insanity is very wide (or at least is very wide for the purposes of the defence of automatism)[9] whereas the Scottish definition is believed to be more restrained and better grounded in common sense.[10] The basis of the Scottish approach seems to be that insanity must relate to genuine mental illness; and from that basis, it would be exceedingly odd to have to regard persons suffering from the effects of a disease such as diabetes or epilepsy as insane. Such a standard rule would perforce possess a somewhat unreal, if not fictional quality. In any event, it appears to have been agreed in *Ross v. H.M. Advocate*[11] that Lord Clyde's original dictum in *H.M. Advocate v. Cunningham*[12] was defective rather because of its width than anything else. As Lord Justice-General Hope said[13]: "The conclusion which I invite your Lordships to reach in this case is that *Cunningham* was wrongly decided in so far as it held that *any* [Lord Hope's own emphasis] mental or pathological condition short of insanity is relevant only to the question of mitigating circumstances and sentence." That conclusion (with which the remaining members of the Appeal Court agreed) suggests that there may be a class of mental dysfunction, caused by an internal factor not amounting to mental illness, where a special approach is called for. Although the court in *Ross* did not go on to specify what that special approach should be,[14] it must be plain that two considerations influence the solution. The first of these is that there is a need to cater for future public safety where an internal factor produces a mental condition whereunder the accused is unable to prevent himself acting violently (or perhaps just "criminally"), and especially so where such a mental condition may occur again. Indeed, there is a feeling that internally generated mental dysfunctions are very likely to recur since there is no obvious and understandable external cause for them: thus, the perceived need to consider future public safety in relation to "internal" rather than "external" factors. The second consideration concerns

---

[8]   [1991] 2 W.L.R. 1206, *per* Lord Lane at pp. 1211H to 1212A.
[9]   See, for example, *R. v. Hennessy* [1989] 1 W.L.R. 287, *per* Lord Lane at pp. 291–293; and *R. v. Sullivan* [1984] A.C. 156, *per* Lord Diplock at pp. 170–173.
[10]   See Chap. 8 at para. 8–15 *et seq.*
[11]   1991 J.C. 210.
[12]   1963 J.C. 80 at p. 84; see para. 4–22, above.
[13]   1991 J.C. 210 at p. 222.
[14]   See, for example, Lord McCluskey's opinion at p. 231, quoted at para. 4–34 above.

the frequent references in *Ross* and elsewhere to such mental conditions being "short of" or "not amounting to" insanity. These references emphasise clearly that acquittal on the ground of insanity cannot be a legitimate option in such cases unless resort is had to the grossest of fictions.

The preferred Scottish approach?

What then is the preferred Scottish solution to the problem posed in **4–36** paragraph 4–34, above? Decided cases from the late nineteenth century to the present day suggest that the preferred approach may involve conviction of such persons in respect of crimes factually proved against them, coupled to disposals which cater almost exclusively for future public safety. The emphasis, in other words, lies not on punishment, since in many such cases consideration of penalty would be quite unjust, but rather on what steps should be taken to prevent such persons constituting a danger to others in the future. This approach can be seen in the Scottish cases considered in the paragraphs which follow. Whilst it is true that the persons concerned in these cases may have been more deserving of sympathy than prosecution and criminal conviction, public policy surely requires a realistic solution to a difficult problem. After conviction, of course, a court will usually be able to consider a wider range of criteria as to the future dangerousness of such a person than would have been possible under the rules of evidence which pertain during a trial. Conviction also opens up the widest possible range of disposals as the law presently stands.[15] Whilst recent reforms have greatly enhanced what a court may do after an acquittal on the ground of insanity,[16] the arguments against returning an insanity verdict at all in respect of a person suffering from the disorders mentioned in the following paragraphs remain compelling.[17]

Non-insane internal factors

(1) "Naturally" induced sleep

Whilst it is unusual for "criminal" acts to be performed during natural **4–37** sleep, it is not entirely unknown. In the case of *Simon Fraser*[18] the accused was asleep in bed together with his wife and 18-month-old son (apparently

---

[15] *cf.* a straightforward acquittal, to which no conditions whatsoever can be attached.
[16] See para. 4–18, above.
[17] Powerful arguments have been expressed, however, against this view, and it has been concluded that the English approach — *i.e.*, acquittal on the ground of insanity — has, in terms of certain dicta in the case of *Ross*, already been adopted in Scotland. See in particular, G.T. Laurie *"Automatism and Insanity in the Law of England and Scotland,"* 1995 J.R. 253.
[18] (1878) 4 Coup. 70.

a not-uncommon domestic arrangement in the nineteenth century). According to his own declaration,[19] he dreamt that a white beast flew through the floor and round the back of the bed where the child was lying. He further dreamt that he tried to catch it, and indeed caught something which he dashed against the floor and door of the room. He then came to his senses and found that it was his son he had caught and so treated. The child died shortly afterwards of its injuries. Fraser never denied that he had caused his son's death. In reply to a murder charge brought against him, however, he pled "not guilty" and advanced the defence that he was asleep at the time. At his trial, three medical experts testified that he was not insane but that he did suffer from an abnormal mental condition. According, again, to his own declaration, Fraser had strange dreams every night — usually between midnight and 1 a.m. — but was rarely "outrageous" except every six months or so. By being "outrageous," he apparently meant "violent", since about 18 months prior to the killing of his child, he dreamt that his wife was being attacked by a dog which led him to throw some pieces of furniture at it. In consequence, his wife had received bruising to her arm and eye. The trial judge, Lord Justice-Clerk Moncreiff, told the jury[20] that he supposed they would agree that Fraser was totally unconscious of what he had done to his son and he suggested that they return a finding "that the pannel [a Scots law term for the accused] killed his child, but that he was in a state in which he was unconscious of the act which he was committing by reason of the condition of somnambulism, and that he was not responsible." The jury did so.

4–38   Opinions as to what that verdict meant have varied.[21] However, the preponderance of the evidence points to conviction.[22] The Solicitor-General, for example, who was prosecuting the case in person, successfully requested an adjournment of two days following the jury's verdict — the pannel to be kept in custody during that time. The original court records[23] narrate the fact of the adjournment as follows: "The Court delayed pronouncing sentence in the meantime: Continued the diet against the pannel till Wednesday first the seventeenth current at three o'clock, and ordained him in the meantime to be detained in the prison of Edinburgh." At the resumed diet, the Solicitor-General deliberately refrained from "moving for sentence"

---

[19] S.R.O., J.C. 26/1269.

[20] (1878) 4 Coup. 70 at p. 75.

[21] See, for example, Williams, *Criminal Law: The General Part,* p. 173 — "he ... was not convicted of murder, nor indeed of anything"; *cf.* Walker, *Crime and Insanity in England,* Vol. 1. p. 170, where he questions the "assumption which one finds in later writers, that the result of Fraser's case was an acquittal."

[22] As Lord Justice-General Hope concluded in *Ross v. H.M. Advocate,* 1991 J.C. 210 at p. 217.

[23] S.R.O., J.C. 4/77.

— a privilege he had where a person had been found guilty of a crime. The reason in this case why the prosecutor so refrained was that the pannel and his father had signed an agreement as follows[24]: "I, Simon Fraser, having in view the nature of the attacks to which I am occasionally subject at night, do hereby solemnly promise and undertake that I shall always sleep alone; and I, Simon Fraser, Senior, father of the said Simon Fraser, do hereby solemnly promise and undertake, so far as in my power, to see and take care that my son fulfils the promise before written made by him." Prevention of harm to others in the future was thus thought to have been secured; and the ultimate mitigation of punishment was achieved by the prosecutor's declining to move for sentence at all. It is true, of course, that the court attached no sanction if the undertaking were to be breached by Fraser in the future. But the trial was widely reported in the press[25] and the public thus placed on its guard. In *Ross v. H.M. Advocate*[26] Lord Justice-General Hope opined that the approach taken in *Simon Fraser* was "a very special one". Special approaches may well, however, be justified in such unusual situations.

    R. v. Burgess. The outcome in *Simon Fraser* can be contrasted with the **4–39** attitude of the Court of Appeal in the English case of *R. v. Burgess.*[27] There the accused attacked a woman, hitting her over the head with a bottle and a video-recorder. He submitted a defence of non-insane automatism, in that he had been asleep and sleep-walking at the time. The trial judge ruled that his defence amounted to insanity, since there was no external cause for his mental dysfunction at the time of the attack. The jury, therefore, acquitted him on the ground of insanity — thus (as the law then was) automatically securing his detention in a mental hospital. It is difficult to feel completely comfortable with such a decision; but the Court of Appeal endorsed it fully.

(2) Disease — certain types of epilepsy

    Violent, unpredictable behaviour can follow certain types of epileptic **4–40** fit, although the sufferer will probably be totally unaware of what he does. In *H.M. Advocate v. Mitchell*,[28] for example, the accused had savagely killed a woman with blows from a knife and a meat-chopper. His defence was "psychic epilepsy" — that he had experienced the sort of epileptic fit which is not accompanied by the usual outward signs of a *grand mal* seizure (*e.g.* convulsions, tongue-biting, and foam evident at the mouth). As this,

---

[24] S.R.O., AD14/78/166.
[25] See, for example, *The Scotsman*, July 16 and 18, 1878.
[26] 1991 J.C. 210 at p. 217.
[27] [1991] 2 W.L.R. 1206.
[28] 1951 J.C. 53.

therefore, was a wholly "internal" fit and was consistent with a wholly mental condition, he submitted a defence of legal insanity. This was accepted as such by both the judge and the jury. Of course, it does not follow from that case that all types of epilepsy are to be regarded as mental illnesses for the purposes of the criminal law in Scotland[29] and if particular types do not square with the definition of legal insanity, then the result should be conviction accompanied by whatever disposal seems appropriate in the circumstances to secure public safety. This was made quite plain in *H.M. Advocate v. Cunningham.*[30] That case concerned not crimes of violence, but taking and driving away a van without the permission of the owner, causing death by dangerous driving — the van had mounted the pavement and knocked down four pedestrians — and being unfit to drive owing to the consumption of drink or drugs.[31] The accused had tendered a defence of "temporary dissociation" (*i.e.* that he had not been aware of what he had been doing at the critical times) owing to "an epileptic fugue or other pathological condition". Since this had been tendered as a defence which, if established, would lead to the unconditional acquittal of the accused, the prosecutor sought a ruling from the trial judge that acquittal could not follow from it unless the mental condition it referred to was consistent with legal insanity. The trial judge, Lord Wheatley, certified this point to a larger court of three High Court judges who confirmed that the prosecutor's contention was correct. If an epileptic or similar mental condition was not such as to amount to legal insanity, then the result would be conviction (assuming that the Crown's case was otherwise established) tempered by such mitigation of the "normal" sentence as seemed appropriate. There was no suggestion in the court's decision that such an accused person would have to be punished in any usual sense of that word.

4–41   It has sometimes been hinted at[32] that the decision in *Cunningham* is inconsistent with the result of the full bench ruling in *H.M. Advocate v. Hayes,*[33] but this is not really so. Andrew Hayes had been driving a bus when he had some sort of epileptic seizure. The result was that the bus ceased to be under his complete control, collided with two parked lorries and overturned. Several persons were injured (including the drivers of the two parked vehicles) and four passengers in the bus lost their lives. The charge brought against Hayes was one of culpable homicide at common

---

[29]   *cf.* the approach taken by the English courts in *R. v. Sullivan* [1984] A.C. 156.
[30]   1963 J.C. 80, as modified by *Ross v. H.M. Advocate,* 1991 J.C. 210; see paras. 4–22 and 4–23, above.
[31]   All statutory offences, now to be found in ss.178, 1 and 4(1) respectively of the Road Traffic Act 1988, as amended where appropriate by the Road Traffic Act 1991.
[32]   See Gane and Stoddart, p. 69; Gordon, para. 3–20.
[33]   High Court at Edinburgh, November 1, 1949, unreported, but reproduced in Gane and Stoddart at p. 70.

law together with, as an alternative, the less serious statutory offence of dangerous driving. He submitted a defence of "temporary dissociation" (see paragraph 4–40, above) due to "masked epilepsy" or other pathological condition. After trial, the jury found him guilty of culpable homicide but also found his defence of "temporary dissociation" proved. There can be little doubt, therefore, that he had been found guilty of the more serious crime; but his counsel asked the trial judge, Lord Carmont, to inquire if the jury meant by this that they would have found him guilty "if he had been a normal man". When the question was put, it appeared that the jury might have meant just that — and Lord Carmont went on to inquire if they therefore wished to reconsider their verdict. This resulted in the jury's apparently wishing to find him "not guilty", and some confusion as to what was then the proper verdict. The court records[34] clearly reveal that Lord Carmont reinstated the jury's original verdict — such that the accused stood convicted of culpable homicide. Of course, this left the problem of disposal since the conviction had been accompanied by a finding that the defence had also been established. His Lordship, therefore, certified the question of disposal to a full bench of the High Court at Edinburgh (the court consisting of Lord Justice-General Cooper, Lord Justice-Clerk Thomson, and Lords Mackay, Carmont, Jamieson, Russell and Keith). It is highly significant that Hayes had his bail continued during the intervening period. It is also highly significant that the Solicitor-General (who was appearing in person for the Crown) opened the proceedings at Edinburgh by "moving for sentence". These things would have been impossible had Hayes not been convicted.[35] The outcome was that he was not to be punished in any conventional way. Instead, he was to be discharged provided he agreed to surrender his driving licences and promised never to drive vehicles again — undertakings which he found it prudent to make. The seven judges of the High Court seemed keen to stress that this was not to be taken as a precedent — suggesting that all such cases (as indeed all sentencing decisions) should be treated on an individual basis. No formal agreement (as in *Simon Fraser's* case, see para. 4–37, above) was necessary since the licences were presumably at once handed to the court. The licensing authorities were also to be notified accordingly.

(3) Disease — diabetes

A brief description of diabetes has already been given (see para. 4–27, above). It is clearly not a mental illness. It would be absurd to attempt to treat it by psychiatric means. Where the disease itself (as opposed to some

4–42

---

[34] S.R.O., J.C. 5/28, Appendix No. 40.
[35] *cf.* Gane and Stoddart's commentary to their account of this case at p. 72.

drug or similar preparation taken for its treatment) creates a mental dysfunction leading to total lack of control, then it seems plain in England that the resulting condition amounts to legal insanity.[36] In Scotland, it is thought that the result of disease-induced hyperglycaemia or hypoglycaemia (see para. 4–27, above) leading to total loss of control at the time of an alleged offence should be conviction together with such disposal as will minimise future public danger from the person concerned. If this is correct, then the correctness of the decision in *Farrell v. Stirling*[37] must be doubted. There the sheriff had been fully satisfied[38] that the accused "carried out his normal régime as a diabetic so far as injection of insulin and diet were concerned", yet acquitted him of a statutory driving charge where the evidence suggested total lack of control at the time. Where the disease itself randomly creates a situation of total lack of control despite the best endeavours of medicine to stabilise the sufferer's condition, a clear concern for future public safety exists to which neither straightforward acquittal nor acquittal on the ground of insanity provides an adequate or realistic response.[39]

(4) Disease — spontaneous hypoglycaemia

4–43   What pertains to diabetes should also follow in relation to other diseases which produce (of their own accord) similar effects. Thus, in *Stirling v. Annan*[40] the accused was said to suffer from a condition known as "spontaneous hypoglycaemia". That illness caused the sufferer to experience sudden and unexpected diminutions in the level of sugar in his blood from time to time. During such hypoglycaemic episodes, he was reckoned to be totally unaware of what he might in fact be doing — such as (in the case itself) removing and pocketing various items from the shelves of a self-service store, and thereafter walking from the store without attempting to pay for them. Stirling was in fact convicted of theft in respect of the items he had taken — a decision which, it is suggested, was probably correct. On appeal, however, the advocate-depute conceded that a miscarriage of justice might have occurred. The conviction was thus quashed. To date, it remains unclear why such a concession was made. There was certainly no suggestion

---

[36] See, for example, *R. v. Quick* [1973] Q.B. 910, *per* Lawton L.J. at pp. 922H to 923A; *R. v. Hennessy* [1989] 1 W.L.R. 287, *per* Lord Lane at p. 293G.

[37] 1975 S.L.T. (Sh.Ct.) 71.

[38] *ibid.* p. 73, col. 2.

[39] In *MacLeod v. Mathieson*, 1993 S.C.C.R. 488 (Sh.Ct.), the sheriff was prepared for the sake of argument to accept that hypoglycaemia was an external factor — possibly because of doubts as to whether it was caused by insulin or the disease. In rejecting the accused's defence of automatism, he distinguished *Farrell v. Stirling*, 1975 S.L.T. (Sh.Ct.) 71 on the ground that there, the accused had had no prior warning that he was subject to such attacks.

[40] 1984 S.L.T. 88.

that any external factor was involved which might have brought the case (prospectively, of course) within the ambit of *Ross v. H.M. Advocate*.[41]

(5) Disease in general — qualifying conditions

Many diseases, or sudden illnesses for that matter, can lead to total **4–44** unconsciousness or to mental conditions where the patient is totally unable to control his actions. Heart attacks, strokes,[42] arteriosclerosis,[43] and brain tumours[44] may obviously all have such effects. Where an accused person in Scotland elicits some evidence in favour of his having been unconscious or unable to control his actions because of any illness or disease, a court would possibly require to be satisfied that he had truly been totally unable to control his actions at the relevant time and that he had no prior warning that such a lack of control or state of unconsciousness was likely to arise. But since no straightforward acquittal follows in such cases and the major question is really one of disposal to the best advantage of public safety, it is probably unnecessary to insist strictly on the sort of qualifying conditions demanded in *Ross v. H.M. Advocate*.[45] In any event, prosecutorial discretion would obviously enable many such cases to be disposed of in ways other than by prosecution before the courts.

(6) Weak intellect

In *Clark v. H.M. Advocate*[46] a married couple was charged with the wilful **4–45** neglect of a young child in a manner likely to cause it unnecessary suffering and injury — contrary to the Children and Young Persons (Scotland) Act 1937, section 12(1). The defence attempted at the trial to lead psychiatric evidence that both of the accused were "so feckless and incompetent that they did not appreciate what the result of their failure [to provide adequate food and medical aid for the child] would be".[47] In brief, the argument was that they were well aware of what they did or refrained from doing for the child, but were totally unaware of the effects which their conduct or omissions would have because of some congenital weakness of intellect from which they suffered. Whilst it is true that such weakness of intellect is an internal factor, it is also true that such weakness had no effect on the ability of the two accused to control their conduct. It is suggested, therefore, that there was no relevant internal factor in the case, and that the "normal"

---

[41] 1991 J.C. 210; see para. 4–19, above.
[42] See, for example, the English civil case of *Roberts v. Ramsbottom* [1980] 1 W.L.R. 823.
[43] See, for example, the English case of *R. v. Kemp* [1957] 1 Q.B. 399.
[44] See, for example, *R. v. Charlson* [1955] 1 W.L.R. 317.
[45] 1991 J.C. 210; see paras. 4–19 to 4–21, above.
[46] 1968 J.C. 53.
[47] *ibid. per* Lord Justice-Clerk Grant at p. 56.

convictions affirmed by the Appeal Court were correct. Special convictions, for the limited purpose of assessing measures for the future protection of the public, were thus not in contemplation. Weakness of intellect has, therefore, little relevance in this part of the criminal law. Its true role is as a general plea in mitigation of punishment.[48]

(7) Hysterical amnesia

4-46   Loss of memory (amnesia) is also a condition which should have no bearing whatever on criminal liability — assuming that it occurred after the critical event(s) and is not symptomatic of some graver and more long-lasting mental condition. On that assumption, it can have no effect on a person's ability to control his conduct at the time of an alleged offence. There is a suggestion, however, that "hysterical amnesia" at the time of the alleged offence might be pled as at least a mitigatory matter in an appropriate case. In *Russell v. H.M. Advocate*[49] a defence of that description (of which few further details are revealed) was not considered improper except in so far as it paralleled a plea in bar of trial which had already been rejected.[50]

CONCLUSION

4-47   If the suggested approach of Scots law to the problem of non-insane internal factors is accepted (see para. 4–36, above), then Scotland deals with cases of total loss of control (following from total alienation of reason) in relation to proven criminal conduct according to the following categories: (1) where that total loss of control is caused by mental illness, then the accused will be acquitted on the ground of insanity, with all the consequences which such a verdict has (see para. 4–18, above); (2) where that total loss of control is caused by an external factor which meets the qualifying conditions, then the accused will be acquitted unconditionally on the ground of automatism; and (3) where that total loss of control is due to disease or illness not amounting to insanity and especially where it is likely to recur, then the accused should be convicted in order that measures of treatment or restraint may be considered for the purpose of future public safety, there being no such thing as "acquittal with conditions" in Scots law. Difficult issues appear to be raised, of course, where there are two or more causal factors at work. In diabetic automatism cases, for example, the effect of insulin (external) on the accused's mental state may have to be weighed against the causal factor of the disease itself (internal): and in the "lager can" type of case,

---

[48] See, for example, *John McLean* (1876) 3 Coup. 334, *per* Lord Deas at p. 387.
[49] 1946 J.C. 37, *per* Lord Justice-Clerk Cooper at p. 45.
[50] See also the English case of *R. v. Isitt* [1978] R.T.R. 211.

where drugs are allegedly pushed into the accused's chosen drink,[51] the effect of drink knowingly ingested (external, but generally not relevant to the defence of automatism) should strictly be weighed against the effect of the drugs (external, and possibly within the defence) on the accused's mental state. These are, however, issues of fact and degree — and will have to be solved in a common-sense way.

In the case of crimes which require *mens rea*, the method of dealing **4-48** with accused persons who fall within category (3) above may seem unjustifiable — since such accused clearly possess no more subjective *mens rea* than those who fall within category (2). But unless *H.M. Advocate v. Cunningham*[52] and leading decisions which followed it[53] are overturned completely,[54] the preferring of convictions for the main purpose of considering measures of public protection is possibly the best way of reconciling the prior case law with what was said by the Appeal Court in *Ross*. Of course, the opinions in *Ross* do not rule out straightforward acquittals for at least some persons who fall within category (3) — perhaps, for example, for those who suffer a wholly unforeseeable stroke or heart attack whilst driving a mechanically propelled vehicle. And it may be that Scots law will eventually categorise such persons according to a more sophisticated classification. But it is certainly to be hoped, in accordance with a general approach which Scots law has long favoured, that all those — especially police, prosecutors and judges — who influence the practice of the law (and thus the law itself) will approach difficult cases in this area bearing in mind "in a common sense way their sense of fairness".[55]

Further reading

Ferguson, P. R., "The Limits of the Automatism Defence" (1991) 36 J.L.S. 446.

Ferguson, P. W., "The Defence of Automatism," 1991 S.L.T. (News) 415.

Ferguson, P.W., "Automatism, Responsibility and Recklessness," 1992 S.L.T. (News) 375.

Fletcher, G. P., *Rethinking Criminal Law* (1978), pp. 426 *et seq.*

Gordon, G. H., *Criminal Law* (2nd ed., 1978), Chap. 3, paras. 3–08 to 3–27 as altered by the second cumulative supplement, pp. 10–12.

---

[51] *e.g., Ross v. H.M. Advocate,* 1991 J.C. 210; *Sorley v. H.M. Advocate,* 1992 J.C. 102; *Cardle v. Mulrainey,* 1992 S.L.T. 1152.

[52] 1963 J.C. 80.

[53] In particular *Clark v. H.M. Advocate,* 1968 J.C. 53 and *Carmichael v. Boyle,* 1985 S.L.T. 399.

[54] And *Ross v. H.M. Advocate,* 1991 J.C. 210 did not go that far — see Lord Justice-General Hope's opinion at p. 222.

[55] *R. v. Quick* [1973] 1 Q.B. 910, *per* Lawton L.J. at p. 922C.

Gross, H., *A Theory of Criminal Justice* (1979), Chap. 2.

Hart, H. L. A., *Punishment and Responsibility* (1968), Chap. IV — "Acts of Will and Responsibility".

Laurie, G.T., "Automatism and Insanity in the Law of England and Scotland," 1995 J.R. 253.

Mewett, A. W. and Manning, M., *Criminal Law* (2nd ed., 1985), Chap. 3, from p. 69, and Chap. 9.

Williams, G., *Textbook of Criminal Law* (2nd ed., 1983), Chaps. 7 and 29.

CHAPTER 5

CAUSATION

Introduction

The issue of causation is raised by the legal definitions of many different   **5–01**
crimes. For example, as is described in Chapter 10, it is a requirement of
the crime of fraud that there be a causal connection between the false
pretence and the actions of the dupe. There are also many crimes which
contain in their definitions an element of resultant harm. These include
crimes against property, such as malicious mischief or fire-raising, and also
crimes against the person. An example of the latter is the crime of aggravated
assault. This might result in, for example, severe injury or permanent
disfigurement to the victim of the attack. As previously noted, liability for
a result crime, such as an aggravated assault, can only be imposed upon an
individual if it was his conduct which caused the harm to the complainer
(see para. 3–06, above). If the prosecution cannot establish a causal link
between the accused's conduct and the consequences of the assault, then
liability for the aggravating features of the crime will not be imposed upon
him.

In many cases causation can be determined without any great difficulty.   **5–02**
If A attacks B with a hatchet, then there is no problem in attributing the
resultant severe injury to the conduct of A. The problems arise when there
are a number of factors contributing to the result and/or when other events
intervene between the conduct of the accused and the consequential harm.
Without doubt the most complex and difficult problems arise in the law
relating to homicide. Most of the important authorities on causation concern
either murder or culpable homicide. There may have been a considerable
length of time elapsing between the infliction of the original injury and the
death. The explanation for the importance attached to causation in the law
of homicide is that the law strives to determine when a death is attributable
to the conduct of the accused.[1]

---

[1]   Fletcher, *Rethinking Criminal Law*, p. 358.

CAUSATION IN FACT

The "But For" Test

5–03   The first issue to be considered in a result crime, such as homicide, is whether
the accused did in fact cause the victim's death. The issue is frequently
resolved by the application of the "but for" or *sine qua non* test: but for the
conduct of the accused, would the victim have died? It is not necessary that
the conduct of the accused has been the only cause of the harm. Nor is it
necessary that his conduct be a substantial cause, provided that it is a
material, and more than a minimal, cause.[2]

Necessity for Causal Link

5–04   In most cases, proof of causation in fact will not present any major problem
to the prosecution. As in the aggravated assault example outlined above,
the issue will be self-evident. But the existence of a causal link will always
need to be established: it should not be taken for granted.[3] In *Hendry* v.
H.M. Advocate[4] a conviction for culpable homicide was upheld on appeal.
The appellant had assaulted a 67-year-old man, who died as a result of a
heart attack a short while thereafter. Only minor injuries had been caused
to the deceased, but he had a pre-existing heart condition which could have
led to death after any degree of exertion or distress. There were further
complicating factors, in that the deceased had angina, he had consumed a
large amount of alcohol, he had eaten a large meal, and he had climbed a
flight of stairs. All of these were stress factors which could have additionally
contributed to the heart attack. The key issue for the prosecution was to
prove beyond reasonable doubt the existence of a causal link between the
assault and the heart attack.

5–05   In *Lourie* v. *H.M. Advocate*[5] the appellants' convictions for culpable
homicide were quashed by the Appeal Court. Lourie and another youth had
been charged on the basis that they had entered the house of an elderly
woman uninvited and stolen a handbag in her presence. The appeal was
allowed because there was insufficient evidence that the deceased had
observed the theft and it was unclear whether or not the appellants had
entered the house uninvited. The prosecution maintained that the woman
had been put in a state of fear and alarm by the appellants' actions. It was
argued that the deceased's fatal heart attack had been a direct consequence.

---

[2]   See *Watson v. H.M. Advocate* (1978) S.C.C.R. Supp. 192.
[3]   See, for example, *Malone v. H.M. Advocate*, 1988 S.C.C.R. 498.
[4]   1987 J.C. 63.
[5]   1988 S.C.C.R. 634; *cf. R. v. Watson* [1989] 1 W.L.R. 684.

The death had ensued soon after the visit by the appellants. An expert medical witness called by the prosecution testified that a heart attack could have been the result of an increase in strain. The defence argued either that the death could have been a complete coincidence or that she had died as the result of exertion which may have accompanied the events which took place. It was argued that if the latter was indeed the case, the death was not the result of the illegal act in the sense that the act had caused the woman's death. The first point to note about a set of facts such as these is that any doubt would have to be resolved in favour of an accused. If a jury thought that the woman's death might have been coincidental, then there would have to be an acquittal. The defence's second argument is more problematic. Assuming that there had been sufficient evidence to support the prosecution case, the woman had only been required to exert herself because of the unlawful actions of the appellants. But for their actions, the woman would have lived longer. To anticipate the discussion in the rest of this chapter somewhat, there would not then appear to be any difficulties in establishing the necessary causal link between the conduct of the accused and the consequential death of the victim.

CAUSATION IN LAW

CAUSES AND CONDITIONS

Causation is not, however, simply a question of fact. It is necessary, but not **5–06** sufficient, that the accused's conduct be a factual cause of the death or other type of harm. Not every factor which meets the "but for" standard is sufficient for the imposition of criminal liability. If a reckless motorist drives the wrong way down a motorway and collides with another vehicle, killing the occupant, the presence of the other vehicle is a "but for" cause of the crash. Common sense suggests that the presence of the victim on the road should not be regarded by the criminal law as the cause of his death. This could be described instead as a condition, rather than a cause, of the fatality. A condition is a normal event or circumstance which is necessary for the result to occur, but cannot be said positively to have caused it.

PROXIMITY REQUIREMENT

There must be causation in law. The law requires that a cause be "proximate". **5–07** This requirement of proximity reflects the law's concern only with those causal factors which are closely connected with the result. In relation to homicide, the rules of law relating to proximate cause are intended to provide a safeguard against liability attaching to an individual whose acts are remote from the victim's death or where his conduct contributes only minimally. Similar considerations apply in relation to those other crimes in which the issue of causation is implicit.

THE LEGAL PRINCIPLES OF CAUSATION

5–08   The legal principles governing causation in law generally take the form of guidelines rather than strict legal rules. The most significant of these principles are examined in the following sections. The reader should not expect to find a description of rules which will consistently determine questions of causation. Causal analysis relies much upon common sense and moral intuition.

The characteristics of the victim

5–09   It is commonly stated that the accused must "take his victim as he finds him". An example of this principle operating in practice is provided by the civil case of *McDonald* v. *Smellie*.[6] This case arose from an incident in which a young child was bitten by a dog. The child was predisposed to meningitis and the contraction of the disease was directly attributable to the dog bite. It was held that the child's subsequent death had to be regarded as being caused by the dog.

The "thin skull" rule

5–10   This principle is sometimes referred to as the "thin skull" rule. This rule means that the accused will be criminally liable if death results from some pre-existing weakness in the victim. As Lord Jamieson said in *Bird* v. *H.M. Advocate*,[7] it is not a "defence that the victim was an old person, an infirm person, or a person that suffered from a bad heart, and that if he had been young and healthy the consequences would not have happened." The type of situation covered by the rule is where A strikes B on the head in a way that would normally cause only bruising, but because B has an unusually thin skull the blow fractures B's skull and he dies. A cannot then claim that B's unusual physique breaks the chain of causation between his conduct and the death. The basis for this rule is a consideration of public policy: the accused should not have injured the victim in the first place. On a strict analysis, however, it could not really be said that the accused had "voluntarily" caused the death of the victim, since he believed, perhaps quite reasonably, that the victim had a normal skull. It could even be argued that the death was accidental. Nevertheless, the criminal law obliges him to take responsibility for the consequences of his actions.

---

[6]   (1903) 5 F. 955.
[7]   1952 J.C. 23 at p. 25.

Psychological characteristics

This rule operates reasonably enough in relation to the physical   **5–11**
characteristics of the victim, but how far can it be taken? Should it extend
to the psychological characteristics or religious beliefs of the victim? The
English case of *R.* v. *Blaue*[8] indicates that the courts would be unlikely to
make any distinction between physical and psychological characteristics.
The appellant in this case had stabbed the victim, who was a Jehovah's
Witness, numerous times and pierced her lung. At the hospital to which she
had been taken, the victim refused the immediate blood transfusion necessary
to save her life and died from her wounds shortly afterwards. The appellant
contended that the refusal to have the blood transfusion was unreasonable
and, as such, had broken the chain of causation. The Court of Appeal rejected
this argument. Lord Justice Lawton stated:

> "[T]hose who use violence on other people must take their victims as
> they find them. This in our judgment means the whole man, not just
> the physical man. It does not lie in the mouth of the assailant to say
> that his victim's religious beliefs ... were unreasonable. The question
> for decision is what caused her death. The answer is the stab wound.
> The fact that the victim refused to stop this end coming about did not
> break the causal connection between the act and the death."[9]

The case of *Blaue* is a persuasive authority for the view that an assailant
must take his victim as he finds him both physically and psychologically.
On the facts of the case, this conclusion seems to be the correct one. One
view would be that there are dangers in expressing the principle too widely.
Should the conclusion be the same if the refusal had been out of spite for
the assailant?

The conduct of the victim

It thus appears that even an "unreasonable" refusal of medical treatment   **5–12**
by a victim will not break the chain of causation. There are, however, a
number of different ways in which a victim could contribute to his own
demise. The question then arises: Are there any circumstances in which the
conduct of the victim will be held to have broken the causal link? In the
case of *Joseph and Mary Norris*[10] the original wound inflicted by the accused
was trivial. The victim went drinking, removed his bandages and went out
late at night in poor weather. He contracted tetanus and died. Lord Craighill
directed the jury that the question for them to answer was whether the tetanus

---

[8]   [1975] 1 W.L.R. 1411.
[9]   *ibid*. p. 1415.
[10]   (1886) 1 White 292.

would have developed whether or not the victim had acted in the way he did. If the tetanus was the consequence of the conduct of the accused, then they were liable for the result. If, however, the disease had been brought on by the imprudence of the victim, then there should be a verdict of not guilty.

No duty on complainer to mitigate harm

5–13   This charge to the jury is unusual in that, perhaps because of the trivial nature of the original wound, considerable emphasis was placed on the conduct of the deceased. The more commonly expressed view is that a victim is not under any legal duty to mitigate the effects of the injuries inflicted upon him. It would appear that the victim is quite at liberty to neglect his own well-being and the assailant must take the consequences of his actions. This basic principle is restated in many of the relevant authorities. For example, in *James Williamson*[11] Lord Justice-Clerk Inglis said that the fact that a victim "is weaker than his neighbours, either from natural constitution or bad habit, can never make the slightest difference in the question of guilt or innocence."[12]

5–14   Similarly, the accused has to take responsibility for any harm occurring to the victim during an escape. If he causes so much fear in the victim that he dies in the course of a desperate escape attempt, then the accused will be held to have caused the death of the victim. In the case of *Patrick Slaven*,[13] the accused had assaulted a woman with intent to ravish her. They pursued her as she tried to escape, and she fell over a cliff and died. It was held that the conduct of the accused had caused the death.

The "daft" complainer?

5–15   In the English case of *R. v. Roberts*,[14] the victim was a young lady to whom the appellant had given a lift. During the journey he made a number of improper suggestions to her and touched her breasts. The victim jumped from the car, which was travelling at a speed between 20 and 40 miles per hour, suffering grazing and concussion in the escape. The appellant claimed that the victim's action in jumping out of the car had broken the chain of causation and thereby relieved him of liability for her injuries. The Court of Appeal was not impressed by this argument. Lord Justice Stephenson was of the opinion that only if the actions of the complainer had been "daft" would the chain of causation have been broken. In *R. v. Williams and Davis*[15]

---

[11]   (1866) 5 Irv. 326.
[12]   *ibid*. p. 328.
[13]   (1885) 5 Coup. 694.
[14]   (1971) 56 Cr.App.Rep. 95.
[15]   [1992] 1 W.L.R. 380.

the deceased was a hitch-hiker who had jumped from a moving car in order to escape an attempted robbery. The Court of Appeal set out two questions which need to be addressed in such a case: "first, whether it was reasonably foreseeable that some harm ... was likely to result from the threat itself; and, secondly, whether the deceased's reaction ... was within the range of responses which might be expected from a victim placed in the situation which he was."[16] What had to be considered was "whether the deceased's conduct was proportionate to the threat; that is to say that it was within the ambit of reasonableness and not so daft as to make it his own voluntary act which amounted to a novus actus interveniens and consequently broke the chain of causation."[17]

These two decisions support the view that if the victim acts unreasonably, **5–16** then the accused should not be held liable for the harm. The unreasonable behaviour becomes the cause of the harm. This conclusion would appear to be inconsistent with the decision in *Blaue* (see para. 5–11, above) and contrary to the principle underlying the "thin skull" rule. Even if the actions of a victim could be described as "daft", the accused should still be held responsible for the consequences. The accused must take his victim as he finds him, "daftness" and all. It is debatable whether a Scottish court would take the same approach as the Court of Appeal. In a different context, an unreasonable action on the part of the victim — the voluntary ingestion of a drug — has been held not to break the chain of causation.[18]

Induced suicide

A not unrealistic scenario would have a rapist infecting his victim with **5–17** AIDS. She decides to commit suicide rather than suffer a lingering death. Should the rapist be held to have caused the death? There are American cases, such as *People v. Lewis*,[19] and *Commonwealth v. Wright*,[20] which suggest that where the victim has, as a result of the egregious conduct of the accused, become so disturbed as to commit suicide, the accused will be held to have caused the death of the victim. The point has yet to be resolved in a Scottish case. In *John Robertson*[21] Lord Handyside reserved his opinion on the question of whether an induced suicide would break the chain of causation:

"If the act of suicide was the immediate consequence of the violence, I am not prepared to say what such a state of facts might warrant. I do

---

16 [1992] 1 W.L.R. 380 at p. 389D.
17 *ibid.* p. 388H.
18 *Lord Advocate's Reference (No. 1 of 1994)*, 1995 S.L.T. 248.
19 124 Cal. 551 (1899).
20 455 Pa. 480 (1974).
21 (1854) 1 Irv. 469 at p. 470.

not say that it would amount to culpable homicide, although it would certainly come very near to it."

Whether as a matter of principle, or through an application of the "thin skull" rule, it is likely that a court would determine that the rapist should be held to have caused the death of the victim.

Intervening causes

5–18	It is a fundamental requirement of causation in law that the conduct of the accused be a sufficiently direct cause of the consequential harm to the victim. It is quite possible that a number of other "but for" causes will contribute to the eventual result. Some will be more significant than others, but very few will be of sufficient significance to break the causal chain.

The concept of a novus actus interveniens

5–19	The legal term for an event which does break the chain of causation is a *novus actus interveniens*. The example which is frequently given is that of an assault victim left in a field who is subsequently struck by lightning and dies. The initial assault would not then be seen as the proximate cause of that result. In order to break the chain of causation between the assailant and the consequential harm in this way, the *novus actus* must supersede the original conduct. The law takes a very restrictive view of what can constitute a superseding cause significant enough to break the causal link. An individual can even be held responsible for the harms which result from the intervening conduct of his victim (see paras. 5–13 and 5–14, above).

5–20	An informative authority in this regard is *Khaliq v. H.M. Advocate*,[22] the celebrated decision concerning "glue sniffing kits". Here the High Court held that the subsequent voluntary acts of the purchaser of such a kit could not constitute a *novus actus interveniens* relieving the sellers of responsibility for the "real injury" caused. The causal link was not broken merely because a voluntary act on the part of the recipient of the intoxicant was required in order to bring about the harmful consequences. In the *Lord Advocate's Reference (No. 1 of 1994)*[23] this principle was applied in the context of culpable homicide. The fact that the deceased had voluntarily ingested the amphetamine supplied by the accused did not relive him of responsibility for the death.

Assault and subsequent infection

5–21	It is not difficult to envisage many natural events which could intervene between the conduct of the accused and a resulting harm. A straightforward

---

[22]	1984 J.C. 23; applied in *Ulhaq v. H.M. Advocate*, 1991 S.L.T. 614; 1990 S.C.C.R. 593.
[23]	1995 S.L.T. 248.

example would be the non-fatal wound which becomes infected and the victim dies as a result of the infection. There is no difficulty in saying that the individual who inflicted the wound is liable for the death. The immediate cause of death may have been the infection, but the original wound will be cognised by the law to be the proximate cause of death. This situation can be distinguished from that where the victim is exposed to some other, entirely unpredictable, cause of death. It is possible that the victim of an assault might coincidentally contract a fatal disease while lying in hospital. In the American case of *Bush v. Commonwealth*[24] the victim caught a fatal dose of scarlet fever from the hospital physician who treated him. It was held that it was the disease, not the original assault, which had caused the death.

In the case of *James Wilson*,[25] a wound inflicted on the victim developed **5–22** into erysipelas while he was being treated in hospital. There was a dispute as to whether the victim had been infected by another patient or whether it was a direct complication of the original injury. Lord Cockburn charged the jury that the original wound should be regarded as the cause of death provided that the disease was "not altogether new, but a natural consequence of the injury."[26] If, on the other hand, "the disease was ... entirely new — not produced by the wounds, but by infection, or some other external cause" death was caused by the coincidental infection and not by the wound. The *caveat* entered to this principle by Lord Cockburn is most important:

> "Suppose a man to die of apoplexy, but that apoplexy to have been caused by a blow. It will not ... do for the prisoner to say ... I gave you a blow, but I did not give you apoplexy. He must stand the peril of the consequences of his act."[27]

This passage reiterates the basic principle of causation already referred to. It is clear that in order for a subsequent infection to constitute a *novus actus interveniens* it will need to be quite independent of the original wound. As it was put by the Courts-Martial Appeal Court in *R. v. Smith*[28]: "only if the second cause is so overwhelming as to make the original wound merely part of the history can it be said that the death does not flow from the wound." In a homicide case, the focus will be placed on the original wound. The subsequent aggravation will generally be disregarded, unless the later aggravation has clearly arisen from an independent cause.

---

[24] 78 Ky. 268 (1880).
[25] (1838) 2 Swin. 16.
[26] *ibid.* p. 19.
[27] *ibid.* p. 18. *Cf. J. Campbell* (1819) Alison i, 147.
[28] [1959] 2 Q.B. 35 at p. 43.

Medical treatment

5–23   In fact, *Smith* concerned poor medical treatment rather than a subsequent
infection. The general principle in relation to *malregimen*, as it is sometimes
called, is that negligent medical treatment is irrelevant since the accused
must stand the consequences of his unlawful conduct. As was stated in the
case of *James Williamson*,[29]

> "it will never do ... if a wound calculated to prove mortal in itself is
> afterwards followed by death, to say that every criticism that can be
> made of the treatment of the patient after the wound is received is to
> furnish a ground for acquitting the person who inflicted the wound of
> either murder or culpable homicide."

The situation is essentially the same as when the victim unreasonably refuses
medical treatment. The conduct of the accused will still be held to be the
proximate cause of death. The only distinction which might be drawn is
between negligent medical treatment which merely serves to aggravate the
original wound and treatment which is so grossly negligent as to constitute
an independent cause of death. "Ordinary" negligence would not appear to
be sufficient. There would need to be something approaching criminal
recklessness on the part of the doctor. As a matter of policy, a court would
be most unwilling to regard anything done by a doctor in the ordinary course
of medical treatment as constituting a *novus actus interveniens*: "it will
only be in the most extraordinary and unusual case that [medical] treatment
can be said to be so independent of the acts of the defendant that it could be
regarded in law as the cause of the victim's death to the exclusion of the
defendant's acts."[30]

5–24   In *R. v. Smith*[31] the appellant had been convicted of the murder of a
fellow soldier. The two had been involved in a fight, during the course of
which the victim was stabbed a number of times with a bayonet. On the
way to a medical station the victim was twice dropped from a stretcher and
there was a considerable delay before he received treatment. The appellant
contended that these subsequent events had broken the chain of causation.
The court rejected this argument. It held that his conduct would be regarded
as the cause in law since it had been shown that it was the operating and
substantial cause of death. In this case the victim had clearly died because
of the stab wounds. Only if the original wounds could be said to have merely
provided the setting in which some other cause of death operated would the
court have been prepared to say that the chain of causation had been broken.

---

[29] (1866) 5 Irv. 326 at p. 328.
[30] *R v. Cheshire* [1991] 1 W.L.R. 844, *per* Beldam L.J. at p. 851G.
[31] [1959] 2 Q.B. 35.

Discontinuing life support

An approach similar to that in *Smith* can be found in *Finlayson v. H.M.* **5–25**
Advocate,[32] where it was held that switching off a life support machine did
not break the chain of causation. Here an injection of a controlled drug had
caused brain death in the victim. The High Court determined that the effects
of the injection constituted the substantial and continuing cause of death.
This causative link had not been affected by the decision to switch the life
support machine off, which was a reasonable one in the circumstances. The
court decided, in effect, that the life support machine had merely held the
consequences of the injection in abeyance. When the machine was switched
off, the injection continued to be the cause of death.

Reasonable foreseeability

In *Finlayson* the court adopted the dictum of Lord Wright in *The* **5–26**
Oropesa[33]:

"To break the chain of causation it must be shown that there is
something which I will call ultroneous, something unwarrantable, a
new cause which disturbs the sequence of events, something which
can be described as either unreasonable or extraneous or extrinsic".

The finding of the court was that switching off the life support machine did
not pass this test. A further observation made by the court was that switching
off the machine was foreseeable.

The test of foreseeability

This concept of foreseeability is prayed in aid in many of the authorities **5–27**
concerning causation. For example, in *R. v. Roberts*[34] the Court of Appeal
relied upon the fact that the victim's attempt to escape was a reasonably
foreseeable consequence of what the appellant had done. The basic notion
is that whether or not an intervening cause will be held to have broken the
chain of causation depends upon its foreseeability. The test is whether the
harm was due to an intervening event that a reasonable person could have
foreseen. If not, then the superseding cause will be regarded in law as the
proximate one. A possible limit to the test is that identified by Lord Reid in
the civil case of *McKew v. Holland and Hannen and Cubitts (Scotland)
Limited*: "[I]t does not follow that [an accused] is liable for every
consequence which a reasonable man could foresee. What can be foreseen

---

[32] 1979 J.C. 33.
[33] [1943] P. 32 at p. 39.
[34] (1971) 56 Cr.App.Rep. 95; see para. 5–15, above.

depends almost entirely on the facts of the case, and it is often easy to foresee [a] *novus actus interveniens* as being quite likely."[35] This is why the test is better seen as one of *reasonable* foreseeability, rather than one of foreseeability *per se*. The test is an objective one. An example of a situation suitable for an application of the test is that of A striking B and leaving him unconscious on the sea shore. B drowns when the tide comes in. It would be ridiculous if A could escape liability on the basis that he did not cause the death, but the sea did.

5–28   The nature of the foreseeability test is well illustrated by two American cases. In *People v. Fowler*[36] the victim of an assault was left lying unconscious in a road. He was subsequently struck by a car and killed. The action of the driver of the vehicle, being foreseeable, was held not to be a superseding cause and the original assailant was responsible for the death of the victim. The reverse of this type of situation can be seen in *Lewis v. Commonwealth*.[37] Here an individual knocked the victim down, but a third person subsequently kicked him in the head causing death. The conduct of the third party was clearly an unforeseeable superseding cause.

Foreseeability and malregimen

5–29   The foreseeability test could be applied to the *malregimen* cases. One application of the test would be that if the original assault is foreseeably fatal, then subsequent medical maltreatment could not break the chain of causation. An alternative application might be to say that "ordinary" negligence on the part of a doctor is foreseeable: everyone knows that doctors make mistakes. The implication would be that grossly negligent or reckless treatment could break the chain of causation, since that would be unforeseeable.

5–30   In the English case of *R. v. Jordan*[38] it was held that "palpably wrong" medical treatment had broken the chain of causation. As stressed earlier, however, it would be the truly exceptional case where such a conclusion could be reached. In *Jordan* the original wound inflicted on the victim had nearly healed at the time of death. The proximate cause of death was the injection of a drug to which the victim was allergic. The court held that the original injury was merely the setting within which another cause of death operated. In this case the court reached the conclusion described by Lord Justice-Clerk Inglis in the case of *James Williamson*[39]:

---

[35]   1970 S.C. (H.L.) 20 at p. 25.
[36]   178 Cal. 657 (1918).
[37]   19 Ky.L.Rep. 1139 (1897).
[38]   (1956) 40 Cr.App.Rep. 152.
[39]   (1866) 5 Irv. 326 at p. 328; see para. 5–13, above.

"If a person receives a wound ... which is not fatal in itself ... and then afterwards by unskilful and injudicious treatment this wound assumes a more serious aspect, and finally terminates in death, it is possible to say ... that the wound inflicted by the prisoner is not the cause of death, because it would not by itself have produced death but for the bad treatment which followed on it."

This passage needs to be treated with considerable caution. The deceased only received the poor medical treatment because he had been the victim of a life-threatening assault. Why should the assailant not be regarded as having caused the death?

Fatality and foreseeability

The argument is sometimes made that it is possible to draw a distinction **5–31** between an injury which is foreseeably fatal and one which is not. There is no guarantee, however, that a court would consider the foreseeability test as applicable in such a case. It may prefer a simple application of the "but for" or "thin skull" rules. Much may come to depend on the nature of the original assault. Which test a court decides to apply may well depend upon an assessment of the accused's "blameworthiness" (see para. 5–37, following). In *R. v. Blaue*[40] the English Court of Appeal did not apply the principle of foreseeability to the rule that the victim had to be taken as she was found. It will be recalled that there was a refusal to draw any distinction between physical characteristics which, even if unusual, can be argued to be foreseeable, and unusual psychological characteristics. It is surely not reasonably foreseeable that a victim will hold religious beliefs which preclude her accepting life-saving medical treatment (see para. 5–11, above).

FACT, LAW AND POLICY

THE PROBLEM OF CAUSATION

The task which confronts the criminal lawyer in relation to causation is that **5–32** of defining the necessary circumstances for its establishment. Causation is important because without this requirement an individual with a negligible or non-existent connection to a crime could be punished. The law does not engage in a wide-ranging philosophical inquiry about the concept of causation. The practical aim of the law is to identify those causes for which the accused can be held responsible. This involves a normative, as well as a factual judgment. In the simplest of terms, these causes will be those that make some noteworthy contribution to the circumstances surrounding the

---

[40] [1975] 1 W.L.R. 1411.

forbidden harm. Every cause must meet the "but for" test. A helpful definition of what constitutes a cause is that of Fletcher: "Among all the necessary conditions for a particular event, the 'causes' are those conditions that make the difference under the circumstances."[41]

The legal context

5–33   The principle of proximate cause requires that the conduct of the accused must have been the legal cause, as well as the factual cause, of the *actus reus* in order for him to be criminally liable. This concept of a proximate cause is a somewhat obscure one. There is no precise method for identifying a proximate cause. A court will not discover the proximate cause by applying a method derived from logic. It will be faced with two major legal issues of causation to resolve. First, in what circumstances can one say that there is a causal link between the accused's conduct and the harm? Secondly, what can constitute a *novus actus interveniens* breaking the chain of causation? A number of the different tests employed by the courts to resolve these questions have been outlined in this chapter. These principles tend to take the form of guidelines, rather than strict rules.

The factual context

5–34   It should also be emphasised that, because causation is a mixed question of law and fact, it is dangerous to reach dogmatic conclusions independently of the facts of a case. The particular constellation of facts confronting a court may be of primary significance. A judge will be very wary of trespassing on the territory of the jury. In *Finlayson v. H.M. Advocate*, Lord Justice-General Emslie said that:

> "[I]t was not in any event a matter for the Judge to determine *ab ante* whether, as matter of fact, it could be said that the chain of causation had been broken. That was a matter inextricably bound up with the other facts in the case which were for determination by the jury".[42]

5–35   It would, of course, be quite legitimate for a judge to point out that a subsequent event could not in law constitute a *novus actus interveniens*. This might be the case if the victim had refused medical treatment because of his religious beliefs.[43] A judge would be at liberty to direct a jury that the refusal was, as a matter of law, not to be regarded as a superseding cause which had broken the chain of causation.

---

[41] *Rethinking Criminal Law*, p. 595.
[42] 1979 J.C. 33 at p. 36.
[43] See *R. v. Blaue* [1975] 1 W.L.R. 1411; para. 5–11, above.

The policy context

One view of the issue of causation is that the courts do not in fact rely **5–36** upon generally applicable principles of the kind described in this chapter. Gordon's view is that:

> "What often happens in practice is that courts discuss causal theories learnedly and at length, and purport to reach a conclusion by reference to a logical appraisal of these theories; but in fact the causal criterion applied to the case is chosen, not because of its intrinsic logic and correctness, but because it is the one which leads most easily to the same answer as would be given to the question: 'Should A bear the blame for this?'."[44]

The argument seems to be that courts resort to considerations of policy when determining whether the accused has caused a particular harm. (A more limited version of this argument is that a court will utilise a moral judgment in deciding whether or not causation is established.) There are difficulties with this interpretation. It is always dangerous to claim that a court is doing something other than what it says it is. Perhaps a better view would be that the principles in this area of law are both flexible and overlapping. As a consequence, a court will have a choice over which principle or test to apply. For example, the principle of reasonable foreseeability can lead to a different conclusion from an application of the "thin skull" rule (see para. 5–31, above). A further problem with the policy approach is that, even as a purported explanation of what the courts do in practice, it offers precious little guidance for future cases.

Causation and responsibility

Causation cannot simply be judged objectively in terms of physical acts. **5–37** As Gordon states in the passage quoted above, some element of responsibility or blameworthiness must come into the equation. Indeed, one influential view is that an analysis of causation is dependent upon the criterion of blameworthiness.[45] The principle informing this approach is that if blame can be attributed to an accused, the result is proximate and the causal link will be established. This means that if an accused has *mens rea*, one can conclude that he expected, or should have expected, the harm resulting from his unlawful conduct. He is blameworthy and causation will be established. (This is not to say that the presence of *mens rea* can create a causal link which is not already there.) In contrast to the pure policy approach, there is here at least some guidance for resolving future cases.

---

[44] *Criminal Law*, para. 4–01.
[45] Gross, *A Theory of Criminal Justice*, pp. 232–254.

Further reading

Clarkson, C. M. V., and Keating, H., *Criminal Law: Text and Materials* (3rd ed., 1994), Part 4.

Farmer, L., et al., "Scots Criminal Law and Aids," 1987 S.L.T. (News) 389.

Fletcher, G. P., *Rethinking Criminal Law* (1978), pp. 358–372.

Katz, L., *Bad Acts and Guilty Minds* (1987), Chap. 4.

Norrie, A., *Crime, Reason and History. A Critical Introduction to Criminal Law* (1993), Chap. 7.

Sheldon, D., "Dole, Directness and Foresight in Causation," 1996 J.R. 25.

CHAPTER 6

ATTEMPT

Introduction

The question to be addressed in this chapter can be stated quite simply: **6–01**
under what circumstances is it a crime to endeavour to commit a crime?
The key to understanding the law in this area is to appreciate that conduct
prior to the successful completion of a criminal end can itself constitute a
crime. Conduct which is criminalised at this preliminary stage is known as
an "inchoate", or incomplete, crime. There are three such inchoate crimes
recognised in Scots law: attempt; conspiracy; and incitement (sometimes
known as instigation). Conspiracy and incitement are discussed in the next
chapter. This chapter is concerned solely with the law of attempt.

An attempt to commit any crime is criminal.[1] The basic notion of an **6–02**
attempted crime is easy to grasp, but the legal definition of the crime of
attempt tends towards vagueness; different interpretations of the relevant
principles are to be found in the authorities. It is also true to say that some
of the concepts underlying the crime of attempt are somewhat elusive; this
is particularly true in relation to "impossible" attempts.

Why attempts are penalised

The clearest rationale for punishing attempts is that summarised by Hart: **6–03**
"The criminal had gone so far as to do his best to execute a wicked
intention."[2] In particular, the individual who has attempted to commit a
crime may well be equally as dangerous as the one who has succeeded in
his criminal enterprise. The difference between the two attempts in terms
of success or failure could simply be attributable to chance or luck. A further
argument is that the individual who attempts to commit a crime causes
harm worthy of punishment through the creation of public anxiety.

There is also the issue of deterrence to consider. Hart makes the point **6–04**
that "the accused has manifested a dangerous disposition to do all he can to
commit a crime, and the experience of punishment may check him in the

---

[1] Criminal Procedure (Scotland) Act 1995, s.294.
[2] Hart, *Punishment and Responsibility*, p. 128.

future, since it may cause him to attach more weight to the law's threats."[3] As far as more general deterrence is concerned, the same considerations which apply to a completed crime would appear to apply equally in the case of an attempt.

6–05   The criminalisation of attempts is also justifiable as a preventive measure. Without the recognition of inchoate crimes, the police would have no legal basis for intervening at a preliminary stage. After all, one fundamental aim of the criminal law must be to try to prevent would-be criminals from succeeding in their aims. This would become much more difficult if the criminal law was concerned only with completed crimes.

Disguised attempts

6–06   There are a number of substantive criminal law offences which can be seen as "disguised" attempts. There exists a range of statutory offences which are targeted at preventing crimes and which prohibit preparations to commit crimes. For example, the law restricts the carrying of weapons[4] and, in certain circumstances, equipment which could be of use in committing theft.[5] The common law crime of housebreaking with intent to steal is in reality an inchoate offence which penalises conduct in a similar way to the law of attempt, but at an even earlier stage in the criminal endeavour. An example should help to clarify the point: A breaks into a house in order to steal an item of property. He may not, however, have proceeded sufficiently far to be guilty of attempting to commit the intended crime (theft). As Lord Justice-General Normand observed in *Coventry v. Douglas*[6]: "The mere presence of a person in a particular place may be only preparatory to the execution of the criminal intent, and not itself an overt criminal act." The independent crime of housebreaking with intent to steal allows A to be apprehended at the time of gaining entry (or even attempted entry[7]). There is no need to wait on A beginning to perpetrate whatever crime he has in mind.

6–07   Another crime which could be seen as an attempt in disguise is assault. As is described in greater detail in Chapter 9, although the attack on the complainer must be physical in character to constitute an assault, there

---

[3]   Hart, *Punishment and Responsibility,* p. 129.
[4]   See, for example, the Carrying of Knives etc. (Scotland) Act 1993.
[5]   Civic Government (Scotland) Act 1982, s.58 (applicable where the accused has two or more convictions for theft).
[6]   1944 J.C. 13 at p. 20. In *H.M. Advocate v. Forbes*, 1994 S.L.T. 861, the Appeal Court left open the question of whether it constituted attempted assault and rape to enter premises, strip down and prowl around with intent to assault and rape.
[7]   See *Burns v. Allan*, 1987 S.C.C.R. 449; *Heywood v. Reid*, 1996 S.L.T. 378. For a more detailed discussion of this crime, see para. 10–35, following.

need not be a physical result. In *Stewart v. Procurator Fiscal of Forfarshire*,[8] the accused was convicted of assault after he had aimed a blow at the complainer, but had missed. And in *Gilmour v. McGlennan*[9] it was held that to point a toy gun at someone could constitute assault. It might be thought that the charge of attempted assault is redundant, since it could involve libelling that an accused had attempted to attempt to attack the complainer. The charge of attempted assault does, however, sometimes occur in practice.[10]

MENS REA

Just as in relation to a completed crime, the two elements of *mens rea* and *actus reus* are present in an attempted crime. As far as *mens rea* is concerned, the basic rule appears to be quite simple: the *mens rea* for an attempted crime is the same as for the completed crime. Where the crime is one of intention few problems are caused. For example, the requisite *mens rea* for the crime of attempted theft is the same as that for the completed crime: the "essence" of this crime is that there was "an intention to commit the crime of theft."[11]

6–08

RECKLESSNESS

The conceptual problems as regards the *mens rea* of attempt arise in relation to those crimes which can be perpetrated recklessly. If the *mens rea* of an attempted crime is the same as that for the completed crime, does this mean that one can attempt to commit a crime of recklessness? Does the law recognise the possibility of a reckless attempt? The conceptual difficulty raised by this question is whether it should be possible to "blunder" into an attempt.[12] In other jurisdictions,[13] and perhaps in earlier times in Scotland,[14] the answer to these two questions would be in the negative. It is a commonly expressed view that there must be an intention to commit the crime whose attempt is libelled. That is, an essential element of an attempt is that the

6–09

---

8   (1829) 2 S.J. 32.
9   1993 S.C.C.R. 837.
10 See para. 9–11, following.
11 *Coventry v. Douglas*, 1944 J.C. 13, *per* Lord Fleming at p. 19. See also *Johnstone v. Lees*, 1995 S.L.T. 1174 (conviction for attempting to pervert the course of justice dependent upon intention).
12 F. Sayre, "Criminal Attempts" (1928) 41 Harv. L. Rev. 821 at p. 843; T. Arnold, "Criminal Attempts — The Rise and Fall of an Abstraction" (1930) 40 Yale Law Jnl. 53 at p. 68.
13 See *Knight v. The Queen* (1992) 175 C.L.R. 496 (Australia); *R. v. Ancio* (1984) 6 D.L.R. (4th) 577 (Canada); Criminal Attempts Act 1981, s. 1(1); and *R. v. Whybrow* (1951) 35 Cr.App.Rep. 141 (England and Wales).
14 See the references in Hume, i, 27–28, to "criminal purpose" and "criminal resolution".

result required by the definition of a crime should have been intended. The very notion of an attempt appears to necessitate that the accused has "tried" to do something and that there is an intended consequence. In murder, for example, this would be the death of the intended victim.

6–10   Scots law appears to take a rather different approach to the *mens rea* of an attempted crime. There is an objective focus upon what the accused actually did, rather than what he intended at the time. Particular regard must be paid to the decision in *Cawthorne v. H.M. Advocate*.[15] This case determined that the *mens rea* for attempted murder is the same as that for murder[16]; the only difference being that in attempted murder the victim does not actually die. As Lord Brand explained in the course of his charge to jury in *H.M. Advocate v. Blake*[17]: "'Attempt to murder' is the charge brought against a man who is alleged to have made an attack on another in circumstances in which, had his victim died as a result of his attack, the crime would have been murder." Murder can be committed "unintentionally", in the sense that the accused need not foresee the death of the victim as a consequence of his conduct if he demonstrates wicked recklessness. Following *Cawthorne*, one can say that wicked recklessness is sufficient *mens rea* for attempted murder; there need not be an actual intention to kill. An illustration of this approach to the *mens rea* of attempted murder is provided by Lord Keith's charge to the jury in *McGregor v. H.M. Advocate*[18]:

> "If you go out and recklessly fire off a firearm or wave a knife or dagger about and kill somebody, that may be murder. The test of attempted murder is whether, if the actions of the accused had resulted in the death of one of the [complainers] you would have said that was murder or not. If a man drives along with a policeman on his bonnet in such a way that the policeman falls off and is killed ... — if you would have said that was murder, then you would be entitled to convict him [of attempted murder]."

6–11   The approach outlined above, which recognises that one can attempt to commit a crime of recklessness, is at variance with the ordinary concept of an attempt. It is an unnatural use of language to say that A, who is reckless as to the result of his assault upon B, without intending to kill him, attempts

---

[15] 1968 J.C. 32. Alison, i, 163, appears to endorse this approach, but this is because wicked recklessness is there treated as equivalent to an intention to kill. There is no authoritative judicial decision on whether the *Cawthorne* principle applies to crimes other than murder which can be committed recklessly.
[16] Lord Justice-Clerk Ross described this principle as "well settled" in *Brady v. H.M. Advocate*, 1986 J.C. 68.
[17] 1986 S.L.T. 661 at p. 662H.
[18] (1973) S.C.C.R. Supp. 54 at p. 56.

to murder B. The *Cawthorne* approach can, however, be seen as consistent with the prevailing objective approach to the establishment of criminal liability. In Scotland, the accused is to be sanctioned because he nearly committed a crime, that is, came close to perpetrating the *actus reus*. His blameworthy mental state is reflected in this fact.

ACTUS REUS

POLICY ISSUES

The greatest difficulties in the law of attempt relate to the *actus reus*. The **6–12** primary issue is that of determining at what point we can say that the accused's conduct has proceeded sufficiently far towards the commission of a completed crime that it can be classified as a criminal attempt. Where can the line be drawn between a criminal attempt and a non-criminal preparation? There are two fundamental policy concerns which weigh upon this issue. The first is that of facilitating the police in the tasks of crime prevention and law enforcement. The test adopted for establishing the *actus reus* must offer a reasonable chance for intervention before the criminal enterprise reaches its proposed end. One decision which appears to conflict with this requirement is *Guthrie v. Friel*.[19] The Appeal Court held that an appellant who had been apprehended sitting in his car with the seat belt fastened, having started the engine, and with the headlights turned on, could not be said to be attempting to drive. It was stated that the position might have been different had the handbrake been released.

Of equal significance, however, is a concern for civil liberties and the **6–13** rights of the individual. The criminal law should not seek to penalise conduct which is extremely preparatory to the commission of a crime. The law must avoid punishing an individual merely for having undesirable thoughts.[20] Given the inevitable tension between these two concerns, it is not surprising that Scots law does not provide a clear guide as to the *actus reus* of criminal attempts. Although it is clear which is the prevailing test, no single approach to the question has received unequivocal support. The relevant authorities are inconsistent as to what *actus reus* is necessary before preparatory actions by an accused constitute an attempt to commit a crime. It is only on rare occasions that the courts have articulated explicitly a test or theory to identify when a criminal attempt occurs. Nevertheless, it is possible to identify three significant theories by inference from the facts of different cases and the observations of judges. The three theories or tests are: (1) irrevocability; (2) last act; and (3) perpetration. A further problem is that these tests have

---

[19] 1993 S.L.T. 899.
[20] *Morton v. Henderson*, 1956 J.C. 55, *per* Lord Justice-General Clyde at p. 57.

a tendency to overlap one another; nor have the courts always sought to clarify which approach they are adopting.

IRREVOCABILITY THEORY

6–14   There are authorities which appear to suggest that a criminal attempt cannot be committed at a stage before the final chain of events is irrecoverable by the actions of the accused. In *H.M. Advocate v. Mackenzie*,[21] Lord Justice-Clerk Macdonald referred to the "well-established and most just rule of law, which does not allow of punishment for unfulfilled intents and preparations which have not culminated in an irrevocable act of commission or attempt". In *H.M. Advocate v. Tannahill and Neilson*,[22] Lord Wark stated that in order to constitute a criminal attempt there had to be "some overt act, the consequences of which cannot be recalled by the accused". This approach to the *actus reus* was endorsed by Lord Justice-General Clyde in *Morton v. Henderson*.[23] In neither of these latter two cases, however, was there evidence of anything more than a mere suggestion that a crime (fraud in both instances) might be perpetrated. The judicial opinions expressed on both occasions went beyond what was immediately necessary to dispose of the cases and are inconsistent with the views expressed in other authorities. That said, Lord Justice-Clerk Ross appeared to accept the applicability of the irrevocability test in *McKenzie v. H.M. Advocate*.[24]

6–15   What appears to lie behind this approach to criminal attempts is a feeling of disquiet about the very notion of criminalising behaviour prior to the commission of a crime. This general attitude is well summarised in the reported observations of the defence counsel in the case of *Samuel Tumbleson*[25:]

> "Attempts to commit crimes want that character of completeness, of finality, which would make it proper to prosecute them criminally. In many such cases it can hardly be said that the individual has proceeded beyond intention, — that he has done anything partaking, in strictness, of the character of an overt act; and it is of overt acts alone that the law can take cognizance."

---

[21] 1913 S.C.(J.) 107 at p. 111. In *Burns v. Allan*, 1987 S.C.C.R. 449, this case was cited as authority for the perpetration test (see para. 6–19, following). The judgments in *Mackenzie* do say that the accused must have moved beyond the stage of perpetration, but this is in the context of his having performed an irrevocable act.

[22] 1943 J.C. 150 at p. 153.

[23] 1956 J.C. 55.

[24] 1988 S.L.T. 487.

[25] (1863) 4 Irv. 426 at p. 428.

One continues to find echoes of this language even in contemporary decisions.[26]

LAST ACT THEORY

There are old authorities which suggest that a criminal attempt occurs when **6–16** an accused has done all that he believes is necessary to commit the proposed crime. In the case of *Janet Ramage*[27] the accused had placed some poison in a teapot from which the intended victim was expected to drink some tea. A charge of attempted murder was held to be relevant. Similarly, it was emphasised in *Samuel Tumbleson* that, in order to constitute attempted murder by poisoning, it was not necessary that the poison should actually be taken by the intended victim. An application of what has been described as the "irrevocability" test could not support these conclusions. In *Janet Ramage*, for example, the consequences of the accused's act were not incapable of recall: she could have removed the teapot before the victim drank any of the tea. What the accused had performed was the last act required to bring about the murder.

There is little to commend either the "last act" or "irrevocability" theories **6–17** of criminal attempts. The conduct of an accused will commonly provide an adequate foundation for an inference of *mens rea* at a stage prior to the reaching of an irrevocable or the last act. There is also the practical point that an application of either test would severely hamper the police in seeking to prevent crime. It would become well-nigh impossible to effect an arrest during an attempt in order to prevent the commission of the proposed crime.

PERPETRATION THEORY

It is for these reasons that a more flexible approach to the *actus reus* is **6–18** generally thought to be preferable. An application of the "perpetration" theory simply involves asking whether or not the accused has committed an act which is sufficiently proximate to the commission of the completed crime. That is, an attempt involves perpetration rather than preparation. This is the prevailing approach to the *actus reus* of attempts in Scots law: "before a charge of attempting to do something can be established, the individual must have passed from mere preparation to perpetration."[28] The leading authority for this flexible approach to the *actus reus* of criminal

---

[26] See, for example, *McKenzie v. H.M. Advocate*, 1988 S.L.T. 487; *Guthrie v. Friel*, 1993 S.L.T. 899.

[27] Hume, i, 28.

[28] *Guthrie v. Friel*, 1993 S.L.T. 899, *per* Lord Justice-Clerk Ross at p. 901C. See also *H.M. Advocate v. Innes*, (1915) 7 Adam 596, *per* Lord Justice-General Strathclyde at p. 601.

attempts is *H.M. Advocate v. Camerons*,[29] where Lord Justice-General Dunedin charged the jury that the fundamental issue was "to discover where preparation ends and where perpetration begins ... [I]t is a question of degree, and ... it is a jury question."

6–19   In this case the accused were convicted of attempting to defraud an insurance company. The evidence produced at the trial was that the accused had staged a fake robbery, but that no formal insurance claim had been submitted. Clearly, therefore, the accused had not performed the last act necessary for the commission of the fraud. It would also have been possible for the accused to have changed their minds and decided to proceed no further with the proposed fraudulent scheme. This case serves to illustrate the weaknesses of both the last act and irrevocability tests. Their application to the facts in this case could not have led to a conviction.

6–20   Examples of conduct which have been held to be more than merely preparatory include:

1. Joining a queue at a turnstile: statutory offence of attempting to enter a football ground while drunk[30];
2. Menacing a police officer with a machete, without striking him, at the same time as threatening to kill him: attempted murder[31];
3. Disconnecting an external burglar alarm: attempted house-breaking with intent to steal[32];
4. Inserting a hand into a till: attempted theft.[33]

6–21   One possible criticism of the perpetration theory is its vagueness. The great difficulty is that of identifying the point at which an accused has moved from mere preparation towards the commission of a crime. Is it the case that, as one trial judge observed,[34] "the answer to that question can only be intuitive and a matter of impression and degree"? It would be difficult for a workable law of criminal attempts to be very precise. Hume recognised that there is "a great variety of ambiguous cases, with respect to which it is very difficult to say where preparation ends and perpetration begins."[35] In *Coventry v. Douglas*,[36] Lord Justice-General Clyde likewise accepted that:

---

[29] (1911) 6 Adam 456 at p. 485. The Lord Justice-General was adopting this language from Hume, i, 29.
[30] *Barrett v. Allan*, 1986 S.C.C.R. 479 (the statutory offence is now contained in the Criminal Law (Consolidation) (Scotland) Act 1995, s.20(7)(b)).
[31] *Strachan v. H.M. Advocate*, 1994 S.C.C.R. 341.
[32] *Burns v. Allan*, 1987 S.C.C.R. 449.
[33] *Coventry v. Douglas*, 1944 J.C. 13.
[34] *Barrett v. Allan*, 1986 S.C.C.R. 479, *per* Sheriff Hyslop at p. 480.
[35] Hume, i, 29.
[36] 1944 J.C. 13 at p. 20. See also Lord Walker, "The Growth of the Criminal Law," 1958 J.R. 230 at p. 237: "it is needless to say the point when preparation ends and perpetration begins raises a problem of some nicety."

"The line of demarcation between preparation and perpetration cannot be defined in any general proposition".

The perpetration theory approach does, nevertheless, possess the **6–22** inestimable advantages of practicality and workability. Nor should it be thought that Scots law is alone in applying a flexible approach in determining what constitutes a criminal attempt. English law defines the *actus reus* of an attempt as "an act which is more than merely preparatory to the commission of the offence".[37] Other jurisdictions appear to apply equally vague tests.

IMPOSSIBILITY

It would be fair to suggest that no aspect of the criminal law has generated **6–23** more confusion than the law relating to impossible attempts. Throughout the common law world much academic and judicial energy has been expended in efforts to determine in what circumstances an accused can be convicted for an impossible attempt: that is, for an attempt to commit a crime which cannot for some reason succeed. The kind of situation at issue is where the accused has the requisite *mens rea* for the proposed crime and has moved from the stage of preparation to that of perpetration. The only defensive avenue open to him is that of the impossibility of perpetrating the intended crime. Typical examples would be where the pocket which the accused intends to pick is empty or where goods which the accused intends to reset are not in fact stolen.

Following the decision of the Appeal Court in *Docherty v. Brown,*[38] the **6–24** general principle of law is settled. The impossibility of completing the intended crime does not act as a general defence to the charge of a criminal attempt. It is a basic characteristic of an attempted crime that the result has not been brought about. The reason for this would not appear to possess any legal significance. There had, however, been a couple of anomalous occasions on which the High Court had upheld a defence of impossibility on the facts of particular cases (see para. 6–29, following). And it is also true to say that some commentators continue to express disquiet about attributing criminal liability to an accused who has attempted to do the impossible.

There are three principal concerns which lie behind reservations about **6–25** criminal liability in cases of impossible attempts. The first is that many impossible attempts involve conduct which appears innocuous when viewed objectively. In a case of attempted reset, for example, the retention of property which has not been stolen is objectively innocent. Secondly, the

---

[37] Criminal Attempts Act 1981, s.1(1).
[38] 1996 S.L.T. 325.

conduct in impossible attempts cannot always be said to demonstrate criminality as serious as that which an attempt prosecution might suggest. For example, A is under the misapprehension that B has a weak heart and that if subjected to a violent shock will die. He is desirous of causing B's death. To this end, he suddenly jumps out in front of B, shouting loudly. When viewed objectively, this incident would not be described as an attempt to murder B. In subjective terms, of course, A has the *mens rea* of murder and he has clearly tried to begin to perpetrate the intended crime. The reason why the accused failed to commit the intended murder was due to a circumstance for which he was not responsible (that is, the fact that B has a strong constitution). There is, however, an alternative interpretation: A's criminal liability should relate to what he actually did. Adopting this perspective, his conduct would appear to constitute a simple assault or a breach of the peace. There was no outward manifestation of a criminal intention to murder B: A could be punished for an attempt only on the basis of his thoughts.

6–26   A third, related concern could be that permitting convictions in impossible attempt cases increases the risk of convicting those who are innocent. Where the conduct of an accused is objectively innocent, it is much more difficult to infer the presence of the necessary *mens rea*. In an example such as that described in the previous paragraph, the prosecution case will be based primarily on evidence of the accused's internal thought processes and subjective purpose. In endeavouring to prove the accused's guilt, the prosecution will be unusually dependent upon whether there has been a confession. There may also be reliance upon hearsay testimony as to what the defendant said about his purpose to others, and upon other circumstantial evidence. This could mean that there will be a heightened danger of convicting an innocent person or of attributing too much criminal liability to an accused; that is, convicting him of attempting a serious offence (murder) when a conviction for a completed less serious offence (assault or breach of the peace) might be more appropriate.

FACTUAL IMPOSSIBILITY

6–27   A distinction is commonly drawn between cases of "factual" impossibility and "legal" impossibility. The concept of factual impossibility covers the situation where the accused's proposed end would constitute a crime, but he fails to perpetrate it because of some factual circumstance which is unknown to him and outwith his control. The classic question in this context is whether it could constitute attempted murder to shoot at a corpse, thinking that it was a live body.[39] It is now settled that factual impossibility does not

---

[39] This situation arose on the facts of *Collins v. H.M. Advocate*, 1991 S.C.C.R. 898, but did not fall to be determined by the court.

afford a defence to a charge of attempt. In *Docherty v. Brown*[40] the accused had been charged with attempting to possess drugs with intent to supply, contrary to the Misuse of Drugs Act 1971, sections 5(3) and 19. The appellant had taken possession of some tablets in the mistaken belief that they contained a controlled drug, when they did not in fact do so. It was held that in such circumstances an attempt charge was relevant. All five judges were satisfied on this point. Lord Justice-Clerk Ross stated:

> "The fact that something is physically impossible will prevent an accused from being convicted of the complete crime, but it does not prevent him being relevantly charged with attempt to commit that crime provided that he has the necessary mens rea, and does some positive step towards executing his purpose."[41]

An earlier authority is *Lamont v. Strathern*.[42] In this case the High Court **6–28** held it was attempted theft where the accused had placed his hand in an empty pocket with the intent to steal. Lord Sands stated that he was unimpressed "by the metaphysical argument that, whereas one cannot take what is not there, therefore one cannot attempt to take what is not there."[43] He pointed out that it would be unreasonable "to deny to Mother Hubbard the credit of an attempt to fetch a bone for her dog."

In *Docherty v. Brown*[44] the Appeal Court disapproved two earlier cases **6–29** which had suggested that where there was an attempt to procure a criminal abortion, but the prosecution was unable to prove that the woman was pregnant, no criminal liability attached to the attempt. The principal authority for this rule was *H.M. Advocate v. Anderson*,[45] a decision which was followed in *H.M. Advocate v. Semple*.[46] This rule had long appeared to be anomalous and inconsistent with the decision in *Lamont v. Strathern*.[47] There had been attempts to reconcile the two, most recently in *Maxwell v. H.M. Advocate*,[48] but these had not been convincing. It is unrealistic to try and differentiate a case of attempted abortion from one of attempted theft. In *Lamont v. Strathern* Lord Sands distinguished the rule in *Anderson* by stating that in the case of an attempted abortion a "pregnant woman is the condition of the offence", whereas in the case of an attempted theft from the complainer's pocket a "pocket which *may* contain something of value is the only

---

[40] 1996 S.L.T. 325.
[41] *ibid*. p. 331F–G.
[42] 1933 J.C. 33.
[43] *ibid*. p. 36.
[44] 1996 S.L.T. 325.
[45] 1928 J.C. 1.
[46] 1937 J.C. 41.
[47] 1933 J.C. 33.
[48] 1980 J.C. 40.

condition."[49] This attempted distinction was ingenious, but is itself impossible. The presence in the pocket of property to steal could equally be regarded as a condition of an attempted theft, something which the law does not require.[50]

6–30   The common feature to cases of factual impossibility is that had the facts been as the accused believed them to be, he would have perpetrated the intended crime. He has committed the *actus reus* of an attempt and he has the requisite *mens rea*. There would not appear to be any convincing reason why there should be a defence available to the accused simply because he did not utilise the proper means to accomplish the crime or because he was for some reason unable to commit the crime on the instant occasion. His lack of success is not related in any way to his intention to perpetrate the crime.

INHERENT IMPOSSIBILITY

6–31   Accepting that factual impossibility should not ordinarily afford a defence, there remains to be considered the accused who fails to commit the intended crime because he has chosen an "inherently" impossible or unreasonable method of attempting the crime. The example which is generally quoted is that of an attempt to murder by witchcraft. Should the accused in such a case be held to be guilty of attempted murder if it is proved that he believed that the invocation of a spell could kill? The difficulty is in being able to say that the accused is sufficiently dangerous to merit a conviction for attempted murder. In *Docherty v. Brown*[51] Lord Justice-General Hope recognised that:

> "[W]here on the true facts the notion that a crime could have been committed was fanciful ... no good purpose would be served in prosecuting a person who acted in this way, because his actings were so wholly misconceived as to cause no risk of harm to anybody."

LEGAL IMPOSSIBILITY

6–32   The possible distinction between factual and legal impossibility can be illustrated by reference to two familiar examples. The classic example of factual impossibility is that of an attempt to steal from an empty pocket. Legal impossibility is exemplified by an attempt to reset goods which by law have ceased to be stolen goods. The facts of the English case of

---

[49] 1933 J.C. 33 at p. 38.
[50] See *Docherty v. Brown*, 1996 S.L.T. 325, *per* Lord Sutherland at p. 334J.
[51] 1996 S.L.T. 325 at p. 327F–G.

Haughton v. *Smith*[52] provide an instance of legal impossibility. A consignment of stolen meat was repossessed by the police, thereby ceasing to be stolen property (which was a requisite of the statutory offence of handling stolen goods under the Theft Act 1968, section 22). The consignment was allowed to continue to its destination, where it was met by the accused who intended to unload the meat. Their intention, that of handling stolen meat, might be described as legally impossible.

One can identify two kinds of legal impossibility: (1) "absolute" legal **6–33** impossibility; and (2) "composite" legal impossibility. As outlined in the ensuing discussion, it is important to distinguish between these two concepts.[53]

Absolute Legal Impossibility

Absolute legal impossibility arises in cases where the crime which the **6–34** accused thinks he is perpetrating is non-existent. Quite simply, the criminal law does not prohibit either the conduct of the accused or the result which he intends to bring about. Examples of absolute legal impossibility do not arise in practice and are confined to the hypothetical examples of academic authors. People are not prosecuted for adultery or for failing to read the whole of this book, even if the individual concerned believes that his conduct is criminal. Regardless of his intention, an accused cannot be convicted of attempting to commit a non-existent crime. This doctrine of absolute legal impossibility can be interpreted as one aspect of the principle of prospectivity (see para. 14–09, following). The conduct in question is not a crime either at common law or under statute; it cannot be retrospectively criminalised as a result of the accused's blameworthy mental state. If the intention of the accused does not correlate to a recognised crime, his desire to do something criminal is not sufficient for the imposition of criminal liability. It is not for the accused to extend the boundaries of criminal liability in this manner.

Composite Legal Impossibility

Composite legal impossibility arises in cases where the accused intends to **6–35** perpetrate a recognised crime, but this proves to be impossible because of a factual mistake regarding a legal circumstance relevant to his conduct. As the definition implies, this type of impossibility is a composite. The impossibility has both a factual and a legal component. A good example of composite legal impossibility is the familiar one of an attempt to reset

---

[52] [1975] A.C. 476.
[53] For a fuller discussion of this conceptual distinction, see Dressler, *Understanding Criminal Law* (1987), pp. 351–354; I. P. Robbins, "Attempting the Impossible: The Emerging Consensus" (1986) 23 Harv. J.Legis. 377.

property which has ceased to be stolen. Completion of the intended crime is impossible because of the absence of a legal requirement. In this case the accused's error relates to the legal status of the property in question. It is legally impossible for the offence of reset to be committed where the property is not stolen.

6–36   It is difficult to identify a principled basis for distinguishing instances of composite legal impossibility from those of factual impossibility. In cases of composite legal impossibility the accused is in error about a material fact; for example, whether the property which he attempts to reset was stolen. The accused's purpose was a criminal one which failed to be carried into effect because of some detail of which he was unaware. It is reasonable to draw the conclusion that any instance of composite legal impossibility can, with equal conviction, be conceptualised as one of factual impossibility. In terms of legal principle, the two are indistinguishable. If impossibility affords no defence to the attempter of the factually impossible, then neither should it provide an answer to a criminal charge in a case of composite legal impossibility.

Further reading

Duff, R.A., *Intention, Agency and Criminal Responsibility* (1990), Chap. 8.

Gill, B., "Impossibility in Criminal Attempts," 1965 J.R. 137.

Jones, T. H., *Attempted Homicide in English and Scots Law* (University of Manchester Faculty of Law Working Paper No. 15, 1992).

Scottish Law Commission, *Attempted Homicide* (Consultative Memo. No. 61, 1984).

Ullmann, W., "The Reasons for Punishing Attempted Crimes" (1939) 51 J.R. 353.

CHAPTER 7

COMPLICITY AND CONSPIRACY

Introduction

This chapter is concerned with criminal acts which involve more than **7–01**
one individual. It describes both the characteristics of multi-party criminal
conduct and the circumstances in which the criminal law can hold an
individual accused liable for the acts of others. There is an account of how
the accused who associates himself with a criminal actor can be held liable,
even though he does not personally bring about (that is to say, *cause*) the
actus reus.

In the ensuing discussion three types of criminal liability are described. **7–02**
First, the law of complicity penalises all those who participate in the
commission of a crime. Liability of this character is known in Scots law
as art and part guilt. Secondly, there is the crime of conspiracy, which
penalises all those who merely agree to commit a crime. Conspiracy is a
crime in its own right and can form the basis for art and part guilt. That is,
where the conspiracy is put into effect and the crime committed, liability
for complicity can be founded on the accused's conspiratorial relationship
with others. Thirdly, there is the offence of incitement (sometimes known
as instigation), which is committed where the accused solicits another to
perpetrate a crime.

ART AND PART GUILT

The basic principle

Art and part guilt, sometimes described as "acting in concert", has **7–03**
long formed part of the common law. The fundamental principle is
that where two or more people engage together in committing a crime,
each actor is equally guilty of the whole crime irrespective of the
particular role played by each individual. The law recognises that, to
be found guilty of a crime, the accused need not have participated in
every act necessary to constitute that crime. The example which is
commonly given by way of illustration is that the man who keeps watch
during a robbery by standing at the door of a bank is as guilty of the
crime of robbery as the man who actually takes the money from the
safe.

7–04   Naturally, there are certain restrictions to the broad principle of art and part guilt. The law does not recognise guilt by association.[1] The accused must have been aware of what the others involved in the criminal enterprise were doing. Further, in that knowledge, he must have assisted the others to some extent. That is, he must have participated in some way in the acts involved. Both these requirements are described in this chapter.

PARTIES TO CRIME

7–05   There is not, in Scots law, a separate offence of "aiding and abetting" someone in the commission of a crime. The general rule is that no distinction is drawn between the different parties involved in the commission of the crime on the basis of their degree of involvement. This means that anyone who involves himself in even a minor way in a criminal enterprise will be unsure when he is criminally liable and when he is not. This uncertainty is the price to be paid for his immoral actions.[2] It can, nevertheless, sometimes be helpful to visualise a number of different roles where several individuals participate in the commission of a crime: (1) the *instigator*, who intends that the crime be committed and persuades someone else to do so; (2) the *aider*, who assists in the commission of the crime; and (3) the *principal* who is the "actual" perpetrator of the crime.

DIRECT AND DERIVATIVE LIABILITY

7–06   In art and part guilt these different degrees of participation merge into joint liability for the commission of the crime, but it is only the principal who is directly liable; it is only he who is guilty of the whole crime in his own right. The art and part guilt of the instigator and the aider must derive from the commission of the crime (and are dependent upon it), since they only participate in the earlier stages of the criminal enterprise. In terms of the example above, one can say that the look-out derives his criminal liability from the commission of the robbery. He is guilty art and part because he has assisted in the commission of the crime, not because he directly stole anything from the bank.

7–07   It is important to appreciate that art and part guilt does not impose criminal liability for the actions of another simply because of a relationship between the parties. As will be more fully described in succeeding paragraphs, there must be some behaviour on the part of the instigator or aider designed to persuade or assist before the law imposes liability on him for the actions of

---

[1]   See *Khalid v. H.M. Advocate*, 1990 J.C. 37.
[2]   Katz, *Bad Acts and Guilty Minds*, p. 260. In *Docherty* v. *H.M. Advocate*, 1956 J.C. 89 at p. 94, Lord Moncrieff referred to "the doctrine of law which ascribes to associates in crime in certain cases responsibility for the criminal acts of their associate."

the actual offender. What this notion of derivative liability does signify is that the art and part guilt of the instigator or aider (but not that of a joint principal) is dependent upon the crime having been perpetrated. If the crime is not committed, or if the accused cannot properly be said to have participated in its commission, the question of art and part guilt does not arise, although that of conspiracy or incitement may do. Art and part guilt is not a form of inchoate liability.

<h3 style="text-align:center">COMMON PURPOSE</h3>

The starting place for any discussion of the concept of art and part guilt **7–08** must be to consider how an individual who is not directly engaged in the conduct that constitutes the crime can be held liable for the actions of others. The criminal law generally recognises only personal liability: the derivative liability inherent in art and part guilt appears to be inconsistent with this fundamental principle. An individual may become art and part guilty of the crime as the result of personal conduct, but once he is subsumed into the legal category of art and part guilt his criminal liability becomes dependent upon the actions of another person. The justification for this type of derivative liability is that the person involved art and part intends to assist, or participate in, the commission of the crime. In the terminology of art and part guilt, there must be a "common purpose". This requires actual knowledge, or reasonable anticipation, on the part of the aider. A common purpose cannot be established by evidence that the accused "'*may* have known what the other ... *might* have been doing'".[3] If the common purpose or plan cannot be established, then the principle of art and part guilt cannot be invoked and each accused has to be judged on the basis of his own actions and not those of his co-accused or of anyone else.

If there is a common purpose, the particular accused, by providing **7–09** voluntary and intentional assistance, identifies himself with the conduct of the co-accused whom he has assisted (and who may be the "actual" perpetrator of the *actus reus*) and becomes art and part guilty of the crime. The criminal actions of the co-accused can then be imputed to him. The *mens rea* required for the crime in question will be inferred upon proof of the intentional assistance in the commission of the crime. It would, of course, be open to an accused to rebut this inference by pointing to evidence suggestive of a reasonable doubt. Art and part guilt is not based on innocent assistance.

---

[3] *Khalid v. H.M. Advocate*, 1990 J.C. 37, *per* Lord Justice-General Hope at p. 39 (disapproving Sheriff's charge).

DEGREES OF INVOLVEMENT

7–10 Art and part guilt covers a wide range of degrees of involvement in the commission of crimes. It can extend from the offering of relatively minor assistance or advice to full participation in the *actus reus* of the crime. The criminal law regards all conduct within these extremes as constituting art and part guilt. In terms of the example outlined above (see para. 7–03), art and part guilt would include the individual who, with knowledge of the plan, supplied the robber with some piece of information or equipment which was utilised to facilitate entry to the bank. This would still be the case even if the counsellor or supplier was nowhere near the bank at the time of the robbery. Indeed, his physical presence or absence is irrelevant to the question of art and part guilt. The person who supplies a necessary piece of equipment may in fact be of more assistance to the actual perpetrator of the crime than the look-out.

7–11 Clearly it is possible to draw a distinction between the individual who provides some minor assistance or counsel and the individual who fully participates in the commission of the crime itself. Indeed, the criminal law would tend to see the latter as simply a joint criminal enterprise with more than one primary or principal offender rather than as an example of art and part guilt. In terms of the bank robbery example: if two or more people were involved in entering and stealing from the safe in the bank, it would not be strictly necessary to analyse the situation in terms of art and part guilt. Both can be regarded as joint principal offenders. Nevertheless, it is clear that the principle of art and part guilt extends to this situation just as much as when there has been something less than full participation in the crime by an aider or instigator. In practice, however, the criminal law would draw a distinction between these two situations — if only in terms of sentencing.

Assistance and participation

7–12 It bears repeating that, before art and part guilt can be established, the prosecution have to prove that the accused assisted the principal offender to commit the crime. Once assistance has been established, however, the precise extent of it is not really significant. Depending upon the precise facts at issue, almost any type of assistance can suffice. This requirement of assistance is generally described as one of participation. This does not mean, of course, that the accused has to have participated in the perpetration of the *actus reus* of the crime before art and part guilt can be attributed to him. Rather, what is meant is participation in the criminal enterprise which results in the commission of the crime.

7–13 Further, it is not necessary for the prosecution to prove that the crime would not have been committed without the accused's participation. In art and part guilt there is no "but for" requirement: an accused will still be regarded as guilty art and part even if his participation was causally unnecessary to the commission of the crime. That is, it is no defence for the look-out and the supplier of the getaway vehicle to state that the principal offender would have perpetrated the bank robbery regardless of their assistance. This absence of a causation requirement is reflected in the fact that any degree of assistance or participation suffices.

Psychological assistance

The requisite assistance or participation required to establish art and **7–14** part guilt could come in the form of psychological influence. This would occur when the accused has counselled or instigated the commission of the crime. The legal terminology for this state of affairs is "antecedent (or prior) concert". If the accused cannot be proven to have actually participated in the *actus reus* of the crime, he can only be guilty art and part if there is evidence of prior concert.[4]

In a case where antecedent concert is libelled it is necessary for the **7–15** prosecution to establish that the commission of the crime was a likely result of the psychological assistance rendered by the accused. The instigation would have to be such as to induce the criminal conduct. Advice of a very general character would not be sufficient to establish guilt.[5] There would have to be a connection between the instigation and a specific crime. This requirement is illustrated by *H.M. Advocate v. Johnstone and Stewart*.[6] The alleged crime here was that of being art and part guilty in an illegal abortion. The first accused had given the name of an abortionist (the second accused) to another woman. The accused had no connection with the abortionist, whom she knew only by name. Because of this tenuous link, she was acquitted. Lord Moncrieff charged the jury that the mere giving of a name in these circumstances could not constitute participation in the subsequent crime. In order to establish antecedent concert there would have had to have been some communication between the two accused.

Physical assistance

Physical assistance can take a variety of forms. For example, it could **7–16** entail supplying a weapon to be utilised during a bank robbery. As such, it would constitute antecedent concert. Alternatively, art and part guilt could involve participating more directly in the crime by acting as the look-out or by driving the getaway vehicle.

---

[4] *Spiers v. H.M. Advocate*, 1980 J.C. 36. See *Little v. H.M. Advocate*, 1983 J.C. 16, for an example of instigation as the basis for art and part guilt.
[5] Hume, i, 278.
[6] 1926 J.C. 89.

Prior agreement

7–17   Art and part guilt can most easily be proved where there is actual participation in the crime itself. In many such cases there will have been a prior agreement to participate in the commission of the crime. A straightforward example is provided by the facts in the case of *H.M. Advocate v. Fraser and Rollins*.[7] In accordance with a pre-arranged plan a woman lured the victim to a park where two men were waiting to rob him. The victim was assaulted and died of his injuries. All three were equally liable for the man's death and equally guilty of murder.

Spontaneous assistance: mobbing

7–18   The concert necessary to art and part guilt can also arise from a spontaneous coming together at the time of the offence. A classic case on this is the unreported (on this point) decision of *H.M. Advocate v. Gallacher*.[8] This case arose out of a feud between the members of a travelling circus and some of the inhabitants of Hamilton. As is often the case the precise facts are not too clear, but it appears that one of the local men started a fight with the deceased victim, who had been mistaken for one of the circus staff. A number of other men joined in and stood around the victim who was kicked to death. Three members of the crowd were convicted of murder. There was no evidence of antecedent concert. The conviction was based on the fact that they "were in a kicking crowd animated by a common purpose, joining in the attack, assisting and encouraging." It is important to recognise, however, that the accused who joins in an assault which has already commenced does not in any way become responsible by adoption for what has gone on before his intervention.[9] Accession after the fact is not a doctrine which is recognised in Scots law.[10]

7–19   As is described in more detail in the account of the crime of mobbing in Chapter 12, it is in cases involving mobs that the law relating to art and part guilt seems to be taken further than in most other crimes. If a member of a mob can be proven to have participated in some of the actions perpetrated by the mob, he will be guilty art and part of any other acts which are of a broadly similar type. Further, he will still be liable art and part for other actions by the mob committed without his direct participation if these acts are done in pursuance of the common purpose of the mob with which he aligned himself. This guilt is derived from his association with the mob. Through his participation he can be taken to have endorsed the common

---

[7]   1920 J.C. 60.
[8]   1950. Discussed by Gordon, *Criminal Law*, para. 5–33.
[9]   *McLaughlan v. H.M. Advocate*, 1991 S.L.T. 660.
[10] Hume, i, 281; *Collins v. H.M. Advocate*, 1991 S.C.C.R. 898, *per* Lord Allanbridge at p. 903F. See also *Martin v. Hamilton*, 1989 J.C. 101.

purpose and to have foreseen the consequences of any further actions by the mob. In relation to a mob, of course, the concept of a common purpose can be a somewhat elastic and elusive one. This is particularly so when one considers that the common purpose need not be a preconceived one: it can arise spontaneously once the group has come together. Moreover, as was held in the case of *Michael Hart*,[11] the common purpose need not be articulated or even clearly formulated in the minds of the participants.

Participation by omission?

The first principle to note is that "mere presence at the scene of a crime **7–20** is insufficient of itself to constitute art and part guilt."[12] Evidence of active encouragement or assistance is required.[13] In *H.M. Advocate v. Kerr*[14] the three accused were charged with assault with intent to ravish. One of the accused did not actually participate in the attack, but had stood nearby watching. He did not speak to either his co-accused or to the complainer during the attack. His conduct was held not to attract art and part guilt. In such a case, however, the outcome would be different if there was sufficient evidence that the accused had been present as part of a common plan and in order to assist the actual perpetrator(s).[15]

The corollary of this principle is that neither does failure to prevent the **7–21** commission of a crime impose art and part guilt. The fact that this makes the commission of the crime easier would appear to be irrelevant. However, if it could be established that the reason for the "omission" was a desire to assist or encourage the commission of the crime, there would not then appear to be any barrier to art and part guilt. There would then be the necessary common purpose. Similarly, if there is a legal duty to intervene, art and part guilt can arise out of a failure to act. In *Bonar and Hogg v. MacLeod*[16] a senior police officer was held to be guilty art and part in an assault on a prisoner by a junior officer which he had done nothing to prevent and from which he had failed to disassociate himself. The position of the senior officer was stated to have been that of an official standing by and allowing a breach of the law.

LIABILITY FOR THE OUTCOME

The essence of art and part guilt is that the accused either execute a common **7–22** plan or demonstrate a spontaneous common purpose. It is necessary to

---

[11] (1854) 1 Irv. 574.
[12] *Quinn v. H.M. Advocate*, 1990 S.C.C.R. 254, *per* Lord Justice-Clerk Ross at p. 260G. See also *Lawler v. Neizer*, 1993 S.C.C.R. 299.
[13] *Jamieson v. Guild*, 1989 S.C.C.R. 583.
[14] (1871) 2 Coup. 334.
[15] *Stillie v. H.M. Advocate*, 1992 S.L.T. 279. See also *White v. MacPhail*, 1990 S.C.C.R. 578.
[16] 1983 S.C.C.R. 161.

establish the presence of concert, either prior to the commission of the crime or through a coming together at the time of the offence. If the prosecution cannot prove concert, then each individual will be liable only to the extent that his own actions can be proved to the satisfaction of the court.[17] An example of this latter situation is provided by *H.M. Advocate v. Welsh and McLachlan*.[18] The two accused were alleged to have broken into a house where one of them (it was not known which) had killed the owner. There was no evidence of a common plan between the accused to use violence, and the violence was both sudden and unexpected. Lord Young directed the jury that each accused could only be held culpable for his own actions. Since it was not known who had killed the victim, both accused were acquitted of homicide.

7–23 The basic difficulty facing the prosecution in a case such as *Welsh and McLachlan* is an evidential one. The result of this case would have been very different had the prosecution been able to prove a common purpose or plan. In that case one could then apply the basic doctrine of art and part guilt that all the accused are regarded as equally liable for the outcome of the criminal conduct. The particular outcome does not have to be intended by the accused before he can be found guilty art and part. Rather, he will be held responsible for any foreseeable consequence. For example, if during the course of an armed robbery of a bank one accused shot and killed an assistant for refusing to hand over any money, on a strict application of art and part guilt the co-accused would be equally guilty of murder. Although the specific killing may not have been planned, it is a foreseeable consequence of an armed robbery. This rule can operate harshly on occasion. The accused can still be convicted as guilty art and part even though he lacks the *mens rea* of the specific crime of murder. This would particularly be the case if he had played only a small part in the criminal enterprise.

Distinguishing between co-accused

7–24 Perhaps it is in order to alleviate the harshness of the doctrine that the courts are sometimes prepared to distinguish between co-accused in apportioning culpability. In fact, it is conceivable that the minor participant in the bank robbery scenario would be convicted of culpable homicide and the actual killer of murder. Both are guilty of homicide, but their culpability could be assessed separately by reference to their respective *mentes reae* at the time of the offence. Authority for this proposition is provided by *Melvin*

---

[17] *Humphries v. H.M Advocate*, 1994 S.C.C.R. 205.
[18] (1897) 5 S.L.T. 137. See also *H.M. Advocate v. Robertson*, (1896) 2 Adam 92; *Docherty v. H.M. Advocate*, 1945 J.C. 89; *Morton v. H.M. Advocate*, 1986 S.L.T. 622, *per* Lord Justice-General Emslie at p. 623C: "It is undoubtedly true that where two people are charged with a crime and there is no concert and there is no evidence as to which of the two committed the critical act then neither can be convicted."

v. H.M. Advocate.[19] The two accused had been charged with robbery and murder, but there was no evidence of antecedent concert. One accused was convicted of murder and the other of culpable homicide. It was held that it was legitimate to assess the degree of recklessness displayed by each of the accused in this way. In *Malone v. H.M. Advocate*[20] this issue arose in the context of an assault committed jointly by the two accused. It was stressed that only striking differences in the conduct of each assailant could justify convicting one accused of culpable homicide and the other of murder.[21] It is thus not necessary in every case where there are two or more accused of murder art and part to charge the jury that it is possible to find one accused guilty of murder and another guilty of culpable homicide.[22]

Foreseeability and the common purpose

An accused will not be held responsible for any conduct on the part of a   **7–25** co-accused which goes unforeseeably outwith the common plan or purpose. In *Welsh and McLachlan*[23] Lord Young made the point that an unexpected attack need not be foreseeable to anyone other than the actual assailant. Thus, if the reason for the shooting in the bank robbery example had been that the assistant was having an affair with the killer's wife, the homicide would then be unrelated to the planned crime and there would be no art and part guilt for the death.

This issue, as to whether the use of a weapon by a co-accused was   **7–26** foreseeable, is not uncommon in cases of alleged art and part guilt in murder.[24] Lord Justice-Clerk Wheatley identified the essential question in *Walker and Raiker v. H.M. Advocate*[25]: did the accused know or should he have known that use of a weapon was involved in the planned crime? Was it within the scope of the common purpose? As was suggested in *Welsh and McLachlan*, if the use of a weapon by one accused is sudden and unexpected, liability for the consequences of its use will not be imposed on a co-accused.

---

[19] 1984 S.L.T. 365.
[20] 1988 S.C.C.R. 498.
[21] It is possible that one accused might be able to avail himself of a defence of provocation (or diminished responsibility) which would warrant a verdict of culpable homicide despite an equal participation in the attack: *Gray v. H.M. Advocate*, 1994 S.L.T. 1237.
[22] *Moir v. H.M. Advocate*, 1993 S.L.T. 1191.
[23] (1897) 5 S.L.T. 137; see para. 7–22, above.
[24] See, for example, *Kiely v. H.M. Advocate*, 1988 S.C.C.R. 120. A related question which can arise is whether the weapon used by the actual perpetrator is of a similar type to that which the accused had contemplated. In *O'Connell v. H.M. Advocate*, 1987 S.C.C.R. 459, the issue was whether a metre long piece of wood was a lethal weapon of a similar nature to a hammer. It was held that this was a question of fact for the jury to determine.
[25] 1985 J.C. 53. See also *Carrick v. H.M. Advocate*, 1990 S.C.C.R. 286; *Robertson v. H.M. Advocate*, 1990 S.C.C.R. 345; *cf. Mathieson v. H.M. Advocate,* 1996 S.C.C.R. 388.

In *Boyne v. H.M. Advocate*,[26] the Appeal Court reiterated the basic principle that to be found guilty art and part the accused would have to know or "have reasonable cause to anticipate" that a weapon might be used on the victim. This issue had to be addressed "from the appellant's state of knowledge about what was going on."[27] In *Brown v. H.M. Advocate*[28] it was stated that a jury was not bound to convict of murder where two accused had been involved art and part in a knife attack on the deceased. In a case where "the murderous act went beyond the common purpose and there was no evidence to show which of the two assailants had used the knife", one could not exclude the possibility that "all that was in contemplation was to use weapons to inflict serious injury" and that the appropriate verdict was culpable homicide.[29] To secure a verdict of guilt of murder art and part, therefore, the prosecution would have had to prove either that the accused intended the death of the victim or had contemplated, as part of the common purpose, an act of the necessary degree of wicked recklessness.

Distributing liability between the parties

7–27　　Thus it is possible for a co-accused to be guilty of a lesser offence than the actual perpetrator of the crime. Does this mean conversely that someone who assists in the commission of a crime can be guilty art and part of a more serious offence than the actual offender, or that he can be convicted if the actual offender is acquitted? The answer to both these questions is a qualified affirmative. It is arguable whether or not there is a conceptual barrier to a conviction for a more serious offence than that of the actual offender. One difficulty can be mentioned at the outset. Art and part guilt can be derived from the commission of a crime, without "direct" involvement in its perpetration. How can it then be possible to be more guilty art and part than the "actual" offender? How can guilt beyond that of the actual perpetrator be acquired by the person who merely assisted him? One view would be that once it has been established that the actual offender caused the *actus reus*, the liability of any other particular accused should be assessed according to his own *mens rea*. Such an approach would appear to be in accord with the decision in *Melvin v. H.M. Advocate*.[30]

---

[26] 1980 S.L.T. 56. In *Docherty v. H.M. Advocate*, 1945 J.C. 89 at p. 96, Lord Moncrieff alluded to "the doctrine that secondary responsibility for a criminal act arises only in cases of reasonable expectation."

[27] 1980 S.L.T 56, *per* Lord Justice-Clerk Wheatley at p. 59. Lord Wheatley also gave the example of an accused who, as a member of a gang, was involved in an attack on a victim. He sees another member of the gang unexpectedly take out a knife and deliver a fatal blow. If the accused then carried on with the attack on the victim that would constitute art and part guilt of murder.

[28] 1993 S.C.C.R. 382.

[29] *ibid. per* Lord Justice-General Hope at p. 392G. See also *Codona v. H.M. Advocate*, 1996 S.C.C.R. 300.

[30] 1984 S.L.T. 365; see para. 7–24, above.

It is debatable how far outside the law of homicide the approach should **7–28** be taken — given that it does appear to represent a departure from the traditional rule of equality of liability for the outcome among the participants. Further, there are obvious limitations to the *Melvin* doctrine. If A instigates B to commit an aggravated assault on C, but B perpetrates a simple assault only, then it would not be possible to convict A of an aggravated assault. This crime has not been committed. A has the appropriate *mens rea*, but there is no *actus reus*. He can only be guilty art and part of the assault which B actually commits. (He would also be guilty of inciting B to commit an aggravated assault.) In the context of homicide, however, it is submitted that the flexible approach does make sense. If unlawful homicide is regarded as a single crime which has two levels of culpability (murder and culpable homicide), then there is no objection in principle to saying that the liability of the aider or instigator should be founded on his own *mens rea*. For example, the accused, assuming that he has the requisite *mens rea* for murder, could instigate a homicide in circumstances where the actual killer is guilty of culpable homicide only. An example would be where the killer is informed by the instigator that if he returns home he will find his wife committing adultery. As is detailed in Chapter 9, it is likely that the husband will have available the partial defence of provocation which will reduce the crime from that of murder to voluntary culpable homicide. However, the instigator acted with deliberation and premeditation and cannot claim to have been provoked. He could be convicted of murder.

Acquittal of the actual offender

Do the same considerations apply where the actual offender is acquitted? **7–29** Does the acquittal mean that there is no crime of which to be art and part guilty? The fact that the principal offender was acquitted does not necessarily mean that the crime in question has not been committed, nor that the accused did not participate. The actual offender may have been acquitted because he was, for example, insane or coerced. In these two instances a crime would have been committed of which one could still be guilty art and part. There are cases, however, where acquittal of the actual offender would be inconsistent with the establishment of art and part guilt. If in a case of a planned rape the accused who actually had sexual intercourse with the complainer was acquitted of rape because the woman had in fact consented, the co-accused who assisted would also be entitled to an acquittal. There would not have been a crime of which to be guilty art and part.

It appears that the mere fact that it would have been legally impossible **7–30** for a particular accused to have committed the crime in his own right is no bar to a conviction for art and part guilt. This point is illustrated by *Vaughan v. H.M. Advocate*.[31] Vaughan had been accused of acting in concert with the

---

[31] 1979 S.L.T. 49.

mother of a small boy in forcing the child to have intercourse with the mother contrary to the Incest Act 1567.[32] The accused was not related to either the mother or the boy. This meant, of course, that he could not himself have committed incest in this instance. The High Court held that he could still be guilty art and part for acting in concert with the co-accused mother in the commission of the offence. In the same way art and part guilt would attach to an unmarried person who assisted a married person to commit bigamy.

Acquittal of joint principal

7–31   The doctrine of art and part guilt is apt to cover the situation where it would perhaps be more accurate to speak in terms of there being more than one principal offender, rather than a single principal offender and a number of lesser participants in the commission of the crime (see para. 7–11, above). In such a case there is no difficulty in convicting one accused while another is acquitted. The explanation might simply be that there is more probative evidence against one party to the joint enterprise than against the other.[33] This situation is illustrated by *Capuano v. H.M. Advocate*.[34] The appellant had been charged with assault through acting along with others. His two co-accused had been acquitted. The appellant's argument was that, since he was charged with being involved as an accessory, he could not be convicted when the others were acquitted. The Appeal Court stated that there was ample evidence of the appellant's participation in the crime and that this was not a case where the conviction depended upon that of the co-accused principal offenders.

Actual offender acquitted because mens rea absent

7–32   The more difficult case arises where the accused is alleged to have participated in some capacity other than that of a joint principal, but the actual offender is acquitted because he lacks the *mens rea* necessary for the crime. Since Scots law purports to draw no distinction between the parties to a crime this point might seem to be irrelevant. It is sometimes argued, however, that in cases of this nature there is no crime of which to be guilty art and part.

7–33   A case at point here is the much discussed decision of the English Court of Appeal in *R. v. Cogan and Leak*.[35] Here Cogan was acquitted of the rape of Leak's wife on the basis that he lacked the necessary *mens rea*. The

---

[32] See now Criminal Law (Consolidation) (Scotland) Act 1995, s.1.
[33] *Low v. H.M. Advocate*, 1994 S.L.T. 227.
[34] 1985 S.L.T. 196. See also *H.M. Advocate v. Camerons* (1911) 6 Adam 456; *Tobin v. H.M. Advocate*, 1934 J.C. 60.
[35] [1976] 1 Q.B. 217.

"crime" had been instigated by Leak, who compelled his wife to have sexual intercourse with Cogan. Leak falsely told Cogan that his wife would agree to the intercourse. Cogan's "mistake" as to the wife's consent negated his *mens rea*. The question arose as to whether Leak could be convicted as an accessory. The court held that he could and offered two explanations why this was so. The first was that Cogan could perhaps be regarded as Leak's innocent agent. Since Leak caused Cogan to misunderstand the situation, he had used Cogan's "body as the instrument for the necessary physical act."[36]

The concept of innocent agency or instrumentality is an accepted principle of criminal law (see para. 4–03, above). The doctrine can be invoked where the accused has, with the requisite *mens rea*, manipulated an insane person or a child below the age of criminal responsibility to commit a crime. It would not be necessary to have resort to the doctrine of art and part guilt. His guilt does not owe anything to the conduct of a co-accused. He will be convicted because he is regarded as directly liable for committing the crime. In crimes such as theft or housebreaking with intent to steal, the acquittal of an innocent agent does not present a barrier to establishing liability.   **7–34**

The difficulty in applying this doctrine to Leak was the then existence in English law of the marital rape exemption.[37] Similar conceptual difficulties would arise where it was a woman who utilised an innocent agent to have non-consensual sexual intercourse with the complainer. She could not commit the crime of rape herself, so how can the existence of an innocent agent make her directly liable?   **7–35**

The court's second explanation was that there was no reason why Leak could not be viewed as Cogan's accomplice. The fact that Cogan was innocent was held not to alter the fact that the victim was raped.[38] That is, the *actus reus* of rape was committed when Leak's wife was forced to have non-consensual sexual intercourse. The argument would appear to be that the crime of rape was committed by Cogan at Leak's instigation and that this crime can then be imputed to Leak. The difficulty with this approach is in being able to say that the crime of rape was committed where the *mens rea* was absent. One of the constituent elements of the crime of rape was lacking. Cogan's behaviour was immoral and reprehensible, but English law did not regard it as a crime. If Cogan did not commit a crime, then how could one say that Leak was engaged in a criminal act with him? How could there be art and part guilt if there was no crime?   **7–36**

---

[36] [1976] 1 Q.B. 277 at p. 223.
[37] Now no longer accepted in either Scotland (see *S. v. H.M. Advocate*, 1989 S.L.T. 469) or England (see *R. v. R.* [1992] 1 A.C. 599).
[38] Likewise, the fact that Leak himself could not rape his wife would not be a barrier to accomplice liability: see para. 7–30, above.

DISSOCIATION

7–37   One final issue to consider in relation to art and part guilt is whether it is ever possible to assist in a criminal endeavour, but then escape liability through abandoning the enterprise and withdrawing. The basic principle here appears to be that art and part guilt can be avoided where an accused has terminated his relationship with the other participants and communicated this fact to them. If an accused can bring forward evidence of dissociation then this will go to the issue of whether he was in fact acting in concert; that is, whether the prosecution has established art and part guilt. As Lord Justice-General Emslie said in *MacNeil v. H.M. Advocate*[39]: "evidence of 'dissociation' by a participant in the preparation of a crime or offence in contemplation will be highly relevant in any decision as to whether he can be held to be in concert with those who proceed to commit it".

7–38   To accord legal recognition to the existence of dissociation is only sensible. To hold otherwise might deter people from withdrawing from a criminal enterprise and be taken to indicate that there was no point in doing so.

CONSPIRACY

Legal definition

7–39   The definition of conspiracy which has been adopted by the Scottish courts is that of Viscount Simon L.C., in the civil case of *Crofter Hand Woven Harris Tweed Co. Ltd v. Veitch*[40]: "Conspiracy ... is the agreement of two or more persons to effect any unlawful purpose, whether as their ultimate aim, or only as a means to it, and the crime is complete if there is such agreement, even though nothing is done in pursuance of it." The one necessary amendment to this definition is that the word "unlawful" should be read as "criminal": a conspiracy "is constituted by [an] agreement ... to further or achieve a criminal purpose."[41] In *Maxwell v. H.M. Advocate* Lord Cameron went on to define a criminal purpose as "one which if attempted or achieved by action on the part of an individual would itself constitute a crime by the law of Scotland."[42] This means that before a conspiracy can be classified as criminal its purpose necessarily would have had to have been criminal if done by one person.

7–40   It should be stressed that unless the prosecution can prove the existence of an agreement, there cannot be a conviction for conspiracy. There must

---

[39]   1986 J.C. 146 at p. 159.
[40]   1942 S.C. (H.L.) 1 at p. 5.
[41]   *Maxwell v. H.M. Advocate*, 1980 J.C. 40, *per* Lord Cameron at p. 43.
[42]   *ibid.*

be actual agreement. As is the case with instigation as a basis for art and part guilt, matters must go beyond simply putting a suggestion to someone with a view to further discussing the issue and maybe reaching agreement in the future. That would not constitute a conspiracy; there being no "meeting of minds". Rather, it might be an attempted conspiracy or incitement (see para. 7–62, following).

FORMS OF CONSPIRACY

It is possible that the members of an alleged conspiracy actually might **7–41** have met together to agree their plan, but this is not essential to the establishment of conspiratorial liability. Conspiracies can take a variety of other forms. In particular, it is not necessary for every member of a conspiracy to be aware of the existence of every other member.

Chain conspiracies

A "chain" conspiracy can arise where A agrees with B who agrees with **7–42** C and so on. The fact that A is unaware of C's involvement is no bar to saying that they, along with B, are parties to the same conspiracy. The difficulty raised for the prosecution by this type of conspiracy is as to how the individuals in the chain can properly be linked together, particularly where there is a large number of links.

Wheel conspiracies

A conspiracy can also take the form of a wheel. This occurs where there **7–43** are a number of parties who each agree with one central ringleader who forms the "hub" of the wheel. Each agreement between the hub and a party to the conspiracy forms a "spoke". For the wheel conspiracy fully to take shape, however, the prosecution would need to be able to establish the existence of a "rim" around the wheel. This is essential to proving the existence of one large, single conspiracy. If there is no rim, then there are simply a number of conspiracies to which the hub is a party: there are as many conspiracies as there are spokes in the wheel.

CONTROVERSIAL NATURE OF CONSPIRACY

From a prosecution perspective, conspiracy can be a useful way of dealing **7–44** with behaviour considered to be dangerous or undesirable, but which does not constitute a complete or even an attempted crime. Despite this apparent utility to prosecutors, the crime of conspiracy remains controversial. It has long created unease among many observers of the criminal process.

From a defence perspective, the crime of conspiracy is problematic. It **7–45** can be used to penalise conduct which is extremely precursory to the perpetration of the *actus reus* of a complete crime. Further, the crime lays stress upon the mental state of the accused in that the crucial issue is whether there was an agreement between the parties to the alleged conspiracy. There is comparatively little emphasis upon the conduct of an accused. This heightens the danger that an accused will be penalised not for what he himself did, but for consorting with other people who are much more intimately involved in the "conspiracy". The criminal law should be scrupulous in seeking to avoid guilt by association or guilt by confusion; an unscrupulous prosecutor could use conspiracy as a catch-all charge.

PROVING THE CONSPIRATORIAL AGREEMENT

7–46   Proof of the agreement essential to a criminal conspiracy will generally be inferential. Sometimes overt acts will have been committed by some or all of the accused, but this will not always be the case. But even if there have been some such overt acts, the existence of *mens rea*, in the form of an agreement and commitment to the criminal purpose of the conspiracy, will have to be proved by inference. For example, if a group of men is apprehended wearing masks and carrying weapons while sitting in a car outside a bank, there is a clear inference to be drawn that there is an agreement to rob the bank. The group is unlikely to be there for any other purpose!

7–47   Lord Justice-Clerk Grant pointed out to the jury in *H.M. Advocate v. Wilson, Latta and Rooney*[43]:

> "[Y]ou won't often get eye-witnesses of the agreement being made or eavesdroppers who actually heard it being made. Accordingly, in many cases it is a question of judging from the acts of the alleged conspirators whether in fact there was a conspiracy between them in pursuance of which they are acting."

The evidence derived from such a decisional process will not always be as unambiguous as the example in the previous paragraph. An individual who may appear at an early stage of the "conspiracy" to be involved might not be firmly committed and might well have ceased to play any part before the complete crime is committed. This problem is raised in a crucial form by the absence of any requirement of proximity such as is to be found in the law of attempt.

7–48   The cynical view of proof in conspiracy cases would be that the apparent difficulty in proving the agreement is to the advantage of a prosecutor. There is the danger that in stressing to the jury that a conspiracy can be proved inferentially, the judge may neglect to emphasise the necessity of proof *per se*.

---

[43] 1968, unreported, but see Gane and Stoddart, *Casebook on Scottish Criminal Law*, p. 203.

A RATIONALE FOR THE CRIME OF CONSPIRACY?

It is possible to identify two main justifications for criminalising **7–49** conspiracies. The first is that recognition of the crime of conspiracy can serve as an instrument to prevent the commission of crimes. Conspiracy, like attempt, is an "inchoate" or incomplete crime. All that is required to constitute a conspiracy is an agreement. It is not necessary to have done anything in pursuance of it. This means that the law relating to conspiracy becomes operative at an earlier stage than the law of attempt. The agencies of law enforcement are thereby given the opportunity to intervene at an earlier stage than would otherwise be the case. In this sense the criminalisation of conspiracies is justified as a back-up to the law of attempt. The intervention of the criminal law is justified by the fact of the agreement to commit a crime. This agreement and consequent commitment to the criminal enterprise is regarded as sufficient evidence of the threat posed by the accused.

The second justification is concerned with the special dangers which **7–50** are perceived to attend criminal conduct by a group. The rationale here is similar to that underlying art and part guilt. The premise is that a conspiracy poses a greater threat to law and order than a number of individuals working alone. There are various aspects to this perceived dangerousness. If there is a conspiracy, then it would appear to be more likely that the proposed crime will be committed. Even if one individual reneges on the agreement, his co-conspirators can still continue. Psychological factors relating to the nature of groups may make it more likely that the criminal purpose will be achieved. The co-conspirators will provide one another with mutual support and loyalty. Most conspiracies do lead to the commission of the planned crime.

RELATIONSHIP WITH ART AND PART GUILT

In addition to constituting a crime in its own right, conspiracy can provide **7–51** a method of holding one member of a criminal group accountable for the actions of his co-accused. As Lord Justice-Clerk Grant expressed it in *Wilson, Latta and Rooney*[44]: "Normally a man is responsible only for what he himself does, but if he is involved in a conspiracy he may be responsible not only for what he himself does but for what his fellow-conspirators do." That is, a conspiracy can provide the basis for establishing art and part guilt. To give an example: two accused agree together that a particular individual should be murdered. This agreement in itself makes them guilty of conspiracy. If one accused then goes on to perpetrate the killing, the

---

[44] See para. 7–47, above.

conspiratorial agreement can form the basis for holding the other accused guilty art and part of the murder.

7–52   However, art and part guilt can arise without there being a conspiracy. To return to the example of the bank robbery: if a customer were spontaneously to come to the assistance of the robber, there would be art and part guilt. There would not be a conspiracy because there was no agreement between the two individuals. In many instances of art and part guilt, however, there will be sufficient evidence from which to infer the existence of a conspiratorial agreement. An example would be the supplier of a weapon used in the course of the robbery.

Conspiracy in Practice

7–53   The basic legal concept underlying a criminal conspiracy is straightforward, but this does not mean that there are no difficulties in practice. In practical terms, an obvious problem is that caused by a trial involving a potentially large number of accused, each with individual legal representation. The most significant difficulty, however, is caused by the tendency to have over-long and complex indictments. Even a cursory examination of the reported cases in this area of law will show the reader this much.

Agreement pursued by specific crimes

7–54   One category of conspiracy is where specific crimes have been carried out in pursuance of the agreement. The case of *Wilson, Latta and Rooney*[45] provides an example. The indictment contained libels of a conspiracy to pervert the course of justice and the commission of subornation and attempted subornation in pursuance of the conspiracy. The jury was informed that it was still possible to convict of subornation, even if there was an acquittal in relation to the conspiracy.

Agreement pursued by criminal means

7–55   Conspiracy indictments sometimes do not set out any specific crime by means of which the agreement was to be carried out. Rather than charging a specific crime, the indictment will state that the conspiracy was to be effected by "criminal" or "violent" means. An example is provided in the unreported case of *H.M. Advocate v. Walsh*.[46] The charge here was of conspiring to further the purposes of the IRA "by the unlawful use of force and violence ... for the purpose of endangering ... lives ... and destroying property."

---

[45] See para. 7–47, above.
[46] 1921, unreported. Discussed by Gordon, *Criminal Law,* para. 6–62.

If the indictment libels a conspiracy to achieve some purpose by criminal **7–56** means, then the prosecution will have to prove the criminal means. This point was made clear in *Sayers v. H.M. Advocate.*[47] The indictment charged a conspiracy to further the purposes of the Ulster Volunteer Force by criminal means. Sayers was found guilty by the jury, but under deletion of the criminal means detailed in the indictment. On appeal, it was held that there was inadequate specification and that the charge of which Sayers had been found guilty was therefore irrelevant. The crime of conspiracy could not be established in the absence of specification of the alleged criminal means.

Conspiracy and non-proximate preparations

A charge of conspiracy can be utilised as a substitute for one of attempt; **7–57** where there has been an agreement to commit the crime, but the accused has not moved sufficiently far towards perpetration to constitute an attempt. An example of this type of conspiracy charge is provided by *West v. H.M. Advocate,*[48] which concerned a conspiracy to assault and rob people employed in particular premises. The charge was that in furtherance of a conspiracy the accused

> "[D]id loiter in the vicinity of said premises ... and thereafter enter said premises while ... in possession of a blade from a pair of scissors, and ... in possession of an open razor, all with intent to assault said employees with said weapons and rob them of money."

On appeal, it was held that there was sufficient evidence from which the existence of a conspiracy could be inferred.

Impossibility

If the factory outside which the appellant in *West v. H.M. Advocate* was **7–58** apprehended had in fact been deserted, would the "impossibility" of carrying out the agreed crime have afforded a defence? This issue of impossibility in relation to inchoate crimes was addressed in detail in the previous chapter on attempt and the reader is referred to that discussion for a consideration of the theoretical issues. It is not proposed to repeat in substance what was said there. The same conceptual problems which arise in relation to attempting to do the impossible appear also in conspiracy.

In conspiracy, as in attempt, it is difficult to see why mere factual **7–59** impossibility should afford a defence. It should not be relevant to the question of conspiratorial liability that the agreement to carry out the robbery could not be fulfilled because of a mistake in the planning. This appears to have

---

[47] 1982 J.C. 17.
[48] 1985 S.C.C.R. 248.

been the approach taken in the case of *Maxwell v. H.M. Advocate*.[49] Here Lord Cameron stressed that since a conspiracy is an agreement to achieve a criminal purpose, it is the criminality of the purpose and not the result which makes the agreement criminal.

7–60 As in the law of attempt, the picture becomes murkier if one introduces the concept of legal impossibility. An alternative view to that expressed in *Maxwell* could be that, since conspiracy involves an agreement to commit a criminal act, the impossibility of breaking the law should be relevant to the question of criminal responsibility. On the other hand, it is difficult to see why different approaches should be adopted in conspiracy and attempt: impossibility should be (un)available as a defence to the same extent in both inchoate crimes.

Withdrawal as a defence?

7–61 The crime of conspiracy is committed the moment that the agreement is made. This means that there is no such thing in legal terms as "withdrawal" from a conspiracy. But if an accused had signalled his dissociation from the purpose of the conspiracy, this could serve to relieve him of art and part guilt for the subsequent commission of the completed crime by his co-conspirators (see para. 7–37, above).

INCITEMENT

ATTEMPTED CONSPIRACY

7–62 It is a crime to attempt to form a conspiracy. The crime is known as incitement. It is committed where the accused has approached another person and invited him to participate in the perpetration of a crime.[50] An example of an appropriate libel in an indictment might be that of an "attempt by A to induce B to enter the conspiracy and incite him to assist in carrying out a robbery". The crime is complete as soon as the incitement occurs. The law does not insist upon any further action towards committing the *actus reus*. The requisite *mens rea* is that the incitement be motivated by an intention that the party incited commit the relevant crime.

RELATIONSHIP WITH ART AND PART GUILT AND CONSPIRACY

7–63 As in the case with conspiracy, incitement is not only a crime in its own right, but can provide a foundation for art and part guilt. Incitement is one

---

[49] 1980 J.C. 40.
[50] See *H.M. Advocate v. Tannahill and Neilson*, 1943 J.C. 50, and *Morton v. Henderson*, 1956 J.C. 55.

of the ways in which an individual can participate in and assist the commission of a crime. Thereafter he can be called to account for the criminal act (see para. 7–14, above). To give an example: A incites B to murder C. At this stage A is guilty of the crime of incitement. If B does kill C, then A is guilty art and part of the murder. A will not be convicted of incitement, because this crime merges with his art and part guilt for murder. If the murder bid failed, then the incitement would similarly merge with the attempted murder.

In this example, of course, there is an intermediate stage of conspiracy **7–64** when B agrees to A's suggestion. Again, if the murder is perpetrated, this would be treated as a basis for establishing art and part guilt, rather than a crime in its own right. A conspiracy charge would only become appropriate if B agreed to the proposal, but failed to carry it into effect.

POLICY ARGUMENTS

The crime of incitement permits the application of criminal liability at a **7–65** much earlier stage than the law of attempt or the crime of conspiracy. If the accused has invited another to commit a crime, that is sufficient in itself. There is no requirement of agreement and none of moving towards the perpetration of the proposed crime. One argument would be that the crime of incitement is directed at behaviour too remote from the actual commission of the *actus reus*. If A incites B to commit a particular crime, he hopes that B will enter a conspiratorial agreement to commit the crime. Assuming that B agrees, the crime of conspiracy is committed. However, there is no requirement that the proposed conspiracy be proximate even to an attempt to commit the crime which the inciter originally had in mind. Thus one view could be that incitement is an excessively inchoate crime and penalises behaviour which is too preparatory to the commission of the intended crime.

The justification for criminalising the act of incitement is largely the **7–66** same as that for a completed conspiracy. Incitement is regarded as worthy of punishment because it is an attempt to form a conspiracy; conduct which is regarded as sufficiently dangerous in itself to justify the intervention of the criminal law. Particular dangers are seen to flow from the agreement of a number of individuals to commit a crime (see para. 7–50, above). A further rationale is that of protecting the individual who is incited from corruption.

Further reading

Ferguson, P., "Art and part guilt and the 'defence' of dissociation," 1987 J.R. 131.
Forensis, "The Logic of Art and Part Guilt," (1985) 30 J.L.S.S. 230.
Kadish, S., "Complicity, Cause and Blame," in *Blame and Punishment: Essays in the Criminal Law* (1987), Chap. 5.

Katz, L., *Bad Acts and Guilty Minds* (1987), Chap. 5.

Scottish Law Commission, *Art and Part Guilt of Statutory Offences* (Consultation Paper, 1984).

Scottish Law Commission, *Criminal Law — Art and Part Guilt of Statutory Offences* (Scot. Law Com. No. 93, 1985).

CHAPTER 8

DEFENCES

INTRODUCTION

This chapter discusses a wide range of defences which an accused can plead **8–01** in a criminal case. The accused's interest in raising a legally recognised defence is that it can serve either to elide criminal liability altogether or to diminish the seriousness of the crime for which he is convicted. The most significant of this latter category of "partial" defences are diminished responsibility and provocation, which can, for example, operate to reduce the accused's culpability from murder to (voluntary) culpable homicide. These pleas are discussed in the contexts of assault and homicide in Chapter 9.

DEFENCES IN PRACTICE

It is possible to identify two principal ways in which defences can operate. **8–02** First, some defences represent an effort by the accused to raise a reasonable doubt concerning a material element of the prosecution's case. Examples would include the defence of mistake of fact, which negates the *mens rea* of the crime, and the defence of alibi, which establishes that the accused could not have perpetrated the *actus reus* of the crime. These can be described as "failure of proof" defences. They do not provide a ground of defence independent of the definition of the crime. A failure of proof defence is the absence of one or more of the requisite elements of the crime. Secondly, there are those defences which result in the acquittal of the accused even though the prosecution has proved each element in the definition of the crime. Examples of this type of defence include self-defence, coercion and necessity.

Justifications

Some defences — notably self-defence — amount to a justification for **8–03** the accused's conduct. The essence of a justification defence is that it renders a notional infringement of the criminal law lawful. According to Hart,[1] a

---

[1] *Punishment and Responsibility* (1968), p. 13.

justified act is one that "the law does not condemn, or even welcomes". The accused who raises a justification defence claims that he has done nothing wrongful for which he should be punished. For example, if A kills B in self-defence, this act is justified. A may have perpetrated the *actus reus* of unlawful homicide, but, because of the fact that A acted to counter unjustified and life-threatening aggression from B, his use of fatal force becomes justified. The act of killing B is permitted by the criminal law.

Excuses

8–04   An excuse defence exculpates the accused who has satisfied all the elements of a crime but who, because of some excusing condition, cannot be regarded as responsible for his actions. The basic distinction between a justification and an excuse is that the former focuses upon the *conduct* of the accused, whereas the latter concentrates upon his *responsibility*. Unlike a justification, an excuse does not render conduct lawful and proper. An excuse negates the accused's personal responsibility for violating the criminal law. Excuses are recognised by the criminal law in circumstances where an accused has perpetrated an unjustifiable act, but cannot be regarded as morally blameworthy. The accused who pleads the defence of involuntary intoxication to a charge of murder does not claim that the killing was justifiable. His contention is that he should not be regarded as morally blameworthy, and should therefore be excused from criminal responsibility.

MITIGATING CIRCUMSTANCES

Plea in mitigation

8–05   Even if an accused cannot avail himself of a legally recognised defence, he can always ask a court to take what he claims to be mitigating circumstances into account. The fact that he does not fulfil the legal requirements of a defence does not mean that the accused will not be able to persuade a court to impose a lesser punishment upon conviction than would normally be the case. As was stressed in *Falconer v. Jessop*,[2] "one of the rights which an accused person has is to speak in mitigation before sentence is passed."

Evidence of mitigating circumstances

8–06   Further, an accused is entitled to introduce evidence of mitigating circumstances in the course of his trial. This is the case irrespective of the

---

[2]   1975 S.L.T. (Notes) 78.

irrelevance of the evidence as a defence. In *Clark v. H.M. Advocate*[3] Lord Walker stated that "an accused person is entitled as of right to lay before the jury all evidence which might properly induce them to commend him to leniency in the event of his being held guilty." Thus, an accused who wishes to argue that his conduct was not wholly voluntary, but is unable to meet the strict legal test of involuntariness, might be able to lead the self-same evidence at his trial by way of mitigation.[4] Likewise, an accused who is unable to establish a defence of necessity (see para. 8–88, following) may be able to persuade a court that the special circumstances which led to the commission of the crime indicate that a less severe sentence would be appropriate.[5]

SPECIAL DEFENCES

Procedure

"Special defence" is a procedural term of art in Scots law. It refers to certain defences which an accused is not allowed to state unless a written plea has been lodged at least 10 clear days before the trial (where the accused is cited for trial before a High Court), or at or before the first diet (where the accused is cited for trial before a sheriff-and-jury court), except where he is able to satisfy the court that there was cause for his not having done so.[6] There is no definitive list of special defences, but one can identify four generally accepted ones: (1) alibi; (2) incrimination; (3) insanity; and (4) self-defence. **8–07**

The features common to these special defences are those described by Lord Walker in *Adam v. MacNeill*[7]: "Generally speaking, a special defence is one which puts in issue a fact (1) which is not referred to in the libel, and (2) which, if established, necessarily results in acquittal of the accused." There are other defences, most notably accident, error and necessity, which could lead to the acquittal of the accused, but notice need not be given except in the case of the four recognised special defences and the two (coercion and automatism) treated as if they were special.[8] The category of special defences is not an exclusive one in the sense that they are the only defences which can lead to an acquittal. It is a concept of procedural rather than substantive law. **8–08**

---

[3] 1968 J.C. 53 at p. 58.

[4] See paras. 4–19 and 4–31, above; *H.M. Advocate v. Murray,* 1969 S.L.T. (Notes) 85.

[5] See *Morrison v. Valentine,* 1990 S.C.C.R. 692; *Graham v. Annan,* 1980 S.L.T. 28.

[6] Criminal Procedure (Scotland) Act 1995, s.78(1), (3). First diets apply only to sheriff court proceedings: ss.66(6), 71.

[7] 1972 J.C. 1 at p. 5.

[8] Criminal Procedure (Scotland) Act 1995, s.78(2).

ALIBI

8–09   The defence of alibi is quite simply that at the time when the crime is alleged
to have been committed, the accused was not at the place libelled. In order
to be relevant, the special defence lodged as the foundation for the plea of
alibi must be definite.[9] It must specify the place where the accused alleges
that he was, and at what time.

INCRIMINATION

8–10   The defence of incrimination (otherwise known as impeachment) is that
the crime was not committed by the accused but by another person, named
if known. It is not a special defence where the accused utilises a "cut-throat"
defence and incriminates his co-accused, but the same statutory requirement
that notice of intention to lead such evidence be lodged is applicable.

INSANITY

8–11   If the accused was insane at the time of committing the crime charged, he is
entitled to an acquittal. The effect of this defence is that even if the accused
did commit the crime, his insanity relieves him of responsibility for his
actions and he cannot be convicted. In effect, the *actus reus* is admitted but
mens rea is denied. The fact that an accused is found not guilty by reason of
insanity does not mean, however, that he has to be released. An accused
who pleads successfully the special defence of insanity under solemn
procedure will have his case disposed of in terms of statutory provisions
under which he can be ordered to be detained in a mental hospital without
limit of time.[10] Indeed, it is possible for an accused who has been acquitted
on the grounds of insanity to lose his liberty for as long as, or even longer
than, if he had been convicted and sentenced to imprisonment. In this context
insanity would not be operating as a defence in the traditional sense; rather,
it would serve as a mechanism for activating the (potentially indefinite)
confinement of a person who is considered to be a danger to society.

8–12   Attitudes to the insanity defence tend to be ambivalent. The Scottish
legal system attaches great significance to the principle that an accused
should only be regarded as criminally liable when his conduct can be
regarded as that of a responsible actor. If an accused can establish that this
necessary element of rationality did not characterise his conduct by virtue

---

[9]   See *H.M. Advocate v. Laing and Others* (1871) 2 Coup. 23.
[10] Criminal Procedure (Scotland) Act 1995, ss.54(6), 57(1)(a) and (2). Notice that a court has
a range of disposals which are open to it in such a case, but that an acquittal of murder on
the ground of insanity must be followed by a mental hospital detention order, whereunder
the person in question is subject to special restrictions without limit of time: s.57(3).

of his insanity at the time of committing the crime, then he should not be regarded as blameworthy. On the other hand, when the insanity defence is raised it tends to be in a well-publicised and particularly horrific case. It is possible that the desire to punish a wrongdoer may take precedence over the view that punishment of the mentally ill is inappropriate.

Legal and clinical insanity

It is important to emphasise at the outset that insanity is a purely legal concept. It is not a clinical term derived from psychiatry or psychology. Insanity is not synonymous with any medical conception of mental disorder. In *Brennan v. H.M. Advocate*,[11] Lord Justice-General Emslie stated that the legal meaning to be attributed to the concept of insanity for the purposes of the special defence was not "to be resolved upon medical opinion for the time being". His Lordship's view was: "It is, on the contrary, a question which has to be resolved by the law itself as a matter of legal policy in order to set, in the public interest, acceptable limits upon the circumstances in which any person may be able to relieve himself of criminal responsibility."[12]   **8–13**

In this sentence Lord Emslie identifies the practical as well as legal problem in cases where the special defence of insanity is raised. Should the conduct of the accused be excused because of his mental state at the time of an otherwise criminal act? How is the availability of such a defence to be evaluated?   **8–14**

The alienation of reason test

The test applied by the Scottish courts is derived from Hume,[13] who stated: **8–15**

> "To serve the purpose of a defence in law, the disorder must ... amount to an absolute alienation of reason, ... such a disease as deprives the patient of the knowledge of the true aspect and position of things about him, — hinders him from distinguishing friend or foe, — and gives him up to the impulse of his own distempered fancy."

Hume's approach to insanity was approved in *Brennan* and in *Cardle v. Mulrainey*.[14] In *Brennan*, Lord Emslie restated the import of Hume's definition in the following terms: "In short, insanity in our law requires proof of total alienation of reason in relation to the act charged as the result   **8–16**

---

[11] 1977 J.C. 38 at p. 42.
[12] *ibid.* pp. 42–43.
[13] i, 37.
[14] 1992 S.L.T. 1152.

of mental illness, mental disease or defect or unsoundness of mind".[15] This requirement of "a total alienation of the accused's mental faculties of reasoning and of understanding what he is doing" was reiterated by Lord Justice-General Hope in *Cardle v. Mulrainey*.[16] His Lordship explained that if "the accused knew what he was doing and was aware of the nature and quality of his acts and that what he was doing was wrong",[17] the requisite degree of alienation of reason had not been present.

8–17   The issue as to whether the accused's reason was alienated in relation to the crime in question is one for the jury to determine in the light of the evidence and their common sense. In the terms used by Lord Strachan in *H.M. Advocate v. Kidd*, "it is to be judged on the ordinary rules on which men act in daily life."[18] The jurors are the arbiters of insanity. They can take account of any medical evidence given by expert witnesses, but such evidence is not conclusive. The significance of medical evidence is severely limited by the fact that insanity is a legal rather than medical concept. Further, a medical witness can only speculate as to the accused's state of mind at the time of a crime, since the information upon which his judgment is based will have been obtained subsequent to the crime being committed.

"Temporary madness"

8–18   Hume[19] states that

> "although the distemper must ... be absolute in degree, it is not indispensable that it be also continual in respect of time ... [w]hether his malady is constant and unremitting, or only returns at intervals, still his defence shall be equally available, if he was then ... void of reason."

However, as is described subsequently in this chapter, voluntary intoxication can never amount to "temporary madness" sufficient to found the special defence of insanity (see para. 8–72, following).

SELF-DEFENCE

8–19   If an action is done in self-defence it is not criminal. A special defence is available to an accused whose otherwise criminal use of physical force

---

[15]   1977 J.C. 38 at p. 45.
[16]   1992 S.L.T. 1152 at p. 1160E–F.
[17]   *ibid.* D–E. This clarification was made in the context of the defence of non-insane automatism, but it seems clear that the Lord Justice-General saw it as equally applicable to insanity. The phraseology is reminiscent of the English law, founded upon *M'Naghten's Case* (1843) 10 C. & F. 200.
[18]   1960 J.C. 61 at p. 70.
[19]   i, 39.

against the complainer (or deceased) is justifiable because it was necessary to protect himself (or a third party) from an apparent threat of attack by the complainer. Since the defence is premised on the fact that the accused did commit the actions libelled by the prosecution, to be relevantly pled as a special defence the accused will have to admit that he perpetrated the acts libelled, albeit that he claims to have been justified in so acting.[20]

It is possible to identify two principal situations where a plea of self-defence can arise. The first is where it is pled by an accused charged with murder or a related crime such as attempted murder or assault to the danger of life. Secondly, the accused charged with a non-aggravated assault may claim to have been justified in utilising a lesser, non-fatal degree of force. As might be expected, most of the relevant authorities concern the application of the defence in homicide prosecutions. The ensuing discussion reflects this emphasis and is concerned principally with the use of a fatal degree of force in self-defence. The problem which the law has to confront is that of drawing an appropriate line between the state's obligation to protect its citizens and the individual's right to use deadly force to repel an aggressor.[21]

8–20

The rules of self-defence

Since a killing perpetrated in self-defence is not criminal, the parameters of this special defence are severely restricted. There are three conditions which have to be met before an accused can avail himself of the defence. The classic formulation of these requirements is to be found in Lord Keith's charge to the jury in *H.M. Advocate v. Doherty*[22]: (i) "there must be imminent danger to the life or limb of the accused"; (ii) "the retaliation that he uses in the face of this danger must be necessary for his own safety"; and (iii) "if the person assaulted has means of escape or retreat, he is bound to use them."

8–21

Imminency requirement

Unless the threat is imminent, self-defence does not act as a justification. This notion of imminence connotes that unless the accused had acted against his assailant, the assault would have occurred immediately. The conduct of the accused would not fulfil the legal requirement if the assailant had threatened to put his life at risk on some subsequent occasion.

8–22

---

[20] See *H.M. Advocate v. McGlone*, 1955 J.C. 14.
[21] Fletcher, *A Crime of Self-Defence* (1987), p. 18.
[22] 1954 J.C. 1 at pp. 4–5.

Necessity and proportionality

8–23   The second rule of self-defence has two elements to it: the force must be both necessary in the circumstances and proportional to the threat which is being combatted. The moral basis of the common law's approach to self-defence is that human life, including that of an assailant, should not be taken unnecessarily. This means that an accused is not justified in killing an assailant where a non-fatal response would be sufficient to counter the attack. One might say, for example, that, if there is an attempt to stab the accused by an elderly and infirm assailant, it would not be justifiable for the accused to kill in self-defence if he knows that he can avoid his own death by disarming the assailant.

8–24   This example illustrates the requirement that the degree of force used in retaliation by the accused must not be disproportional: it must not exceed what is reasonably necessary in the circumstances. This rule is subject to the clarification which follows, since the courts do not weigh the matter too finely. In *Doherty* Lord Keith told the jury: "You do not need an exact proportion of injury and retaliation; it is not a matter that you weigh in too fine scales ... Some allowance must be made for the excitement or the state of fear or the heat of blood at the moment of the man who is attacked".[23] According to Hume[24]: "In deciding on pleas of this sort the judge will not insist on an exact proportion of injury and retaliation, but rather be disposed to sustain the defence unless the [accused] has been transported to acts of great cruelty or great excess."

8–25   What is necessary in any particular case is a matter for the jury to decide on the evidence, but it will be directed that the benefit of the defence is lost where the force used to counter the attack is excessive. As Lord Cameron observed in *Fenning v. H.M. Advocate*[25]: "[T]he protection which the law affords to the victim of an attack is not a licence to use force grossly in excess of that necessary to defend himself. ... This is the foundation upon which the plea itself is based."

8–26   In *Doherty* Lord Keith emphasised that the jury had "to consider the question of proportion between the attack made and the retaliation offered."[26] The nature of the attack which is being countered is of particular relevance in determining the proportionality or otherwise of the degree of retaliatory force used by the accused. The law appears to be that an accused can never be justified in using fatal force to combat what he knows to be a non-fatal attack, even if the only means of countering the attack is to kill the assailant.[27]

---

[23] 1954 J.C. 1 at pp.4–5.
[24] i, 335.
[25] 1985 J.C. 76 at p. 81.
[26] 1954 J.C. 1 at p. 5.
[27] The one exception to this strict rule appears to be in the case of rape; see para. 8–39, following.

In *McCluskey v. H.M. Advocate*,[28] Lord Strachan stated: "Speaking generally, homicide will not be justified by self-defence unless it is committed of necessity in the just apprehension on the part of the killer that he cannot otherwise save his own life." In *Doherty* Lord Keith gave the following example: "[i]f a man was struck a blow by another man with the fist, that could not justify retaliation by the use of a knife, because there is no real proportion at all between a blow with a fist and retaliation by a knife".[29]

In *McCluskey* the accused was charged with murder. He claimed that the killing arose out of his defending himself from an attempt by the deceased to commit sodomy upon him. Lord Strachan, the trial judge, refused to charge the jury that if they believed the accused's story they could acquit on the basis of self-defence. In the event, he was convicted of culpable homicide. On appeal, the court stressed danger to life as a necessary condition to a successful plea. Lord Justice General-Clyde was firmly of the opinion that there could be "no justification at all for extending this defence to a case where there is no apprehension of danger to the accused's life ... but merely a threat ... of an attack on the appellant's virtue."[30] *McCluskey* was followed in *Elliott v. H.M. Advocate*,[31] where the evidence was that the accused had killed not in fear of his life, but in fear that he would be subjected to homosexual assaults. The trial judge's withdrawal of the plea of self-defence from the jury was upheld on appeal. **8–27**

The duty to retreat

If there are means of escape from the attack available, then there is an obligation to use them. There is a duty to retreat rather than use fatal force against the assailant. The proviso to this rule is that it should be a safe avenue of retreat. Hume[32] points out that, "though the party ought to retire from the assault, yet this is always said under provision, that he can do so without materially increasing his own danger, or putting himself to an evident disadvantage with respect to his defence." **8–28**

The rationale for this rule is that it is consistent with the general principle that, out of proper respect for the value of human life, fatal force should not be inflicted other than when absolutely necessary. Imposing a duty to withdraw does not increase the risk of harm to the victim of an attack, because, as the quotation from Hume suggests, retreat is not insisted upon where it might place the would-be self-defender in danger. **8–29**

---

[28] 1959 J.C. 39 at p. 40.
[29] 1954 J.C. 1 at p. 5. See also *Moore v. MacDougall*, 1989 S.C.C.R. 659.
[30] 1959 J.C. 39 at p. 42.
[31] 1987 S.C.C.R. 278.
[32] i, 229.

The self-defender's belief

8–30   Where there has been an apprehension of danger by an accused, a plea of self-defence is not necessarily defeated by the fact that he was in error. The availability of the special defence is based on reasonable appearances rather than objective reality. An accused is justified in using fatal force in self-defence where he reasonably believes that his assailant poses an imminent danger to his life and that fatal force is necessary to protect himself. Self-defence is permissible where the accused makes a reasonable error of fact regarding the material conditions of the defence. In *Owens v. H.M. Advocate*[33] Lord Justice-General Normand stated:

> "[S]elf-defence is made out when it is established to the satisfaction of the jury that the [accused] believed that he was in imminent danger and that he held that belief on reasonable grounds. Grounds for such belief may exist though they are founded on a genuine mistake of fact."

This statement of law was affirmed in *Jones v. H.M. Advocate*.[34] Lord Justice-Clerk Ross observed: "The question is whether the assault by the appellant was justified, and whether the evidence discloses that what he did was for his own safety in order to ward off danger actually threatened or which he reasonably *apprehended* was threatened."[35]

8–31   In *Crawford v. H.M. Advocate*,[36] Lord Justice-General Cooper emphasised that, "when self-defence is supported by a mistaken belief rested on reasonable grounds, that mistaken belief must have an objective background and must not be purely subjective or of the nature of a hallucination." This issue as to the reasonableness or otherwise of a would-be self-defender's error is discussed further in the subsequent account of error of fact (see paras. 8–57, 8–61 and 8–62, following).

Defence of others

8–32   The special defence extends to the use of reasonable force to protect another person from an unjustified attack. Lord Wheatley stated in *H.M. Advocate v. Carson*[37]: "If a man sees another man being unlawfully attacked, he is entitled to stop that unlawful attack." Where the accused has come to the assistance of a third party, the defence will be available even though he need not have become involved and could have retreated from the situation.[38]

---

[33] 1946 J.C. 119 at p. 125.
[34] 1990 J.C. 160.
[35] *ibid.* p. 172 (emphasis added).
[36] 1950 J.C. 67 at p. 71.
[37] 1964 S.L.T. 21.
[38] *Fitzpatrick v. H.M. Advocate*, 1992 S.L.T. 796.

Self-generated self-defence

It seems unlikely that a self-generated necessity to kill could support a   **8–33**
claim of self-defence. If A picks a fight with B and threatens to kill him, he
is not justified in killing B if the latter responds to A's original attack by
attacking him. One cannot say, however, that a person who starts a fight
can never plead self-defence: "in a case in which there is a struggle, the
right of self-defence may be invoked by the original assailant as well as by
a man who was at the outset his victim."[39] It is possible to conceive of
circumstances where A could be justified in using a fatal degree of force
against B even though he perpetrated some wrongful act which initiated
the chain of events leading to the fatal outcome for which he is being
prosecuted. If A perpetrated a minor assault upon B, causing the latter to
become unreasonably provoked and to attempt to kill A, the original assailant
would appear to be justified in killing B, even though he is not free from
fault. In *H.M. Advocate v. Robertson and Donoghue*, Lord Justice-General
Normand observed that if "the victim, in protecting himself or his property,
uses violence altogether disproportionate to the need, and employs savage
excess, then the assailant is in turn entitled to defend himself against assault
by his victim."[40]

In *Boyle v. H.M Advocate*,[41] the accused admitted committing a breach   **8–34**
of the peace through being part of a mob which had threatened another
group of people. He had joined in the subsequent fight, armed with a knife,
and had killed a member of the opposing mob. He pled self-defence, claiming
that he had acted to protect a third party. The Appeal Court regarded it as

> "a misdirection for the trial judge to tell the jury that the appellant
> could not plead self defence if he was a willing participant in the
> sense that he joined in the fight willingly. Even if he was a participant
> in the sense that he stepped forward into the fight, it would all depend
> on the circumstances whether self defence could be pleaded."[42]

This approach to the issue was followed in *Burns v. H.M. Advocate*.[43] The
important issue is whether the victim's retaliation to the accused's initial
assault is such that the latter is entitled to defend himself. This "depends
upon whether the violence offered by the victim was so out of proportion to
the accused's own actings as to give rise to the reasonable apprehension
that [the accused] was in an immediate danger from which he had no other
means of escape, and whether the violence which [the accused] then used

---

[39] *H.M. Advocate v. Robertson and Donoghue*, October 17, 1945, unreported, *per* Lord-Justice
General Normand, quoted in *Boyle v. H.M. Advocate*, 1993 S.L.T. 577 at p. 587D–E.
[40] *ibid* at p.587D.
[41] 1993 S.L.T. 577.
[42] *ibid*. at p. 588A.
[43] 1995 S.L.T. 1090.

was no more than was necessary to preserve his own life or protect himself from serious injury."[44]

Self-defence and provocation

8–35   Provocation is discussed in detail in the next chapter, but it bears stressing at this juncture that the issues of self-defence and provocation are quite different in substance and effect and are conditional upon distinct factual circumstances. It is not uncommon for an accused in a murder trial to plead both, but they are not matters of concurrent consideration: the issue of provocation only comes into play once the jury has rejected the claim of self-defence.

8–36   Self-defence is a special defence which, if successfully pled, results in an acquittal. A killing in self-defence is justified. Provocation does not lead to an acquittal. If established, it will result in a verdict of guilty of culpable homicide rather than of murder. It is not a justification for the killing, rather it lessens the accused's culpability. The rationale is that an accused who has been provoked into losing his self-control should not be judged by the same standards as the person who kills "in cold blood".

Women and self-defence

8–37   A woman kills her male partner who has physically and sexually abused her over a long period of time, but who is not about to attack her on the occasion in question. Has she acted in self-defence? It is possible to identify two different scenarios.[45] The first is where the man is killed as a pre-emptive move on the part of the woman while he is asleep or otherwise innocently occupied. It would then be difficult for the wife to satisfy the rules of self-defence, particularly the imminency requirement. As a matter of principle it would be difficult to justify such a killing. The abuser has not lost his right to life through being violent on other occasions. He is still entitled to the same legal protection as any other victim of a would-be self-defender. In the event that self-defence is not available, there may be the possibility of a verdict of culpable homicide rather than murder on the basis of "cumulative" provocation.[46]

8–38   The second possibility is that the woman may misinterpret an innocent movement on the part of the man as an attack to the danger of her life. She will want to rely upon the fact that she had been "battered" on previous occasions to support the reasonableness of her erroneous view that she was about to be attacked. This is an evidential problem.[47] The general rule is

---

[44]   1995 S.L.T. 1090, *per* Lord Justice-General Hope at p. 1093I.
[45]   See Dressler, *Understanding Criminal Law* (1987), pp. 203–205.
[46]   See para. 9–62, below.
[47]   Field, *The Law of Evidence in Scotland*, para. 12.4.

that while an accused can lead evidence concerning the victim's general character, it is not competent to lead evidence of specific acts of violence alleged to have been committed by the deceased upon the accused some time previously.[48] The difficulty posed by this evidential rule concerns how the accused can establish that the deceased was a violent person unless she is permitted to cite specific actions on the part of the man. There have been occasions, however, when courts have been prepared to depart from a strict application of this doctrine. In *H.M. Advocate v. Kay*,[49] the accused had killed her husband and pled self-defence. Lord Wheatley admitted evidence of assaults upon her by the deceased on five previous occasions as relevant to her claim that she reasonably believed her life to be in danger on the instant occasion. The basis for this decision was that the indictment libelled that the accused had herself demonstrated malice towards the deceased on previous occasions. In the interests of fairness, therefore, the accused was allowed the opportunity to prove in turn by detailed evidence that she had reason to apprehend danger from the deceased.

The one exception to the danger to life requirement for killing in self-defence is in the case of rape (see paras. 8.26–8.27, above). In his opinion in *McCluskey v. H.M. Advocate*, Lord Clyde specifically makes allowance for the availability of the plea to a woman who has killed in the course of resisting an attempt to rape her.[50] This privilege is not available to the male victim of a homosexual attack. There is a clear discriminatory inconsistency in the law. **8–39**

OTHER DEFENCES

ACCIDENT

One can envisage many different circumstances where an accused could be responsible for accidentally bringing about the *actus reus* of a crime. If a result has been brought about accidentally, that would be inconsistent with the existence of *mens rea*. No criminal responsibility can rest upon an accused for an accident. In *Mackenzie v. H.M. Advocate*, Lord Avonside pointed out that the defence of accident is always open and that "however tenuous the evidence may have been, 'accident' is a question of fact and must be left to the decision of a jury."[51] **8–40**

---

[48] See *H.M. Advocate v. Fletcher* (1846) Ark. 171; *Brady v. H.M. Advocate*, 1986 J.C. 68.
[49] 1970 S.L.T. (Notes) 66; described as "a very special case" by Lord Justice-Clerk Ross in *Brady v. H.M. Advocate, supra,* at p. 74.
[50] 1959 J.C. 39 at pp. 42–43.
[51] 1983 S.L.T. 220 at p. 224.

Objective test

8–41   It bears pointing out that the fact that a result was accidental from the accused's perspective does not mean that the criminal law will regard it as such. In *McGregor v. H.M. Advocate*[52] Lord Keith gave the example of an accused who had driven his car along with a policeman on the bonnet in such a way that the policeman had fallen off and was killed. He pointed out that "it is a matter of more or less accident whether he is killed or not, whether he happens to land on his head or some other part of his body." Nevertheless, the motorist would still be regarded as criminally responsible for causing this "accidental" death. It is necessarily an objective test and a court will take cognisance of the principle, outlined by Macdonald, "that where the result ... was likely to occur, the perpetrator is answerable."[53] Likewise, the doctrine of transferred intent operates to penalise a result of the accused's conduct which he might regard as accidental (see para. 3–35, above).

Crimes of recklessness

8–42   Crimes of recklessness and negligence can function in a similar manner. The fact that an accused has been involved in a road traffic "accident" does not mean that he will not be convicted of dangerous or careless driving. Worthy of note is *H.M. Advocate v. Pearson*,[54] where the accused was charged with the murder of one woman and the assault of another. He claimed that he had "accidentally" stabbed the two women while swinging a knife about recklessly. In the course of his charge to the jury, Lord Cameron stated: "If you on the evidence came to the conclusion that ... the accused ... whilst recklessly swinging that knife about stabbed this unfortunate woman, that would not in law be accident entitling him to an acquittal."[55]

Accident and self-defence

8–43   It is not unknown for an accused to lodge a special defence of self-defence and then to introduce evidence supportive of a claim of accident at his trial. The relationship between these two defences is a complex one. It has been held by the Appeal Court that the two pleas will not always be mutually exclusive.[56] But, in order to succeed in the plea of self-defence, it is necessary for an accused to admit bringing about the *actus reus* of the

---

[52] (1973) S.C.C.R. Supp. 54 at p. 56.
[53] Macdonald, *Criminal Law of Scotland* (5th ed.), p. 2; see also *Roberts v. Hamilton*, 1989 J.C. 91.
[54] (1967) S.C.C.R. Supp. 20.
[55] *ibid.* p. 21.
[56] See *Surman v. H.M. Advocate*, 1988 S.L.T. 371, *per* Lord Justice-Clerk Ross at p. 374L; *H.M. Advocate v. Woods*, 1972 S.L.T. (Notes) 77.

alleged crime (see para. 8–19, above). This will ordinarily give rise to an inference of *mens rea* and may be difficult to reconcile with a claim that the *actus reus* was brought about accidentally. This might seem to suggest that an accused should have to make a choice between the defences of accident and self-defence. However, in practice, accused persons can be inclined to make claims such as: "I was acting in self-defence when I killed him, but it was an accident anyway"; or "I killed him accidentally, but I acted in self-defence". If the accused adduces any evidence, however improbable, his claim will go to the jury. Nevertheless, it is arguable that the issues of accident and self-defence should be regarded as distinct in conceptual terms. It is submitted that the proper basis of self-defence is that the crime may have been committed with *mens rea*, but that the accused was justified in acting as he did. (If the accused lacks *mens rea*, perhaps because it was an accident, he is not guilty, irrespective of circumstances suggestive of self-defence.) That is, the defence operates even though the prosecution can prove all the elements of the crime. As Lord Morison stated[57] in his charge to the jury in *Surman*: "Self defence is a *deliberate act intended by the victim of an attack* for his own protection and an act which has been reasonably committed for ... the protection of the person who is accused." Lord Morison went on to say that a person who kills in self-defence lacks "wicked intent".[58] In this second quotation the judge is using the notion of intent in a broad sense to indicate that there is a difference in moral terms between a "wicked" killer and one who kills in self-defence. That there is such a moral difference is unarguable, but the criminal law caters for this difference through the existence of the doctrine of self-defence. It seems to be an unnecessary complication or qualification to merge the concepts of self-defence and *mens rea* in the way Lord Morison indicates. It is certainly not the case that an accused's plea of self-defence will be defeated because he possessed *mens rea*. Self-defence, unlike accident, is not a failure of proof defence.[59] By way of contrast, reference can be made to Lord Cameron's charge to the jury in *H.M. Advocate v. Brogan*,[60] where he simply observes that an act done in self-defence lacks a "criminal quality". That is to do no more than to restate the basic principle that criminal conduct will not be regarded as such if perpetrated in self-defence and is consistent with the approach adopted here. If the plea of self-defence is applicable, it is difficult to see how the *actus reus* can have been brought about accidentally. If it was brought about accidentally, the accused lacks the requisite *mens rea* and should be acquitted.[61] The issue of self-defence is pre-empted by

---

[57] *Surman, supra*, at p. 372K (emphasis added).
[58] *ibid*. p. 372L.
[59] See para. 8–02, above.
[60] 1964 S.L.T. 204.
[61] See *H.M. Advocate v. Woods, supra* at n. 56, *per* Lord Justice-Clerk Grant at p. 78.

the defence of accident and, it is argued here, is superfluous, since it has no effect upon the accused's intention to bring about the *actus reus* (intention here being used in a narrow sense, specific to a particular crime, in contrast to Lord Morison's view in *Surman*).

ERROR

Error of law

8–44   The fact that an accused has the requisite *mens rea* for a particular crime does not mean that he must have been aware of the illegality of his behaviour. Subject to very limited exceptions, ignorance or error of law is no defence. This doctrine is deeply embedded in Scottish criminal jurisprudence. According to Hume,[62] even though the accused "thought that it was a lawful act, and liable to no punishment, ... he still has no defence in this sort of imperfect and corrupt belief."

8–45   In *Clark v. Syme*,[63] the accused was charged with malicious mischief after he had killed his neighbour's sheep. His defence was that he believed that he had a legal right to do so after giving due warning to the neighbour about sheep damaging his crops. In rejecting this defence of error of law, Lord Justice-General Clyde[64] said: "The mere fact that his criminal act was performed under a misconception of what legal remedies he might otherwise have had, does not make it any the less criminal."

The rationale for the rule

8–46   Various reasons have been given for the rule that error of law does not affect criminal responsibility. Sometimes it is said that there is a powerful presumption that citizens have knowledge of the criminal law, but there can be little justification for such a presumption. Most people have only a vague idea of the content of the criminal law. A pragmatic justification for the rule is that accused persons would raise fraudulent claims of error which the prosecution would find difficult to disprove. But is an error of law claim any more difficult to judge than any other matter (such as insanity) which the criminal courts deal with on a regular basis?

8–47   The more plausible justification for the general rule of law is a utilitarian one. It is in the interests of society for citizens to educate themselves regarding the criminal law so that they will obey it. The best way to achieve this end is to apply a strict rule that errors of law will not be excused. As

---

[62] i, 26.
[63] 1957 J.C. 1.
[64] *ibid.* p. 5. See also paras. 11–15 to 11–17, following.

Holmes describes in *The Common Law*[65]:

> "The true explanation of the rule is the same as that which accounts
> for the law's indifference to a man's particular temperament, faculties,
> and so forth. Public policy sacrifices the individual to the public good
> ... It is no doubt true that there are many cases in which the criminal
> could not have known that he was breaking the law, but to admit the
> excuse at all would be to encourage ignorance where the law-maker
> has determined to make men know and obey, and justice to the
> individual is rightly outweighed by the larger interests on the other
> side of the scales."

Common law and error of law

At the root of the common law's approach is the thesis that it is impossible **8–48**
to make a reasonable error of law. The law is presumed to be both settled
and readily comprehensible. Anyone who purports to have made an error
of law is blameworthy for not having made the effort to become acquainted
with the law. Whether this approach can be justified must be open to serious
doubt. Of course, everyone knows that the traditional common law crimes
such as theft or fire-raising are illegal. But the common law is made by the
courts on an ad hoc, case-by-case basis. Judicial law-making is necessarily
retroactive (see Chapter 14). For the person punished for a new crime created
by the judiciary, or for committing an old crime in a new way, the law can
hardly be said to be either settled or comprehensible (see para. 2.57, above).

Error of law and mens rea

The typical error of law case is that exemplified by *Clark v. Syme*[66]: the **8–49**
accused claims that he made an error regarding the criminal law for which
he is being prosecuted. The law's analysis of this situation is that if the
accused, with *mens rea*, brings about the *actus reus* of a crime, he is
criminally liable and it is no defence for him to say that he did not know
that the *actus reus* was proscribed by the criminal law. A far less common
alternative is that an accused will admit awareness of the criminal law for
which he is being prosecuted, but will instead claim to have been in error
about the civil law. It is arguable that in some circumstances a mistake
regarding the civil law could operate to negative the *mens rea* in the
definition of the crime. For example, if A is charged with malicious mischief
arising out of an incident where he has intentionally damaged property
belonging to B, an error of the civil law which led him to believe that the
property was his own should be a defence.[67] In *Roberts v. Inverness Local*

---

[65] (1881), p. 48.
[66] 1957 J.C. 1.
[67] A persuasive authority to this effect is the English case of *R. v. Smith (David)* [1974] Q.B. 354.

Authority,[68] the accused was acquitted of moving a cow from one district to another without the requisite licence. Acting upon the advice of a local official, he believed that the two districts had been amalgamated into one. He had made an error of civil law as to the boundaries of the districts. It is unclear, however, what the outcome would have been had the accused made the error of law himself.

8–50   The limitation to this principle is that it could not apply where the criminal law sets a standard which is not the same as that by which the accused chooses to abide. The principle is confined to the civil law and to concepts such as the ownership of property or the boundaries of a district. It was no defence for the accused in *Clark v. Syme*[69] to assert that he believed the law permitted him to kill his neighbour's sheep. In *Andrew Ewart*,[70] the accused, together with his victim, had been guarding a churchyard. The accused mistook his colleague for a "body-snatcher" and shot and killed him. He was held guilty of murder, since it would have been murder to kill someone who had in fact come to remove dead bodies. His error was as to the criminal law. (The error as to the victim's identity was similarly irrelevant.)

Erroneous claims of right

8–51   The defence of claim of right in crimes of dishonesty is said to be a recognised exception to the general rule as to the irrelevancy of error of law.[71] If that is so, then an error as to a belief in a legal right to appropriate will exclude the *mens rea* of theft, as it eliminates the requisite element of "dishonest" appropriation. If A appropriates B's property under the misconception that it is lawfully his, A's action is not theft. This conclusion is in accord with the general principle described above, under which an error of civil law can operate as a defence by preventing the accused from having *mens rea* in acting as he did. Again, however, the accused's error must be one which leads him to believe that he has a right to act as he did. It is not sufficient that he simply believes that his act of appropriation does not constitute a crime. The distinction between an error of civil law (the law of property) and criminal law (the law of theft) is fundamental. An error as to the former can give rise to the defence of claim of right; an error as to the latter never can.

Dewar v. H.M. Advocate

8–52   In *Dewar v. H.M. Advocate*[72] the accused was the manager of a crematorium who was convicted of the theft of a large quantity of coffin

---

[68]   (1889) 2 White 385.
[69]   1957 J.C. 1.
[70]   (1828) Syme 315.
[71]   Gordon, *Criminal Law*, para. 14–83.
[72]   1945 J.C. 5; 1945 S.L.T. 114.

lids and a number of coffins. His defence was that he believed that the coffin lids were his to keep or use as he saw fit: to treat as scrap. His belief was that he was merely following the general and accepted practice in crematoria. It was conceded that this belief was unfounded in fact. The jury was charged in terms of the law of erroneous claim of right. On appeal, however, the view was taken that the law of error was inapplicable. The basis for this opinion was that the accused claimed an error of law which was supported only by his belief that his actions were merely in accord with common practice. The court accepted that a defence of claim of right *could* succeed where it was based on an error of fact, but stressed that the error must be founded on "rational and colourable grounds" and could not be based on the "singular" idea of the accused himself.[72a] (For a discussion as to whether the accused's belief need be reasonable, see para. 8–57, following.)

An alternative approach to *Dewar* would be to concede that the accused **8–53** may have been making an error about the law of property, in which case it could have constituted a relevant error of law (serving to negative the *mens rea* of theft). On this view the issue would become whether Dewar had acted as he did because of a belief that it was not contrary to the criminal law to appropriate the coffin lids; or whether his behaviour had been actuated by an error of the law of property. One imagines that it would have proved difficult for Dewar to have satisfied a court that the latter had been the case. Nevertheless, it is difficult to agree with the conclusion of Lord Justice-General Normand that the answer to the question was so obvious that there was no need for Dewar's claim to be put before the jury.

Error of fact

Error of fact can affect an accused's criminal responsibility in two ways. **8–54** First, he may claim to have been in error about a fact that would justify his conduct. For example, A erroneously believes that he is about to be subjected to a fatal attack by B, so he kills him in self-defence (see paras. 8–30 and 8–31, above). Secondly, an accused may claim to have been in error about a fact relevant to an ingredient of the definition of the crime for which he is being prosecuted. The present discussion is concerned principally with this second category of error.

A shoots and kills B because of his mistaken belief that he is shooting at **8–55** a deer. A has perpetrated the *actus reus* of the crime of murder. Applying an objective test one can draw an evidential inference of the presence of the requisite *mens rea* (see paras. 3–18, 3–25 and 3–26, above). The accused was in error about the fact that he was shooting at a human being: a fundamental element of the law of murder. Does this mean that he is not guilty of murder?

[72a] *per* Lord Justice-General Normand at p. 12 (J.C.); p. 115 (S.L.T.).

Mens rea *and error of fact*

8–56   The answer to this question is in the affirmative. His error of fact will operate to negative the constituent of *mens rea* included in the crime of murder (an intention to kill, or wicked recklessness as to the death of, a human being). A will be found not guilty of murder because the prosecution will be unable to prove one of the prerequisites of the crime; the *mens rea* of murder cannot be satisfied by an intention to kill a deer. It should be stressed that error of fact operates as a defence in this manner only to the extent that it can be demonstrated to have affected A's *mens rea*.[73] Indeed, it might be thought misleading to utilise the term "defence" in this context. The issue could be interpreted as simply whether or not the accused had the *mens rea* required by the definition of the crime for which he is being prosecuted.[74]

8–57   Need A's error of fact as to his target's identity be a reasonable one in order to provide an answer to a criminal charge? At one time an unequivocally affirmative response would have been given to this question. By analogy from the law of erroneous self-defence the conclusion would have been drawn that the accused's erroneous belief must be subjected to a reasonableness test (see paras. 8–30 and 8–31, above). Authority would also have been derived from *Dewar v. H.M. Advocate*, where Lord Justice-Clerk Cooper charged the jury that the accused's error as to a claim of right had to be an "honest and reasonable belief, based on colourable grounds."[75]

Meek *v.* H.M. Advocate

8–58   The decision in *Meek v. H.M. Advocate*[76] appears to represent a new common law approach to the issue. It was held that an erroneous belief that the complainer was consenting need not be reasonable in order to constitute a defence to a charge of rape.[77] The reasoning behind this approach seems to be that where an error as to the complainer's consent exists, even if it is unreasonable, it prevents the formation of the requisite *mens rea*. This leads to the conclusion that an accused acting under such a misconception cannot be guilty. The import of *Meek* may thus be that where an error of fact relates to a definitional element of a crime, it need not be held on reasonable grounds before it constitutes a defence.

8–59   In terms of the error of fact doctrine *Meek* is then an explicable decision: an accused either possesses the *mens rea* required by the definition of a

---

[73] See *McIver v. H.M. Advocate*, 1991 S.L.T. 81.
[74] In this case, murder. A conviction for culpable homicide, however, would not be precluded.
[75] 1945 J.C. 5 at p. 8; see also para. 8–52, above.
[76] 1983 S.L.T. 280; followed in *Jamieson v. H.M. Advocate*, 1994 S.L.T. 537.
[77] The definition of the crime of rape has to be taken as intentionally or recklessly having sexual intercourse without consent for the following argument to succeed; *cf.* the account of rape given in Chapter 9.

crime or he does not. Nevertheless, *Meek* has proved to be a controversial decision. This is only to be expected, given that it appears to stand for the proposition that a man who has forcible intercourse with a non-consenting woman can be acquitted of rape. But it seems unlikely that an accused would be acquitted where the woman had physically resisted or otherwise clearly demonstrated that she was not consenting; indeed, the appeal in *Meek* was not allowed. It is doubtful that a jury composed of reasonable people would conclude that the accused in such a case had been genuinely, as opposed to recklessly, in error about the woman's lack of consent. Lord Justice-General Emslie pointed out: "The absence of reasonable grounds for such an alleged belief will ... have a considerable bearing upon whether any jury will accept that such an 'honest belief' was held."[78] It is unnecessary for a trial judge to give a full *Meek* direction in every rape case. If the evidence presents the jury with a "simple choice" between violence and consent, with "no room for any halfway house", the honest belief of the accused does not arise as an issue.[79]

The law in transition?

It still remains to be seen whether *Meek* portends a new trend and lays **8–60** down a general principle applicable in contexts other than the law of rape. The Appeal Court has hinted that it may not.[80] But if it does, the observations of Lords Normand and Cooper in *Dewar v. H.M. Advocate*[81] will have to fall by the wayside. One interpretation of *Meek* would be that it signifies that an erroneous belief in a claim of right need not be held on reasonable grounds in order to provide a defence. The issue is simply as to the presence or otherwise of the *mens rea* of theft.

Meek *and self-defence*

The decision in *Meek* raises the question of whether it is logical to say that **8–61** the accused's belief need not be reasonable in cases of rape where consent is erroneously believed to exist, but must be in cases of self-defence where a danger to life is erroneously believed to exist. One commentator has remarked:

> "[I]t seems unarguable that if one believes one is being attacked (whether the belief is reasonable or not ...) one can scarcely be said to intend to commit [a criminal] assault. Is it not manifest that the belief prevents the formation of *mens rea* ... regardless of whether a definitional element is involved or the defence raises a new issue."[82]

---

[78] 1983 S.L.T. 280 at p. 281.
[79] *Quinn v. H.M. Advocate*, 1990 S.C.C.R. 254, *per* Lord Justice-Clerk Ross at p. 263D.
[80] See *Jamieson v. H.M. Advocate*, 1994 S.L.T. 537, *per* Lord Justice-General Hope at p. 541I–J.
[81] 1945 J.C. 5.
[82] J. W. R. Gray, "With or Without Reason?" 1983 S.L.T. (News) 154 at p. 156.

In this passage Gray points to the theoretical distinction between an error as to a definitional element in a crime and an error as to a fresh issue, such as the necessity of self-defence (see para. 8–02, above). He is of the opinion that such a distinction "is wholly at variance either with even-handed justice or mere common sense."[83] But Gray himself concedes that such a distinction can be drawn, albeit (as he opines) an undesirable one. It appears that the courts would wish to maintain this distinction. This is the clear implication of the decision in *Jones v. H.M. Advocate*.[84] On the question of a plea of self-defence founded on an error of fact, the opinions of Lord Justice-Clerk Ross and Lord Wylie both include a requirement that the danger to life should be "reasonably apprehended".[85] There is no reference to *Meek*.

8–62   One further point is that even if *Meek* were held to be applicable to cases of erroneous self-defence, the courts would not concede to an accused the privilege of using an unreasonable degree of force in self-defence. That is, even if the accused's unreasonable belief in the necessity for self-defence and the absence of an opportunity to withdraw were held not to affect the availability of the special defence, it would be excessively subjectivist to say that an accused could be allowed to judge for himself what amounted to a reasonable degree of force in those imagined circumstances. The courts must uphold standards of reasonableness in this regard at least.

INTOXICATION

8–63   The ensuing discussion is concerned with examining whether and in what circumstances an accused can avoid the imposition of criminal liability for his wrongdoing as a result of his intoxication from either drink or drugs. The law relating to intoxication can be divided into two general categories: voluntary and involuntary. Different considerations apply according to which classification of intoxication is under discussion.

Voluntary intoxication

8–64   Intoxication can be said to be voluntary where the accused is blameworthy in becoming intoxicated. This fault element will exist where he has voluntarily consumed a substance which he either knew or should have known would cause him to become intoxicated. (An exception to this rule is necessary for the circumstance where the intoxicant has been medically prescribed.)

---

[83] 1983 S.L.T. (News) 154 at p. 157.
[84] 1990 J.C. 160; an approach endorsed in *Jamieson v. H.M. Advocate*, 1994 S.L.T. 537, *per* Lord Justice-General Hope at p. 541I–J.
[85] 1990 J.C. at pp. 172 and 174.

The general rule is that voluntary intoxication is not an excuse for a **8–65** criminal act. As Hume describes,[86] if Scots law "does not consider the man's intemperance as an aggravation, it at least sees very good reasons why it should not be allowed as an excuse, to save him from the ordinary pains of his transgression." The rationale underlying this approach is one of public policy: it arises from a recognition of the potential for harm which can follow from the ingestion of alcohol or drugs. In the English case of *Director of Public Prosecutions v. Majewski*[87] Lord Elwyn-Jones observed:

> "Self-induced alcoholic intoxication has been a factor in crimes of violence, like assault, throughout the history of crime in this country. But voluntary drug taking with the potential and actual dangers to others it may cause has added a new dimension to the old problem with which the courts have had to deal in their endeavour to maintain order and to keep public and private violence under control. To achieve this is the prime purpose of the criminal law."

A further policy consideration is that alcohol is a factor in the commission of many crimes. The implications of accepting voluntary intoxication would be open-ended.[88]

Voluntary intoxication and mens rea

There have been attempts in the past to raise a defence on the basis that **8–66** intoxication can negative the mental element in an alleged crime. The contention has been that an accused's mind can be so affected by alcohol or drugs that he is incapable of forming the requisite *mens rea* of the crime. Scots law does not recognise any such defence. As exemplified by the decision in *Brennan v. H.M. Advocate*,[89] the High Court takes the view that a voluntarily intoxicated accused is responsible for the consequences of his actions. He can be held responsible for anything that happens while he is intoxicated. The potential consequences of becoming intoxicated are widely known; an accused can be blamed for taking the risks which everyone knows to be involved in becoming intoxicated.

In *Brennan* the court was facilitated in adopting this approach by the **8–67** fact that it was a crime of recklessness which was at issue. Murder need not be committed intentionally; wicked recklessness suffices. Even if intoxication could negative the presence of an intention to kill, it was of no avail unless it could also negative wicked recklessness. The crucial question in *Brennan* was whether his conduct displayed wicked recklessness. The

---

[86] i, 45.
[87] [1977] A.C. 443 at p. 469.
[88] See Alison, *Principles*, p. 661.
[89] 1977 J.C. 38; 1977 S.L.T. 125.

court's view was that voluntary intoxication was sufficiently reckless in itself: "[I]t is extremely difficult to understand how actings may lose the quality of ... recklessness because the actor was in an intoxicated state brought about by his own deliberate and conscious purpose."[90]

8–68   Did Brennan know what he was doing? He had ingested between 20 and 25 pints of beer, a glass of sherry and a quantity of LSD. Is his claim that he did not know what he was doing when he stabbed his father to death implausible? The answer to this question is surely in the negative: one can become so intoxicated as to lose appreciation of what one is doing. But this is somewhat beside the point in a crime which can be committed recklessly. The act of getting intoxicated is culpable in itself. As *Brennan* indicates, if the crime is one of recklessness the accused's attempt to negative his *mens rea* will necessarily fail.

The extent of the no-excuse rule

8–69   It is unclear from *Brennan* whether the rule that voluntary intoxication does not negative *mens rea* applies to all crimes or only to those which can be committed recklessly. There are some crimes, including assault and theft, which can only be committed intentionally. Does this mean that it is a defence for the accused to show that he was so drunk as to be unable to form the requisite intention to assault or steal? It seems not. The no-excuse rule appears to apply to all crimes, irrespective of the particular *mens rea* required by any definition of the crime. In *Brennan*, the court took a robust view of the purported excuse of intoxication, concluding: "There is nothing unethical or unfair or contrary to the general principle of our law that self-induced intoxication is not by itself a defence to any criminal charge, including in particular the charge of murder."[91] This approach was re-affirmed in *Ross v. H.M. Advocate*.[92] Lord Justice-General Hope explained[93] that, "where the condition which has resulted in an absence of *mens rea* is self induced ... the accused must be assumed to have intended the natural consequences of his act." This "exception" to the normal rule of criminal responsibility requiring *mens rea* is justified on "grounds of public policy".[94]

8–70   A possible conceptual difficulty with this no-excuse rule is that it equates the wrongful act of becoming intoxicated with the degree of culpability required by the definition of the crime. In *Brennan* voluntary intoxication was equated with wicked recklessness. Getting intoxicated may be reckless, but is it "wickedly" so? This conceptual problem becomes more acute in

---

[90] *Brennan v. H.M. Advocate,* 1977 J.C. 38 at p. 50; 1977 S.L.T. 125 at p. 157.
[91] *ibid.* p. 51 (J.C.); p. 158 (S.L.T.).
[92] 1991 J.C. 210.
[93] *ibid.* p. 214 (J.C.).
[94] *ibid.*

crimes with a special degree of intention, such as theft. When the courts insist upon a particular *mens rea* in the definition of a common law crime they do so because it is that particular mental element which renders the accused more blameworthy than when that element is absent. A refusal to regard as relevant any claim that the accused lacked the requisite *mens rea* appears to defeat the purpose of including the specific mental element in the definition of the crime.

A plea in mitigation?

It is clear that voluntary intoxication is not a defence to a criminal charge. **8–71** It is not uncommon, however, for it to be led by way of a plea in mitigation, particularly in cases of minor breaches of the peace and similar offences. Hume himself observes[95] that intoxication might be used in mitigation of sentence in relation to crimes "which are neither attended with any profit to the delinquent or immediate damage to one's neighbour, or to society; and which are chiefly reputed criminal, on account of the violation of order and decency, and the *possible* evil influence on the minds of others." If A has been shouting and bawling in the street, intoxication offers at least some explanation as to his conduct. It may allay the fear that he is a dangerous individual, rather than simply an annoying drunk. (This is not to suggest, of course, that drunks cannot sometimes be dangerous; the line between drunkenness as an explanatory or mitigating factor and as an aggravating factor is a fine one.)

Temporary insanity

The law does not recognise a defence of temporary insanity resulting **8–72** from the voluntary ingestion of alcohol or drugs. In *H.M. Advocate v. McDonald*,[96] Lord Justice-Clerk Macdonald pointed out:

> "In ordinary language we talk of a man being mad with drink because at the time when he has got drink in him he acts like a madman; but he is not in these circumstances a madman recognised by the law as irresponsible for his actions. It would be a very dangerous and a very sad thing indeed if it ever came to be laid down as a principle of law that a man was not responsible for his actions because he had brought himself to a state like that of a madman by pouring a quantity of alcohol down his throat. That is not the law; that has never been the law."

---

[95] i, 46.
[96] (1890) 2 White 517 at p. 519.

In *Brennan* it was stressed that the transitory effects of the alcohol and LSD were not sufficient in law to amount to insanity. Even if the accused's mental faculties had been substantially impaired that could not amount to insanity and he had to be regarded as legally responsible for his actions.

"Real" insanity

8–73   In *McDonald*, Lord Macdonald drew a distinction between an isolated act of drinking, which might cause an individual to act like a "madman," and the prolonged imbibing of excessive drink which had caused actual brain disease. He regarded the latter as exculpatory. He spoke of a defence of insanity caused by alcohol as applying when "the man's reason is overthrown, either permanently or for a course of time." In such a case the accused does not know "the quality of what he is doing, and he is not responsible."[97]

8–74   As Lord Macdonald realised, habitual and excessive indulgence in alcohol or drugs can result in permanent brain damage and a mental disorder sufficient to amount to insanity. (In *Brennan* there was no evidence of brain damage.) Insanity caused by alcohol or drugs is not regarded as different to any other kind of insanity. In the case of *Alexander Milne*, Lord Justice-Clerk Inglis observed[98]:

> "[I]f the mind is diseased — ... then that is insanity, which will take away criminal responsibility. If there be such insanity, it matters not ... what was the exciting cause of that insanity. It may be drunkenness — or it may be indulgence in any other vicious propensity — it is of no consequence which it is, if insanity is actually proved and is present at the time."

Thus a mental disorder caused by the long-term use of intoxicants is not inconsistent with an insanity defence. If the accused does meet the requirements of the insanity defence he is entitled to an acquittal.[99]

Involuntary intoxication

8–75   Intoxication might be said to be involuntary where the alcohol or drug has been consumed as the result of an honest error or another person has used fraud or coercion to cause the accused to consume it (see paras. 4–16 and 4–25, above). In *McGregor v. H.M. Advocate*,[1] Lord Keith's charge to the jury suggested that involuntary intoxication could result in an incapacity

---

[97] *H.M. Advocate v. McDonald* (1890) 2 White 517, at pp. 521–522.
[98] (1863) 4 Irv. 301 at p. 344.
[99] See para. 8–11, above.
[1] (1973) S.C.C.R. Supp. 54 (see para. 8–41, above).

to form the *mens rea* and could therefore be a defence. He drew an analogy between involuntary intoxication and somnambulism. On appeal, however, the view was expressed that this direction had been too favourable to the accused.

In *H.M. Advocate v. Raiker*,[2] Lord McCluskey suggested that an accused **8–76** would lack "the criminal state of mind that is a necessary ingredient of any crime" where he had acted "wholly and completely under the influence of some drug which was administered by force or by stealth without his consent." This view would appear to be correct, but for coerced intoxication to afford a defence it would be necessary to show that the acts were the product of the involuntary intoxication and that "it was a drug which like hypnosis put his will as it were under the control of another."[3]

Following the decision in *Ross v. H.M. Advocate*,[4] it is clear that **8–77** involuntary intoxication can operate as a defence where it constitutes non-insane automatism (see paras. 4–19 *et seq.*, above). The preconditions for the availability of the defence, as described by Lord Justice-General Hope,[5] are: "that the external factor [the intoxication] ... must not be self-induced, that it must be one which the accused was not bound to foresee and that it must be one which resulted in a total loss of control of his actions in regard to the crime with which he is charged." In *Sorley v. H.M. Advocate*[6] it was stressed that there are strict limits to the availability of the defence. There is a requirement of clear evidence of the accused's state of mind and also of the "causative link" between the involuntarily consumed intoxicant and his behaviour.[7]

COERCION

The character of the defence

To establish the defence of coercion in relation to a serious crime an **8–78** accused must show that he violated the criminal law in order to avoid imminent death or serious injury at the hands of a coercer. A classic example for an application of the defence would be the motorist who is forced at gunpoint to transport an armed robber away from the scene of the crime and is subsequently charged with being art and part of the robbery. In a situation such as this, the doctrine of coercion recognises that for the driver

---

[2] 1989 S.C.C.R. 149 at p. 154.
[3] *ibid.*
[4] 1991 J.C. 210.
[5] *ibid.* p. 222 (J.C.).
[6] 1992 J.C. 102.
[7] *ibid. per* Lord Justice-General Hope at p. 107 (J.C.), and p. 870E–F (S.L.T.); see also *Ebsworth v. H.M. Advocate*, 1992 S.L.T. 671; *MacLeod v. Napier*, 1993 S.C.C.R. 303.

to violate the law is less serious than to adhere to the letter of the law and thereby risk death or serious injury.

8-79   If the accused has been coerced into committing a crime, he avoids the harm which has been threatened to him, but does so at the expense of contravening the law and possibly injuring an innocent third party. Unlike the person who has acted in justifiable self-defence, he does not promote a value supported by the law. The common law imposes strict limits upon its availability as a defence. In *H.M. Advocate v. McCallum*,[8] Lord Allanbridge pointed out to the jury:

> "When you come to consider this defence [coercion], I think it is right — and I am sure you will appreciate — that it would make life very easy for criminals and very difficult for law enforcement if, whenever a criminal was actually caught, he could turn round and say, 'I admit I committed the crime but I was coerced into doing it by someone else.' That being so, any such defence must be very carefully considered indeed."

The rationale of the defence

8-80   The basis of the defence of coercion in Scots law is that identified by Lord Hunter in *Thomson v. H.M. Advocate*[9] when he says "that the will and the resolution of the accused must have been overborne by threats which he believed would be carried out so that he was not at the material time acting of his own free will." Similarly, in *H.M. Advocate v. Docherty*,[10] Lord Keith told the jury:

> "It can happen that the will of an individual is overborne by the will of another in certain circumstances so he is not acting of his own free will. ... The essence of the matter is that the will of the accused should be overborne by the threats which he believed would be carried out."

8-81   Statements such as these can be misleading. A coerced individual retains free will in the sense that he can choose how to conduct himself. If he decides to break the criminal law in order to avoid death or serious injury, then he makes a choice. The law's emphasis on this purported lack of free will is more a reflection of the fact that the accused's opportunity to exercise his capacity to choose will have been substantially undermined by the coercer's threats. The reason for not imposing criminal liability on the coercee is the recognition that it is unfair to punish the blameless person

---

[8] (1977) S.C.C.R. Supp. 169.
[9] 1983 J.C. 69 at p. 74.
[10] (1976) S.C.C.R. Supp. 146.

whose only choice was the morally unacceptable one between either self-sacrifice or breaking the law.

Coercion and *mens rea*

It is sometimes suggested that a coerced accused should be found not **8–82** guilty on the basis that he lacked *mens rea* at the time of committing the crime. An observation to this effect can be found in Lord McCluskey's charge to the jury in *H.M. Advocate v. Raiker*[11]:

> "[T]he law is that where a person has ... a justifiable fear that if he does not act in accordance with the orders of another person, that other person will use life-threatening violence against him ... , and if as a result of that fear ... he carries out acts which have all the typical external characteristics of criminal acts ... then in that situation ... he lacks the criminal state of mind that is a necessary ingredient of any crime."

This view of the effect of coercion is misconceived. If A is threatened **8–83** by B that he (A) will be killed unless he assaults C, A has the requisite intent for the crime of assault against C when he hits him. A may be excused for having *mens rea* because he was coerced, but the intention to assault is present. If A does not have the requisite *mens rea*, he is not guilty of assault, irrespective of whether he was subjected to coercion.

The rules of coercion

The rules governing the availability of the defence of coercion are still **8–84** largely those outlined by Hume.[12] He identifies four "qualifications": (1) "an immediate danger of death or great bodily harm"; (2) "an inability to resist the violence"; (3) "a backward and inferior part in the perpetration"; and (4) "a disclosure of the fact, as well as restitution of the spoil, on the first safe and convenient occasion." Following the decision of the High Court in *Thomson v. H.M. Advocate*,[13] it appears that the first two "qualifications" remain preconditions for the availability of the defence, but that the extent of participation in the crime and/or restoration of the spoils go only to the credibility of the accused's plea. As regards the nature of the coercer's threat, it is thought that something less than one of death or serious injury would be insisted upon by a court where the crime committed by the coercee was not a particularly serious one: the rule laid down in *Thomson* should be read in the context of a case of armed robbery.

---

[11] 1989 S.C.C.R. 149 at p. 154.
[12] i, 53.
[13] 1983 J.C. 69.

Threats of present and future violence

8–85   In his initial opinion in *Thomson* Lord Hunter states that "all the Scottish authorities are based on the principle that a defence of coercion, in order to be successful, requires that the danger must be immediate."[14] This requirement of imminency will be familiar from the discussion of self-defence (see para. 8–22, above). It was explained in the following terms by Lord Justice-Clerk Wheatley in the same case[15]: "[I]t is only where, following threats, there is an immediate danger of violence, in whatever form it takes, that the defence of coercion can be entertained, and even then only if there is an inability to resist or avoid that immediate danger."

8–86   One question which arises is whether the defence can ever be founded on present threats of future harm. In general terms the answer has to be in the negative, because of the immediacy requirement. In Lord Wheatley's terms, there must be an "immediate danger of the threat being implemented in the event of non-compliance at the point of time when the decision had to be made."[16] As Lord Allanbridge charged the jury in *H.M. Advocate v. McCallum*[17]:

> "It is one thing to force a man to commit a crime by actually holding a pistol to his head ... — that is an immediate threat. It is another thing to threaten a man that if he does not commit a crime he ... can be killed or injured in the future — that is a future threat. ... [W]hen you are considering in law the question of the defence of coercion it is to immediate and not to future threats that you look."

The reason for discounting threats pertaining to the future is that the individual threatened is expected to seek the protection of the police. In *Thomson*, however, Lord Wheatley[18] does concede that "even in the ordinary condition of a well-regulated society there may be a circumstance where a person is exposed to a threat of violence ... from which he cannot be protected by the forces of law and order and which he is not in a position to resist." In this passage Lord Wheatley appears to be suggesting that there could be an exceptional case where threats of future danger could be admitted as evidence of coercion, if recourse to the police would be ineffective. His Lordship goes on to say that: "If such a situation arose it would have to be determined on its facts and no profit can be gained from an exercise in hypothetical cases."

[14] *Thomson v. H.M. Advocate* 1983 J.C. 69 at p. 74.
[15] *ibid.* p. 77.
[16] *ibid.* p. 80.
[17] (1977) S.C.C.R. Supp. 169.
[18] 1983 J.C. 69 at p. 78.

A defence to murder?

In his charge to jury in *Collins v. H.M. Advocate*,[19] Lord Allanbridge **8–87** stated that "as a matter of law coercion is not a defence in Scotland to the crime of murder". His explanation was:

> "It is because of the supreme importance that the law affords to the protection of human life. It is repugnant that the law should recognise in any individual in any circumstances however extreme the right to choose that one innocent person should be killed rather than any other person including himself."

NECESSITY

A residual defence

The defence of necessity is a residual one. It exculpates conduct contrary **8–88** to the criminal law that dictates of common sense and moral fairness suggest is excusable or justifiable, but which does not fall within the categories of a recognised defence such as self-defence or coercion. The defence is problematic in Scots law due to Hume's evident disapproval of the plea and a lack of direct High Court authority. Nevertheless, the High Court has not been prepared to say that the defence does not exist — despite having had opportunities to do so[20] — and as a matter of legal principle the desirability of a defence of necessity is clear.

A system of criminal law which did not recognise such a defence would **8–89** be irrational and unjust. Cases do arise in which none of the specific defences apply, but where the accused's conduct does appear to be excusable or justifiable. It is possible to identify two broad types of situation for an application of the defence: (1) altruistic necessity; and (2) self-interested necessity.

Altruistic necessity

Someone who commits a crime out of necessity can be acting as society **8–90** would wish him to and be promoting a value supported by the law, in that he is contravening the letter of the law in order to secure some greater good. His conduct is justifiable. A straightforward example would be the person who breaks into a house in order to gain access to a telephone in order to report a serious road traffic accident. Another example could be

---

[19] 1991 S.C.C.R. 898 at p. 902C. See to like effect *H.M. Advocate v. Peters* (1969) 33 J.C.L. 209.

[20] See, for example, *McLeod v. MacDougall*, 1989 S.L.T. 151; *Morrison v. Valentine*, 1991 S.L.T. 413.

that of the disqualified motorist who drives his seriously-ill child to hospital (on the assumption that there is no reasonable alternative means of conveying the child; see para. 8–92, following).

Self-interested necessity

8–91   An accused who acts out of necessity may be avoiding harm to himself at the expense of contravening the law. He would not then be regarded as promoting a value supported by the law. This form of necessity can be described as coercion by circumstances: the accused is constrained by circumstances to act as he did. It is exemplified by the sheriff court decision in *Tudhope v. Grubb*.[21] The accused was charged with an offence of attempting to drive with an excess of alcohol in his blood. He had attempted to drive in order to escape further injury after he had been assaulted by a number of men. The sheriff decided that in these circumstances a defence of necessity was available and the accused was acquitted.

When should the defence be available?

8–92   Although the defence may be available in both these categories of case, it is only to be expected that the courts will look more favourably on the first category. It was stated by Lord Justice-Clerk Ross in *McNab v. Guild*[22] that the "defence could only be made out if the findings showed that at the material time [there was an] immediate danger to life or of serious injury." The corollary of this requirement is that there would have to be no alternative means of preventing the threatened harm.[23] Assuming that these two conditions are met, one can give little more guidance other than to say that the availability of the defence is going to turn on whether those sitting in judgment deem that the conduct of the accused can be exculpated. A significant part of this assessment will be a determination of whether the harm avoided was greater than that incurred by choosing to contravene the criminal law. As in relation to coercion, it is most unlikely that necessity could ever afford a defence to a murder charge.[24]

---

[21] 1983 S.C.C.R. 350 (Sh.Ct.).
[22] 1989 S.C.C.R. 138; followed in *Morrison v. Valentine, supra* at n. 20.
[23] *Morrison v. Valentine, supra* at n. 20, at p. 414K (S.L.T.).
[24] See para. 8–87, above; *R. v. Dudley and Stephens* (1884) 14 Q.B.D. 273.

Further reading

Ferguson, P., "Murder, Provocation and Self Defence," 1986 S.L.T. (News) 38.

Gray, J.W.R., "The Expulsion of Beard from Scotland: Murder North of the Border" [1979] Crim. L. R. 369.

Jones, T. H., "The Defence of Necessity in Scots Law," 1989 S.L.T. (News) 253.

Norrie, A., "The Defence of Coercion in Scots Criminal Law," 1984 S.L.T. (News) 13.

Smith, J. C., *Justification and Excuse in the Criminal Law* (1989).

CHAPTER 9

CRIMES AGAINST THE PERSON

Introduction

9–01 The crimes considered in this chapter all deal with readily identifiable harms caused to particular victims. They all thus fall within John Stuart Mill's "harm principle" (see para. 1–07, above), and require no further justification. "Harm" here means physical injury (including death) as well as the fear and alarm caused by the threat of such injury.

1. ABDUCTION

9–02 Hume[1] discusses abduction under the description: "Of forcible abduction and marriage". This suggests that the crime might be rather limited both as to victim and purpose; but this is not the modern approach. A charge of abduction of a child of six has been received without objection,[2] as has such a charge relating to an adult male.[3] Burnett's remark[4] would, therefore, seem to have been accepted, namely: "[w]here the abduction is neither with a view to marriage, nor rape, it is punishable *tanquam* [sic] *crimen in sua genere* [*i.e.* as a crime in its own right] as an unjust oppression, and restraint." It is thus thought that Sheriff Mitchell correctly stated the law when he said: "the essence of abduction [is] to carry off a person against his or her will without lawful authority. It humbly [seems] to me that abduction for any purpose is criminal. I refer to Macdonald and to the 5th edn. at p. 124."[5] Thus, a man wrongfully arrested by a police officer on a wholly spurious charge of breach of the peace was criminally abducted by that officer, according to the decision in *Elliot v. Tudhope*, where it was also accepted by Sheriff Mitchell[6] that "unlawful detention was a recognised crime at common law." The *mens rea* element of abduction is uncertain,

[1] *Commentaries*, i, 310.
[2] *M. v. H.M. Advocate* (1980) S.C.C.R. Supp. 250.
[3] *Elliot v. Tudhope*, 1987 S.C.C.R. 85.
[4] *A Treatise on Various Branches of the Criminal Law of Scotland* (1811), p. 109.
[5] *Elliot v. Tudhope*, 1987 S.C.C.R. 85 at p. 93.
[6] *ibid.*

but probably amounts to intention rather than recklessness on common sense grounds.

2. ASSAULT

Introduction

The crime of assault covers a very wide spectrum of harmful or alarm-   **9–03** producing behaviour. As was said by Lord Justice-Clerk Hope in *Kennedy v. Young*[7]: "[t]he word assault is one of the most flexible terms." In Hume's time, however, it seems that "assault" was just one of a number of expressions used to denote criminal forms of "real injury". As he puts the matter[8]:

> "the law is provided with sundry ... terms ... such as assault, invasion, beating and bruising, blooding and wounding, stabbing, mutilation, demembration, and some others. But although the injury do not come under any of those terms of style, nor be such as can be announced in a single phrase ... [l]et the libel ... give an intelligible account of it in terms at large; and, if it amount to a real injury, it shall be sustained to infer punishment."

Despite its undoubted width, assault in modern Scots law is a more specific crime than the foregoing quotation would tend to imply, and, in particular, can be distinguished from other forms of "real injury".

DEFINITION OF ASSAULT

Until recently, twentieth-century criminal courts in Scotland have tended   **9–04** to favour the account of assault given by Macdonald at pages 115 to 119.[9] The following working definition is, therefore, based on Macdonald's central concept of an "attack": thus, an assault is committed when one person makes an attack upon another with the intention of effecting the immediate bodily injury of that other person or producing the fear of immediate bodily injury in his mind. The details of this definition will be explained in the following paragraphs.

The *actus reus*: an attack

Use of the term "attack" may seem strange in view of the great variety   **9–05** of conduct which the common law has accepted as sufficient for assault

---

[7] (1854) 1 Irv. 533 at p. 539.
[8] i, 327–328.
[9] *Criminal Law of Scotland* (5th ed.); see, for example, *Smart v. H.M. Advocate*, 1975 J.C. 30 at p. 33; *cf. Lord Advocate's Reference (No. 2 of 1992)*, 1993 J.C. 43.

(see paras. 9–06 to 9–11, below). But it is submitted that the sense of an unjustified, hostile, direct approach to the victim, which the word carries, is apt to describe the vast majority of assault situations encountered in practice. Whilst it is true that spitting on someone has been described as an assault,[10] as has the cutting-off of a woman's hair whilst she was asleep,[11] and the forcible stopping of a man's horse,[12] and that arguably some of these situations may not amount to "attacks" in any usual sense of that term, it is also clear that the law's acceptance of them as criminal assaults is highly exceptional, if not remarkable. It is also remarkable that a "verbal attack" on another seems not to amount to an assault. "[M]ere words cannot constitute an assault," says Macdonald at page 115; and this seems to be tacitly accepted. There is, however, no authority to vouch that rule, other than a passage in Alison[13] where that author appears to be expounding English rather than Scots law.

Attacks producing injury

9–06   Although Macdonald[14] emphasises that the conduct sufficient for an assault need not injure the victim at all, bodily harm is very often the result of an attack. Such harm may be slight or serious. Examples of the former have included the marks produced by compressing the victim's arm[15] or seizing him by the throat in order to march him rapidly to a police interview-room,[16] or even the disfigurement effected by cutting off some of her hair.[17] But examples of trivial injuries are seldom included in the law reports, which tend to feature more serious matters. Thus, at the other end of the scale, are found the results of holding someone's head under water,[18] blocking the air supply to a critically-ill patient in intensive care,[19] and pouring petrol over someone whose clothing then caught fire.[20] It will be plain, therefore, that it matters not whether an injury is serious or utterly trivial, so long as it was produced by a deliberate attack upon the victim; and it will also be plain that it matters not whether the victim was conscious or not at the time of the attack made upon him. Thus, it made no difference at all that a man, who had part of his nose bitten off, had been insensible

---

[10]   *James Cairns* (1837) 1 Swin. 597, *per* Lord Justice-Clerk Boyle at p. 610.
[11]   *Charles Sweenie* (1858) 3 Irv. 109, *per* Lord Cowan at p. 145.
[12]   *Kennedy v. Young* (1854) 1 Irv. 533.
[13]   *Principles*, i, 176.
[14]   *Criminal Law of Scotland*, p. 115.
[15]   *Aitken v. Wood*, 1921 J.C. 84.
[16]   *Bonar v. McLeod*, 1983 S.C.C.R. 161.
[17]   See para. 9–05, above.
[18]   *Kepple v. H.M. Advocate*, 1936 S.L.T. 294.
[19]   *Atkins v. London Weekend Television Ltd*, 1978 J.C. 48.
[20]   *Williamson v. H.M. Advocate*, 1984 S.L.T. 200.

through drink at the time[21] or that a person had been asleep when paper was stuffed into his hand and ignited.[22]

Those entitled to use reasonable force

"It happens from time to time that charges of assault are made against officials and others who are entitled in virtue of their offices to exercise in certain circumstances physical force. I may cite as examples police officers, prison warders, asylum attendants, railway servants and ships' officers."[23] This is undoubtedly true; but such persons will not be seen as carrying out attacks, provided the force they use is no more than is necessary, for example, to arrest a suspect,[24] or to foreclose disruptive behaviour by mentally-handicapped children.[25] They will thus escape conviction for assault since there is no hostile use of force, although it can also be said, of course, that they lack the necessary *mens rea* for the crime (see paras. 9–12 to 9–16, below).[26] In a similar way, parents (or those in *loco parentis*)[27] may discipline their young children by slapping or smacking, and will not be seen to be "attacking" them unless tempers are lost and reasonable chastisement becomes excessive punishment. That, of course, is a matter of degree in all the circumstances of each case.[28] Teachers of young children in schools may also impose reasonable, corporal chastisement to keep discipline[29]; but such cases are now unlikely to trouble the criminal courts at all due to the effect of section 48A of the Education (Scotland) Act 1980, which effectively removed the civil law defence of "reasonable discipline" from teachers in the public sector. Finally, those who play sports, such as rugby or ice-hockey, which allow physical tackling of opponents in the course of play, will also escape conviction for criminal assault, provided that they confine themselves to what the rules of the game allow by way of physical contact with members of the opposing team. There will then be no question of there being any "attack".[30]

9–07

---

[21] *Charles McEwan* (1824) in Hume, *Commentaries*, i, 331 n.a.
[22] *Lachlan Brown* (1842) 1 Broun 230.
[23] *Brown v. Hilson*, 1924 J.C. 1, *per* Lord Sands at p. 6. The list may now include stewards or "bouncers" whose responsibilities extend to the maintaining of order at events attended by large numbers of people — see, *e.g. H.M. Advocate v. Harris*, 1993 J.C. 150.
[24] *cf. Marchbank v. Annan*, 1987 S.C.C.R. 718; *Codona v. Cardle*, 1989 J.C. 99.
[25] *Skinner v. Robertson*, 1980 S.L.T. (Sh.Ct.) 43; *cf. Norman v. Smith*, 1983 S.C.C.R. 100.
[26] See, *e.g. H.M. Advocate v. Harris*, 1993 J.C. 150, *per* Lord McCluskey (diss.) at p. 161B–C.
[27] See, *e.g. Stewart v. Thain*, 1981 J.C. 13.
[28] Contrast *Guest v. Annan*, 1988 S.C.C.R. 275, and *Peebles v. MacPhail*, 1990 S.L.T. 245. See also *Kennedy v. A*, 1993 S.L.T. 1134.
[29] See, *e.g. McShane v. Paton*, 1922 J.C. 26; *cf. Gray v. Hawthorn*, 1964 J.C. 69.
[30] See, *e.g. Lord Advocate's Reference (No. 2 of 1992)*, 1993 J.C. 43, *per* Lord Justice-Clerk Ross at p. 48E. *Cf. Dobbs and Macdonald v. Neilson* (1899) 3 Adam 10, where an inferior criminal court quite unaccountably convicted two professional boxers for what they did to each other during the course of a friendly contest, fought according to that sport's normal rules.

Attacks producing fear

9–08   "Gestures threatening violence so great as to put another in bodily fear, whether accompanied by words of menace or not, constitute assault."[31] This statement was impliedly approved by Lord Justice-Clerk Ross in *Atkinson v. H.M. Advocate*[32] where the masked accused burst into a shop and vaulted a counter, thus placing a cashier in a state of fear and alarm for his safety. This was considered quite sufficient by itself for conviction, and confirms the conclusion derivable from earlier authorities that actual injury is not required. All that is necessary is that the accused should have made some unjustified, hostile, direct approach to the victim which led him to fear that he was about to be injured. Thus, if a weapon such as a firearm is directed threateningly towards another, that will be enough, even if the accused himself knows that no injury can actually be caused by it.[33] Similarly, where the victim is menaced with a cutting, striking or stabbing instrument, assault may well be made out at that stage.[34] It would be a mistake, however, to imagine that presenting a weapon at another is always sufficient for assault; it has been held, for example, that producing a knife during an interlude in a fight, and holding it out towards one's opponent whilst saying "fuck off", could be a legitimate method of trying to avoid the resumption of hostilities rather than a hostile act itself.[35] No weapons, however, are necessarily required for this form of assault. In *John Irving*,[36] for example, the accused had repeatedly shaken his fist in the face of his victim; and that, accompanied by threatening words, was clearly sufficient.

9–09   The question arises in relation to attacks which produce fear rather than actual injury whether the victim has to be conscious of the attack made upon him. Must he have been personally aware of the menaces and threats to his safety? Although the matter is not free from difficulty, it is suggested that it should be unnecessary to show that he was so aware. On any other view, it would be no assault to brandish an axe in anger at a person who was asleep or intoxicated, which surely cannot be right. There is no authority on the point, however. Where the victim has actually been alarmed, it is equally unclear whether his alarm must be considered reasonable in the

---

[31]   Macdonald, p. 115.
[32]   1987 S.C.C.R. 534 at p. 535.
[33]   *Gilmour v. McGlennan*, 1993 S.C.C.R. 837; *Lord Advocate's Reference (No. 2 of 1992)*, 1993 J.C. 43.
[34]   *Norval v. H.M. Advocate*, 1978 J.C. 70, where a sword, hammer and knife were presented; *Bryson v. H.M. Advocate*, 1961 S.L.T. 289, where a candlestick was brandished at a policeman and a threat made to strike him with it. See also *Strachan v. H.M. Advocate*, 1995 S.L.T. 178 (where the charge was actually one of attempted murder).
[35]   *Mackenzie v. H.M. Advocate*, 1983 S.L.T. 220, *per* Lord Justice-Clerk Wheatley at p. 223.
[36]   (1833) Bell's Notes 88.

circumstances. The point was raised, but not decided, in *Gilmour v. McGlennan.*[37]

Indirect attacks

The classic example of an indirect attack is the setting of some animal **9–10** upon one's victim. Naturally, the animal would have to be one generally regarded as amenable to human control, such as a dog. In *Kay v. Allan*[38] it was indeed said that encouraging a boxer-dog to attack two young boys trespassing in the accused's garden was an assault; but the decision of the Appeal Court proceeded on a concession by the Crown to the effect that it had to be shown in such a case, "that the person accused caused the dog in some way to move at the alleged victim with the intention that the dog in so moving would at least frighten him."[39] It appears, then, that it is not necessary for the dog (or similar animal) to attack and injure the victim. An unusual instance of an indirect attack occurred in *David Keay*,[40] where the accused, who was riding in a carriage, whipped a pony as he overtook it. This caused the frightened animal to bolt and throw its young rider, who was seriously injured. The court seemed to entertain no doubt that this was an assault on the person who was hurt. It has been held to be no answer to a charge relating to an instruction to a dog that it should "fetch" another person that the instruction was intended as a joke, since a dog cannot distinguish between a jocular command and a hostile one.[41]

The immediacy of the attack

It would seem that an attack, as described above, should be followed, or **9–11** be capable of being followed, by immediate injury if assault is to be made out. If a significant temporal gap exists between the conduct of the accused and some resultant injury, then the crime (if any) is probably not one of assault. So, in *Charles Costello*[42] a separate, innominate offence was significantly charged (and upheld) where the accused had sent the victim a box of gunpowder, so ordered as to explode in his face when the package was delivered and opened. On the other hand, in *Smith v. Paton*[43] the accused was charged with attempted assault, in that he had sent to his victim a postal packet so designed that concealed razor blades would lacerate the

---

[37] 1993 S.C.C.R. 837.
[38] (1978) S.C.C.R. Supp. 188.
[39] *ibid.* p. 190.
[40] (1837) 1 Swin. 543.
[41] *Quinn v. Lees,* 1994 S.C.C.R. 159.
[42] (1882) 4 Coup. 602.
[43] June 1986, Dundee Sheriff Court, unreported.

fingers of anyone opening it. He pled guilty, however, and thus no matter of principle was discussed.[44]

The *mens rea* of assault

9–12   The overwhelming preponderance of authority points to assault being a crime of intention.[45] Although Hume's treatment of assault is somewhat superficial, he does refer to intent being required—in particular the intent to hurt and wound[46]; and in the case of *John Roy*[47] it is plain that the prosecutor gave up the case because he could not show any intention to injure. It had been suggested by him that assault covered all injuries causally connected to a criminal act of the accused (in this case, the kicking-in of a house window—malicious mischief) but the court would have none of that. Again, in the later case of *H.M. Advocate v. Phipps*[48] Lord Ardwall told the jury that they could not convict of assault unless they found that the accused had had evil intent or an intention to do bodily injury. This was a curious way to present the matter in the context of that case, since the accused (the two sons of the shooting tenant on a Scottish estate) conceded that they intended to frighten the victims by the device of firing off loaded shotguns. They had heard voices from the far banks of a river, and had assumed that they were having to contend with poachers. At the pitch-black of midnight, therefore, they fired off their weapons in the direction of the voices they had heard, their object being to scare off the men in question and secure their poaching gear. It did not occur to them that anyone on the far bank would be within range; but such was the case. Two of the "poachers" were injured. Clearly the accused had no intention of injuring anyone, but they did intend to frighten off the men concerned by causing them to be alarmed for their personal safety. As actions on the part of one person which cause another to feel alarm for his safety are undoubtedly sufficient for the *actus reus* of assault, an intention to produce such alarm must certainly form the correlative *mens rea*. Lord Ardwall's virtual direction to the jury to acquit the accused must, therefore, be based on his belief that it was lawful to frighten off persons supposed to be engaged in poaching.[49]

---

[44] Paton's case is doubly curious in that it is often stated that in view of the width of the concept of "attack", there is no such thing in practice as attempted assault—see Ferguson, *Crimes Against the Person*, para. 1.02; Gordon, *Criminal Law*, para. 29–02. See also para. 6–07, above.

[45] See *Lord Advocate's Reference (No. 2 of 1992)*, 1993 J.C. 43, *per* Lord Justice-Clerk Ross at p. 48C–D, Lord Cowie at p. 51B–C, and Lord Sutherland at pp. 52I to 53A; *H.M. Advocate v. Harris*, 1993 J.C. 150, *per* Lord Justice-Clerk Ross at p. 154D–E (quoting Gordon, *Criminal Law*, para. 29–30), and Lord Murray p. 156C.

[46] i, 328.

[47] (1839) Bell's Notes 88.

[48] (1905) 4 Adam 616 at p. 630.

[49] *ibid.* p. 634.

It must follow, therefore, that two forms of *mens rea* are sufficient for **9–13** assault. The first relates to an intention to do bodily harm, and the second to an intention to place someone in a state of fear and alarm for his personal safety.

Must the intent be evil?

According to Macdonald,[50] "Evil intention [is] of the essence of assault." **9–14** A similar remark was made by Lord Ardwall in the case of *H.M. Advocate v. Phipps*,[51] although he seemed to explain there that "evil" intent meant "an intention to do bodily injury". In the leading case of *Smart v. H.M. Advocate*[52] the Appeal Court said: "If there is an *attack* on the other person *and it is done with evil intent*, that is, intent to injure and do bodily harm, then ... the fact that the person attacked was willing to undergo the risk of that attack does not prevent it from being the crime of assault." Discounting for the present what the court said about the role of consent (see para. 9–18, below), it seems that the relevant form of the *mens rea* here is really a straightforward "intent to do bodily injury" rather than an "evil intent" to do so. And this, with some degree of hesitation, appears to be the present law. In the leading modern authority on this precise issue,[53] the trial judge directed the jury that whether or not there was evil intent was at the heart of the case.[54] The accused had burst into a shop, held out a handgun in front of him, and given the startled assistants a command to hand over the contents of the till. The assistants were alarmed for their own safety. The accused's story was, however, that he had then begun laughing, announced it was all a joke, and left the premises. At his trial for (*inter alia*) assault, he submitted that he had had no evil intent, the whole episode having been an essay in the art of the practical joke. The trial judge told the jury that if they believed the accused's story, they should acquit since there would indeed be no evil intent. The accused was duly acquitted (on a not proven verdict) and in the course of a subsequent Lord Advocate's reference, Lord Justice-Clerk Ross opined as follows:

> "It has often been said that evil intention is of the essence of assault (Macdonald's *Criminal Law*, p. 115). But what that means is that assault cannot be committed accidentally or recklessly or negligently (Gordon's *Criminal Law* (2nd ed.), para. 29–30). In the present case, it is plain that when the accused entered the shop, presented the handgun at Mrs Daly and uttered the words which he did, he was

---

[50] p. 115.
[51] (1905) 4 Adam 616 at p. 630.
[52] 1975 J.C. 30 at p. 33 and 1975 S.L.T. 65 at p. 66 (emphasis added).
[53] *Lord Advocate's Reference (No. 2 of 1992)*, 1993 J.C. 43.
[54] *ibid.* quoted by Lord Justice-Clerk Ross at p. 46D.

acting deliberately. That being so, in my opinion, he had the necessary intent for his actions to amount to assault …".[55]

It appears to follow, therefore, that the epithet "evil" is an unnecessary, if not misleading, one, and that the proper recension of the *mens rea* is indeed what is stated at para. 9–13, above. A difficulty with this view, however, is that it was not necessarily shared by the other two judges in the case. Lord Cowie, for example, was of the opinion that "evil intent" was an essential element in the crime,[56] and that it was necessary to establish that the act of the accused had indeed been evil. As he put it: "[h]aving established that the act is an evil one [based on its quality], all that is then required to constitute the crime of assault is that that act was done deliberately and not carelessly, recklessly or negligently."[57] Equally, Lord Sutherland in his opinion indicated that "[t]he words 'evil intent' have an eminently respectable pedigree."[58] It is true too in other recent cases that some judges continue to favour "evil intention" as the proper description of the *mens rea* of assault.[59] The conclusion is that one cannot entirely be certain whether "evil intent" is simply an outmoded way of referring to "intent" or whether (for some judges at least) "evil intent" has a meaning distinct from simple intent. It is suggested that the former is the better view.

9–15   There may be some advantage, nevertheless, in requiring an intention to be "evil". Sportsmen playing a physical contact sport where heavy tackling, or even punching is permitted within the rules; police arresting unwilling suspects; nurses subduing violent patients; and parents and others disciplining unruly children (on all which, see para. 9–07, above), may all be said in a quite literal sense to intend the force they use. But, provided that the force used is no more than that permitted within the rules of the sport or than that necessary for the legitimate aim pursued, there is no evil intention in respect of it. If only bare intent is required for the crime, rather than evil intent, then a game of, say, rugby must inevitably be analysed as a continuous sequence of assaults, which will then require justification or excuse. Even more telling is the effect upon surgical or dental treatment. It is very odd somehow to have to regard a surgical operation, say, for the amputation of a limb, as a theoretical assault requiring justification by way of "necessity" or "the ultimate good of the patient"; and yet it is certainly arguable that the surgeon involved intends to do what he does, and that that

[55] *Lord Advocate's Reference (No. 29 of 1992)*, 1993 J.C. 43 at p. 48C–D.
[56] *ibid.* p. 51B.
[57] *ibid.* p. 51C–D.
[58] *ibid.* p. 52H.
[59] See, *e.g. Boyle v. H.M. Advocate*, 1993 S.L.T. 577, Lord McCluskey's charge to the jury at p. 579K to 580C; *H.M. Advocate v. Harris*, 1993 J.C. 150, *per* Lord Justice-Clerk Ross at p. 154D–E (quoting directly from Macdonald, p. 115), *per* Lord McCluskey (diss.) at pp. 158I to 159B; *Kennedy v. A*, 1993 S.L.T. 1134 at p. 1137A.

involves bodily harm. But a surgeon (or indeed any other professionally trained medical operative) will not lightly be assumed to have any evil intent. Insistence on an evil intention will thus avoid the awkward notion of a prima facie, but justifiable, assault in relation to medical treatment. As against all this, of course, is the inherent vagueness of the moral concept "evil". Vague concepts within a criminal justice system are perfectly capable of giving rise to unexpected, and even unwanted submissions — such as, that practical joke scenarios do not qualify as assaults since they cannot be thought of as "evil". There may, however, be something to be said in favour of terms which allow discretion to the court to deal with awkward situations sensibly. It cannot always be wise to rely solely on the exercise of restraint on the part of the prosecutor.[60]

Is recklessness sufficient for assault?

There is no evidence in favour of recklessness, still less negligence, being a sufficient form of *mens rea* for assault, and indeed a considerable body of evidence against. Quite apart from the authorities referred to at paragraph 9–12, above, the court in *David Keay*[61] was at some pains to avoid concluding that an assault might have been recklessly committed. Where the accused had whipped a pony because it was apparently in the path of his carriage, thus causing it to throw and injure its rider, Lord Moncreiff said: "I cannot see what purpose the pannel could have, except either to do him a direct injury, or to put him in alarm."[62] His Lordship also remarked there that it would not amount to an assault if a person were to throw a stone heedlessly out of a window and thus injure some innocent passer-by.[63] Further evidence is provided by the decision of the Appeal Court in *Roberts v. Hamilton*.[64] There, the accused was charged with assault in that she had aimed a blow with a stout pole at A but had in fact missed and hit B, who happened to be within range. The accused had had no intention to injure B at all; and, in fact, it would seem to have been an act of recklessness or carelessness that had resulted in the injury. But the court held[65] that as long as there was intent to hit someone, then that intent was

9–16

---

[60] See *Lord Advocate's Reference (No. 2 of 1992)* 1993 J.C. 43, *per* Lord Justice-Clerk Ross at p. 48E–F.
[61] (1837) 1 Swin. 543.
[62] *ibid.* p. 545.
[63] It could, however, amount to some crime involving culpable and reckless behaviour—as in *R.H.W. v. H.M. Advocate*, 1982 S.L.T. 420. Such crimes are dealt with separately in this chapter (see paras. 9–24 to 9–33, below); and their very existence underlines the fact that recklessly caused injuries are not assaults.
[64] 1989 S.L.T. 399.
[65] *ibid.* p. 401F–H (S.L.T.).

transferred to the person actually struck. Thus assault has been zealously preserved as a crime of intention in Scots law.[66]

9–17 An assault charge may be aggravated, or made more serious in various ways. Prime amongst these are statements in the indictment of ultimate intentions which the accused is alleged to have had. Hume,[67] mentions particularly in this context the intent to kill,[68] the intent to ravish,[69] and the intent to rob. The mode of perpetration of the assault is also often encountered as an aggravation, particularly if a weapon such as a firearm was used.[70] It is also common, even up to the present day, to find the results of the attack specified as aggravations—for example, that they were "to the danger of life",[71] "to severe injury, permanent disability and permanent disfigurement",[72] or even "to severe internal injury".[73] The place of the assault may be taken as an aggravation. It has always been regarded as more heinous, for example, to attack a person violently in his own home — and especially so if his home had been entered by the accused for that very purpose. (This used to be regarded as the separate offence known as "hamesucken"[74]; but that is not the present practice.[75]) An assault may also be aggravated by indecencies; but it surely goes too far to say that every indecent assault is simply an ordinary assault so aggravated.[76] Punching a woman and then fondling her breasts is clearly an aggravated assault; but such fondling unaccompanied by such violence or intimidation[77] is either an indecent assault or it is no crime at all, depending upon whether such familiarities were consented to (see para. 9–19, below).

---

[66] Compare the position in England, as shown in *R. v. Venna* [1976] Q.B. 421.

[67] i, 328–329.

[68] See, for example, *Mysie or Marion Brown or Graham* (1827) Syme 152; *cf.* Ferguson, *Crimes Against the Person*, para. 1.04.

[69] *James Gibbs* (1836) 1 Swin. 263; *Rodgers v. Hamilton*, 1994 S.L.T. 822.

[70] Macdonald, p. 118.

[71] Which can be added whether or not there were actual injuries. See *Peter Leys* (1839) 2 Swin. 337; *cf. Jane Smith or Thom* (1876) 3 Coup. 332; *Kerr (Stephen) v. H.M. Advocate*, 1986 S.C.C.R. 91; *H.M. Advocate v. O'Donnell*, 1996 S.L.T. 563, *per* Lord Justice-Clerk Ross at p. 565H.

[72] Which may appear separately, or together as in *Williamson v. H.M. Advocate*, 1984 S.L.T. 200.

[73] As in *Kirkwood v. H.M. Advocate*, 1939 J.C. 36, where the shaft of a hammer was thrust into the victim's "private parts".

[74] See Hume, i, pp. 312 *et seq.*; Alison, *Principles*, p. 199 *et seq.*; *cf.* Macdonald, p. 118.

[75] See *H.M. Advocate v. Forbes*, 1994 S.L.T. 861, *per* Lord Justice-General Hope at p. 862J–L (also 1994 S.C.C.R. 163 at p. 164).

[76] See Gordon, *Criminal Law*, para. 29–24; *cf.* Macdonald, p. 119.

[77] See, *e.g. Turner v. Scott*, 1996 S.L.T. 200.

CONSENT AS A DEFENCE

No current version of the definition of assault in Scotland includes the phrase **9–18** "without his consent" among its terms.[78] "Lack of consent" is not, therefore, a definitional element. "Consent of the victim" might nevertheless be considered as a defence to an assault charge. But in the few cases where consent has been tendered as a defence, the courts have generally reacted unenthusiastically. Where, for example, what is involved is the deliberate physical injury of another, in pursuance of a quarrel at least, it is no defence that that other person agreed to accept the risk of injury, as in *Smart v. H.M. Advocate*[79] where both parties to a consensual, "no holds barred" fight stood to be successfully prosecuted for assault. It may be too that where a person agrees to be injured for his own (perhaps sexual) gratification, his consent will not prevent his injurer's conviction for assault. If that is so, then Scots and English law would be at one in this matter, namely, that for reasons of public policy, persons cannot be permitted to consent to their own injury.[80] It remains uncertain whether or not consent would be a defence where the victim agreed to be placed in a state of fear and alarm for his personal safety.

Consent and indecent assault

"If A touches B in a sexual manner and B consents to him doing so (and **9–19** there is nothing else involved which would constitute a crime under statute or at common law) there is no assault because there is no evil intention to attack the person of B."[81] But, with respect, what elides assault there is the consent of the person being touched, or rather, A's knowledge of that. Indeed, if that person consents to straightforward fondlings, touchings, embracings and the like, there is no need to consider the intent of the other person at all—a good argument, it is suggested, for considering "indecent assault" to be an offence of its own type.[82] If there was in fact no consent on the part of the victim, an honest belief in consent on the part of the accused should be sufficient to secure his acquittal of a "pure" indecent assault, on analogy with the decision in *Meek v. H.M. Advocate*[83] relating to rape. And in the one case which so far has raised this issue,[84] the advocate-depute maintained

---

[78] *cf.* the definition of theft at para. 10–02, below.

[79] 1975 J.C. 30 at p. 33.

[80] *R. v. Brown* [1994] 1 A.C. 212 (H.L.); *cf. Att.-Gen.'s Reference (No. 6 of 1980)* [1981] Q.B. 715, which appears to preserve consent as a "defence" in relation to minor injuries—a distinction which the court in *Smart v. H.M. Advocate*, 1975 J.C. 30, considered wrong.

[81] *per* Lord Justice-Clerk Wheatley in *Smart v. H.M. Advocate*, 1975 J.C. 30 at p. 32.

[82] *cf.* para. 9–17, above.

[83] 1983 S.L.T. 280, confirmed in *Jamieson v. H.M. Advocate*, 1994 S.L.T. 537.

[84] *Young v. McGlennan*, 1991 S.C.C.R. 738.

that such a belief might secure an acquittal if based on reasonable grounds.[85] At the end of the day, however, the Appeal Court was content to declare that the victim had not consented, that the appellant had gone further than had been justified by the general conviviality of the occasion, and that he had taken advantage of the victim by "touching her in a sexual manner deliberately and without her consent".[86] Whether an honest belief *not* based on reasonable grounds would have been sufficient was not commented upon. If consent is obtained by fraud, then that probably precludes conviction for indecent assault[87]; but a medical practitioner cannot claim that a patient's consent to medical examination for a specific complaint permits him to explore the patient's body entirely as he wishes until the patient expressly demurs.[88] For their greater protection, it appears to be accepted that girls under the age of 12 can give no valid consent to sexual "indecencies".[89] That safeguard for girls under puberty is presumably derived from the correlative common law offence of "lewd, indecent and libidinous practices and behaviour", a protection which has been extended by statute to girls under 16.[90]

Lewd, Indecent and Libidinous Practices

9–20　　　　This offence is a type of indecent assault possibly reserved for cases where the victim is a child under the age of puberty (*i.e.* under 14 for boys, and under 12 for girls).[91] Where the victim is under the age of puberty, any apparent consent by the child can then be discounted.[92] This would, therefore, provide another exception to the rule that a true indecent assault, as opposed to an assault aggravated by indecencies, is elided by consent. But it is perhaps noteworthy that Macdonald[93] states: "In the case of boys, there are obvious reasons why mere puberty should not be made the limit of a charge of this sort"; and, in *McLaughlan v. Boyd*[94] lewd practices were indeed charged in respect of males who were clearly over the age of 14. The charge was not held irrelevant, although the question of the victims' consent, and the

---

[85] *Young v. McGlennan*, 1991 S.C.C.R. 738 at p. 742F (as précis-ed by Lord Justice-General Hope).

[86] *ibid.* p. 743F.

[87] See the civil case of *Gray v. Criminal Injuries Compensation Board*, 1993 S.L.T. 28, where the "victim" was the innocent partner in a bigamous marriage. Fraud itself would remain a legitimate charge, however.

[88] *Hussain v. Houston*, 1995 S.L.T. 1060.

[89] See *C. v. H.M. Advocate*, 1987 S.C.C.R. 104, where the point was strongly urged by the Crown and conceded by the appellant.

[90] Criminal Law (Consolidation) (Scotland) Act 1995, s.6.

[91] See *R.L. v. H.M. Advocate*, 1969 J.C. 40; *Hogg v. Normand*, 1992 S.L.T. 736; *Meredith v. Lees*, 1992 J.C. 127.

[92] See Gordon, *Criminal Law*, para. 36–09.

[93] p. 150.

[94] 1934 J.C. 19.

relevance of that consent in the circumstances, were left unanswered. The best modern opinion seems to be that "the balance of authority is now in favour of the view that the age of the complainer is not of the essence of the crime of lewd, libidinous and indecent practices and behaviour",[95] although the point was not conclusively decided in that case. If this is so, then the issue of consent may become a live one where the complainer is above the age of puberty; but the statutory offence[96] or the common law crime of shamelessly indecent conduct[97] may be used to render the issue irrelevant.

PROVOCATION

The treatment of provocation by both Hume[98] and Macdonald[99] strongly suggests that it is available as a complete defence. It is now clear from authorities relative to homicide[1] and breach of the peace[2] that provocation does not exculpate; its function is hopefully to "have a very considerable bearing upon the penalty which ought to be imposed in respect of [a] finding of guilt."[3] Provocation, therefore, cannot have any higher effect in relation to assault. The expectation is that it will lessen the sentence which might otherwise be imposed.   **9–21**

It seems that a wide variety of matters may be raised as provocation at a trial for assault. These obviously include a violent attack made on the accused to which he responds there and then in the heat of the moment[4]; but the response must keep some sort of proportion to the original violence offered. As Hume put it: "[t]he general rule being once announced, that the person assaulted must keep within the bounds of an allowable resentment, the application is matter of common sense; and little aid is to be derived from any thing that books can teach on the subject."[5] But finding one's spouse in the throes of homosexual passion has also been considered sufficiently provoking,[6] as have insulting words and behaviour. Thus, in the old case of *Ensign Andrew Monro*[7] the accused was understandably moved to violence on being called a "bougar" and "son of a whore"; and in *James McEwen*[8]   **9–22**

---

[95] *Batty v. H.M. Advocate,* 1995 S.L.T. 1047 (where the female victims were aged between 12 and 16 years), *per* Lord Justice-General Hope at p. 1051G–H.

[96] Criminal Law (Consolidation) (Scotland) Act 1995, s.6 (girls over 12, and under 16 years).

[97] See paras. 12–23 *et seq.*, below; and *Batty v. H.M. Advocate,* 1995 S.L.T. 1047.

[98] i, 333–337.

[99] pp. 116–117.

[1] *Fenning v. H.M. Advocate,* 1985 J.C. 76, *per* Lord Cameron at pp. 79–80.

[2] *MacNeill v. McTaggart* (1976) S.C.C.R. Supp. 150 at p. 151.

[3] *ibid.*

[4] See Hume, i, 334–335.

[5] i, 335; and see *Lennon v. H.M. Advocate,* 1991 S.C.C.R. 611.

[6] *H.M. Advocate v. Callander,* 1958 S.L.T. 24.

[7] (1700) Hume, i, 334, n. 2.

[8] (1838) Bell's Notes 91.

provocation was found in a newspaper article which was libellous of the accused's mother. In all cases, however, the assault must follow soon after the provocation, whatever it be. The intention is to make suitable allowance for incidents and events which excite the accused to a state of retaliatory passion, and not to cater in any way for a long-nurtured thirst for vengeance. Hume[9] mentions the 1746 case of *Alexander Lockhart* who was permitted to adduce evidence of provocation by insulting words given him by the victim in the morning of May 4, in alleviation of an assault perpetrated by him on the evening of the same day; but that must surely be the limit of the law's toleration. It is probable, however, that the rules for provocation are less strictly applied in assault than they are in homicide cases.[10]

DIMINISHED RESPONSIBILITY

9–23	This matter is again a mitigatory plea rather than a complete defence, and operates in the same way as provocation (see para. 9–21, above). It was probably first used at some stage in the second half of the nineteenth century, as a palliative to a conviction for murder with its capital punishment consequences.[11] What diminished responsibility means is some weakness of mind falling short of insanity but providing a degree of excuse for the crime committed. This is neither very scientific nor precise but it is probably wholly proper for the law to give such a concept an open-ended significance. The most frequently quoted account of the matter is to be found in a dictum of Lord Justice-Clerk Alness in *H.M. Advocate v. Savage*[12] which is set out in full at paragraph 9–69, below. It emphasises that there must be some form of mental disease, if this mitigatory issue is to be considered at all, a conclusion which continues to be upheld.[13] There have been opinions from the Bench that a plea of diminished responsibility is confined to a murder indictment,[14] but there is no good reason for such a restriction, and it is suggested that Macdonald[15] is correct when he states: "On principle, weakness of mind not amounting to insanity would appear to be available in mitigation of guilt of assault."

---

[9] i, 337.

[10] See paras. 9–60 *et seq.*, below.

[11] See *Alexander Dingwall* (1867) 5 Irv. 466, discussed in para. 9.67, below.

[12] 1923 J.C. 49.

[13] *Connelly v. H.M. Advocate*, 1990 S.C.C.R. 504; *Williamson v. H.M. Advocate*, 1994 S.L.T. 1000; *Martindale v. H.M. Advocate*, 1994 S.L.T. 1093.

[14] *H.M. Advocate v. Cunningham*, 1963 J.C. 80, *per* Lord Justice-General Clyde at p. 84; *Brennan v. H.M. Advocate*, 1977 J.C. 38 at p. 47.

[15] p. 117.

3. NON-INTENTIONAL INJURY

Introduction

Using Hume's concept of "real injury" (see para. 9–03, above) as an **9–24**
established general principle[16] the Scottish courts have developed a series
of related crimes. These differ from assault in that injuries suffered by the
victim are not caused intentionally by the accused. Rather they are the
product of recklessness on his behalf. It has been said frequently by the
judiciary that non-intentionally caused injuries are not criminal at common
law unless the conduct of the accused went well beyond carelessness. A
very significant derogation from the standard of care expected of a person
of ordinary understanding and competence has to be shown. In the leading
case of *H.M. Advocate v. Harris*,[17] three of the five judges emphasised this
point,[18] and indeed considered that the standard referred to in *Quinn v.
Cunningham*[19] was essentially correct. That standard was itself derived from
an earlier culpable homicide case[20] where the requirement was stated to be
"gross, or wicked, or criminal negligence, something amounting, or at any
rate analogous, to a criminal indifference to consequences".[20a] A high
standard of recklessness of this nature is, therefore, essential, and forms the
mens rea of each such crime.[21] It was also held to be correct in *Harris* that
actual injury was not always necessary — that there was a crime, or class
of crimes, of which the essence was causing danger to the "lieges" by the
recklessness of one's conduct.[22] Although criticised by Lord McCluskey,[23]
Lord Prosser was surely correct when he opined that recklessness (in this
context at least) consists of a failure in one's duty to so conduct oneself that

---

[16]   See *Khaliq v. H.M. Advocate*, 1984 J.C. 23, *per* Lord Justice-General Emslie at pp. 31–32.
[17]   1993 J.C. 150.
[18]   *ibid. per* Lord Murray at p. 155H–I, Lord Morison at p. 162A–C, and Lord Brand at pp.
       168E and 169B (where he sought to distinguish between recklessness of the required high
       standard, and "mere" recklessness).
[19]   1956 J.C. 22 — overruled in other respects by *H.M. Advocate v. Harris.*
[20]   *Paton v. H.M. Advocate,* 1936 J.C. 19.
[20a] *per* Lord Justice-Clerk Aitchison at p. 22.
[21]   It has to be noted, however, that in some cases, the Appeal Court has criticised judges who
       directed juries that a high degree of recklessness was required. Criticism was based on the
       view that such directions introduced unnecessary complications where the simple distinction
       to be made was between negligent or accidental conduct (which was not criminal) and
       reckless behaviour (which was): see, *e.g. Carr v. H.M. Advocate,* 1995 S.L.T. 800, *per*
       Lord Justice-General Hope at pp. 903K–L and 904A (reckless fire-raising).
[22]   This was conceded by counsel for the respondent in the case, a concession which all five
       judges considered to have been correctly made. Notice that Lord Prosser sensibly objected
       to the use of the archaic expression "lieges"; as he put it, at p. 166C: "danger to others can
       be referred to as danger to others without obsolete terms which need explaining."
[23]   *H.M. Advocate v. Harris,* 1993 J.C. 150, at p. 159H–I. The basis of his criticism was that
       complex accounts of the *mentes reae* appropriate to particular crimes will simply create
       difficulties for judges and confusion for juries.

foreseeable danger of significant injury to others as a consequence of one's actions is set at an absolute minimum.[24] Clearly the nature of the activity and the degree of risk involved are important considerations in the assessment of conduct as "reckless"; but Lord Prosser appears to emphasise that recklessness and danger to others are interdependent in crimes of this nature — and that it makes sense to consider whether there had been danger to others even where injury is actually caused.[25] Certainly, where unintentional injury does result from the conduct of the accused, it is plainly necessary to categorise that injury as accidentally, negligently or recklessly caused — only the last of the three being relevant from the point of view of the criminal law. Equally, if significant unintentional injury has been caused by one's conduct, a strong inference arises that one's conduct probably was dangerous to others. It may be sufficient in fact that the conduct was dangerous in respect of the victim alone. The existence of danger to others, due to one's conduct, is thus a useful (if not essential) guide to separating the relevant from the irrelevant in crimes of this sort. The essential elements of the best known of these offences are discussed in the paragraphs which follow.

OFFENCES INVOLVING A RELATIONSHIP BETWEEN ACCUSED AND VICTIM

Cruel and barbarous treatment

9–25   Indictments for offences of this description were found frequently in the nineteenth century. Very often such a charge would be combined with an allegation of "Wilful and Culpable Neglect"[26]; but a composite charge of that nature was regarded as containing one offence only.[27] It seems, since it is difficult to be certain about this, that the offence is aimed at those who are close relatives or guardians of the victim, or at any person who can be said to have undertaken his care and custody.[28] Thus, in *John McRae*, the accused was alleged to have confined his weak-minded wife in a space no longer than three-and-a-half feet, and no higher than two-and-a-half feet for almost four months. This was further alleged to have caused the unfortunate woman serious injury to her mind and body. He was convicted— as was his co-accused, a female servant within the household. It is to be noted that a close, personal relationship existed between victim and accused,

---

[24] *H.M. Advocate v. Harn's*, 1993 J.C. 150 at p. 165C–D.

[25] *ibid.* p. 165E–F.

[26] The epithets "culpable" and "wilful" are possibly mere surplusage in indictments and complaints — see, *e.g.*, *H.M. Advocate v. Harris*, 1993 J.C. 150, *per* Lord Justice-Clerk Ross at p. 154C–D, Lord McCluskey (diss.) at p. 158A–C, Lord Prosser at pp. 165H to 166A–B.

[27] See the form of indictment in John McRae's case.

[28] *John McRae* (1842) 1 Broun 395, *per* Lord Cockburn at p. 399.

and that the injurious consequences of their actions featured prominently in the charge. Where these features were found to be absent from an apparently similar indictment, the High Court found the charge to be irrelevant.[29]

Cruel and unnatural treatment

Nineteenth-century indictments[30] often alleged cruel and unnatural, or just cruel treatment; but it is difficult to see how that varied (if at all) from the "cruel and barbarous" variety. In *William Fairweather*,[31] for example, a father was accused of confining his weak-minded daughter in a small hutch in an outhouse for about a month, whereby her life was endangered and she was reduced to a state of almost total idiocy. He pled guilty to the charge, which factually looked identical to that in *John McRae* (see para. 9–25, above). In both cases, it is very likely that the accused meant the victims no harm. They probably thought, given nineteenth-century standards, that what they did was as good a method as any of coping with mental illness. But they all exhibited utter disregard for the health and safety of the persons concerned. Very much the same might be said of the inn-keeper and his assistant in *McManimy and Higgans*.[32] Those two accused evicted a man suspected of typhoid from an inn in Stirling, and carried him by rail (on the outside part of a carriage) to a Glasgow station where he was abandoned for the police to discover. Although the unfortunate victim died shortly thereafter in hospital, the accused pled guilty to reckless, cruel and culpable removal of a sick person from his bed whilst he was helpless, to his injury and the danger of his life, and to reckless and cruel treatment involving desertion of a sick person. Their pleas were accepted; and it is to be noted that they were designed as persons entrusted with the care of a sick person, or who had assumed custody and charge of him. Such ascriptions would be unnecessary, of course, where the accused was a parent of the victim. Thus, in *Rachel Gibson*[33] a mother was alleged, amongst other things, to have treated her new-born child cruelly and unnaturally by putting it in a basket and sending it, suitably labelled, by rail as an ordinary parcel. It was her clear intention to desert the child in that somewhat novel way, by which it "was seriously injured in its health". (She pled guilty after the indictment had been held relevant.)

9–26

---

[29] See *Robert Watt and James Kerr* (1868) 1 Coup. 123, where the accused was alleged to have forced young, ill-clad stowaways to leave his ship and find their way as best they could across ice floes towards land, which was many miles distant.

[30] For a more modern example, see *Lambert v. H.M. Advocate,* 1993 S.L.T. 339.

[31] (1842) 1 Broun 309.

[32] (1847) Ark. 321, which also involved homicide.

[33] (1845) 2 Broun 366.

OFFENCES INVOLVING INJURY, OR DANGER OF INJURY TO ONE OR MORE OF THE
LIEGES

Reckless Injury

9–27   It has recently been made clear that there is a discrete offence of
unintentionally but recklessly causing injury to another. In *H.M. Advocate
v. Harris*,[34] a steward at a night club was charged with recklessly seizing
hold of the victim, pushing her on the body and causing her to fall down a
flight of steps onto the roadway outside the premises, where she was run
over by a vehicle to her severe injury and permanent disfigurement. This
was one of two alternative charges in the indictment, the other being one of
assault. It was objected firstly that the non-assault charge was not a crime
known to the law of Scotland since it had not been specifically stated that
what the steward had done was also "to the danger of the lieges". It was
held on this point that such an addendum was unnecessary, and, in so far as
prior authority[35] had required such an additional formula, that prior authority
would be overruled. Secondly, it was claimed that since the facts were
identically stated in both alternative charges, there was no difference between
those charges, and that both, therefore, amounted to assault. (No doubt
since it was possible that the accused had not intended to do more than
carry out his duty of ejecting the complainer from the premises, using no
more than reasonable force, it was also possible that the prosecutor would
not succeed in proving that the accused had intended to injure her. It was
thus to the accused's possible advantage to have the "recklessness" charge
removed, since he might remain vulnerable to that.) Four of the five judges
supported the prosecution's view that recklessly causing injury was a distinct
type of crime, and that it was properly posited here as an alternative to
assault.[36] It was emphasised that although a steward may be entitled
intentionally to manhandle persons attending a night club and to eject them
using reasonable force without being criminally liable for assault, yet "if
reasonable force is not exceeded, ejection may ... be culpably reckless ...
if insisted upon in face of danger to the person being ejected or to that
person's actual severe injury."[37] As a result of the clarification of the law in
Harris, this particular crime probably now embraces former cases relating
to injuries caused by the reckless driving of a horse and cart[38] or a

---

[34] 1993 J.C. 150.

[35] *Quinn v. Cunningham,* 1956 J.C. 22.

[36] 1993 J.C. 150, *per* Lord Justice-Clerk Ross at p. 154D–E, Lord Murray at p. 156E, Lord
     Morison at p. 162G, and Lord Prosser at p. 167H–I. (Lord McCluskey dissented on this
     point.)

[37] *ibid. per* Lord Murray at p. 156E.

[38] *Alexander Lawson* (1829) Bell's Notes 76.

locomotive,[39] the reckless navigation of a ship,[40] the reckless disposal of a glass bottle,[41] and the like. There must, of course, be a causal link established between the accused's reckless conduct and the injury to the complainer, but that link seems easily drawn. In *Kimmins v. Normand*,[42] for example, a person being legitimately searched for drugs by the police was asked if he had about his person any needles or similar sharp instruments. It was held on appeal that his denial of having any such object, when he well knew that he had an unprotected hypodermic needle in his pocket, provided the necessary causal link to the injury of a policeman who subsequently placed his hand in that pocket in the course of the search.[43] The charge was thus fully relevant as one of "recklessly causing injury". (That charge also alleged that the unfortunate policeman had been "exposed to the risk of infection" when the needle entered his hand; but this is probably a matter of aggravation rather than any necessary element in the description of the crime.)

Reckless endangerment of the lieges

Where no injury is caused by reckless behaviour, but that behaviour is objectively dangerous to others, a distinct offence of recklessly causing such danger is available.[44] Modern examples may be seen in *Normand v. Robinson*,[45] where the accused organised a mass entertainment known as "a rave" in derelict premises which were completely unsafe for the holding of such an event, and in *Normand v. Morrison*,[46] where the accused allegedly denied to police officers who were about to search her that she had an unprotected hypodermic needle in her handbag — thus exposing those officers (or any one of them who undertook the search) to the risk of infection. It does not seem essential to the relevancy of such a charge that the words "to the danger of the lieges [or others]" should actually appear on it, provided that such danger can readily be inferred[47]: and it does not seem to be (nor could be) an objection to such a charge that injuries were actually caused. In *MacPhail v. Clark*,[48] for example, the accused set fire to stubble in a field in such a reckless manner that smoke in great quantity drifted over the carriageway of a nearby road thus causing acute problems of visibility for drivers of vehicles there. Whilst the accused unconcernedly

9–28

---

[39] *Thomas Smith* (1853) 1 Irv. 271.
[40] *Archibald Grassom* (1884) 5 Coup. 483.
[41] *R.H.W. v. H.M. Advocate*, 1982 S.L.T. 420.
[42] 1993 S.L.T. 1260.
[43] *per* Lord Justice-General Hope at p. 1261H.
[44] *H.M. Advocate v. Harris*, 1993 J.C. 150.
[45] 1994 S.L.T. 558.
[46] 1993 S.C.C.R. 207 (Sh.Ct.).
[47] See the complaint in *Normand v. Morrison, supra* at n. 45.
[48] 1983 S.L.T. (Sh.Ct.) 37.

continued with other tasks in the same field, road accidents occurred because of the smoke. There were injuries as a result of those accidents; but the charge appears to have been one of reckless endangerment to which the accounts of accident and injury were added by way of aggravation. In a case where the causal link between the accused's reckless conduct and actual injury to another is weak or difficult to prove, treating the injury as an aggravation is obviously a sensible course of action for the Crown to adopt.

Administration of noxious substances

9–29   It has been clear since the early nineteenth century that the deliberate and reckless (in the sense of having complete disregard for the consequences) administration of deleterious substances to anyone, to his injury, is criminal.[49] Thus Hume makes mention that the administration of a powerful aphrodisiac (cantharides) to three women, such that they were injured in their health, was considered a relevant crime.[50] Nor did it matter that the motive was merely one of sport or jest: in *Henry Inglis, Andrew and Robert Colvilles*,[51] for example, the administration of snuff in a draught of liquor to the victim as something of a joke was clearly criminal (although charged as culpable homicide, since the person who drank it died in consequence). It will be plain, therefore, that it is not necessary to show that the accused forced the noxious substance into the mouth or body of the victim. It is quite enough that he caused the victim to take it, the self-administration, so to speak, not representing any *novus actus interveniens* (see paras. 5–19 *et seq.,* above). In *Robert Brown and John Lawson*[52] it seems to have been quite sufficient that the accused gave a quarter of a pint of whisky to a seven-year-old child, who then, as far as one can determine, proceeded to drink it off by himself (the child suffered from epileptic fits thereafter). Naturally, whether a substance is truly noxious or not will depend on the age and disposition of the victim; but substances prescribed by a doctor, or having apparent medicinal properties, are unlikely to be regarded as "deleterious", unless the circumstances are special.[53] It is possible too that consent might be a defence to a charge of administration of things having such medicinal properties.[54]

---

[49] *Alexander Mitchell* (1833) Bell's Notes 90.
[50] i, 237, n.b.—the case of *John Ferguson and John Edie* (1822).
[51] (1784) Hume, i, 237.
[52] (1842) 1 Broun 415.
[53] *Peter Milne and John Barry* (1868) 1 Coup. 28, *per* Lord Cowan at p. 31.
[54] *ibid.*

Supplying of potentially noxious substances

A state of intoxication has always held a considerable fascination for   **9–30**
human beings of all ages, and the obtaining of substances which will effect
such a state has been seen at all times as a desirable goal. Those who are
excluded by virtue of youth or lack of means from having ready access to
"normal" and readily safe intoxicants have proved peculiarly inventive in
exploiting substances really intended for some harmless, household purpose.
Boot-polish, lighter fuel, paint thinners, and various glues, for example,
can be turned to use as highly dangerous intoxicants when inhaled or ingested
instead of being utilised for their intended purposes. It was indeed the desire
to control abuse of such substances which lead the Appeal Court in *Khaliq
v. H.M. Advocate*[55] to invent or perhaps "discover" the crime referred to
here as "supplying potentially noxious substances". The offence itself is
rather more complex, however, than that somewhat simple title would
suggest.

The charge in *Khaliq*[56] contained at least five elements: (1) that the   **9–31**
accused shop-keepers wilfully and recklessly supplied (*i.e.* sold, or perhaps
bartered) substances capable of giving off toxic fumes (*e.g.* "Evo-stik" glue);
(2) that they did so to customers who were children, aged between eight
and 15 years; (3) that the substances were specially supplied in, or with,
containers (*e.g.* otherwise empty plastic bags) to facilitate the inhalation of
those toxic fumes; (4) that the accused did so, well knowing that those
customers intended to inhale the fumes and that such inhalation would or
could be injurious to their health and a threat to their lives; and (5) that by
virtue of their conduct, the accused caused those customers to inhale the
fumes to the danger of their health and lives (on which, see para. 5–20,
above). That complex indictment was found relevant before the trial court,
and the accused were convicted. Both findings were upheld on appeal.
Although Lord Justice-General Emslie said[57]: "that the persons supplied
were children is not ... essential to the relevancy of the charge", it was
widely felt that his remarks were mere *obiter*, since public concern at the
time had centred on glue-sniffing by children. Indeed, when Parliament
eventually placed a virtual embargo on sales of such substances to children,[58]
it did not extend the legislation to Scotland, since it apparently was of the
persuasion that that was already the law in this country due to the decision
in *Khaliq*. It was also widely felt that it had been very significant that the

---

[55] 1984 J.C. 23.
[56] *ibid.*
[57] *ibid.* p. 33.
[58] See the Intoxicating Substances (Supply) Act 1985. See also the indictment in *Khalid v.
H.M. Advocate*, 1990 J.C. 37.

substances had been supplied in "user-friendly" "kits". These "feelings" thus enabled the decision in *Khaliq* to be limited in a sensible way, so that it would not be seen as extending to the supply of whisky to a known alcoholic or cigarettes to a known sufferer from lung cancer.[59] But the subsequent decision in *Ulhaq*[60] (see para. 9–32, below) has demonstrated that such perceived limitations were wrong.

9–32	In *Ulhaq v. H.M. Advocate*[61] a shopkeeper was again charged with the same type of offence first seen in *Khaliq*. Significant differences existed, however, between the two fact situations. In *Ulhaq*, the customers were not children. They were all between 20 and 29 years of age, and could thus be described accurately as adults. What they had bought from the store in question were vast quantities of lighter fuel and glue—but all in their original cartons, tins and tubes. No inhalation-assisting "kits" were supplied at all. It was argued in vain, however, that those issues made any significant difference. It was enough that the store-keeper knew that his customers intended to use the substances for no proper purposes, that he supplied them on that basis, and that he thus caused them to abuse the substances in question to their injury and danger. This decision then resurrects the spectre of criminality surrounding, for example, the sale of significant quantities of alcohol to a known alcoholic. It may be that the case depends solely on its own facts, and is confined to volatile substances such as lighter fuel and glues. If that, however, is felt to be an essentially naive view, then the decision may only be rescued from uncontrolled expansion by reference to this: that the crime ought to be limited to the kind of substances which are potentially noxious if used in a way that their manufacturers never intended as proper (*e.g.* by being inhaled or swallowed), and which are not otherwise regulated in terms of sale, purchase or possession by Parliament.[62] The signs are, however, that the courts are not persuaded that such limitations upon the offence would be justified.[63] It might be thought, of course, that there is a problem with establishing a causal link in such cases since the person supplied must choose to use the substance in a way that its manufacturer

---

[59]	See *Skeen v. Malik* (1977) unreported, in Gane and Stoddart, *Casebook on Criminal Law* (2nd ed.), pp. 453–457.

[60]	1991 S.L.T. 614.

[61]	*ibid.*

[62]	*cf.* cigarettes and ethyl alcohols. See the Children and Young Persons (Scotland) Act 1937, s.18, as amended by the Protection of Children (Tobacco) Act 1986 and by the Children and Young Persons (Protection from Tobacco) Act 1991.

[63]	See *Lord Advocate's Reference (No. 1 of 1994)*, 1995 S.L.T. 248, where the "supplying" of drugs (controlled under the Misuse of Drugs Act 1971) was considered equivalent to the offence fashioned in *Khaliq* and *Ulhaq* for the purposes of culpable homicide where the person supplied died after ingesting those drugs. The "rules" pertaining to the "reckless supply of potentially noxious substances" were thus made available against the supplier in a culpable homicide prosecution, and enabled objections there to the establishing of a causal link to be swept aside.

did not intend, and that, therefore, the exercise of such choice amounts to a *novus actus interveniens*[64] which thus breaks the chain of interlinking events between the supplying and the abuse. In *Khaliq,*[65] however, such an argument was dismissed by the Appeal Court. The view was taken that the abuse of the substances was the "known, intended and expected purpose"[66] of their being supplied at all, and that there was such a close connection between supplying and administration in such circumstances that it was legitimate to treat the supply as analogous to administration (and thus criminal) "even in the absence of words of instigation on the part of the suppliers."[67]

Discharge of firearms

It is certainly criminal to discharge firearms recklessly to the danger or **9–33** actual injury of the lieges.[68] That no one need actually be injured is understandable given the lethal nature of such weapons; but in the absence of real injury, it seems necessary that there were people within range at the time, as in *David Smith and William McNeil,*[69] where much emphasis was placed on the fact that the accused shot through the glass window of an inhabited house, to the imminent danger of those living there. There seems little to be gained by treating this as an offence separate from "reckless injury" (see para. 9–27, above) or "reckless endangerment of the lieges" (para. 9–28), although an especially dangerous *modus*, of course, is involved in this instance of those crimes.

4. HOMICIDES

Introduction

There are two forms of criminal homicide recognised by Scots common **9–34** law—murder and culpable homicide. The *actus reus* of both of those crimes is identical. It consists of positive conduct by the accused, or a failure by him to act where he had a legal duty to do so, which causes the death of

---

[64] See para. 5–19 *et seq.*, above.
[65] loc. cit. in n. 55, *supra.*
[66] *per* Lord Justice-General Emslie, at p. 33.
[67] *ibid.* This method of establishing a causal connection was used *a fortiori* in *Lord Advocate's Reference (No. 1 of 1994)* (see n. 63, above), where prohibited (and thus dangerous *per se*) drugs were supplied to a person who had voluntarily sought them, voluntarily selected a particular dose of them, voluntarily taken that dose, and then died from the effects.
[68] See, for example, *Robert Anderson* (1832) Bell's Notes 73; *Gizzi v. Tudhope*, 1983 S.L.T. 214.
[69] (1842) 1 Broun 240.

another human being.[70] "Failures to act" have already been explored in Chapter 3,[71] and "causation" issues in Chapter 5. But the question of when a person is dead raises some nice issues of its own. Before a "person" can be killed, he must have been alive. In a sense (and for some, a very real sense), a human foetus is alive from the moment of its conception onwards. If that were so for the purposes of the criminal law, then it would be homicide to end a foetus's "life" by destroying it in its mother's womb. That is not, however, the approach taken. Hume makes it plain that the destruction of life in the womb is not homicide but the separate crime of abortion.[72] The criterion for homicide thus appears to be that the victim had been a "self-existent human life".[73] At the very least, the victim must have been born alive at one point in time, and killed at another, because of some action or inaction on the accused's part. As Hume colourfully indicates,[74] until a foetus is born alive, it is merely *pars viscerum matris* (*i.e.* part of its mother's viscera). It seems, however, that the Appeal Court has accepted that a child born alive can be subsequently killed by some injury which was caused to it in the womb.[75]

Abortion

9–35   The crime of abortion at common law consists of intentionally causing or procuring the termination of pregnancy and consequently the destruction of a developing foetus.[76] The method of achieving such an end is probably of little moment, but the cases on the subject generally refer to the use of instruments or the administration of drugs.[77] It is also essential that there had been a criminal purpose, since it may have been necessary to cause the abortion[78]—to save the life of the mother, for example. Since the Abortion Act 1967, however, the common law crime has ceased to be of any real significance. The import of the Act[79] is that an abortion carried out by a qualified doctor will not be criminal, provided that two independent doctors certify that there would be greater risk to the physical or mental health of the mother or any of her existing children in carrying the foetus to term

---

[70] Gordon, *Criminal Law*, paras. 23–04 to 23–08.
[71] See paras. 3–09 *et seq.*
[72] i, 186; see para. 9–35 below.
[73] As Macdonald puts it at p. 87, although this has to be seen simply as a useful way of referring to the demarcation line between a foetus and a child born alive. A newly-born infant, and indeed a person in a coma or persistent vegetative state (see para. 9–72, below) can hardly be said to be 'self-existent', yet are clearly not beyond the protection of the law of homicide.
[74] i, 186.
[75] *McCluskey v. H.M. Advocate*, 1988 S.C.C.R. 629 at p. 632.
[76] Macdonald, p. 114.
[77] See *Minnie Graham* (1897) 2 Adam 412.
[78] Macdonald, p. 114.
[79] See s.1(1), as amended by the Human Fertilisation and Embryology Act 1994, s.37.

than in terminating the pregnancy (which may be done on these grounds until the end of the 24th week of the pregnancy only); or (and the following are without time-limit), that there would be grave permanent injury (mental or physical) to the mother (or risk to her life) if the pregnancy were allowed to continue, or that there would be substantial risk of serious handicap to the child if the foetus were allowed to be born.

Death

There is no particular legal definition of death. In modern times, it is **9–36** clear that the cessation of breathing or heart-beat does not conclusively show that a person is dead. Medical science has in any event invented the technological means of sustaining breath and pulse in situations where a person has lost the means of sustaining them for himself.[80] It is thought, therefore, that an appropriate legal test for death must now involve the permanent cessation of brain activity. But the courts have not commented on the matter, although at least one reported case presented the opportunity for them to do so.[81]

Res judicata

Homicides are often caused by actions which are crimes in their own **9–37** right, for example, by assaults or by administration of noxious substances such as active poisons. Since Scots law has no rule equivalent to that of the English "year and a day" rule[82] it can happen that an accused is convicted and sentenced for an assault upon a person who later, much later, dies of his injuries. The view taken, however, is that the original conviction for any such crime less than homicide does not prevent a new trial for homicide, if the victim subsequently dies.[83] From this point of view, homicide is not just an aggravated form of assault or other offence of real injury, but a separate class of crime.

Casual Homicide

The older text-writers emphasise that some killings are not criminal, **9–38** and that in particular some may be described as "casual". Hume indicates that such a killing occurs "when a person kills unintentionally, who is lawfully employed, and neither means bodily harm to any one, nor has failed in the due degree of care for preventing danger to his neighbour."[84]

---

[80] See, *e.g.*, para. 9–72, below (Persistent Vegetative State).
[81] See *Finlayson v. H.M. Advocate*, 1979 J.C. 33; para. 5–25, above.
[82] See *R. v. Dyson* [1908] 2 K.B. 454.
[83] *Tees v. H.M. Advocate*, 1994 S.L.T. 701.
[84] i, 194.

What he seems to mean by this is simply that accidental homicides are not criminal (as in the case of *John Leper*,[85] where a prisoner insisted on running ahead of his guard, despite warnings that the castle which they were traversing was in part ruinous and dangerous; the prisoner having become lost and fallen 20 feet to his death, it was held that no blame for the death could be attached to his escort).

Justifiable homicide

9–39   Other killings which are not criminal are those which are justifiable. Hume,[86] for example, mentions homicides effected by soldiers with good cause (in war, perhaps, or in the quelling of a riot), or police officers. It is thought, however, that police officers would only be justified in killing where it was necessary to do so in self-defence—a broad category open to anyone (see paras. 8–19 *et seq.* above), and also, it seems, to women in particular in avoidance of rape (see para. 8–39, above). Despite some dicta to the contrary,[87] it is not thought that homicide in defence of property alone can ever be justifiable.

Excusable homicide

9–40   It is not clear whether there is any such class as that of "excusable homicide"[88] but it remains possible that the Scottish courts will not follow English authority, and will not rule out a defence of coercion to a homicide charge (see para. 8–87, above[89]). If that happens, then, as coercion is an excuse personal to the accused, this class would have at least one member.

Penalties for homicide

9–41   The two forms of criminal homicide are distinguishable from one another by reference to their *mens rea* requirements and also according to the penalty which follows conviction. For murder, there is a fixed sentence of life in prison, with appropriate provision for those who are under 18 and those who are under 21.[90] The trial judge may make a recommendation as to the minimum number of years to be served before the person concerned may be released by the Secretary of State for Scotland; but even when such a

---

[85]   (1682) Hume, i, 194.

[86]   i, 195.

[87]   *e.g., Edward Lane* (1830) Bell's Notes 77, *per* Lord Moncreiff, that a servant might be justified in killing an intruder found in his master's house "if he thought he could not otherwise protect his master's property."

[88]   See paras. 8–03 and 8–04, above, for the difference between an excuse and a justification.

[89]   Which refers to Lord Allanbridge's direction to the jury in *Collins v. H.M. Advocate*, 1991 S.C.C.R. 898 at p. 920C.

[90]   Criminal Procedure (Scotland) Act 1995, s.205.

person is released from prison, he is released only on licence.[91] Culpable homicide, on the other hand, carries no maximum sentence other than that which the trial court has for any common law crime (see Appendix D). It follows then that a wide range of sentencing options exists for those convicted of culpable homicide, and instances can easily be found of very lenient disposals which reflect the circumstances involved. In *Robert Bruce*,[92] for example, where the death was something of a mischance occasioned during the course of a consensual fight, the accused was convicted and fined one shilling (although he was also required to find caution to keep the peace for one year); and in the controversial case of *H.M. Advocate v. Sherman*[93] the accused was admonished after having been convicted of the culpable homicide of his wife and child by shooting. The implication of the penalty differences between the two crimes is that all murders are taken to be equally morally bad, whereas culpable homicide cases vary enormously in moral culpability. It is also implied, of course, by reference to sentence that only a High Court can deal with a case of murder; and it is a matter of law that a district court can never deal with a case of murder or culpable homicide.[94]

MURDER

Definition of murder

The accepted definition of murder in current Scots law is that given by **9–42** Macdonald.[95] It runs: "[m]urder is constituted by any wilful act causing the destruction of life, whether intended to kill, or displaying such wicked recklessness as to imply a disposition depraved enough to be regardless of consequences." In other words, it consists of the *actus reus* proffered at paragraph 9–34, above, together with two alternative forms of *mens rea*.

Actus reus

Murder is a result crime (see para. 2–40, above). From this point of **9–43** view, it is certainly correct to say that the type of conduct which causes death is of little consequence (see para. 3–05, above). But the conduct in

---

[91] Criminal Procedure (Scotland) Act 1995, s.205(4). A "minimum years" recommendation should not be made for less than 12 years, and generally should be made only where there were circumstances of exceptional brutality in effecting the killing and/or the accused is considered a danger to the public: *Casey v. H.M. Advocate*, 1993 J.C. 102; *cf. McGuire v. H.M. Advocate*, 1995 S.C.C.R. 776 (where such a recommendation was set aside on appeal).

[92] (1855) 2 Irv. 65.

[93] February 27, 1990, Aberdeen High Court, unreported.

[94] 1995 Act, s.7(8)(b)(i).

[95] p. 89.

question must be capable of raising an inference that *mens rea* of either type existed. What might reasonably be said at present, therefore, is that the range of conduct capable of raising such an inference is vast. It extends, for example, to the use of severe physical violence, as in *Charles McDonald*[96]—using fists, stones and bottles; the employment of weapons, as in *Cawthorne v. H.M. Advocate*[97]—rifle firing high-velocity bullets; the administration of poisons, as in *Christian Gilmour*[98] and *Madeleine Smith*[99]; setting fire to the victim's clothing, as in *H.M. Advocate v. Kennedy*[1]; boring holes in a ship's bottom, as in *H.M. Advocate v. Monson*[2]; throwing the victim twice from a fourth floor window, as in *McGuire v. H.M. Advocate*[3]; and deserting a young child as in *Elizabeth Kerr*[4] or a seriously injured adult, as in *H.M. Advocate v. McPhee*.[5]

Mens rea: intent

9–44   Macdonald's definition (see para. 9–42, above) includes an intention to kill as a sufficient form of *mens rea*, and that smacks of plain common sense. It is also founded on Hume's requirement of an "absolute purpose to kill"[6] or an absolute resolve "to dispatch [one's] victim on the spot."[7] The question arises, however, whether or not it is necessary that the intent to kill should be "evil" or "wicked". In *Fenning v. H.M. Advocate*, for example, Lord Mayfield told the jury that they could not convict of murder if they thought there was an absence of "wicked intent or recklessness".[8] It is thought, however, that a simple intent to kill is sufficient, whether accompanied by a wicked motive or not.[9] If it were otherwise, intentional killings based on good ulterior motives, such as euthanasia, would not be capable of analysis as murders; but that is contrary to what most commentators believe.[10] How prosecutors in the exercise of their discretion

---

[96] (1867) 5 Irv. 525.
[97] 1968 J.C. 32.
[98] (1844) 2 Broun 23.
[99] (1857) 2 Irv. 641.
[1] (1907) 5 Adam 347.
[2] (1893) 1 Adam 114.
[3] 1995 S.C.C.R. 776.
[4] (1860) 3 Irv. 645, though she pled guilty to culpable homicide.
[5] 1935 J.C. 46.
[6] i, 191 and 256.
[7] i, 238.
[8] 1985 S.C.C.R. 219 at p. 220.
[9] See *Scott v. H.M. Advocate*, 1996 S.L.T. 519, where the Appeal Court thought it inappropriate to refer to the "wickedness" of intentional murder as opposed to the degree of wickedness required by the alternative form of *mens rea*. It was sufficient and less confusing for juries to refer simply to Macdonald's classic definition (see para. 9–42, above) without adding to it.
[10] See Gordon, *Criminal Law*, paras. 25–02 and 25–03; Ferguson, *Crimes Against the Person*, para. 3.02.

deal with such killings is, of course, beside the point, as far as the *mens rea* of the crime is concerned. It seems that it is possible for the Crown to peril its case on an intent to kill, such that recklessness is not an issue at all.[11]

Mens rea: wicked recklessness

What is plain in relation to the alternative form of *mens rea* for murder **9–45** is that "wicked" recklessness is more than "simple" recklessness. More is required than the usual "utter disregard of what the consequences of the act in question may be, so far as the public are concerned."[11a] That may be enough for some instances of culpable homicide; but it clearly cannot also be sufficient for murder, if the two crimes are to be distinguished successfully. The difference, of course, may simply be one of degree; that recklessness for murder is morally a more reprehensible form than normal. It is thought, however, that it is possible to be more specific than that. In particular, from the accounts of this alternative form of *mens rea* given by Hume,[12] three issues seem to be involved: first, that the accused should have meant to perpetrate some great and outrageous bodily harm; secondly, that that harm was such as might well have resulted in death; and thirdly, that that harm showed an absolute or utter indifference as to whether the victim lived or died. Hume requires, then, an assault (or something close to it) of such seriousness that it might easily have resulted in death and which shows in the circumstances a complete indifference to the life of the victim. That sort of approach will certainly suit most of the reported cases, though not all of the judicial dicta on the matter.

Intent to do outrageous or excessive bodily harm

It must be remembered, of course, that "wicked recklessness" is an **9–46** alternative form of *mens rea*, and that it applies where the accused is assumed not to have had any intent to kill. Hume's initial requirement of an intent to "do him an excessive and outrageous bodily harm"[13] will itself, however, be objectively assessed, such that it can be deduced not only from actual physical violence[14] but also, for example, from setting fire to a house, known to be inhabited, in the early hours of the morning.[15] It is more difficult to

---

[11] *Whiteside v. H.M. Advocate,* 1996 S.L.T. 299.

[11a] *Quinn v. Cunningham,* 1956 J.C. 22, *per* Lord Justice-General Clyde at p. 24.

[12] i, 191, 238 and 256.

[13] i, 238.

[14] As in *H.M. Advocate v. Fraser and Rollins,* 1920 J.C. 60, or *Brennan v. H.M. Advocate,* 1977 J.C. 38.

[15] See the facts in the English cases of *R. v. Nedrick* [1986] 1 W.L.R. 1025; *Hyam v. D.P.P.* [1975] A.C. 55.

make such a deduction in some cases, such as that of *Cawthorne v. H.M. Advocate*.[16] There, the accused fired several rounds of high-velocity bullets into a room where, as he well knew, a number of people had taken refuge from him. No attempt was made to avoid hitting anyone there by, for example, firing towards the ceiling. On the assumption that his intent was merely to frighten those people and not to injure or kill them at all, the Appeal Court still determined that he had shown the wicked recklessness necessary for murder. It may be that this is a maverick decision; or it may be that Hume's initial requirement would be better phrased as "an intent to do the victim any great and outrageous harm", so as to accommodate frightening persons in such a way. It is difficult, however, to see that *Cawthorne's* case was one of wicked recklessness at all. Anyone doing what he did might reasonably be supposed to have intended to kill.

9–47   Hume, of course, made an intent to do outrageous bodily harm only one of three necessary requirements if murder was to be brought home to a person who did not have an intent to kill. An intent to do serious bodily harm is not by itself, therefore, a sufficient form of *mens rea* for murder. Unfortunately, it is clear that some judges have taken the view that it was. This must be a clear misreading of what Hume intended. Certainly Hume did write the following: "[o]ur practice ... does not distinguish between an absolute purpose to kill, and a purpose to do any excessive and grievous injury to the person."[17] But, after quoting some illustrations, he continued:

> "Because, in committing any such desperate outrage on the body [i.e. any one of the examples he had just quoted], the pannel shows an utter contempt of the safety and the life of his neighbour, and if not a determination to kill him, at least an absolute indifference whether he live or die."[18]

His illustrations (hamstringing the victim, cutting out his tongue, beating him to within an inch of his life) clearly support the three-fold approach detailed above (see para. 9–45), and thus give no support for the view that death following *any* deliberate infliction of grievous bodily harm is automatically murder.

9–48   In any event, a *mens rea* for murder in terms of "an intent to do serious bodily injury" is part of the English account of this crime[19]; and the Appeal Court has soundly rejected the view that the Scots and English definitions of murder are the same.[20] Beyond that, the vagueness of the phrase "serious

---

[16] 1968 J.C. 32.
[17] i, 256.
[18] i, 257.
[19] See, for example, *R. v. Moloney* [1985] A.C. 905, *per* Lord Bridge of Harwich at p. 927H.
[20] *Brennan v. H.M. Advocate*, 1977 J.C. 38.

bodily injury" makes for uncertain and possibly unfair decisions. In the event of someone dying, for example, after having had his arm deliberately broken by the accused, it would have to follow that the crime was murder,[21] notwithstanding that death was not reasonably to be anticipated from such an injury, and that the actions of the accused might not have shown utter indifference whether the victim lived or died. It is submitted, therefore, that Scots cases, where judges have opined that an intent to do serious injury is an independent form of *mens rea* for murder, are wrong.[22] Such a submission can be supported by reference to the House of Lords Select Committee on Murder and Life Imprisonment.[23] Not only did many prestigious contributions from advocates, solicitors and academics in Scotland deny the existence of such a form of *mens rea*, but so also did evidence from the Lord Justice-Clerk, Lord Ross and the then Lord Justice-General, Lord Emslie. Lord Emslie in particular[24] implied that Lord Sutherland in *H.M. Advocate v. Hartley*[25] had been incorrect to tell the jury that an intent to do serious bodily harm was enough by itself to constitute the *mens rea* of murder; and he also said[26] in relation to the opinion of the court in *Brennan v. H.M. Advocate*, which was apparently compiled by him, that he had merely been careless in expressing himself there, when he had written: "[o]ur definition of murder includes the taking of human life by a person who has an intent to kill or to do serious injury or whose act is shown to have been wickedly reckless as to the consequences."[27] Alternatively, he thought that perhaps the second "or" in the quotation should have appeared as "and".

Lethal weapons and particular crimes

Some judicial dicta, and Hume,[28] appear to support the view that death **9–49** causally connected to the use of certain weapons or the perpetration of certain crimes, will automatically be classed as murder. The authority for

---

[21] *R. v. Cunningham* [1982] A.C. 566, *per* Lord Edmund Davies at pp. 582–583.
[22] See, for example, *Margaret Robertson or Brown* (1886) 1 White 93, *per* Lord McLaren at p. 104; *William Marshall* (1897) 4 S.L.T. 217, *per* Lord Young at p. 217; *George Paterson* (1897) 5 S.L.T. 13, *per* Lord Young at p. 13; *Kennedy v. H.M. Advocate*, 1944 J.C. 171, *per* Lord Justice-General Normand at p. 177; *H.M. Advocate v. Kidd*, 1960 J.C. 61, *per* Lord Strachan at p. 74; *Cawthorne v. H.M. Advocate*, 1968 S.L.T. 330, *per* Lord Avonside at p. 330 and Lord Guthrie at p. 332; *Brennan v. H.M. Advocate*, 1977 J.C. 38 at p. 47; and *H.M. Advocate v. Hartley*, 1989 S.L.T. 135, *per* Lord Sutherland at p. 135.
[23] H.L. 78–I to III, session 1988–89.
[24] *ibid.* at 78–III, Q. 2017.
[25] 1989 S.L.T. 135 at p. 135.
[26] Q. 2020.
[27] 1977 J.C. 38 at p. 47.
[28] i, 24 and 25.

this is sparse, however. Lord Sands in *H.M. Advocate v. Fraser and Rollins*[29] certainly told the jury that if there was an attempt at a crime of serious violence, then any resultant death of the victim was murder. He further gave as examples an abortion involving the use of instruments which ended with the death of the woman concerned,[30] and any rape or robbery in which the victim was killed.[31] His conclusion then followed: "if a man uses reckless violence that may cause death, and uses that violence in perpetrating a crime, it is murder. You do not require the deliberate intention to kill, but you must have reckless use of force without any consideration of what the result of that use of force may be." It is submitted that this is either a rather loose form of Hume's tripartite requirement (see para. 9–45, above) or is simply wrong.[32] Similarly, it would be wrong to imagine that murder is automatically relevant if death follows upon a crime in which a certain type of weapon was employed. In *H.M. Advocate v. McGuinness*,[33] for example, Lord Justice-Clerk Aitchison told the jury: "If people resort to the use of deadly weapons of this kind [knives, pokers, hatchets], they are guilty of murder whether or not they intended to kill." That, however, is not really the point. The true issue is that the more dangerous to life a particular weapon is, the more likely its deployment will show that the accused meant to perpetrate some outrageous bodily harm, that his actions were very likely to result in death, and that those actions showed an absolute indifference as to whether his victim lived or died. In other words, dangerous or lethal weapons will often make it simpler to fulfil Hume's requirements for non-intentional murder.[34]

Examples of "wicked recklessness"

9–50   Cases of murder correctly founded on "wicked recklessness" are easily found amongst the law reports. Amongst the clearest of these must figure the ancient case of *Patrick Stewart*.[35] In the belief that the victim had had sexual intercourse with his daughter, the accused had him bound with cords, his penis cut off, his scrotum filled with ashes, his leg broken with a blow from an axe, and his person then carried off to a close confinement—where death ensued. An equally clear application of the "wicked recklessness"

---

[29] 1920 J.C. 60 at p. 62.
[30] *ibid.* pp. 62–63.
[31] *ibid.* p. 63.
[32] Gordon, *Criminal Law,* paras. 23–24 to 23–26; Ferguson, *Crimes Against the Person*, paras. 2.19 and 2.20.
[33] 1937 J.C. 37 at p. 40.
[34] See para. 9–45 above; *Parr v. H.M. Advocate*, 1991 J.C. 39, *per* Lord Justice-General Hope at p. 47; and *Broadley v. H.M. Advocate*, 1991 J.C. 108.
[35] (1602) Hume, i, 260; Pitcairn's *Criminal Trials*, Vol. II, p. 392.

test can be found in *George Paterson*[36] where the drunken accused not only violently struck the unfortunate female victim, but also thrust a red-hot poker into her rectum and private parts. The test was also considered to be fulfilled in the case of *John McCallum and William Corner.*[37] These two accused partially severed the cable which lowered men in a bucket to the bottom of a pit. Their intention was to cause some injury to the victim, who they knew would be next to be lowered on that particular cable. He fell violently to the bottom of the mine shaft when the cable broke under the strain—just as the accused had intended. They had not intended his death, however. On their own admissions, they had simply intended to injure him to a certain degree, to the extent of a broken leg, for example. In the whole circumstances of the case, there could be little doubt that wicked recklessness was displayed there.[38]

Consent and murder

In *H.M. Advocate v. Rutherford*,[39] where the accused had strangled a woman, part of the defence case involved the plea that the victim had desired him to do so—that she had wanted to be killed. Lord Justice-Clerk Cooper simply told the jury that consent was not a defence to murder, apparently as a matter of law. He made no attempt to justify his ruling, although the accused in that case would have faced almost insuperable difficulties in establishing that the woman had indeed consented. Even if cast-iron proof had been available, however, it seems unlikely in the extreme that it would have been treated as having any relevance to the outcome of the trial.   9–51

CULPABLE HOMICIDE

Definition of culpable homicide

There is no single, simple definition of culpable homicide. Essentially (and admittedly unhelpfully) it covers any killing of a human being brought about by another in circumstances where that other should be accounted criminally responsible for it. It clearly excludes murder, and both casual and justifiable homicides (see paras. 9–38, 9–39, and 9–42 *et seq.*, above); and it is common enough for juries to be told that culpable homicide "means unlawful killing of a human being in circumstances which don't amount to murder."[40] The *actus reus* of the crime is plainly the same as that for murder,   9–52

---

[36] (1897) 5 S.L.T. 13.
[37] (1853) 1 Irv. 259.
[38] See also *John Campbell* (1836) 1 Swin. 309; *Andrew Ewart* (1828) Syme 315; and *Miller and Denovan v. H.M. Advocate*, 1960, unreported, noted at 1991 S.L.T. 211.
[39] 1947 J.C. 1 at pp. 5–6.
[40] *Berry v. H.M. Advocate* (1976) S.C.C.R. Supp. 156, *per* Lord Keith at p. 156.

although the conduct would presumably be less than that capable of raising an inference of murderous *mens rea*, except where there is virtually murder but for the existence of provocation or diminished responsibility (see paras. 9–60 *et seq.*, and 9–67 *et seq.*, below). The *mens rea* of culpable homicide depends on the category of the crime.

9–53　　　Hume deals with four categories of culpable homicide. The first of these clearly relates to an assault which results in death, yet does not display either an intent to kill or the excessive violence, the great likelihood of death, and the utter indifference to the life of the victim that are the hallmarks of murder (see paras. 9–44 and 9–45, above). As he puts it:

> "[w]here there is a wrongful purpose to do any bodily harm, though not outrageous or excessive, yet still if death unfortunately ensue, the invader is not free of guilt ... He is so far blameable, as he did a thing which was wrong and unlawful in itself, and which might [in the sense of 'did'?] end in the death of his neighbour."[41]

The second covers a situation "where the homicide is done in prosecution, generally, of any wrong and unlawful act, though without malice to any individual,"[42] and seems to involve offences of recklessly caused real injury. Thirdly, Hume mentions that "some punishment is due, though the slaughter happen in the performance even of a lawful act, if there be great heedlessness and indiscretion, or a want of due caution and circumspection, in the way of doing the thing."[43] This may be termed "recklessly-performed, lawful-act" culpable homicide. Fourthly, and finally, Hume considers virtual murders, where the killing is preceeded by provocation,[44] to be culpable homicide. To that fourth category now must be added killings which would be murders but for the diminished responsibility of the accused or the attitude taken by the prosecuting service in Scotland. All these categories are illustrated in the paragraphs which follow.

Voluntary and involuntary culpable homicide

9–54　　　Gordon has popularised in Scotland the use of the terms "voluntary" and "involuntary" to denote the different categories of culpable homicide, and that classification has been adopted here. It is important, however, to bear in mind that these terms are not used to indicate whether the accused was aware of his conduct at the time. "Voluntary culpable homicide ... is murder under mitigating circumstances, comparable to what is known in

---

[41]　i, 191; see also i, 234 at "3".
[42]　i, 192; see also i, 234 at "2".
[43]　i, 192; see also i, 233 at "1".
[44]　i, 239 *et seq.*

parts of the United States as second-degree murder."[45] Consequently, "voluntary culpable homicide" applies to the fourth of the categories mentioned above, and "involuntary culpable homicide" to the remaining three.[46]

INVOLUNTARY CULPABLE HOMICIDE

Assault type

Where death is causally related to an assault, but is not the readily **9–55** foreseeable result of it, it will not generally be possible to infer the *mens rea* for murder; but the perpetrator of the assault is not guiltless, nor is he guilty only of assault. He is taken as a matter of law to be guilty of culpable homicide, irrespective of how trivial the assault may have been.[47] Of course, the more serious the assault is in real terms, the more likely that the *mens rea* for murder may be inferred, as in the border-line case of *Patrick Slaven*[48] where the victim was twice assaulted by men who were intent on ravishing her, and, having made her escape, was chased by them until she fell over a precipice to her death. As it was put in *John McCallum and William Corner*[49]: "[i]f one purposes to inflict a very slight injury, which he has no right to inflict, and death unexpectedly and out of all reasonable calculation ensues, that is culpable homicide; if a more serious injury was intended, the case may be one of murder." This is clearly capable of being a very harsh rule, bearing in mind the great width of the crime of assault (see para. 9–03 *et seq.*, above). In *Robert Vance*,[50] for example, the accused who was fighting another, threw back his arm and struck the victim, causing him to fall over and hit his head. The victim died from the resultant injury. It was not even clear from the facts that the accused knew the victim had been standing behind him, but as Lord Moncreiff[51] was reported to have said:

> "in so far as the misfortune which befell [the victim] was concerned, it was clear that it was undesigned on the part of the pannel, yet ... it could not be said that the pannel was free from blame, inasmuch as he was engaged in an illegal act at the time, and the blow was given in the course of the fight ... [and] it must be held to be culpable homicide."

---

[45] Gordon, *Criminal Law*, para. 25–01.
[46] *ibid.* paras. 26–01 to 26–03.
[47] See, for example, *H.M. Advocate v. Delaney*, 1945 J.C. 138; *Bird v. H.M. Advocate*, 1952 J.C. 23; *McDermott v. H.M. Advocate*, 1973 J.C. 8; *cf. H.M. Advocate v. McGinlay*, 1983 S.L.T. 562.
[48] (1885) 5 Coup. 694.
[49] (1853) 1 Irv. 259, *per* Lord Justice-General McNeill at p. 270.
[50] (1849) J. Shaw 211.
[51] *ibid.* p. 214.

The jury, however, found the accused not guilty (as is always their privilege).

Unlawful act type

9–56   What is thought to be involved here is the perpetration of a crime other than assault which might reasonably involve personal injury, and in fact ends in death. Crimes of real injury, where the *mens rea* requirement is recklessness, are prime candidates. The causal connection between the crime itself and the death must, of course, be established; but once it is established, the result is culpable homicide, even though there was no question of there being any intent to kill. There are many reported cases which support this type. For example, in *James Niven*[52] the accused discharged a firearm in a public street. An innocent passer-by was killed due to, according to the accused's story, a piece of metal having by accident been included with the gunpowder. The court had no doubt that this was culpable homicide (although the jury acquitted Niven of the charge). The offence involved there was clearly the reckless discharge of firearms to the danger of the lieges (see para. 9–33, above). A very similar offence is involved in the hypothetical situation spoken of by Lord Moncreiff in *David Keay*.[53] There, his Lordship said that if a person threw a stone out of a window, and the stone happened to hit someone causing his death, then that would be culpable homicide. Similarly again, in *Mathieson v. H.M. Advocate*[54] the accused committed the crime of reckless fire-raising by setting some cans of paint alight. The paint was stored at the rear entrance of a building which itself caught fire, thus resulting in the deaths of four persons. And in *Sutherland v. H.M. Advocate*,[55] even wilful fire-raising of the accused's own property with intent to defraud insurers was considered appropriate, since the way in which the operation had been carried out exhibited the necessary recklessness in relation to the death which occurred. There have also been cases of culpable homicide where the unlawful activity consisted of the administration of noxious substances to the victim in a reckless fashion. Thus, in *Elizabeth Hamilton*[56] the accused nursery maid gave ten drops of laudanum to her 10-month-old charge to quieten him, even though she had been distinctly told by the child's mother to administer nothing of that nature to him at all; and again in *Adam Philip*[57] the accused gave 10 full glasses of whisky to a 10-year-old boy, thus occasioning his death. It has also been recently held that supplying a controlled drug (amphetamine) to a person

---

[52] (1795) Hume, i, 192.
[53] (1837) 1 Swin. 543 at p. 545.
[54] 1981 S.C.C.R. 196.
[55] 1994 S.L.T. 634.
[56] (1857) 2 Irv. 738.
[57] (1818) Hume, i, 237, n.a.

who died after ingesting it provided a proper basis for culpable homicide.[58] Equally, therefore, the reckless supply of potentially noxious substances (see para. 9–30 *et seq*, above) should merit a charge of culpable homicide, where death resulted.

The *mens rea* element for culpable homicide of this sort is presumably **9–57** the recklessness generated by, or associated with, the primary crime, which recklessness is carried forward as it were to the death itself. If that is so, then it may be possible to charge culpable homicide in relation to primary crimes (unlawful acts) which would not normally be expected to cause personal injuries at all, but where the crime itself was carried through in such a reckless manner as to make a resulting death not entirely unforeseeable. An example of such a crime would be theft. Unlike robbery (for which see Chapter 10), theft would seldom be linked with injury, let alone death; but Gordon refers to the unreported case of *Finnigan*[59] where the accused was convicted of culpable homicide for having stolen a gas meter by wrenching it away from its supply pipe, thus causing the death of a person who occupied another part of the same building. A more modern version of the same thinking may be found in *Lourie v. H.M. Advocate*[60] where two youths, who were alleged to have pushed their way into an elderly woman's house and there stolen her handbag in her presence, were convicted of culpable homicide, on the basis that their behaviour had caused her fatal shock. (Their convictions were quashed on appeal on the ground of insufficiency of evidence.)

Recklessly-performed, lawful-act type

The essence of this form of culpable homicide is that the accused in fact **9–58** caused the death of another because of the grossly careless way in which he performed some otherwise not-unlawful (*i.e.* not-criminal at common law) activity. Hume[61] gives the example of a building being demolished in such a fashion that debris is carelessly cast into the street below, to the fatal injury of some passer-by. He also mentions the careless felling of a tree,[62] the careless driving of a coach[63] and also the presenting of a gun at another, apparently in jest.[64] The lack of care which must be shown, however, is high. In the "driving" case of *Paton v. H.M. Advocate*[65] Lord Justice-Clerk Aitchison remarked: "[i]t is now necessary to show gross, or wicked, or

---

[58] *Lord Advocate's Reference (No. 1 of 1994)*, 1995 S.L.T. 248.
[59] 1958, Glasgow High Court, noted in Gordon, *Criminal Law*, para. 26–26.
[60] 1988 S.C.C.R. 634.
[61] i, 192.
[62] *Mathew Graham* (1813) Hume, i, 192, n. 2.
[63] *Thomas Clerk* (1805) Hume, i, 192, n. 2.
[64] *David Buchanan* (1817) Hume, i, 192, n. 2.
[65] 1936 J.C. 19 at p. 22.

criminal negligence, something amounting, or at any rate analogous, to a criminal indifference to the consequences." It now appears to be accepted that this standard is that of recklessness; not wicked recklessness, of course, but the sort of simple recklessness set out in *Allan v. Patterson*.[66]

9–59   Reported cases involving this form of culpable homicide are legion. They include deaths caused by the grossly careless navigation of a boat,[67] folding up of a bed which had a child in it at the time,[68] and preparation of a headache remedy.[69] The unreported case of *Ross Fontana*[70] is also not without interest. He was convicted of culpable homicide because of the grossly improper way in which he had installed a gas fire. He had recklessly failed to provide flues for the removal of fumes, with the result that two people were poisoned by carbon monoxide when the fire was turned on.

VOLUNTARY CULPABLE HOMICIDE

Provocation

9–60   It is a common human failing to lose one's self-control if one is suddenly attacked or insulted or taunted by another; and that loss of control often manifests itself in violence, sometimes with fatal consequences for the victim. Such a victim is hardly blameless himself, of course, and may be said to have played some part in his own demise. For that reason, the law makes some concession to "human infirmity in those difficult and agitating situations, which require a more than ordinary strength of mind, and command of temper to withstand them."[71] That concession is a modest but nevertheless significant one. As Lord Cowie once put it to a jury: "[i]f ... you find that all the factors were present for a verdict of murder, but ... you take the view ... that he was provoked ... then for that reason also you could reduce the offence of murder to culpable homicide."[72] Much the same was said by Lord Cullen to a jury in *Graham v. H.M. Advocate*.[73] Where the

---

[66]   1980 J.C. 57. The test there was applied in *Sutherland v. H.M. Advocate*, 1994 S.L.T. 634. But that test is not necessarily appropriate for all crimes where recklessness is sufficient as the *mens rea* — see, *e.g. Thomson v. H.M. Advocate*, 1995 S.L.T. 827 (involving reckless fire-raising).

[67]   *Angus MacPherson and John Stewart* (1861) 4 Irv. 85.

[68]   *Williamina Sutherland* (1856) 2 Irv. 455.

[69]   *Edmund Wheatley* (1853) 1 Irv. 225, where a medical student who was learning the art of dispensing medicines in a chemist's shop, and who had no authority to do what he did, prepared a potion for a friend, thus causing his death. His actions were treated as having gone well beyond a mere careless error in dispensing—*cf. George Armitage* (1885) 5 Coup. 675 and *H.M. Advocate v. Wood* (1903) 4 Adam 150.

[70]   March 1990, Kirkcaldy High Court.

[71]   Hume, i, 249.

[72]   *Stobbs v. H.M. Advocate*, 1983 S.C.C.R. 190 at p. 199.

[73]   1987 S.C.C.R. 20 at p. 22.

facts and circumstances in relation to a killing show, therefore, that the intention to kill or wicked recklessness for murder was probably present, provocation can have a mitigatory or palliative effect in securing a conviction for the lesser offence of culpable homicide. The initial inference of murderous *mens rea* is thus offset. "[T]here would be an absence of a wicked intent or recklessness because the provocation provoked the act and deprived it of the element of murderous intent."[74] Provocation, therefore, does not exculpate; it provides a partial excuse for what was done, and thus justifies a conviction for culpable homicide on an original murder charge, so that an appropriately mitigated sentence may be considered.

Immediacy of retaliation

Hume[75] requires there to be a "sudden impulse of resentment" in retaliation of provocation "suffered upon the spot". Macdonald puts the same point even more forcefully: "[p]rovocation, although great, will not palliate guilt if any interval have elapsed between the provocation and the retaliation."[76] The point is that provocation is a concession to human infirmity and not an excuse for cold-blooded vengeance-taking. Once passions have been allowed to cool, provocation no longer applies. Thus, in *Walter Redpath*[77] the accused was attacked by his eventual victim, and made efforts there and then to lift a stone in order to retaliate. He thought better of it, however, and instead went indoors to look out a firearm. Not long after, he returned to the scene of the initial attack with a gun and shot the victim. Although afterwards convicted of culpable homicide only, he should have been convicted of murder, according to Hume, since an interval for "cooling-off" had been allowed to elapse prior to the fatal conduct. It seems, then, that instant retaliation to a provoking incident is to be taken quite literally. Although the courts have not been quite as strict as Hume might have wanted them to be, any significant gap between provocation and retaliation is certainly such as to elide the plea.[78]

9–61

Cumulative provocation

Linked to the requirement of immediacy of retaliation is the rule that there must be a specific, provoking incident. There must be such an incident, sufficiently provoking in itself in the eyes of the law, just before the fatal violence was delivered by the accused. If there had been a course of incidents of a provocative nature over a series of days, weeks or even years, but no

9–62

---

[74] *Fenning v. H.M. Advocate*, 1985 S.C.C.R. 219, *per* Lord Mayfield at p. 220.
[75] i, 239.
[76] p. 94.
[77] (1810) Hume, i, 252, n. 1.
[78] See *Parr v. H.M. Advocate*, 1991 J.C. 39.

final incident to which the accused responded then no provocation exists in law, and the crime will be murder. This has consistently been upheld by the courts.[79] In particular, this means that a wife, who for years has been subjected to violence by her husband, and who one day "snaps" at the end of her tether and kills him as he lies sleeping in a chair, must be convicted of murder (but see para. 8–38, above). In practice, of course, it may be possible for particular judges to direct juries in appropriate cases to ignore this rather harsh rule.[80]

Recognised provocation

9–63   *Violence.* According to Macdonald,[81] the usual form of acceptable provocation is violence. "The defence of provocation is of this sort—'Being agitated and excited, and alarmed by violence, I lost control over myself, and took life, when my presence of mind had left me, and without thought of what I was doing'." This statement has been specifically approved on several occasions.[82] However, the degree of violence visited upon the accused is of considerable importance. As Lord Cooper once said: "[i]t takes a tremendous amount of provocation to palliate stabbing a man to death ... A blow with the fist is no justification for the use of a lethal weapon. Provocation, in short, must bear a reasonable retaliation to the resentment which it excites."[83] It is now clear that there must indeed be a reasonable or proportionate relationship between the accused's reaction and the victim's provocative conduct.[84] There must not be a gross disproportion between that reaction and the conduct,[85] for it is accepted that an equality or fine balance between the two cannot be looked for in such situations where there is loss of control.[86] Thus, in *Thomson v. H.M. Advocate*[87] the accused stabbed his victim repeatedly with a knife (which he had taken the precaution

---

[79]   See *Thomson v. H.M. Advocate*, 1986 S.L.T. 281; *Graham v. H.M. Advocate*, 1987 S.C.C.R. 20; *Parr v. H.M. Advocate, supra,* n. 78.

[80]   See, for example, *Crawford v. H.M. Advocate*, 1950 J.C. 67; but *cf. H.M. Advocate v. Greig*, High Court, November, 1979, noted in Gane and Stoddart, *Casebook on Scottish Criminal Law* (2nd ed.), p. 526.

[81]   p. 94.

[82]   See, *e.g., Cosgrove v. H.M. Advocate,* 1990 J.C. 333 at p. 339; *Low v. H.M. Advocate,* 1994 S.L.T. 277, *per* Lord Justice-Clerk Ross at p. 285L.

[83]   *Smith v. H.M. Advocate*, 1952, Glasgow High Court, noted in Gordon *Criminal Law*, para. 25–19. Notice that in *Robertson v. H.M. Advocate* 1994 S.L.T. 1004, Lord Justice-Clerk Ross (at p. 1005H–I) thought that "retaliation" in the quotation should read "relation".

[84]   *McCormack v. H.M. Advocate*, 1993 J.C. 170; *Robertson v. H.M. Advocate*, 1994 S.L.T. 1004.

[85]   *Low v. H.M. Advocate*, 1994 S.L.T. 277, *per* Lord Justice-Clerk Ross at p. 286D–G (where it is stated that the self-defence threshold of "no cruel excess" should be confined to that defence, and not applied also to provocation).

[86]   *Robertson v. H.M. Advocate,* 1994 S.L.T. 1004. See the directions to the jury by Lord McLean at p. 1004H–I, which seem to have been approved by the Appeal Court.

[87]   See above, n. 79.

of bringing with him to a meeting) after a trivial assault, which consisted in no more than the victim's physically attempting to stop him leaving the room where they both were. There was a gross disproportion between the violence and the retaliation, and the plea of provocation was ruled out. In the same way, it was ruled out in *Fenning v. H.M. Advocate*[88] since it was a gross over-reaction to counter a drunken man's random gesticulations with a knife by beating his brains out with a stone or rifle butt. *Ensign Hardie*[89] was on firmer ground, however, since he had been struck with a "tree" (*i.e.* a baulk of wood) and beaten by the eventual victim, who had been on horseback at the time.

Sexual infidelity. Since well before the time of Hume, it has been **9–64** recognised that a man who found his wife in the very act of adultery with another man might be convicted of culpable homicide rather than murder if he killed him, her or them on the spot.[90] Presumably, this would apply to a wife who had found her husband in similar adulterous circumstances. The basis was (and is) that such a spouse had been sorely provoked. The issue has not been confined, however, to cases where the adultery was discovered as it actually took place. In *H.M. Advocate v. Gilmour*[91] Lord Justice-Clerk Aitchison told the jury:

> "If you are satisfied that the accused found his wife in the act of adultery, or in circumstances that reasonably conveyed to his mind that his wife had just committed adultery, or was just about to commit adultery when discovered, you are entitled ... to acquit the accused of murder and to find him guilty of culpable homicide only."

And further, in *H.M. Advocate v. Hill*[92] it was accepted that provocation could be made out where a man's wife and her lover confessed to having committed adultery. This was all the more surprising since "words" are not generally accepted as sufficient for the plea of provocation to be upheld; and, of course, a confession refers to some incident which has taken place in the past. Still further, however, it has been decided that this form of provocation is open to a person merely cohabiting with another.[93] There is no requirement, therefore, that sexual infidelity should be confined to married or even heterosexual couples. Recently, indeed, Lord MacLean directed a jury that provocation was open to a woman who killed the man who, as she had been informed, had been sharing a bed with her lesbian partner.[93a] But the Appeal Court has made very plain that the words used

---

[88] 1985 J.C. 76.
[89] (1701) Hume, i, 244, n. 2.
[90] *James Christie* (1731) Hume, i, 245.
[91] 1938 J.C. 1 at pp. 2–3.
[92] 1941 J.C. 59.
[93] See *McKay v. H.M. Advocate*, 1991 J.C. 91.
[93a] See *H.M. Advocate v. McKean*, 1996 S.C.C.R. 402.

must go beyond mere insults in the course of a quarrel: they must "disclose in clear and unequivocal terms that the deceased had been committing adultery".[94]

Words not sufficient

9–65   The general consensus has always been that words however "foul or abusive," or, "signs or gestures, how contemptuous or derisive so ever" cannot operate as provocation in relation to a murder charge.[95] This represents a conspicuous difference between the application of provocation in homicide and in assault (see para. 9–22, above). In *William Aird*[96] the accused was denied provocation in relation to his killing of a woman who had thrown the contents of a chamber pot in his face; and that being so, abusive words and taunts could scarcely hope to fare any better. The Appeal Court, therefore, continues to uphold the orthodox view,[97] whilst recognising that there may be occasions when that view should yield.[98] It is not clear when that might legitimately happen, however, since each case appears to turn on its own facts and circumstances; but sexual insults and taunts were left to the jury as provocation in *Berry v. H.M. Advocate*,[99] as were (alleged) threats to tell the accused's wife of an adulterous association clandestinely enjoyed by the accused in *Stobbs v. H.M. Advocate*.[1]

Effect on attempted murder

9–66   If provocation is capable of converting murder to culpable homicide, then provocation relative to a charge of attempted murder should logically result in a conviction for attempted culpable homicide. But the courts appear to have taken the view that attempted culpable homicide does not exist. The appropriate verdict, therefore, appears to be assault to severe injury under provocation.[2] As provocation has the effect of mitigating punishment, it seems quite unnecessary for the courts to have bothered with such logical niceties; attempted murder carries no fixed sentence, and a conviction for

---

[94] *McKay v. H.M. Advocate,* 1991 J.C. 91, *per* Lord Justice-General Hope at pp. 90 and 96; see also *McCormack v. H.M. Advocate,* 1993 J.C. 170, Lord Justice-General Hope at p. 179F–G.
[95] Hume, i, 247, 249; Macdonald, p. 93.
[96] (1693) Hume, i, 248.
[97] See *Thomson v. H.M. Advocate,* 1986 S.L.T. 281; *Cosgrove v. H.M. Advocate,* 1990 J.C. 333; *McCormack v. H.M. Advocate,* 1993 J.C. 170, *per* Lord Justice-General Hope at p. 179D–E.
[98] See *Thomson v. H.M. Advocate, supra, per* Lord Hunter at p. 286; *Cosgrove v. H.M. Advocate, supra, per* Lord Cowie at p. 339.
[99] (1976) S.C.C.R. Supp. 156.
[1] 1983 S.C.C.R. 190.
[2] *Brady v. H.M. Advocate,* 1986 J.C. 68; *Salmond v. H.M. Advocate,* 1992 S.L.T. 156.

attempted murder would not have precluded the court from making an appropriate adjustment in penalty to take account of the provocation.

Diminished responsibility

In a similar way to provocation, diminished responsibility can result in a conviction for culpable homicide rather than murder, so that an appropriately mitigated sentence can be considered.[3] Hume does not deal with this matter, however, since it was scarcely recognised in law until the second half of the nineteenth century. The case usually credited with its inception is that of *Alexander Dingwall*.[4] There, the accused had stabbed his wife and killed her. He was charged with murder. He had delivered only one blow whilst his mind was apparently occupied with totally different matters. Insanity was raised at the trial as a possible defence, but the medical evidence was generally against it. But it was established that Dingwall was an alcoholic, suffered frequently from *delirium tremens*, and had had heat stroke in India, which left him with epileptic-type fits. Lord Deas is reported as having said to the jury: "if weakness of mind could be an element in any case in the question between murder and culpable homicide, it seemed difficult to exclude that element here." A verdict of culpable homicide was returned.

9–67

Requirements for diminished responsibility

Diminished responsibility is not insanity, and thus, unlike insanity, does not lead to a complete acquittal. But because it can result in a verdict of culpable homicide rather than murder, it has been kept under tight control. There must be mental weakness. Bad temper which was not controlled is insufficient[5] and the temporary effects of voluntary intoxication are certainly excluded.[6] Psychopathic personality, where the sufferer is lacking in emotion and normal inhibition, has, perhaps, not been entirely ruled out; but great reservations were expressed in respect of it in the Appeal Court in the case of *Carraher v. H.M. Advocate*[7] although that may have been because of the way in which the medical evidence was presented there. Nevertheless, the Appeal Court has also emphasised that the doctrine of diminished responsibility must not be applied too flexibly.[8]

9–68

---

[3] *Strathearn v. H.M. Advocate,* 1996 S.C.C.R. 100.
[4] (1867) 5 Irv. 466.
[5] *Braithwaite v. H.M. Advocate,* 1945 J.C. 55.
[6] *Brennan v. H.M. Advocate,* 1977 J.C. 38 at pp. 45–46.
[7] 1946 J.C. 108.
[8] *Williamson v. H.M. Advocate,* 1994 J.C. 149 *per* Lord Justice-Clerk Ross at p. 153E–F, in rejecting a "severe personality disorder" as sufficient (also 1994 S.L.T. 1000 at p. 1003I–J).

9–69   The accepted legal definition of diminished responsibility dates from 1923. In *H.M. Advocate v. Savage*[9] Lord Justice-Clerk Alness stated:

> "It is very difficult to put it in a phrase, but it has been put in this way: that there must be aberration or weakness of mind; that there must be some form of mental unsoundness; that there must be a state of mind which is bordering on, though not amounting to insanity; that there must be a mind so affected that responsibility is diminished from full responsibility to partial responsibility — in other words, the prisoner in question must be only partially accountable for his actions. And I think one can see running through the cases that there is implied ... that there must be some form of mental disease."

The accused in *Savage* derived no benefit from that formulation of the test, however, since he was convicted of murder and executed. But the *Savage* test was affirmed as correct in *Connelly v. H.M. Advocate*[10] where an attempt to suggest that Lord Justice-Clerk Alness had set up four alternative forms of diminished responsibility was rejected. His test must be read as a whole. *Connelly* also emphasises that mental disease is at the basis of diminished responsibility, and that without medical evidence to support such disease, the plea is unlikely ever to be successful.[11]

Effect on attempted murder

9–70   In a similar way to provocation (see para. 9–66, above), diminished responsibility does not reduce an attempted murder charge to one of attempted culpable homicide. The appropriate verdict in such a case is one of assault.[12]

Discretionary culpable homicide

9–71   There are said to be particular types of homicide which fulfil the requirements for murder, but which are invariably dealt with as culpable homicide because of the view taken of them by the prosecution service in Scotland. These types are fully dealt with by Gordon under the title, "The Unofficial Categories"[13] and include cases of euthanasia and suicide pacts. Although cases of euthanasia seem rare in this country, instances of suicide pacts, where one of the parties has survived a mutual suicide attempt, do

---

9   1923 J.C. 49 at p. 51.
10 1990 J.C. 349, *per* Lord Justice-General Hope at p. 358.
11 *ibid. Connelly* was approved in *Williamson v. H.M. Advocate,* 1994 J.C. 149, and *Martindale v. H.M. Advocate,* 1994 S.L.T. 1093.
12 *H.M. Advocate v. Blake,* 1986 S.L.T. 661, *per* Lord Brand at p. 662.
13 Paras. 25–02 to 25–07.

occur from time to time. Thus in *H.M. Advocate v. Carter*[14] a couple had intended to commit suicide by inhaling carbon monoxide gas. They thus ran a hose-pipe from the exhaust of a car to its interior, where they shut themselves in. The one who survived pled guilty to a charge of culpable homicide in relation to the other's death.

Persistent vegetative state

It has recently been declared by the Lord Advocate[15] that doctors who **9–72** withdraw life-sustaining "treatment" (in its widest sense, to include feeding and hydration) from patients who are in a "persistent vegetative state" will be immune from prosecution for homicide (murder or culpable homicide) in respect of such a patient provided that the Court of Session has first agreed to such withdrawal. The procedure to be employed before that Court was laid down in *Law Hospital N.H.S. Trust v. The Lord Advocate,*[16] where Lord President Hope described such a state as follows:

> "This is the result of irreversible damage to the cerebral cortex. The function of consciousness has been lost completely and for ever. The patient is wholly unaware of her surroundings. She cannot see, hear, feel pain or pleasure, communicate by word or movement or make voluntary movements of any kind. The brain stem structures are preserved and, so long as this continues, she remains clinically alive. The vegetative reflexes which control such functions as breathing, cardiac action and digestion are maintained. Involuntary movements of the eyes and the ability to make sounds give the impression of apparent wakefulness ... But she is now permanently insensate, and she remains alive only because feeding and hydration are provided to her artificially and because of the nursing care which she continues to receive in the hospital."[17]

5. RAPE

DEFINITION OF RAPE

The definition of rape has been developed somewhat in recent years. The **9–73** *actus reus* consists of a male person having vaginal sexual intercourse with a female person "by force" (as that has been interpreted) where that sort of intercourse is also "against her will" — meaning that at the relevant time

---

[14] May 1990, Glasgow High Court, unreported.
[15] Policy statement, made on April 11, 1996, noted at 1996 S.C.L.R. p. 518F–G.
[16] 1996 S.C.L.R. 491; see in particular the opinion of Lord President Hope at pp. 507–508.
[17] *ibid.* at p. 494D–E.

her consent to it had expressly or impliedly been refused.[18] It is obviously implicit in this that the female must have been capable of refusing her consent at the material time. The *mens rea* of the offence "includes the intention to have intercourse with the woman without her consent"[19] or recklessness as to the matter of consent.[20] The elements of the crime are considered in the paragraphs which follow.

General

9–74   Rape is a gender-specific crime. In Scotland, it can only be committed by males upon females, which appears to mean by persons biologically male at birth upon persons born biologically female.[21] Persons who undergo "sex change" operations can probably neither rape nor be raped—one of the presumed implications of the European Court of Human Rights' ruling in *Rees v. United Kingdom*.[22] It is, therefore, a crime of specific personal violence perpetrated on females. In historical times, the crime was thought to be an off-shoot of abduction.[23] The view then taken was that the carrying off and defiling of a female was of greater offence to her husband or father than to the female herself, a view which would now be regarded as outrageous. Echoes of it could still be heard in the nineteenth century, however, as in the case of *Charles Sweenie*[24] where Lord Ivory listed the evil consequences of rape as: "the danger of impregnation — the loss of status, — the taint to her family."

Vaginal intercourse

9–75   Abduction is now totally unnecessary in relation to rape; and the old rule that the victim must register her complaint within 24 hours of the act has long ceased to apply.[25] Long delay in making a complaint is, however, unlikely to be propitious for a successful prosecution. But the act must

---

[18] See, *e.g.* the definition given by Lord Justice-General Hope in *Jamieson v. H.M. Advocate,* 1994 J.C. 88, at p. 92E, and the account given to the jury by Lord Penrose in *W. v. H.M. Advocate,* 1995 S.L.T. 685, at p. 686B–C. Notice that in both, the archaic expression "carnal knowledge" is used to denote sexual intercourse.

[19] *Jamieson v. H.M. Advocate,* 1994 J.C. 88, *per* Lord Justice-General Hope at p. 92E, see para. 9–82, n. 55, *infra*.

[20] *ibid.* p. 93F; para. 9–82, *infra*.

[21] *cf.* current English law, as contained in the Criminal Justice and Public Order Act 1994, s.142.

[22] (1987) 9 E.H.R.R. 56.

[23] See para. 9.02, above; Mackenzie, *The Laws and Customs of Scotland in Matters Criminal* (2nd ed., 1699), I, 16.

[24] (1853) 3 Irv. 109 at p. 142.

[25] *Captain Charles Douglas* (1697) Maclaurin's Cases, p. 13, No. 12.

consist of penetration of the victim's vagina by the accused's penis. Penetration need not be more than slight[26] but it must occur. Most authorities correctly say that ejaculation is unnecessary[27] but prosecutions are likely to be difficult without ejaculate to examine and submit to DNA profiling. Unlike the previous law in England, in this country there has never been any set age below which male sexual potency is presumed impossible. If a youngster in fact proves himself capable of penile penetration, then he can be prosecuted (all other things being equal).[28] What have come to be known graphically as "oral-sex" and "anal-sex" do not qualify as rape, however astonishing this may appear.[29] The essence of rape may well be considered popularly as the unwanted, violent invasion of any body orifice by any means, but major law reform would be required to make that a reality in Scotland. At present, nothing short of, or different from, penile penetration of the vagina will suffice. Sexual activity short of, or different from that amounts to indecent assault.[30]

By force and against her will

Hume was an avid reader of contemporary English legal works, and **9–76** was especially impressed it seems by the writings of William Blackstone. Blackstone's *Commentaries on the Laws of England* were first published in 1769, and rape is described therein as: "the carnal knowledge of a woman forcibly and against her will."[31] Unsurprisingly, Hume uses much the same description,[32] Alison follows suit[33] and Burnett treads the same well-worn path.[34] Macdonald, whether he realised it or not, reproduces Blackstone's words exactly.[35] The courts too have been unusually conservative in their description of rape, mainly, it appears, preferring a definition which features the formula "forcibly and against her will".[36]

Some commentators have pointed out that force is simply one way of **9–77** demonstrating that the intercourse was against the victim's will. If the

---

[26] *Alexander Macra or Macrae* (1841) Bell's Notes 83.

[27] *Duncan Macmillan* (1833) Bell's Notes 82; *Archibald Robertson* (1836) Bell's Notes 82–83.

[28] See *Robert Fulton Jnr* (1841) 2 Swin. 564.

[29] *Barbour v. H.M. Advocate*, 1982 S.C.C.R. 195.

[30] *ibid.*

[31] Vol. IV, Chap. 15, p. 210.

[32] i, 302.

[33] i, 209.

[34] *Treatise*, 101.

[35] p. 119.

[36] See, *e.g. Stobbs v. H.M. Advocate*, 1983 S.C.C.R. 190, *per* Lord Cowie at p. 200; *C. v. H.M. Advocate*, 1987 S.C.C.R. 104, *per* Lord Mayfield at p. 105; *S. v. H.M. Advocate*, 1989 S.L.T. 469 at pp. 471L–472E; *Jamieson v. H.M. Advocate*, 1994 J.C. 88, *per* Lord Justice-General Hope at p. 92E and para. 9–82, *infra. Cf. W. v. H.M. Advocate*, 1995 S.L.T. 685, Lord Penrose's charge to the jury at p. 686B–C.

accused was compelled to use force, then it seems obvious that the female must have been unwilling and refused her consent. Therefore, it is argued, the *actus reus* can more accurately be represented as: "the carnal knowledge of a woman against her will".[37] The authoritative writers, however, place the emphasis on "force". Hume, for example, puts it this way:

> "The knowledge of the woman's person must be against her will and by force ... The resistance must be ... continued to the last; so that it is by main force only and terror that the violation is accomplished."[38]

It cannot be said, however, that a description in terms of force alone would suffice, since it is always possible that forcible intercourse might be willingly enjoyed by both parties. It seems preferable, then to refer to both force and unwillingness, as indeed the courts continue to do.[39]

Constructive force

9–78   Violence applied to the person of the female is the most obvious manifestation of force, but not the only one. Hume clearly considers that significant threats of injury will suffice, such as a dagger held to her breast or a pistol to her head.[40] These acts amount to constructive force, since they are just as effective as actual force in subduing her contrary will — her will to resist to the utmost. Similarly, if such be her will, it does not cease just because she faints during the struggle, or is unable to give real effect to it because of her infirmity or youth.[41] Indeed, in the case of young girls (taken to be those under the age of 12), force (and unwillingness) is always to be presumed, whether they in fact show signs of resistance or not. Hume also mentions drugging as equivalent to actual force; if an unwilling female is plied with drugs or potions to overcome her unwillingness, then that is rape,[42] although Burnett[43] was highly sceptical of this. Hume's view has prevailed, however (see para. 9–81, below). The conclusion here is that submission through fear should not be confused with a willingness to have intercourse; a lack of resistance may still be compatible with the use of "force" though never a blow was struck. A modern example occurs in *Barbour v H.M. Advocate*[44] where the accused threatened to break the victim's legs, to use a knife on her, and batter her head against a wall. Although she put up no actual resistance to his sexual advances, it is plain

---

[37] Ferguson, *Crimes Against the Person*, para. 4.07.
[38] i, 302.
[39] See para. 9–76, above.
[40] i, 302.
[41] i, 303.
[42] *ibid.*
[43] *Treatise*, 103.
[44] 1982 S.C.C.R. 195.

that he would have been convicted of rape in these circumstances had there been sufficient evidence of vaginal penetration.

The role of consent

If the female consents to the intercourse, then naturally rape is out of the **9–79** question (unless she is very young, when apparent consent is ignored, in favour of a presumption of unwillingness). A female who consents cannot be said to have had intercourse forced upon her against her will. In any event it is now clear that "against her will" carries the connotation that the victim had refused her consent.[45] The refusal of consent is, therefore, part of the definition; and it would be incorrect to say that "consent of the victim" is simply a matter of defence. As a definitional element, however, consent is treated rather differently in Scotland from the way in which it has been interpreted in English law.

Consent as a definitional element

In the early nineteenth century, the English courts seem to have accepted **9–80** Blackstone's account of the crime in terms of "force" and "against the victim's will". But in the middle of that century, a series of cases radically altered the traditional definition.[46] The effect was that rape came to be defined as the having of sexual intercourse without the female's consent. The view was taken that "without her consent" meant just that — without her positive (or implied) consent. No longer was it necessary to show that the victim had resisted (even if only constructively) and thus shown her manifest unwillingess. This had a marked effect on the attitude of the English courts to insensible victims (see para. 9–81, below). But in modern Scots law, the requirement that the intercourse should have been against the victim's will limits the ambit of consent to the express or implied refusal of it by the female. In Scotland, a definition in terms of 'sexual intercourse without the victim's consent' would simply be too broad. It would fail to give effect to the law relating to insensible victims.

Insensible victims

Where a female is unconscious, for example, by reason of drink, drugs **9–81** (including anaesthetics) or natural sleep, and she is taken sexual advantage of by a male, the Scottish definition of rape requires the prosecutor to show that she was unwilling to have intercourse with that male prior to her insensibility. Further, it is necessary to show that her unwillingness was

---

45   See para. 9–73 and n. 19, above.
46   See *R. v. Camplin* (1845) 1 Den. 89; *R. v. Fletcher* (1859) 8 Cox. C.C. 131.

overcome by his administering drugs or drink to her.[47] His actions in doing so are, therefore, tantamount to "force". But where the accused has no hand at all in producing her state of insensibility, where he happens upon her by chance and has sexual intercourse with her when she is totally unaware of his presence and intentions, then it cannot be established that she demonstrated unwillingness. It obviously cannot be shown that any force was used to overcome unwillingness which never existed in fact; and, therefore, there is no rape.[48] Scots law thus sets the prosecutor in such a case the difficult task of proving that the principal role in effecting the female's unconsciousness was performed by the accused, and that he performed that role in order to overcome her known unwillingness to have intercourse with him. Difficult enough in intoxication cases, that task is completely impossible where the female was in a state of natural sleep at the time.[49] It remains the law in Scotland, therefore, that a female, who had not made plain her refusal of consent to intercourse with the accused prior to becoming insensible, cannot be raped by him if he later takes sexual advantage of her whilst she is so insensible. This is, of course, the inevitable consequence of defining the crime in terms of "unwillingness" and "refusal of consent". Had the definition taken the form of that which pertains in England — namely, "sexual intercourse with a person ... who at the time of the intercourse does not consent to it",[50] it would have been relatively simple to conclude, for example, that a male who happened by chance on an insensible female (whom he did not know) and had sexual intercourse with her, should be convicted of rape. She clearly would not at the time have consented to such activity with him, and his actions would, in popular and in English terms, be considered as rape. The intercourse would have been "without her consent". But under the present law in Scotland he could be guilty of no higher a crime than indecent assault or clandestine injury.[51] Such a female victim could not be shown to have been unwilling, or to have refused her consent, at any material time. Indeed, she would not have met the basic threshold of having the capacity at that time either to refuse or to be unwilling. It is submitted, therefore, that from this point of view, the English approach to rape is clearly superior, and should be considered for adoption in this country.[52]

---

[47] See, *e.g.*, *H.M. Advocate v. Logan*, 1936 J.C. 100.

[48] *Sweeney v. X.*, 1982 S.C.C.R. 509.

[49] *Charles Sweenie* (1858) 3 Irv. 109.

[50] Sexual Offences Act 1956, s.1, as substituted by s.142 of the Criminal Justice and Public Order Act 1994.

[51] See para. 9–87, below.

[52] As very nearly happened in any event, in terms of the majority of the opinions cast in *William Fraser* (1847) Ark. 280; see para. 9–84, below.

The *mens rea* of rape

The *mens rea* of rape has been most recently commented upon in **9–82** *Jamieson v. H.M. Advocate*,[53] where the trial judge told the jury that the accused's "defence" of error as to the victim's consent was not sustainable unless based on reasonable grounds. The Appeal Court held that this was a clear misdirection, since the trial judge had been wrong not to follow a prior ruling by the court in 1982.[54] But the court also took the opportunity of explaining why reasonable grounds were not required in such cases. This was due to the form of the *mens rea* in rape. As Lord Justice-General Hope put it:

> "The crime of rape consists in the carnal knowledge of a woman forcibly and against her will. Thus the *mens rea* of this crime includes the intention to have intercourse with the woman without her consent. The absence of a belief that she was consenting is an essential element in it. If a man has intercourse with a woman in the belief that she is consenting to this he cannot be guilty of rape."[55]

If Scots law is to sustain its view that sexual intercourse with an insensible female is not rape, then the *mens rea* of the crime must be an intention to have vaginal intercourse with a female where the male knows that she has refused, and continues to refuse, to have such intercourse with him, or, perhaps, where he knows that she had so refused up to the last moment she was capable of doing so. But the Lord Justice-General did not insist that such knowledge on the part of the accused was always essential. In fact he went on to imply that it would be sufficient in the alternative "if he acted without thinking or was indifferent as to whether or not he had her consent".[56] If a man had intercourse with a woman who in fact had refused her consent, but he had ignored the signs of refusal since he did not care one whit whether she consented or not, then he could be said to have a sufficient form of *mens rea* for the crime of rape. The two alternate forms of *mens rea* are thus intention (involving knowledge of her refusal to consent) or recklessness (involving indifference as to the issue of her consent). It had to follow, then, that an honest belief in the consent of the victim would, if believed by the jury, be sufficient to acquit, since it would negative both recognised forms of the *mens rea* of the crime.[57]

---

[53] 1994 J.C. 88.

[54] *Meek v. H.M. Advocate*, 1983 S.L.T. 280, which had apparently been followed in many similar (unreported) cases, such as that of *H.M. Advocate v. Stevenson*, Appeal Court, July 5, 1985.

[55] *Jamieson v. H.M. Advocate*, at p. 92E.

[56] *ibid.* p. 93F–G.

[57] In so doing, the Court in *Jamieson* (as in *Meek*), were following the earlier English decision of the House of Lords in *D.P.P. v. Morgan* [1976] A.C. 182 — even though the account of rape given by English law is not identical to that accepted in Scotland.

Marital rape

9–83   Hume hinted, rather than advanced as a definite rule, that a married man could not be convicted of raping his wife if he had sexual intercourse with her himself, by force and against her will.[58] What this was based on is hard to imagine, other than totally unacceptable views such as that a man had some "right" of property in his wife's body, or a "right" to expect that she would not deny him the means of acquiring legitimate heirs. In any event, if there ever was a soundly based "rule" of that nature in Scots law, it was laid to rest in *S. v. H.M. Advocate*.[59] The Appeal Court decided there that a married man was in no better position than any other man *vis-à-vis* the rape of his wife, thus culminating a process of attrition in respect of the "rule" begun by *H.M. Advocate v. Duffy*[60] and *H.M. Advocate v. Paxton*.[61] English law has since followed the Scottish lead on this issue.[62]

Fraud and rape

9–84   Since consent to sexual intercourse clearly elides rape, the question arises: "what is the law if consent is obtained by deception?" Relevant deceits here might include promises of marriage, promotion or other reward. If these promises were never intended to be fulfilled, then fraud could certainly be made out.[63] In a slightly different way, fraud would also be relevant if a man deceived a woman into thinking that he was someone with whom she would have been happy to have intercourse, as where he pretended to be her husband[64] or lover. Such a case of "husband impersonation" arose in *William Fraser*.[65] Fraser was alleged to have inserted himself into the bed of a married woman, and there, by behaving familiarly with her, made her believe that he was her husband. It was on that basis that she allowed him to have intercourse with her. Three offences were charged as alternatives in the indictment against him, namely—rape; assault with intent to ravish; and the innominate crime of "fraudulently obtaining access to a married woman". The main debate centred on whether rape or the innominate offence was relevant in the circumstances. Four of the six judges opined that the proper definition of rape was the having of sexual intercourse without the woman's consent (see the opinions of Lord Justice-Clerk Hope, and Lords Mackenzie, Moncreiff and Cockburn). That being so (and later authorities

---

[58] i, 306.
[59] 1989 S.L.T. 469.
[60] 1983 S.L.T. 7.
[61] 1984 J.C. 105.
[62] See *R. v. R.* [1992] 1 A.C. 599.
[63] See paras. 10–67 *et seq.*
[64] *cf. Gray v. Criminal Injuries Compensation Board*, 1993 S.L.T. 28 (Court of Session, Lord Weir).
[65] (1847) Ark. 280.

have *not* accepted that it is so—see para. 9–81, above), it seemed irrefutable that the victim had consented. Therefore, there could be no rape. Only Lord Cockburn, however, accepted the logic of that. The other three all maintained that Fraser was guilty of rape, since the victim's consent had not been an "informed" consent, owing to the element of deception. This interesting, if not bold, view was regrettably not shared by the remaining three judges, who sided with Lord Cockburn in deciding that consent obtained by fraud was nevertheless consent. In the final analysis, then, there was no rape here.

Disquiet over the decision in *William Fraser's* case (and similar cases in England)[66] led in 1885 to a change in the law. Under the Criminal Law Amendment Act of that year, it was declared to be common law rape in both Scotland and England to pretend to be a married woman's husband and thus obtain intercourse with her. The rule is now contained in section 7(3) of the Criminal Law (Consolidation) (Scotland) Act 1995. It has no application, however, to any case of deception other than that relating to a married woman's husband. Now that it cannot be presumed that a married woman would necessarily have consented had the rogue really been her husband, this specific statutory exception probably has little to justify it. **9–85**

Mentally ill victims

It is possible to argue that females suffering from certain mental illnesses or defects should be protected by the same rule which pertains to young children. It would then be the case that intercourse with them could be assumed to be by force and against their wills. Any consent apparently given could be ignored (although this could be harsh indeed where the victim exhibited no outward signs of mental illness). Despite some isolated dicta, however, such as that by Lord Cockburn in *William Fraser*,[67] there is no authority for treating mentally ill females any differently from females of normal mental capacities and abilities.[68] Instead, statutory provision of a limited nature has been made.[68a] **9–86**

Clandestine injury to women

In *Charles Sweenie*,[69] as an alternative to rape, the indictment contained the innominate offence of "wickedly and feloniously having carnal knowledge of a woman whilst asleep, and without her consent." Four of the six judges eventually decided that the accused was guilty of the innominate offence, in that he had climbed into bed with a sleeping woman **9–87**

---

[66] *R. v. Clarke* (1854) 6 Cox C.C. 412; *R. v. Barrow* (1868) 11 Cox C.C. 191.
[67] (1847) Ark. 280 at p. 308.
[68] See Gordon *Criminal Law*, para. 33–16.
[68a] *e.g.* the Mental Health (Scotland) Act 1984, s.106; see para. 9–88, *infra.*
[69] (1858) 3 Irv. 109.

and had intercourse with her. She did not wake until he was withdrawing, it appears. Rape was out of the question since a sleeping victim could not be shown to have been actively unwilling. Gordon, following Macdonald, refers to that innominate offence as "clandestine injury to women".[70] It may well be correct to regard such an offence as simply an example of indecent assault,[71] but the specific innominate offence continues to be used by some prosecutors.[72]

Alternative verdicts

9–88   A case of rape must be tried in a High Court[73] but under section 14 of the Criminal Law (Consolidation) (Scotland) Act 1995, a jury may convict of something other than rape, where that alone has been charged but the essentials of rape have not been established. The jury may instead convict of the statutory offences of procuring a woman or girl to have intercourse with a man by threats, false pretences or drugging,[74] of attempting to have intercourse with a girl under the age of 13,[75] or of having (or attempting to have) intercourse with a girl who is older than 13 but under 16 years of age.[76] They may also convict of the common law offence of indecent assault. Also, under section 106(5) of the Mental Health (Scotland) Act 1984, a jury may convict the accused of having sexual intercourse with a woman suffering from a state of arrested or incomplete development of mind, if that is what is established rather than rape.

6. THREATS AND EXTORTION

Introduction

9–89   Since it is accepted that words cannot amount to an assault (see para. 9–05, above), it still seems necessary to deter in some other way the using of words in such a manner as to cause fear and alarm. The method adopted by the common law is to recognise that it is sometimes criminal to threaten to do things to the detriment of the person threatened. Depending on what is said, some threats are criminal as soon as they are communicated, irrespective of why they were said, as long as the accused meant to communicate them to the victim. With respect to other threats, they are not

---

[70] para. 33–21, following Macdonald, p. 120.
[71] See Gordon, *Criminal Law* (Second Cum. Supp.), entry for para. 33–21.
[72] It is also recognised as a distinct crime in the Criminal Procedure (Scotland) Act 1995, s.274(2)(c). See also *Rodgers v. Hamilton,* 1994 S.L.T. 822, Lord Justice-Clerk Ross at p. 823C.
[73] See Criminal Procedure (Scotland) Act 1995, s.3(6).
[74] Criminal Law (Consolidation) (Scotland) Act 1995, s.7(2).
[75] *ibid.* s.5(2).
[76] *ibid.* s.5(3).

reckoned as criminal at all, unless they are made with the object of forcing the victim to do something he otherwise would not have been willing to do. In both cases, the *mens rea* element appears to be intention.

Threats criminal by themselves

Hume[77] made a distinction between verbal threats and written ones. On the apparent view that what is said is usually as transient as hot-air, verbal threats were only criminal if they related to burning down the victim's house or the like.[78] If they related only to "personal mischief", then the most that could be hoped for was an action for caution to keep the peace. This was apparently so even where there had been a threat to kill.[79] Written threats, however, were more serious—possibly since they could be read and re-read. If they related to personal violence or property damage, and demanded something as the price of non-implementation of the threat, then there was proper criminality.[80] As can be seen, however, all Hume's authorities are old and the law on this matter did not fully develop until much later in the nineteenth century.

9–90

The leading case on criminal threats is still that of *James Miller*.[81] It is important not for its facts, but for the light thrown on the whole subject by Lord Justice-Clerk Inglis.[82] His view was that it was wrong to make any distinction between what had been spoken and what had been written. (This is clearly correct. The effect on the victim is what really matters, rather than the method of communication.) He also opined that certain threats, however made, were criminal by themselves. He listed those as threats to burn down a house, to put someone to death, to do someone serious bodily harm, and (perhaps less understandably) to do someone serious injury as to his property, fortune, or reputation. With all of those, it did not matter whether the accused ever intended to carry out what he threatened; nor did it matter that he had no particular purpose to serve in making the threat at all. Thus, in the later case of *Elizabeth Edmiston*[83] the accused tried in vain to show that written threats to blow out the victim's brains and burn his house about his ears were at worst a thoughtless frolic. The court, following *James Miller*, ruled that it was of no consequence whether or not the accused really intended to cause serious alarm. It was enough that threats of that description

9–91

---

[77] i, 135 and 442.
[78] *Grizzel Sommerville* (1686) Hume, i, 135; *Laird and Lady Grant* (1712) Hume, i, 135.
[79] *Captain Andrew Nairne* (1712) Hume, i, 442.
[80] See *John Fraser* (1759) Hume, i, 439; *James Gray* (1737) Hume, i, 441.
[81] (1862) 4 Irv. 238.
[82] *ibid.* pp. 244–245.
[83] (1866) 5 Irv. 219, approved (*quoad* the principle it espouses) in *Lord Advocate's Reference (No. 2 of 1992)*, 1993 J.C. 43.

had been communicated at all. Also in the still later case of *Margaret McDaniel*[84] there was a verbal threat to tear the victim in pieces and "do for her". Although there was an ulterior purpose of discouraging the victim from giving evidence at a criminal trial, it is significant that that purpose was libelled as an aggravation of the threat—strongly suggesting that the threat was criminal by itself. A less usual, but still criminal, threat consisted of part words, part conduct in *H.M. Advocate v. Hayes*.[85] There, the accused sent a package containing explosives to the victim along with a letter. The note indicated that an electric detonator would be sent next time, thus threatening that the next package would blow up as soon as it was opened. Lord Cameron had no doubt at all that a threat criminal by itself was involved there, and that such a threat constituted a crime as soon as it was uttered, or placed with the postal authorities for onward transmission to the victim. There can be little doubt then that *James Miller* has been followed in subsequent cases, and must be taken to represent the modern law.

Extortion

9–92   Also in *James Miller*, Lord Justice-Clerk Inglis intimated that threats, insufficient to be thought criminal by themselves, could become criminal if "used for an unlawful purpose such as extorting money".[86] Here, both the nature of the threat and the demand must be considered. In *Marion Macdonald*,[87] for example, the female accused wrote to the victim and threatend to expose his alleged immoral activities to his family and friends unless he agreed to pay her £10. The court had no doubt that a relevant charge had been made out when that sort of threat was allied to that sort of demand; and it was also opined that any offer by such an accused to show the truth of what she threatened to expose would be entirely irrelevant.[88] A similar type of decision can also be seen in *Hogg v. H.M. Advocate*.[89]

9–93   There must, of course, be an actual threat—express or implied—for extortion to be made out. In *H.M. Advocate v. Donoghue*[90] the accused told an agent for the owner of five stolen paintings that for £1200 he would probably be in a position to secure their return. This was charged as attempted extortion; but clearly it could not succeed, since no threat (such as to destroy the paintings) had been made. It did constitute a suitable threat, however, for the accused to affix a notice to a car which had been parked on private property without permission, where that notice indicated that a wheel clamp

---

[84] (1876) 3 Coup. 271.
[85] 1973 S.L.T. 202.
[86] (1862) 4 Irv. 238 at p. 246.
[87] (1879) 4 Coup. 268.
[88] *ibid. per* Lord Deas at p. 273.
[89] 1954 S.L.T. (Notes) 82.
[90] 1971 S.L.T. 2.

had been secured to the vehicle, and that it would not be removed until a "levy on trespass parking" of £45 had been paid.[91] The threat, of course, must be accompanied by a demand. That demand generally is for the payment of money[92] but it is not necessarily restricted to that. Thus, in *George Jeffrey*,[93] the demands made were sometimes for goods; and in *Rae v. Donnelly*[94] the price demanded for silence as to alleged sexual impropriety was the giving up of a claim for unfair dismissal on the part of one victim, and the tendering of his resignation on the part of the other.

Status of the threat and the demand

The crime of extortion must obviously not be so widely drawn that it **9–94** prevents, say, a creditor from threatening to sue his debtor as a means of obtaining repayment of what is lawfully due. There, the demand for money would be quite legitimate, assuming that the due date for payment had come, as would the threat employed to pressurise the debtor. In the same way, it might be thought wrong for the law to penalise as extortion some matter which was ultimately for the victim's own benefit. If, for example, an employee had been caught with his hand in the till, it would clearly be to his benefit to take advantage of an offer from his employer to accept his resignation, even if pressurised into that by the threat of bringing in the police.[95] It was possibly to cater for situations such as these that Lord Justice-Clerk Thomson said of the type of threat made: "when the pressure consists in creating in the victim fear that, unless he yields, his position will be altered for the worse, it is criminal unless the pressure sought to be exerted is regarded by the law as legitimate."[96] He then continued: "legal process is such a form of pressure. So too ... is the pressure exerted by one contracting party on another contracting party. I need not consider whether these are exhaustive of legitimate forms of pressure." But more modern authority has emphasised that to enforce payment of a debt by any means other than those the law regards as legitimate is extortion, and that the only legally acceptable methods of enforcement are due process in a court of law, or lien (or retention) in relation to specific contracts.[97] Thus, irrespective of whether what is demanded is lawfully due or not (and that, of course, may be a matter which can only be resolved in court), a threat, for example, to

---

[91] *Black v. Carmichael; Carmichael v. Black,* 1992 S.L.T. 897.
[92] See *Priteca v. H.M. Advocate* (1906) 5 Adam 79; *Black v. Carmichael; Carmichael v. Black, supra.*
[93] (1840) 2 Swin. 479.
[94] 1982 S.C.C.R. 148.
[95] See *Hill v. McGrogan*, 1945 S.L.T. (Sh.Ct.) 18.
[96] *Silverstein v. H.M. Advocate*, 1949 J.C. 160 at p. 163.
[97] *Black v. Carmichael; Carmichael v. Black, supra, per* Lord Justice-General Hope at p. 900D–E.

detain (or injure) the 'debtor's' person or property[98] would lead to a relevant charge of extortion.

Further reading

Ferguson, P. R., "Criminal Liability for the Supply of Solvents," 1990 S.L.T. (News) 301.

Ferguson, P.R., "Controversial Aspects of the Law of Rape: An Anglo-Scottish Comparison" in Hunter, R. F. (ed.), *Justice & Crime* (1993), pp. 180 *et seq.*

Ferguson, P. W., "Rape and Reasonable Belief," 1983 S.L.T. (News) 89.

Ferguson, P. W., "Murder, Provocation and Self-Defence," 1986 S.L.T. (News) 38.

Ferguson, P. W., "The Doctrine of Provocation," 1986 S.L.T. (News) 171.

Ferguson, P. W., "Wheel Clamping and the Criminal Law," 1992 S.L.T. (News) 329.

Goff, Lord "The Mental Element in the Crime of Murder" (1988) 104 L.Q.R. 30.

Gordon, G. H. "Cawthorne and the *Mens Rea* of Murder," 1969 S.L.T. (News) 41.

Gordon, G. H., "The *Mens Rea* of Murder," 1967 S.L.T. (News) 89.

Jones, T. H., & Griffin, S., "Serious Bodily Harm and Murder," 1990 S.L.T. (News) 305.

McCall-Smith, A., "Brain Death" (1980) 25 J.L.S. 113.

Ness, G., "Assault and Reasonable Chastisement," 1995 S.L.T. (News) 185.

Norrie, K. McK., "Abortion in Great Britain: One Act, Two Laws" [1985] Crim.L.R. 475.

Phillips, A. F., "Beyond the Limits of Assault: A Duty of Care?" 1995 S.L.T. (News) 115.

Ross, J., "Unlawful Act Culpable Homicide," 1996 S.L.T. (News) 75.

---

[98] *ibid.* p. 900E.

CHAPTER 10

CRIMES OF DISHONESTY

1. THEFT

Introduction

Scots law recognises a right of property or ownership in many different **10–01** things. It subsists, for example, in relation to land, buildings, jewellery, farm and domestic animals, vehicles, foodstuffs, crops, money, debts, stocks and shares, copyright, patents and so on. A right of property is a complex one, under which the owner, depending on the precise nature of what he owns, may normally use, consume, destroy, keep, conceal from public gaze, transfer to another (for a price or by way of gift), pawn, mortgage or otherwise deal with the subject of the right. At any one time, an owner may or may not have possession; he may indeed be temporarily debarred from possession, as where, for example, he has pawned or hired out the thing that he owns. His ownership, however, will normally continue to exist notwithstanding a loss of possession. Theft is designed to help protect the right of property in things. It protects more than mere possession, but less than the whole gamut of things in which ownership is legally recognised.

GENERAL DEFINITION OF THEFT

In the modern law, it is theft to appropriate moveable, corporeal things **10–02** belonging to another person, without the consent of that person, where the accused knows that those things belong to another and intends to deprive him of them or their use permanently, indefinitely, or (in certain circumstances) temporarily. No Scottish authority shows that any additional requirement of "dishonesty" (despite the title of this chapter) has to be shown or inferred — unlike the situation in current English law under the Theft Act 1968, section 1(1). It is also unnecessary to show that the accused made any material gain from the appropriation. "[I]t is the owner's loss and not the other's gain which is important."[1]

---

[1] *Black v. Carmichael; Carmichael v. Black,* 1992 S.L.T. 897, *per* Lord Justice-General Hope at p. 902F, quoting with approval from Gordon, *Criminal Law*, para. 14–63.

THE *ACTUS REUS* OF THEFT

Appropriation

10–03 It is thought[2] that this term now more accurately represents the essential element in the *actus reus* than the "taking" referred to by Hume. His views[3] were somewhat eccentric and can be seen clearly in the following extract:

> "All the necessary characters seem to be set forth in that short description of it, given in the civil [*i.e.* Roman] law ... the felonious taking and carrying away of the property of another, for lucre.
>
> I. The fundamental circumstance here ... is this of the *taking* ... In which it is implied, that the thing has not been previously in the possession of the thief, but in that of the owner, or some person for him, out of which the thief, without the consent of the owner, removes it."

For Hume, then, it was necessary to show that the accused had deprived the owner of the possession of the thing, provided that the accused had the necessary *mens rea* at the very moment of deprivation. If the accused had been given possession of the thing with the consent of the owner, and only later formed the intention of keeping it for himself and treating himself as if he were its owner, that was not theft. If a person hired a horse, took a watch on loan, or agreed to carry goods to a certain destination, then as a matter of fact he would have had possession with the owner's consent and it would be assumed that he had originally meant to act honestly, unless the contrary was clearly proved. If that was not proved and he subsequently converted the horse, watch or goods to his own purpose (for example, by selling it or them), "he only breaks his contract, and abuses his powers as possessor."[4] In brief, a person already in possession of the thing with the consent of the owner would (somewhat generously) be presumed to be in honest possession of it. A later manifestation of dishonest intention might result in a wrong being committed, but it would not amount to theft.[5]

10–04 That Hume was strongly of the persuasion that theft protected the owner's possession is further illustrated by his treatment of a finder of things which had been lost.[6] The person who lifts a wallet from the street where its owner has accidentally dropped it is plainly from that moment onwards in possession

---

2 *Black v. Carmichael; Carmichael v. Black, supra* at p. 901H.
3 i, 57.
4 i, 58–9.
5 i, 58 at "2".
6 i, 62.

of it. In Hume's estimation, it could not be theft for him subsequently to "keep it to himself":

> "Because there is no felonious intention, nor even a *trespass* in the first occupying of the thing, which is lying vacant, and inaccessible to the owner, and may lawfully be taken possession of for the sake of custody, or till offer of a reward. So much is this the case, that though caught in the very act of laying hold of the thing, the man could not be punished or found fault with."[7]

The assumption of initial honesty in such a case[8] seemed, indeed, to be decisive; on the premise that theft required a dishonest taking of possession, no subsequent dishonesty could count since no-one could again take what he had already taken.

Attractively logical though Hume's views were, the premise on which **10–05** they were founded was openly doubted by the judiciary even before his death on August 30, 1838. The leading reported case in this respect is that of *John Smith*,[9] although earlier cases in which Hume was not followed are referred to in the pleadings and opinions. Smith was alleged to have found a pocket book, £112 in bank notes and a bill of exchange — all of which having been accidentally dropped by the owner on or near a public road. The name of the owner appears to have been contained in the pocket book, and thus Smith could have had no doubt to whom the items belonged. He was charged with theft since, having found these things, he "did then and there, or at some other time and place ... appropriate the same to his own uses and purposes." The words "at some other time and place" plainly covered a situation which Hume would not have counted as theft; but the court of six judges unanimously found the whole indictment relevant. As Lord Meadowbank trenchantly remarked,[10] "it is of no consequence of what character the original possession of the property is. The moment the intention of appropriating the property of another is formed, then the theft is committed." Lord Mackenzie was equally forthright[11] in that he stated:

> "We have determined that in the case of carriers, servants, clerks, shopmen, the appropriation of goods held on a limited title for behoof of the owner is theft; and of course all these decisions apply with greater force to the case of a finder, who took the goods honestly, and subsequently formed the felonious intention of appropriating them."

---

[7] Hume, i, 62.

[8] *cf.* Burnett, 123, where the assumption is put the other way.

[9] (1838) 2 Swin. 28, decided on March 12, 1838. For a modern example of a charge of theft by finding, see *MacMillan v. Lowe,* 1991 J.C. 13, where in the special circumstances of the case, possession of the goods a mere four hours after they were found was sufficient to justify the conclusion that the finder had appropriated them.

[10] *John Smith* (1838) 2 Swin. 28 at p. 52.

[11] *ibid.* pp. 53–54.

The words of Lord Cockburn[12] are are also worthy of notice:

> "The definition which our law gives of theft, is, that it is ... fraudulent taking of the property of another for the sake of lucre. Now what is meant by this word *taking*? I know no authority, and no principle, for confining it to the act of first possessing ... I don't conceive that there can be any taking, in the sense of this definition, without an intention to take. It means appropriation."

10–06   If "appropriation" is what is required, and it is submitted that it is, then it covers a number of different situations. Certainly it includes Hume's dishonest taking possession of a thing and carrying it away. It has also been held to apply where a car found on private land without permission to be parked there was "wheelclamped", thus immobilising it and depriving the owner of its use and enjoyment as a vehicle.[13] This would not be the case, however, if property had been incidentally (as opposed to deliberately) immobilised — for example, "as a result of some legitimate act such as the closing or locking of a gate for security."[14] Appropriation also extends more widely to a manifest change in attitude towards things that the thief originally possessed lawfully and honestly, as where he subsequently applies or converts those things to his own use,[15] or claims them as his own.[16] That "appropriation" is indeed what is required is the only plausible explanation of the judiciary's rejection of Hume's view[17] that a footman could not steal his livery in cases such as *Elizabeth Anderson*,[18] where a discharged poorhouse inmate committed theft by purporting to sell the petticoat, shawl and shift given into her temporary possession by the relevant parochial board, and *John Martin*,[19] where again an inmate committed theft by purportedly selling his poorhouse "uniform". It also explains Lord Mackenzie's remarks in *George Brown*[20] that "in the case of a horse hired without any felonious purpose, and afterwards carried off by the hirer, we have decided that a theft is committed."[20a] But that decision is contrary to the opinion of Baron Hume. Thus Hume had become "greatly qualified"[21]

---

[12] *John Smith* (1838) 2 Swin. 28 at p. 56.
[13] *Black v. Carmichael; Carmichael v. Black*, 1992 S.L.T. 897, *per* Lord Justice-General Hope at p. 902B–C. Notice, however, that Lord Allanbridge considered that the facts amounted to a case of theft by finding: p. 903B–C.
[14] *ibid. per* Lord Justice-General Hope at p. 902D–E.
[15] *John Smith* (1838) 2 Swin. 28, *per* Lord Cockburn at pp. 56–57.
[16] *John Waugh* (1873) 2 Coup. 424, *per* Lord Ardmillan at p. 427.
[17] i, 60.
[18] (1858) 3 Irv. 65.
[19] (1873) 2 Coup. 501.
[20] (1839) 2 Swin. 394 at p. 428.
[20a] *cf.* Alison, i at pp. 259–260 for possible authorities.
[21] *John Smith* (1838) 2 Swin. 28, *per* Lord Moncreiff at p. 54.

or "seriously modified".[22] No doubt, the courts felt less need than usual to follow that authoritative writer since he himself had admitted[23]: "[t]hus much of the taking which [sic] is essential to the crime of theft. Upon the whole of which inquiry ... it may be proper to remark, that our practice has not yet attained to sufficient maturity in these matters."

Moveable, corporeal things

Things can be stolen if they can be physically possessed and can be **10–07** moved from place to place. As Alison[24] narrates: "[t]heft may be committed of every inanimate thing, which is either moveable or capable of being severed from that which is naturally or artificially attached to it." It follows then that a growing crop becomes moveable property when cut from the field or dug up from the earth, and thus at that stage can be possessed and stolen.[25] Even a piece of land might gradually be stolen (all things being equal) by excavating its substance[26]; that could not, however, exhaust the right of property involved in land ownership, since that is a metaphysical entity said to extend a *coelo usque ad centrum*.[27] Such a right of property in land is, of course, created and evidenced by title deeds or land certificates. Once again, whilst it is possible to steal such deeds or certificates,[28] what is stolen is not the right of property in the land itself but the documents themselves, considered as miscellaneous collections of paper and parchment. The right to the land cannot in fact be stolen because it is the incorporeal (*i.e.* intangible, non-possessable) property of a particular individual.

Corporeal moveables are referred to by Bell[29] as including **10–08**

> "all things which, being themselves capable of motion or of being moved, may be perceived by the senses — seen, touched, taken possession of: as ships, household furniture; goods and effects of all kinds; farm stock and implements; horses, cattle and other animals; corn, money, jewels, wearing apparel."

Such moveables, it is said,[30] are the only things which can be stolen, since they are the only things capable of being physically possessed and carried away in accordance with Hume's account of theft (see para. 10–03, above).

---

[22] *Elizabeth Anderson* (1858) 3 Irv. 65, *per* Lord Ardmillan at p. 68.
[23] i, 69–70.
[24] *Principles*, i, 278.
[25] See, for example, *James Miln* (1758) Hume, i, 79 (grain); and *Andrew Young* (1800) Hume, i, 79–80 (potatoes).
[26] i, 80.
[27] *i.e.* "from the heavens right to the centre of the earth," see Bell, *Prin.*, 10th ed., s.940.
[28] See *Patrick Eviot* (1614) Hume, i, 80.
[29] *Prin.*, s.1285.
[30] Gordon, *Criminal Law*, para. 14–29.

Since his account has been departed from somewhat in modern law,[31] the need to confine theft to moveable, corporeal property is questionable. An extension of the crime to cover the appropriation of at least some types of incorporeal property would, therefore, seem worth considering. No reported case has endorsed such an extension, however, and so called "intellectual property" (*e.g.* copyrights, patents and designs) is protected either by civil law remedies or by particular statutory offences.[32] On the other hand, no reported case has ruled out such an extension, such authorities as there are having been concerned with innominate offences rather than theft.[33]

10–09   As is obvious from the passage quoted from Bell, animate things can also meet the test of being moveable and corporeal. Thus animals may be stolen,[34] as also "infant" children.[35] The conventional view is that an "infant" child is one below the age of puberty,[36] which means a boy under 14 or a girl under 12,[37] and the authorities certainly support the view that a young child must be involved.[38] The Scottish Law Commission, however, has recommended that such children should cease to be considered as "stealable", and that an appropriate statutory offence should be substituted.[39] Adults (*i.e.* apparently anyone beyond the age of pupillarity) cannot be stolen; but the crime of abduction substitutes for theft where such persons are forcibly taken away.[40]

10–10   Some things are difficult to perceive as moveable and corporeal in the required sense. Currency, for example, in the form of banknotes can certainly be stolen, although the notes themselves appear to represent some ill-defined, intangible right. Prosecutions for thefts of money assume, however, that the face value of what has been appropriated is involved, and not just such value as mere pieces of paper attract.[41] The reason for this is that such promise (an incorporeal matter) as is contained in a banknote is made to the bearer, and not to any particular person. Electricity is also thought to pose conceptual difficulties,[42] but it is clearly moveable and corporeal. The

---

[31] See paras. 10–05 *et seq.*
[32] See, for example, the Copyright, Designs and Patents Act 1988, s.107.
[33] See *John Dewar*, Burnett, 115; S.R.O. J.C.13/21, October 3, 1777 (erroneously, it seems, referring to as a case of theft in Macdonald, p. 20); *H.M. Advocate v. Mackenzie*, 1913 S.C. (J.) 107; *Grant v. Allan*, 1987 J.C. 71.
[34] Hume, i, 81.
[35] i, 84. See para. 10–15, below.
[36] Macdonald, p. 21; Gordon, para. 14–43.
[37] See Child Abduction (Scot. Law Com. No. 102, 1986), Pt. III, para. 3.3.
[38] *Rachel Wright* (1808–9), Hume, i, 84, n. 2 (child aged between two and three); *Mary Millar or Oates* (1861) 4 Irv. 74 (child aged nine years nine months).
[39] *supra*, Pts. III and IV.
[40] *Barbour v. H.M. Advocate*, 1982 S.C.C.R. 195.
[41] *John Mooney* (1851) J. Shaw 496.
[42] Gordon, *Criminal Law*, para. 14–34.

fact that it cannot as easily be possessed and taken away as many other forms of stealable property is probably not of great importance once it is recalled that appropriation is what is required in the modern law.

Belonging to another person

Since theft protects an owner's right of property, stealable things must **10–11** be owned — and owned by someone other than the accused. As Macdonald puts the matter[43]: "[a] person is not guilty of theft for irregularly taking that which is his own, although he may thereby commit some offence other than theft." It is not possible in Scotland, therefore, for a person to steal his own car, by driving it off clandestinely from a repair-garage in order to avoid paying for work done on it.[44] Although the garage proprietor would have had a lien (*i.e.* a right to retain possession) over such a car until the work had been paid for, such a lien does not amount to any right of ownership. It has been declared that a pawnbroker has some form of ownership in relation to things which are pawned — certainly a form sufficient to save him from conviction for theft if he disposes of such things before the conclusion of the redemption period,[45] — but this is at odds with the tenor of the present legislation,[46] and Gordon[47] is surely correct to say that the view taken in that case must be wrong.

In contracts of sale involving "stealable property", ownership passes to **10–12** the buyer according to the rules contained in the Sale of Goods Act 1979,[48] sections 17, 18, 19, 20A and 21. But in lesser contracts than sale, such as loan, where the subject of the loan is money, or anything else which is consumed by use and is intended to be so consumed (*e.g.* a jar of coffee), ownership must pass on delivery by the lender. As Bell remarks[49]: "[p]ossession in this, as in the case of ordinary moveables, presumes property." The obligation of the recipient is thus to return an equivalent sum of money, together with any interest charged, or an equivalent amount of the thing consumed. It is difficult to see that failure to do so could be more than a breach of contract. Theft must be negatived by his ownership of the thing lent. In a similar way, if a banknote is tendered for change into coin or notes of smaller denomination, or is tendered in payment for a purchased item, it seems that ownership of the note must pass on delivery.

---

[43] p. 16.
[44] *cf. R. v. Turner (No. 2)* [1971] 1 W.L.R. 901, which depended on the extended meaning given to "belonging to another" by the (English) Theft Act 1968, s.5(1).
[45] *Catherine Crossgrove or Bradley* (1850) J. Shaw 301, *per* Lord Moncreiff at p. 305.
[46] Consumer Credit Act 1974, especially ss.116(3), 117(2), 118(1), 119(2) (though not applicable to Scotland), 120, 121, and 122.
[47] *Criminal Law*, para. 14–46.
[48] As amended by the Sale of Goods (Amendment) Act 1995, s.1.
[49] *Prin.*, s.1333.

Failure either to give change at all or to give the correct change would, therefore, seem to be a breach of contract rather than theft. The original note and the pool of cash from which change might be had are both in the possession, and thus ownership of the defaulting party. Yet in *John Mooney*,[50] where a banknote was indeed tendered in payment for goods of considerably less value, and no change given, Lord Justice-Clerk Hope directed the jury that: "[i]f there was theft at all, it was theft of the one-pound note." Although that direction might have had the merit of granting relief to the "innocent" party from having to pursue a claim according to the vagaries and expense of the civil law, his Lordship advanced no justification for considering that theft could be relevant there at all. Nevertheless, Mooney was convicted of theft of the banknote and transported for seven years. If that was a "just" result, it was certainly not arrived at by any principled argument.

10–13   Almost all moveable, corporeal property in Scotland is owned by someone — either by a particular person or, by way of fiction, by the Crown. If such property is truly abandoned by its modern-day owner, then the Crown fills any hiatus in ownership between abandonment and, say, its collection as waste by a local authority.[51] It thus remains stealable at every step. It is also the case under feudal theory that treasure hidden or abandoned in antiquity belongs to the Crown[52] and can, therefore, be stolen by its finder. As Bell puts it[53]: "[t]he rule is, *quod nullius est fit domini regis.*" No doubt, neither that maxim nor its import is widely known to the general public; but where a crematorium manager espoused an honest belief that coffins delivered to his premises to be burnt were ownerless scrap, lawfully capable of being appropriated by anyone including himself, the Appeal Court rejected his defence of error on the grounds that it did not rest on reasonable grounds.[54] Temporarily-lost property is, of course, not abandoned by its owner; and its finder is not even entitled to claim ownership where the original owner remains untraced.[55]

10–14   The case of indigenous animals living naturally in the wild is special, although the rule is one of considerable antiquity. They form a conspicuous exception to what was stated at the beginning of the preceding paragraph. According to Hume[56]:

> "Our practice acknowledges, of course, the exception of those animals which are wild, and in no degree *sub domino* [*i.e.* within anyone's

---

[50] (1851) J. Shaw 496 at p. 497.
[51] *Mackenzie v. Maclean*, 1981 S.L.T. (Sh.Ct.) 40; see also Environmental Protection Act 1990, s.45(9), noting that "waste" is defined by s.75(2) as substituted by the Environment Act 1995, Sched.22, paras. 88; *cf.* the offence under s.60(1).
[52] *Lord Advocate v. University of Aberdeen and Budge*, 1963 S.C. 533.
[53] *Prin.*, s.1291.
[54] *Dewar v. H.M. Advocate*, 1945 J.C. 5; see paras. 8–52 *et seq.*, above.
[55] See the Civic Government (Scotland) Act 1982, s.73.
[56] i, 81.

ownership], such as game in the fields, or fish in a lake or river: There may be a trespass in taking these without leave of the owner of the grounds, but they are not his property, to be stolen."

In fact they are no one's property until killed or taken into captivity. Then ownership follows possession[57] and they may then be stolen. The Theft Act 1607,[58] as it has come to be known,[59] is the sole survivor of a number of pieces of legislation passed by the Scots Parliament to clarify doubtful cases relating to wild animals.[60] It states (using modern orthography): "[w]hosoever steals bees, and fishes in proper stanks and lochs shall be called and convened therefor as a breaker of the law." Since the penalty was (and is) a small fine, it is difficult to be confident that "these offences are raised to the rank of theft."[61] Nevertheless, "proper stanks and lochs" have been interpreted as "fish ponds belonging entirely to one proprietor and used for the purpose of keeping fish therein."[62] It also appears that the Act only applies to fish caught within the stank or loch and not to those which have escaped and are caught elsewhere.[63]

Since "infant" children are stealable property (see para. 10–09, above), **10–15** they would apparently require to be owned by their parent(s) or guardian, if the usual rules for theft are applicable. This would involve a very odd conception of ownership since it clearly could not involve the usual property rights of, for example, destruction or sale. The essence of child theft has, however, been described as:

"the deliberate taking of a child from the custody of a parent or other person who has for the time being the parental right of custody in terms of the statute[64] or under an order made by the court. The matter does not depend on the natural relationship which exists between a father and his child. It depends entirely upon interference with the parental right of custody, by virtue of which the child is in the care and possession of the person from whom it has been taken."[65]

Consequently, a parent may be excluded from having lawful custody, and may be able to steal his own child simply because he is excluded from

---

[57] *Prin.*, s.1290.
[58] A.P.S. IV, c.6, p. 373.
[59] Statute Law Revision (Scotland) Act 1964, Sched. 2.
[60] Hume, i, 82.
[61] *ibid.*
[62] *Pollok v. McCabe* (1909) 6 Adam 139, *per* Lord Ardwall at p. 143.
[63] See *Valentine v. Kennedy*, 1985 S.C.C.R. 89, which concerned the taking of rainbow trout (non-indigenous, farmed fish) from waters outside a stocked reservoir.
[64] See now the Children (Scotland) Act 1995, ss.1–4 and 11.
[65] *Hamilton v. Wilson*, 1994 S.L.T. 431 (father of illegitimate child convicted of theft of the child from its mother), *per* Lord Justice-General Hope, at p. 433E.

possession.[66] It might be advantageous, therefore, to treat child-stealing as a special crime of its own kind — as is more or less admitted by the authoritative writers in their description of it as "plagium".[67]

10–16 A similar problem is encountered with the "theft" of human corpses. This is partly solved by the existence of the special crime of violation of sepulchres. It is committed by raising the body of a deceased person from its grave; but ceases to apply once the process of dissolution of the corpse has reached a rather ill-defined stage.[68] That crime does not depend, however, on the recognition of any person's ownership of the remains. Between death and burial (or cremation), it is presumed that theft may still apply to the corpse[69]; but the early case of *Mackenzie*,[70] mentioned in the report of *H.M. Advocate v. Coutts*,[70a] does not seem to provide authority for this, since the charge was not one of theft.[71] In the case of *Dewar v. H.M. Advocate*[72] a conviction for stealing coffins (or at least their lids), which had been delivered to a crematorium to be burnt, was upheld on appeal. There was no discussion which addressed the question of who owned these items at the time. But ownership here may be clearer than in the other situations outlined above, for the executors in each case must have authorised payment for the coffin and lid out of funds in respect to which they stood as trustees.[73] They were, therefore, the true owners[74] until such time as the whole coffin (along with its contents) was reduced to ashes in the crematorium's furnace.[75]

> "[T]he charge of theft is competent ... though the case should be such in which it is difficult precisely to describe the owner, or the quality of the immediate interest in the thing ... We are ... content with such a description of the thing, as makes the title of possession or management clear, and excludes all pretence of right in the pannel to take it away."[76]

---

[66] *Hamilton v. Wilson, supra.* See also *Downie v. H.M. Advocate,* 1984 S.C.C.R. 365 (Sh.Ct.); *Hamilton v. Mooney,* 1990 S.L.T. (Sh.Ct.) 105.

[67] Hume, i, 82; Alison, i, 280; J. M. Fotheringham, "Plagium: The Sins of the Father v. The Rights of the Parent," 1990 J.L.S. 506.

[68] *H.M. Advocate v. Coutts* (1899) 3 Adam 50.

[69] Hume, i, 85, n. 1.

[70] Unreported, but partial account at (1733) Burnett, 124.

[70a] (1899) 3 Adam 50 at p. 57, n. 1.

[71] Gordon, *Criminal Law*, para. 14–44.

[72] 1945 J.C. 5.

[73] See Gordon, *Criminal Law*, para. 14–49 (ownership by trustees of trust property).

[74] See the Succession (Scotland) Act 1964, s.14(1).

[75] See also *Herron v. Diack and Newlands*, 1973 S.L.T. (Sh.Ct.) 27, a macabre case where it was assumed that an American funeral casket was stealable until committed with its contents to the waters of the River Clyde.

[76] Hume, i, 78.

Thus, it is sufficient in a charge of theft to allege that the property is owned by someone unknown, as long as it is made clear that that someone could not have been the accused.[77]

Where the alleged thief asserts a belief that the property in question was **10–17** his own, or at least was available for him to deal with as he pleased, this is an admissible defence[78]:

> "[t]he person must however be excusable for believing, that the thing which he has taken is his own. For as to that sort of belief ... which is directly in the face of law, and is grounded only in the violent passions of the man, or his blind prejudices in his own favour, it is what the Judge can have no regard to, and what none of the lieges can be allowed to entertain."[79]

Such a belief must, therefore, be more than honestly held; it must be based on reasonable grounds, as in *Dewar v. H.M. Advocate*,[80] and the evidential burden of establishing that appears to lie with the accused.[81] This may or may not amount to what Gordon refers to as a "Claim of Right"[82] or the defence of "Entitlement".[83]

Without the consent of the owner

What was done must have been done without the consent of the owner **10–18** or his authorised agent or representative. This is usually obvious from the facts and circumstances. Plainly there is appropriation without the owner's consent if foodstuffs or beverages given to the accused for safekeeping are consumed or destroyed by him. Similarly, a person entrusted with valuables whilst the owner travels abroad has no authority to sell or pawn them, or indeed to devote them to some worthy charity. To do so is to arrogate to himself the rights of the owner and that amounts to appropriation in the absence of error as to consent, or a contract allowing him such rights (*e.g.* sale or gift). It probably also amounts to appropriation to sell such a valuable opportunistically for a far greater price than would normally have been commanded, even if the accused believed in good faith that he was thus benefiting the owner.[84] Retrospective consent might, of course, be given in such a case.

---

[77] See the statutory styles in the Criminal Procedure (Scotland) Act 1995, Scheds. 2 and 5.

[78] Hume, i, 73.

[79] *ibid.* i, 74.

[80] 1945 J.C. 5, *per* Lord Justice-Clerk Cooper at p. 9.

[81] *ibid. per* Lord Justice-General Normand at p. 12.

[82] Gordon, *Criminal Law*, para. 14–83; see also para. 8–51, above.

[83] *ibid.* para. 14–85.

[84] *ibid.* para. 14–64.

10–19   Whether appropriation within Hume's category of "taking and carrying away" is without the owner's consent is also usually obvious from the facts. Indeed, very little is required to satisfy the notion of "taking and carrying away",[85] and thus it may be crucial to discover what consent, if any, the owner actually gave. According to Hume[86]:

> "[i]n general, the law intends that the thing must be removed from the place and state of keeping in which it had been" ... [but] ... [a]lthough there be but a very slight removal in respect of place, it seems also in every instance to be a theft, if the thing is thereby lost to the owner, so that he has to seek for and knows not where to find it...".

An illustration he gives (translated into modern terms) concerns a hotel guest who places an item of hotel property in his own case. Plainly, hotel managements intend that towels, televisions, kettles and the like should be used by guests; but they give no consent to their being removed from their possession and control in such a manner. In a similar way, there is probably appropriation where a person removes goods from a supermarket shelf (to which the management does presumably consent) but places them at once in his own bag or coat-pocket instead of the receptacle provided by the store.[87] Whether such appropriations amount to theft will, of course, depend on whether the *mens rea* element is satisfied (see paras. 10–21 to 10–28, below).

Error as to consent

10–20   According to Alison[88]:

> "[i]f the taker believed on rational grounds, that the owner would not object to his taking the goods, the crime will not be theft. This presumed consent may be inferred from the near relationship of the parties, or their intimate connexion, in the way of friendship, partnership, or business."

Although Alison provides no examples, it must be plain that a house guest might well consider that he would have the consent of his host to assuage

---

[85] See, *e.g., John Paterson and Alexander Glasgow* (1827) Syme 174 — bed clothes removed from beds and rolled in a counterpane to await later collection; *Cornelius O'Neill* (1845) 2 Broun 394 — accused arrested as he drew a pile of clothes with a stick towards an open window outside which he was standing.

[86] i, 70 and 71.

[87] See *R. v. McPherson* [1973] Crim.L.R. 191, a case under the (English) Theft Act 1968, wherein "appropriation" is given an interpretation at s.3(1) similar to that which is probably now favoured in Scotland; see also *Barr v. O'Brien*, 1991 S.C.C.R. 67.

[88] *Prin.*, i, 273.

nocturnal pangs of hunger or thirst by visiting the larder, fridge or wine cellar. It is to be noted that Alison requires such a belief to be based on reasonable grounds; and it may be thought that an honest but unreasonable belief would not be sufficient here (despite the decision to the contrary effect in the context of rape, in *Jamieson v. H.M. Advocate*[89]). But it is certainly possible to argue that the law is currently in a state of transition (see paras. 8–58 to 8–60, above), and indeed, if it is correct that lack of consent of the owner (or custodier) is part of the definition of the crime, then it may be difficult to avoid the conclusion that since an honest error as to consent suffices in rape, then *a fortiori* it must also do so in theft. On the other hand, if "consent" in relation to theft is really a matter of defence — then reasonable grounds may on principle continue to be required.[90]

THE *MENS REA* OF THEFT

Knowledge and intention

Hume's view of the *mens rea* of theft is encapsulated in the following **10–21** quotation[91]: "[the appropriation] must be with a felonious purpose; by one who knows that the thing belongs to another, and who means to deprive him of his property." It follows that if the accused does not know that the property is owned by another, then he ought to be acquitted, provided (most probably) that the court takes the view that his lack of knowledge is reasonably understandable. Thus in *Fraser v. Anderson*,[92] by a majority of two to one, the High Court decided that where a person who had sold cattle to another (on a promise—that appeared not to have been honoured—to pay at a fixed future date), he might well not have understood that a breach of contract did not retransfer the right of property in them to himself. Consequently, where he had retained possession of the animals throughout, it was not theft for him to have purported to resell them to a third party.

Hume did not expressly say whether an intent to deprive the owner of **10–22** his property permanently was required, but since he gave examples where only temporary deprivation was involved and plainly stated that these did not suffice for theft, it is highly probable that permanency was indeed what he had in mind.[93] Even as late as 1976, the conventional view remained that, "the essential feature of the *mens rea* of theft is an intention to

---

[89] 1994 S.L.T. 537, following *Meek v. H.M. Advocate,* 1983 S.L.T. 280.
[90] *cf. Jamieson v. H.M. Advocate,* 1994 S.L.T. 537, *per* Lord Justice-General Hope at p. 541J.
[91] i, 73.
[92] (1899) 2 Adam 705.
[93] His examples, at i, 73, include a servant riding his master's horse at night without permission, and a farmer finding his neighbour's plough and putting it to his own, unauthorised, temporary use.

appropriate, and that appropriation involves an intention to deprive the owner permanently of his goods."[94]

10-23   That view had been given added veracity by the decision in *Strathern v. Seaforth*.[95] In that case, the accused had taken a car from where it had been parked in a Glasgow street in order to have the pleasure of driving it for a limited period. He was charged with clandestinely taking the vehicle where he knew that he did not have, nor could have expected to have the permission of the owner. The charge did not libel theft; nor did the court consider it as a case of stealing. It was a separate crime of its own kind. Macdonald[96] considers the case to illustrate that a kind of theft — *furtum usus* — had been accepted in Scotland. But *furtum usus* (theft of use) involves unauthorised use of what one possesses by consent of the owner,[97] which is clearly rather different from the true situation in the case. In the following year, the same crime featured in the case of *Murray v. Robertson*,[98] where an acquittal was entered on appeal since the taking of fish boxes for unauthorised use had been openly rather than clandestinely done. A description of the essentials of the offence,[98a] therefore, in terms of clandestine "taking and using"[99] (for a limited period) seems peculiarly apt — and distances the crime from the conventional view of theft, that there must be intent to deprive permanently.

10-24   Of course, at the precise moment when a car is taken away without authority, it is impossible to say what the exact intention of the taker is. Indeed, it might well be inferred from his actions that his intent was to deprive the owner of it permanently. In any event, where any "taking and carrying away"[99a] is involved it is sufficient for inferring the *mens rea* of theft if the thing is left in a place where the owner would not be liable to find it by his own investigative efforts. For these reasons, then, in *Kivlin v. Milne*[1] it was decided that theft was legitimately charged where a "joy-rider" of a motor vehicle had abandoned it in such a place that the owner would not have found it. As joy-riders may be assumed seldom to return the vehicle to the precise spot from which it was taken, *Kivlin v. Milne*[2] substantially undermines the need for a separate crime of "taking and using" in such cases. In any event, such cases now fall under the terms of the statutory offence presently contained in section 178 of the Road Traffic Act

---

[94]   *Herron v. Best*, 1976 S.L.T. (Sh.Ct.) 80, *per* Sheriff Macphail at p. 81.

[95]   1926 J.C. 100.

[96]   pp. 19–20.

[97]   See D. Matthaes, *De Criminibus: Text and Translations*, eds. M. L. Hewett and B. C. Stoop (1987), i.i.6.

[98]   1927 J.C. 1.

[98a]   *cf.* unlawfully taking and using the property of another; *cf.* Gordon, paras. 15–29, *et seq.*

[99]   Gordon, paras. 15–29 to 15–32.

[99a]   Hume, i, 73.

[1]   1979 S.L.T. (Notes) 2.

[2]   *supra*, in which no formal opinion was delivered by the Appeal Court.

1988. Recently, the Appeal Court has decided that an intention to deprive someone of his property "indefinitely" would be sufficient in an appropriate case. In *Fowler v. O'Brien*,[3] the accused had been refused permission to have a "shot" of the victim's bicycle, but decided to take the bike away in any event. This was not done clandestinely but quite openly. The accused gave no indication when it would be returned, nor did he state any conditions which would have to be fulfilled before its return. The victim did eventually recover his cycle — several days later. In upholding the conviction for theft, Lord Justice-General Hope concluded that this was not a case where an intent to deprive permanently might be inferred, since the victim had been able to recover the bike through his own efforts. Equally, however, it was not one of those cases where an intent to deprive temporarily might be sufficient — since the accused had not laid down any conditions relative to the return of the goods. There was thus no clear "nefarious purpose".[4] Instead he said this: "it appears to us that it would be more accurate to say that the owner was deprived of his bicycle indefinitely, since it was not made clear to him whether and, if so, when it would be returned to him."[5] On the assumption then that an intent to deprive indefinitely can be distinguished from an intent to do so permanently, and can be applied generally, there must be at least two forms of the *mens rea* for theft.

There is, however, yet another possibility for the *mens rea* of theft. This **10–25** was pointed out by Lord Justice-Clerk Macdonald, but lay dormant for many decades. In *H.M. Advocate v. Mackenzie*[6] the male accused was charged with the theft of a book of secret chemical formulae. He had apparently "borrowed" the book just for the limited purpose of making copies of its contents. Was this truly theft? Lord Justice-Clerk Macdonald had no doubt that it was:

> "That such a taking, although there is no intention to retain the article, may be theft is, I think, clear. The article is taken from its owner for the serious purpose of obtaining something of value through the possession of it ... In this case ... if [the prosecutor] can make out by his evidence that the book was taken, and taken for a nefarious purpose, he may be able to obtain a direction in law from the Judge at the trial that what was done constituted a theft of the book."[7]

In the current edition of Macdonald it is declared that temporary deprivation for an "illegitimate" purpose can constitute theft.[8] It seems, therefore, that

---

[3]   1994 S.C.C.R. 112.
[4]   Hume; paras. 10–25 to 10–27, below.
[5]   1994 S.C.C.R. 112, at p. 115C.
[6]   1913 S.C.(J.) 107.
[7]   *ibid.* at p. 110 — a view in which Lord Dundas concurred.
[8]   p. 20.

the intent required for this crime might be either an intention to deprive the owner permanently, or an intention to deprive him temporarily provided that a nefarious or illegitimate purpose lay behind it.

10–26   But what was a nefarious or illegitimate purpose? The temporary removal of a car to drive around in it did not seem to qualify[9]; nor did the unauthorised but temporary taking and using of fish boxes.[10] Removal of a book to copy out its secret and valuable contents was, however, sufficient, provided that the thief had no authority to have the book in his possession.[11]

10–27   The Appeal Court eventually seems to have endorsed Macdonald's view. In *Milne v. Tudhope*[12] the accused had been paid in advance for certain house improvements. When these were completed, the owner of the house expressed dissatisfaction, and required further work to be done. The accused was unwilling to do so unless he obtained a promise of further payment. In the absence of such a promise, he removed a significant number of fittings from the house in order to force the owner to allow him to carry out the further work and to agree to pay him for it. The fittings were thus taken and held hostage temporarily to force the owner's hand. At the appeal against conviction for theft, counsel for the appellant seems to have conceded that intent to deprive temporarily for a nefarious purpose was sufficient. The main part of the debate thus focused on whether there had been a nefarious purpose in this case. The court held that there had been: "the appellant was trying to achieve something by a scheme which he must have known was unlawful. Whether 'nefarious' means 'criminal' in this context or unlawful does not matter for present purposes."[13] Additionally, in *Kidston v. Annan*[14] the Appeal Court determined that where the accused was in possession of a television set with the consent of the owner, it was "nefarious" for him to refuse to return it until an unwanted repair was paid for. Once again, there was no argument as to whether this alternative form of intent was valid or not. In the absence of contrary authority, therefore, its validity must be accepted, as Lord Stewart in *Sandlan v. H.M. Advocate*[15] seemed to when he informed the jury that there were now two types of theft — the ordinary sort where there was intention to acquire things for personal benefit or profit, and the more unusual sort where things were taken:

> "not for the enjoyment or profit of the accused, but [as in this case] simply ... to give verisimilitude to the pretence of a robbery. The intention would not be to deprive Hamilton Laidlaw permanently of

---

[9] *Strathearn v. Seaforth*, 1926 J.C. 100.
[10] *Murray v. Robertson*, 1927 J.C. 1.
[11] *H.M. Advocate v. Mackenzie*, 1913 S.C. (J.) 107, *per* Lord Salvesen at p. 113.
[12] 1981 J.C. 53.
[13] *ibid*. p. 57. This point remains unsettled.
[14] 1984 S.L.T. 279.
[15] 1983 S.C.C.R. 71.

their property in the jewellery, but simply to take it for a time as a manoeuvre to save [the accused's] face so that the true stock position could be concealed ... The law is that such a taking of the goods of another, aimed at achieving a nefarious purpose, constitutes theft even if the taker intends all along to return the thing taken when his purpose has been achieved."[15a]

Intention may be inferred

Two fairly recent cases of theft have emphasised that although theftuous **10–28** intent will normally be inferred from the facts and circumstances (in the usual Scottish manner, see paras. 3–25, 3–26, above), such an inference need not always be drawn, and sometimes is not to be drawn where evidence to the contrary is believed; as in *Petrovich v. Jessop*[16] where a law student and alleged shoplifter had maintained that he had simply forgotten to pay for two books, on the basis that he had not slept for two nights and had been under examination and business stress; and *Mason v. Jessop,*[17] where it was held that an intent to steal could not be inferred from the mere breaking of panes of glass in a church window by a drunken person looking for a place to consume a can of beer.

For lucre

Despite the inclusion of these words in Hume's definition of theft it is **10–29** obviously unnecessary for the thief to make any economic gain from his crime. What matters is the owner's loss. Indeed, Hume concedes as much when he states that the phrase "for lucre" simply implies detention from its owner, or destruction of the thing taken.[18] For this reason, it cannot matter what actual value the thing appropriated has[19]; and prosecutions for thefts of items of minimal value are not uncommon.[20] It might be noted, however, that the value of items stolen does have a bearing on the jurisdiction of the district court.[21] The fact that the *de minimis* rule (see para. 2–54, above) plays an especially small part in this crime may reflect the lasting feeling that theft is a peculiarly heinous offence — having once, of course, been punished by hanging.[22] It is also obviously of no benefit to the thief for him

---

[15a] *Sandlan v. H.M. Advocate,* 1983 S.C.C.R. 71 at pp. 82–83.
[16] 1990 S.L.T. 594, as explained in *Ivers v. Normand,* 1994 S.L.T. 317.
[17] 1990 S.C.C.R. 387.
[18] i, 75. See para. 10–03 above.
[19] i, 76.
[20] See, *e.g., Walker v. MacGillivray* (1980) S.C.C.R. Supp. 244, where newspapers valued at 38p were allegedly stolen.
[21] Criminal Procedure (Scotland) Act 1995, s.7(4).
[22] See *James Joss* (1821) Shaw 29; *cf.* the Criminal Procedure (Scotland) Act 1887, s.56 (now repealed).

to change his mind and return what he had taken. Provided that he had at one time appropriated the property with the required sort of *mens rea*, the crime has been committed and cannot thereafter be uncommitted. In this connection, Hume quotes the case of *Finlay MacGibbon*,[23] where the accused stole six horses, and was prosecuted for their theft notwithstanding that he ultimately had returned them to their owner along with 200 merks by way of "compensation".

AGGRAVATIONS

10–30 Since theft ceased to be in any way a capital crime,[24] aggravations have ceased to be of great importance; but two still figure prominently in charges, namely "housebreaking" and "opening lockfast places". According to Lord Justice-General Hope in *Peter Alston and Alexander Forrest*,[25] the old custom was to charge housebreaking as a separate crime. If that was ever so, however, it had certainly been abandoned by the time of Hume.[26]

Housebreaking

10–31 This aggravation applies where a theft was committed after the thief entered any "shut and fast building",[27] provided he effected entry by forcing a way past "the ordinary obstacles" placed there by the owner or occupier to deny access to those not entitled or invited to enter.[28] Despite its title, "housebreaking" is applicable to any building, whether a dwelling-house (occupied or not) or a commercial establishment (such as an office or shop). In the case of *John Fraser*[29] it was held that a hen-house was a sufficient building for this purpose; and the statutory styles for theft mirror that exactly.[30] Of course, the most obvious instance of housebreaking occurs where a door or window has been broken or smashed by the prospective thief. The concept extends, however, rather more widely than that.

10–32 It seems to be well established that the security of a building can be overcome in a variety of ways which do not involve destructive measures at all. Thus, if a key to a door is stolen, or a skeleton key carried and used to obtain unauthorised entry, that will be quite sufficient.[31] There is a suggestion

---

[23] (1669) Hume, i, 79.
[24] Criminal Procedure (Scotland) Act 1887, s.56 (now repealed).
[25] (1837) 1 Swin. 433 at p. 473.
[26] i, 98 *et seq.*
[27] Hume, i, 103.
[28] *ibid.* i, 98.
[29] (1831) Bell's Notes 41.
[30] See the Criminal Procedure (Scotland) Act 1995, Sched.5 — "You did break into a poultry house and steal three fowls."
[31] Hume, i, 98 and the case of *Colin Fraser and Daniel Gunn* (1827) there at n. 2.

in some cases that such housebreakings can be taken to the ultimate degree. So in *John Maclean*,[32] and also in *Crown v. Devin and Polin*,[33] placing one's hand through a hole in a door and sliding back a bolt on the other side was considered sufficient; and in *John Dewar*[34] it seems that the court was prepared to accept that pressing a key out of a lock and winkling it out from a gap under the door in question constituted housebreaking. The more extreme decisions of this sort, however, have been put in doubt since the case of *Peter Alston and Alexander Forrest*.[35] There, by a narrow majority of four to three, the High Court decided that it was not housebreaking to obtain entry by turning a key left in a door-lock. As Lord Gillies put it[36]: "the object of the law is to protect the property of those who show due regard to their own property. The law cannot protect the careless and negligent." Still less, then, can it be housebreaking to enter a building through an unlocked door or an open (or unfastened) window.[37]

Unusual routes of entry may also be described as housebreaking, even **10–33** where the owner or occupier has taken no steps at all to make such routes secure. The view taken is that there is no need to secure chimney vents and sewer pipes since access to a building via them is hardly to be anticipated, or, in modern times, thought to be possible.[38]

Opening lockfast places

Once a thief has gained entry to a building, he may be confronted by **10–34** further obstacles to his theftuous progress. Individual rooms may themselves be locked, and it is then moot whether "breaking" into them constitutes housebreaking[39] or the opening of lockfast places.[40] Since it will certainly constitute either one aggravation or the other, the issue is probably academic. But it is certainly not housebreaking to force open chests, safes, cupboards or vehicles. These do not constitute "buildings" of any sort, and the appropriate aggravation will be the opening of lockfast places.[41]

---

[32] (1828) Bell's Notes 36.
[33] (1829) 5 Deas & Anderson 145.
[34] (1777) Burnett 115; S.R.O. J.C. 13/21, loose papers Box 213.
[35] (1837) 1 Swin. 433.
[36] *ibid*. p. 466.
[37] Hume, i, 98; *Lafferty v. Wilson*, 1990 S.C.C.R. 30.
[38] But see *Rendal Courtney* (1743) Hume, i, 99 and *John Hunter* (1801) Hume, i, 99 n. 5.
[39] Hume, i, 101.
[40] See *Mary Young or Gilchrist and Cecilia Hislop* (undated) Bell's Notes 34.
[41] See Hume, i, 98 and the statutory styles for theft in the Criminal Procedure (Scotland) Act 1995, Sched. 2.

Housebreaking with intent to steal

10–35   According to Hume[42] this was recognised as a crime separate from, and of a lower order than theft in *Charles Macqueen and Alexander Baillie*.[43] This is still the case today.[44] The Appeal Court has determined that disconnecting a burglar-alarm system can amount to attempted housebreaking with intent to steal.[45] The view taken was that the alarm system was an integral part of the security of the building. It has also been decided that such an attempt could (depending upon the precise circumstances) be shown by smashing a security light.[46] Logically too, the separate crime of "opening lockfast places with intent to steal" might be anticipated; and it certainly exists.[47]

THEFT IN OTHER PARTS OF THE UNITED KINGDOM

10–36 If property is stolen in another part of the United Kingdom and brought to Scotland by the thief, he may be dealt with as if the theft had been effected in Scotland.[48] This represents an extension of the normal, geographically limited jurisdiction of the Scottish Courts (see para. 2–42, above).

2. EMBEZZLEMENT

Introduction

10–37   The *Oxford English Dictionary*[49] gives the following as the only modern definition of "embezzlement": "the fraudulent appropriation of entrusted property". This is not at all at odds with the meaning of "embezzlement" as a crime, despite the curious way in which nineteenth-century indictments were framed. In *John McLeod*,[50] for example, the accused was charged in terms that he did "embezzle and fraudulently appropriate to [his] own uses and purposes" one pound sterling entrusted to him. Such tautology, however, was not unusual in the florid styles employed at that time, and does not imply that embezzlement had some meaning radically different from the accepted dictionary definition.

---

[42] i, 102.
[43] (1810) Hume, i, 102 n. 2.
[44] See, *e.g.*, *Mason v. Jessop*, 1990 S.C.C.R. 387.
[45] *Burns v. Allan*, 1987 S.C.C.R. 449.
[46] *Heywood v. Reid*, 1996 S.L.T. 378.
[47] See, *e.g.*, *Thompson v. Carmichael*, 1990 S.C.C.R. 51.
[48] See the Criminal Procedure (Scotland) Act 1995, s.11(4)(a). This also appears to apply if the accused has simply received property stolen in any other part of the United Kingdom: s.11(4)(b).
[49] 1989 ed.
[50] (1858) 3 Irv. 79.

In the time of Hume and Alison, an important distinction lay between **10–38**
"theft" on the one hand and "breach of trust and embezzlement" (as
embezzlement was then known) on the other. Theft was a capital offence,
whereas the other crime was not.[51] Because of this important practical
difference, fine lines often required to be drawn and "many nice cases
require[d] to be distinguished."[52] This did not lead to a clear contrast being
drawn between the two crimes. Today, neither offence being capital, it may
seem unnecessary to distinguish between them at all; and the very real
difficulty of attempting to do so is revealed in the Criminal Procedure
(Scotland) Act 1995[53] which allows a conviction for theft to be returned on
a breach of trust and embezzlement charge, and vice versa. From this point
of view, then, it would not seem to matter which of the two was in fact
charged. There are also very few modern, reported cases which comment
on the essential features of embezzlement; and some modern texts on
criminal law omit any reference to this crime at all.[54] But there is a definite
role for it — separate from theft. Indeed, it covers dishonest appropriations
where theft cannot operate, as where, say, a trustee or executor appropriates
the trust or executry funds. He cannot steal these, since he stands as owner
towards them[55]; but he can certainly embezzle them. It may also be possible
to embezzle property which is incorporeal and, therefore, cannot be the
subject of theft.[56]

General definition

A general definition in terms of Hume's[57] and Alison's[58] accounts is **10–39**
made difficult by their view that theft only applied to a dishonest taking
possession of goods from the owner, or other person legally entitled to
such possession. For them, appropriation where there was no such taking
was at best a breach of trust. Thus the appropriation by a servant of his
uniform, by a watchmaker of the watch given him to repair, or by the finder
of lost property was a breach of trust[59]; but such appropriations are now
clearly thefts (see paras. 10–05 and 10–06, above). In modern times,
therefore, it would be better to regard embezzlement as the deliberate
appropriation to one's own use and purpose of property entrusted to one by
the owner (or person otherwise entitled) in such a way as to confer the
status of a quasi-owner, for the purposes of dealing with that property and

---

[51] Hume, i, 61.
[52] Alison, i, 354.
[53] Sched. 3, para. 8(3),(4).
[54] See, *e.g.*, Harper and Hamilton, *A Fingertip Guide to Criminal Law* (3rd ed., 1994).
[55] Gordon, *Criminal Law*, paras. 14–49 and 17–28.
[56] *ibid.* para. 17–01; but *cf. Grant v. Allan*, 1987 J.C. 71; 1988 S.L.T. 11.
[57] Chap. II.
[58] *Principles*, Chap. XII.
[59] Alison, i, 354, 359 and 360.

accounting for one's dealings with it to that owner (or person otherwise entitled). The various facets of this definition are developed below.

ACTUS REUS

Entrusted by the owner to the accused

10–40   The "owner" may be an individual, or the partners of a firm,[60] or a co-executor or trustee[61]; and he (or they) must have given the accused authority to deal with the property in question on a quasi-owner basis.[62] Naturally, that authority must not have been rescinded before the act of appropriation. If it had been, then such appropriation would be theft (all other things being equal).[63] The range of persons entrusted with quasi-ownership status might include trustees, executors, factors, agents, managers, administrators, distributors and collectors, according to J. W. Angus[64]; but much depends on what persons answering to such descriptions are entitled to do with the property in question.[65] They should be authorised to avail themselves of some of the powers which an owner might have — such as the selling of the property, or its investment (speculatively or otherwise) or the using of it to raise money — all subject to an obligation to account to the owner for what has been done. A stock-broker, for example, may be given wide-ranging powers to "play the market" with a specific sum of money; in the course of his dealings with that money, he may in fact reduce the value of the capital sum to naught (since all investors are on notice that the value of investments may go down as well as up). And yet, provided he honestly discloses to the owner all that he has done (however incompetently) in the way of dealing, and has not pocketed any of the proceeds thereof without authority, there will be no question of embezzlement. Bad management or incompetence is not criminal; pocketing or otherwise appropriating the results of authorised dealings may well be.

10–41   If the accused lacked the powers which could be described as those of a quasi-owner, if he had been handed the property for a specific purpose and for a limited time (say, a broken watch to be repaired), then his appropriation of that property may well be theft rather than embezzlement.[66] If a painting

---

[60] See *Peter A. Sumner*, Appeal Court, November 1983, noted in Gordon, *Criminal Law*, (Second Cumulative Supplement), para. 17–28.

[61] *John Lawrence* (1872) 2 Coup. 168.

[62] *cf. Kent v. H.M. Advocate*, 1950 J.C. 38, where there was no evidence that such authority had ever been given and thus no prospect of a claimed appropriation being one of embezzlement.

[63] See *Alexander Mitchell* (1874) 3 Coup. 77.

[64] *A Dictionary of Crimes and Offences* (1st ed., 1895), under "Embezzlement".

[65] See, *e.g.* Hume's account of the powers of a farm steward at i, 60.

[66] *cf. William Keith* (1875) 3 Coup. 125, especially Lord Ardmillan at p. 133.

or a book, for example, is loaned by its owner to another, it is plainly theft for that other person to sell it or destroy it or give it away.[67]

On the other hand, if an accused person had powers of dealing with the **10–42** property, and had indeed dealt with it, the appropriation to his own use and purpose of any of the proceeds of that dealing would almost certainly identify him as an embezzler. The fact that his obligation was to account for those proceeds to the owner, and that he had failed to do so, might provide sufficient proof of his appropriation of them.[68] Were he to have had such "dealing" powers, but appropriated the property in the form in which it was received, or at least before any authorised "dealing" with it was entered into at all, there is precedent for the resulting crime being one of theft.[69] From this point of view also, the accused in *Catherine Crossgrove or Bradley*[70] should have been convicted of theft. Thus, if a stock-broker is given a sum of money by a client, with instructions to invest it as he sees fit for the best profit of that client, it would probably be theft for the broker to use the money to pay off his most pressing, personal creditors. It would certainly not amount to embezzlement since he had never begun the dealing he had been authorised to do.

THE *MENS REA* OF EMBEZZLEMENT

It is difficult to deduce from the case authorities what is the precise *mens* **10–43** *rea* element of embezzlement. In *Edgar v. Mackay*[71] what seemed to be looked for was evidence from which "the inference of dishonesty" might be drawn, so that it could be concluded "that the money in question was fraudulently appropriated". This is not very helpful; but what may have been meant is that a deliberate intent to appropriate has to be proved or inferred. This would involve forms of *mens rea* similar to those required in theft (see paras. 10–21 to 10–27, above). Nevertheless, whereas "dishonesty" does not seem particularly relevant in theft, it was made almost the rationale of embezzlement in the decision in *Allenby v. H.M. Advocate*.[72] There, a fish salesman sold the catches brought to port by several different trawler skippers, and placed the proceeds in one undivided account, as was his known, normal practice. He then advanced money from the pooled account to trawler skippers other than those entitled to it, and was charged with embezzlement. But since this was all done openly, and according to the custom pertaining at that port (Aberdeen), the Appeal Court felt that there

---

[67] See the statutory styles for theft in the Criminal Procedure (Scotland) Act 1995, Sched. 5.

[68] See, *e.g., Edgar v. Mackay*, 1926 J.C. 94.

[69] *J. D. Wormald* (1876) 3 Coup. 246.

[70] (1850) J. Shaw 301; see para. 10–11, above.

[71] 1926 J.C. 94, *per* Lord Justice-Clerk Alness at p. 97.

[72] 1938 J.C. 55.

was a basic lack of dishonesty and acquitted him. It is also noteworthy that in *H.M. Advocate v. Wishart*[73] an intent to place clients' money at risk, or perhaps just a reckless course of action involving funds owing to them, was considered sufficient for conviction.[74]

DIFFICULT CASES

10–44 Since the Criminal Procedure (Scotland) Act 1995 (see para. 10–38, above) virtually allows charges of theft and embezzlement to be interchanged, it will be obvious that in some cases there is uncertainty as to which of the two would be more appropriate. Indeed, some offences which clearly fit the definition of theft have been prosecuted to conviction as embezzlement — and vice versa. For example, in *Edgar v. Mackay*[75] a solicitor was instructed to obtain payment of a debt for one of his clients. He apparently did succeed in obtaining the money; but did not forward it to the client or indeed communicate with him on the subject at all. After months of fruitless inquiries, that client instructed a second solicitor to pursue the matter. It was then discovered that the original solicitor had indeed secured possession of the moneys in question, but had unaccountably refused to hand them over. Eventually, the arrest of the first solicitor was effected on a charge of embezzlement. On appeal against conviction, it was held that conviction for embezzlement was justified in the circumstances. But since the lawyer in question had no authority to deal with the money, the conviction should probably have been one for theft. It may be said that a lawyer collecting such a debt is entitled to deduct his expenses and fees from the money received. But it is highly questionable whether such deductions would amount to "dealing by a quasi-owner". It may be, however, as Gordon aptly states, that professional persons embezzle rather than steal, theft being reserved for non-professional appropriators of property.[76]

3. ROBBERY

Introduction

10–45 This crime might loosely be described as "theft achieved by violence".[77] On that sort of description, robbery would appear to be no more than an aggravated theft. However, the tradition has always been to treat it as a

---

[73] (1975) S.C.C.R. Supp. 78.
[74] It might also have involved an intent to deprive the true owners temporarily for a nefarious purpose — see paras. 10–25 to 10–27, above.
[75] 1926 J.C. 94.
[76] See Gordon, *Criminal Law*, paras. 17–06, 17–16, 17–17 and 17–25.
[77] Or as "forcible theft" — Hume, i, 104.
[78] See Alison, i, 227 and 236.
[79] See *O'Neill v. H.M. Advocate*, 1934 J.C. 98, *per* Lord Justice-Clerk Aitchison at p. 101.

crime separate from theft.[78] It is, however, often difficult to make such a distinction in an individual case.[79] Because of such difficulty, it is permissible to convict of theft on a robbery charge.[80] Nevertheless, one significant difference between the two offences is that a later appropriation of property already in one's possession can never be robbery (since a taking of possession is of the essence of robbery). It may also be true that violent efforts to retain what has already been snatched without force are not such as to convert a simple instance of theft to one of robbery.[81]

The force or violence involved in robbery tends to associate it with the **10–46** crime of assault but the violence used need not amount to an assault at all and robbery is regarded as independent of it.[82] In *O'Neill v. H.M. Advocate*,[83] where assault and robbery were both apparently charged, the accused was found guilty of robbery only, the assault having been found "not proven". The Appeal Court affirmed that that verdict had been competent and correct; but two of the Appeal Judges (Lords Hunter and Anderson) were of the persuasion that the "assault" mentioned in the indictment had been libelled as a mere aggravation of the robbery rather than as a separate crime.[84] Where specific acts of violence (or threats of violence) are narrated in the indictment or (less likely) complaint, and those acts (or threats) are not proved, there may be no other evidence from which it can be established that there was any violence associated with the taking of the property at all — and without violence, there can be no robbery.[85]

DEFINITION OF ROBBERY

Robbery may be considered as the deliberate taking of moveable and **10–47** corporeal property from another by force and against his will. The "taking" referred to means the seizing of physical possession of the article in question. All other things being equal, "as soon as any article has fully passed into the hands of the invader",[86] the crime is complete. It is even considered a "taking" for the purposes of this crime if the victim is so intimidated that he hands the things over himself, or stands passively by whilst the accused helps himself to what might be had.[87] Equally, if there is a struggle and the victim drops some article, there is a sufficient "taking" if the accused immediately picks it up.[88] There is little need to show that the things taken

---

[80] Criminal Procedure (Scotland) Act 1995, Sched. 3, para. 8(3).
[81] See *Thomas Innes and Ann Blair* (1834) Bell's Notes 42; *Daniel or Donald Stuart* (1829) Bell's Notes 42–43.
[82] See, *e.g., James Campbell* (1824) Hume, i, 107 n.a.; *James Fegen* (1838) 2 Swin. 25.
[83] 1934 J.C. 98.
[84] *ibid.* pp. 102 and 103.
[85] See, *e.g., Flynn v. H.M. Advocate,* 1995 S.L.T. 1267.
[86] Hume, i, 105.
[87] *ibid.*
[88] *Anderson, Paul and Bannatyne* (1791) Hume, i, 105.

were then actually carried away; for even if the accused is arrested as soon as he has taken possession of them, or hands them back almost at once, the *actus reus* of the crime is still considered complete.[89]

10–48   It is probably popularly supposed that robbery involves the taking of things which were about the victim's person or being carried by him at the time. Whilst that is often the case, it is not necessary that it should be so. As Hume puts it[90]: "[robbery is applicable to] any thing which is under the immediate care and protection of the person invaded; so that unless by force or terror applied to him, it cannot be taken away." A fair example of this point occurs in the case of *Thomas Kelly*[91] where a girl left in charge of a house was compelled to rush from it because of the accused's swearing and abusive, threatening words. Thus, the coast was left clear for the accused to take what he desired from the building. That, however, was no less a crime than robbery.[92]

The taking must be by force and against the victim's will

10–49   The important consideration is that the seizing or snatching should be contrary to the wishes of the victim. This can be exhibited in various ways. There might, for example, have been the application of real, physical force. The accused might have struggled with the victim for mastery of some article that he had, or might have beaten him senseless in order to overcome his resistance.[93] Alternatively, "constructive" force or intimidation might be applied; and that would usually be quite sufficient. In *Samuel Riccards*,[94] for example, the accused made verbal threats of violence to a woman who at once handed over money and other goods. Again in *William Macmillan and Spence Gordon*,[95] repeatedly shaking a stick over a woman's head eventually achieved the desired result — *i.e.* she opened her lock-fast repositories from which the robbers could then help themselves. Even aggressive demands for money, coupled with "gripping" the victim, have been held sufficient.[96] Hume[97] is at pains to point out, however, that such intimidation has to make the victim fear reasonably for his immediate, personal safety and thus overcome his will to prevent the property being taken. What will reasonably achieve that is obviously a question of fact, but the number of persons involved, the weapons that they display, their

---

[89]   Hume, i, 105; Alison, i, 235.
[90]   i, 106.
[91]   (1837) Bell's Notes 44.
[92]   Or "Stouthrief", as that form of robbery was then known — although that term does not appear to be quite obsolete: see *Mongan v. H.M. Advocate*, 1989 S.C.C.R. 25 at p. 25F.
[93]   See, for example, *William Adams or Reid* (1829) Bell's Notes 43.
[94]   (1710) Hume, i, 107.
[95]   (1829) Alison, i, 231.
[96]   *Hugh Lundie* (1754) Hume, i, 107.
[97]   i, 108.

demeanour and language are all of some significance. In one modern case, where two employees were told by an agent for an alleged creditor of their employer that they would not be allowed to leave their employer's premises until they had handed over the contents of the till (to help repay an alleged debt), their proven alarm was considered sufficient for robbery in relation to what they consequently handed over.[98] If the threat is other than one of immediate, personal violence — for example, to set fire to a building, or to make false accusations of crime — Hume doubts its effectiveness to render the crime one of robbery; but Alison[99] is surely correct to point out that much will depend on the precise circumstances of each case. Who or what is liable to be consumed by a blazing building must obviously figure in the analysis. The evidential presumption applicable to theft and to reset that very recent possession of stolen property may, if there are other criminative circumstances, point to the possessor's being guilty of theft or reset (as the case may be),[1] would seem to be applicable also to robbery.[2] This is somewhat surprising, however, for the mere possession of property — no matter how recently taken from the owner or custodier — can raise no reasonable presumption as to the use or threat of violence, which is an essential feature of the crime of robbery.

Moveable and corporeal property

Robbery probably extends to the same sort of property as can be stolen **10–50** (see paras. 10–07 to 10–10, above), the value of what is taken being of little importance.[3] It is unclear if one can commit robbery in respect of property one owns but is not entitled at the material time to possess. The close links with theft would suggest, however, that a negative answer should be given.[4] It must be the case, however, that the property in question has to be owned by someone at the material time. This might pose problems if the accused intended to kill his victim, and only after he had succeeded in that purpose decided to make off with property from the body. Since no force would then have had to be applied, the subsequent taking would probably be theft rather than robbery; but to whom would the property then have belonged? Benjamin Bell, the author of the notes to the 1844 edition of Hume, points to this very problem and makes reference to the case of *James Blair*.[5] There, apparently, no objection was made to a charge of robbery from a dead body,

---

[98] *Harrison v. Jessop,* 1992 S.L.T. 465.
[99] i, 231–33.
[1] See, *e.g., Steele v. H.M. Advocate,* 1992 J.C. 1.
[2] See *L. v. Wilson,* 1995 S.L.T. 673.
[3] See *James Brodie* (1842) 1 Broun 341, where a conviction for robbery was obtained in respect of coin worth two pence.
[4] *cf.* Alison, i, 239.
[5] (1830) Bell's Notes 43 and 44.

where it was asserted that what had been taken was "the property or in the lawful possession of his [*i.e.* the deceased's] heirs and executors."

THE *MENS REA* OF ROBBERY

10–51 This is uncertain, but appears to encompass the intent to use force and the intent to devote things taken by force to one's own uses and purposes. Hume unhelpfully refers to the *mens rea* as felonious intent — that is, "a purpose to appropriate the thing."[6] Presumably, there must also be knowledge that the thing taken by force is not one's own. If that is so, then the position (apart from the matter of force) must be analogous to that which pertains in theft (see paras. 10–21 to 10–28, above). It seems, however, that an assault, which in fact results in the accused's coming into possession of some property that the victim then had about his person, will raise the presumption that the *mens rea* for robbery exists — although that presumption may be rebutted.[7]

4. RESET

Introduction

10–52 The crime of reset in its traditional form is straightforward and easy to understand. It exists to provide a strong disincentive to theft[8] by providing that those who knowingly receive stolen property will themselves be guilty of an offence. Since reset applies to property obtained by robbery, fraud or embezzlement too,[9] it provides a disincentive to those crimes also. Unfortunately, the traditional form of the crime has been thrown into confusion by Lord Justice-Clerk Macdonald. As will be seen below, he added to its scope in a way which might be regarded as "unjustified" or even "unauthorised", but which certainly detracted from its clarity. For that reason, the text below discusses "traditional" and "Macdonald" resets separately.

Traditional reset

10–53 The definition of the traditional form is succinctly given by Hume[10] as follows: "Reset of theft, is the receiving and keeping of stolen goods,

---

[6] i, 108.
[7] See Hume, i, 108 and the case of *Edgar Wright* (1788) mentioned there.
[8] Hume, i, 113.
[9] See Criminal Law (Consolidation) (Scotland) Act 1995, s.51; Criminal Procedure (Scotland) Act 1995, Sched. 3, para.8(1).
[10] At i, 113.

knowing them to be such, and with an intention to conceal and withhold them from the owner." Alison[11] reproduces that formula exactly, and indeed it admirably encapsulates the essence of the crime. The only addition is necessitated by the fact that reset is not now confined to the fruits of theft or robbery. It extends in modern times to property obtained by embezzlement and fraud as well.[12] The identification, let alone conviction, of the thief, robber, fraudster or embezzler is not a prerequisite for prosecution[13]; nor is it now necessary[14] to give details of the original theft, robbery, embezzlement or fraud in the complaint or indictment.[15] The crime, moreover, appears to apply to *plagium*.[16]

THE *ACTUS REUS* OF RESET

"It is the fundamental circumstance in the description of this crime, that the **10–54** stolen goods are *received into the offender's possession* ... [There must be] *a handling* of the things themselves, for the purpose of detention and concealment."[17] There is little doubt, then, that the traditional form of the crime requires the accused to have received possession of the property in question. It does not seem to matter greatly how that possession is acquired — Hume mentioning pledge, barter, safe-keeping (for the thief) and purchase (even for a fair price). It has to be noted, however, that the fairer the price, the more difficult it will be to show that the accused possessed the required *mens rea*. Possession, of course, is not confined to personal handling. Goods delivered by others to one's house and placed somewhere within its rooms are as much possessed as if one had done the carrying and locating oneself — always provided that one knew they were to be so delivered and placed. It is within this context that Hume[18] refers to the "privity and connivance" of the house owner. If he permits the property to be so deposited, then he possesses it.[19] It is not, however, necessary for the accused to have received possession directly from the original thief, robber or whoever; but, naturally, the greater the number of hands through which it has passed en route to the accused, the greater will be his chances of casting doubt on his ever having known that it had been dishonestly come by in the first place.[20] It is, for

---

[11] *Principles*, i, 328.
[12] See para. 10–52, above.
[13] Hume, i, 119–120.
[14] *cf.* Alison, i, 335.
[15] Criminal Procedure (Scotland) Act 1995, Sched. 3, para. 8(1).
[16] See para. 10–15, above, and *Margaret Cook* (1897) 2 Adam 471 at p. 474, which concerned an eight-year-old child.
[17] Hume, i, 113 — emphasis added; see also Alison, i, 328.
[18] i, 114.
[19] *cf. John and Elizabeth Bell* (1736) Hume, i, 114.
[20] See Alison, i, 329.

example, clearly not unknown for stolen goods eventually to find their way back to legitimate retail outlets.

THE *MENS REA* OF RESET: KNOWLEDGE

10–55 There are two parts to the *mens rea* of reset. The first concerns "knowledge of the vicious quality of the thing".[21] Presumably this should mean knowledge that the goods one receives were originally obtained from their true owner by theft, robbery, fraud or embezzlement. But strict adherence to that would often make the crime impossible to substantiate; and it is thought that knowledge that the goods were not honestly come by would suffice, provided that they were in fact stolen, or obtained by robbery, fraud or embezzlement. The requisite knowledge need not exist when possession is first taken. Macdonald[22] is surely correct to point out that knowledge can arise at a later point than that, and indeed this is borne out by case law, as in the case of *Latta v. Herron*[23] where it was held that the accused, a lawyer, must have come to realise that two antique guns were stolen property when he reflected later on the suspicious circumstances of their sale to him.

10–56 Hume is adamant that anything less than "knowledge" will not do. Thus, he rules out "bare suspicion" or "indiscretion".[24] Negligent inattention to the possibility that the goods are tainted by a dishonest mode of acquisition is, therefore, insufficient; but the Appeal Court has, in recent times, accepted that deliberately shutting one's eyes to the obvious is equivalent to knowing the true position.[25] It will be clear, then, that knowledge can be inferred from the circumstances. If that were not so, then again it would be difficult to substantiate the offence in the absence of the theft, robbery, fraud or embezzlement having been observed by the accused, or the person from whom possession was obtained having confessed to the dishonest mode of acquisition. Such an inference will not, however, inevitably be drawn[26] since otherwise the whole notion of *mens rea* would be very substantially defeated.

10–57 Circumstances which Hume[27] considered valid in relation to the inference of knowledge are still in use today. They may be enumerated as follows (though most seem to be plain applications of common sense):

1. Concealment of the property in hidden places, which would include "under a seat" — for example, see *MacLennan v.*

---

[21] Hume, i, 114.
[22] *Criminal Law*, p. 68.
[23] (1967) S.C.C.R. Supp. 18.
[24] i, 114.
[25] See, *e.g., Latta v. Herron, supra*, and *Friel v. Docherty*, 1990 S.C.C.R. 351.
[26] See, *e.g., Shannon v. H.M. Advocate*, 1985 S.C.C.R. 14.
[27] i, 114.

Mackenzie[28] where this was held not to be a usual place for the location of a car radio-cassette player — but not, in respect of carpet-laying tools, a bathroom cupboard[29];

2. False denial of having the goods at all[30];

3. Attempts to disguise or efface identification marks on the property, as, for example, the scraping-off of the serial number on a piece of electrical equipment[31];

4. Payment of a low price for the property — less than half the true value, for example, in *Latta v. Herron*[32] — provided that the accused would or ought to have been aware of their true worth[33];

5. "Awkward" (as Hume puts it) stories of how the goods had been acquired, as in *MacLennan v. Mackenzie*,[34] where the accused told the police that a stolen radio-cassette player had been taken by him from a car being repaired in his boss's premises, and that with the full permission of his boss; as in *Watt v. Annan*,[35] where the accused claimed to have bought a valuable saw two-and-a-half years earlier from one "Doddy Boyle" who had subsequently, and conveniently, died; as in *McKellar v. Normand*,[36] where it seems that the accused implied that it would be quite usual to buy a bed and a blanket at the door of one's house; or as in *Forbes v. H.M. Advocate*,[37] where the accused, in respect of a substantial package partially concealing a valuable art-work, in an obvious position in the back of his vehicle, denied knowing that it was there at all, because he never checked the vehicle (which was normally left unlocked) for strange objects that might have been left there by persons unknown;

6. Where the quality of the property, in view of the circumstances and station in life of the accused, suggests that it could not have been come by honestly — a matter raised by the prosecutor, but not accepted by the Appeal Court, in *Craigie v. H.M. Advocate*[38] in relation to two holdalls of expensive carpet-fitter's tools found

---

[28] 1987 S.C.C.R. 473.
[29] See *Craigie v. H.M. Advocate,* 1989 S.L.T. 631.
[30] See, *e.g., Davidson v. Brown,* 1990 S.C.C.R. 304; *cf. Girdwood v. Houston,* 1989 S.C.C.R. 578, where knowledge was more or less admitted.
[31] *MacLennan v. Mackenzie, supra.*
[32] (1967) S.C.C.R. Supp. 18.
[33] See *Latta v. Herron, supra,* where the accused was a knowledgeable collector of antique firearms. *Cf. Murray v. O'Brien,* 1993 S.C.C.R. 90.
[34] 1987 S.C.C.R. 473.
[35] 1990 S.C.C.R. 55.
[36] 1992 S.C.C.R. 393.
[37] 1995 S.L.T. 627.
[38] 1989 S.L.T. 631.

in the bathroom cupboard of a house where no one followed the profession of carpet-fitting, as was evident from the way in which the only carpet in that house had been laid; and

7.   Where the pannel or his "author"[39] is a reputed thief or resetter.

To Hume's list, it may be prudent to add that it is a suspicious circumstance if the property found in the accused's possession has been very recently stolen, as in *Davidson v. Brown*,[40] where garments and toiletries had been stolen just a few hours before they were found by the police in a plastic swing-bin balanced on the accused's knees as she sat in the back seat of a car.

10–58   Knowledge that the property in question was stolen or otherwise dishonestly come by is, of course, insufficient by itself as the *mens rea* of reset. The second part of the mental element is that the accused must have intended to detain the property from its true owner,[41] though he need not propose to do so by keeping it permanently himself.[42] If this second requirement were not to be insisted upon, then police and court clerks, who happen to have known stolen property in their possession for legitimate reasons connected with the administration of justice, would be guilty of reset. Such an intention to detain may be established by confession, or by inference from the same sorts of circumstances as figure in the establishing of knowledge. Where such an inference can be drawn from the circumstances, the accused will have to provide some evidence to the contrary if it is not then to be drawn.[43] That does not imply, however, that some burden lies on the accused to show his innocence.[44]

TRADITIONAL RESET AND THEFT

10–59   Statute has permitted a conviction for reset to be returned on a theft charge.[45] This is because of the close connection that there can be between the two crimes. In *O'Brien v. Strathern*,[46] for example, a serving soldier sold his regimental kilt (his uniform) to a shopkeeper who knew perfectly well that that amounted to theft on his customer's part. The shopkeeper was convicted of reset. But considering that the soldier's appropriation could be evidenced in no other way than by the sale itself, to which the shopkeeper was a party, the purchaser might as well have been convicted of theft, art and part, as of

---

[39]   Or now, apparently, the company that he keeps — *Davidson v. Brown*, 1990 S.C.C.R. 304.
[40]   *Davidson v. Brown, supra.*
[41]   Hume i, 115.
[42]   Alison, i, 333.
[43]   Hume, i, 115.
[44]   See *McDonald v. H.M. Advocate*, 1989 S.C.C.R. 559.
[45]   The Criminal Procedure (Scotland) Act 1995, Sched. 3, para. 8(2).
[46]   1922 J.C. 55.

reset. (It would not be possible, of course, for the same person to be convicted of both theft *and* reset in respect of the same property.[47]) The instances which Hume[48] gives in illustration of the close connection between theft and reset tend to be ones where the "resetter" could well have been art and part guilty of theft in the circumstances. But conviction of reset on a theft charge does not require any suspicion of complicity in the original stealing.[49] It has also been held that although the original theft charge must specify with some precision when the alleged theft took place, this does not bind the Crown to establish that the implied alternative of reset occurred within the same stated time period (although, of course, no other time period will appear in the complaint or indictment).[50]

There is no provision, however, for a conviction for theft to be returned **10–60** on a complaint or indictment which specifies reset.[51] This is probably because reset was seen historically as the lesser of the two crimes, and it would have been unfair to convict of an offence more serious than the one actually charged. Nevertheless, where the prosecutor has evidence which supports reset rather than theft, he may still charge theft, where there is evidence of possession of recently stolen property and of other "material" circumstances, and where the accused is reckoned as being unable to show a fair way of coming by that property.[52] It is impossible to be certain what will be acceptable as "recent" in this connection but possibly a matter of hours or days is the limit.[53] Obviously, the shorter the time period involved, the more likely it is that the person found in possession of the property is also the person who stole it. But there must be more to it than that. There must be "other material circumstances" leading to the inference that the possessor is the thief. What are material circumstances or, as they now tend to be called, "criminative circumstances",[54] will depend on the facts of the individual case. In *Cassidy v. McLeod,*[55] for example, the accused were found in possession of beer (cans and bottles) and plastic crates in a house not far from an inn where a theft of such things had occurred the night before. The fact that the bottles and cans were similar to those stolen, and

---

[47] See, *e.g., Druce v. Friel,* 1994 S.L.T. 1209.
[48] i, 115–116.
[49] See, *e.g., MacLennan v. Mackenzie,* 1988 S.L.T. 16; *Watt v. Annan,* 1990 S.C.C.R. 55.
[50] *MacLennan v. Mackenzie, supra.*
[51] *cf.* Criminal Procedure (Scotland) Act 1995, Sched. 3, para. 8(2), (3), (4)
[52] See, *e.g., Young v. Webster,* 1993 S.L.T. 349; *Druce v. Friel,* 1994 S.L.T. 1209.
[53] See *Watt v. Annan, supra* — six months too long after the theft; *MacLennan v. Mackenzie, supra* — two-and-a-half months too long; *Craigie v. H.M. Advocate, supra* — where a sheriff directed a jury that six weeks was too long; *Tudhope v. Smellie* (1977) S.C.C.R. Supp. 186, where 19 to 20 days was held sufficient, although it was emphasised that it depends ultimately on the circumstances of each case.
[54] See, *e.g., Fox v. Patterson,* 1948 J.C. 104.
[55] 1981 S.C.C.R. 270.

of such a mixed variety and type as to suggest that it was unlikely that they had been purchased, made it easy to infer that the accused were in possession of the very property that had recently been stolen, and indeed that was conceded when the case was argued before the Appeal Court. It was further established that the crates were not generally sold to the public, that one of the accused had telephoned the inn the previous evening and had asked for a "carry-out" on credit (which had been refused), and that a trail of cans and crates led across some waste-ground from the scene of the theft towards the very house occupied by the accused. The Appeal Court, therefore, considered that other criminative circumstances had indeed been established, that the accused had been unable to show an honest way of coming by the beer, and that therefore the charge of theft in the complaint had been fully substantiated.

MACDONALD RESET

10–61 Macdonald[56] narrates that there is another form of reset, namely: "being privy to the retaining of property that has been dishonestly come by." No attempt, however, is made to explain what is meant by "being privy". The *Oxford English Dictionary*[57] definitions of "privy" suggest that it might mean "participating in the knowledge of something secret" or "being an accessory to some secret transaction". If these suggestions are taken to be what Macdonald had in mind, then he surely refers to nothing more than a form of art and part guilt in relation to traditional reset. There would be nothing objectionable in that, save perhaps the undue widening of the offence to property that had been "dishonestly come by". Although that would include property obtained by theft, robbery, embezzlement or fraud, it might also cover property acquired in some non-criminal way which could nevertheless be stigmatised as "dishonest".[58] But it is thought that there is no warrant for such an extension to traditional reset. In any event, Macdonald gives this alternative form of the crime without reference to authority of any kind. In 1968, however, the Appeal Court decided that it represented a correct statement of the law,[59] although it remains unclear what the alternative form is supposed to mean. It is plain, however, from Macdonald's own example of its use, that it is by no means confined to art and part guilt of traditional reset.

---

[56] p. 67.
[57] 1931 ed.
[58] *cf.* the situation in *Grant v. Allan*, 1987 J.C. 71.
[59] See *McNeil v. H.M. Advocate*, 1968 J.C. 29, following *McCawley v. H.M. Advocate* (1959) S.C.C.R. Supp. 3.

The example that is given in Macdonald's text runs as follows: "It is **10–62** reset for a person to connive at a third party possessing or retaining the stolen goods, even if the person charged never laid a finger on the property stolen." Again, this might refer to a form of art and part guilt. If so, it would be wholly acceptable and unexceptionable. But the example is derived, and obtains whatever authority it possesses, from a direction to a jury made by Lord Justice-Clerk Macdonald himself in 1903 in *H.M. Advocate v. Browne*.[60] In the course of that direction, he said:

> "If a man steals a bundle of notes out of a man's pocket, and after that informs another man that he has got these notes, that he has stolen them, or if the other man saw him stealing them and knew that they were stolen, then if the other man connived at it remaining in the possession of the thief or being put in any place for safe custody, such as hiding it in a cupboard, he is guilty of receiving feloniously even although he never puts his fingers on the notes at all. Reset consists of being privy to the retaining of property that has been dishonestly come by."

This must be taken along with a later passage in Macdonald's text book[61] which reads: "If the first offender with his knowledge hide the property, even in a hole in a wall, and he connive at this, he is guilty." There are a number of objections to this.

First, Macdonald thus makes dispensable what both Hume and Alison[62] **10–63** state is essential, that is, that the resetter should have received (handled, taken possession of) the property in question. This point was well taken by both Lord Justice-Clerk Grant and Lord Strachan in *Clark v. H.M. Advocate*[63] and made them doubt that Macdonald could possibly have been correct. Their doubts were dismissed, however, by the Appeal Court in *McNeil v. H.M. Advocate*,[64] apparently on the basis that the Macdonald alternative had appeared in his text book without objection for a very long time. Secondly, it is clear from his examples that Macdonald did not have in mind any mere "art and part" form of guilt. The person who sees or knows of the thief's concealment of the property and "connives at" that is simply guilty of reset as actor. There is no other person, by hypothesis, who is guilty of reset and in respect of whose crime he might be art and part guilty; and Macdonald does not suggest that the accused might be art and part guilty of the theft itself. Thirdly, Macdonald makes no attempt to explain what is meant by "connive at", and this caused great difficulty to the trial

---

[60] (1903) 6 F. (J.) 24 at p. 26.
[61] p. 68.
[62] *Crimes*, i, 113; *Principles*, i, 333.
[63] 1965 S.L.T. 250 at pp. 252 and 253.
[64] 1968 J.C. 29.

judge and jury in *Clark v. H.M. Advocate*.[65] The sheriff there, in fact, directed that the accused would be guilty if he knew that stolen property was being disposed of, yet did nothing to inform the police; but there had to be more to it than proof that the accused was merely in the company of the thief when the property happened to be disposed of. This somewhat inconsistent direction was clearly enough to confuse any jury, as the Appeal Court conceded when quashing the conviction for reset. But their Lordships did little to clarify the meaning of "connive at" other than to agree with both counsel that acts of a positive nature would have to be shown. No doubt this better accords with the philosophy that a person should not be convicted of a crime because of his mental attitude alone[66] but it gives little guidance as to the scope of Macdonald's examples. For these reasons alone, it can be suggested that the Macdonald form of reset should be abandoned by Scots law. His examples are also probably contrary to principle, in that they seem to require a person who knows of, or observes a crime to inform the authorities,[67] in the absence of any of the accepted legal duties discussed in Chapter 3.

MISCELLANEOUS MATTERS

10–64 If property was stolen in any part of the United Kingdom other than Scotland, receiving of that property in this country can still be dealt with by the Scottish courts.[68] This privilege does not extend, however, to property obtained outwith Scotland by fraud or embezzlement. It is also the case that a district court can deal with a case of reset, theft, fraud or embezzlement on complaint provided that the value of the property in question does not exceed level 4 on the standard scale.[69] Such a court cannot try cases of robbery at all, however. It may follow then that the reset of the proceeds of a robbery must be tried in a sheriff or High Court.

5. FRAUD

Introduction

10–65   The common law crime of fraud helps protect persons from their own gullibility. Modern advertising techniques exploit the psychological fact that most persons can be imposed upon and influenced in ways they might

---

[65] 1965 S.L.T. 250.
[66] *cf. Girdwood v. Houston*, 1989 S.C.C.R. 578.
[67] *Pace* the view taken in *McNeil v. H.M. Advocate, supra.*
[68] Criminal Procedure (Scotland) Act 1995, s.4(b); *cf.* the now replaced original wording in the Criminal Procedure (Scotland) Act 1975, ss.7(2), 292(2).
[69] 1995 Act, s.7(8)(b)(iii).

hardly suspect. But the common law, knowing nothing of the advertising agent's skills, generally does not seek to prevent "bad bargains" or decisions taken on misleading information. Rather it seeks to proscribe deliberate falsehood, and not "legitimate" persuasion techniques, in interpersonal and business dealings. Such protection as the law gives to consumers short of deliberate falsehood is a modern development under statutory law.[70] Fraud is archaically called "falsehood, fraud and wilful imposition" in the Criminal Procedure (Scotland) Act 1995,[71] and "swindling" in Hume.[72] It is also an alternative verdict where theft has been charged,[73] presumably to cater for cases where consent to the appropriation is discovered in the course of the evidence.[74] It is further the case that a conviction for theft or reset can be returned on a fraud charge.[75]

Working definition

Currently, a working definition of the crime might run as follows: that **10–66** fraud consists of a false pretence made to another person in the knowledge of its falsity and with the intention that that other person should be deceived by it into acting in a way in which he would not otherwise have acted, provided that that other person *is* so deceived and does so act on account of it.[75a] It will be noted that the proviso reveals fraud to be a result crime (see para. 2–40, above); a false pretence is of no avail for the completed crime unless it causes the specified result. More detailed consideration of this definition will be found in the following paragraphs.

Actus Reus: False Pretence

What may be pretended falsely, and what may be the methods of conveying **10–67** falsehoods to another are matters upon which it is difficult to generalise. As Hume puts it[76]: "It would be a vain, and a tedious attempt, to enumerate all the manifold shapes of cheating or fraud, in which falsehood is one of the chief ingredients of the guilt." Yet, whatever it be that is expressed or implied, it has to be verifiably false there and then. If it happens to be true, then there can be no question of fraud. Of course, what is true or false is generally

---

[70] See, *e.g.*, the Trade Descriptions Act 1968.

[71] *e.g.* Sched. 3, para. 8.

[72] i, 172.

[73] 1995 Act, Sched. 3, para. 8(4).

[74] Consent obtained by falsehood is regularly taken in Scotland to be a proper consent — *William Fraser* (1847) Ark. 280 — although this would seem to be objectionable on moral grounds.

[75] 1995 Act, Sched. 3., para. 8(2), (3).

[75a] See *MacDonald v. H.M. Advocate,* 1996 S.L.T. 723, *per* Lord Justice-Clerk Ross at p. 726B, quoting with approval from Gordon, *Criminal Law* (2nd ed.), para. 18–02.

[76] i, 177.

easy to establish. Whether a person is really who he says he is, whether the goods he has for sale are truly as he describes them, or whether he is really entitled to claim what he presently seeks, can usually be proved one way or the other without much difficulty. But if a person is, for example, induced to buy or to sell by reason of some future intention expressed by another, how can fraud ever be a relevant charge? It stands to reason that a person's future intentions relate to things that he would wish or hope to be able to undertake. But the best-intentioned hopes or wishes may never be fulfilled. They may turn out to have been over ambitious, or to be frustrated by events; and it is their very uncertainty that leads to the conclusion that future intentions cannot form part of the province of fraud. A person's intentions cannot generally be described as false when they are made. But it does not follow that express or implied statements of intent can never be false.

10–68   Scots law takes the view that a statement of intention which its maker never plans to fulfil is false when it is made. Thus, where goods are obtained on credit by one who secretly plans not to pay for them at all, and indeed does not pay for them, there is a false pretence, since he has allowed the person delivering the goods to believe that the normally implied intent to pay at a future date applies in this case *comme toujours*.[77] In the same way, one who orders a meal in a restaurant implies that his intention is to pay for it after it has been consumed; but if he plans all along to walk out without paying and eventually does so walk out, the impression he creates in relation to his intentions is plainly false throughout. Similarly, booking a room in a hotel for a few days' stay does not normally involve payment in advance, but does involve the implied undertaking that the guest in question will pay in the future when his account is presented. If he plans from the moment of booking onwards not to pay at all, then he impliedly makes a false pretence, as has been recognised in the statutory styles of charge.[78]

10–69   In the case of *John Hall*[79] Lord Young rejected the view that future intentions or promises could ever amount to false pretences for the purposes of fraud. As he put it:

> "A purchaser without intention to pay may afterwards think better of it and pay, or his creditor may succeed in compelling payment. Again a purchaser intending to pay may subsequently change his mind and dishonestly refuse. Shall the former (who in fact pays) be punished as a criminal, and the latter (who does not) go free? A crime committed cannot thereafter be uncommitted."

---

[77] See, *e.g.*, charge 2 in the indictment in *Drew v. H.M. Advocate*, 1995 S.C.C.R. 647.
[78] See the Criminal Procedure (Scotland) Act 1995, Sched. 5, — "You did obtain from A.N. board and lodging to the value of £16 without paying and intending not to pay therefor."
[79] (1881) 4 Coup. 438 at p. 447.

This interesting dilemma ignores, however, the practicalities — and Scots law is a very practical system. A crime cannot be committed by intention alone; the person who initially intends not to pay, but thereafter does pay, will be guilty of nothing since his secret intentions are ultimately unfulfilled. The law does not usually concern itself with unfulfilled intentions. Although there may well be a theoretical fraud in such a case, it is unlikely to be discovered, there are no outward signs of criminality, and no harm or prejudice has been caused.[80] On the other hand, the person who initially intends to pay but ultimately changes his mind may well be charged with fraud, for it is impossible to see into a person's mind and detect such subtle changes in intent. If no payment is ever tendered, it may well be justifiably assumed that that person never intended to do so. That would not prevent, of course, the acceptance of some plausible excuse tendered on his part, for example, that he entered a restaurant and ordered a meal in good faith, thinking erroneously that he had his wallet or credit card in his pocket.

In any event, Lord Young's views were rejected in the more modern **10–70** case of *Richards v. H.M. Advocate*[81] where the sale of a mansion house and ornamental grounds was induced by the accused's (or rather his nominee's) professed intention to live in it with his family and retain it entirely in its then current state. The seller's desire was that the property should not be built upon and should therefore not be bought by any entrepreneur attracted by the lure of its development potential. The prosecutor's case was that the professed intention of the purchaser was false from the beginning; and on that basis, the Appeal Court affirmed the correctness of the conviction for fraud. What matters then is a person's present intent as to his future conduct. It is his present intent which can be described as false for the purposes of fraud.

Examples of false pretences

Pretences may be express or implied. Under the "express" banner, **10–71** examples would include the written or spoken assumption of a false name or address, provided that gave the impression of wealth, status or just credit-worthiness[82]; assumption of a false status[83]; assertion that goods for sale

---

[80] Lord Young's example, where payment is compelled by civil process, may, however, be different.

[81] 1971 J.C. 29.

[82] See, *e.g.*, *Thomas Macgregor and George Inglis* (1846) Ark. 49, where the first-named accused passed himself off as "Captain" Macgregor and managed to obtain on credit a carriage, two gold watches, cattle and a grand piano.

[83] See, *e.g.*, *Tapsell v. Prentice* (1910) 6 Adam 354, where a woman gave a false name and address but also passed herself off as the manageress of a group of travelling people and thus able to purchase large quantities of groceries on the group's behalf.

were of much greater merit than was actually the case[84]; assertion that services rendered were of much greater value than was in fact true (provided, of course, that their true value is also stated in the charge)[85]; assertion that a named person was guilty of a crime[86]; making of false claims to be owed money and raising court actions to recover what was said to be due[87]; or, making of false insurance claims.[88]

10–72 Pretences may be implied by what the accused does without any words being spoken or written at all. In *James Paton*,[89] for example, bulls to be displayed at a prize show were made more attractive for the judges by having their skins inflated with air and their horns enhanced with false extensions; and in the English case of *R. v. Morris*[90] the accused switched price labels on goods displayed on a supermarket shelf so that the goods intended to be purchased then displayed a lower price than that originally attached by the store. Note might also be taken of *William Fraser*[91] where the accused was alleged to have tricked a married woman into believing that he was her husband. His behaviour towards her was said to have had that effect and, on that basis, she was said to have permitted him to have sexual intercourse with her. The majority of the court held that if the prosecutor's case could be substantiated, then the crime committed would be one of fraud rather than rape. Also, in *Strathern v. Fogal*[92] the accused's failure to disclose on a rates return to the local assessor that he had obtained substantial premiums from tenants as a condition of his renewing their leases was considered to be sufficient for common law fraud. A failure to reveal what there is a legal duty to disclose can, therefore, be a sufficient false pretence.[93]

---

[84] See, *e.g., Hood v. Young* (1853) 1 Irv. 236, where two knackery-ready horses were glowingly described as "good workers" at an auction sale, the only reason for sale being given (falsely) that the seller was going abroad.

[85] See, *e.g., H.M. Advocate v. McAllister*, 1996 S.L.T. 220, where the accused pretended to an 87-year-old woman that roof repairs (actually worth no more than £50 — the cost of replacing one slate) had been done to the value of £2,000; *cf. Bennett v. Houston*, 1993 S.L.T. 1182, where the actual value of the work done was omitted from the charges — which were, therefore, dismissed as irrelevant charges of fraud.

[86] See, *e.g., Elliot Millar* (1847) Ark. 355, where the accused misinformed the police that his wife was trying to murder him — even providing a cup of poisoned coffee and a bowl of his "own" vomit as real evidence.

[87] See, *e.g., George Kippen* (1849) J. Shaw 276; *McKenzie v. H.M. Advocate*, 1988 S.L.T. 487.

[88] See, *e.g., Maciver and Macallum* (1784) Hume, i, 176.

[89] (1858) 3 Irv. 208.

[90] [1983] Q.B. 587.

[91] (1847) Ark. 280 and 329.

[92] 1922 J.C. 73.

[93] *cf. Buchmann v. Normand*, 1994 S.C.C.R. 929, where, although the charge was brought under s.7(4) of the Civic Government Act 1982, the failure to reveal previous convictions by leaving blank the space intended for them in a licence application form, had clear affinities with common law fraud.

Cheque and "plastic money" transactions

It is probably clear (bearing in mind the relative dearth of Scottish **10–73** authority) that false pretences can be involved in transactions where cheques or credit cards are tendered in payment for goods or services. Since no one generally makes any statement concerning his relationship with the bank or credit card company where the account in question is held, what is in fact being asserted when a cheque or "plastic money" is tendered must be a matter of implication. In the nineteenth-century case of *Rae v. Linton*[94] it was held that handing over a cheque in payment involves the following implied statements — that the person drawing the cheque has an account with the bank or other financial institution in question (which will not be true if, for example, that person has stolen the cheque book); that he has authority from that bank to draw a cheque for such an amount; and that there is good reason to believe that that cheque will be met when presented to that bank. It is not implied necessarily that the account holder has currently a credit balance in his account of at least the amount for which the cheque has been drawn; for it has to be accepted that in modern times, banks and similar institutions have a distinct interest in allowing customers to overdraw on their accounts — even where no special arrangements have been made. For that reason, it may be better to conclude that the important implied assertion is that "the present state of affairs is such that, in the ordinary course of events, the cheque will on its future presentment be duly honoured."[95] This is better since it takes into account the normal delay in clearing a cheque which is presented for payment in the ordinary way. Special presentations apart, a person with no funds in his account may thus still draw a cheque without making any (implied) false pretence. The normal delay in clearance would provide a period of grace during which to make overdraft arrangements with his bank, or to pay money into his account.

Where a cheque card is also tendered along with one's cheque, it would **10–74** appear that "the main implicit assertion"[96] will always be true. Provided that the conditions for the use of such a card are observed[97] then the bank or other issuing institution is obliged to honour the cheque in question, as a matter of commercial reality, if nothing else. However, it has been held in England that there is an extra implied assertion involved when such a card is used, namely, that the person tendering the card has authority from the issuing bank or other institution to use it and has not had that authority cancelled.[98] The rationale of this is that if the person accepting a cheque

---

[94] (1874) 3 Coup. 67.
[95] *R. v. Page* [1971] 2 Q.B. 330, *per* Phillimore, L.J. at p. 333.
[96] See para. 10–73, above.
[97] See *R. v. Charles* [1977] A.C. 177.
[98] *R. v. Charles, supra.*

backed by such a card knew that the person tendering it was not authorised to use it, he would still be paid by the bank in question if he nevertheless proceeded with the transaction; but he would then be art and part guilty of that other person's fraudulent scheme. He cannot, therefore, be taken to have treated such a consideration as irrelevant. The same implied assertion of "authority to use it" applies in England to credit card transactions[99]; and it is thought that the same sort of reasoning would find favour with Scottish courts in relation to the use of both sorts of cards.

Result of the false pretence

10–75   According to Macdonald[1]: "Fraud involves a false pretence made dishonestly in order to bring about some definite practical result." That the addressee of the pretence must be deceived by it in such a way that there is a "definite practical result" has received support in the cases of *Adcock v. Archibald*[2] and *H.M. Advocate v. Wishart*[3]; but those words provide little guidance as to what is in fact a sufficient result. For that reason, the working definition proffered above (at paragraph 10–66) draws on part of the opinion of Lord Hunter in *Adcock v. Archibald*[4] to the extent that the person deceived must be induced to do what he otherwise would not have done. It is thought that this provides a reasonable guide to what is required, provided that it is borne in mind that "doing what one otherwise would not have done" includes doing nothing at all, that is, "taking no steps to do what one otherwise would have done." It is also important to bear in mind that a conviction for fraud does not depend on the accused having gained anything as a result of his deception,[5] nor upon anyone having made any economic loss.[6] It is further important to note that where prejudice is suffered as a result of a false pretence, it may be so suffered by a person other than the very person deceived.[7]

Examples of results

10–76   Illustrations of "results" are numerous in the law reports and include a court ordering the arrestment of sums in the accused's hands and owing to

---

[99] *R. v. Lambie* [1982] A.C. 449.
[1]   p. 52.
[2]   1925 J.C. 58, *per* Lord Justice-General Clyde at p. 61.
[3]   (1975) S.C.C.R. Supp. 78, *per* Lord McDonald at p. 85.
[4]   *supra*, p. 61.
[5]   *Alexander Bannatyne* (1847) Ark. 361, *per* Lord Justice-Clerk Hope at p. 380.
[6]   See *Adcock v. Archibald, supra*, where, because of a minimum wage agreement, neither the mining company nor any of its employees made any loss as a result of the accused's successful deceit.
[7]   See, *e.g.,* the subject matter of para. 10–74, above; since there a retailer will be held to be deceived by any cheque or credit card fraud but only the bank or other institution will be prejudiced by having to pay out on the transaction.

his own creditors, the accused having initiated completely false actions for debt in fictitious names against those creditors "to delay payment of a debt which was due from him"[8]; a mining company being induced to credit 1s. 3¹/₂d. to a team of miners who had not worked the load of coal it represented at all[9]; police being forced to investigate a false accusation of murder[10]; a purchaser being induced to purchase, and thus come under an obligation to take and pay for, a misdescribed horse[11]; a woman refraining from preventing sexual intercourse since she had been induced to think her assailant was her husband[12]; a person sending a money order for £2, having been induced to do so by a forged letter, even though the accused never obtained possession of the order[13]; a prize being awarded to a bull, the meritorious condition of which being the result of cheating[14]; a firm of stock-brokers having been able to demonstrate substantial credit balances to the auditors appointed to inspect their accounts, after a solicitor had drawn cheques on his clients' account payable to the stock-brokers for that purpose alone — the understanding being that the stock-brokers would return the moneys to the solicitor as soon as the auditors had been deceived[15]; and solicitors being induced to raise actions for debt based on fabricated documents and false information.[16] Of course, the result must be caused by the false pretence, otherwise there can be no completed fraud.[17] If the person in receipt of the deception would have acted as he did in any event, then again there can be no fraud, although attempted fraud might then be considered.

THE *MENS REA* OF FRAUD

The accused must know that what he says or writes or implies is false, and **10–77** must intend thereby to deceive. It seems unlikely that recklessness as to the truth of statements made to another would be sufficient, as is apparently borne out by the decision of the Appeal Court in *Mackenzie v. Skeen.*[18] There the accused showed the utmost carelessness in weighing offal intended

---

[8] *George Kippen* (1849) J. Shaw 276, *per* Lord Justice-Clerk Hope at p. 286.
[9] *Adcock v. Archibald*, 1925 J.C. 58.
[10] *Elliot Millar* (1847) Ark. 355.
[11] *Hood v. Young* (1853) 1 Irv. 236 — see in particular the reply to counsel by Lord Justice-Clerk Hope at p. 239.
[12] *William Fraser* (1847) Ark. 280.
[13] *Daniel Taylor* (1853) 1 Irv. 230.
[14] *James Paton* (1858) 3 Irv. 208.
[15] *H.M. Advocate v. Wishart* (1975) S.C.C.R. Supp. 78.
[16] *McKenzie v. H.M. Advocate*, 1988 S.L.T. 487 — though charged as attempt to defraud the alleged debtors.
[17] See, *e.g., Mather v. H.M. Advocate* (1914) 7 Adam 525; *Tapsell v. Prentice* (1910) 6 Adam 354.
[18] 1971 J.C. 43.

to be sold to a pet-food manufacturer by weight, but was nevertheless acquitted of fraud. Of course, it could not be shown in the circumstances that he had any intention to deceive either his own employers or the pet-food company — obviously a matter of some importance to this crime.[19]

JURISDICTION

10–78 In a country as small as the United Kingdom, it is inevitable that fraudulent schemes will not always be respecters of borders. This may pose nice problems of jurisdiction. For example, if letters containing false pretences and orders for goods on credit are sent from Scotland to suppliers in England, as in *Thomas Macgregor and George Inglis*,[20] and these suppliers are induced to send the goods in question, there is an immediate problem. Fraud, as was stated at paragraph 10–66, is a result crime and is not complete until someone is made to do what he otherwise would not have done (see paragraph 10–75, above). No crime, therefore, would seem to have been completed in Scotland. Do Scottish courts, then, have jurisdiction over the whole crime? And what of the converse situation, as in *William Bradbury*[21] where goods were sent from Scotland in response to "false pretence" letters originating in England. If some definite rule was operated in Scots law, then one might be able to conclude that the Scottish courts had jurisdiction where, for example, the fraud was actually completed in Scotland, but not otherwise. In fact, in the two cases referred to above, the High Court affirmed that jurisdiction existed in Scotland over both situations as completed frauds; and it now seems clear that provided a material part of any fraudulent scheme can be said to have a Scottish domicile, the whole crime can competently be dealt with in Scotland, irrespective of whether the courts of any other country might also have had jurisdiction.[22] This is curious but is wholly in keeping with Scots law's intensely pragmatic approach to crime. If the courts of this country were to shackle themselves to a particular jurisdictional rule in such cases, then clear criminality might well go unpunished.

6. UTTERING AS GENUINE

DEFINITION OF THE CRIME

10–79 Uttering as genuine is a specialised type of fraud. It is closer to attempted fraud than to fraud itself, since no result of the false pretence is required. The false pretence is also very specific. It has to amount to a forged document

---

[19] See, *e.g.*, *Paterson v. Ritchie*, 1934 J.C. 42.
[20] (1846) Ark. 49.
[21] (1872) 2 Coup. 311.
[22] *Laird v. H.M. Advocate*, 1985 J.C. 37.

(or instrument, as the older authorities tend to call it). In the words of Lord Neaves in *Michael Hinchy*[23]:

> "the wicked and felonious using and uttering of a forged instrument is a completed crime. Whether the party succeeds is of no consequence; the essence of the crime is not the success but the perpetration of the act, of giving it forth from the party to another ... The document must have gone forth to the world; the forgery is not committed unless this is done."

The *mens rea* element is probably very similar to that of fraud. Drawing the various facets of the crime together, an acceptable definition might read: a person is guilty of uttering as genuine if he deliberately exposes a forged document to another person, as if it was genuine, where he knows that it is forged and intends that that other person should be deceived by it.

A forged document

The classic example of such a document is one which bears a forged **10–80** signature. However, it is not necessary that the forgery should amount to a passable imitation of the signature of the person in question, nor is it necessary for the document even to purport to be signed by that person.[24] In *Daniel Taylor*,[25] the accused claimed to be the brother of the person to be deceived. He sent her a note in which he requested her to send money "poste restante" since he was in some kind of unexplained trouble. There was also an assertion that he had injured his hand. The note, he explained, had therefore been written at his request by another who had also had to adhibit his signature for him. It concluded with the words: "your afflicted brother Andrew Muir, signed for me — I cannot." The note was nevertheless held to be a forgery, Lord Justice-General McNeill stating[26]: "I do not think it necessary that the signature of Muir should be there. It is enough that the letter professes to be signed by a person authorised to sign Muir's name." It would, of course, have been monstrous if so crafty a ruse had been successful in removing the finished article from the ranks of forgeries.

A document with a genuine signature on it may, however, also be a **10–81** forgery. The point here concerns the authority given or intended by the person who signed it. If one party gives a cheque to another in payment of an account for £6, careless drawing of that cheque might well give scope for the recipient to alter "six" to "sixty" and 6 to 60, as in the case of *William*

---

[23] (1864) 4 Irv. 561 at pp. 565–566.
[24] Compare with Hume's definition of this crime at i, 140 at para. 2.
[25] (1833) 1 Irv. 230.
[26] *ibid*. p. 234.

Mann.[27] But the altered cheque then does not have the authority of the person who signed it, and must be regarded in total as a forgery. The same conclusion follows if a person, for example, were to sign a cheque in blank, leaving the recipient on trust to fill in the name of the payee and the amount. If the recipient, say a shop assistant, were to enter his own name on that cheque, instead of the store-name, as intended, or deliberately to double the agreed amount, there would certainly be a forgery.[28]

Deliberate exposure to another

10–82   The essence of this crime is not the forging of the document itself, but the deliberate communication of that document to another as if it was genuine. As Lord Neaves aptly put it in *Michael Hinchy*[29]: "A man may ... fabricate a series of the most nefarious documents, but if he keeps them in his desk and never uses them, he has committed no crime." Were a thief, therefore, to break open such a desk and discover the forgeries, there would obviously be no crime of uttering as genuine; but if that thief were to take them and try to pass them off as genuine himself, the crime of uttering would then be committed thus far by him, and not by the original forger. It will be obvious, then, that the "utterer" need not himself be the manufacturer of the forgery[30] but that the *actus reus* is complete when the document is deliberately placed in the hands of a third party as genuine.[31] If the forgery is sent by post to another, it seems that the uttering might be complete when the packet containing it is delivered to the postal authorities.[32] This would entail, however, completion of the crime before such a packet was ever opened and scrutinised by any third party. This odd rule, however, may simply represent a blurring of the edges of the crime to enable the Scottish courts to retain jurisdiction in cases where the addressee is domiciled outwith Scotland.[33] Such blurring is not unusual in fraud cases, however.[34] If a forged document were to be handed to another as forged, then the present crime cannot possibly be committed; but, depending on the facts, there might be evidence of attempted fraud or a criminal conspiracy.[35]

---

[27]   (1877) 3 Coup. 376.
[28]   *cf. Simon Fraser* (1859) 3 Irv. 467, where there could be no such forgery since the accused had written above a signature on an originally blank sheet of paper only that which the person signing it had expected would appear.
[29]   (1864) 4 Irv. 561 at pp. 564–565.
[30]   See *John Smith* (1871) 2 Coup. 1, *per* Lord Ardmillan at p. 12.
[31]   *John Smith, supra, per* Lord Justice-General Inglis at p. 8.
[32]   See *William Jeffrey* (1842) 1 Broun 337, in particular Lord Mackenzie at p. 341.
[33]   As in *William Jeffrey* itself, *supra*.
[34]   See para. 10–78, above.
[35]   Or even an entirely separate, common law crime — see *John Horne* (1814) Hume, i, 150 at n. 1.

MENS REA

The accused must, of course, be aware that the document he communicates **10–83** to another is forged.[36] He must also intend to deceive that other person[37] and, possibly, to prejudice the person whose name was forged.[38] But he need have no success in his intentions. "It is sufficient, therefore, to complete the crime, if the forged instrument has been uttered ... though it was challenged immediately as a forgery, and returned to the prisoner."[39] In *John Smith*,[40] for example, a forged cheque crudely signed in the name of "Frankie Yewls" was sent by the accused to a "friend" to encash. The recipient, however, immediately reckoned it a forgery and handed it to the police. The fact that he was not himself deceived was held to be entirely irrelevant. A good or even understandable motive will also not suffice to acquit the accused. If, for example, goods were purchased and a receipt forgotten to be obtained from the seller, it might be understandable for the purchaser to write out an appropriate receipt so as not to trouble the seller — but use of such a receipt would certainly amount to uttering as genuine according to Hume.[41] Whether such a case would ever actually be prosecuted would, of course, depend on the whole circumstances.

Further reading

"Theft and Conditional Intention," 1985 S.L.T. (News) 77.
Gordon, G. H., *Criminal Law* (2nd ed.), Chaps. 14–18 and 20.
Jones, T. H., "Temporary Appropriation as Theft" (1989) 34 J.L.S. 343.
Ross, J., "Housebreaking with Intent," 1994 S.L.T. (News) 315.
Scott, P. F., "Computer Hacking," 1989 S.L.T. (News) 323.
Scottish Law Commission, *Computer Crime* (Scot. Law Com. No. 106, 1987) Cmnd. No. 174.

---

[36] See *John Smith, supra, per* Lord Justice-General Inglis at p. 9; *Barr v. H.M. Advocate*, 1927 J.C. 51, *per* Lord Justice-General Clyde at p. 53.
[37] Hume i, 154; *John Smith, supra, per* Lord Justice-General Inglis at pp. 9 and 10.
[38] Hume, i, 154; *John Smith, supra*, at p. 10.
[39] Alison, i, 402.
[40] (1871) 2 Coup. 1.
[41] i, 154–155.

CHAPTER 11

CRIMES AGAINST PROPERTY

11–01 The crimes in this chapter are mostly common law ones relating to the protection of property, other than incorporeal property, from encroachment, damage or destruction.

1. TRESPASSING ON HERITABLE PROPERTY

Introduction

11–02 "Unless by virtue of some special statutory provision ... prosecution does not lie under Scottish law merely for unauthorised entry on another's land."[1] This is undoubtedly true; and as far as the common law of crime is concerned, a trespasser "may indeed jeer at the time-honoured placard, which threatens him with rigorous prosecution, as *brutum fulmen* [a harmless thunderbolt]."[2] As long as he does no harm to property,[3] no common law accusation will lie. The protection of heritable property from trespass is normally, therefore, a civil law matter.[4] But the civil law is not noted for its alacrity in dealing with, say, squatters, or those occupying heritable property in order to make some protest; and a better remedy may lie where the terms of certain statutes are applicable. The best known of these statutes are dealt with below.

(1) THE TRESPASS (SCOTLAND) ACT 1865

11–03 The offences contained in the Trespass (Scotland) Act 1865 as amended, most recently by the Roads (Scotland) Act 1984, are contained in section 3 and currently stand as follows:

> "Every person who lodges in any premises [as defined — see below], or occupies or encamps on any land, being private property, without the consent and permission of the owner or legal occupier of such

---

[1] Smith, *A Short Commentary on the Law of Scotland* (1962), p. 526.
[2] Rankine, *A Treatise on Land-Ownership* (4th ed., 1909), p. 140.
[3] *cf.* malicious mischief at paras. 11–08 *et seq.*, below.
[4] Rankine, *op cit.*, Chap. IX.

premises or land, and every person who encamps or lights a fire on or near any road [as defined in s.2] or enclosed or cultivated land, or in or near any plantation, without the consent and permission of the owner or legal occupier of such road, land or plantation, shall be ... punishable as hereafter provided."

According to Rankine[5] this Act "was passed for the purpose chiefly of preventing strolling tinkers, gipsies, and others from squatting without permission on private property or private roads." But the offences are certainly not confined to such persons, the most significant limitation being concerned rather with the type of premises involved. In terms of section 2, premises "shall mean and include any house, barn, stable, shed, loft, granary, outhouse, garden, stackyard, court, close, or inclosed space". It must, therefore, be doubted whether this Act can appropriately be invoked where strikers occupy their employer's factory or students stage a "sit-in" protest within the administration block of their college or university. This may be a matter for regret in some quarters, since those found committing an offence under the Act may be "apprehended and detained" by the police under section 4 — patently a more rapid and effective way of restoring possession of the premises to the owner or legal occupier than can be provided by the civil law. On the other hand, it may be said that such powers of arrest are remarkable, given that the maximum penalty for those convicted of such offences is a mere fine of level 1 on the standard scale (see Appendix C).

Rankine[6] believed that the Trespass (Scotland) Act 1865 had been "found **11–04** very useful in putting a stop to much petty pilfering and wanton destruction of woods and fences in country districts." That may well be so; but there are very few reported cases on such offences. Indeed, searches in the usual repositories suggest that *Paterson v. Robertson*[7] is probably the only reported case. There, subtenants of a furnished house had been given appropriate notice to quit. Whilst they were absent from the premises, the furniture was removed, the house securely locked, and the keys returned by the tenant to the house factors who acted as agents for the owners. Nevertheless, the subtenants returned to the property and gained access by obtaining a key from a neighbour. According to Lord Justice-General Normand, from that time on "they were doing what they knew was wrong, and from that moment they were no better than squatters who had effected a lodgment in the house at their own hands." It would seem from this opinion that the *mens rea* of the crime might be knowledge on the accused's part that he had no entitlement whatsoever to lodge in the premises or encamp on the land; and, if that is so, then Gordon is possibly correct to say that a person who

---

[5] *ibid.* p. 144.
[6] *ibid.* p. 145.
[7] 1944 J.C. 168.

believed himself entitled, at least on reasonable grounds, would have a good defence.[8]

(2) THE CRIMINAL JUSTICE AND PUBLIC ORDER ACT 1994

(a) Trespasser failing to obey a police direction to leave

11–05   The complex offence contained in section 61 of the Criminal Justice and Public Order Act 1994 is applicable to Scotland.[9] In essence, it applies where at least two people "trespass" on land (where trespassing is defined[10] as entering or remaining upon land — which does not include buildings, other than agricultural ones or scheduled monuments, or roads, other than footpaths, cycle tracks and bridleways[11] — without lawful authority and without the occupier's[12] consent) and where they have the common purpose of residing[13] on that land for a period of time. That, however, is nowhere near sufficient for the offence to be committed. Not only must the occupier of the land have taken reasonable steps to ask them to leave, but he must also (apparently) have summoned the police. The senior police officer attending the *locus* must then reasonably believe that the people concerned are trespassers and that the occupier has indeed taken reasonable steps to persuade them to depart from his land; he must also reasonably believe that one at least of the following is satisfied, namely — that the trespassers (or any of them) have caused damage to the land or to property (defined as heritable property other than land, or corporeal moveable property[14]) on it; that the trespassers (or any of them) have used threatening, abusive or insulting words or behaviour to the occupier, any member of his family, his employee or his agent; or, that the trespassers have brought six or more vehicles[15] on to the land. If he is so satisfied as to these points, the police officer may then direct the trespassers, all or some of them, to leave and to remove their vehicles and other property. The offence is committed where such a trespasser, in the knowledge of the police direction, fails to leave as soon as reasonably practicable, or, having once left in obedience to the direction, returns to the same land as a trespasser within a period of three

---

[8]   *Criminal Law*, para. 15–50.
[9]   See s.172(8).
[10] s.61(9), *s.v.* "trespass" at (b).
[11] s.61(9).
[12] Occupier is defined, by s.61(9), as the person in Scotland entitled to natural possession of the land.
[13] It is not a bar to being considered as having a purpose of "residing" there that one has a home elsewhere: s.61(9).
[14] s.61(9).
[15] Vehicles need not be roadworthy, and the term includes a chassis, a caravan, or a load carried in, by or attached to such a conveyance: s.61(9).

months from the day when the direction was first given.[16] (Failure to remove vehicles or other property seems to be excluded from the offence; but the police may seize such property in terms of section 62.) There is also a statutory defence available. A person accused of a contravention of this section may try to show that he was not in fact trespassing at the relevant time, or, he may try to show that he had a reasonable excuse either for not leaving as soon as reasonably practicable or for returning as a trespasser within the specified period.[17] In the one case so far reported on the operation of this offence in Scotland,[18] it appeared that the land in question was subject to a dispute. There were two possible occupiers. That being so, the sheriff who heard the case took the view that it was necessary for the police to make enquiry as to which of the competing parties was the true occupier, since only that person could give instructions (or, possibly, have instructions given on his behalf) to the trespassers to depart. This might have been a question of some difficulty if only one of the two claimants had been prepared to ask the trespassers to leave: but that was not the case. The contending occupiers were entirely at one in wishing and instructing the departure of the persons in question, and consequently the Appeal Court had no difficulty in rejecting the sheriff's view. (This offence is obviously one of fairly limited scope, since it does not apply in general to buildings and is hedged about with qualifying conditions.)

(b) Aggravated trespass

The offence of "aggravated trespass"[19] requires that a person should **11–06** trespass[20] on land[21] in the open air, and deliberately conduct himself there so that those engaged (or about to be engaged) there (or on adjoining land) in "lawful activities"[22] will be intimidated and thus deterred from engaging in those lawful activities. It is also sufficient if he so conducts himself as to obstruct or disrupt those activities. This offence is aimed at those who set out to disrupt activities such as "field sports", and who do so (or attempt to do so) by trespassing on land. There is clearly a "public order" dimension to this offence; but the device of linking the crime to trespassing secures its place in this section of the text.[23]

---

[16] s.61(4).

[17] See s.61(6).

[18] *Neizer v. Rhodes,* 1995 S.C.C.R. 799.

[19] See s.68.

[20] The term "trespass" is not defined for the purposes of this section.

[21] Land does not include highways or roads; see s.68(5)(a).

[22] As defined in s.68(2).

[23] Where a person is committing, intends to commit, or has committed an offence under s.68, or where two or more persons are trespassing with the common purpose of disrupting, etc., lawful activities there, it is also an offence for him or them to refuse to leave the land when directed to do so by a police officer: see s.69. A statutory defence is provided at s.69(4).

(c) Trespassory assembly offences

11–07   Equally, the "trespassory assemblies" offences[24] have public order connotations; but they too entail the protection of land from trespass. For such offences to exist, there are a number of qualifying conditions. First the chief officer of police must reasonably believe that an assembly of 20 or more persons[25] is intended to be held in a particular local authority area, at a place in the open air on land to which the public either has no right of access, or a very limited right of access.[26] He must also believe that that assembly is to be held there without the permission of the occupier,[27] or in excess of such permission as had been granted, or beyond the limited right of public access which exists. If he has such beliefs, he must also be of the reasonable persuasion that that assembly will effect "serious disruption to the life of the community" or significant damage to the land itself or to a building (or monument) erected on it — where that land or building is of historical, architectural, archaeological or scientific importance.[28] Provided that he has been satisfied in these ways, he may then apply to the council of the relevant local authority for an order to prohibit the holding of all trespassory assemblies within a specified area for a specific period.[29] Provided further that the relevant council sees fit to make such an order, the holding of any such assembly will be forbidden, *i.e.* one which

> "(a) is held on land to which the public has no right of access or only a limited right of access, and (b) takes place in the prohibited circumstances, that is to say, without the permission of the occupier of the land or so as to exceed the limits of any permission of his or the limits of the public's right of access."[30]

Once such an order has been made, it will be an offence to organise or take part in an assembly which contravenes the terms of the order — provided the organiser or the participant is aware of that order.[31] It will also be an offence under certain conditions to disobey a direction from a police officer that a particular person, reasonably believed to be *en route* to such an assembly, should not continue in a direction which would lead him there.[32]

---

[24]   Sections 14A to 14C of the Public Order Act 1986, added thereto by ss.70 and 71 of the 1994 Act.

[25]   s.14A(9).

[26]   Section 14A(9) suggests that a limited right of access would apply to a highway or a roadway.

[27]   *i.e.* the person in Scotland lawfully entitled to natural possession of that land: s.14A(9), *s.v.* "occupier", at (b).

[28]   s.14A(1)(b).

[29]   See s.14A(6) for the maximum area and time-period allowed to such an order.

[30]   s.14A(5)(a),(b).

[31]   The offences are contained in s.14B.

[32]   See s.14C.

2. MALICIOUS MISCHIEF

Introduction

Malicious mischief might well be taken to be a result crime (see para. **11–08** 2–40, above) since the actions of the accused must normally be shown to have destroyed or damaged property belonging to another. However, there are up to four different versions of the crime, and one of these appears to require no result at all (see para. 11–23, below). Hume's account of malicious mischief[33] is particularly confusing and perplexing, and lends itself to misconstruction, as is evident in the case of *H.M. Advocate v. Wilson*.[34] In an attempt to allay further confusion, four accounts of this crime are set out separately below, namely: Riotous and Wilful Mischief; Traditional Malicious Mischief; "Wilson" Malicious Mischief; and "Stewart" Malicious Mischief.

RIOTOUS AND WILFUL MISCHIEF

Hume[35] deals with a variety of cases which seem characterised by a form of **11–09** mobbing.[36] Certainly, the essence of these appears to be "violent or tumultuous molestation, intrusion, or invasion of property,"[37] in the course of which damage may be very slight, or even non-existent as in *Mungo Grant*.[38] There, the rightful possessor was simply denied access to his house by the intrusion of the accused with an armed force. In other examples in this series, the damage that did occur was predicated upon the vindication of some alleged civil wrong, such as the raising of turf for a bowling green from a disputed piece of land[39] or the encroachment upon the accused's loft in the parish church.[40] Further in *Glass of Sauchie v. Monro of Auchinbowie*,[41] although the accused was alleged to have broken down dam-dykes and thus stopped the machinery at a mill, it was claimed that he enjoyed at least the privilege of doing so in order to draw water for mills on his own property. That all of these cases were essentially civil matters is clearly admitted by Hume,[42] when he writes: "These judgments may serve as a specimen of the

---

[33] i, 122–125.
[34] 1984 S.L.T. 117; see particularly the opinions of Lord Justice-Clerk Wheatley and Lord McDonald.
[35] i, 122–123; see Alison, i, 449.
[36] See paras. 12–02 *et seq.*, below.
[37] i, 124.
[38] (1712) Hume, i, 122.
[39] *Trotter of Mortonhall* (1716) Hume, i, 123.
[40] *Henry Trotter of Mortonhall* (1730) Hume, i, 123.
[41] (1712) Hume, i, 122.
[42] i, 124.

course of practice in former times, (for of late years the Civil Courts have more commonly been resorted to for the redress of such injuries)". Their rationale as criminal causes was consequently not dependent on the damage done but rather on "the due regard to the order and tranquillity of society". Of course, it is correct that Hume thought true (or "traditional") malicious mischief depended upon significant damage, in the absence of violence or tumult; but these strange, civil-dispute, insignificant-damage cases are really of their own kind, and Hume's "grounds of relevancy in such cases" must be employed with caution in other types of malicious mischief.[43]

11–10   That they have not been employed with caution[44] means that Hume's "grounds of relevancy" and other comments cannot entirely be ignored. In particular he comments that: "It does not serve to acquit the pannel ... that he proceeded in the belief of a civil wrong, previously committed by the pursuer [*sic*] against him: He is not excusable when he forgets that the courts of law are open to his complaint."[45] Further, he notes that in this type of case, "the pannel shall equally be convicted, whether he interferes with the property of another, or with his state only of peaceable and lawful possession."[46] But that his comments here are confined to a special form of the crime is revealed in his final remark, namely: "That which the law chiefly regards in such debates, is not so much the patrimonial damage, which in most of these instances was but trifling, as the insult to the public and the individual, by the violence and tumult attending the execution."[47]

Actus reus and *mens rea*

11–11   So far as it can be determined, the *actus reus* of this type of the crime depends upon unauthorised interference with, and not necessarily physical damage to, the property of another, in circumstances of violence, tumult and public disturbance.[48] The *mens rea* appears to be "wilfulness"[49]; and it is not a defence that the accused acted out of a misapprehension of his civil law rights.[50]

---

[43]   *ibid.*
[44]   See, *e.g., H.M. Advocate v. Wilson*, 1984 S.L.T. 117.
[45]   i, 124. In practice the courts have vacillated between giving effect to, and ignoring this remark in relation to examples of "traditional" malicious mischief; see paras. 11–15 to 11–17 below.
[46]   Reliance on these words has produced a novel type of malicious mischief in recent years; see *H.M. Advocate v. Wilson, supra, per* Lord Justice-Clerk Wheatley at p. 119 and Lord McDonald at pp. 120 to 121.
[47]   i, 124.
[48]   See, *e.g., Archibald Barr* (1834) Bell's Notes 47.
[49]   Hume, i, 122.
[50]   Hume, i, 124.

TRADITIONAL MALICIOUS MISCHIEF

Traditional malicious mischief consists in the intentional or reckless **11–12** damaging of property belonging to another, without that other's consent or permission.[51] Hume clearly recognised this form of the crime[52] but required the damage to be "great" or considerable if conviction was to follow in the absence of violence and tumult. The modern law, however, does not appear to insist on any such restriction, since even the "injury" done to grass by walking over it has been held sufficient for this form of the crime.[53]

Actus reus

It has been said that "an omission could never be an act of malicious **11–13** mischief"[54] and this is probably correct in this form of the crime. The accused must, therefore, bring about the damage or destruction by positive acts on his part. Certainly, all of the reported cases are of that description. In relation to inanimate things, these include the cutting of leather hosepipes[55]; or a horse's harness[56]; the breaking of window panes[57]; the burning of a "chariot" by pouring acid on it[58]; the tearing down of a fence[59]; the knocking away of pit-props such that the roof of a mine fell in[60]; the ruination of several thousand gallons of oil by opening containers and letting the liquid run to waste[61]; and the setting fire to growing trees and plants.[62] The injury or killing of animals is also relevant. Thus in *Thomas Bellie*[63] poisoned feed-stuffs were thrown into a neighbour's yard where they killed some of her hens; and in *Archibald Thomson*[64] the accused killed a cow in calf by inserting the handle of a pitch-fork into the animal's vagina. Likewise, trampling plants or pulling them out by the roots must be sufficient for this form of malicious mischief.[65] If, however, property is not destroyed or

---

[51] Gordon, *Criminal Law*, paras. 22–01 and 22–03.
[52] i, 122 and 124.
[53] *Ward v. Robertson*, 1938 J.C. 32.
[54] *H.M. Advocate v. Wilson*, 1984 S.L.T. 117, *per* Lord Stewart (dissenting) at p. 122, commenting on a Crown concession there.
[55] *Robert Hall* (1837) 1 Swin. 420.
[56] *Speid v. Whyte* (1864) 4 Irv. 584; though this was later thought to be too trivial by Lord Justice-General Clyde in *Clark v. Syme*, 1957 J.C. 1 at p. 6.
[57] *Ann Duthie* (1849) J. Shaw 227.
[58] *Colin Campbell* (1823) Alison, i, 450.
[59] *Black v. Laing* (1879) 4 Coup. 276.
[60] *Nicolson Muir* (1825) Alison i, 450.
[61] *David Munro* (1831) Bell's Notes 48.
[62] *Archibald Phaup* (1846) Ark. 176, although the charge there might more appropriately have been one of culpable and reckless fire-raising.
[63] (1600) Hume, i, 124.
[64] (1874) 2 Coup. 551.
[65] See, *e.g., Samuel Wallace and Thomas Ferguson* (1839) Bell's Notes 47.

damaged where it is found, but first taken away from where the owner or legal possessor left it, that would normally be theft rather than the present crime.[66] It is, therefore, surprising that one of the three charges of malicious mischief in *Samuel Wallace and Thomas Ferguson*[67] referred to the removal of a gate and the dumping of it in a canal, unless, of course, the time interval involved had been so slight as to be considered irrelevant.[68]

Mens rea

11–14   The title of the crime here is, of course, malicious mischief, which suggests that the *mens rea* required is "malice". Malice, indeed, was said by Lord Justice-Clerk Wheatley[69] to connote "the evil intent deliberately to do injury or damage to the property", though no authority was advanced to justify such a view. Nevertheless, that interpretation allied to Hume's insistence[70] that the damage or destruction be "wilful" suggests that the appropriate *mens rea* is intention.[71] If intention to damage or destroy can be shown or inferred from the circumstances, then that is certainly sufficient for conviction, and there is no need to show any further intent to spite the owner.[72] However, such intention is not necessary for conviction. As Lord Justice-Clerk Aitchison laid down in *Ward v. Robertson*[73]:

> "It is not essential to the offence of malicious mischief that there should be a deliberate wicked intent to injure another in his property. I am prepared to take the case upon the footing, although it may involve some departure from the law as laid down by Hume, that it is enough if the damage is done by a person who shows a deliberate disregard of, or even indifference to, the property or possessory rights of others."

This strongly suggests that simple recklessness is an alternative form of *mens rea* for the crime[74]; and indeed Lord Justice-Clerk Aitchison's above quoted remarks were specifically approved by Lord Justice-General Clyde in *Clark v. Syme*.[75] Consequently, if the damage or destruction can be shown to have been the product of the accused's recklessness (see paras. 3–28 *et seq.*, above), then conviction must follow. Such recklessness cannot always

---

[66]   See Alison, i, 273–274.
[67]   *supra.*
[68]   See Burnett, p. 116, n. *.
[69]   *H.M. Advocate v. Wilson*, 1984 S.L.T. 117 at p. 119, col. 2.
[70]   i, 122.
[71]   *cf.* Alison, i, 448, where mention is made of "the wanton or reckless destruction of property".
[72]   *Archibald Thomson* (1874) 2 Coup. 551, *per* Lord Deas at p. 553.
[73]   1938 J.C. 32 at p. 36.
[74]   See Gordon, *Criminal Law*, para. 22–03.
[75]   1957 J.C. 1 at p. 5.

be inferred, however. Thus, in *Ward v. Robertson*[76] *mens rea* could not be inferred from the mere fact that the appellant had walked in a straight line through a field of ordinary grass, causing some trivial damage thereto. No reasonable person would have considered any real or lasting harm to have been so caused. But the matter would have been different, as Lord Justice-Clerk Aitchison emphasised,[77] if a stroll had been taken through a more obvious crop (the grass here having been intended merely for sheep grazing), or, as Lord Mackay put it,[78] if the appellant had deliberately trampled the grass by taking many more steps than were necessary to traverse the field or by walking round and round in circles. It is also clear, however, that carelessness will not be sufficient, even apparently if gross.[79]

Vindication of rights

Hume appears to remark generally that if damage or destruction is done **11–15** under a "misapprehension of right", that will not secure an acquittal.[80] This was undoubtedly upheld in *Clark v. Syme*[81] where a farmer shot a sheep belonging to a neighbour on the basis that that neighbour had refused to prevent his animals straying into the farmer's fields and consuming turnips there. He shot the sheep in the belief that he was entitled to do so to protect his own property. His acquittal on a charge of malicious mischief was reversed on appeal, however, Lord Justice-General Clyde[82] holding: "The respondent in this case acted deliberately. He knew what he was doing and he displayed in his actings a complete disregard of the rights of others." The fact that the respondent had acted under a mistake of law did not afford him a defence.[83] The approach of the courts to this defence in relation to malicious mischief has not, however, been entirely consistent.

In *Speid v. Whyte*[84] the condition on which timber was to be auctioned **11–16** was that the price should be paid before removal. Because some of the timber was located too far from a road to make extraction of it economic, the auctioneer purported to sell it to a neighbouring farmer who insisted that he be allowed to remove it forthwith. When the owner of the timber realised that this particular lot of wood was being removed without the price having been first paid, he remonstrated with the farmer's men who

---

[76] 1938 J.C. 32.
[77] *ibid*. p. 36.
[78] *ibid*. p. 38.
[79] See *Archibald Phaup* (1846) Ark. 176, *per* Lord Justice-Clerk Hope's charge to the jury at p. 177.
[80] i, 122.
[81] 1957 J.C. 1.
[82] *ibid*. p. 5.
[83] See para. 8–45, above.
[84] (1864) 4 Irv. 584.

were even then loading it up, and eventually he cut the harness securing a horse to a cart. For this he was convicted of malicious mischief — but acquitted on appeal. As Lord Neaves put the matter[85]:

> "[The appellant] was undoubtedly the proprietor of the wood till the conditions of sale were implemented, which they had not been; and although he may not have acted judiciously, or even legally, in the course he adopted to vindicate his property, still he did act in vindication of his supposed rights, and not merely from a desire to injure or destroy the property of another."

Whether the essence of this case can be distinguished from that in *Clark v. Syme* must be doubted[86] but Lord Neaves also said: "[the acts done] do not amount to that reckless and wilful destruction of property which is essential to the constitution of malicious mischief." These words can be construed so as to rest the acquittal on the *de minimis* principle (see para. 2–54, above); and indeed Lord Justice-General Clyde in a much later case considered that the acquittal there had been right on that basis, namely, that the trivial nature of what had been done was not consistent with the correct degree of recklessness or wilfulness required by the crime.[87] Significantly, it was not considered to have been correct on the grounds that a proprietor is entitled to damage the property of another in order to safeguard his own.

11–17   Again, in *Black v. Laing*[88] a father and son were eventually acquitted of malicious mischief on appeal. They had torn down a fence, recently erected by another along the boundary of a piece of land they possessed, on the basis that it had blocked the only access to their land. Although no formal opinion was delivered by the court, it does appear that the appellants were felt to be justified in destroying the fence in these circumstances.[89] In a later case with not dissimilar facts, however, the accused was convicted and his appeal dismissed.[90] Either, as Gordon suggests,[91] these cases cannot be relied upon and there is no defence of acting in vindication of supposed rights, or each such case must be dealt with individually and decided according to its own facts and circumstances, a not uncommon way for Scots criminal courts to deal with awkward issues. Even if Gordon is correct, it is still possible that vindication of supposed rights might be pled in mitigation of sentence.[92]

---

[85] *ibid.* p. 586.
[86] See Gordon, *Criminal Law*, para. 22–10.
[87] *Clark v. Syme*, 1957 J.C. 1 at p. 6.
[88] (1879) 4 Coup. 276.
[89] *ibid.* p. 278.
[90] See *Forbes v. Ross* (1898) 2 Adam 513.
[91] *Criminal Law*, paras. 22–09, 22–11.
[92] See *McDonald v. Mackay* (1842) 1 Broun 435.

Provocation

It would seem on principle that provocation should be able to be pled in **11–18**
mitigation in a malicious mischief case (involving damage to property) just
as it may be in a case of assault (involving injury to the person). In practice,
this appears to be true. In *Andrew Steuart*[93] the accused, who had had his
gun with him for sporting purposes on the day in question, shot a horse
belonging to a tenant farmer of his who had provoked him by removing
most of the crops before the rent due for his property had been met. As
Lord Deas remarked[94]: "It is not in the least surprising that you were much
offended and angry at what was going on. That, however, only goes to
mitigate the offence. It does not take it away."

"WILSON" TYPE MALICIOUS MISCHIEF

This type of malicious mischief was recognised in the case of *H.M. Advocate* **11–19**
v. Wilson[95] and may generally be described as the unauthorised interference
with another's property such as to cause deliberate consequential loss to
the owner or lawful possessor. In this form of the crime, no physical damage
need be caused to existing property at all.

In *Wilson* the accused was charged with malicious mischief in that he **11–20**
had pressed the emergency stop-button of a turbine at a power station

> "whereby the full generation and feeding of electricity into the national
> electricity grid was brought to a halt for 28 hours or thereby and
> 12,113,800 kilowatt hour units of electricity ... were lost and had to
> be replaced and fed into the national grid from other sources at a cost
> of £147,000 or thereby."

The accused objected to the relevancy of this charge in that no physical
damage had been caused either to the stop-button or to the turbine itself.
This argument succeeded before Sheriff D. B. Smith but was rejected by a
majority of the Appeal Court. Lord Justice-Clerk Wheatley[96] considered
that physical damage was not essential to this type of charge, either because
it accorded with Hume's views or because there was "a wider cover to be
given to the earlier view of the nature of the offence." However, his Lordship
could only achieve congruity with Hume by importing from "Riotous and
Wilful Mischief" the conclusion that "the pannel shall equally be convicted,
whether he interfere with the property of another, or with his state only of

---

[93] (1874) 2 Coup. 554.
[94] *ibid*. p. 555.
[95] 1984 S.L.T. 117.
[96] *ibid*. p. 120, col. 2. See also p. 120, col. 1.

peaceable and lawful possession."[97] It will be recalled, however, that mere interference with, as opposed to damage to, property was only to be considered criminal where there was also violence and tumult. As no violence or tumult was adverted to in the indictment, then it must follow that Lord Justice-Clerk Wheatley and Lord McDonald were really here extending the notion of traditional malicious mischief so as to create a novel form of the crime. It is thus criminal to interfere deliberately with the property of another with the intention of causing its owner or legal possessor financial loss, where such loss is actually incurred and where the property interfered with remains itself entirely undamaged.

11–21   Extending the ambit of a crime by judicial decision is not, of course, entirely illegitimate or unknown in a common law based system; and there is indeed something illogical in concluding that had the stop-button in *Wilson* been operated by being hit with a hammer then malicious mischief would have been a relevant charge, whereas that would not have been so if an undamaging finger had been used to operate it instead. That type of illogicality clearly weighed heavily with Lord Justice-Clerk Wheatley[98] and Lord McDonald.[99] But, as Lord Stewart[1] pointed out in his dissenting judgment:

> "if the infliction of damage is an essential element of the crime then the absence of such damage takes the actings, however reprehensible, out of the category of criminality ... The distinction may seem narrow and artificial but it is nevertheless a distinction which in my opinion the law has made."

A dissenting judgment, however, can have no bearing on the outcome of the case — which is that a new form of malicious mischief has been conceived by the majority in *Wilson*. It differs from "Riotous and Wilful Mischief" in that no violence or tumult need be shown; and it differs from "Traditional Malicious Mischief" in that no physical damage to property need be caused.

Mens rea

11–22   It is as yet not entirely clear whether this new form of the crime can be committed recklessly. Although the indictment certainly referred to "wilfully, recklessly and maliciously" activating the emergency stop-button, Lord Justice-Clerk Wheatley's opinion[2] refers to the deliberate nature of the initial

---

[97] Hume, i, 124; *Wilson, supra, per* Lord McDonald at p. 120, col. 2.
[98] *Wilson, supra*, p. 119, col. 2.
[99] *ibid.* p. 121, col. 1.
[1] *ibid.* p. 122, col. 1.
[2] *ibid.* p. 119, col. 2.

act, and to the Crown's proper concession that "consequential injury has to be intended", as also elsewhere to the libel's being "habile to carry the inference that the initial positive, wilful, reckless and malicious act was intended to harm the employer by causing patrimonial injury." This is admittedly rather confusing[3] and scarcely settles the matter.

"STEWART" MALICIOUS MISCHIEF

Lord Stewart's interesting dissenting opinion in *H.M. Advocate v. Wilson*[4] **11–23** contains the following passage:

> "The term [*i.e.* malicious mischief] also includes maliciously placing any obstruction on a railway or wilfully and recklessly doing so in a manner calculated to obstruct [this being a quotation from Macdonald, p.84] (see *Miller* and *Murdoch*). Actual damage to property may not be necessary if the malicious act is clearly intended to cause such damage."

As stated above at paragraph 11–21, the content of a dissenting judgment can hardly be taken as a statement of law; but since Lord Stewart here envisages a form of malicious mischief without physical damage (apparently contrary to his own view of the crime) and refers for support to two nineteenth-century cases, his views merit some consideration.

Of the two cases to which Lord Stewart referred, only that of *David* **11–24** *Miller*[5] is truly relevant. There the accused placed a stone on the rails of a railway line at a time when he knew a train carrying passengers was due. In fact, the danger of damage to the train and of injury to passengers was averted, since some unknown third party removed the stone before the train could make contact with it.[6] Miller pled guilty to a charge at common law of "Wilfully, maliciously and unlawfully placing [that stone] ... in a manner calculated and intended to obstruct such train and carriages and to endanger the lives and safety of the passengers and others travelling thereby." If this was genuinely an instance of malicious mischief, then, since the case has never been overruled or questioned, it was understandable that Lord Stewart should wish to consider it along with his account of the crime. But the case contains no discussion of malicious mischief at all. Nor does the reporter (Arkley) refer to it, or index it as an example of such a crime. Indeed, it seems closer to the crime of endangering the lieges[7] than to malicious mischief.

---

[3] See also Lord McDonald's opinion at pp. 120, col. 2 to 121, col. 1.
[4] *supra*, pp. 121 to 122, and at p. 122, col. 1, repeated at p. 122, col. 2.
[5] (1848) Ark. 525.
[6] *cf. John E. Murdoch* (1849) J. Shaw 229, where a similarly placed stone was not removed and much actual damage ensued.
[7] See para. 9–28, above.

11–25   In short, it is submitted that *Miller* does not disclose an exceptional form of malicious mischief at all. Rather at best it is, or would now be treated as, an example of attempted "traditional malicious mischief" — distinguishable from the completed crime by the very fact that no damage transpired. It seems to follow then that conduct which does not result in actual damage and which is not accompanied by violence and tumult or consequential loss cannot amount to the completed crime of malicious mischief, no matter how clear the intention to cause physical damage may appear to be. If this is correct, then the statutory form of charge in Schedule 5 to the Criminal Procedure (Scotland) Act 1995 — "You did maliciously place a block of wood on the railway line and attempt to obstruct a train" — may simply be an example of attempted malicious mischief, or, if not that, then an example of an attempt to commit a distinct crime of obstruction.

3. VANDALISM

11–26   A statutory crime with a specification similar to that of "traditional malicious mischief" was created in 1980,[8] but now appears in section 52 of the Criminal Law (Consolidation) (Scotland) Act 1995. In terms of that section: "any person who, without reasonable excuse, wilfully or recklessly destroys or damages any property belonging to another shall be guilty of the offence of vandalism." This offence is plainly close to "traditional malicious mischief" in that it insists that there be actual damage caused to property and specifies that the *mens rea* required may be either wilfulness or recklessness. But there are some differences too. The Appeal Court, for example, in *Black v. Allan*[9] emphasised that the statutory offence was not a mere echo of malicious mischief, but a separate crime in its own right. In particular, where recklessness is advanced as the appropriate form of *mens rea*, *Black v. Allan* holds that part (at least) of the test for that in *Allan v. Patterson*[10] is to be applied. Consequently, where one youth jumped on another's back in the course of horseplay in a public street and was somehow thrown or shrugged-off into a nearby glass window-pane (which broke), it was wrong for justices of the peace in a district court to conclude that there had been recklessness simply because there was always some danger of breakage when youths "fooled around" in such ways. What the justices should have asked themselves was whether the actions of the accused created such an obvious and material risk of damage to the window as to be considered reckless.[11]

---

8   Criminal Justice (Scotland) Act 1980, s.78(1).
9   1985 S.C.C.R. 11 at pp. 12–13.
10 1980 J.C. 57; see para. 3–29, above.
11 It has, of course, not been determined whether the *Allan v. Patterson* notion of recklessness (or any part of it) is applicable to "traditional malicious mischief".

Vandalism also differs from its common law equivalent in that the damage **11–27** or destruction must be "without reasonable excuse". It seems clear from the opinion of the Appeal Court in *MacDougall v. Yuk-Sun Ho*[12] that if the accused raises the issue that there may have been a reasonable excuse, the burden is then on the Crown to show that the tendered excuse was unreasonable. Failure to show that will inevitably result in acquittal — not something which can be affirmatively stated in relation to "traditional malicious mischief". Maximum penalties are also different. As usual, conviction of the common law crime exposes the accused to the maximum range which the trial court possesses (see Appendix D); but the statutory offence[13] carries a maximum fine of level 3 on the standard scale (see Appendix C) or a maximum prison sentence of 60 days, or both of these, in a district court, and maxima of the "prescribed sum" (see Appendix C) and/ or 3 months (6 months for a second or subsequent conviction) in a sheriff court. In addition, summary procedure is mandatory for vandalism whereas malicious mischief in its common law manifestations can be, and often is, taken on indictment.

4. FIRE-RAISING

Introduction

In essence, the crime of fire-raising involves the intentional or reckless **11–28** damaging or destroying of corporeal property belonging to another without his consent or permission. As such, it is simply a serious form of "traditional malicious mischief" where the damage or destruction is achieved in a specific way.[14] In modern times, therefore, there is probably little justification for treating fire-raising as a separate common law crime; but it does in fact continue to be so treated.[15] It will be appreciated that in historical times there was considerable reason for impressing upon people the dangers of fire, most buildings, certainly dwelling-houses, then being constructed of wood and roofed with thatch. The absence of effective fire-brigades must also have weighed in the balance. Because of these considerations, the Scots Parliament in 1526[16] declared that setting fire to houses and corns (presumably because of their then very great importance as staple food-stuffs), burning houses known to have people in them at the time, and "wilful fire-raisings" were to be "constructive treasons". Not only were those crimes

---

[12] 1985 S.C.C.R. 199 at p. 203; see also *Murray v. O'Brien,* 1994 S.L.T. 1051.
[13] See the Criminal Law (Consolidation) (Scotland) Act 1995, s.52(3).
[14] See *John Mackirdy* (1856) 2 Irv. 474, *per* Lord Justice-Clerk Hope at p. 475.
[15] See, *e.g., Carr v. H.M. Advocate,* 1995 S.L.T. 800.
[16] A.P.S. II, 316, c. 10.

to be capital offences, but they were also to be attended by the special penalties associated with treason — for example, forfeiture of all the convicted person's property. According to Burnett,[17] the mention of "wilful fire-raisings" in the Act did not mean that all intentional setting-fire to things was to be considered as treason. Rather, his opinion was that this signified only that fire-raisings relative to the particular types of property specified in the statute had themselves to have been intentional before the treason penalties attached. This is almost certainly how the Act was interpreted, as were the later Acts of 1540[18] and 1592.[19] These measures respectively enacted that the burning of corn in barnyards and in stacks was treasonable, and that the burning of "coilheuchis" (coal pits)[20] for vengeance or spite was to be similarly treated. Fire-raising in respect of houses (with people in them or not), corn (including corn standing in fields),[21] or coal pits was, therefore, to be punished with exceptional severity.[22]

11–29 The Scots law of treason was more or less abolished at the time of the Union with England; and the opportunity was then taken to reduce the "constructive treason" offences to "mere" capital offences.[23] The "wilful" burning of houses, corn or coal pits was thus made punishable with death; whereas non-wilful burnings of such things or fire-raisings of any sort in respect of other types of property (where criminal at all) were not. Parliament eventually added the malicious burnings of woods, underwoods and coppices to the ranks of capital fire-raisings[24] and thus the overall picture was tolerably understandable — at least until the close of the nineteenth century. In 1887,[25] capital punishment for "wilful" fire-raising of houses, corn, coal pits and woods was abolished, and the status of those crimes as "High Court only" was cancelled. Henceforth, instances of "wilful fire-raisings" (as wilfully setting fire to any of those specific types of property had come to be known)[26] might be dealt with in sheriff courts, but only on indictment there. "Wilful fire-raising" had thus become a "technical" term[27] connoting the "wilful" setting of fire to houses, corn, coal pits or woods. These particular fire-

---

[17] *Treatise*, p. 214.
[18] A.P.S. II, 377, c. 38.
[19] A.P.S. III, 575, c. 68.
[20] *Pace* Gordon, *Criminal Law*, para. 22–23, n. 58.
[21] Hume, i, 129, 131.
[22] See, *e.g., Sir James Makconeill* (1608) Pitcairn's Criminal Trials, III, p. 5; *Johnne Henrie* (1615) Pitcairn's Criminal Trials, III, p. 361.
[23] See the Treason Act 1708.
[24] The Act of 1 Geo I, c.48, s.4.
[25] See the Criminal Procedure (Scotland) Act 1887, s.56 (now repealed).
[26] See *Angus v. H.M. Advocate* (1905) 4 Adam 640, *per* Lord Justice-General Dunedin at p. 644.
[27] *ibid. per* Lord Adam at p. 646.

raisings had to be tried on indictment, whereas all other criminal fire-raisings might be prosecuted in whatever way seemed merited by the circumstances.

There have been further developments. Under section 5(4) of the Criminal **11–30** Procedure (Scotland) Act 1995, it is competent to try even those technical "wilful fire-raisings" summarily — but not in a district court.[28] Conversely, under section 52(2) of the Criminal Law (Consolidation) (Scotland) Act 1995, it is declared incompetent "to charge acts which constitute the offence of wilful fire-raising as vandalism." As a result of those provisions, it is still necessary to consider "wilful fire-raising" as something technically different from ordinary fire-raisings; and this in turn leads to the conclusion that there are up to three different forms of the crime. These are "wilful fire-raisings" (meaning intentionally setting fire to houses, corn, coal pits, or woods), intentional fire-raisings, and culpable and reckless fire-raisings. Gordon[29] suggests that some of the understandable confusion in nomenclature observable in some nineteenth-century cases might be eliminated by referring to just two categories — namely "heritable" and "non-heritable" fire-raisings, "'heritable' fire-raising being the setting fire to any of the specified subjects, whatever the *mens rea.*" It is thought, however, that this whole issue is more than sufficiently complicated already, and that the injection of fresh terms would make this crime even more impenetrable than it regrettably now is.

WILFUL FIRE-RAISING

This may be defined as the intentional setting fire to houses, corn, coal pits, **11–31** or woods owned by another without his permission. It will be noted that the choice of subjects for this crime is dictated entirely by historical criteria. It can hardly be said in modern times, for example, that this form of the offence covers only items of the maximum value that can be imagined. Thus, deliberately setting fire to bank notes worth millions would probably be criminal, but it could not strictly amount to "wilful fire-raising".[30]

Actus reus

Of the types of property specified by this offence, "houses" seems **11–32** somewhat vague. According to Hume,[31] what is meant is "every sort of house, whether a dwelling-house, work-house [presumably meaning a factory or office, in modern times], or warehouse, or a barn, stable, or other out-house; so it be what is commonly understood to be a house, and not a

---

[28] 1995 Act, s.7(8)(b)(i).
[29] *Criminal Law*, para. 22–23.
[30] See Hume, i, 131.
[31] i, 132.

bare hovel or temporary place of shelter." To that list can be added shops,[32] hotels[33] and labourers' huts.[34] All of this suggests that Gordon's conclusion, that all heritable buildings are within the purview of this offence, is probably accurate.[35] Alison is also clearly correct to remind his readers that "house" includes any part of it or any of its "fixtures".[36] The building need not be inhabited or occupied at the time it is ignited[37] but it is sufficient if any of the types of property here relevant has been burnt to any degree, no matter how small.[38] Provided the fire has "taken effect", as nineteenth-century indictments put it,[39] then the *actus reus* of the crime is complete, even if the fire is extinguished by a "well disposed person" or of its own accord before any great damage has been done.[40]

Belonging to another

11–33   The property set on fire must belong to another[41]; and in one nineteenth-century case, it was declared that an indictment was defective in that it failed to state that the shop set on fire was the property of someone other than the accused, notwithstanding that he had been designed as a mere tenant of the premises.[42] It is clear, therefore, that a tenant who sets fire to premises let to him has fulfilled the *actus reus* of the crime.[43] Curiously, the older text-writers state that although it is generally not criminal for an owner of property to set fire to it, since, of course, it is his own, it may be "wilful fire-raising" for him to do so if that property has been let to a tenant or is subject to a liferent interest at the time.[44] It is, thus, not sufficiently his own, if subject to a tenancy; yet not sufficiently the tenant's own, if the tenant sets fire to it. According to Alison[45] it is not the existence of the tenancy or liferent right that matters, but rather whether the tenant or liferenter has taken occupancy or possession. This may be a just way of looking at these complex cases since it focuses attention on the danger to property or persons

[32] See, *e.g.*, *John Arthur* (1836) 1 Swin. 124.
[33] *cf. H.M. Advocate v. Bell*, 1966 S.L.T. (Notes) 61.
[34] See *John Vallance* (1846) Ark. 181, where the huts seemed indeed to be very close to "bare hovels".
[35] *Criminal Law*, para. 22–23 at n. 57.
[36] i, 430. See also Walker, *Principles of Scottish Private Law* (4th ed.), Vol. III, pp. 11 *et seq.*
[37] *John Vallance, supra, per* Lord Justice-General Hope at p. 186.
[38] Alison, i, 429; *John Arthur, supra, per* Lord Justice-Clerk Boyle at p. 152.
[39] And see Hume, i, 127–128.
[40] See, for example, *John Arthur, supra*, where due to the prompt action of a passer-by, a door was burnt only to the extent of one-twentieth of an inch, according at least to the accused's counsel at p. 149; see also *Peter Grieve* (1866) 5 Irv. 263.
[41] Hume, i, 132–133.
[42] *John Mackirdy* (1856) 2 Irv. 474.
[43] Hume, i, 132; *Margaret Drysdale* (1826) Alison, i, 435.
[44] Hume, i, 132; Alison, i, 437; *Walter Buchanan* (1728) Hume, i, 133.
[45] i, 437.

rather than on ownership; but there is no other warrant for it[46] and it strays rather far from the concept of "belonging to another".

Mens rea

The fire must be raised "wilfully", and Hume[47] leaves his reader in no **11–34** doubt that that means "with a purpose to destroy the thing to which it is applied." Provided that there is such a purpose, then setting fire to something other than the property meant to be burned, in the knowledge that the fire will naturally and inescapably spread to that property, is sufficient.[48] Thus, for example, to set fire to a pile of furnishings (moveable property) within a house, meaning and expecting it to take effect on the fabric of the house itself, will be enough if the house or any of its fixtures is actually burnt to any degree. Even setting fire to one's own property will suffice, if the fire spreads to a neighbour's property — if that had been one's intention all along.

The *mens rea* of "wilful fire-raising" is thus intention — intention to **11–35** damage or destroy the property burned. Hume,[49] however, went further than that and considered a form of transferred *mens rea* to be applicable. If a person, for example, set fire to moveable property A owned by another, intending to destroy or damage A only, but the fire spread to heritable property B also owned by that other, then that person would be guilty of wilful fire-raising in respect of B, all other things being equal, provided that the spread of the fire to B was

> "not of quite a fortuitous and extraordinary nature, but such as might naturally and not improbably ensue ... What has ensued is a mischief, though higher, of the very same sort as that which he intended, and so likely to happen, that, when he did the one, he must have been utterly indifferent whether this damage also should or should not ensue".[50]

Gordon[51] was of the opinion that Scots law did not accept the concept of transferred *mens rea* at all; but, since the airing of his opinion in 1978, the Appeal Court has accepted that that concept does apply to assault (see paras. 3–35 to 3–37, above). It was possible, therefore, that it might also apply to "wilful fire-raising". The Appeal Court has subsequently determined,

---

[46] *cf.* Hume, i, 133.
[47] i, 128.
[48] Hume, i, 129–130.
[49] i, 130.
[50] i, 130.
[51] *Criminal Law*, para. 22–26; but see now the entry for this para. in Second Cum. Supp. (1992).

however, that that is not so. In *Blane v. H.M. Advocate*,[52] the accused set fire to a quilt in the room he occupied in a hostel. His intention was to create smoke so that he could inhale the same and thus commit suicide. He did not intend that flames should be caused, and did not intend, or apparently even foresee, that any fire so created should, or might, spread to the hostel building itself. In the event, fire did take hold on the building — some £15,000 worth of damage being caused. The accused was charged with wilful fire-raising in relation to the premises and convicted (the sheriff having directed the jury in accordance with Hume's notion of transferred intent). On appeal, the court considered that an intention, directly or indirectly, to set fire to the hostel building was essential for conviction, and that a fulfilled intention to set fire only to moveable property which just happened in turn to set fire to heritable property was insufficient. It might, however, have been possible to obtain a conviction for "wilful fire-raising" if the accused had deliberately set fire to the furnishings in the room in such a way as to demonstrate his utter indifference whether the fire might spread to the building itself or not. As the sheriff had not put the matter to the jury in that way, however, the conviction had to be quashed. Mention of the terms "utter indifference" does suggest, of course, that the court may have had recklessness in mind as an alternative form of *mens rea*. The opinions cast, however, do not support such a conclusion. At best, "utter indifference" was seen as one way, an objective way, of proving the requisite intent.[53] And this view has been borne out by the dicta in *Carr v. H.M. Advocate*.[54]

11–36   Motive is, as usual, of no moment in ascertaining the *mens rea* for the crime.[55] If one intended to burn part of a house, such as a door, in order to obtain unauthorised entrance or exit, then the *mens rea* for "wilful fire-raising" would be present whatever was the ulterior reason for so intending. In *Jean Gordon or Bryan*[56] Lord Mackenzie expressed great doubt as to whether escapees from a prison at Banff could be guilty of capital fire-raising by burning a hole in the prison door to gain their liberty. His view appears to have been that their intention was to escape and not to harm the prison itself. But if they could not effect their escape other than by burning the prison door, then surely they must have intended to damage that part of the prison by fire? In any event, Lord Mackenzie's views are obiter, since the charge was one of prison-breaking aggravated by setting fire to the doors and other parts of Banff Prison, and further are contrary to Hume's opinion, namely that "it does not mend the case for the pannels, that this act [burning doors and other parts of a gaol] has been subservient to the other,

---

[52] 1991 S.C.C.R. 576.
[53] See, *e.g.*, the opinion of Lord Justice-General Hope at pp. 581E to 582B.
[54] 1995 S.L.T. 800.
[55] See *Robert Smillie* (1883) 5 Coup. 287, *per* Lord Young at p. 290.
[56] (1841) 2 Swin. 545 at pp. 546–547.

and also felonious offences of mobbing, breaking gaol, and setting prisoners at large."[57]

INTENTIONAL FIRE-RAISING

The existence of this form of fire-raising, dealing with the intentional burning **11–37** of subjects other than those relevant for "wilful fire-raising", seems well enough vouched. As Hume notes:

> "it does not ... seem to be capital as a fire-raising, that a mob after rifling a house, collect the effects and burn them in the street; or even that within the house, they burn the owner's title deeds, bank-notes and bonds, or other goods, however valuable, gathered into a heap in the fire-place, or upon the hearth."[58]

Alison also seems to be of the same persuasion,[59] although his examples of non "wilful fire-raising" property as "a milk-house in the corner of a field, a dovecot in an orchard, or the like" look suspiciously as if they might qualify as "houses" for the "wilful" form of the crime.[60] Some older cases,[61] too, lend their support to the existence of a crime of intentional fire-raising, independent of the "wilful" variety.

Gordon begs to differ, however. He writes[62]: **11–38**

> "The setting fire to any other subjects [*i.e.* other than those for wilful fire-raising] was known as culpable and reckless fire-raising, even if it was committed intentionally. 'Culpable and reckless' fire-raising, however, was also used to denote cases in which the specified subjects were set on fire but without the *mens rea* necessary for wilful fire-raising".

Such a view is not without support. In the Criminal Procedure (Scotland) Act 1995, for example, the statutory style of charge in Schedule 2 offers only "wilful" or "culpable and reckless" fire-raising in relation to the alleged setting-fire to a warehouse. Again in *Angus v. H.M. Advocate* Lord Justice-General Dunedin,[63] after considering the crime of "wilful fire-raising", said:

> "But there was always another crime known to the law — an innominate crime, and visited by an arbitrary penalty — which consisted in setting fire, or attempting to set fire to anything. It is true

---

[57] i, 131.
[58] *ibid.*
[59] i, 432.
[60] See also Alison, i, 442.
[61] See, *e.g., Alexander Pollock* (1869) 1 Coup. 257.
[62] *Criminal Law*, para. 22–23.
[63] (1905) 4 Adam 640 at p. 644.

that the epithet in that case was not 'wilful,' but of doing so 'culpably and recklessly'. "[64]

Further, in the more modern case of *Wither v. Adie*[65] the charges concerned the setting-fire to a dozing man's shoelaces. That can hardly have been other than intended, yet the charge was one of recklessly setting fire to those items. On balance, however, it is submitted that it is unnecessarily confusing to refer to intentional fire-raisings as culpable and reckless ones; and that if this form of the crime is truly innominate, then it is best to refer to it in a meaningful and rational way as was clearly done by the Appeal Court in *Blane v. H.M. Advocate*[66] where the accused was convicted of the substituted offence of "setting fire to the bedding in his room wilfully".[67]

Actus reus and *mens rea*

11–39   The *actus reus* of this crime consists in the setting fire to corporeal property other than that included within the range appropriate for "wilful fire-raising" but is otherwise similar to that for the "wilful" form of the offence. The *mens rea* is very clearly intention, again as in the "wilful" form of the crime.

CULPABLE AND RECKLESS FIRE-RAISING

11–40 Both Hume and Alison[68] clearly advert to such a crime. Alison in particular states[69] that "if the burning the pannel's own house be attended with obvious risk to adjoining tenements, and one of them be actually burned in consequence, the guilty party as for *culpable and reckless fire-raising*, is amenable to a severe punishment." The *actus reus* is thus similar to that of each of the other forms of this crime but, obviously, without restriction as in "wilful fire-raising" to particular types of property. If fire in fact takes effect on the property of another, and it is causally related to an act on the part of the accused, then that is sufficient.

Mens rea

11–41   This form of the offence is, therefore, readily distinguishable from the other two in terms of *mens rea*. Neither "wilful" nor intentional fire-raising can be committed recklessly; and the sole issue here is what recklessly

---

[64] *cf.* the views of Lord Adam at p. 646 and of Lord McLaren at p. 647.
[65] 1986 S.L.T. (Sh.Ct.) 32.
[66] 1991 S.C.C.R. 576.
[67] *ibid. per* Lord Justice-General Hope at p. 584C.
[68] *Crimes*, i, 128, *Principles*, i, 433.
[69] i, 438.

means in this context. In *Robert Smillie*[70] Lord Young opined: "If a man, while engaged in some illegal act, raises a fire, he is guilty of wicked, culpable and reckless fire-raising." That, however, is most doubtful. It would mean that a careless or unlucky thief would automatically be guilty of reckless fire-raising if he happened to cause a fire whilst engaged in the act of stealing property. That such automatic guilt is frowned upon in Scots law seems apparent from the case of *James Stewart and John Walsh*.[71] There, the accused were stealing whisky from a cask on a railway waggon, and one of them "allowed" his lamp to come into contact with the spirit (or the fumes emanating from it), and thus caused a fire which destroyed the whisky, two casks, a chest of tea, six chairs and the railway waggon itself. There was no question of his having intentionally set fire to those items of property, of course; but because of grave doubts voiced by the court that he had scarcely done so recklessly either (in spite of having been engaged in an "illegal act" at the time) the Solicitor-General was compelled to withdraw the charge of reckless fire-raising. It thus does not resolve the issue to inquire whether the accused was engaged in illegality at the time. The question as to whether or not he was "reckless" remains entire and unanswered even after such inquiry has been completed.

There have, until recently, been few judicial pronouncements on the **11–42** meaning of recklessness in this form of fire-raising. In *George MacBean* Lord Justice-Clerk Hope said[72] that it would be sufficient if a person set a house on fire "in such a state of reckless excitement, as not to know or care what he was doing, but who had no deliberate intention of setting fire to the house." It now seems that that is the correct approach, and that, for example, directing a jury that the test for recklessness in such a crime can be taken from the road traffic case of *Allan v. Patterson*[73] would be wrong. In *Thomson v. H.M. Advocate,*[74] therefore, Lord Justice-Clerk Ross said this:

> "[I]n a case of fireraising it is not the manner of doing an act which would otherwise be lawful which is in issue [as in *reckless* driving], but the question whether the accused had the mens rea necessary for the commission of a crime. It would have been appropriate for the sheriff therefore to confine his definition to the question whether the accused's actions showed a complete disregard for any dangers which might result from what he was doing and in particular of the fire taking effect on the premises."[75]

---

[70] (1883) 5 Coup. 287 at p. 291.
[71] (1856) 2 Irv. 359.
[72] (1847) Ark. 262 at p. 263.
[73] 1980 J.C. 57 (a case of "reckless" driving in terms of the law then current).
[74] 1995 S.L.T. 827 at p. 829D–E.
[75] This accords (*mutatis mutandis*) only with the last part of the test for recklessness given in *Allan v. Patterson*, 1980 J.C. 57, *per* Lord Justice-General Emslie at p. 60.

In so saying, Lord Ross was agreeing entirely with the view expressed by Lord Justice-General Hope in *Carr v. H.M. Advocate*.[76]

Further reading

Forensis, "Vandalism & Malicious Mischief" (1986) 31 J.L.S. 232.
Gane, C. H. W. & Stoddart, C. N., *Casebook on Scottish Criminal Law* (2nd ed., 1988), notes on *H.M. Advocate v. Wilson*, pp. 633–638.
Gordon, G. H., commentary to *H.M. Advocate v. Wilson*, 1983 S.C.C.R. 420 at pp. 428–431.

---

[76] 1995 S.L.T. 800, at p. 803K–L. See also pp. 803L to 804A, where Lord Hope opined that it was wrong for the sheriff in that case to have told the jury that a high degree of recklessness was what was required. As in other crimes where recklessness was sufficient for the *mens rea* element, the true contrast was a simple one — between carelessness on the one hand and recklessness on the other.

CHAPTER 12

CRIMES RELATING TO PUBLIC ORDER AND MORALITY

General introduction

This chapter introduces the best known crimes which attempt either to **12–01** prevent disorder in the community or to uphold current notions of acceptability in individual behaviour. It must be noted at the outset that it is not easy to justify all of the offences which presently fall within such parameters. Whilst public disorder can fairly easily be seen as a "harm" which requires discouragement (although it may sometimes be a somewhat vague "harm" against the community in general rather than particular individuals), it is much more difficult to justify the compelling of persons to behave, or not to behave, in specified ways because of the annoyance, nuisance or distress otherwise caused to other persons. The difficulty here is that individuals vary enormously in their sensitivity to the behaviour of others. It is far from easy, therefore, to establish what is acceptable and what is not acceptable, in the sense of being offensive, to the community in general. This is particularly so in sexual or quasi-sexual matters, where the identification of what is indecent or obscene is the true issue. In Scotland, and indeed elsewhere, such identification is usually left to the good sense of the judge or jury, and little attempt is made to specify in advance what will be indecent or obscene as a matter of law; and arguably that is the best method of resolving moral dilemmas, where these are found within the criminal law. Where the moral issue at stake is a much more "public" one involving, for example, one's duty to tell the truth (perjury) or to refrain from betraying the security of one's country (treason), then some form of identifiable "harm" is more readily apparent.

1. CRIMES RELATIVE TO PUBLIC ORDER

MOBBING

Definition of mobbing

The common law crime of mobbing is committed when persons combine **12–02** together to achieve a commonly-shared purpose by violence or intimidation (that is, by unlawful or criminal means), where their combined conduct causes alarm to the community and disturbance of the public peace. Everyone in a crowd or mob who, by his presence and behaviour, adopts and seeks to promote such a common purpose is guilty of this crime. In the very full indictments found in nineteenth-century case reports, accused persons (usually a mere fraction of the total mob) were always charged as having been part of a riotous and disorderly crowd which, acting of common purpose, did various alarming and disorderly things in implementation of that purpose. Thus was their guilt to be brought home; they had been part of a larger design — assisting, aiding and abetting it by their culpable presence.[1] This indeed is essentially still the way in which the crime is charged.[2] In addition to their being guilty of mobbing, the accused could also (and still can) be guilty art and part of particular crimes, if such had been committed by individual members of the mob other than themselves — provided that such particular crimes were genuinely foreseeable, given the commonly-shared purpose and its method of implementation.[3] This, however, might be a very serious business if, say, someone had been killed as a result of the mob's conduct. Whereas mobbing in the nineteenth century was not itself a capital crime,[4] murder certainly was, even for one found guilty art and part.[5] Although murder is no longer, of course, a capital-punishment offence it is still today a serious matter for those accused of mobbing to face the prospect of conviction for murder or other offences which they did not personally commit; but that is certainly still the law.[6] Modern charges tend to be so drawn that particular offences can be brought home to the accused either as members of the mob or as individuals (if evidence exists that they were individually responsible for committing them).[7]

Actus reus of mobbing

12–03   There must be a number of persons present before a "mob" can be constituted. It is uncertain, however, what the minimum acceptable number might be. Hume[8] unhelpfully refers to the necessity of there being "a great

---

[1]   See, for example, *James Cairns* (1837) 1 Swin. 597 at pp. 597–600; *Daniel Blair* (1868) 1 Coup. 168 at pp. 169–171.

[2]   See the Criminal Procedure (Scotland) Act 1995, Sched. 2 and para. 12–06, n. 22, below; see also the indictment in *Kilpatrick v. H.M. Advocate,* 1992 J.C. 120, as quoted by Lord Justice-General Hope at p. 122.

[3]   See, *e.g., Myles Martin* (1886) 1 White 297, *per* Lord Mure's charge to the jury at pp. 304–306.

[4]   Hume, i, 426.

[5]   See, *e.g., William Gibson* (1842) 1 Broun 485.

[6]   See, *e.g., Hancock v. H.M. Advocate*, 1981 J.C. 74.

[7]   See *Kilpatrick v. H.M. Advocate*, 1992 J.C. 120, *per* Lord Justice-General Hope at pp. 125–126.

[8]   i, 416.

host or multitude", whereas Alison[9] adopts the number "12" from the Riot Act 1714.[10] In terms of reported cases, the size (often estimated) of a mob has varied from some 1,300[11] to eight[12]; and in *Sloan v. MacMillan* Lord Salvesen hinted[13] that five might be too few. Clearly, however, the fewer the number involved, the more likely it is that all can be identified and charged directly with their individual offences, thus rendering resort to "mobbing" unnecessary. It may be of interest here that the analogous English offence called "Riot" requires a minimum of 12 persons.[14]

Commonly-shared purpose

There must be a common purpose. That, however, is hardly the most **12–04** important issue in rendering a crowd's activities criminal, since a common purpose may well be a quite lawful one, as where persons gather to greet the return of a successful sporting team or to protest in a silent and peaceful manner over the imposition of some disliked fiscal measure. The crux of the matter is, therefore, that the common purpose itself should be a violent and mischievous one[15] or, if more peaceful in concept, should be implemented in a violent or intimidatory way.[16] It certainly does not matter that the crowd considered that it was acting in vindication of some supposed public or legal right in, say, preventing fish being landed on a Sunday[17] or pulling down a wall thought to have been erected over a public footpath.[18] If there is believed to be infringement of a legal right, then the remedy of those disaffected is clear. They must resort to the civil courts. If they choose not to do so, but resort to main force and violence, that will certainly be construed as an appropriate common purpose for mobbing.[19]

Although it is natural to think of a common purpose as something planned **12–05** and known well in advance of the actual incidents constituting mobbing, this need not be so. Provided that such a purpose can be shown, then it is of

---

[9]   i, 510.
[10] Now repealed; see the Statute Law (Repeals) Act 1973, s.1(1) and Sched. 1, Pt. 5.
[11] *John G. Robertson* (1842) 1 Broun 152.
[12] *Hancock v. H.M. Advocate, supra.*
[13] *Sloan v. MacMillan*, 1922 J.C. 1 at p. 7.
[14] Public Order Act 1986, s.1.
[15] See, *e.g.,* the violent obstruction of officers of law in the execution of their duty in *Alexander McLean* (1886) 1 White 232.
[16] *e.g.* the fraudulent intimidation used by the "mob" to persuade voluntary workers in a coal mine to cease pumping operations during an industrial dispute — *Sloan v. MacMillan, supra*; the violence used by those intent on upholding the Sabbath as a day of rest in *Alexander Gollon or Gollan* (1883) 5 Coup. 317.
[17] *Alexander Gollon or Gollan, supra.*
[18] *Alexander Macphie* (1823) Alison, i, 512, where the wrongous and illegal erection of such a wall was later affirmed by the jury court (civil) and the House of Lords.
[19] See, *e.g., Thomas Wild* (1854) 1 Irv. 552, *per* Lord Cowan's charge to the jury at p. 558.

no moment whether it was conceived in advance or arose spontaneously at the relevant time.[20] In *George Smith*,[21] for example, a large crowd assembled to communicate to the magistrates of Glasgow their demands for food, money and work. There seemed to be no pre-arranged plan to do anything beyond that but, following dissatisfaction with the magistrates' response to their demands, the crowd instantly became a mob by forming and implementing, there and then, a purpose to steal and rob.

12–06   Modern indictments and complaints do not have to specify the exact common purpose,[22] but failure by the Crown to show a specific common purpose or to prove facts from which one might be inferred will inevitably spell the end of any prosecution for mobbing.[23] Certainly, proof of a series of random acts of violence and depredation, carried out by varying sets of persons who alighted from time to time from a transit van at different locations in a Scottish town, was held insufficient to raise an inference as to any common purpose at all.[24]

Alarm and disturbance

12–07   It also seems essential to this crime that the conduct of the mob should cause public alarm and disturbance.[25] Hume suggests too[26] that the level of such disturbance should be "significant", which, it is thought, must be correct. In *John G. Robertson*, Lord Justice-Clerk Hope stated[27]: "If, as in this case, a crowd collect and act together, with intent to oppose the entrance of a Presbytery into a church where duty is to be performed, and oppose such entry by dense numbers, and by refusing to move, though there were no noise nor other acts, — that would be mobbing." Were this dictum to be received as law, then peaceful protestors, who sit down in a road in order to block the entrance of traffic to some premises or other, would be guilty of mobbing for doing no more than that — which seems wholly inappropriate. Indeed, in *Robertson*, there was substantial violence, damage and disturbance, such that Lord Justice-Clerk Hope's remarks are no more than *obiter dicta*. As such, they should not be followed. That is not to suggest, of

---

[20]   Alison, i, 513.

[21]   (1848) Ark. 473.

[22]   See the Criminal Procedure (Scotland) Act 1995, where the appropriate style in Sched. 2 is: "You formed part of a riotous mob, which, acting of common purpose, obstructed A.B., C.D., and E.F., constables of the Northern constabulary on duty, and assaulted them, and forcibly took two persons whom they had arrested from their custody."

[23]   *Francis Docherty* (1841) 2 Swin. 635; *Hancock v. H.M. Advocate*, 1981 J.C. 74; *Kilpatrick v. H.M. Advocate*, 1992 J.C. 120.

[24]   *Hancock v. H.M. Advocate, supra.*

[25]   Hume, i, 416.

[26]   i, 419–420.

[27]   (1842) 1 Broun 152 at p. 192.

course, that a crowd of persons could not cause alarm by intimidatory behaviour. But if that were claimed, much would depend on what was done or said.[28]

Mere presence in a mob

It is possible to find some judicial opinions which suggest that those **12–08** who follow a crowd out of idle curiosity may be considered part of that crowd by their very presence there. Such persons might then become guilty of mobbing, and of anything else the crowd cares to do in pursuance of its common design, by presence alone, or rather by failing to remove themselves from that crowd once its common purpose of violence or intimidation had become clear.[29] The overwhelming preponderance of authority, however, shows that such fears are groundless; and it is thought that Lord Young was correct in *John Nicolson*,[30] when he said to the jury:

> "If the prisoners, or any of them, were there from idle curiosity, that would not make him or them one of the mob. He would have to take the consequences, and when violence is used to disperse a mob, it frequently happens that those present out of curiosity suffer from that violence. But if in point of fact the prisoners were there not as participants in the conflict, not assenting to it, and not aiding it, they would not be guilty of mobbing ... although they were physically present."[31]

Mens rea

None of the reported cases seems to deal with the issue of *mens rea* in **12–09** mobbing; but the clear implication is that no one can be convicted of this crime unless he knew what the common purpose of the mob was, and intended to aid and abet it by whatever means he could.

---

[28] See, *e.g.*, *Sloan v. MacMillan*, 1922 J.C. 1, where the mob claimed (falsely) that there were hundreds of disaffected, striking miners outside the pit, whose anger it would be difficult to contain if those working in the mine itself did not instantly cease their labours.

[29] See *James Farquhar* (1861) 4 Irv. 28, *per* Lord Ardmillan at pp. 40–41; *John G. Robertson, supra, per* Lord Justice-Clerk Hope at pp. 194–195.

[30] (1887) 1 White 307 at pp. 314–315.

[31] See also Hume, i, 422; *John Urquhart* (1844) 2 Broun 13, *per* Lord Justice-Clerk Hope at p. 15; *Hancock v. H.M. Advocate*, 1981 J.C. 74, *per* Lord Cameron at pp. 83–84 and Lord Justice-General Emslie at p. 86; and the similar directions given to the jury by Lord McCluskey in a case of breach of the peace by a crowd of persons in *Boyle v. H.M. Advocate*, 1993 S.L.T. 577 at p. 579I.

Rioting

12–10   Many of the older cases refer to this crime as mobbing and rioting. But "rioting" was the general description of fighting between two or more persons[32] in breach of the public peace, and featured commonly before the inferior courts in Scotland from the seventeenth century onwards.[33] Although rioting was still being described as a viable offence in its own right as late as 1838,[34] it is now thought to be in desuetude. Particular examples of it would now be dealt with as assaults or breaches of the peace. In any event, it would be inaccurate to describe the crime currently being explored as mobbing and rioting, since fighting is very far from being an indispensable feature of it.

BREACH OF THE PEACE

Introduction

12–11   According to Hume,[35] a breach of the public peace is a mere brawl which goes the length of disturbing and alarming the neighbourhood. However, the modern crime of breach of the peace is very much wider than that. Essentially, it now extends to any conduct which actually has one of a number of effects on others, or any conduct which might reasonably be expected to have such an effect. The range of those effects is considered further in the paragraphs which follow; but since "disturbance" and "alarm" are certainly included, it seems to follow that the commission of almost any existing crime might well be described as a breach of the peace. If taken to its limit, then, breach of the peace might be capable of swallowing up the whole of the criminal law of Scotland, with the exception of some esoteric statutory crimes perhaps. And of that sort of development, there is indeed some sign. Thus, assault may be considered as a breach of the peace[36] and charged as such; malicious mischief and vandalism may be similarly regarded[37]; and even inconsiderate driving, under the Road Traffic Act 1988, section 3, now appears to be prosecutable as such.[38] As breach of the peace is a common law crime, and can thus be prosecuted summarily or on indictment according to circumstances, then the non-availability of an adequate penalty would hardly be a bar to such development. The case against this, however, is overwhelming.

---

[32] *cf.* Alison, i, 510.
[33] See especially the baron court and justice of the peace court records of the 17th and 18th centuries.
[34] See *John McCabe* (1838) 2 Swin. 20.
[35] i, 439.
[36] *Johnstone v. Lindsay* (1906) 5 Adam 192, *per* Lord Justice-Clerk Macdonald at p. 195.
[37] See, *e.g., Winnik v. Allan*, 1986 S.C.C.R. 35; *Buchanan v. Hamilton*, 1990 S.L.T. 244.
[38] *Smillie v. Wilson*, 1990 S.L.T. 582.

Whilst the major part of the criminal law of Scotland could indeed be **12–12** expressed in some facile, breach-of-the-peace-type phrase, such as "doing things (or refraining from doing things) which cause, or could reasonably cause alarm or disturbance", this would lead inevitably to complete uncertainty as to what exactly the law did prohibit. At present, there is considerable uncertainty as to what breach of the peace itself properly covers[39]; and it would thus be most unwelcome to extend that uncertainty by enlarging the scope of breach of the peace at the expense of other, fairly well-defined offences. But this is, of course, something of a vicious circle. It is precisely because breach of the peace has become so ill-defined that it has proved possible for it to stray into fields occupied by other offences. The only way to halt this process is for breach of the peace to be defined in a clearer and more limited fashion than is currently the case. Regrettably, however, there is little indication that that is likely to be so.

Definitions

Two judicial "definitions" of this crime are currently much referred to. **12–13** In *Raffaelli v. Heatly*[40] Lord Justice-Clerk Thomson said that the offence was a species of disorderly conduct, and "where something is done in breach of public order or decorum which might reasonably be expected to lead to the lieges being alarmed or upset or tempted to make reprisals at their own hand, the circumstances are such as to amount to breach of the peace." Again, in *Wilson v. Brown*[41] Lord Dunpark stated that

> "a test which may be applied in charges of breach of the peace is whether the proved conduct may reasonably be expected to cause any person to be alarmed, upset or annoyed or to provoke a disturbance of the peace. Positive evidence of actual alarm, upset, annoyance or disturbance created by reprisal is not a prerequisite of conviction."

Neither of the above accounts claims to be a complete definition of the **12–14** crime, and it may be that a complete definition would be impossible of attainment, given the extraordinarily wide scope of the offence. Nevertheless, it seems to be evident from those accounts that the actual effect on any human "victim" of the accused's conduct is irrelevant unless that victim's reaction would have been shared by a reasonable person; and this does appear to have been borne out by the authorities. In *Mackenzie v. Normand,*[42] for example, the accused (who had his eyes hidden behind

---

[39] See, *e.g.,* Lord McCluskey in *MacDougall v. Dochree,* 1992 J.C. 154 at p. 160 where he stated that breach of the peace had "no consistently necessary common core".
[40] 1949 J.C. 101 at p. 104.
[41] 1982 S.L.T. 361 at p. 362, col. 2.
[42] 1992 S.L.T. 130 at p. 131I–J, where the stress is laid on the conduct being "calculated" to cause alarm and distress.

reflective sunglasses) repeatedly entered a queue inside a liquor store, repeatedly left it before he reached the sales point, and repeatedly stared at the assistants both from inside and outside the store — all over a period of some two hours. The assistants were alarmed by such conduct, and the Appeal Court, in confirming the conviction for breach of the peace, concluded that it "would not be at all surprising" for them to be so. By way of contrast, in *Farrell v. Normand*,[43] a 10-year-old girl (the victim of the accused's attentions) was thoroughly alarmed and upset by his behaviour; but that behaviour amounted to no more than beckoning her over at a leisure centre and asking her if she would like a drink. Although the Appeal Court thought it a narrow point, it determined that such conduct as had been proved would not have caused alarm and distress to a reasonable person and that the conviction for breach of the peace had to be quashed.[44] The impression is also had from the "definitions" (see paragraph 12–13, above) that something positive has to be done by the accused; but this is not necessarily so. In *Montgomery v. McLeod*,[45] for example, a youth, who refused to leave the scene of an earlier disturbance and thus was in point of fact doing nothing, was convicted of breach of the peace since the police feared that his continued presence might lead to a fresh disturbance.

12–15   It would be erroneous to conclude from the foregoing "definitions" (see para. 12–13, above) that the range of "effects" reasonably to be expected from the conduct is restricted to alarm, upset, annoyance or provocation. In *Sinclair v. Annan*,[46] for example, conviction was affirmed on the basis that a witness had been "embarrassed" by what the accused had said to her; and in *Young v. Heatly*[47] a deputy headmaster was convicted on the basis that any reasonable person would have been disgusted by his indecent remarks to adolescent boys. It is also clear that conduct which generally creates a disturbance, rather than anything else, will be sufficient.[48] It will be appreciated, therefore, that a wide range of possible effects of conduct is subsumed by the offence. Indeed it is possibly those effects which are of crucial importance rather than the type of conduct itself, or where it takes place. Thus, in *Montgomery v. McLeod*[49] it was stated:

---

[43] 1993 S.L.T. 793.

[44] *ibid.* at p. 796A. Lord Justice-Clerk Ross did opine that the decision might have been different if the conduct had been persisted in once the girl had clearly registered her alarm and upset. *Cf. Shannon v. Skeen* (1977) S.C.C.R. Supp. 180, where the Appeal Court quite unaccountably quashed the convictions of two men who persistently followed, and thus caused considerable alarm to, a woman who was collecting money from vending machines.

[45] (1977) S.C.C.R. Supp. 114.

[46] 1980 S.L.T. (Notes) 55.

[47] 1959 J.C. 66.

[48] See, *e.g., Derrett v. Lockhart*, 1991 S.C.C.R. 109, where two men had fought violently in a public place in front of eyewitnesses.

[49] (1977) S.C.C.R. Supp. 164 at p. 165.

"There is no limit to the kind of conduct which may give rise to a charge of breach of the peace. All that is required is that there must be some conduct such as to excite the reasonable apprehension [that mischief may ensue], or such as to create disturbance and alarm to the lieges in fact."

And it has been held in several cases that it is of no moment whether the conduct takes place in public or in private; what really matters is the effect which ensues, or the reasonably apprehended effect which might have ensued.[50] Of course, it may be taken as read that if the conduct was truly in private, then no one could reasonably have been expected to have been affected by it. As Lord Justice-Clerk Ross put the matter: "If the respondent had been in a locked cubicle into which no one outside the locked door could see, unless the door was unlocked, I would accept that whatever he did within the locked cubicle could not amount to a breach of the peace."[51] What he appears to have meant there was that conduct which is accidentally discovered (as, for example, where a person stumbles and falls against a toilet cubicle door, thus bursting it open) should not amount to breach of the peace. Only if conduct is reasonably discoverable should its actual discovery be criminal. (This may well depend, however, on the nature of the conduct and whether it could amount to some other crime — such as shamelessly indecent conduct — where the privacy of the occasion is truly irrelevant.[52]) It is also worth emphasising here that the courts may ignore the evidence of witnesses that they were *not* alarmed, annoyed or tempted to make reprisals, and instead base conviction on their own views of what reasonable persons might have felt or been tempted to do.[53]

Actus reus of breach of the peace

As indicated above, the conduct of the accused must have had, or been **12–16** considered likely to have had, one of a number of possible effects on the "victim" (if breach of the peace can be said to have "victims") or at least on eye-witnesses — who include potential eye-witnesses. The relative unimportance of the precise form of conduct employed can easily be seen

---

[50] See, *e.g., Ferguson v. Carnochan* (1889) 2 White 278; *Matthews and Rodden v. Linton* (1860) 3 Irv. 570; *Young v. Heatly, supra.*

[51] *MacDougall v. Dochree,* 1992 J.C. 154 at p. 159; see also *Thompson v. MacPhail,* 1989 S.L.T. 637.

[52] See *MacDougall v. Dochree, supra, per* Lord McCluskey at p. 161.

[53] See, *e.g., Young v. Heatly, supra; Wyness v. Lockhart,* 1992 S.C.C.R. 808 (polite, and uncomplained of, begging in the streets of Aberdeen); *Cameron v. Normand,* 1992 S.C.C.R. 866 (kicking a football in the streets of Glasgow in such a way as to cause vehicles to swerve and pedestrians to take avoiding action, although no one in fact made any complaint on the relevant occasion — the view being taken that this was a "possibility of reprisal type" case).

by reference to some illustrative cases. Thus, in *Derrett v. Lockhart*[54] the behaviour consisted of fighting to the disturbance of the vicinity; in *Palazzo v. Copeland*[55] it consisted of firing a shot-gun in the air at an early hour in the morning, to the alarm and consternation of those who heard it; in *Butcher v. Jessop*[56] it was a seven-second flaring of tempers by players at a Celtic-Rangers football match, which might reasonably have caused a riot amongst the 43,000 spectators; in *McLean v. McNaughton*[57] the conduct amounted to throwing a lighted firework down the centre aisle of a bus to the great alarm of the passengers; in *Whitchurch v. Millar*[58] it consisted of marching through the streets of Hamilton on the sabbath at the head of a singing, shouting crowd of some 40 persons — all to the alleged annoyance of residents of the town; in *Dougall v. Dykes*[59] the accused marched from a church in a noisy and irreverent manner whenever, during divine service, a particular minister, whom he disliked, entered the pulpit — to the great annoyance and insult of the minister and congregation; in *Turner v. Kennedy*[60] the conduct amounted to no more than distributing pamphlets advocating liberal educational views to school pupils — to the annoyance and distress of some of those pupils' parents; in *Stewart v. Lockhart*[61] the accused (male) attired himself in women's clothing and walked through an area of Aberdeen usually frequented by female prostitutes — all to the alarm of the police, who felt that the accused might be mistaken for a woman by potential prostitute-clients, and thus be visited with violence when the error was discovered; in *Saltman v. Allan*[62] the conduct consisted of aggressive shouting and swearing at the police and refusing to desist when called upon to do so — all to the annoyance of the constables who heard it; in *Carey v. Tudhope*[63] a police constable threatened to push a suspect's face through a grille, kick him through it instead, or drive over him with his van — all to the evident alarm of the suspect and an eye-witness; in *Raffaelli v. Heatly*[64] the behaviour amounted to twice, late at night, peering through a gap in curtains drawn across a window — which the Appeal Court considered to be a clear breach of decorum, which, if discovered, might have led to reprisals being taken against the accused; and, in *Alexander v.*

---

[54] 1991 S.C.C.R. 109.
[55] 1976 J.C. 52.
[56] 1989 S.L.T. 593.
[57] 1984 S.C.C.R. 319.
[58] (1895) 2 Adam 9.
[59] (1860) 4 Irv. 101.
[60] (1972) S.C.C.R. Supp. 30.
[61] 1991 S.L.T. 835.
[62] 1989 S.L.T. 262.
[63] 1984 S.C.C.R. 157.
[64] 1949 J.C. 101; see also *MacDougall v. Dochree*, 1992 J.C. 154.

Smith[65] it was the accused's repeated attempts to sell an ultra right-wing newspaper to unsympathetic football supporters which amounted to breach of the peace, the police having formed the view that those supporters might exact reprisals against him unless he desisted forthwith.

Consideration of the various types of conduct in a random selection of **12–17** breach of the peace cases suggests that there is no unifying feature to be discerned there whatsoever. Rather, the common thread running through such cases is the effect, or reasonably likely effect, of what the accused did, namely actual disturbance of the neighbourhood, or an unlooked for and unwelcome psychological response (for example, alarm, distress, concern, embarrassment, desire to respond violently) in the minds of those present (or most likely to be present) at the time.

Mens rea

The *mens rea* of breach of the peace has never been determined in any **12–18** reported case. It is, therefore, uncertain what the *mens rea* might be. As breach of the peace is a common law crime, it must be assumed that strict liability (see Chapter 13) is not applicable, since "[t]here is a presumption that all common law crimes require *mens rea*."[66] Probably if the accused's conduct, whatever it be, is deliberate or even reckless, and is causally connected, or reasonably could be so connected, to one of the recognised "effects", then that will suffice. It does not seem to be necessary for the accused to intend or even appreciate the effect (actual or likely) on others. This seems to be borne out by *Hughes v. Crowe,*[67] where the claim was made that the accused had had no *mens rea* at the relevant time. What had happened was that the occupants of the lower flat in a building were "entertained" to banging sounds and the playing of loud music from the flat above — all at 7.15 on a Saturday morning. The noises (all exceedingly loud) continued for about one hour, until put a stop to by the police. It was claimed that the accused had had no knowledge that there was anyone in the lower flat at the time, and that he had not been warned about his conduct before being charged. The Appeal Court, however, took the view that although *mens rea* was required for breach of the peace, it was to be inferred from the nature and quality of the actings. Here, it would have been obvious in a four-flatted building that persons were likely to be at home at that hour on a Saturday, and that the acts of the appellant, persisted in for a considerable period, thus showed a "gross lack of consideration for others who might be present in the other flats in the block at the time."[68] This does not exactly

---

[65] 1984 S.L.T. 176.
[66] Gordon, *Criminal Law,* para. 7–12.
[67] 1993 S.C.C.R. 320.
[68] *ibid. per* Lord Justice-General Hope at p. 323F.

settle what the precise *mens rea* element for the crime might be; but certainly a "good" or understandable motive for one's deliberate conduct seems to be of no moment at all, as in *Ralston v. H.M. Advocate*[69] where a prisoner's deliberate roof-top protest caused complete disruption to the running of the prison, and was thus a breach of the peace — irrespective of the merits of his desire to publicise alleged poor prison conditions. On the other hand, in *MacDougall v. Dochree*,[70] it appeared to be accepted by all three judges in the Appeal Court that it would not be breach of the peace for persons, who were suspicious that "peeping-tom" activities might be taking place in a locked toilet cubicle (which by exercise of ingenuity provided viewing access to a next-door solarium), to test their suspicions by peering under a gap at the bottom of the cubicle door whilst the toilet was occupied by the suspect. This suggests that a "good" motive (for example, crime detection by persons other than the police) may provide a defence.

Particular defences

12–19   It is apparently not a good defence that the accused committed a breach of the peace in order to bring to an end an existing breach, even one being committed outside his own house by some troublesome youths,[71] presumably on the basis that two wrongs do not make a right. But self-defence is definitely applicable to a "fighting" or assault type of the crime.[72] It may be a defence that only the police heard or saw the accused's conduct, unless the police, inured as they must be to reprehensible behaviour, were entitled to be (and, possibly, actually were) annoyed or alarmed thereby.[73]

Statutory forms of charge

12–20   The three statutory forms of this offence in the Criminal Procedure (Scotland) Act 1995[74] are deemed to be relevant without further

---

[69] 1989 S.L.T. 474 and para. 3–20, above.

[70] 1992 J.C. 154. See also *Cardle v. Murray,* 1993 S.L.T. 525 (resisting unlawful detention by struggling, shouting and swearing), and *cf. Woods v. Normand,* 1992 S.C.C.R. 805 (attempting to end what was mistakenly thought of as an assault on a friend by use of threatening words and behaviour, where the Appeal Court opined that even if there had been a "good motive", the tactics adopted went far beyond what was justified): these two decisions, however, could also be explained as examples of self-defence (see para. 12–19, below).

[71] *Palazzo v. Copeland,* 1976 J.C. 52.

[72] *Derrett v. Lockhart,* 1991 S.C.C.R. 109.

[73] See *Cavanagh v. Wilson,* 1995 S.C.C.R. 693, applying the decision in *Logan v. Jessop,* 1987 S.C.C.R. 604; but *cf. Norrie v. McLeod,* 1988 S.C.C.R. 572, *Saltman v. Allan,* 1989 S.L.T. 262, and *Lochrie v. Jessop,* 1992 S.L.T. 557, which all seemed to discredit *Logan v. Jessop* as having any value as a precedent.

[74] Sched. 5.

specification,[75] even the astonishing: "You did conduct yourself in a disorderly manner and commit a breach of the peace." What is astonishing there is the total lack of information conveyed to the accused of the case he has to meet, bearing in mind the enormously wide range of conduct which suffices for this crime. However, the Appeal Court has confirmed that no more than that is usually required.[76] Can it be just to require the accused to ascertain for himself the precise charge against him?

Analogous statutory offences

Failing to leave, etc., a rave after police direction

There are a number of statutory offences covering ground similar to **12–21** some instances of breach of the peace.[77] One of the most complex of these is to be found in section 63 of the Criminal Justice and Public Order Act 1994. The marginal note to that section refers to a "rave"; but the substance of the offence explains that the crime relates to an actual or planned gathering of more than 100 persons (whether trespassers or not[78]) on land in the open air,[79] where amplified music[80] is played at night (whether with intermissions or not) and is of such duration and loudness as to be likely to cause serious distress to inhabitants of the locality.[81] If a police officer of at least the rank of superintendent reasonably believes that two or more persons are on that land making preparations for such a "rave", and/or that 10 or more persons are there attending it or waiting for it to begin, he can give direction that all such persons[82] are to leave the land and remove whatever vehicles or other property they may have brought to it. The offence is committed by failing to leave that land as soon as reasonably practicable, or returning to it within seven days of the direction being given[83] — both without reasonable

---

[75] Criminal Procedure (Scotland) Act 1995, s.138(2).

[76] *Anderson v. Allan*, 1985 S.C.C.R. 399.

[77] See, *e.g.,* the Civic Government (Scotland) Act 1982, ss. 46 (*inter alia* prostitute soliciting in a public place); 49(2) (*inter alia* permitting any creature to give any other person reasonable cause for alarm or annoyance), 54(1) (*inter alia* failing to desist from playing a musical instrument so as to give any other person reasonable cause for annoyance), and 55(1) (touting for trade so as to give any other person reasonable cause for annoyance).

[78] This is not, therefore, predominantly a trespassory offence (see paras. 11–05 *et seq.*, above). "Trespasser" is defined as in s.61(9): see s.63(10).

[79] This includes a place partly open to the air, such as a sports stadium (s.63(10)), but not in Scotland a place which has been licensed as a place of public entertainment (s.63(9)).

[80] This includes "sounds wholly or predominantly characterised by emission of a succession of repetitive beats": s.63(1)(b).

[81] s.63(1).

[82] Under s.63(2), this is not applicable to exempt persons, *i.e.* the occupier of the land, members of his family, or his employee or agent, as also those who have homes situated there: see s.63(6) and (10). "Occupier" is defined as in s.61(9): see s.63(10).

[83] s.63(6). "Vehicle" is defined as in s.61(9): see s.63(10).

excuse.[84] Before there can be a conviction, it must be shown that the accused was aware of the direction; but the direction is deemed to have been properly communicated if reasonable steps have been taken to bring it to the attention of those concerned.[85] Within a defined distance of such a "rave", a police officer can stop persons he reasonably believes are on their way to it and require that they should proceed in a "non-rave" direction; it is also an offence to fail to comply with such a requirement.[86]

2. CRIMES RELATIVE TO MORALITY

General introduction

12–22   The crimes dealt with under the above heading are those which generally cannot be justified on the basis of direct harm done to another. Certainly no harm in any conventional sense need be caused by them. Rather the badge of criminality is borne because what is done offends against the currently accepted standards of moral behaviour or against the tenets of the "honour-code" which all upstanding citizens are presently expected to observe. Examples of the former kind consist of various sorts of "shamelessly indecent conduct" (including incest, which is usually dealt with separately), and examples of the latter are the crimes of treason, sedition, perjury, giving false information to the criminal authorities, and various "attempts" to pervert or hinder the course of justice.

SHAMELESSLY INDECENT CONDUCT

Introduction

12–23   It is now accepted as a principle of Scots law[87] that "all shamelessly indecent conduct is criminal"[88]; and that principle has been used to justify or generate a number of particular offences at common law (see paras. 12–25 to 12–28, below). It also probably justifies the criminal nature of incest, but that offence must be dealt with separately since it is statutorily based. Strictly, statutory offences require no other justification than that they have been properly enacted by the accepted legislative process. Incest is dealt with at paras. 12–29 *et seq.*, below.

---

[84]   The *onus* of showing such an excuse is on the accused (s.63(7)).
[85]   s.63(4).
[86]   s.65.
[87]   Although see this chapter's "Further reading" section for academic criticism.
[88]   *R. v. H.M. Advocate*, 1988 S.L.T. 623, *per* Sheriff Macphail at p. 624C–D, approved on appeal at p. 625E–F.

General points

With the exception of incest, therefore, the following general points can **12–24** be made about shameless indecency offences. First, charges usually allege that the accused conducted himself in a shamelessly indecent manner in that he did things which themselves were indecent or obscene to the annoyance of others, or that he directed indecent or obscene things at others in the full knowledge of their nature. Secondly, it does not matter whether the accused so conducted himself in public or in private; or at least there is no rule that the conduct ceases to be criminal just because it was done in a non-public place.[89] Thirdly, the indecency or obscenity of the conduct itself or of what was directed at others is to be determined not by the accused's opinion of it, nor by the opinions of expert witnesses, but by the judge or jury alone.[90] In coming to a decision on that, such a judge or jury is to consider whether the conduct or the things directed at others were liable to deprave and corrupt those others, or the persons likely to be affected, since that is what "indecent or obscene" means in this context.[91] "Indecent or obscene", then, and for that matter the synonymous expression "indecent and obscene", convey the single idea of that which is liable to corrupt others.[92] Fourthly, it is necessary in charges of this nature to specify not only the conduct of the accused, but also facts from which the "shamelessness" of it can be inferred.[93] This serves to emphasise that "it is not the indecency of the conduct itself which makes it criminal but it is the quality of 'shamelessness'."[94] What precisely amounts to that quality seems to depend on the particular form which the offence takes, as will be seen in the paragraphs which follow. It was the view of both Lords Stott and Maxwell, however, in *Dean v. John Menzies (Holdings) Limited*[95] that "shamelessness" connotes a subjective human quality, and that where knowledge as an aspect of that quality is required to be shown on the part of the accused, it should be actual knowledge or knowledge he must have had in the circumstances.[96] "Shamelessness" probably, therefore, denotes the *mens rea* element of these offences. Fifthly, such offences are not

---

[89] *Watt v. Annan*, 1978 J.C. 84, *per* Lord Cameron at p. 89.
[90] *Ingram v. Macari*, 1983 J.C. 1.
[91] *Ingram v. Macari*, 1982 J.C. 1.
[92] 1983 J.C. 1 at p. 3.
[93] *Robertson v. Smith*, 1980 J.C. 1, *per* Lord Cameron at p. 4.
[94] *Watt v. Annan*, *supra*, *per* Lord Cameron at p. 88.
[95] 1981 J.C. 23 at pp. 36 and 38 respectively.
[96] See *Tudhope v. Barlow*, 1981 S.L.T. (Sh.Ct.) 94 at p. 99, where Sheriff Macphail acquitted the temporary manageress of a shop on the grounds that she did not know what sort of magazines were on sale there, although the sheriff had been persuaded that the magazines which were the subject of prosecution would have been liable to deprave and corrupt a significant proportion of the shop's regular customers.

precisely limited to any particular fact situations or categories — apparently as a matter of public policy.[97] The instances of shameless indecency offences which follow, therefore, are typical rather than exhaustive of the genre.

Indecent exposure

12–25   One of the leading authorities on this form of shameless indecency is *McKenzie v. Whyte*.[98] Lord Justice-Clerk Inglis explained there[99] that there were two forms of indecent exposure of the "person" (almost always meaning exposure of the penis). One of these concerned deliberate exposure to another with a view to corrupting his or her morals — an offence he described as "lewd, indecent and libidinous conduct" (see para. 9–20, above); and the other related to a more indiscriminate form, namely: "[Exposure] in a reckless and indecent way, so as to be seen by a number of people in some public place." The latter form is certainly illustrated in the more modern authorities, where "shamelessness" is invariably specified in the charge.[1] "Shamelessness" in this type of offence is probably, therefore, satisfied by intentional or reckless exposure to others, assuming them to be alarmed, annoyed or disgusted by it.[2] But clearly, conduct which is liable to deprave and corrupt others is not always involved. There are, however, considerable similarities with breach of the peace.[3]

Indecent exhibitions

12–26   It is certainly an offence of shameless indecency to exhibit an "indecent or obscene" film or videotape to others[4] or to provide "indecent or obscene" live entertainment by strip-tease artistes at a public house or hotel[5]; and it does not matter whether those watching the performance, or attending the exhibition consented to it or not.[6] "Shamelessness" is made out in such circumstances if the accused knew, or clearly must have known, the nature of what was to be seen by others, and the material was deliberately shown in order to deprave and corrupt those exposed to it, or was deliberately shown and reasonably likely to have that corrupting effect.[7]

---

[97]   See *Watt v. Annan, supra, per* Lord Cameron at p. 89.
[98]   (1867) 4 Irv. 570.
[99]   *ibid.* p. 575.
[1]   See *Niven v. Tudhope*, 1982 S.C.C.R. 365; *MacDonald v. Cardle*, 1985 S.C.C.R. 195.
[2]   *cf. Niven v. Tudhope, supra.*
[3]   See paras. 12–11 *et seq.*, above.
[4]   See *Watt v. Annan*, 1978 J.C. 84.
[5]   See *Lockhart v. Stephen*, 1987 S.C.C.R. 642, although Sheriff Stewart found the "cabaret" there not liable to deprave and corrupt an audience of adults.
[6]   See *Watt v. Annan, supra; Lockhart v. Stephen, supra.*
[7]   *Watt v. Annan, supra, per* Lord Cameron at pp. 88–89; *cf.* the Indecent Displays (Control) Act 1981, ss.1 and 5(4)(a).

Selling, etc., indecent or obscene things

There appears to be a common law offence of "publishing, vending or **12–27** circulating, or causing to be published, vended or circulated or exposing for sale any lewd, impure, gross or obscene book devised, contrived and intended to vitiate and corrupt the morals of the lieges."[8] It also appears to be still used, since that was the substance of the charge in *Robertson v. Smith*[9] which dealt with magazines, books, films and playing-cards. There, Lord Cameron concluded that although the charge referred to "shameless indecency", the complaint did not in fact include an offence of shameless indecency. Indeed, it did not specify any facts from which the "shamelessness" of the conduct could be inferred.[10] But he went on to say[11]: "I would ... be disposed to regard the offence of exposure of obscene material for sale as one which may competently be comprehended within the general category of shameless and indecent conduct according to the common law of Scotland." Since that dictum was pronounced, prosecutors have charged the selling, or exposing for sale of indecent or obscene material as either a *Henry Robinson*[12] type crime, or as a "shameless indecency" one.[13] As far as "shameless indecency" is concerned, the shamelessness here is represented by "the deliberate act of exposing for sale and selling the indecent and obscene [materials] in question in full knowledge that they were [indecent and obscene]."[14] Hiring out of such material is also within the scope of the offence but not wholesale stocking of such things, even with an eventual intention to circulate them to retail shops which might then sell them on to the public.[15] Direct contact with the public as consumers of books, magazines, films, videocassettes, and so on is thus essential, so that just "having" such materials with a view to future sale will possibly not be sufficient, unless the material represents reserve stock for replenishing items of a similar nature already exposed for sale.[16] It is not a defence that the accused took precautions to exclude children from access to the material and to attract only those adults with an interest in such wares; indeed, such precautions only serve to point-up the accused's "shamelessness" in the

---

[8]   *Henry Robinson* (1843) 1 Broun 590 and 643.
[9]   1980 J.C. 1.
[10] See para. 12–24 above at "Fourthly".
[11] *Robertson v. Smith, supra* at p. 4.
[12] (1843) 1 Broun 590.
[13] Unless a statutory provision may be used instead — see, *e.g.,* the Civic Government (Scotland) Act 1982, s.51(2).
[14] *Tudhope v. Taylor*, 1980 S.L.T. (Notes) 54 at p. 55.
[15] *Smith v. Downie*, 1982 S.L.T. (Sh.Ct.) 23; *Tudhope v. Sommerville*, 1981 J.C. 58, although itself involving a "Henry Robinson" type crime.
[16] See *Robertson v. Smith*, 1980 J.C. 1, *per* Lord Cameron at pp. 5–6.

above sense.[17] It is also not a defence that the accused was at the time running a licensed "sex shop".[18]

Sexual behaviour of an incestuous quality

12–28   In *R. v. H.M. Advocate*[19] the accused indulged in overtly sexual behaviour with his 16-year-old daughter. This did not involve sexual intercourse, and thus could not have been charged as incest.[20] Nevertheless, it was prosecuted as "shameless indecency". The accused objected to the relevancy of the indictment on the basis that it was not criminal for a father to so behave towards his daughter where she was over 16 and had not (at least for the sake of this argument) objected to his doing so. Such matters are irrelevant in incest, however, and Sheriff Macphail regarded them as irrelevant here also, since the conduct was "incestuous in quality".[21] The Appeal Court upheld Sheriff Macphail's views and arguments in sustaining the charge as relevant, and significantly added[22]:

> "we observe that he [*i.e.* the Sheriff] seems to be saying what has been said by jurists since the time of Hume, namely, that a sexual relationship between a parent and child is in the law of Scotland regarded as behaviour which is repugnant to society."

The "shamelessness" here, therefore, was represented by the incestuous quality of the accused's deliberate conduct towards his daughter. It has also been held (though not on appeal) that a man who had sexual intercourse (and who behaved in other sexually intimate ways) with his foster child, apparently with her consent and whilst she was above the age of 16, was relevantly charged with shameless indecency for doing so, notwithstanding that Parliament had not — and arguably had deliberately not — criminalised such behaviour.[23]

Incest

12–29   The crime of incest has been largely statutory since the Reformation; but references in the standard texts[24] to the Incest Act 1567 must now be

---

[17]   *ibid.* p. 5.
[18]   See the Civic Government (Scotland) Act 1982, s.45 and Sched. 2, para. 1, as amended by the Local Government etc. (Scotland) Act 1994, Sched.13, para. 129, although few such shops have been so licensed in Scotland; see also the Video Recordings Act 1984, s.12.
[19]   1988 S.L.T. 623.
[20]   See paras. 12–29 and 12–30, below.
[21]   *R. v. H.M. Advocate, supra* at p. 624K.
[22]   *ibid.* p. 625H.
[23]   *H.M. Advocate v. R.K.,* 1994 S.C.C.R. 499, opinion on relevancy of charge (3) therein by Lord MacLean. The statutory section considered in the case is now to be found in s.3 of the Criminal Law (Consolidation) (Scotland) Act 1995.
[24]   See, *e.g.,* Hume, i, 447 *et seq.*; Alison, i, 563 *et seq.*

replaced by references to the Criminal Law (Consolidation) (Scotland) Act 1995. In terms of the modern law, it is incest for a person to have sexual intercourse with a close relative of the opposite sex, where he knew of the relationship at the time.[25] It is of no moment what age the closely related sexual partner is at the time (although sexual intercourse with girls under 16 is, of course, also penalised in other ways — see para. 9–88, above). If the sexual partner consents to the intercourse, and he or she also knew of the close relationship, then both parties will be guilty.

The crime is confined to sexual intercourse, which, although not defined **12–30** in the Act, must be taken to mean penetration of the vagina by the penis. It follows then that any lesser or different form of sexual behaviour cannot be incest. It may, however, be a form of shamelessly indecent conduct.[26] The close relatives of the opposite sex with whom one is not permitted to have sexual intercourse are clearly set out in tables in the Act.[27] Most are blood relatives, but it is to be noted that half-blood relationships are included. Thus, it would be incest for a brother to have sexual intercourse with his half-sister — for example, where they were both born of the same mother but had been sired by different fathers. Legitimacy or illegitimacy is of no consequence in assessing relationships in the table. It is also to be noted that two adoptive relationships are within the ambit of the crime. It is, therefore, incest for a man to have sexual intercourse with his adoptive mother (or former adoptive mother) or with his adopted daughter (or former adopted daughter); and vice versa for a female, of course. Adoption is the process by which a person's ties with his natural parents are legally terminated. But for the purposes of incest, his relationship with his natural parents is deemed to continue.[28] It is a defence if the accused proves that he did not know of the close relationship and had no reason to suspect it, or that he did not consent to the sexual intercourse, or that he was married to the other person at the time.[29] Such a marriage would have had to have been contracted outwith Scotland, since the marriage and incest laws have been harmonised in this country, but be recognised as valid under Scots law.[30]

Rationale and related offences

The present formulation of incest is founded on a Scottish Law **12–31** Commission Report[31] which considered several reasons for maintaining it

---

[25] 1995 Act, s.1.
[26] See para. 12–28, above.
[27] 1995 Act, s.1(1), Table, paras.1 and 2.
[28] Adoption (Scotland) Act 1978, s.41(1).
[29] 1995 Act, s.1(1)(a)–(c).
[30] On which, see Anton and Beaumont, *Private International Law* (2nd ed., 1990), Chap. 16.
[31] No. 69 of 1981, Cmnd. 8422.

as a crime. These included protection and maintenance of the family unit,[32] genetic fault (in that the offspring of intercourse between persons closely related are more likely to suffer from mental or physical abnormalities than the children of non-closely related unions),[33] and moral repugnancy.[34] In modern society, however, where traditional family units are not as conspicuous as they once were, contraceptive measures are well understood and practised, techniques for the prediction and detection of foetal abnormalities are highly advanced, and abortions available widely, it is suggested that the only convincing rationale for the retention of incest in the criminal law is moral repugnancy. If that is accepted, then incest must indeed be a special form of "shamelessly indecent conduct". The crime is limited, however, in the sense that it does not extend to step-relationships, although moral repugnancy might well be thought to apply there also. If a man marries a woman who already has a daughter by a prior partner, it is not incest under the Act for him to have sexual intercourse with his wife's daughter — now his stepdaughter. For that reason, the 1995 Act contains the separate offence of "intercourse with step-child",[35] and also the crime of "intercourse of person in position of trust with a child under 16", which amongst other things covers the case of a man who lives with, rather than marries, a woman who already has a young daughter from a prior relationship.[36] These provisions, however, are complex, and must be read carefully to appreciate their full impact.[37]

"Honour-code" Offences

Introduction

12–32   The crimes, briefly dealt with below, can be classified as "honour-code" offences, meaning those where the accused was in breach of his plain duty to behave as an upright citizen of his country should. They can also, of course, be classified in other ways — for example, as "offences against the state", "offences against public welfare", or "offences against the course of justice".[38] But none of these classifications has any official status; and, in the interests of economy, the one title which appears to cover all of those selected here has been preferred.

---

[32] *ibid.* paras. 3–10 to 3–16.
[33] *ibid.* paras. 3–19 to 3–23.
[34] *ibid.* paras. 3–17 to 3–18.
[35] 1995 Act, s.2.
[36] 1995 Act, s.3.
[37] See also the cases mentioned in para. 12–28, above, on shameless indecency.
[38] See Gordon, *Criminal Law*, Pts. 6, 7 and 8.

Treason

Since the Union with England, the Scots law of treason has been replaced **12–33**
by that which pertains in England.[39] There is consequently nothing
particularly Scottish about it. Hume[40] and Gordon[41] both more than
adequately describe the law; and reference to these standard texts should
be made when details of the crime are required. It must be seldom, however,
that such details will be required. The crime of treason is of importance
only in wartime, or in time of rebellion, when the aspect of it known as
"adhering to the Queen's enemies" may assume importance. At basis, as
Hume narrates, treason "includes all such offences as are more immediately
directed against the person and government of the [Queen]; and amount to
a violation of that fidelity and allegiance which is due to [Her] Majesty
from all [her] subjects." Offences against state security in peace time are
generally not regarded as treasons, but as specific statutory offences where
the requirements of the statutes in question can be met.[42]

Sedition

Like treason, sedition is a crime of little importance in times of peace **12–34**
and stable government, and, therefore, of little importance today. Certainly,
Hume's account of the crime[43] suggests that almost any serious criticism of
the monarchy, the government or the church might be appropriate for a
charge of sedition, if "suited and intended to disturb the tranquillity of the
State — for the purpose of producing trouble or commotion, and moving
[Her] Majesty's subjects to the dislike, resistance, or subversion of the
established government and laws, or settled form and order of things."[44]
The major part of Hume's text was, however, written during the period
characterised by the French Revolution and the Napoleonic adventures in
Europe, and is clearly coloured by contemporary fears for the stability of
the British state. Further details of this crime, if required, may be found in
the standard texts.[45]

Perjury

This common law crime consists of "the judicial affirmation of falsehood **12–35**
upon oath."[46] When a witness is called upon to give evidence under oath

---

[39] See the Treason Act 1708.
[40] i, 512 *et seq.*
[41] *Criminal Law*, paras. 37–01 to 37–25.
[42] See, *e.g.*, the "Official Secrets Acts 1911 to 1989" as they are now referred to under the
    Official Secrets Act 1989, s.16(2).
[43] i, Chap. XXVII.
[44] i, 553.
[45] See, *e.g.* Gordon, *Criminal Law,* paras. 39–01 to 39–08.
[46] Hume, i, 366.

(or affirmation) in any judicial proceedings, then he promises to tell the truth, and clearly is on honour to do just that. If he gives evidence which he knows is not true, then he is in breach of the faith reposed in him and can be prosecuted for perjury if the evidence he gave was "pertinent to the point at issue".[47] The *actus reus* of the offence is thus complete when the false evidence is uttered; and the *mens rea* is satisfied if the accused can be shown to have known that that evidence was false at the time he gave it. It has been held to be perjury where the accused gave evidence that he had been with A at the relevant time, when in truth he knew he could not recall whether he had been with A or with B.[48] As far as the "pertinence" of the evidence to the proceedings in which it was given is concerned, the following statements by Alison have been approved by the High Court:

> "The falsehood must be in a matter pertinent to the issue, and competent to be asked of the witness; but if this be the case, it matters not in how trivial a matter the falsehood may consist, or how far from the original relevant matter the witness may have been led before he makes the false [statement]."[49]

It has also been held to be perjury for an accused person to give false evidence denying his guilt at his own trial.[50] There also exists the related offence of "Subornation of Perjury", which consists in the deliberate "seducing" of someone to commit perjury by, for example, promises of reward, actual bribery or threats of violence, provided that false evidence is eventually given by the "victim".[51]

Attempt to pervert or defeat or hinder the course of justice

12–36   It is thought that an "attempt to pervert the course of justice" is not a distinct common law offence, but is either a general principle used to generate a variety of related, specific offences,[52] or a convenient description for a series of innominate crimes.[53] As a principle or a description, it can take a number of different formulations, such as "attempt to defeat the course

---

[47] Hume, i, 369.

[48] *Simpson v. Tudhope*, 1988 S.L.T. 297.

[49] i, 469 at "4"; approved in *Lord Advocate's Reference (No. 1 of 1985)*, 1987 S.L.T. 187 at p. 192J.

[50] See *H.M. Advocate v. Cairns*, 1967 J.C. 37, where Cairns had been acquitted of murder on a verdict of not proven, at a trial where he himself had given evidence denying that he had stabbed the victim.

[51] See Hume, i, Chap. XII.

[52] See *Bernard Greenhuff* (1838) 2 Swin. 236, *per* Lord Cockburn at p. 274.

[53] See *H.M. Advocate v. Martin*, 1956 J.C. 1, *per* Lord Cameron at p. 3, where both views appear to have been advanced, the former ultimately being favoured.

[54] See, *e.g.*, the charge in *H.M. Advocate v. Martin, supra*.

of justice",[54] "hindering the course of justice",[55] or "hinder and frustrate the course of justice and attempt to defeat the course of justice."[56] Where a complaint or indictment of such a nature uses a form which includes the word "attempt", this is generally not to be understood as a reference to an attempt to commit the crime. "Attempt" is used in this context as a mere word of style, as must be obvious from cases of "escaping from lawful custody" where the prisoner did indeed escape,[57] and of "hiding oneself away to avoid giving evidence for the Crown" where the accused did successfully spirit himself away.[58] These are completed crimes, and not attempts in the normal sense. Indeed it is equally common in such circumstances for the word "attempt" to be dropped altogether such that the charge simply narrates the perversion of the course of justice.[59] The course of justice must, of course, have been running in order to have been perverted; but not much seems necessary to satisfy this element, since in one case it was held sufficient that police officers, having been shown an arrest warrant for a particular person, had set off to find him.[60] The *mens rea* element of these offences appears to be behaviour deliberately aimed at perverting the course of justice.[61] It is suggested that what unites cases classifiable under the heading of this paragraph is the accused's failure to obtemper his public, moral duty to allow the criminal justice system to run its appointed course, once set in motion. Witnesses should thus recognise their duty to give evidence when called upon to do so, or, at least, to make themselves available to give evidence when they suspect that that will be required of them; persons in lawful custody should seek only lawful methods of securing their liberty; witnesses should tell the truth when under oath to do so in judicial proceedings; and so on. Where a specific named crime exists, however, it is customary to charge that rather than an "attempt to defeat the course of justice", as happens plainly in the case of perjury.[62]

Giving false information to the criminal authorities

The crime of giving false information to the criminal authorities could **12–37** be seen as an example of "attempting to defeat the ends of justice". But

---

[55] See, *e.g.*, the charge in *Turnbull v. H.M. Advocate*, 1953 J.C. 59.
[56] See *H.M. Advocate v. Mannion*, 1961 J.C. 79.
[57] See, *e.g.*, *H.M. Advocate v. Martin*, *supra*.
[58] See *H.M. Advocate v. Mannion*, *supra*.
[59] See, *e.g.*, *McElhinney v. Normand*, 1996 S.L.T. 238.
[60] *McElhinney v. Normand*, *supra*, opinion of Lord Sutherland at p. 242D. The police had in fact spotted the person named in the warrant and were chasing him down the street when the accused in this case intervened by picking up the wanted man in a car and carrying him "safely" away.
[61] See, *e.g.*, *Carney v. H.M. Advocate*, 1995 S.L.T. 1208; *Johnstone v. Lees*, 1995 S.L.T. 1174.
[62] See para. 12–35, above; but *cf. Waddell v. MacPhail*, 1986 S.C.C.R. 593, where lies told to the police were dealt with under the present general principle.

since the giving of such false information usually applies to the setting in motion of an investigation rather than contributing something negative to one already in train, the tendency is to charge it as a crime of its own kind. There are two distinct aspects. The first relates to the making of a false accusation of crime against a particular, named individual, where the accusation is, of course, known by its maker to be false. This is recognised as criminal by Hume[63]; and the case of *Simpkins v. H.M. Advocate*[64] provides a modern example (although reported only on sentence). Hume[65] requires that there be special malice shown by the accused, although it is probably now sufficient that he plainly knew the story to be untrue when he uttered it. Negligence or perhaps even recklessness in assembling the facts on which such an accusation is based would probably not be enough, since there is clearly a public need not to discourage the reporting of crimes to the police or fiscal.

12–38   The second aspect relates to the giving of false information to the police (or perhaps the local prosecutors) which makes them commence an investigation. This is certainly criminal, and is sometimes referred to as "wasting police time".[66] Whilst the information must be known to be false,[67] there is no need here for any person to be named as a culprit or for any suggestion to be made that a crime has been committed at all. In *Kerr v. Hill*,[68] for example, the accused merely told the police that he had seen a collision between a bus and a cyclist, and left it entirely open as to whether a crime had been involved. As Lord Justice-General Normand put it[69]: "The point is that the criminal authorities were deliberately set in motion by a malicious person by means of an invented story. That is the essence of the crime". This plainly appears to be confirmed by the decision in *Bowers v. Tudhope*[70] where a false allegation was made to the police that a giro cheque had been lost (not stolen). Once again, it seems sufficient that the accused knew that the information was false. In practice, malice on his part does not appear to be required.[71]

Further reading

Christie, M. G. A., *Breach of the Peace* (1990).
Ewing, K., "Obscene Publications," 1982 S.L.T. (News) 55.

---

[63] i, 341–343.
[64] 1985 S.C.C.R. 30.
[65] i, 342.
[66] See, *e.g.*, Gane and Stoddart, *Casebook on Scottish Criminal Law*, p. 710.
[67] See *Walkingshaw v. Coid*, 1988 S.C.C.R. 454 (Sh.Ct.).
[68] 1936 J.C. 71.
[69] *ibid.* p. 75.
[70] 1987 J.C. 26.
[71] See, *e.g.*, *Gray v. Morrison*, 1954 J.C. 31.

Ferguson, P. W., "Perjury and Material Lies," 1986 S.L.T. (News) 312.

Forensis, "Wasting the Time of the Police — Is It a Crime?" (1987) 32 J.L.S. 353.

Gordon, G. H., "Crimes Without Laws," 1966 J.R. 214.

Gordon, G. H., "Shameless Indecency and Obscenity" (1980) 25 J.L.S. 262.

Maher, G., "The Enforcement of Morals Continued," 1978 S.L.T. (News) 281.

Scottish Law Commission, *Mobbing and Rioting* (Consultative Memorandum No. 60, 1984).

CHAPTER 13

STATUTORY OFFENCES

Introduction

13–01   The major part of this book has been concerned with non-statutory offences, since Scotland still places considerable reliance upon the common law to generate and define its criminal law. Whether this is a defensible position to adopt in the late twentieth century will be considered in Chapter 14. But it is not possible, even in this country, to ignore or underestimate the considerable importance and impact of statutory crimes. Much of the time of the criminal courts is taken up, for example, in dealing with a wide range of particular offences set out in the Road Traffic Act 1988 and in the Misuse of Drugs Act 1971. It can hardly be expected, of course, that an introductory text on criminal law would deal in detail with all of the crimes to be found within those two Acts, let alone the many offences set out in literally hundreds of statutes currently in force. Indeed, adequate consideration of road traffic and of drugs offences would require the construction of individual volumes of some length devoted entirely to those subjects. In any event, such volumes already exist — see the "Further reading" at the end of this chapter. It must also be borne in mind that there has never been a period since its inception when Parliament has not been active in the promulgation of new crimes. The range of statutory offences is, therefore, likely to increase rapidly in relation to issues and matters which can hardly at this time be imagined. As far as the Scottish courts are concerned, Parliament may do as it pleases. If a new offence has been created in an enactment which has passed both Houses and received the Royal Assent, then it is formally valid and cannot be questioned on the basis that it is otherwise unconstitutional.[1]

INTERPRETATION I

13–02 Although a statutory crime cannot, then, be struck down on the basis of its unconstitutionality (unlike, say, the position in the United States), the

---

[1]   See *Sillars v. Smith*, 1982 S.L.T. 539.

criminal courts may still make a substantial contribution to the way in which that crime is received. This is achieved by the device of interpretation. A court has a duty to interpret the bare words used by Parliament. In theory, anyone with a reasonable command of English should be able to understand the import of any statutory crime. It will after all have been laid out in a particular section of the statute in question in plain English words. But initial appearances can be deceptive. A particular word may be found to have no plain, simple significance at all. Again, the plain meaning of a particular word may not have been intended. If that was not intended, then one would expect Parliament to have made that clear; and generally it does, by allocating a particular meaning in an "Interpretation section" — which may be far removed from the very section which contains the word in focus. In section 28(1) of the Road Traffic Act 1988 (as substituted by the Road Traffic Act 1991, section 7), for example, it is stated: "A person who rides a cycle on a road dangerously is guilty of an offence." Relative to that, Parliament has seen fit to give particular meanings to "dangerously" (in section 28(2) and (3)), and to "cycle" and "road" (both defined in section 192(1) of the Road Traffic Act 1988, as amended by the Road Traffic Act 1991, Schedule 4, para. 78(2)). It will be noted that with respect to "road", the inquirer is directed to a completely different Act — namely, the Roads (Scotland) Act 1984 — for part of the desired definition. Such definitions, however, may themselves require more particular interpretation when they are considered in relation to an actual case.[2] Where given definitions require more particular interpretation, or where statutory words have not been defined at all, it is judges in courts, in actual criminal cases before them, who must so interpret or assign meanings. When they do so, their decisions may be considered authoritative,[3] in which event the interpretations and assigned meanings become part of the statutory law itself. In relation to statutory road traffic offences, for example, what it means to "drive" a mechanically propelled vehicle is often crucial; but the Road Traffic Acts have never defined "driving" at all. The courts have, therefore, had to decide the meaning of that word, and its correlatives.[4] Clearly these interpretations and meanings do not appear in the bare text of the statutory crime. They will have to be searched for by the inquirer, using, for example, the *Current Law Statute and Legislation Citator* volumes.[5]

---

[2] See *Beattie (John M.) v. Scott*, 1990 S.C.C.R. 435, and *Young v. Carmichael*, 1991 S.C.C.R. 332, in relation to the definition of "road" under the Roads (Scotland) Act 1984. See also *Dick v. Walkingshaw*, 1995 S.L.T. 1254 (as to whether and in what circumstances the deck of a ferry can be considered as a "road").

[3] See para. 2–10, above.

[4] See *Ames v. MacLeod*, 1969 J.C. 1; *McArthur v. Valentine*, 1990 S.L.T. 732; *Guthrie v. Friel*, 1993 S.L.T. 899 (attempt to drive), and para. 13–03 below.

[5] Covering 1948 to 1988, with subsequent years in individual volumes — see the prefaces to each volume for full instructions on use.

Decisions by English courts

13–03   When the precise meaning of a particular word or phrase in a statutory crime is an issue in criminal proceedings, a court will look for interpretation sections within the Act itself, and also for interpretations laid down in authoritative decisions in the past. It is to be noted here that decisions by English criminal courts, no matter how eminent, are never more than "persuasive" in Scotland[6]; they are never required to be followed in this country, where judges may take an entirely different view. This certainly does happen — however regrettable it may be in relation to statutory offences which Parliament intended to be applied uniformly on both sides of the border. In many offences under the Road Traffic Act 1988, for example, that the accused was "driving" a motor vehicle at the time is of some importance. But, where a person is standing outside a broken-down car, pushing it along a road by muscle power and making occasional adjustments to its direction by reaching for the steering-wheel, he is definitely "driving" that car under Scots law[7] but probably would not be doing so in England.[8] Again, in *Kelly v. MacKinnon*[9] Lord Justice-General Emslie refused to entertain the view of the Lord Chief Justice of England in *Cafferata v. Wilson*[10] that, for the purposes of section 57(1)(b) of the Firearms Act 1968, a starting-pistol or similar "gun" was a component part of a lethal weapon and thus a "firearm" since it could, by boring out the barrel and carrying out certain other operations, be made capable of firing live ammunition; and indeed the Lord Justice-General described the views expressed in the English case as "manifestly absurd" and "not only unsound but patently unsound".[11]

Repealed versions of the same crime

13–04   In *Kiely v. Lunn*[12] a boy of 15 had had many absences from school. Consequently his father was charged with the offence under section 35(1)

---

[6]   They may, of course, be regarded as "highly persuasive", usually meaning that they are well worth following — see, *e.g.*, *Davies v. Smith*, 1983 S.L.T. 644 (which adopts the reasoning given in *Federal Steam Navigation Company Ltd v. Department of Trade and Industry* [1974] 1 W.L.R. 505).

[7]   *Ames v. MacLeod*, 1969 J.C. 1; *McArthur v. Valentine*, 1990 S.L.T. 732.

[8]   *R. v. MacDonagh* [1974] Q.B. 448.

[9]   1982 J.C. 94 at pp. 98 and 99.

[10]   [1936] 3 All E.R. 149.

[11]   In one case it was said: "The result may be that different constructions are placed upon the Act of 1988 [Road Traffic Act] in Scotland and in England but this is the result of different police procedures in the two countries": *Simpson v. McClory*, 1993 J.C. 110, *per* Lord Justice-Clerk Ross at p. 119D.

[12]   1983 J.C. 4.

of the Education (Scotland) Act 1980,[13] namely: "Where a child of school age ... fails without reasonable excuse to attend regularly at ... school, his parent shall be guilty of an offence." The reason for the boy's protracted absence was that he was chronically addicted to glue sniffing, and showed no willingness to accept help in breaking the habit. In terms of section 42(1)(b) of the same Act, there would be deemed to be a reasonable excuse if "the child had been prevented by sickness from attending school." The question which arose for decision was, therefore, whether a self-inflicted and self-perpetuated disability could be construed as "sickness". Since no interpretation was offered by the Act itself, and no previous cases could be found to shed light on the matter, the Appeal Court looked at previous versions of the same crime. In particular, they looked at the Education (Scotland) Act 1883, and at section 11, which held out as a reasonable excuse: that "the child had been prevented from attending school by sickness or any other unavoidable cause." Although the last five words had been dropped from section 42(1)(b) of the 1980 Act, the Appeal Court took the view that these words still provided an excellent guide as to how "sickness" was to be interpreted, namely that it meant "an unavoidable cause of absence, at least in the sense that it cannot be construed to include a state of ill health brought about by the deliberate actings of the child concerned."[14] The conclusion is, then, that it is legitimate to use the original wording of repealed but re-enacted statutory crimes as an aid to the construction of the latest re-enacted form, provided, of course, that it was not Parliament's clear intention to alter the substance of the original crime.

Use of dictionaries

Where all else fails, and the meaning to be assigned to a particular word **13–05** in a statutory offence is crucial to the determination of a case, the courts will often turn to dictionary definitions. Where several meanings are proffered by a dictionary, the court will generally adopt the one that best accords with the word in its statutory context. In *Patchett v. MacDougall*,[15] for example, the accused had shot a collie dog in the head and killed it. There was no evidence that it had survived the shooting for any significant length of time, or at all. Nevertheless, the accused was charged with causing "unnecessary suffering to [the] animal" by wanton or unreasonable conduct, in terms of section 1(1)(a) of the Protection of Animals (Scotland) Act 1912. As he had shot the dog deliberately and without reason, his guilt or innocence plainly depended upon whether he had caused it to "suffer" or not. To determine this issue, Lord Justice-Clerk Wheatley examined the definition

---

[13] c.44, but given erroneously as c.20 in the report.
[14] 1983 J.C. 4 at p. 7.
[15] 1983 J.C. 63.

of "suffering" as given in the *Shorter Oxford English Dictionary* (a favoured work amongst the judiciary, presumably because of its convenient, two-volume size). He chose the second of the meanings offered there, namely "the bearing or undergoing of pain", and concluded that there was no evidence that the unfortunate animal had undergone any such thing. The accused, therefore, had his conviction quashed, the Lord Justice-Clerk dismissing the argument that the dog had suffered by losing its life as metaphysical, and not what the Act envisaged at all.[16]

13–06   Similarly, in *White v. Allan*[17] a woman was convicted of the offence specified in section 46(1) of the Civic Government (Scotland) Act 1982, which states that: "A prostitute (whether male or female) who for the purposes of prostitution ... (c) importunes any person who is in a public place, shall be guilty [of an offence]." She was charged, then, as a person possessing a certain qualification, *i.e.* that she was a prostitute. She challenged the applicability of that special capacity to her.[18] It thus became necessary for the Crown to demonstrate that she had possessed that qualification at the time of the alleged importuning. The main thrust of the argument was that this offence had originally been enacted in 1892[19] and was then committed only if the accused was a "common prostitute". Since Parliament had changed the wording of the offence in 1982 by dropping the adjective "common", this was claimed to have opened the way for a different interpretation, namely that if a person, such as the accused, behaved on the occasion in question as a prostitute might (as indeed the accused had), then she fell within the qualification and thus within the ambit of the offence. The Appeal Court, however, rejected that contention. It considered that the elision of the word "common" in the re-enacted offence made no difference, and that the standard meaning of "prostitute" in the *Concise Oxford Dictionary* ("a woman who offers her body to promiscuous sexual intercourse, especially for payment") still applied. Further, the court interpreted the statutory offence such that the accused had to possess the title of "prostitute", with that dictionary meaning, prior to the incidents which had led to the prosecution. Since the Crown had been quite unable to show that, then the conviction had to be quashed.[20]

---

[16]   *ibid.* p. 64.
[17]   1985 S.C.C.R. 85.
[18]   See now the Criminal Procedure (Scotland) Act 1995, s.255.
[19]   Burgh Police (Scotland) Act, s.381(22).
[20]   Where the meaning of legislation is ambiguous or obscure, it may be possible to use material from Hansard, or other reports of Parliamentary debates to assist in interpretation: *Pepper v. Hart* [1993] A.C. 593 (H.L.).

Common law alternatives

If by way of interpretation (or otherwise) it is decided that the statutory **13–07** offence charged cannot be established on the facts admitted or proved, all is not necessarily lost for the Crown. In terms of paragraph 14(b) of Schedule 3 to the Criminal Procedure (Scotland) Act 1995, "where the facts proved under the indictment or complaint do not amount to a contravention of the enactments but do amount to an offence at common law, it shall be lawful to convict of the common law offence." This rather useful provision was taken advantage of by the sheriff in *Buchanan v. Hamilton*[21] where he decided that vandalism had not been proved but that breach of the peace had. Although his decision to convict of the common law crime was overturned on appeal, this was simply on the basis that it was not for the sheriff to do so on his own, in the absence of a specific submission to invoke the provision from the Crown. The Appeal Court did not decide that it was incompetent to convict of breach of the peace in such circumstances.[22]

INTERPRETATION II

There is also a wider dimension to a court's interpretative powers. This **13–08** relates to a court's ability to decide whether *mens rea* will have to be proved, or facts from which it can be inferred will have to be established, by the Crown in relation to a particular statutory crime. It is usually taken that *mens rea* must be proved, or facts from which it can be inferred must be established in relation to all common law crimes as a matter of principle[23] but it is accepted in modern criminal law that some statutory offences do not, and need not, conform to that principle. These form the class of "strict liability" crimes within the general field of statutory offences. These "strict" offences and the courts' role in identifying them are considered in the paragraphs which follow. Also briefly considered below is the subject of "vicarious liability". This sort of liability — where one person is deemed liable for the criminal act or omission of another — is again thought to be peculiar to statutory offences. It is peculiar to those Acts of Parliament which expressly allow it, or to those where the courts, by dint of interpretation, deem it to apply. Careful note must be taken, however, that in the totality of statutory offences, strict liability or vicarious liability is unusual, and certainly does not represent the norm.

---

[21] 1990 S.L.T. 244.
[22] See, *e.g.*, *Horsburgh v. Russell*, 1994 S.L.T. 942, for conviction of breach of the peace on statutory charges of dangerous or careless driving.
[23] See, *e.g.*, Gordon, *Criminal Law*, para. 7–12.

How strict liability arises

13–09   Offences created by Parliament have precisely worded definitions. Every word which appears in a statutory crime must, therefore, be taken to be meaningful. Equally, it can be argued that what does not appear is also meaningful (see para. 13–10, below). As far as *mens rea* is concerned, many statutory offences expressly refer to some form of that concept. Thus, in the Criminal Law (Consolidation) (Scotland) Act 1995, it is stated in section 48(2)(a) that: "Any person ... who intentionally obstructs a constable in the exercise of the constable's powers under subsection (1) [*i.e.* powers to search suspects for offensive weapons] ... shall be guilty of an offence". There, the central element of the *actus reus* of the offence is "obstruction", and clearly it will have to be shown by the Crown that the obstruction was "intentional" on the accused's part. A similar conclusion follows from the way in which the statutory offence of vandalism has been defined.[24] The central element of that crime relates to the destruction or damaging of property, and it is expressly stated that that must be shown to have been wilful or reckless on the part of the accused. The Misuse of Drugs Act 1971 also contains a further instance of the same idea. Section 8, for example, indicates that: "A person commits an offence if, being the occupier or concerned in the management of any premises, he knowingly permits or suffers any of the following activities to take place on those premises". It will not be sufficient if any of the forbidden activities (which include producing a controlled drug or smoking cannabis) happens to take place on the premises concerned. To be convicted, an accused person must be shown to have known that they were taking place, and allowed them to do so in that state of knowledge.

13–10   Relative to crucial (or central) elements of the offences in question, the express use of words such as "intentionally", "recklessly", "wilfully", or "knowingly" demonstrates that these statutory crimes are to be treated similarly to common law ones — namely, that the specified form of *mens rea* must be proved by the Crown. If it cannot be proved, or if facts from which it might be inferred[25] cannot be established, then the prosecution's case will founder. But what is to be made of offences where Parliament has not made specific provision for any *mens rea* concepts? In section 47(1) of the Criminal Law (Consolidation) (Scotland) Act 1995, for example, it is laid down that: "Any person who without lawful authority or reasonable

---

[24] See para. 11–26, above.
[25] See, *e.g.*, *Lees v. Haig*, 1993 S.L.T. (Sh.Ct.) 76, where the inference was drawn that a concealed, rusty meat cleaver was intended by the accused for use by him for causing personal injury (relative to what is now s.47(4) of the Criminal Law (Consolidation) (Scotland) Act 1995).

excuse, the proof whereof shall lie on him, has with him in any public place any offensive weapon shall be guilty of an offence". Quite apart from the difficulties of construing "public place"[26] and "offensive weapon"[27] it would seem that conviction could follow on mere proof that the accused had an offensive weapon about his person, whether he knew it was there or not. That would appear to be a fair reading of the subsection, taking the words used in a completely literal sense; but whether it would be a fair interpretation in relation to an accused person, who had had an offensive weapon slipped surreptitiously into his coat pocket by another, is a different matter; and that is where the difficulty lies. It certainly can be argued that if Parliament had wanted the courts to insist on *mens rea* being shown, then it would have made appropriate provision. It may, therefore, be meaningful that Parliament has chosen here to exclude any reference to intention, recklessness, knowledge or the like; and so the conclusion may well follow that *mens rea* is not required to be shown by the Crown. Thus, on this argument, if an offensive weapon had really been slipped into the accused's pocket without his having been aware of it, then he would still have "had it with him" as a matter of fact, and must be convicted — his lack of knowledge being an irrelevant consideration, since knowledge did not have to be shown. This is clearly a harsh, but tenable, interpretative argument. On the other hand, if there is some principle at work, even in statutory crimes, that *mens rea* is to be presumed to be part of the definition of all offences, then *mens rea* ought to be required even in the case of statutory offences which are silent on the matter. Were the courts to adopt that principle, then all statutory crimes would require some form of *mens rea*, unless Parliament had made it abundantly clear that that was exceptionally not to be so in relation to a particular offence. The question faced by courts which do espouse that view is, of course: "What form of *mens rea* is to be required in the absence of Parliament's having given any plain directions?"[28]

Presumption in favour of *mens rea*

It seems well established in England that there is a presumption in favour **13–11** of *mens rea* being required even in the kind of statutory offences where the text is silent as to intention, recklessness, knowledge, wilfulness or the like.[29] That presumption yields, however, where a court is satisfied that

---

[26] See 1995 Act, s.47(4) and, *e.g., Normand v. Donnelly,* 1994 S.L.T. 62.
[27] See again s.47(4), and, *e.g., McGlennan v. Clark,* 1993 S.L.T. 1069; *McKee v. MacDonald,* 1995 S.L.T. 1342; and *Lees v. Haig,* 1993 S.L.T. (Sh.Ct.) 76.
[28] For the answer given by English courts in relation to what is now s.47(1) of the Criminal Law (Consolidation) (Scotland) Act 1995 Act, see *R. v. Cugullere* [1961] 1 W.L.R. 858, *per* Salmon J. at p. 860.
[29] See *Sweet v. Parsley* [1970] A.C. 132, *per* Lord Reid at p.148G–H; *Gammon (Hong Kong) Ltd v. Att.-Gen. for Hong Kong* [1985] A.C. 1, *per* Lord Scarman at p. 14B.

Parliament really did not wish *mens rea* to be considered. Since Parliament probably never makes that plain, the courts must look for signs and hints within, or even outwith, the Act itself in order to deduce Parliament's intention. As can be imagined, this is a somewhat arbitrary process. But it does result in some such statutory offences being considered as of *mens rea* quality[30] and others acquiring "strict liability" status,[31] where "strict liability" means that no *mens rea* need be proved or inferred in respect of an issue crucial for conviction.

13–12   In Scotland, it is uncertain whether or not that presumption in favour of *mens rea* is accepted. Gordon[32] hints that it is but his authorities are mostly English. Nevertheless, some minimal acceptance may be detected in the opinions of Lord Justice-General Normand and Lords Wark, Moncrieff and Mackay in *Mitchell v. Morrison*.[33] Lord Cameron, in *Swan v. MacNab*,[34] was also moved to consider it as "a general proposition". The view usually taken in this country, however, is that the problem of *mens rea* or no *mens rea* is resolved by the application of straightforward, common-sense interpretation, rather than by the application of any presumptions, signs and hints. But in both countries it must be emphasised that the threshold for the identification of "strict liability" is the existence of a statutory offence which omits any of the usual references to *mens rea*, at least in relation to the central element of the crime.[35] Without such references such a statutory offence may be received by the courts as "strict"; but this need not be the inevitable conclusion at which the courts arrive.[36] Certain criteria, however, may sometimes be invoked to assist with the interpretation of such troublesome statutory crimes, and these criteria are considered at paragraphs 13–14 *et seq.*, below.

Strict or absolute liability

13–13   Two terms of art have been employed to denote criminal liability which does not depend upon proof of *mens rea*. "Absolute liability" is the older, and now less fashionable of the two. It was certainly used extensively in Scotland during the first half of the twentieth century[37] and is indeed not

---

[30] *ibid.*

[31] See, *e.g.*, *Strowger v. John* [1974] R.T.R. 124.

[32] *Criminal Law*, paras. 8–01 and 8–02, n. 9.

[33] 1938 J.C. 64 at pp. 71, 87, 72–73 and 81–82, respectively.

[34] 1977 J.C. 57 at p. 61.

[35] See *Wings Ltd v. Ellis* [1985] A.C. 272, in relation to the Trade Descriptions Act 1968, s.14(1)(a).

[36] See, *e.g.*, *R. v. Cugullere* [1961] 1 W.L.R. 858.

[37] See, *e.g.*, *Gordon v. Shaw* (1908) 5 Adam 469, where Lord McLaren refers to "absolute prohibition" at p. 478; *Howman v. Russell*, 1923 J.C. 32, *per* Lord Cullen at p. 36; *Mitchell v. Morrison*, 1938 J.C. 64, *per* Lord Justice-General Normand at p. 71.

yet dead.[38] With its connotation of criminal liability not only without proof of *mens rea* but also without benefit of any form of defence, the term is probably much too sweeping, and is best reserved perhaps for those peculiar, "states of affairs" statutory offences which are sometimes encountered.[39] Better, probably, is the term "strict liability". It means criminal liability where the central element of the *actus reus* of the offence does not require proof of *mens rea* on the part of the accused, but does not exclude the possibility of there being some form of defence or indeed the possibility of some form of *mens rea* being required in relation to subsidiary elements. It sounds fairer, in other words, to assert that liability is "strict" rather than "absolute", and indeed may more accurately reflect the true situation. In *Alphacell Limited v. Woodward*,[40] for example, Viscount Dilhorne pointed out that the statutory offence of "causing" polluting matter to enter a stream was not absolute. If it had been absolute, then mere accidental pollution of a stream might result in conviction, which he did not think to have been Parliament's intention at all. Rather, if the accused had been intentionally carrying on some industrial process, in such a way that the natural consequence would have been the pollution of a stream, and such pollution had in fact occurred, then he could be convicted — even though he had neither intended nor known about such pollution at all.[41] *Alphacell Limited v. Woodward* is, of course, an English case, but was specifically approved in *Lockhart v. National Coal Board*.[42]

Criteria for identifying strict liability

It is rare for Scottish courts to discuss, let alone follow, specific criteria **13–14** for the identification of strict liability, statutory offences. The tendency in fact is to follow English precedents, if such exist[43] or to treat such problems of identification as meriting little more than the application of well-known interpretative techniques in a common-sense way.[44] There is the usual tendency also to treat each statute as a separate entity and to avoid laying down rules which might be generally applicable to other statutory offences. It would seem, therefore, fairly academic to attempt to consider what sort of criteria might carry weight with a Scottish court. But certain trends are discernible; and failure to consider these would make it impossible to predict how new or untested statutory offences, which made no express reference to *mens rea*, were to be received. In any event, the sort of criteria to be

---

[38] See, *e.g., MacNeill v. Wilson*, 1981 J.C. 87 at p. 91.
[39] See para. 3–14, above, and *Strowger v. John* [1974] R.T.R. 124.
[40] [1972] A.C. 824.
[41] *ibid.* pp. 839F, 839H–840C.
[42] 1981 S.L.T. 161.
[43] See, *e.g., Lockhart v. National Coal Board, supra.*
[44] See, *e.g., Smith of Maddiston Ltd v. MacNab*, 1975 J.C. 48, where nine judges sat.

borne in mind were hinted at by Lord McLaren in the early twentieth century case of *Gordon v. Shaw*.[45]

Gordon v. Shaw

13–15   In this case, the Sea Fisheries Regulation (Scotland) Act 1895,[46] by virtue of section 10(4) and associated byelaws,[47] made it an offence for any person to use certain trawl-fishing methods in the Moray Firth (*i.e.* within a line drawn between Duncansby Head in Caithness and Rattray Point near Peterhead). The accused was not the master of the vessel concerned, but an ordinary member of the crew. The court was prepared to accept that he might have been quite unaware of the exact location of the boat when the prohibited fishing took place; and the question lay whether his lack of such knowledge would be of any moment, given the non-*mens rea* wording of the offence. In deciding that it would not, and that the accused should be convicted, Lord McLaren mentioned four possible criteria which might be used to decide if such statutory offences were "absolute". These consist of the "policy of the statute", its "language", whether or not a requirement for *mens rea* might make it "very difficult to get a conviction against anyone", and "the duty of those who engage in the fishing industry to inform themselves, and to take care that they do not fish where they are not entitled to fish."[48] They are considered further in the paragraphs which follow.

Policy of the statute

13–16   This criterion involves a court deciding that the aim which a particular statutory offence sets out to achieve is of such importance that it ought to prevail over the maxim *actus non facit reum nisi mens sit rea*.[49] In other words, some statutory offences promote such things as the safety of the public[50] or the protection of the environment, and the securing of these aims may be considered to justify conviction without proof of *mens rea*. That this sort of thinking may figure in the deliberations of Scottish judges can be seen by considering such cases as *Mitchell v. Morrison*,[51] where Lord Justice-General Normand referred to the "safety of the public" in the context of the statutory requirement to maintain records of truck-drivers' hours; *Anderson v. Rose*,[52] where the prohibition against selling a heifer in

---

[45] (1908) 5 Adam 469.
[46] Now repealed by the Inshore Fishing (Scotland) Act 1984, s.10, Sched. 2.
[47] See paras. 2–14 *et seq.*, above.
[48] *Gordon v. Shaw* (1908) 5 Adam 469 at pp. 477–478.
[49] See para. 3–01, above, for translation.
[50] See, *e.g. Gammon (Hong Kong) Ltd v. Att.-Gen. for Hong Kong* [1985] A.C. 1.
[51] 1938 J.C. 64 at p. 71.
[52] 1919 J.C. 20.

calf for slaughter was clearly designed as a wartime measure to protect scarce food resources (as was hinted at by Lord Justice-Clerk Scott Dickson)[53]; *MacNeill v. Wilson*,[54] where the prohibition against having an insecure load on a truck was obviously designed to prevent danger to the public; and *Lockhart v. National Coal Board*,[55] where the protection of water supplies from pollution could be said to have taken precedence over the coal board's understandable claim to have done all that could reasonably have been expected of it in the circumstances.

Language used

Although it is unwise to rely too strongly on this, because of the very **13–17** varied nature of expression found in statutory offences, some words do appear to carry a similar significance relative to criminal liability, irrespective of the statute in which they appear. Thus, where liability depends on "possession" of some article, it is usual to regard the offence as requiring *mens rea* in the form of knowledge, whether the statute specifically mentions knowledge or not. One cannot "possess" what one does not know one has; and further, as Lord Justice-Clerk Ross" said in *Gill v. Lockhart*[56]: "Before there can be possession in terms of the Act [*i.e.* the Misuse of Drugs Act 1971, section 5(2)], it is well established that there must be, on the part of an accused, both knowledge and control."[57] The word "use", however, seems to be given a "strict" interpretation. Thus, where it was criminal to "use" on a road a motor vehicle which did not comply with prescribed regulations, it was not necessary to show that the user knew that his vehicle did not so comply at the relevant time.[58] On the other hand, where a statute forbids someone to "cause or permit" the "use" of something whilst it does not comply with prescribed regulations, both "causing" and "permitting" appear to require knowledge on the part of the accused that the thing was being so used in contravention of those regulations.[59] The "knowledge" need not be actual, however, where the court is satisfied that the accused deliberately avoided informing himself of the obvious.[60] But, where a statute forbade "causing or knowingly permitting" the entry of pollutants into a stream, the "causing" alternative was considered to be "strict".[61] In that case, however,

---

[53] *ibid.* p. 22.
[54] 1981 J.C. 87.
[55] 1981 S.L.T. 161.
[56] 1988 S.L.T. 189 at p. 190G.
[57] See also *Black v. H.M. Advocate*, 1974 J.C. 43.
[58] See *Swan v. MacNab*, 1977 J.C. 57, *per* Lord Cameron at p. 63.
[59] See *Smith of Maddiston Ltd v. MacNab*, 1975 J.C. 48. *Cf. MacDonald v. Howdle*, 1995 S.L.T. 779.
[60] *Brown v. W. Burns Tractors Ltd*, 1986 S.C.C.R. 146.
[61] *Lockhart v. National Coal Board*, 1981 S.L.T. 161.

English authority existed, which was accepted by both counsel and eventually the Appeal Court as being correct. Presumably also, the deliberate attachment of "knowingly" to the "permitting" was seen as significant. With reservations, then, it would seem worthwhile to argue by way of analogy that the interpretation given to a particular word in one statute ought to be decisive of its meaning in another.

Prosecution difficulties

13–18   That the insistence upon proof of *mens rea* would lead to the ineffectiveness of an offence is occasionally voiced as a reason for holding that offence to be of strict liability. The argument is that such insistence would make things just too difficult for the Crown, and that that would be disastrous given the aim which the statute seeks to achieve. Under the Road Traffic Regulation Act 1984, section 89(1), for example, "A person who drives a motor vehicle on a road at a speed exceeding a limit imposed by any enactment ... shall be guilty of an offence." Clearly, if the prosecution were required to prove that a motorist knew he was exceeding a particular speed limit (the central element of the offence), there would be very few convictions and the purpose of the provision (presumably connected with road safety) would be substantially undermined. Similar thinking probably lies behind the view that offences of possessing or supplying controlled drugs do not require the Crown to show that the accused knew that some package or other actually contained controlled drugs. It is enough if an accused person can be shown to have had the knowledge necessary to establish his possession of the package — which happens to contain such drugs.[62] If he claims that he did not know what the contents of the package were, that is a matter for him to establish by way of defence.[63] "Prosecution difficulty" seems, however, to be a somewhat specious way of arguing for the imposition of strict liability. No doubt the Crown can experience similar difficulty in relation to the proof of some common law crimes; but few would suggest that those common law crimes should accordingly be treated as "strict".

Trade regulation

13–19   It is often argued too that statutory offences which bear no express reference to *mens rea* and which are basically designed to impose standards for the carrying on of particular trades or activities should be prime candidates for strict liability. This is particularly so, apparently, where the

---

[62]   See *Tudhope v. McKee*, 1988 S.L.T. 153, in relation to the Misuse of Drugs Act 1971, s.4(3)(b).
[63]   See 1971 Act, s.28.

offence can be regarded as dealing with acts which "are not criminal in any real sense, but are acts which in the public interest are prohibited under a penalty."[64] Such *mala prohibita*,[65] it might be argued, are the price which has to be paid for participating in that trade or activity. Those who do so must simply observe strictly the standards imposed. If they fail to do so, even unknowingly, then they should be convicted.[66] Much the same might be said of motorists, of course, in relation to many offences found in the Road Traffic Act 1988.[67]

Criteria in general

It would be wrong to imagine that the various criteria mentioned above **13–20** form an exhaustive list or are applied on any consistent basis. It is also far from clear whether Scottish courts apply them at all.[68] Of far greater importance, probably, is the court's "feeling" for the particular offence in question; if it seems trivial, from the point of view of its maximum penalty,[69] and regulatory, as measured from the point of view of its content, it will probably be taken as "strict". Otherwise, it is much more difficult to predict how a court will react. It may be safest to conclude that the only strict liability offences are those which have already been recognised as such by a competent court in Scotland. Although that gives little insight into the likely treatment by the courts of new statutory offences, it should be borne in mind that most genuinely new offences, as opposed to re-enacted former ones,[70] do specify some form of *mens rea*.[71]

Defences to "strict" offences

If a particular statutory offence has been recognised as "strict", this does **13–21** not preclude the possibility of a defence. This is obviously so in relation to

---

[64] See Wright J. in *Sherras v. De Rutzen* [1895] 1 Q.B. 918 at p. 922, quoted by Viscount Dilhorne in *Alphacell Ltd v. Woodward* [1972] A.C. 824 at p. 839G, and by Lord Scarman in *Wings Ltd v. Ellis* [1985] 1 A.C. 272 at pp. 293D–294E–F.

[65] See, *e.g.*, *Beattie v. Waugh*, 1920 J.C. 64, and the opinion of Lord Justice-Clerk Scott Dickson at p. 69 that the offence there was "a clear case of *malum prohibitum*"; see also para. 2–41, above.

[66] See, *e.g.*, *Dickson v. Linton* (1888) 2 White 51; *Gordon v. Shaw* (1908) 5 Adam 469, *per* Lord McLaren at p. 478.

[67] See, *e.g.*, *Howman v. Russell*, 1923 J.C. 32 — the present law pertaining to the situation in that case now being found in the Road Traffic Act 1988, s.42 as substituted by the Road Traffic Act 1991, s.8, and S.I. 1989 No. 1796, reg. 24(1)(a).

[68] *cf.* the approach of English courts, as in *R. v. Bradish* [1990] 1 Q.B. 981.

[69] Although the matter of maximum punishment is very far from being decisive, in England, at least — see *Gammon (Hong Kong) Ltd v. Att.-Gen. of Hong Kong* [1985] A.C. 1, *per* Lord Scarman at p. 17F.

[70] See, *e.g.*, the Food Safety Act 1990.

[71] See, *e.g.*, the Computer Misuse Act 1990, ss.1, 2 and 3.

statutes which themselves cater for such defences. In the Food Safety Act 1990, for example, section 8(1) narrates that "any person who sells for human consumption ... any food which fails to comply with food safety requirements ... shall be guilty of an offence." There is nothing to suggest that this would not be considered as a crime of strict liability.[72] But the Act provides specific defences to that crime. In section 21, for example, it is stated that it shall "be a defence for the person charged to prove that he took all reasonable precautions and exercised all due diligence to avoid the commission of the offence by himself or by a person under his control." It will be noted, however, that the burden of establishing such due diligence on the balance of probabilities lies on the accused himself.

13–22 Where no specific defences are provided by an Act to a strict liability offence, it was at one time thought that there might nevertheless be a defence of "excusable ignorance" in relation to matters central to that offence. In particular, a defence of that nature seemed to be recognised by Lord McLaren in *Gordon v. Shaw*[73] when he said: "where a person in the position of the respondent comes forward, and is able to satisfy the Sheriff that he was excusably ignorant of the position of the fishing vessel ... his case will always receive indulgent consideration." Lord Kinnear, however, reserved his opinion on the correctness of that view,[74] which was in turn doubted by Lord Justice-Clerk Scott Dickson in *Beattie v. Waugh*,[75] and ignored in *Howman v. Russell*.[76] On balance, it probably must be accepted that there is no such general defence to strict liability offences in this country; and that the concept of "excusable ignorance" can be given effect to, if at all, only as an aspect of prosecutorial discretion before commencement of proceedings,[77] or in mitigation of sentence following conviction.

Vicarious liability

13–23 In the criminal law, vicarious liability means the responsibility which A might be considered to have for the criminal conduct of B in the absence of any question of complicity (see Chapter 7, above). This is bound to be unusual, since it involves imposing punishment on A where the *actus reus* of the crime in question was not committed by him and where he personally had no *mens rea*. For it to arise at all, therefore, there requires to be some relationship between A and B. In terms of the case law, that relationship is usually that of employer (A) and employee (B), or principal (A) and agent (B); but other relationships could be involved, if these were expressly catered

---

[72] See, *e.g., Dickson v. Linton, supra, per* Lord McLaren at p. 58.
[73] (1908) 5 Adam 469 at p. 479.
[74] *ibid.* p. 481.
[75] 1920 J.C. 64 at p. 68; *cf.* Lord Salvesen (diss.) at p. 69.
[76] 1923 J.C. 32.
[77] *Howman v. Russell, supra, per* Lord Sands at p. 36.

for in a particular Act of Parliament.[78] The criminal conduct of B, however, must occur within the scope of the employment or agency agreement concerned.[79] If it does not, then only the actor (B) is criminally liable for what was done or omitted. The basis for this unusual form of responsibility is thought to be that those who employ others about a particular trade or business are responsible for the way in which those others conduct themselves in relation to the regulations which apply to that trade or business. The employer or principal will certainly avail himself of the rewards of that business; so it is not totally unfair to make him stand the risks — including vicarious criminal liability, where that is considered to exist. In any event, it may well make him more vigilant in relation to the law's requirements.

Presumption against

It seems to be well accepted that this form of liability does not exist in **13–24** relation to common law crimes.[80] Even in the field of statutory offences, there is a presumption against it[81]; and it is clearly for the Crown to show that it ought to exist in relation to a particular crime.[82]

Ambit

Vicarious liability will certainly apply if Parliament has expressly said **13–25** that it should. In such cases, the prosecutor will have no greater task than to point to the plain words of the statute. Thus, in terms of the Licensing (Scotland) Act 1976, many offences there may be committed by the licence-holder, his employee or agent; but where the offence was in fact committed by an employee or agent, the licence-holder may also be held vicariously liable, where Schedule 5 (under column 3) specifically directs that. Express imposition of that sort is, however, unusual; and indeed the licence-holder in such a situation is permitted a defence. He is invited to show that the offence occurred without his knowledge or connivance, and that he exercised all due diligence to prevent its happening.[83] If he can convince a court that

---

[78] See Gordon, *Criminal Law*, para. 8–41.

[79] See, *e.g., City and Suburban Dairies v. Mackenna*, 1918 J.C. 105, *per* Lord Justice-Clerk Scott Dickson at p. 110.

[80] See, *e.g., Haig v. Thompson*, 1931 J.C. 29, *per* Lord Ormidale at p. 33; *Dean v. John Menzies (Holdings) Ltd*, 1981 J.C. 23, *per* Lord Cameron (diss.) at pp. 33–34, Lord Stott at p. 36 and Lord Maxwell at p. 39.

[81] See, *e.g., Haig v. Thompson, supra, per* Lord Anderson at p. 33: "the general rule is that an employer cannot be made constructively or vicariously liable for the criminal act of an employee."

[82] See *City and Suburban Dairies v. Mackenna, supra, per* Lord Dundas at p. 110; *Duguid v. Fraser*, 1942 J.C. 1, *per* Lord Mackay at p. 6.

[83] 1976 Act, s.67(1) and (2).

he had done his best to make his staff comply with the regulations pertaining to that trade, then he will probably escape conviction.[84]

13–26   In the absence of express imposition, vicarious criminal liability has been recognised in relation to regulatory offences concerned with various business transactions normally conducted by employees. Examples include selling things at prices beyond what the law permits,[85] using motorvehicles which do not comply with "construction and use" regulations,[86] and keeping records of hours worked by drivers.[87] In each of these cases, of course, it may be said that the selling, or the using or the keeping of records was something the employer could have done by himself as well as by the hands of his employees, and that that demonstrates that the employer was meant to "share" liability. It may be, therefore, that such liability will not be recognised where the wording of the offence makes it difficult to show that anyone other than the employee himself was intended to be responsible as, for example, where an offence is expressly aimed at those "driving" as opposed to "using" motorvehicles in contravention of regulations.[88]

Compared with corporate liability

13–27   Since employers may be not only sole traders but also public limited companies or partnerships, which have separate legal personality yet are incapable of doing or intending anything save through their management and employees, the whole subject of vicarious liability is easily confused with "corporate criminal responsibility". The topic of such corporate responsibility concerns a direct criminal liability. It is not concerned with the vicarious liability of a company for crimes actually committed by its employees or agents, but rather with the criminal liability of the company itself. There, the actions and *mentes reae* of particular managers or senior employees are imputed to the company (according to the prevailing "controlling mind" theory)[89]; these become the actions and *mentes reae* of the company. In vicarious liability, on the other hand, the company becomes liable for what individual employees have done. The conduct remains that of the employees involved, the only question then being whether the company, as employer, should also be criminally liable on a vicarious basis.

---

[84] *cf.* the system to ensure compliance set up by the employer in *Readers' Digest Association Ltd v. Pirie*, 1973 J.C. 42, which was concerned with the Unsolicited Goods and Services Act 1971.

[85] See *Duguid v. Fraser, supra.*

[86] See *Swan v. MacNab, supra.*

[87] See *Mitchell v. Morrison*, 1938 J.C. 64.

[88] *cf. Swan v. MacNab, supra*; see also *Docherty v. Stakis Hotels Ltd; Stakis Hotels Ltd v. Docherty*, 1991 S.C.C.R. 6, where the Appeal Court decided that certain food regulations were aimed only at those who actually had management and control of the premises in question, and, further, that a company could not have actual management and control.

[89] See *Purcell Meats (Scotland) Ltd v. McLeod*, 1987 S.L.T. 528.

The above distinction must be borne in mind where a statutory offence **13–28** imposes liability not only on the actor but also on any person who "caused or permitted" the offence to occur. If an employer, for example, is charged with "permitting" the contravention of a statutory rule by an employee, then that is a direct liability attaching to the employer. As Lord Justice-Clerk Grant put it in *Mackay Brothers v. Gibb*[90]:

> "It is true that the general rule is that a person is not vicariously liable for the criminal acts of another. This, however, is not a case of vicarious liability and is not so charged. [It was in fact a "permitting" case.] The appellants, being a firm, act by the hands of their partners and employees... . Like a limited liability company, they are a separate legal *persona* and have no mind. The question accordingly is not whether they are vicariously liable for what their garage controller did [*i.e.* hire out a car which had an insufficient depth of tread on one of its tyres], but whether, through him, knowledge of the defect is brought home to them."

Whether or not knowledge is required to be imputed to a company or partnership in a true case of vicarious liability is a moot point. It can certainly be argued that it is not so required, even where the offence in question is not "strict". That, however, would tend to suggest that all vicarious liability was a form of "strict" liability, which probably goes further than present case law or thinking will allow.

Further reading

Bovey, K. S., *Misuse of Drugs* (1986).
Bell, J. and Engle, Sir G., *Cross on Statutory Interpretation* (2nd ed., 1987).
LaFave, W. and Scott, A. W., *Criminal Law* (2nd (Students) ed., 1986), paras. 2.10 *et seq.*, "Constitutional Limitations on the Power to Create Crimes" (USA).
Mewett, A. W. and Manning, M., *Criminal Law* (2nd ed., 1985), Chap. 5, "Offences of Strict Liability" (Canada).
Shiels, R.S., *Controlled Drugs: Statutes and Cases* (1991).
Shiels, R.S., *Offensive Weapons* (1992)
Wheatley, J., *Road Traffic Law in Scotland* (2nd ed., 1989).

---

[90] 1969 J.C. 26 at p. 31.

CHAPTER 14

CONCLUSION

Introduction

14–01   As the preceding chapters have detailed, the broad sweep of the criminal law, including both general principles and specific offences, is governed by the common law. It is true that there is a myriad of statutory offences and that much of the time of the criminal courts is spent dealing with these, specifically under road traffic legislation. Nevertheless, the articulation of the criminal law continues to be a significant function of the Scottish judiciary. Rather than a criminal code or a collection of statutes, it is a body of case law which defines most of the more serious crimes, as well as the fundamental concepts, including attempt and complicity. Moreover, many of the statutory offences are not strictly necessary, since the conduct in question is already punishable at common law. Nor does the fact that Parliament has chosen not to treat a given kind of behaviour as a statutory offence preclude it being regarded as a common law offence.[1]

THE SCOTTISH ORTHODOXY

14–02   There is little evidence of any great pressure among Scots lawyers for more reliance on statute law or for codification. The orthodox view is that the common law allows the courts a desirable flexibility in dealing with the cases that come before them. As Lord Avonside commented in *Khaliq v. H.M. Advocate*[2]: "The great strength of our common law in criminal matters is that it can be invoked to fill a need. It is not static." And indeed the law has been driven forward with considerable boldness in recent years. In particular, reference may be made to decisions such as *Normand v. Robinson*,[3] *S. v. H.M. Advocate*,[4] *H.M. Advocate v. Wilson*,[5] *R. v. H.M. Advocate*,[6] and *Khaliq v. H.M. Advocate*[7] itself. With only occasional

---

[1]   See *H.M. Advocate v. R. K.*, 1994 S.C.C.R. 499.
[2]   1984 J.C. 23 at p. 26.
[3]   1994 S.L.T. 558.
[4]   1989 S.L.T. 469; see para. 9–83, above.
[5]   1984 S.L.T. 117; see paras. 11–19 to 11–22, above.
[6]   1988 S.L.T. 623; see paras. 12–23 and 12–28, above.
[7]   See paras. 9–30 to 9–32, above.

exceptions[8] there has been no question of a court's waiting for a parliamentary solution when novel problems have been set before it.

This tradition owes much to the continuing influence of Hume, who **14-03** was a strong advocate of a flexible, common law system. He recognised that the criminal law had "to be bent and accommodated to the temper and exigencies of the times".[9] Hume saw this as a judicial function. Not all have shared this perspective. A century before Hume, Mackenzie was arguing that "it were to be wisht, that nothing were a crime which is not declared to be so by a statute; for this would ... prevent the arbitrariness of judges".[10] In a review of the 1844 edition of Hume, Lord Ardmillan commented[11]:

> "The proper function of judges is *jus dicere*, not *jus dare*; and nothing is more perilous to constitutional government and public liberty, than the confusion of the judicial and legislative departments of the State. The voice of the judge is but the voice of the existing law, statutory or common, which it is his part to declare and administer. New laws must proceed from the Legislature ... in whom alone rests the power of enacting what all subjects are bound, as subjects, to obey."

Thus whilst the Humean approach may have prevailed, there has long been a competing tradition in Scots law. There has continued to be voiced dissatisfaction with the expanded role accorded to the judiciary in the development of the criminal law under what remains predominantly a common law system.[12]

Is Reliance on the Common Law Desirable?

In other jurisdictions, particularly in England, it has increasingly been felt **14-04** that the defining of crimes is beyond the competence of the courts. In respect of English law, Ashworth identifies it as a "constitutional principle ... that the reach of the criminal law should be declared by the legislature".[13] On this view, it is not felt to be appropriate for the judiciary to play a leading role in formulating the criminal law. Such formulation is generally thought to be the prerogative of the legislature, in view of the policy considerations

---

[8]   See, for example, *Quinn v. Cunningham*, 1956 J.C. 22; *Grant v. Allan*, 1987 J.C. 71; *H.M. Advocate v. Forbes*, 1994 S.L.T. 861.
[9]   Hume, i, 2.
[10] *Law and Customs* (2nd ed., 1699), p. 2.
[11] "Scottish Criminal Law," (1846) IV *North British Review* 313.
[12] See, for example, W. A. Elliott, "Nulla Poena Sine Lege," 1956 J.R. 22; G. H. Gordon, "Crimes Without Laws," 1966 J.R. 214.
[13] *Principles of Criminal Law* (2nd ed., 1995), p. 61.

inevitably involved. As Lord Kilbrandon (an eminent Scottish judge elevated to the House of Lords) stated in *Director of Public Prosecutions for Northern Ireland v. Lynch*[14]:

> "It will not do to claim that judges have the duty — call it the privilege — of seeing to it that the common law expands and contracts to meet what the judges conceive to be the requirements of modern society. Modern society rightly prefers to exercise that function for itself, and this it conveniently does through those who represent it in Parliament."

This view, however, has not been taken by Lord Kilbrandon's brethren sitting in the High Court of Justiciary. Indeed, it has been known even in modern times for a Scottish judge to take a position quite opposed to this. In *Watt v. Annan,*[15] Lord Cameron wished to place the responsibility on Parliament not to create a crime, but to restrict the extent of the common law crime of shameless indecency:

> "It would be impracticable as well as undesirable to attempt to define precisely the limits and ambit of this particular offence .... If it were considered desirable or necessary that this was a chapter of the criminal law in which precise boundaries or limits were to be set then the task is one which is more appropriate for the hand of the legislator."

14–05   It perhaps just as well that contemporary Scottish judges have tended not to apply an unalloyed version of Lord Cameron's philosophy. They recognise that there are limits to their powers and that there are some issues best left to Parliament. It is too early to reach any definite conclusion, but important decisions such as those in *H.M. Advocate v. Forbes*[16] and *Grant v. Allan*[17] may indicate a greater reluctance on the part of the judges of the High Court to exercise their traditionally asserted powers. These two decisions demonstrate a greater sensitivity to the separation of functions between Parliament and the courts and to the principle of *nullum crimen sine lege*.

14–06   There has been no separate Scottish legislature since 1707; and, given its generally unenthusiastic attention to matters of Scottish law reform, the present Westminster Parliament is viewed with a somewhat jaundiced eye north of the border. In itself, of course, this state of affairs cannot justify an extended role for the judiciary in the articulation of the criminal law. It could equally lead to an argument for a reform of the legislative process in respect of Scots law. That said, the prevailing tradition in Scotland has been that judges are to be intimately involved in the shaping and defining

---

14   [1975] A.C. 653 at p. 700.
15   1978 J.C. 84 at p. 89.
16   1994 S.L.T. 861.
17   1987 J.C. 71.

of crimes. It would, therefore, be no argument at all to assert that the traditional Scottish position ought to be discontinued just because the traditions are different elsewhere. There is, nevertheless, a constitutional and democratic dimension to Scottish criminal law. Since the criminal law is society's most important form of sanction, it can be argued that decisions on its scope should be taken by elected representatives in Parliament, rather than by past and present judges. It should not be thought that this is a characteristically modern thesis. Writing extra-judicially a century-and-a-half ago, Lord Cockburn rejected with scorn the notion, "that on the question, whether any action is held to be indictable or not, the *community is safer under the absolute wisdom of two or three individuals*, no matter how great their wisdom and virtue, *than under the wisdom of Parliament!*"[18] It is undeniable that there are policy considerations involved in formulating the criminal law. But a counter-argument to Lord Cockburn might be that in a small, relatively homogeneous country such as Scotland, the judiciary is as much in touch with public opinion as the group of men and women elected to Parliament. The lack of public criticism of the inherent flexibility of Scots criminal law in the hands of the judiciary, and the apparent parliamentary acquiescence in the role played by Scottish criminal judges are not insignificant matters. The difficulty with this argument is that it is premised on the idea that judges are qualified to discern and represent societal values. Lord Cockburn was in no doubt that on this issue: "Parliament is a better, and infinitely more extended representation of public sentiment."[19]

DEVOLUTION

It is quite possible that Scotland will acquire a legislative assembly with **14–07** devolved powers during this decade. If so, this may have a profound impact upon the criminal law. Under the repealed Scotland Act 1978, the Scottish Assembly was to have been given the legislative responsibility for, *inter alia*: principles of criminal liability; offences against the person and against property; sexual offences; offences of dishonesty; offences against public order, decency and religion; offences against the administration of justice; penalties; and criminal evidence and procedure. If a similar model were to be implemented in the future, the general principles and almost all the crimes detailed in this book would come within the domain of the new legislature. It would then be seen whether the extended role assumed by the judiciary has been a response to legislative neglect, or whether it continues to be a supportable feature of the Scottish legal system.

---

[18] "Scottish Criminal Jurisprudence and Procedure," (1846) 83 *Edinburgh Review* 196 at p. 198.
[19] *ibid.* at p. 215.

JUDICIAL DEVELOPMENT OF THE LAW

14–08 It is well understood that the courts in any jurisdiction have an important role in the development of the law through their decisions. It is generally recognised, however, that the opportunities for doing so are much greater in a common law system than in one based on a code or on statutes. Of course, a judge can effectively develop law through his interpretation of a statutory or code provision. But there he simply considers the detailed meaning of what has already been given clear shape by a distinct policy-making body. A Scottish judge of the High Court of Justiciary, of course, may go much further than that. He may, in relation to non-statutory matters, act as a policy maker and give shape to the law in the very case before him. Objections to this judicial role can be based not so much on the usurpation of a parliamentary function as on the principles of prospectivity and certainty.

Prospectivity

14–09   The principle of prospectivity stands for the proposition that criminal liability should only attach to conduct which has previously been declared to be criminal. It is reflected in Article 7 of the European Convention on Human Rights, which sets out the fundamental freedom from retroactive criminal offences and punishment. The European Court of Human Rights has interpreted this provision as not being confined to prohibiting the retrospective application of the criminal law to an accused's disadvantage. It has been taken to embody the more general principles that only the law can define a crime and that the criminal law should not be extensively construed to an accused's detriment, for instance by analogy.[20] The freedom appears to have considerable significance for any common law system. The common law method appears to preclude the requisite degree of forewarning: a judicial decision will apply to the case immediately before the court, as well as forming a precedent for the future. To some extent the same is true if the decision called for is the interpretation of a statutory provision; but the problem is raised in a crucial form by judicial creativity in the common law, where there is no legislative framework. The particular issue which will face a court is the fairness of deciding a case on the basis of a rule articulated after the conduct in question took place.

14–10   In a general sense all judicial decisions in the criminal law are retrospective, in that "it is the subsequent decision which reaches back into time and places the authoritative stamp of criminality upon the prior conduct."[21] This is so whether the case is one of common law adjudication or statutory interpretation (although the task being attempted by the court

---

[20] *Kokkinakis v. Greece* (1994) 17 E.H.R.R. 397 at para. 52.
[21] Hall, *General Principles of Criminal Law* (2nd ed., 1960), p. 61.

will be different according to which category is involved). But, as Hall points out[22]: "the inevitability of a slight, 'normal' degree of retroactivity in judicial decisions provides no ground for tolerating it in its obvious manifestations." Thus, the issue is the "quality of the adjudication" rather than an absolute compliance with the principle of prospectivity and the crucial question to be asked is whether a particular decision is "retroactive only in ... [an] unavoidable way or is it also unexpected and indefensible by reference to the law which had been expressed prior to the conduct in issue?"[23] A similar approach has been adopted by the European Commission and Court of Human Rights. Both have accepted that it is consistent with Article 7 of the Convention for a court to clarify the existing elements of a common law offence and to adapt it "to new circumstances which can reasonably be brought under the original conception of the offence."[24] The key issue is whether the judicial development of the common law is "consistent with the essence of the offence and could reasonably be foreseen".[25] The fundamental freedom from retroactive criminal offences should "not be read as outlawing the gradual clarification of the rules of criminal liability through judicial interpretation from case to case".[26]

On the face of things, the decisions in *S. v. H.M. Advocate*[27] and *Khaliq* **14–11** *v. H.M. Advocate*[28] might appear to have been unexpected and thus indefensible in relation to the principle of prospectivity. On the law believed to have been current when each of the accused in these cases performed deliberate actions, neither of them could have anticipated that his actions would have been criminal (according to the argument). That argument assumes that the prior law applicable to each of those cases was itself precisely expressed. But the prior law applicable to marital rape, for example, was not in fact clearly expressed at all. It had been referred to obliquely by Hume[29] and eroded by the decisions in *H.M. Advocate v. Duffy*[30] and *H.M. Advocate v. Paxton.*[31] The European Court of Human Rights accepted an argument to this effect in deciding that the judicial abrogation of the exception in English law was compatible with Article 7.[32] It is not in the

---

[22] *ibid.* p. 61.
[23] *ibid.*
[24] *X. Ltd and Y. v. United Kingdom* (1982), case no. 8710/79, para. 9.
[25] *S. W. v. United Kingdom; C. R. v. United Kingdom* (1996), 21 E.H.R.R. 393 at para. 36/34.
[26] *ibid.*
[27] 1989 S.L.T. 469.
[28] 1984 J.C. 23.
[29] i, 306.
[30] 1983 S.L.T. 7.
[31] 1984 J.C. 105; see para. 9–83, above.
[32] *S. W. v. United Kingdom; C. R. v. United Kingdom, supra.*

nature of common law that its individual proscriptions are expressed with particular precision. Rather, the common law proceeds from a set of principles of a plain, moral nature. From that point of view, it rings hollow for the accused person in *S. v. H.M. Advocate*, for example, to claim that he forced sexual intercourse on his wife because he knew that the criminal law of rape granted immunity to husbands who behaved in that way; or for the accused in *Khaliq v. H.M. Advocate* to claim that he knowingly supplied children with vast quantities of life-threatening substances since he knew the criminal law could not touch him for that sort of thing at all. Naturally, if the accuseds' views of the pre-existing law had been correct, then one would have concluded that the criminal law was grossly defective. Indeed, the European Court of Human Rights has observed that the marital rape exemption was itself inconsistent with fundamental objectives of the Convention, the very essence of which was respect for human dignity and human freedom.[33] The only question then concerns the *method* by which such defects should be rectified. Scots law has to date chosen a method which entails conviction of the person whose conduct highlights the need for change, or, in the language appropriate to common law, clarification; and the persons so convicted, at least in the two cases cited, could hardly claim to be outraged on any moral considerations.

Certainty

14–12   It would appear, then, that any failure on the part of Scots law to observe the principle of prospectivity is predicated on the basic uncertainty of common law rules. There can be no doubt that common law is inherently uncertain and that the *actus rei* of a number of offences, such as shameless indecency and breach of the peace, have been defined by the courts in very broad terms. The objection to uncertain rules of criminal law is, of course, the subsequent inability of persons to be wholly confident that their proposed conduct will not fall foul of the law; and that is an objection which no system of common law can fully hope to meet. That could lead one to the conclusion that a common law based system is fundamentally flawed and must be replaced by a code or a collection of statutes. But this conclusion is not inevitable: much depends on the degree of uncertainty, and whether that degree of uncertainty can be tolerated. Much depends also on the extent to which uncertainty is absent from codified or statutory regimes.

14–13   The common law of crimes in Scotland is by no means completely uncertain. If it were, it would not have been possible for this book to have been written. But there always remains a degree of uncertainty as to the precise boundaries of rape, theft, malicious mischief and indeed any other such crime. It is the acceptability of that degree of uncertainty which is the

---

[33] *ibid.*, para. 44/42.

true issue here. That is not to deny or ignore the very real problem posed by the power of the High Court of Justiciary to declare new crimes[34]; but that power is anachronistic, unlikely to be used overtly in modern circumstances, and, in any event, a separable issue. Certainly, in relation to crimes already recognised by the common law, one feels scant sympathy for those who attempt to exploit "blurred edges" for their own advantage — if that does, indeed, happen. In reality, it seems that few people ever take steps to ascertain whether or not their proposed conduct would definitely constitute a crime. Even if they did take such steps, they would still find a degree of uncertainty in a statute or code based system of criminal law. The English Theft Act 1968, for example, has attracted a considerable body of interpretative case law, and, without access to those cases, the exact extent of what is forbidden cannot properly be appreciated. That body of case law is also constantly expanding. This is true also of offences found within the Road Traffic Acts, and indeed any other enactments which flow from Parliament. What matters to individuals, it seems, it that they should be able to have a fairly good outline of what the law is and what is expected of them; and it is on that sort of basis that most people are able to avoid criminality fairly successfully in the course of their daily business. From that argument of pragmatism, rather than principle, then, it does not greatly matter on what basis (judicial or legislative) the criminal law rests.

Effectiveness and fairness

The effectiveness of the criminal law is only partly determined by the **14–14** way in which crimes are defined or brought into existence. It is rather a function of the whole of the criminal justice system in question. Thus, where flexible, common law methods define crimes and their extent, the system of criminal law can still be effective and fair provided that flexibility extends to the prosecutor and to the judge. In Scotland, prosecutors are trusted to proceed only where they perceive a need to do so in the public interest. Judges too are trusted in the same public interest to ensure that charges which come before them on complaint or indictment answer properly to the moral principles embedded in the common law. These public trusts reposed in prosecutors and judges amount to checks and balances to ensure that the Scottish criminal justice system operates fairly and effectively. That criminal justice system may not secure absolute compliance with all desirable principles of abstract criminal law but, in the real world, compromises probably have to be made if the system is to function at all. And the Scottish system does seem to work, and to enjoy a high level of public confidence.

---

[34] See paras. 2–21 *et seq.*, above.

LAW REFORM

14-15 There is no system of criminal law, however, which could not benefit from frequent scrutiny and re-appraisal. Whilst it is true that the Scottish system is gradually re-appraised by judges of the High Court, the weakness of that method lies in the random way in which that service is performed. It can only be done on a case by case basis, and is thus dependent to a large extent on matters of pure chance. Leaving to one side the judiciary's suitability to perform this function, an accusatorial court case is far from the best forum in which to consider the wider policy issues involved in the development of the criminal law. The provision of a systematic re-appraisal programme would be better, such as has been mounted, in effect, by the Scottish Law Commission in relation to the civil law. Whilst it is true that matters affecting the criminal law have from time to time been referred to that Commission, these have been *ad hoc* and rather limited in scope. There is, therefore, a good case to be made for more active appraisal, either by the Scottish Law Commission or by a new body, perhaps a Scottish equivalent to the Criminal Law Revision Committee. A Scottish Assembly, if created, would have a key role to play in this process.

Further reading

Colvin, E., "Criminal Law and the Rule of Law," in Fitzgerald, P. (ed.), *Crime, Justice and Codification* (1986).

Farmer, L., "The Boundaries of Scottish Criminal Law" (1989) 148 SCOLAG 9.

Farmer, L., "'The Genius of our Law . . .': Criminal Law and the Scottish Legal Tradition" (1992) 55 M.L.R. 25.

Gordon, G. H., "Judicial Creativity in a Common Law System" (1993) 27 *Israel Law Review* 118.

Jones, T. H., "Common Law and Criminal Law: The Scottish Example" [1990] Crim. L. R. 292.

Nicholson, G., "Codification of Scots Law: A Way Ahead, or a Blind Alley?" [1988] *Statute Law Review* 173.

Styles, S. C., "Something to Declare: A Defence of the Declaratory Power of the High Court of Justiciary," in Hunter, R.F. (ed.), *Justice and Crime* (1993), pp. 211–231.

Willock, I., "Scottish Criminal Law — Does it Exist?" (1981) 54 SCOLAG 225.

Willock, I., "The Declaratory Power — Still Indefensible," 1996 J.R. 97.

APPENDIX A

SELECT BIBLIOGRAPHY OF SCOTS CRIMINAL LAW

1. Works accorded authoritative status

Alison, Archibald J., *Principles and Practice of the Criminal Law of Scotland* (2 vols.: Vol. i, *Principles* (1832); Vol. ii, *Practice* (1833): reprinted 1989).

Hume, David, *Commentaries on the Law of Scotland Respecting Crimes* (4th ed., by B. R. Bell (2 vols., 1844 (with Bell's Notes), reprinted 1986)).

Macdonald, J. H. A., *A Practical Treatise on the Criminal Law of Scotland* (5th ed., 1948, reprinted 1986).

2. General texts

Anderson, A. M., *The Criminal Law of Scotland* (2nd ed., 1904).

Burnett, John, *A Treatise on Various Branches of the Criminal Law of Scotland* (1811).

Gordon, G. H., *The Criminal Law of Scotland* (2nd ed., 1978, and Second Cumulative Supplement, 1992).

Mackenzie, Sir George, *The Laws and Customs of Scotland in Matters Criminal* (2nd ed., 1699).

Renton, R. W. and Brown, H. H., *Criminal Procedure According to the Law of Scotland* (6th ed., edited by G. H. Gordon, 1996).

Smith, T. B., *A Short Commentary on the Law of Scotland* (1962), particularly Chapters 5, 6 and 7.

Stair Memorial Encyclopaedia, The Laws of Scotland, Vol. 7, *s.v.* "Criminal Law" (1995).

3. Texts on particular subjects

Bovey, K. S., *Misuse of Drugs* (1986).

Bradley, I., *Firearms* (1995).

Christie, M. G. A., *Breach of the Peace* (1990).

Gane, C.H.W., *Sexual Offences* (1992).

Ferguson, P. W., *Crimes Against the Person* (1990).

Nicholson, C. G. B., *Sentencing: Law and Practice in Scotland* (2nd ed., 1992).

Rowan-Robinson, J., et al., *Crime and Regulation: A Study of the Enforcement of Regulatory Codes* (1990).

Shiels, R. S., *Offensive Weapons* (1992).
Wheatley, J., *Road Traffic Law in Scotland* (2nd ed., 1993).

4. Casebooks (Excluding standard case report volumes)

Gane, C. H. W. and Stoddart, C. N., *A Casebook on Scottish Criminal Law* (2nd ed., 1988).
Gane, C. H. W. and Stoddart, C. N., *Criminal Procedure in Scotland: Cases and Materials* (2nd ed., 1994).
Shiels, R. S., *Controlled Drugs: Statutes and Cases* (1991).

Appendix B

CRIMINAL LAW CASE REPORTS

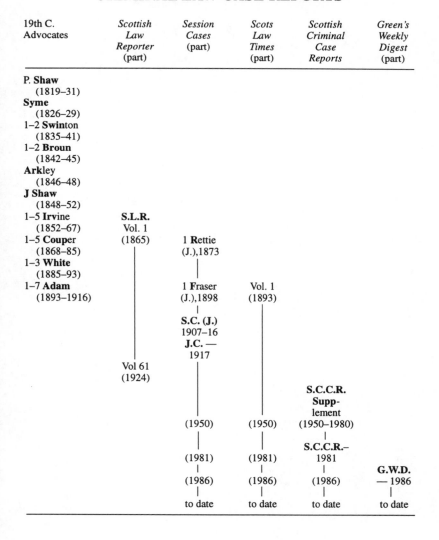

19th C. Advocates	Scottish Law Reporter (part)	Session Cases (part)	Scots Law Times (part)	Scottish Criminal Case Reports	Green's Weekly Digest (part)
P. Shaw (1819–31)					
Syme (1826–29)					
1–2 Swinton (1835–41)					
1–2 Broun (1842–45)					
Arkley (1846–48)					
J Shaw (1848–52)					
1–5 Irvine (1852–67)	S.L.R. Vol. 1 (1865)				
1–5 Couper (1868–85)		1 Rettie (J.),1873			
1–3 White (1885–93)					
1–7 Adam (1893–1916)		1 Fraser (J.),1898	Vol. 1 (1893)		
		S.C. (J.) 1907–16			
		J.C. — 1917			
	Vol 61 (1924)				
				S.C.C.R. Supplement (1950–1980)	
		(1950)	(1950)		
				S.C.C.R.– 1981	
		(1981)	(1981)		
					G.W.D. — 1986
		(1986)	(1986)	(1986)	
		to date	to date	to date	to date

N.B. The same case may be found in more than one set of Reports. It is traditional to regard a "Session Cases" version as superior; but in practice, modern sets of Reports tend to be equally reliable. The S.C.C.R. has the advantage of having Commentaries written by Sheriff G.H. Gordon; G.W.D. contains only short summaries of cases.

THE STANDARD SCALE OF FINES

Almost all statutory criminal offences triable only by summary procedure refer for their maximum fines to the standard scale. This was introduced by the Criminal Justice Act 1982 (c. 48) which, by virtue of section 54, added section 289G to the now repealed Criminal Procedure (Scotland) Act 1975 (c. 21). That Act of 1982, by section 53(a), also amended section 289D of the 1975 Act such that by new subsections 289D(1) and (1A), the Secretary of State for Scotland might alter the various sums appearing on the standard scale if a change in the value of money seemed to necessitate this. In fact, the present scale values were set by Parliament itself, under section 17(1) of the Criminal Justice Act 1991 (c. 53) but now appear in the Criminal Procedure (Scotland) Act 1995 (c. 46) at section 225(2), and, of course, remain alterable by the Secretary of State if there has been a change in the value of money since the last occasion they were altered by order under section 289D(1) of the repealed Act of 1975 (see the 1995 Act, section 225(4)). Those current scale values are as follows:

Level 1	£ 200
Level 2	£ 500
Level 3	£1,000
Level 4	£2,500
Level 5	£5,000

THE PRESCRIBED SUM

Many statutory criminal offences refer to the "prescribed sum" as their maximum available fine. That term was introduced by the Criminal Law Act 1977 (c. 45), s. 63, Sched. 11, para. 5 which inserted section 289B into the Criminal Procedure (Scotland) Act 1975 (c. 21). That provision is now repealed; and the present value of the prescribed sum can be found in section 225(8) of the Criminal Procedure (Scotland) Act 1995 (c. 46) — although the value is unchanged from the monetary figure dictated by section 17(2) of the Criminal Justice Act 1991 (c. 53). The value, shown below, is alterable by the Secretary of State in the same way indicated above for levels on the standard scale.

Prescribed sum £5,000

THE STATUTORY MAXIMUM

The maximum fine for some statutory offences is expressed as "the statutory maximum". In Scotland this is to be taken as a reference to the "prescribed sum" (see above) by virtue of the Interpreptation Act 1978 (c. 30), Sched. 1 (definition of *inter alia* the statutory maximum — as inserted by the Criminal Justice Act 1988 (c. 33), Sched. 15, para. 58), as amended by the Criminal Procedure (Consequential Provisions) (Scotland) Act 1995 (c. 40), Sched. 4, para. 17(b).

SCOTTISH CRIMINAL COURTS

1. District courts

Founded in 1975 to replace the older Burgh, Justice of the Peace and other minor courts, these are local criminal courts with limited jurisdiction — both territorially and by crime: see generally the District Courts (Scotland) Act 1975 (c. 20) and the Criminal Procedure (Scotland) Act 1995 (c. 46) ss.6 and 7. The judges (called "justices of the peace") are not legally qualified but are assisted by qualified clerks (employed by Scottish local authorities). Procedure is always summary (*i.e.* non-jury, if matters proceed to trial). In relation to such common law crimes as can be heard in these courts, maximum powers of punishment extend to imprisonment for 60 days or a fine of level 4 on the standard scale: see the Criminal Procedure (Scotland) Act 1995, s.7(4),(6),(8)–(10) and Appendix C, above. Statutory offences (*i.e.* those which are triable by summary procedure) are punishable according to similar maxima, unless the enactment in question specifically allows a wider or different range (Criminal Procedure (Scotland) Act 1995, s.7(7)). Justices of the peace have important roles in the granting of preliminary and incidental warrants. The proceedings of district courts are never reported (except in the press). Appeal lies only to the Scottish Court of Criminal Appeal.

2. Stipendiary magistrates' courts

Any local authority in Scotland may have these if it has the permission of the Secretary of State to do so. Such a court is a district court presided over by a legally qualified "stipendiary magistrate" who has all the criminal powers of a justice of the peace and of a sheriff in summary criminal proceedings: see *3.*, below; and see the District Courts (Scotland) Act 1975 (c. 20), s.5 and the Criminal Procedure (Scotland) Act 1995 (c. 46), s.7(5). Proceedings of such a court are never reported (except in the press). Appeal lies to the Scottish Court of Criminal Appeal.

3. Sheriff courts

Founded probably in the twelfth century, these are local courts (with both civil and criminal law functions). They have limited territorial jurisdiction but extensive jurisdiction by crime. Of the commonly encountered common law crimes, only murders and rapes cannot be dealt with in these courts (see the Criminal Procedure (Scotland) Act 1995 (c. 46), s.3(6)). Judges are called sheriffs of various descriptions (*e.g.* sheriff principal, floating sheriff, honorary sheriff, temporary sheriff) but all are of equal authority in criminal proceedings. They must be legally qualified and experienced in practice as either advocates or solicitors. Procedure may be either summary or on indictment (*i.e.* non-jury or jury if matters proceed to trial). In relation to common law crimes, Scottish prosecutors decide whether an offence merits jury trial or not. The choice exercised determines the maximum punishment available — *i.e.* in a solemn or indictment case, three years in prison (or more if the sheriff chooses to remit for sentence to the High Court: see the Criminal Procedure (Scotland) Act 1995, ss.3(3), 195, 219(8))) and/or a fine of any amount; in a summary case, three months (sometimes six months: see the Criminal Procedure (Scotland) Act 1995, s.5(2)(a),(d),(3)) *or* a fine not exceeding the prescribed sum: see Appendix C, above. Statutory offences (triable summarily, either way, or on indictment only) may be punished according to the maximum laid down by the enactment in question (but if the maximum laid down is more than three years in prison, a sheriff's powers are restricted to three years (the Criminal Procedure (Scotland) Act 1995, s.3(4),(5)) — though, once again, he might choose to remit for sentence to the High Court. Proceedings before sheriff courts are occasionally reported (in S.C.C.R. or in the Sh.Ct. part of S.L.T.). Appeals of whatever nature may be taken only to the Scottish Court of Criminal Appeal.

4. High Courts of Justiciary

Founded as the court of the Justiciar in the twelfth century, a modern high court consists (normally) of one judge. Such a court has territorial jurisdiction throughout Scotland, and can deal with all common law offences (and indeed is the only court competent to conduct rape and murder trials — see the Criminal Procedure (Scotland) Act 1995 (c. 46), s.3(6)) in addition to all statutory offences (other than those designated as "summary procedure" only). Judges (who are said to belong to the high court considered as a "college") are professional advocates of great experience and are called "Lords Commissioners of Justiciary". (They are also the judges of the civil law court known as the Court of Session.) The effective president is titled "the Lord Justice-General", and the vice-president has the title of "Lord Justice-Clerk". Procedure is always solemn (*i.e.* involving a jury if matters proceed to trial). Maximum powers of punishment extend to life in prison and/or a fine of any amount (for common law crimes), or to the maximum laid down in the enactment in question (in the case of statutory crimes). Proceedings are quite regularly reported (in S.L.T., J.C., S.C.C.R. and G.W.D.: see Appendix B, above), and appeals of whatsoever nature lie to the Scottish Court of Criminal Appeal. Difficult matters arising during a trial may be referred (by a process called "certification") to a larger body of high court judges.

5. The Appeal Court

The Scottish Court of Criminal Appeal (to give it a title which is increasingly in use) was founded in 1926 and consists of a minimum of two or three judges of the high court (considered as a "college" of all high court judges): see the Criminal Procedure (Scotland) Act 1995 (c. 46), ss.103 and 173. All appeals from all lower courts are dealt with by such a bench of judges (which is called a "full bench" if more than three are present — although the exact number comprising such a full bench has always in modern times been an uneven one). Decisions are by a simple majority (where that is possible) of those present, and such decisions are final unless a bench of two judges cannot agree (see the Criminal Procedure (Scotland) Act 1995, ss. 103(3) and 173(2)). There is *no* further appeal to (say) the English House of Lords. (Individual petition to the European Commission on Human Rights is, however, recognised by the United Kingdom.)

6. Nobile Officium Court

This court consists of a minimum of three judges of the high court (considered as a "college" of all high court judges). It may provide a solution on an equitable basis where petitioned in relation to a matter of injustice which is truly unexpected and unforeseeable and where the law provides no alternative remedy. See the index for further information on the *nobile officium*.

INDEX

ABDUCTION,
  actus reus, 9.02
  mens rea, 9.02
  substitute for theft, 10.09
Abortion, 9.34–9.35
Absolute Liability, 13.13,
  and see Strict Liability.
Accident, 8.40–8.43,
  see Casual Homicide.
Act of Adjournal, 2.13
Actus Non Facit Reum Nisi Mens Sit Rea, 3.01
Actus Reus,
  "bare" human acts, 4.06
  committing by ommitting, 3.09
  conscious acts, 4.07
  essential for conviction, 3.03
  failure in contractual duty as, 3.10
  failure in moral duty as, 3.13
  failure to remedy a dangerous
    situation as, 3.11, 3.12
  generally, 3.01
  involuntary act, 4.08–4.09, 4.11–4.14
  legally relevant acts, scope of, 4.12,
    4.13
  mental process in, 4.08
  omissions as, 3.09–3.13
  positive conduct as, 3.03, 3.08
  "responsible" human acts, 4.06
  state of affairs as, 3.14
  voluntary act, 4.01, 4.08
  willed movement, 4.08
    see also Automatism,
      Coincidence, Hypnotism,
      Innocent Agent, Control; and
      under names of individual
      crimes.
Administration of Noxious Substances,
  9.29, 9.56
Advocate, Her Majesty's,
  see Lord Advocate.
Advocate Depute, 2.58
Alibi, 8.09,
  and see Defences, special.

Appeal,
  against sentence, 2.65
  generally, 2.65
Art and Part Guilt,
  aiding another, 7.05, 7.12
  common purpose in, 7.08, 7.09, 7.18,
    7.19, 7.21–7.23
  concert,
    antecedent 7.14–7.16, 7.22
    at time of crime, 7.18, 7.19, 7.22
  conspiracy and, 7.51, 7.52
  degree of participation in crime, 7.10,
    7.11, 7.13
  dissociation from enterprise, 7.37–
    7.38
  foreseeability of events, 7.23–7.28
  generally, 7.02
  incitement and, 7.05, 7.14, 7.15, 7.63,
    7.64
  instigating another, 7.05, 7.14, 7.15
  joint principal offenders, 7.11, 7.31
  legal impossibility, 7.30
  liability compared with that of
    principal, 7.05, 7.06, 7.11, 7.17,
    7.23–7.30, 7.32–7.36
  mens rea and, 7.23–7.28
  merger of charges, 7.63, 7.64
  omission and, 7.20, 7.21
  physical assistance, 7.16
  presence at scene of crime
    unnecessary, 7.10
  psychological assistance, 7.14, 7.15
    and see Mobbing.
Assault,
  actus reus, 9.05–9.11
  aggravated, 9.17
  attempted, 9.11
  breach of the peace and, 12.11
  by means of an animal, 9.10
  consent and, 9.18–9.20
  diminished responsibility and, 9.23
  generally, 9.03, 9.04
  indecent, 9.17, 9.20, 9.87
  injury unnecessary, 9.06

justified use of force, 9.07
mens rea of, 9.07, 9.12–9.16
provocation and, 9.21, 9.22
robbery and, 10.46
sport and, 9.07, 9.15
surgery and, 9.15
threatening gestures and, 9.08, 9.09
unintentional injury, 9.24
verbal "attack" insufficient, 9.05
Attempt,
  actus reus of, 6.12, 6.13
  applicable to any crime, 6.02
  generally, 6.01, 6.06, 6.07
  impossibility and, 6.23–6.36
  last act test, 6.16, 6.17, 6.19
  mens rea of, 6.08–6.11, 6.26
  perpetration (proximity) test, 6.18–6.22
  point of no return test, 6.14, 6.15, 6.17, 6.19
  rationale, 6.03–6.05
  to pervert, defeat or hinder the course of justice, 12.36
  see also Culpable Homicide.
Authoritative Texts,
  Alison, *Principles*, 2.07
  Hume, *Crimes*, 2.05
  Macdonald, *Treatise*, 2.07
Automatism,
  as defence, 4.10, 4.19, 4.47
  concussion and, 4.32
  conditions for, 4.20, 4.21
  diabetes and, 4.42
  epilepsy and, 4.40, 4.41
  fairness and, 4.48
  hyperglycaemia and, 4.27
  hypoglycaemia and, 4.27–4.29
  hysterical amnesia and, 4.46
  in England, 4.11, 4.24, 4.33–4.35, 4.39, 4.42, 4.44
  in Scotland, 4.19–4.46
  ingestion of drugs and, 4.25–4.29
  insanity and, 4.11, 4.18, 4.22, 4.34, 4.35, 4.40
  internal causes of, 4.34–4.46
  non-insane, 4.11, 4.19, 4.20, 4.21, 4.36–4.46
  public safety and, 4.35
  sleep and, 4.37–4.39
  spontaneous hypoglycaemia and, 4.43
  stress and, 4.33
  temporary dissociation and, 4.30, 4.40, 4.41
  toxic fumes and, 4.30, 4.31
  weak intellect and, 4.45

BIBLIOGRAPHY, *see* Appendix A.
Books of Adjournal, 2.13
Breach of the Peace,
  actus reus, 12.16, 12.17
  definitions of, 12.13–12.15
  generally, 12.11
  good motive irrelevant, 12.18
  mens rea, 12.18
  on Vandalism charge, 13.07
  police and, 12.19
  relevancy of charge, 12.20
  scope of, 12.12, 12.15
  self-defence and, 12.19
Byelaw, 2.14, 2.15

CARELESS DRIVING,
  breach of the peace and, 12.11
  see Driving without Due Care.
Casual Homicide, 9.38
Causation,
  "but for" test, 5.03–5.06
  "condition" and cause contrasted, 5.06
  forseeability and, 5.26–5.31
  generally, 3.06, 5.01–5.02, 5.32
  in Art and Part guilt, 7.13, 7.15
  malregimen, 5.23–5.25, 5.29
  novus actus interveniens, 5.19–5.31, 5.35
  policy and, 5.36
  proximity requirement, 5.07, 5.33
  suicide and, 5.17
  taking the victim as found, 5.09–5.11, 5.16
  victim's own contribution, 5.12–5.16
Cause, meaning in statutes, 13.17
Cause or Permit, meaning in statutes, 13.17
Causing Death by Dangerous Driving, 4.02
Certainty, principle of, 14.12
Children,
  minimum age for prosecution, 2.46
  special arrangements for, 2.47
Children's Hearing, 2.47, 2.48
Clandestine Injury to Women, 9.87
Clandestine Taking and Using of Property, 10.23
Coercion,
  basis of, 8.80–8.83
  general, 8.78
  immediacy of threat requirement, 8.85, 8.86
  intoxication effected by, 8.76
  limitations upon, 8.79, 8.84–8.87

murder and, 8.87
Coincidence of *Actus Reus* and *Mens Rea*, 3.33, 3.34
Common Law, 14.01
case law development of, 14.01
flexibility of, 14.02, 14.03
Hume and the, 14.03
judicial development of, 14.03
legislation contrasted with, 2.10
meaning of, 2.03–2.09
moral principles of, 14.11
procedure followed under, 2.39
random development of, 14.15
uncertainty of, 14.12, 14.13
vicarious liability not applicable to, 13.24
Complaint, 2.53
Complicity, *see* Art and Part Guilt, Conspiracy, Incitement.
Concert, Acting in, 7.03,
and see Art and Part Guilt.
Conspiracy,
actus reus of, 7.45, 7.49
agreement necessary, 7.40
art and part guilt and, 7.51, 7.52
as substitute for inchoate attempt, 7.57
attempted, *see* Incitement.
"chain" type, 7.42
crimes pursuant to the agreement, 7.54
criticism of, 7.44, 7.45, 7.47
dissociation, 7.61
effected by criminal means, 7.55, 7.56
generally, 7.02, 7.39
impossibility in, 7.58–7.60
indictment complexities, 7.53–7.56
justification for, 7.49, 7.50
mens rea, 7.46
merger of charges, 7.63, 7.64
proof of agreement, 7.46–7.48
"wheel" type, 7.43
Control, events beyond human, 4.03, 4.15
Conviction,
effect, 1.11
meaning, 1.10
when justified, 1.12, 1.13
Corporate Bodies,
as accused, 2.49
controlling mind theory, 2.49
vicarious liability of, 13.27, 13.28
Crime,
classification of, 2.37–2.41
conduct and result crimes, 2.40, 3.05, 5.01

definition of,
generally, 2.19
Hart, 1.10
identification of conduct or situation as, 2.19, 2.20, 2.26–2.29, 2.36, 12.01
innominate, 2.53
malum in se, malum prohibitum, 2.41, 13.19
offence and, 2.37
once committed cannot be uncommitted, 10.69
state of affairs, 2.40
Criminal Cases,
reports series, 2.09,
and see Appendix B.
Criminal Code, 14.01, 14.02
absence of in Scots law, 2.01, 2.02
proposed for England, 4.01
model penal (USA), 4.01, 4.09
Criminal Courts,
generally, *see* Appendix D.
High Court of Justiciary, 2.03, 2.04, 2.09, 2.13, 2.23,
power to declare the common law, *see* Declaratory Power.
Rules Council, 2.13
Criminal Evidence,
relation to criminal law, 1.20
Criminal Law,
aims of,
deterrence, 1.15
public protection, 1.18
reformation, 1.17
retribution, 1.16
boundaries of, 1.04–1.08, 1.14
checks and balances in, 14.14
clarity of, 14.11
development of by analogy, 14.09, 14.10
distinguished from private law, 1.02, 1.03
effectiveness of, 14.14
enforcement of morals by, 1.04, 12.22–12.31
conservative thesis, 1.04
disintegration thesis, 1.04, 1.08
fairness of, 14.14
flexibility of, 14.14
harm principle and, 1.07, 1.08, 12.01, 12.22
judicial development of, 14.03–14.06, 14.08
legislative development of, 14.04
meaning of, 1.01

moral principles and, 1.01, 1.04–1.06
political policies and, 1.01
public confidence in, 14.14
public law and, 1.02, 1.03
public policy and, 14.06
punishment and, 1.09–1.11
Criminal Letters, 2.59
Criminal Procedure,
accusatorial form, 2.55
adversarial form, 2.57
complementary to criminal law, 1.19
summary and solemn, 2.39
Criminal Prosecutions,
generally, 1.03
how conducted, 2.58, 2.60, 2.61
Criminal Responsibility,
principles of, 1.13, 3.01
Crown Office, 2.58
Cruel and Barbarous Treatment, 9.25
Cruel and Unnatural Treatment, 9.26
Culpable Homicide,
actus reus, 9.52
attempted, 9.66, 9.70
cumulative provocation, 9.62
death resulting from assault, 9.55
from lawful act, 9.58, 9.59
from unlawful act, 9.56, 9.57
diminished responsibility and, 9.67–9.70
discretionary, 9.71
generally, 9.34, 9.52–9.54
mens rea, 9.57, 9.58, 9.60–9.70
provocation and, 9.60–9.66
voluntary and involuntary, 9.54
Cumulative Provocation, *see* Culpable Homicide.

Dangerous driving, 4.02
De Minimis **Principle**, 2.54
Death, legal meaning of, 9.36
Declaratory Power,
meaning of, 2.20, 2.21
origins of, and authority for, 2.22
reasons for retention of, 2.24–2.26
scope of, 2.23, 2.27–2.36, 14.13
Defences,
excuses, 8.04
in general, 8.01, 8.02
justifications, 8.03
mitigatory, 8.05, 8.06
special, 8.07, 8.08,
and see Alibi, Automatism (non-insane), Incrimination, Insanity, Self-Defence.
see also names of particular defences.

Devolution, 14.07
Diminished Responsibility, *see* Culpable Homicide.
Dole, *see Mens Rea*.
Driving,
meaning of, 4.04, 13.03
without Due Care, 4.02
see also Careless Driving.

Embezzlement,
actus reus, 10.40–10.42
definition of, 10.37, 10.39
dishonesty in, 10.43
mens rea, 10.43
theft and, 10.38, 10.40, 10.44
Endangering the Lieges, 9.28
Error,
claim of right, 8.51, 8.53, 8.60
of fact, 8.54–8.62
of law, 8.44–8.53
reasonableness of, 8.57–8.62
European,
Convention on Human Rights, 2.18, 2.21, 14.09, 14.10
Court,
precedents of, 2.17
preliminary rulings from, 2.17
Court of Human Rights, 14.09–14.11
law, 2.17
Evidential Burden of Proof,
on prosecutor, 2.55
on accused, 2.57
Excusable Homicide, 9.40
Extortion, 9.92–9.94

Failing to leave a rave, 12.21
Failing to Stop after an Accident, 4.02
Fire-raising,
culpable and reckless type,
actus reus, 11.40
mens rea, 11.41, 11.42
generally, 11.28–11.30
intentional type,
actus reus, 11.39
general, 11.37, 11.38
mens rea, 11.39
wilful type,
actus reus, 11.32, 11.33
definition, 11.31
mens rea, 11.34–11.36
Fraud,
actus reus, 10.67–10.76
cheque and credit cards, 10.73, 10.74
consent and, 10.65
false pretences, 10.71, 10.76

future intentions and, 10.67–10.70
gain unnecessary, 10.75
generally, 10.65, 10.66
jurisdiction, 10.78
loss unnecessary, 10.75
mens rea, 10.77
practical result, 10.75, 10.76
theft and, 10.65
Fraudulently Obtaining Access to a Married Woman, 9.84
Furtum Usus, 10.23

GIVING FALSE INFORMATION TO THE POLICE, 12.37

HAMESUCKEN, 9.17
Homicide, 9.34–9.37,
    and see Abortion, Casual Homicide, Culpable Homicide, Excusable Homicide, Justifiable Homicide, Murder, Persistent Vegetative State.
Housebreaking, *see* Theft, aggravations of.
Housebreaking with Intent to Steal, 10.35
Hypnotism,
    acts under, 4.16

INCEST, 12.29–12.31
Inchoate crime, *see* Attempt, Conspiracy, Incitement.
Incitement,
    actus reus, 7.62, 7.65
    criticism of, 7.65
    generally, 7.02, 7.40, 7.62
    justification of, 7.66
    mens rea, 7.62
    merger of charges, 7.63, 7.64
Incrimination, 8.10,
    and see Defences, special.
Indecent Exhibitions, 12.26,
    and see Shamelessly Indecent Conduct.
Indecent Exposure, 12.25,
    and see Shamelessly Indecent Conduct.
Indictment, 2.53
Innocent Agent, 4.03, 4.15, 7.34, 7.35
Insane Persons, as accused, 2.51
Insanity,
    generally, 8.11, 8.12
    legal concept of, 8.13, 8.14
    sufficient if temporary, 8.18
    test for, 8.15–8.17
Instigation, *see* Incitement.

Intention, *see Mens Rea.*
Intoxication,
    coerced, 8.76
    insanity and, 8.72–8.74
    involuntary, 8.75–8.77
    mens rea and, 8.66–8.70
    mitigatory plea, 8.71
    public policy and, 8.65, 8.69
    voluntary, 8.64–8.74

JOY-RIDING, 10.24
Judicial Legislation,
    criticism of, 14.03
Jurisdiction, 2.42
Jury, 2.62, 2.63
Justifiable Homicide, 9.39

LEGAL AID, 2.66
Legislation,
    European, 2.17
    interpretation of, 2.10
    meaning of, 2.10
    non-parliamentary, 2.12–2.16
    pre-Union, 2.11
    where found, 2.11
Lewd, Indecent and Libidinous Practices, 9.20
Locus, 2.42
Lord Advocate,
    Lord Advocate's Reference, 2.65
    law officer, 1.03, 2.58

MALICIOUS MISCHIEF,
    breach of the peace and, 12.11
    generally, 11.08
    riotous and wilful type,
        actus reus, 11.11
        Hume's view, 11.09–11.10
        mens rea, 11.11
    "Stewart" type, 11.23–11.25
    traditional type,
        actus reus, 11.13
        general, 11.12
        mens rea, 11.14
        provocation and, 11.18
        where misapprehension of rights involved, 11.15–11.17
    "Wilson" type,
        actus reus, 11.20–11.21
        general, 11.19
        mens rea, 11.22
Malum in se, *see* Crime.
Malum prohibitum, *see* Crime.
Management Rules, 2.16

Mens Rea,
   burden of proof of, 4.19
   dole and, 3.16
   generally, 3.15, 3.16, 3.21
   intention as, 3.23, 3.24
   motive and, 3.19, 3.20
   negligence as, 3.32
   objective assessment of, 3.18, 4.06
   proof of intention, 3.25, 3.26
   recklessness as, 3.28–3.31
   subjective assessment of, 3.18
   transferred intent, 3.35–3.37
      see also Coincidence; and under
         names of individual crimes.
Mobbing,
   actus reus
      common purpose, 12.04–12.06
      number required, 12.03
      presence in crowd, 12.08
      public alarm, 12.07
      vindication of supposed right
         irrelevant, 12.04
   art and part liability and, 12.02
      see also Art and Part Guilt
   generally, 12.02
   mens rea, 12.09
Model Penal Code, *see* Criminal Code.
Murder,
   actus reus, 9.43
   consent and, 9.51
   diminished responsibility, effect on,
      see Culpable Homicide.
   generally, 9.42
   mens rea, 9.44–9.50
   provocation, effect on, *see* Culpable
      Homicide.
   punishment for, 9.41

NECESSITY,
   coercion of circumstances, 8.91
   general, 8.88
   greater good, securing of, 8.90
   murder and, 8.92
Negligence, *see* Mens Rea.
New Prosecution, 2.52
Nobile Officium
   petition to *nobile officium* of High
      Court, 2.67, 2.68
Not Proven, 2.63
Nullum Crimen Sine Lege, 2.21, 2.32,
   14.05

OFFENCE, 2.19, 2.37,
   and see Crime.
Omission, *see Actus Reus.*

Opening Lockfast Places, *see* Theft,
   aggravations of.
**Opening Lockfast Places with Intent to
   Steal,** 10.35

PANNEL, 4.37
Perjury, 12.35
Persistent Vegetative State, 9.72
Persuasive Burden of Proof, 2.55
Plagium, 10.15
Plea in Bar of Trial, 2.51, 2.52
Possession, meaning, 13.17, 13.18
Prescription, *see* Time-bar
Presumption of Innocence, 2.55
**Pretending to be a Married Woman's
   Husband,** 9.85
Private Prosecution, 2.59
Pro Loco et Tempore **Desertion,** 2.56
Procurator Fiscal,
   public prosecution official, 1.03, 2.58
Proof Beyond Reasonable Doubt, 2.55
Proof on Balance of Probabilities, 2.57
Prosecutor's Powers,
   master of the instance, 2.56
   moving for sentence, 2.56
Prospectivity, 6.34, 14.09
Provocation,
   assault and, 9.21, 9.22
   murder and, 9.60
      see also Culpable Homicide.
Psycopathic Personality, 9.68
Publishing Obscene Material, 12.27
Punishment,
   civil penalty, contrasted with, 2.19
   criminal law and, 1.09–1.11
   deterrent, 1.15
   for homicide, 9.41
   involuntary acts and, 4.09
   proportionality of, 1.16
   retributive, 1.16
   victim's views of, 1.16, 1.17
      and see Standard Scale.

RAPE,
   abduction unnecessary, 9.75
   actus reus, 9.75–9.78
   alternative verdicts, 9.88
   consent, 9.79, 9.80, 9.84
   fraud and, 9.84
   generally, 9.73, 9.74
   insensibility of victim, 9.81
   marital, 9.83, 14.11
   mens rea, 9.82
   mental illness and, 9.86
Rave, 12.21

Reckless Discharge of Firearms, 9.33
Reckless Endangerment, *see*
Endangering the Lieges.
Reckless Injury, 9.27
Recklessness, *see Mens Rea.*
Reflex Movements, 4.07, 4.15
Relevancy of a Charge, 2.53, 12.20
Res Judicata, 2.52, 9.37
Reset,
  committed outwith Scotland, 10.64
  generally, 10.52
  jurisdiction, 10.64
  "Macdonald" form of,
    actus reus, 10.61–10.63
    mens rea (connivance), 10.63
  traditional form of,
    actus reus, 10.54
    definition, 10.53
    identification of thief etc.
    unnecessary, 10.53
    mens rea, 10.55–10.58
    recent possession of stolen
    property, 10.60
    theft and, 10.59, 10.60
Rioting, 12.10
Road, meaning of, 13.02
Robbery,
  actus reus, 10.47–10.49
  assault and, 10.46
  definition of, 10.47
  mens rea, 10.51
  relevant property, 10.50
  stouthrief form of, 10.48
  theft and, 10.45

SCOTTISH ASSEMBLY, 14.06, 14.07, 14.15
Scottish Law Commission, 14.15
Sedition, 12.34
Self-defence,
  accident and, 8.43
  accused as original assailant, 8.33,
    8.34
  cumulative abuse and, 8.37, 8.38
  defence of others as, 8.32
  duty-to-retreat requirement, 8.28, 8.29
  error as to need for, 8.30, 8.31, 8.38
  generally, 8.19–8.21
  homicide and, 8.26
  imminent threat requirement, 8.22
  necessary force requirement, 8.23,
    8.29
  proportional retaliation requirement,
    8.24
  provocation and, 8.35, 8.36

  rape and, 8.39
  sodomy and, 8.27, 8.39
    and see Defences, special.
Sentencing, 2.64
Separation of Powers, 14.05
Sex Shops, 12.27
Shamelessly Indecent Conduct,
  actus reus, 12.24, 12.25–12.28
  consent and, 12.26
  generally, 12.23
  mens rea, 12.24
  publishing and, 12.27
  quasi-incestuous behaviour, 12.28
  see Indecent Exposure.
Simpliciter Desertion, 2.56
Solicitor General for Scotland, 2.58
Standard Scale, *see* Appendix C.
Statutes,
  constitutionality of, 13.01
  necessity for interpretation of, 14.13
Statutory Instrument, 2.13
Statutory Offences,
  common law alternatives, when
    competent, 13.07
  dictionary definitions, 13.05, 13.06
  generally, 13.01
  interpretation by courts, 13.02, 13.03
  interpretation sections, 13.02
  mens rea, 13.08–13.12
  repealed provisions, 13.04, 13.06
  vicarious liability, 13.23–13.28
    and see Strict Liability.
Strict Liability, 3.01, 4.06, 4.19, 13.08–
  13.22
Subornation of Perjury, 12.35
**Supplying Potentially Noxious
  Substances**, 9.30–9.32, 9.56

THEFT,
  actus reus
    appropriation, 10.03, 10.06, 10.18,
      10.19
    economic gain unnecessary, 10.29
    finding as, 10.04, 10.05
    Hume's view of, 10.03–10.06,
      10.19
  aggravations of,
    generally, 10.30
    housebreaking, 10.31–10.33
    opening lockfast places, 10.34
    and see Robbery.
  consent and, 10.18, 10.19
  embezzlement and, 10.38, 10.40,
    10.44

error as to consent, 10.20
fraud and, 10.65
generally, 10.02
mens rea,
    Hume's view of, 10.21, 10.22
    indefinite intention to deprive,
      10.24
    inference of, 10.28
    intention permanently to deprive,
      10.22–10.24
    intention to deprive temporarily
      for a nefarious purpose 10.25–
      10.27
    knowledge, 10.21
outside Scotland, 10.36
property,
    children, 10.09, 10.15,
     and see Plagium.
    corpse, 10.15
    electricty, 10.10
    error as to, 10.17
    land, 10.07
    ownership of by another, 10.11–
      10.13, 10.16
    right of, 10.01
    stealable, 10.07–10.16
    treasure, 10.13
    wild animals, 10.14
Threats,
    criminal *per se*, 9.90, 9.91
    generally, 9.89
Time-bar,
    common law crimes, 2.43

    re custody and trial, 2.45
    statutory crimes, 2.44
Tholed Assize, *see Res Judicata.*
Transferred Intent, *see Mens Rea.*
Treason, 12.33
Trespass on Heritable Property,
    generally, 11.02
    statutory Offences, 11.03–11.07
Triviality of Charge, 2.54

UTTERING AS GENUINE,
    actus reus, 10.79–10.82
    deception not required, 10.83
    definition, 10.79
    forgeries, 10.80, 10.81
    mens rea, 10.79, 10.83
    passing off as genuine, 10.82

VANDALISM,
    breach of the peace and, 12.11
    statutory offence, 11.26, 11.27, 13.09
     see also Malicious Mischief.
Verdicts, 2.63
Vicarious Liability, 13.08,
    and see Statutory Offences
Violation of Sepulchres, 10.15
Voluntariness, 3.16, 4.10,
    and see Actus Reus

WASTING POLICE TIME, 12.37